Introduction to Soft Computing

Neuro-Fuzzy and Genetic Algorithms

Introduction to Soft Computing

Neuro-Fuzzy and Genetic Algorithms

Samir Roy

Professor and Head
Department of Computer Science and Engineering
National Institute of Technical Teachers' Training and Research
Kolkata

Udit Chakraborty

Associate Professor
Department of Computer Science and Engineering
Sikkim Manipal Institute of Technology
Rangpo

Pearson

Associate Editor—Acquisitions: Neha Goomer
Associate Editor—Production: V. Pavithra

ISBN 978-81-317-9246-9

First Impression, 2013
Eighth Impression, 2023
Ninth Impression, 2024

Published by Dorling Kindersley (India) Pvt. Ltd, licensees of Pearson Education in South Asia.

Head Office: 1st Floor, Berger Tower, Plot No. C-001A/2, Sector 16B, Noida - 201 301, Uttar Pradesh, India.
Registered Office : Featherlite, 'The Address' 5th Floor, Survey No 203/10B, 200 Ft MMRD Road, Zamin Pallavaram, Chennai – 600044.
Website :in.pearson.com;Email:companysecretary.india@pearson.com

Compositor: BeSpoke Integrated Solutions, Puducherry.
Printed in India Pushp Print Services

In the loving memory of my elder brother Sri N. K. Roy

—Samir Roy

To Dudun (my maternal grandmother)

—Udit Chakraborty

CONTENTS

PREFACE

This book is the result of our desire to provide a learner-friendly text on soft computing. With the growing importance of computational intelligence in diverse application areas, soft computing is fast gaining importance and popularity in the academic world. Nowadays, this subject is included as a full paper, either elective or core, in various undergraduate and graduate curricula in computer science and engineering, information technology, master of computer applications, and related courses. This book covers the syllabi of the soft computing papers in these curricula. We hope that this book will cater the requirements of the students and researchers interested in this field.

The purpose of this book is to introduce the reader to the fundamental concepts of soft computing as a methodological tool. We assume that the reader has rudimentary knowledge of computing and computer programming. Requirement of prior mathematical knowledge is kept at bare minimal. After reading this book, the reader will be able to

- Analyze a given computational task to recognize the appropriateness, or otherwise, of applying soft computing techniques for a solution,
- Design a soft computing system required to address a computational task,
- Implement a soft computing system for a computational task,
- Explain the principles and techniques of soft computing to a learner with knowledge of computer basics.

Compared to other papers of computer science and engineering, information technology, master of computer applications, and related courses, there are very few textbooks on soft computing available in the market. We have tried to provide a truly learner-friendly textbook on the subject. With this purpose in mind, we have adopted an approach of presenting the contents in a manner which is characterized by the following features:

- Clarity of concepts, rather than mathematical rigour, is given priority.
- The concepts are presented, as far as practicable, in an inductive manner rather than being deductive.
- Topics are explained with an ample number of illustrative examples.
- Numerous solved problems are provided at the end of each chapter to help the learner develop problem-solving skills in the area of soft computing.
- Each chapter is augmented with a section entitled 'Test Your Knowledge' in which adequate number of MCQ-type test items are given. This will help the learner to review the knowledge acquired.

For the sake of enhanced learning experience and efficient attainment of learning objectives, other features are incorporated including a list of key concepts as well as the chapter outline at the beginning of each chapter, a summary, bibliography and historical notes at the end of each chapter, and the exercises, of course.

There are thirteen chapters in this book. Apart from Chapter 1 (Introduction), the contents are presented in the rest of the twelve chapters. These twelve chapters can be structured in four modules as detailed below:

Module I (*Fuzzy Systems and Rough Set Theory*): Containing Chapters 2, 3, 4, and 5 on Fuzzy Sets, Fuzzy Logic, Fuzzy Inference Systems, and Rough Sets, respectively.

Module II (*Artificial Neural Networks*): Containing Chapters 6, 7, 8, 9, and 10 on Artificial Neural Networks: Basic Concepts, Elementary Pattern Classifiers, Pattern Associators, Competitive Neural Nets, and Backpropagation, respectively.

Module III (*Intelligent Search Strategies*): Containing Chapters 11 and 12 on Elementary Search Techniques and Advanced Search Techniques, respectively.

Module IV (*Hybrid Systems*): Containing Chapter 13 on Hybrid Systems.

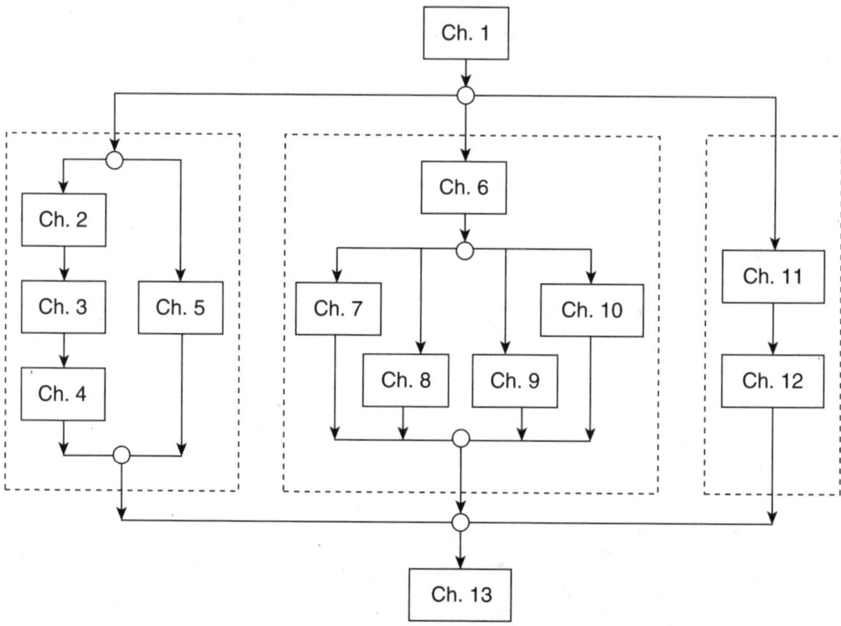

Dependency relations among the chapters of the book

Modules I, II, and III can be studied almost independently. However, there are dependencies among the chapters within a module. These dependencies are depicted in the above figure. The learner may choose the most convenient learning path on the basis of the dependencies depicted in this figure.

While writing this book, we have consciously adopted a learner-centric approach of content delivery. The challenge was to present the text lucidly without diluting the subject matter, so that the book becomes an effective learning material on the subject. Whether this is achieved can only be judged by the reader.

Kolkata
Dec. 31, 2012

Samir Roy
samir.cst@gmail.com

Udit Chakraborty
udit.kc@gmail.com

ACKNOWLEDGEMENTS

This book is a result of the collective efforts of many individuals. We thank Pearson Education for their positive response to the initial book proposal and eventual publication of the book on time. In particular, we are grateful to Neha Goomer (Assistant Editor, Acquisitions), Anita Sharma (Senior Executive, Rights and Contracts), and V. Pavithra (Associate Editor, Production) for their efforts to expedite the execution of the project. We also thank the editorial board and Deepti Goel (Assistant Designer, Production) for the impressive cover design they created for this book. Our individual acknowledgements are given below:

At the outset, I want to express my sense of gratitude to my students whose interactions have kept me alive, intellectually and spiritually, for all these years. It is my privilege to remain in touch with the fresh minds I encounter in the classrooms. I am immensely grateful to my colleagues at the National Institute of Technical Teachers' Training and Research (NITTTR), Kolkata. I especially thank Prof. R. Dasgupta, Head, Department of Computer Science and Engineering, NITTTR, Kolkata, for his understanding, encouragement, and support. I also thank Sri R. Chatterjee, Assistant Professor, Department of Computer Science and Engineering, NITTTR, Kolkata, for the many, many hours of invigorating discussion sessions, and Indra, Mainak, and Utpal for creating a friendly atmosphere and for their readiness to help. I also thank my fellow academicians, researchers, and students at various other educational institutions including the University of Calcutta, Bengal Engineering and Science University (Shibpur), and West Bengal University of Technology.

I thank my wife Sukla for taking me for granted. Thanks to my son Biswaroop and my daughter Deepshikha for accepting the unavoidable hazards of being my children.

Samir Roy
samir.cst@gmail.com

I thank my friends and colleagues at the Sikkim Manipal Institute of Technology for their inspiration. Special thanks to Brig. (Dr) S. N. Misra (Retd), Hon'ble Vice Chancellor, Sikkim Manipal University, Maj. Gen. (Dr) S. S. Dasaka, SM, VSM (Retd), Director, Sikkim Manipal Institute of Technology and Prof. M. K. Ghose, Head, Department of Computer Science and Engineering, Sikkim Manipal Institute of Technology for their continuous support and encouragement. I am also obliged to the students of MCSE 105 (Aug–Dec 2012) with whom a large part of the text was discussed.

I cannot thank my parents enough, for the pain they have endured and the sacrifices they had made to grant me good education. I hope this brings a smile on their faces. My wife has been really tough on me when I relaxed more than planned. The low deadline miss count goes to her credit. I must thank my elder sister for standing like a rock and taking all the blows on the family front so that I could concentrate on my work.

Finally, my apologies, to Doibee, my daughter of two-and-half years, for bearing with the compromise on the quality of her bedtime stories.

Udit Chakraborty
udit.kc@gmail.com

About the Authors

Samir Roy is presently working as a Professor and Head, Dept. of Computer Science & Engineering, National Institute of Technical Teachers' Training and Research, Kolkata, an autonomous institution under the Ministry of Human Resource Development, Government of India. He graduated with honours in Physics from the Presidency College, Kolkata, in 1985, and subsequently obtained the bachelors, masters, and doctoral degrees in computer science and engineering. After serving as a Scientific Officer for a brief period at IIT Kharagpur, he took up teaching as his primary occupation. He has about twenty years of teaching experience in different areas of computer science both at the undergraduate and postgraduate levels at various engineering colleges and training institutes. He has written and presented more than forty articles in international and national journals and in conference proceedings. His areas of interest include artificial intelligence, soft computing, mathematical logic and educational informatics.

Udit K. Chakraborty obtained his bachelors and masters in computer science and engineering from the North Eastern Regional Institute of Science and Technology and the Sikkim Manipal University of Health, Medical and Technological Science, respectively. He is currently working with the Sikkim Manipal Institute of Technology as an Associate Professor in the Department of Computer Science and Engineering and has about ten years of teaching experience. His areas of interest include soft computing, natural language processing and algorithms. He has published several research papers in national and international conferences.

1

INTRODUCTION

Key Concepts

Ant colony, Artificial neural networks (ANN), Belief propagation, Boundary regions, Curve fitting, Darwin, Evolutionary search, Fuzzy control, Fuzzy-evolutionary, Fuzzy inference, Fuzzy systems, Genetic algorithms (GAs), Hybrid systems, Imprecision, Inexactness, Information systems, Law of excluded middle, Learning, Measurement, Natural selection, Neuro-fuzzy, Neuro-genetic, Optimization, Pattern association, Pattern classification, Pattern clustering, Perception, Probabilistic reasoning, Rough sets, Simulated annealing (SA), Soft computing, State space search, Supervised learning, Survival of the fittest, Swarm optimization, Training pairs, Unsupervised learning, Vagueness

Chapter Outline

What is soft computing? How does it differ from traditional 'hard' computing? What are its main components and how do they relate to each other? What are the basic traits of a soft computing technique? These are relevant questions that any inquisitive mind will ask while approaching a text on the subject. While clear answers to these questions can only emerge out of careful study and practice of the subject, some indicators need to be available to the sincere learner at the very outset. This chapter is intended to provide some ideas about the spirit of soft computing as a computational process.

1.1 WHAT IS SOFT COMPUTING?

Well, the obvious answer to this question is, '*soft computing is computing which is not hard*'. But this candid answer might not satisfy some people who are so inherently skeptic as to ask further, '*then what is hard computing*?' The rest of this chapter is dedicated to these skeptics.

The phrase 'soft computing' was coined by Lotfi A. Zadeh, a pioneer in this field, in the early 1990s. The question 'What is soft computing?' can be answered from various perspectives, e.g., its methodological traits, problem solving abilities, constraints, and so on. In fact a complete understanding of the term 'soft computing' is possible only when all these perspectives are taken into consideration. In this introductory text, we will certainly try our best to build this holistic view of soft computing, but presently we start by focusing our attention on what is readily available to us, the phrase 'soft computing'.

The term 'soft computing' consists of two words, 'soft' and 'computing'. Assuming that we have a fairly good idea of what 'computing' is, let us focus our attention on the remaining keyword, i.e., 'soft' which is opposite to 'hard'. Table 1.1 presents certain characteristics that we tend to associate with these two contrasting words.

Table 1.1. *Hard vs. soft*

Hard	Soft
Rigid	Flexible
Fixed	Movable/Adjustable
Systematic	Random
Well-defined	Vague
Exact	Inexact/Approximate
Precise	Imprecise
Measurable	Perceivable
Solid	Porous/fluid
Deterministic	Non-deterministic
...	...

Taking a cue from the words closely associated with 'hard' and 'soft', we may expect that soft computing somehow relates to flexibility, imprecision, inexactness, vagueness, randomness, non-determinism and so on either as computational process, or the computational problems they try to solve. Indeed, these traits distinguish soft computing from hard computing.

In real life we keep on confronting and handling situations characterized by soft qualities. Let us consider a few.

(a) *Parking a car on a narrow parking space.* You want to park a car within a narrow parking space. The available space is just enough to keep the car. You don't need to measure the exact length or breadth of the space. Nor you need to know the exact coordinates of the car's final position. However, you successfully assess the situation and maneuver the car in a way such that the car is finally parked properly.

(b) *Recognition of handwritten characters.* There are infinite variations in the shape of an alphanumeric character written by people. None of them exactly match the printed character. In printed form too, the same character have different shapes in different fonts. Add to this the variation due to size, writing material, colour, the surface on which the characters are written etc. In spite of all these deviations from the 'ideal' shape, we have no difficulty in recognizing a handwritten character. It seems that our brain do not process the image of such an entity pixel by pixel but as a whole. This is again in sharp contrast with the conventional hard computing paradigm.

(c) *Collection of food by ants.* When the ants look for food they start by traveling in random directions. Many ants go out of the ant-hill simultaneously and individually search for food in various directions. However, when the source of food is discovered by one or a few ants, they return to their ant-hill and convey this message to other ants. Gradually, the movements of the entire population of the ants (i.e. those who are engaged in searching and collecting food) converge to a line joining the source of food and the ant-hill. And, this line is usually along the shortest distance between the source and the destination.

Situation (a), that of parking a car on a narrow parking space, is an instance of a problem whose description is imprecise in the sense that the exact measurement of the dimensions of the parking space is not available. In fact, such exact values are neither necessary, nor desirable because it is not a precision job at all. Also unavailable are the dimensions of the car (we do not bother about those figures while parking), and the coordinates of the wheels when the car is finally parked. This is a typical situation where exactitude, or precision, in the description of the problem as well as the solution is neither available, nor necessary.

Situation (b), that of recognition of handwritten characters, exemplify the distinctive nature of human perception as opposed to traditional computational process based on instruction fetch and execute cycle. It seems that the human brain perceives a pattern as a whole, not pixel by pixel. Moreover, small deviations, or incompleteness of description, or similar aberrations from the ideal pattern do not prevent us from recognizing the pattern correctly. This remarkable capacity of human brain is the result of the structure of the brain that allows immense parallelism. There is another important phenomenon called learning. Conventional computation does not model learning. Rather, it is based on the idea of an algorithm as an embodiment of procedural knowledge already learnt by the programmer.

The third situation, the behaviour of ants while searching for food, is an instance of nature's wisdom to achieve betterment over time. This is similar to an optimization process. A more elaborate optimization process undertaken by nature is the evolution of higher order species from lower ones over millions and millions of years by means of natural selection. Randomness is a necessary ingredient of these processes. However, such randomness is not unconstrained. Randomness is necessary to explore possibilities, but at the same time, it must be supported by direction. This is ensured by various mechanisms. For example, in biological evolution the upthrust is provided by natural selection guided by Darwinian principle of survival of the fittest. In ant colonies, this is provided by accumulation of a chemical called pheromone deposited by the ants along the frequently visited paths. Moreover, the target of optimization is also 'softened' in these processes. This is because, unlike traditional optimization, here we do not insist on 'the' optimal solution because we may have to wait too long to receive the best solution. Rather, a near-optimal solution available at a convenient time is accepted. The fact is that certain problems are computationally so complex that finding the best solution would take ages by even the fastest computer. For most practical purposes, a quickly available near-optimal solution at the expense of a slight, probable, compromise in quality is acceptable.

What is soft computing then? It is not a single computational technique. Soft computing is a family of techniques with capacity to solve a class of problems for which other conventional techniques are found to be inadequate. The principal components of soft computing, as on today, includes fuzzy systems (fuzzy set theory, fuzzy logic, fuzzy inference systems etc.), rough set theory, artificial neural networks, probabilistic reasoning, and evolutionary search strategies (including genetic algorithms, simulated annealing, ant colony optimization, swarm optimization etc.). Table 1.2 provides a summary of the domains of these components of soft computing.

Table 1.2. *Soft Computing Techniques*

#	Technique	Application domain
1	Fuzzy systems	Vagueness / imprecision / inexactness / Approximate reasoning
2	Rough sets	Vagueness / inexactness in information systems
3	Artificial neural networks	Learning and curve fitting / Pattern classification, association, clustering
4	Probabilistic reasoning	Uncertainty and belief propagation
5	Evolutionary searches	Complex optimization

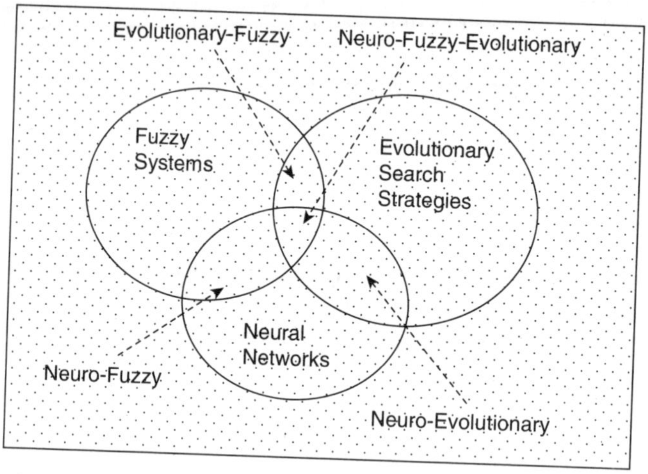

Fig. 1.1. *Synergy among the principal components of soft computing*

It should be noted that while each of these techniques can be applied in isolation to solve problems of related domains, they can work together synergistically. The fact is, soft computing is not just a collection of several techniques, but is a family of highly interacting and complementary techniques.

For instance, artificial neural networks generally lack certain characteristics that are present in fuzzy logic. On the other hand, fuzzy systems cannot learn, adapt, or support parallelism though these are clearly present in neural nets. This observation prompted researchers to develop neuro-fuzzy systems that are highly successful hybrid systems. The complementary role of fuzzy logic and neuro-computing helps a neuro-fuzzy system overcome the limitations of both constituents. Actually, hybridization is a central theme of soft computing. Various hybrid soft computing systems, e.g., neuro-fuzzy systems, fuzzy neural networks, genetic fuzzy systems, fuzzy-evolutionary algorithms, genetic-neural networks etc. have been developed in past years and are being developed. Fig. 1.1 gives a graphical view of hybridization in soft computing.

What are the essential properties that bring all these diverse methodologies together under the common umbrella named 'soft computing'? We can safely say that a computation that deliberately incorporates imprecision on one or more levels of computation resulting either in a change, in fact decrease, in the 'granularity' of the problem, or relaxing the goal of optimization at some stage, is a kind of soft computing. So the effect of including imprecision is a relaxation either at the level of description of the problem, or the level of achievement of the goal. However, it should be noted that the imprecision is not a target. It is a means to achieve practical solution to a given complex problem.

Soft computing can also be considered as a tool to tackle imprecision and uncertainty. As stated by Zadeh, the guiding principle of soft computing is to exploit the tolerance for imprecision, uncertainty, partial truth, and approximation to achieve tractability, robustness, low cost etc. Real life problems are full of uncomfortable characteristics due to partial, vague, noisy, and incomplete information. Under such circumstances, hard computing techniques are not appropriate. In this context, it is worthwhile to ponder over the difference between measurement and perception. While measurements are exact, perceptions are vague. We, the humans, have a wonderful capacity to perform numerous tasks, physical as well as mental, without any measurement or calculations. While science has been motivated to progress from perception to measurement, soft computing perhaps will enable us to return to perception. Hence soft computing may lead in future to computing with words and perceptions.

In the rest of this chapter, we will try to appreciate the spirit of soft computing by a quick review of the basic principles of its components.

1.2 FUZZY SYSTEMS

Fuzzy set theory is an extension, or generalization, of the classical, occasionally referred to as crisp, set theory. Our everyday conversation is full of vague and imprecise concepts, e.g., 'Uncle Sam is tall' or 'It is very cold today'. It is difficult if not impossible to translate such statements into more precise language because such an effort results in losing some of their semantic values. If, instead of saying 'It is very cold today' someone says 'Today's temperature is 5°C', or, instead of saying 'Uncle Sam is tall' we say 'Uncle Sam's height is 5 ft 10 inch', aren't we losing some of the meanings of the statements mentioned above? It seems that in real life, vagueness is not only unavoidable but also desirable to some extent.

As stated earlier, science tries to replace perception with measurement. However, more and more we are facing situations in science and technology where there is a need to retain perception into the system. For instance, consider the case of designing an expert system to embody the diagnostic power of a physician. In his effort to codify the physician's decision making process, the designer discovers that the physician's approach to diagnosis or medication is largely intuitive though supported by various test results and measurements. Accepting vagueness as a valid element of model of reality, instead of trying to mould reality into crisp measurements, is the natural way to implement such applications.

Fuzzy set theory, which effectively models vagueness in its mathematical formulation, is naturally extended to logic. Logic is the study of the structures and principles of reasoning and sound argument. Classical logic is based on the famous 'law of excluded middle'. This law states that every statement must be either true or false. There was strong opposition to this view even in ancient times. Greek philosopher Heraclitus opined that statements could be simultaneously true and false. The central theme of fuzzy logic was upheld by Plato who indicated that there was a third region beyond true or false. In recent past, the systematic alternative to bi-valued logic of Aristotle was proposed by Lukasiewicz in early 1900s. Lukasiewicz proposed a 3-valued (true, false, and 'possible') logic, followed by 4-valued and later 5-valued logics. The modern, infinite-valued fuzzy logic was proposed by LA Zadeh in 1965. In real life we face situations where there is no sharp distinction between truth and falsehood. Rather, there are infinite shades of truths between absolute truth and absolute falsehood. Fuzzy logic accepts this state of affair and builds a system of reasoning on the basis of infinite shades of truth. Fuzzy logic is one of the most successful theories in terms of practical applications. An important class of applications is based on the idea of fuzzy inference system. This is a kind of input-output mapping based on fuzzy logic.

These systems have been applied in machine control and are popularly known as fuzzy control systems. The advantage of fuzzy inference systems is that here the solution to the problem can be cast in terms of familiar human operators. Hence, the human experience can be used in the design of the controller. Engineers developed numerous fuzzy controllers for industrial applications and consumer products.

1.3 ROUGH SETS

Fuzzy sets and fuzzy logic have modeled vagueness in terms of partial membership and partial truth respectively. Another model of vagueness has gained importance in recent past. The concept of rough sets, proposed by Z Pawlak, considers vagueness from a different perspective. Here vagueness is expressed, instead of set membership, in terms of *boundary regions* of a set of *objects*. In large reservoir of multidimensional data, occasionally it is not possible to decide with certainty whether a given object belongs to a set or not. Such objects are said to form a *boundary regions* for the set. If the boundary region is empty, then the set is crisp, otherwise it is *rough*. A non-empty boundary region exists due to insufficient knowledge to define the set with certainty. There are many interesting applications of the rough set theory including knowledge acquisition, decision analysis, knowledge discovery from databases, expert systems, inductive reasoning etc.

1.4 ARTIFICIAL NEURAL NETWORKS

A computer program embodies a ready made procedural knowledge that the programmer has acquired and then translated with the help of a programming language. Superiority of the brain over computer is largely ascribed to brain's capacity to learn from experience. The slow process of learning enables man to perform certain tasks, e.g., recognition, classification, association, clustering etc. in a highly efficient manner.

Artificial neural networks (ANNs) are inspired by the structure and functionality of the brain. There are nearly 100 billion neurons in a normal human brain. Each neuron is locally connected to its neighbouring neurons. The neurons have elementary capacities like summing up the incoming signals and then passing it on to the neighbours conditionally. Human consciousness is the outcome of the collective activities of these 100 billion neurons. In a computer information is stored as localized bits. An ANN preserves information as weights of interconnections among its processing units. Thus, as in the brain, information in ANNs too resides in a distributed manner, resulting in greater fault tolerance. Moreover, multiple data may be superimposed on the same ANN for storage purpose. Like the human brain, ANNs also perform computation in terms of patterns rather than data.

Pattern classification is the task of deciding whether the input pattern, usually a vector, belongs to a certain class or category. In real life, we encounter pattern classification tasks quite often. For instance, we may need to classify a cell, on the basis of its image, as cancer-affected or otherwise.

Another common human experience is pattern association. It takes place when we relate a given pattern to one already stored in memory. We do associate patterns in our daily life almost without any conscious effort. Examples are, recognition of a known face from an image (either distorted, or undistorted), visualizing a flower from its fragrance, remembering a distant past on hearing a particular tune etc. In computing, retrieval of a stored pattern corresponding to an input pattern is known as pattern association. Associative memory neural nets are those which store a set of pattern associations. There are two kinds of associative memory neural nets. The associations may be auto (the input and the stored patterns are identical), or hetero (the input and the stored patterns are different).

Neural nets are trained by providing sample classification data over and over again and making adjustments in their weight vectors so that they become 'experienced' enough to classify unknown patterns successfully. Learning is either supervised or unsupervised. When learning takes place in presence of a teacher the learner has the opportunity to get corrected by the teacher when he commits a mistake. This is supervised learning. A self-learner, in contrast, does not have a teacher and therefore he has to identify an error as well as get it corrected all by himself. Similarly, learning by ANN is either supervised or unsupervised, depending on the availability of training data. By training data we mean a set of pairs of input–output vectors. In presence of such data, the ANN can measure the deviation from desired output values when the net is presented with an input pattern. Supervised learning by an ANN takes place in this way. However, in the absence of such training pairs, the ANN has to adjust itself on its own. Usually some kind of competition facilitates unsupervised learning. There are various ANNs, e.g., Kohonen's self organizing map (SOM), learning vector quantization (LVQ), etc. that act on the basis of unsupervised learning. This text contains discussions on the fundamental ANNs including Hebb nets, Perceptrons, ADALINE, MADALINE etc. as pattern classifiers, Hopfield nets and bidirectional associative memory (BAM) as associative networks, Kohonen's self organizing map (SOM), learning vector quantization (LVQ), adaptive resonance theory (ART) as competitive networks, back propagation networks, etc.

1.5 EVOLUTIONARY SEARCH STRATEGIES

Quite often, intelligent computing takes the form of a state space search. A state space is a graph where the nodes represent the 'states' relating to a computational problem and the directed edges represent possible moves from one problem state to another. Starting with the initial state, the requirement is to reach a 'goal' state by traversing a suitable path through the graph. The state spaces are often huge in size and finding a solution, or a path to the solution, may prove to be highly computation intensive process. In this text we discuss the exhaustive search techniques, e.g., breadth-first search, depth-first search, depth-first iterative deepening etc., as well as various heuristic search strategies.

Complex optimization problems require advanced search techniques to obtain workable solutions within reasonable time frame. Classical optimization techniques can be used only on continuous and differentiable functions. However, often such well behaved functions are not available for certain optimization problems. Moreover, classical search techniques have a tendency to settle down at local optima instead of the global best. There are computational problems which require tremendous computational efforts to find the best solution. Intelligent search strategies like hill climbing may be employed to obtain reasonably good solutions to such problems. However, hill climbing suffers from the serious problem of settling to sub-optimal solutions remaining in the search space as local optimal points. Genetic Algorithms (GAs) and Simulated Annealing (SA) are two search strategies that are inspired by natural evolutionary processes and have the capacity to overcome the problem posed by the existence of local optima in large search spaces. GAs are inspired by the process of natural evolution. The mechanism applied by nature in evolution is natural selection based on the Darwinian principle of survival of the fittest. It is essentially a maximization process. Simulated Annealing (SA) mimics the process of physical annealing. In physical annealing a metal is initially heated to a molten state and then gradually cooled to get a uniform crystal structure. This uniform crystal structure corresponds to a minimal energy level. Hence annealing is a minimization process. The GAs and SAs are extensively applied to solve optimization problems of highly complex nature.

CHAPTER SUMMARY

The forgoing introductory discussion on the nature and constituents of soft computing can be summarized in the following way.

- The term 'soft computing' was coined by LA Zadeh in early 1990s and can be interpreted from various perspectives, e.g., its methodological traits, problem-solving abilities, constraints, and so on. A complete understanding of the term 'soft computing' is possible only when all these perspectives are taken into consideration.
- Soft computing is a family of techniques with capacity to solve a class of problems for which other conventional techniques are found to be inadequate. The principal components of soft computing include fuzzy systems, rough set theory, artificial neural networks (ANNs), probabilistic reasoning, and evolutionary search strategies including genetic algorithms (GAs), simulated annealing (SA), ant colony optimization, swarm optimization etc.
- Fuzzy systems are systems built on fuzzy set theory and fuzzy logic. These systems try to model vagueness, or inexactness, which is a necessary ingredient of everyday interactions and activities. Fuzzy set theory accommodates vagueness by allowing set membership values to lie anywhere between 0 and 1, both inclusive. Fuzzy logic violates the Aristotelian law of excluded middle and allows a statement to be true to any extent between absolute falsehood and absolute truth.
- In rough set theory, vagueness is expressed, instead of set membership, in terms of boundary regions of a set of objects. If the boundary region is empty, then the set is crisp, otherwise it is rough.
- Artificial neural nets are networks of processing elements that follow a computational paradigm akin to that of the human brain. These are efficient structures to classify, associate and cluster patterns. Like human brain, the artificial neural nets need to be trained to carry out the designated task. Learning by ANN could be either supervised, or unsupervised. Supervised learning is assisted by training data and unsupervised learning takes place in absence of any training data.
- Complex optimization problems require advanced search techniques to obtain workable solutions within reasonable time frame. Genetic Algorithms (GAs) and Simulated Annealing (SA) are two search strategies that are inspired by natural evolutionary processes and have the capacity to overcome the problem posed by the existence of local optima in large search spaces. While GA is a maximization process, SA is a minimization process.

✓ TEST YOUR KNOWLEDGE

1.1 Which of the following traits is expected in a soft computing technique?
  a) Precision measurement b) Exactitude
  c) Absolute truth/falsehood d) None of the above

1.2 Which of the following traits is not expected in a soft computing technique?
  a) Randomness b) Softening of goal
  c) Vagueness d) None of the above

1.3 Fuzzy logic is a soft computing technique to deal with
  a) Vagueness b) Learning
  c) Optimization d) None of the above

1.4 Which of the following soft computing techniques is employed to solve complex optimization problems?
   a) Fuzzy logic b) Artificial neural nets
   c) Rough sets d) None of the above
1.5 Simulated annealing is a soft computing technique to deal with
   a) Vagueness b) Learning
   c) Optimization d) None of the above
1.6 Which of the following is associated with artificial neural nets?
   a) Vagueness b) Learning
   c) Optimization d) None of the above
1.7 The soft computing technique to deal with vagueness in information systems is
   a) Artificial neural nets b) Rough set theory
   c) Genetic algorithms d) None of the above
1.8 Which of the following is based on the law of excluded middle?
   a) Predicate Logic b) Rough set theory
   c) Fuzzy logic d) None of the above
1.9 Which of the following theories models vagueness in terms of boundary regions?
   a) Probability theory b) Rough set theory
   c) Fuzzy set theory d) None of the above
1.10 Which of the following search techniques has the capacity to overcome the problem of local optima?
   a) Genetic algorithms b) Simulated annealing
   c) Both (*a*) and (*b*) d) None of the above

Answers

1.1 (d)	1.2 (d)	1.3 (a)	1.4 (d)	1.5 (c)
1.6 (b)	1.7 (b)	1.8 (a)	1.9 (b)	1.10 (c)

EXERCISES

1.1 The vagueness we are accustomed to in our everyday conversation is not just lack of exact measurement but has a semantic content. Critically assess the above statement.
1.2 Identify the basic traits of soft computing as computational process and briefly explain how these traits help us in problem solving.

BIBLIOGRAPHY AND HISTORICAL NOTES

The history of soft computing dates back to the early stages of digital computers when scientists were probing human brain and neural systems in an effort to develop machines on the basis of the brain model. However, as stated earlier, the term 'soft computing' is the brainchild of L A Zadeh who coined it in early 1990s. Consolidation of soft computing as a collection of various synergistically complementary computational techniques is a phenomenon of the last two decades. A selected list of pioneering literature on this emerging field of computer science is presented below.

Goldberg, D. E. (1989). *Genetic algorithms in search, optimization and machine learning.* Addision–Wesley.

Grossberg, S. (1982). *Studies of mind and brain.* Boston, Reidel.

Holland, J. H. (1975). *Adaptation in natural and artificial systems.* Ann Arbor: University of Michigan Press.

Hopfield, J. J. and Tank, D.W. (1986). Computing with neural circuits. *Science*, Vol. 233, pp. 625–633.

Kirkpatrik, S., Gelatt, C. D., and Vecchi, M. P. (1983). Optimization by simulated annealing. *Science*, Vol. 220, pp. 671–680.

Li, X., Ruan, D. and Van der Wal, A. J. (1998). Discussion on soft computing at FLINS96. *International Journal of Intelligent Systems*, Vol. 13, No. 2-3, pp. 287–300.

Magdalena, L. (2010). What is soft computing? Revisiting possible answers. *International Journal of Computational Intelligence Systems*, Vol. 3, No. 2, pp. 148–159.

Pawlak, Z. (1982). Rough sets. *International Journal of Computer and Information Sciences*, Vol. 11, pp. 341–356.

Skowron, A. and Rauszer, C. (1992). *The discernibility matrices and functions in information systems.* In *Intelligent Decision Support - Handbook of Applications and Advances of the Rough Sets Theory*, R. Slowiński (ed.). Dordrecht: Kluwer, pp. 331–362.

Von Neumann, J. (1958). *The computer and the brain*. New Haven: Yale University Press.

Zadeh, L. A. (1994). Soft computing and fuzzy logic. *IEEE Software*, Vol. 11, No. 6, pp. 48–56.

Zadeh, L. A. (2001). Forward. *Applied Soft Computing*, Vol. 1, No. 1, pp. 1–2.

Zadeh, L. A. (2002). From computing with numbers to computing with words – From manipulation of measurements to manipulation of perceptions. *International Journal of Applied Mathematics and Computer Science*, Vol. 12, No. 3, pp. 307–324.

2

FUZZY SETS

Key Concepts

α-cut, α-cut decomposition theorem, Classical/Fuzzy sets, Composition, Concentration, Contrast intensification, Core, Dilation, Fuzzification, Fuzziness/Vagueness/Inexactness, Fuzzy cardinality, Fuzzy Cartesian product, Fuzzy extension principle, Fuzzy membership, Fuzzy membership function, Fuzzy relations, Gaussian function, Height, Level set, Max-min composition, Membership functions, Normality, Normalization, Relation matrix, Restricted scalar multiplication, S-function, Singleton, Support, Trapezoidal function, Triangular function

Chapter Outline

This chapter presents the basic concepts of fuzzy set theory. The fuzzy set theory is an extension, or generalization, of the classical, occasionally referred to as crisp, set theory in the sense that the latter can be considered as a special case of the former. Hence the chapter starts with a review of the fundamentals of the classical set theory. Elementary concepts of fuzzy set theory, e.g., membership functions, transformations on membership functions, linguistic variables, fuzzy set operations etc. are presented along with illustrative examples in sections 2.2, 2.3 and 2.4. This is followed by a discussion on fuzzy relations and related matters in Section 2.4. The chapter ends with a presentation of the fuzzy extension principle that provides a technique to map a function from the crisp domain to its equivalent in the fuzzy domain.

2.1 CRISP SETS: A REVIEW

The notion of a set is of fundamental importance in Mathematics. It can be informally defined in the following way.

Definition 2.1 (*Set*) A set is a collection of distinct *elements*, or *members*, without repetition and without ordering.

Example 2.1 (*Set*)

Consider the set *atomic particles* = {*electron, proton, neutron*}. Since a set is defined by its members without regard to ordering or repetitions, the set of atomic particles cited above is identical to the set {*proton, neutron, electron*}, or the set {*neutron, proton, neutron, electron, proton, proton*}

There are two ways to describe a set. The most obvious one is by enumerating the members of the set. However, occasionally it is convenient to describe a set by citing a property common to all the members of the set. Both of these kinds of set notations are exemplified below.

Example 2.2 (*Set Notations*)

The sets A, B, C, D given below are described by enumeration of its members.

A = {*Jack, Jill, hill, pail, water*}
$B = \{+, -, \times, \div\}$
C = {*Socrates, toothbrush, loneliness*, 235}
D = {*Monday, Tuesday, Wednesday, Thursday, Friday, Saturday, Sunday*}

The set D of all days of a week can be equivalently expressed by citing the property shared by its member. Thus,

$D = \{x \mid x \text{ is a day of the week}\}$

A few other sets described in similar way are

$E = \{x \mid x \text{ is an integer, and } -1 \le x \le +1\}\} = \{-1, 0, +1\}$
$F = \{x \mid x \text{ is a prime number}\}$
$G = \{x \mid x \text{ is a polygon}\}$
$H = \{x \mid x \text{ is an element having 8 electrons in its outermost shell}\}$

The elementary concepts of classical set theory are presented in the following section.

2.1.1 Basic Concepts

This subsection provides the basic set theoretic concepts, e.g. cardinality of a set, the null set, the universal set, belongingness to a set, subset, superset and so on.

Definition 2.2 (*Cardinality of a Set*) The number of elements in a set S is termed as its cardinality and is denoted as $|S|$.

Example 2.3 (*Cardinality of a set*)

A set can be finite or infinite, depending on whether it has a finite or infinite number of elements. For example, the sets A, B, C, D and H in Example 2.2 are finite sets with cardinalities $|A| = 5$, $|B| = 4$, $|C| = 4$, and $|D| = 7$. What is the size of H ? Among the sets mentioned in Example 2.2 the sets F and G are infinite sets.

The Null Set and the Universal Set There are two specially interesting sets, viz. the **null (empty)** set and the **universal** set. These are usually represented by the symbols $\varnothing$ and U, respectively. The null set is the set without any member, so that $|\varnothing| = 0$. The universal set, on the other hand, is the set of all possible elements in a certain context.

Example 2.4 (*The null set and the universal set*)

Let X be the set of all natural numbers that are divisible by 4 but not divisible by 2. As there is no such integer which is divisible by 4 but not divisible by 2, $X = \varnothing$. Similarly, the set of positively charged electrons is also the null set. Moreover, we may define a set $S = \{x \mid x$ is blue-eyed$\}$ in the context of the universal set of all human beings. Then S is the set of all blue-eyed persons and U is the set of all human beings. However, if U is the set of all living creatures, then S is the set of all blue-eyed creatures including, but not limited to, all blue-eyed human beings.

An element x is said to **belong** to a set S, expressed as $x \in S$, if x is included in S. Otherwise x does not belong to S, written as $x \notin S$. For example, for the set $F = \{x \mid x$ is a prime number$\}$, $3 \in F$, as 3 is a prime number, but $4 \notin F$.

Definition 2.3 (*Subset*) A set T is said to be a subset of set S, written as $T \subseteq S$, if every element of T is in S, i.e., $\forall x$ if $x \in T$, then $x \in S$. Equivalently, S is superset of T, symbolized as $S \supseteq T$, if and only if T is a subset of S.

T is a **proper subset** of S, denoted as $T \subset S$, if $T \subseteq S$ and $T \neq S$. Hence, if $T \subset S$, then there is at least one member x such that $x \in S$ but $x \notin T$. For an arbitrary set S the following properties are obvious from the definitions cited above.

(i) $\varnothing \subseteq S$
(ii) $S \subseteq U$
(iii) $S \subseteq S$

Moreover, the chain rule applies to set inclusion operation, i.e., for any three sets A, B, C, if $A \subseteq B$ and $B \subseteq C$, then $A \subseteq C$.

Definition 2.4 (*Equality of Sets*) Two sets S and T are equal if every element of S is in T and vice versa. In other words, $S = T$, if and only if, $S \subseteq T$ and $T \subseteq S$.

Definition 2.5 (*Power Set*) Given a set S, the power set of S, denoted as $P(S)$, or 2^S, is the set of all subsets of S.

Example 2.5 (*Power Set*)

Let us consider the set $S = \{black, white\}$. Then $P(S) = 2^S = \{\varnothing, \{black\}, \{white\}, \{black, white\}\}$. Obviously, if $|S| = n$, then $|P(S)| = |2^S| = 2^n$. Similarly, if $S = \{electron, proton, neutron\}$, then $P(S) = 2^S = \{\varnothing, \{electron\}, \{proton\}, \{neutron\}, \{electron, proton\}, \{proton, neutron\}, \{electron, neutron\}, \{electron, proton, neutron\}\}$.

2.1.2 Operations on Sets

There are three basic operations on sets, viz. *union* ($\cup$), *intersection* ($\cap$), and *complementation* ($'$).

Definition 2.6 (*Set Union*) Given two sets P and Q, the union of P and Q, denoted as $P \cup Q$, is the set of all elements either in P, or in Q, or in both P and Q.

$$P \cup Q = \{x \mid x \in P \text{ or } x \in Q\}$$

Definition 2.7 (*Set Intersection*) Given two sets P and Q, the intersection of P and Q, denoted as $P \cap Q$, is the set of all elements both in P, and Q.

$$P \cap Q = \{x \mid x \in P \text{ and } x \in Q\}$$

Definition 2.8 (*Complement of a Set*) The complement of P, denoted as P', $\overline{P}$, $\neg P$, or $\sim P$, is the set of all elements (of U) outside P.

$$P' = \{x \mid x \notin P\}$$

There are various notations for complementation, as indicated in the definition. However, in this book we shall denote the complement of P as P'.

Definition 2.9 (*Difference between Sets*) The difference of set P from Q, denoted as $P - Q$, is the set of all elements in P but not in Q.

$$P - Q = \{x \mid x \in P \text{ and } x \notin Q\}$$

It is easy to prove that $P - Q = P \cap Q'$

Definition 2.10 (*Symmetric Difference*) The symmetric difference of P and Q, denoted as $P \oplus Q$, is the set of all elements that are either in P, or in Q, but not in both P and Q.

$$\begin{aligned} P \oplus Q &= \{x \mid (x \in P \text{ and } x \notin Q), \text{ or } (x \in Q \text{ and } x \notin P)\} \\ &= (P - Q) \cup (Q - P) \\ &= (P \cap Q') \cup (P' \cap Q) \end{aligned}$$

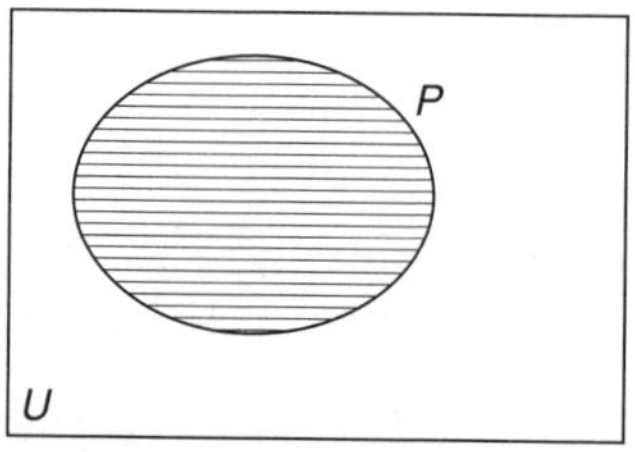

Fig. 2.1. *Venn diagram of set P*

Venn Diagrams Quite often it is convenient to represent a set theoretic expression visually with the help of a diagram called Venn diagram. Usually, a Venn diagram consists of a rectangle presenting the universal set U with other sets presented with the help of circles / ovals inside the rectangle. For example, the Venn diagram of a set S is presented in Fig. 2.1. The region inside the oval is the set P. The Venn diagrams for union, intersection and complementation are shown in Figures 2.2, 2.3 and 2.4 respectively. Fig. 2.5 depicts the difference of two sets while Fig. 2.6 presents the operation of symmetric difference.

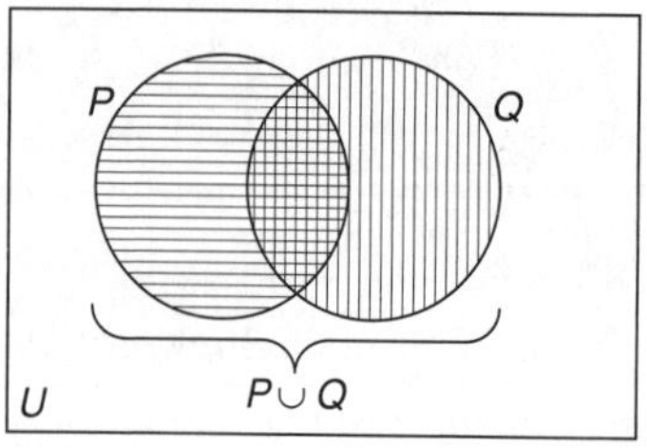

Fig. 2.2. *Union*

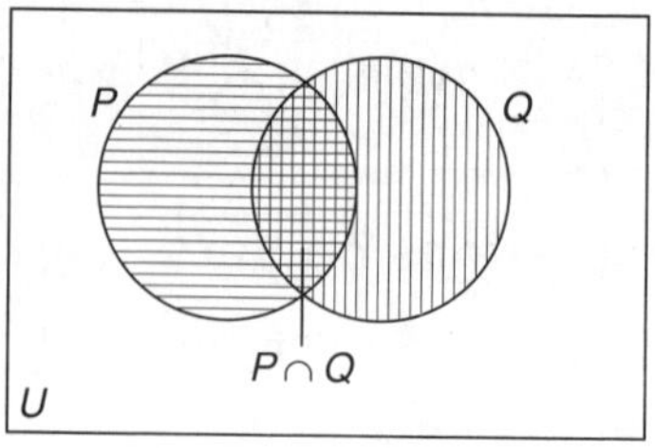

Fig. 2.3. *Intersection*

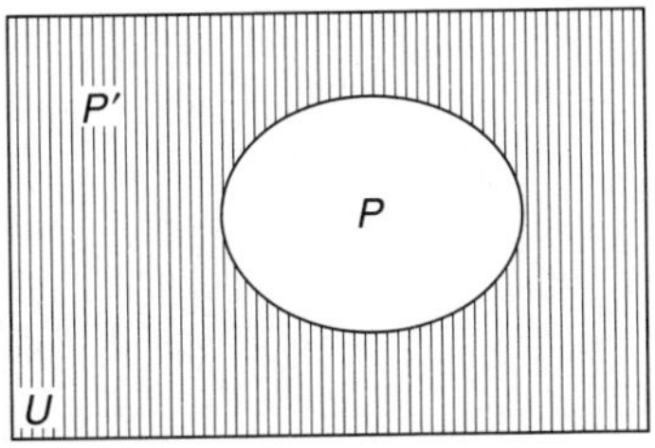

Fig. 2.4. *Complement of a set*

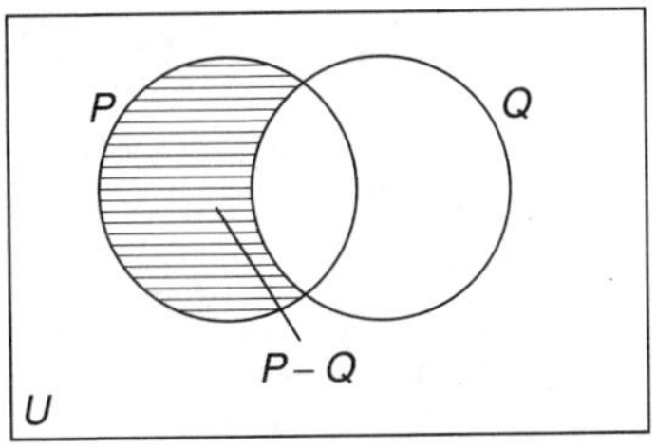

Fig. 2.5. *Set difference*

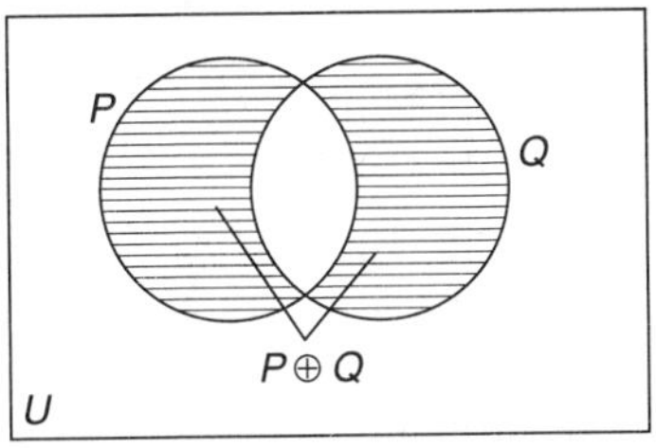

Fig. 2.6. *Symmetric difference*

Definition 2.11 (*Cartesian Product*) Let P and Q be two sets. The Cartesian product of P and Q, denoted as $P \times Q$, is the set of all ordered pairs (x, y) such that $x \in P$ and $y \in Q$.

$$P \times Q = \{(x, y) \mid x \in P \text{ and } y \in Q\}$$

2.1.3 Properties of Sets

Certain properties are obeyed by the set theoretic operations of union, intersection, complementation, symmetric difference etc. These properties are summarized below.

Idempotency
$A \cup A = A$
$A \cap A = A$

Commutative
$A \cup B = B \cup A$
$A \cap B = B \cap A$
$A \oplus B = B \oplus A$

Associative
$A \cup (B \cup C) = (A \cup B) \cup C$
$A \cap (B \cap C) = (A \cap B) \cap C$
$A \oplus (B \oplus C) = (A \oplus B) \oplus C$

Distributive
$A \cup (B \cap C) = (A \cup B) \cap (A \cup C)$
(Left distributivity of union over intersection)
$(A \cup B) \cap C = (A \cap C) \cup (B \cap C)$
(Right distributivity of intersection over union)
$A \cap (B \cup C) = (A \cap B) \cup (A \cap C)$
(Left distributivity of intersection over union)
$(A \cap B) \cup C = (A \cup C) \cap (B \cup C)$
(Right distributivity of union over intersection)

De Morgan's law
$(A \cap B)' = A' \cup B'$
$(A \cup B)' = A' \cap B'$

Identity	$A \cup \varnothing = \varnothing \cup A = A$ $A \cap \varnothing = \varnothing \cap A = \varnothing$ $A \cup U = U \cup A = U$ $A \cap U = U \cap A = A$
Involution	$(A')' = A$
Law of excluded middle	$A \cup A' = U$
Law of contradiction	$A \cap A' = \varnothing$
Universal compliment	$U' = \varnothing$ $\varnothing' = U$
Absorption	$A \cup (A \cap B) = A$ $A \cap (A \cup B) = A$

A set theoretic identity of the form L.H.S. = R.H.S. may be proved by showing that L.H.S. $\subseteq$ R.H.S. and simultaneously L.H.S. $\supseteq$ R.H.S. Example 2.6 illustrates the technique by proving the absorption properties. Also, the properties mentioned above may be applied to prove set theoretic identities. A few such examples are given in the section Solved Problems.

Example 2.6 *(Proof of Absorption Properties)*

The absorption properties state that for arbitrary sets A and B, the identities $A \cup (A \cap B) = A$ and $A \cap (A \cup B) = A$. This can be proved as follows.

Let us take an arbitrary element x of A. Now

Let $x \in A$	Assumption
$\therefore x \in A \cup B$	By definition of union
$\therefore x \in A \cap (A \cup B)$	By definition of intersection
$\therefore A \subseteq A \cap (A \cup B)$	By definition of set inclusion

Now,

Let $x \in A \cap (A \cup B)$	Assumption
$\therefore x \in A$ and $(A \cup B)$	By definition of intersection
$\therefore x \in A$	
$\therefore A \cap (A \cup B) \subseteq A$	By definition of set inclusion

Hence $A \cap (A \cup B) = A$

Again,

$A \cup (A \cap B) = (A \cup A) \cap (A \cup B)$ Distributive law

$= A \cap (A \cup B) = A$

2.2 FUZZY SETS

Fuzzy set theory is a generalization of the classical set theory. Unlike the later, fuzzy set theory recognizes and incorporates in its formalism the natural vagueness that we the human beings are habituated to deal with in our practical, daily, life. This section presents the fundamental concepts of the fuzzy set theory.

2.2.1 Fuzziness/Vagueness/Inexactness

It is quite normal to utter sentences like 'He is a *rich* man', or 'The car is *very expensive*', or '*Old* people tend to be *weak*' and so on in our everyday conversation. While such expressions as *rich*, *very*, *expensive*, *old*, *weak* etc. are extremely convenient in practical communication they are characteristically inexact in the sense that there are no well-defined demarcations between *rich* and *poor*, *very* and *little*, *expensive* and *cheap*, *old* and *young*, or *weak* and *strong*. A person can be rich as well as poor simultaneously, of course to different extents. This vagueness is desirable because otherwise everyday conversation would have been impossible. However, the classical set theory is not equipped to handle such vagueness as it does not allow an element to be a partial member, or a partially non-member, of a set simultaneously. Therefore classical set theory is inadequate to model our intuitive notion of a *set* in general.

As stated earlier, Fuzzy set theory is a generalization of the classical set theory so that the classical set theory is a special case of the fuzzy set theory. It takes into consideration the natural vagueness that we the human beings deal with in our practical, daily, life. As an example, let us consider the data related to a family as described in able Table 2.1.

Table 2.1 *A family data set*

#	Family member	Age	Gender
1	Grand-pa	72	Male
2	Grand-ma	63	Female
3	Dad	41	Male
4	Mom	38	Female
5	Daughter	15	Female
6	Son	13	Male
7	Aunty	52	Female

It is customary to refer to a classical set as *crisp* in order to differentiate it from a *fuzzy* set. The crisp set of the family members $U = \{Grand\text{-}pa, Grand\text{-}ma, Dad, Mom, Sister, Brother, Aunt\}$ may be treated as the *reference set*, or the *universe of discourse*. Now, consider the sets M and F of the male family members and female family members respectively. These are crisp sets because for any arbitrary element x of U, it is possible to decide precisely whether x is member of the set, or not. There is no intermediate status regarding the membership of x to the respective set. However, deciding the membership of an arbitrary $x \in U$ to the set of *senior* persons of the family is not as straightforward as in case of M or F. The status of membership of an element x with respect to a given set S is expressed with the help of a *membership function* μ. A set, crisp or fuzzy, may be defined in terms of membership function.

2.2.2 Set Membership

Description of a set in terms of its membership function is presented in this subsection. We first define crisp membership which is followed by the fuzzy membership function.

Definition 2.12 (*Membership Function*) Given an element x and a set S, the membership of x with respect to S, denoted as $\mu_S(x)$, is defined as

$$\begin{aligned} \mu_S(x) &= 1, \quad \text{if } x \in S \\ &= 0, \quad \text{if } x \notin S \end{aligned}$$

Example 2.7 *(Set Membership)*

Let us consider the set M of male family members and set F of female family members with reference to the family presented in Table 2.1. We see that $\mu_M(Dad) = 1$, and $\mu_M(Mom) = 0$. Similarly, $\mu_F(Dad) = 0$, and $\mu_F(Mom) = 1$. Membership values of the other family members in M and F can be ascertained in similar manner.

Now, consider A to be the set of *senior* persons in the family. *Seniority* is a familiar and frequently-used attribute to a person. But is there any clear and unambiguous way to decide whether a person should be categorized as senior or not? Let us see with reference to U, the universe of discourse.

We may agree without any hesitation that Grand-pa, being 72 years old, is a senior person, so that *Grand-pa* $\in A$. On the other hand the brother and the sister are both too young to be categorized as senior persons. Therefore, we may readily accept that *Daughter* $\notin A$ and *Son* $\notin A$. What about *Mom*, or *Dad*? They are not as aged as Grand-pa but neither as young as the daughter or the son. Moreover, Grand-ma is almost a senior person, being at 63 years, but she might be categorized as a middle-aged person as well.

The point is, the concept of a senior person is not as clearly defined as the gender of the person. In fact, there is a whole range of gray area between total inclusion and total exclusion, over which the degree of membership of a person in the set of senior persons varies.

This intuitive notion of partial membership of an element in a set can be formalized if one allows the membership function to assume any real value between 0 and 1, including both. This means that an element may belong to a set to any extent within the range [0, 1]. Hence it is now possible for an element x to be 0.5 member, or $1/\sqrt{2}$ member of a set S so that we may say $\mu_S(x) = 0.5$, or $\mu_S(x) = 1/\sqrt{2}$.

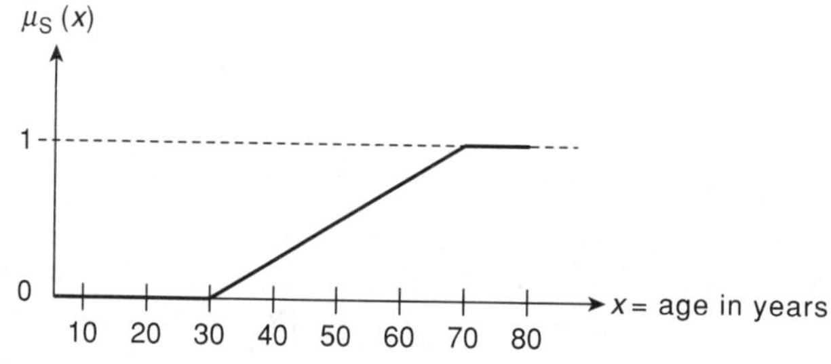

Fig. 2.7. *Membership function for the fuzzy set of senior family members*

Membership profiles/functions Quite often it is convenient to express the membership of various elements with respect to a fuzzy set with the help of a function, referred to as the **membership function**. Take for example the fuzzy set A of senior persons on the universe of discourse U described in Table 2.1. For any $x \in U$, we may determine the membership value of x in A with the help of the following membership function.

$$\mu_A(x) = \begin{cases} 0, & if \quad x < 30 \\ \dfrac{x-30}{40}, & if \quad 30 \le x < 70 \\ 1, & if \quad x \ge 70 \end{cases} \tag{2.1}$$

Here x represents the age of the concerned person. The nature of the membership function is shown graphically in Fig. 2.7.

Formula 2.1 may be applied to find to what extent a person is a member of the fuzzy set A of senior persons. For example, as Grand-pa is more than 70 years old, he is a full member of A, μ_A (*Grand-pa*) = 1.0. However for Grand-ma we have μ_A (*Grand-ma*) = (63 – 30) / 40 = 33 / 40 = 0.825. Hence Grand-ma is a senior person to a large extent, but not as fully as Grand-pa. Table 2.2 shows the membership values of all the family members.

Table 2.2. *Membership values of the senior family members*

#	Family member	Age	$\mu_A(x)$
1	Grand-pa	72	1.0
2	Grand-ma	63	0.825
3	Dad	41	0.275
4	Mom	38	0.200
5	Daughter	15	0.0
6	Son	13	0.0
7	Aunty	52	0.55

If we want to describe such a fuzzy set by explicitly enumerating its members we need to indicate the membership value of each element along with the element itself. Therefore, the fuzzy set A of senior persons can be expressed as a set of ordered pairs A = {(*Grand-pa*, 1.0), (*Grand-ma*, 0.825), (*Dad*, 0.275), (*Mom*, 0.2), (*Aunty*, 0.55)}. *Daughter* and *Son* are not in the list because it is customary not to mention the members with zero membership value. Thus fuzzy sets can be formally defined as given below.

2.2.3 Fuzzy Sets

This subsection presents the definition of a fuzzy set along with a few illustrative examples.

Definition 2.13 (*Fuzzy set*) A fuzzy set F on a given universe of discourse U is defined as a collection of ordered pairs $(x, \mu_F(x))$ where $x \in U$, and for all $x \in U$, $0.0 \leq \mu_F(x) \leq 1.0$.

$$F = \{(x, \mu_F(x)) \mid x \in U, 0.0 \leq \mu_F(x) \leq 1.0\}$$

Classical sets, often referred to as *crisp* sets to distinguish them from fuzzy sets, are special cases of fuzzy sets where the membership values are restricted to either 0, or 1. Each pair $(x, \mu_F(x))$ of the fuzzy set F is known as a **singleton**.

Notation (Fuzzy sets) Apart from enumerating the singletons as described above, fuzzy sets are frequently expressed as the union of all singletons where a singleton is denoted as $\mu_F(x) / x$. Using this notation

$$F = \sum_{x \in U} \mu_F(x)/x \tag{2.2}$$

Here the summation sign Σ is to be interpreted as union over all singletons, and not arithmetic sum. Formula 2.2 is appropriate for discrete sets. For continuous sets, the summation notation is replaced by the integral sign $\int$, as shown below.

$$F = \int_U \frac{\mu_F(x)}{x} \tag{2.3}$$

Example 2.8 (*Fuzzy Membership*)

Let *a*, *b*, *c*, *d*, and *e* be five students who scored 55, 35, 60, 85 and 75 out of 100 respectively in Mathematics. The students constitute the universe of discourse $U = \{a, b, c, d, e\}$ and a fuzzy set *M* of the students who are *good in Mathematics* is defined on *U* with the help of the following membership function.

$$\mu_M(x) = \begin{cases} 0, & \text{if} \quad x < 40 \\ \dfrac{x-40}{40}, & \text{if} \quad 40 \le x < 80 \\ 1, & \text{if} \quad x \ge 80 \end{cases} \tag{2.4}$$

The membership function is graphically shown in Fig. 2.8. Computing the membership value of each student with the help of the Formula 2.4 we get $M = \{(a, 0.375), (c, 0.5), (d, 1.0), (e, 0.875)\}$, or equivalently

$$M = \frac{0.375}{a} + \frac{0.5}{c} + \frac{1.0}{d} + \frac{0.875}{e}$$

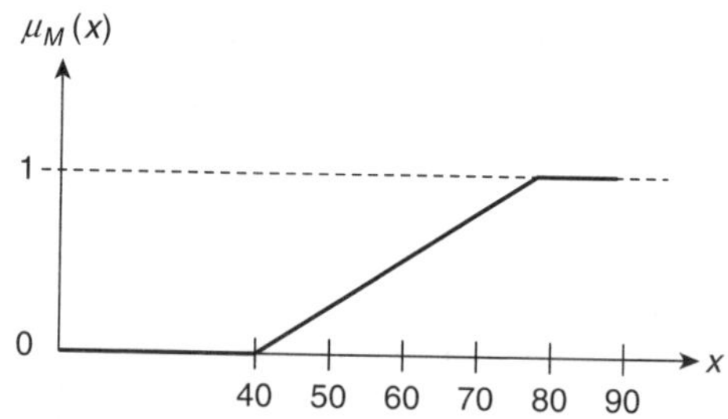

Fig. 2.8. *Membership function for students good in Mathematics.*

Example 2.9 (*Fuzzy Membership*)

Let us consider the infinite set of all real numbers between 0 and 1, both inclusive, to be the universe of discourse, or, the reference set, $U = [\,0, 1\,]$. We define a fuzzy set *C*0.5 as the set of all real numbers in *U* that are *close* to 0.5 in the following way

$$C0.5 = \{x \in [\,0, 1\,] \mid x \text{ is } close \text{ to } 0.5\}$$

The highest membership value would be attained by the point $x = 0.5$ because that is the number closest to 0.5, and the membership is understandably 1. On the other hand since both 0 and 1 are furthest points from 0.5 (within the interval [0, 1]) they should have zero membership to *C*0.5. Membership values should increase progressively as we approach 0.5 from both ends of the interval [0, 1]. The membership function for *C*0.5 may be defined in the following manner.

$$\mu_{C0.5}(x) = 1 - |\,2x - 1\,|, \qquad \forall x \in [\,0, 1\,] \tag{2.5}$$

Since *C*0.5 is a fuzzy set in a continuous domain it can be expressed with the help of the notation

$$C0.5 = \int_{x\in[0,1]} \frac{\mu_{c0.5}(x)}{x} = \int_{x\in[0,1]} \frac{1-|2x-1|}{x} \tag{2.6}$$

2.2.4 Fuzziness vs. Probability

It must be appreciated that the membership of a fuzzy set relate to *vagueness* and not to probability which is a measure of *uncertainty*. The difference between fuzziness and probability is nicely explained with the help the following story. A man is wandering for long hours in a desert and he is now dying for a glass of water. Someone offered him two glasses, glass *A* and glass *B*, of water with the condition that he can not drink from both the glasses and he has to choose only one of the two for drinking. The man has been informed that the water of glass *A* is poisonous *to a degree of* 0.1, which is not fatal. On the other hand glass *B* contains water which is poisonous with a *probability of* 0.1. Which glass of water should the thirsty man choose to quench his thirst, and of course, remain alive? If he drinks from glass *B* he has 90% chance of having pure drinking water but there is 10% chance that the water may be poisonous and in that case he would certainly die. On the other hand if he drinks from glass *A*, he would fall ill due to the fact that the water is partially poisonous. However there is no chance of him dying because the degree of poisoning is not fatal. Glass *A* symbolizes fuzziness while glass *B* symbolizes probability.

2.2.5 Features of Fuzzy Sets

Fuzzy sets are often characterized with certain features, *e.g.*, *normality, height, support, core, cardinality* etc. These features reveal the nature and structure of a fuzzy set. These features are briefly explained in this subsection.

Definition 2.14 (*Normality*) A fuzzy set *F* is said to be normal if there exists an element *x* that completely belongs to *F*, $\mu_F(x) = 1$. A fuzzy set which is not normal is said to be sub-normal.

Definition 2.15 (*Height*) The height of a fuzzy set is defined as the maximal membership value attained by its elements.

$$height\ (F) = \underset{x \in U}{Max}\ \mu_F(x) \tag{2.7}$$

U is the universe of discourse, or, the reference set, for *F*, and *height* (*F*) is the height of the fuzzy set *F*. Obviously, *F* is a normal fuzzy set if *height* (*F*) = 1.

Definition 2.16 (*Support*) The support of a fuzzy set *F*, denoted by *supp* (*F*), is the set of all elements of the reference set *U* with non-zero membership to *F*.

$$Supp\ (F) = \{x \mid x \in U, \text{ and } \mu_F(x) > 0\} \tag{2.8}$$

Definition 2.17 (*Core*) The *core* of a fuzzy set *F* is the set of all elements of the reference set *U* with complete membership to *F*.

$$Core\ (F) = \{x \mid x \in U, \text{ and } \mu_F(x) = 1\} \tag{2.9}$$

Both *supp* (*F*) and *core* (*F*) are crisp sets. It is easy to see that *core* (*F*) $\subseteq$ *supp* (*F*).

Definition 2.18 (*Cardinality*) The sum of all membership values of the members of a fuzzy set *F* is said to be the cardinality of *F*.

$$|F| = \sum_{x \in U} \mu_F(x) \tag{2.10}$$

Example 2.10 *(Cardinality)*

Let us consider the fuzzy set M defined on the reference set $U = \{a, b, c, d, e\}$ as described in Example 2.8.

$$M = \frac{0.375}{a} + \frac{0.5}{c} + \frac{1.0}{d} + \frac{0.875}{e}$$

The fuzzy set M is normal, because we have $\mu_M(d) = 1.0$. Its height is 1.0. Moreover, as we see, *supp* $(M) = \{a, c, d, e\}$, *core* $(M) = \{d\}$, and the cardinality of M is $|M| = 0.375 + 0.5 + 1.0 + 0.875 = 2.750$.

2.3 FUZZY MEMBERSHIP FUNCTIONS

Theoretically any function $\mu_F : U \rightarrow [0, 1]$ may act as the membership function for a fuzzy set F. The nature of the membership function depends on the context of the application. For example, what is hot with respect to human body temperature is certainly very cool for a blast furnace. Hence the membership function for the concept *hot* must differ in the two contexts mentioned above. Fuzzy sets are usually described with simple membership functions. A few parameterized functions that are quite frequently used for this purpose are given below along with their graphical representations.

2.3.1 Some Popular Fuzzy Membership Functions

This subsection presents the Triangular function, Trapezoidal function, Gaussian function and S-function as the widely used fuzzy membership functions. In the subsequent discussion, all of these are assumed to be normal.

(a) Triangular function Perhaps the most frequently used membership function is the triangular function. Equation 2.11 provides the definition of a triangular function. The function is graphically shown in Fig. 2.9.

$$\mu(x) = \begin{cases} 0, & \text{if} \quad x \le a \\ \dfrac{x-a}{m-a}, & \text{if} \quad a \le x \le m \\ \dfrac{b-x}{b-m}, & \text{if} \quad m \le x \le b \\ 0, & \text{if} \quad x \ge b \end{cases} \tag{2.11}$$

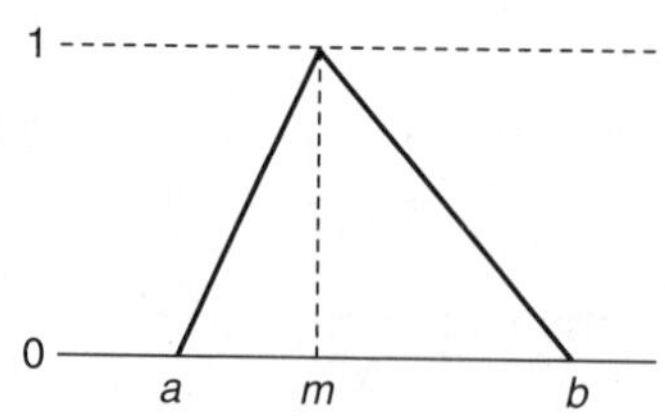

Fig. 2.9. *Shape of a triangular function*

(b) Trapezoidal function The trapezoidal function is defined in Equation 2.12. As shown in Fig. 2.10, its shape is similar to that of a triangular function except that instead of a sharp peak, it has a flat peak.

$$\mu(x)=\begin{cases}0, & if \quad x\leq a\\ \dfrac{x-a}{m-a}, & if \quad a\leq x\leq m\\ 1, & if \quad m\leq x\leq n\\ \dfrac{b-x}{b-n}, & if \quad n\leq x\leq b\\ 0, & if \quad x\geq b\end{cases} \tag{2.12}$$

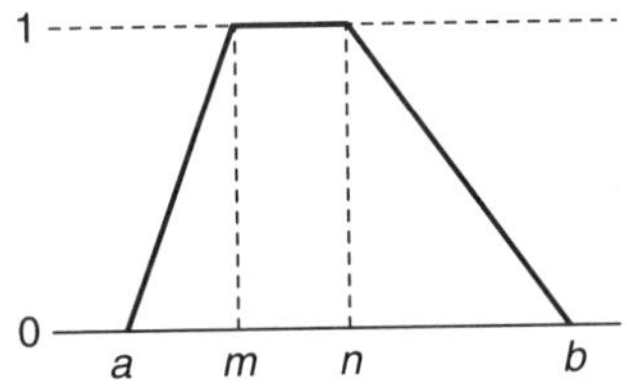

Fig. 2.10. *Trapezoidal function*

(c) Gaussian function Another widely used membership function is the Gaussian function. The advantage of Gaussian function is it is differentiable everywhere. Equation 2.13 provides the formula for Gaussian function and Fig. 2.11 shows its shape.

$$\mu(x)=e^{-k(x-m)^2} \qquad where \quad k>0 \tag{2.13}$$

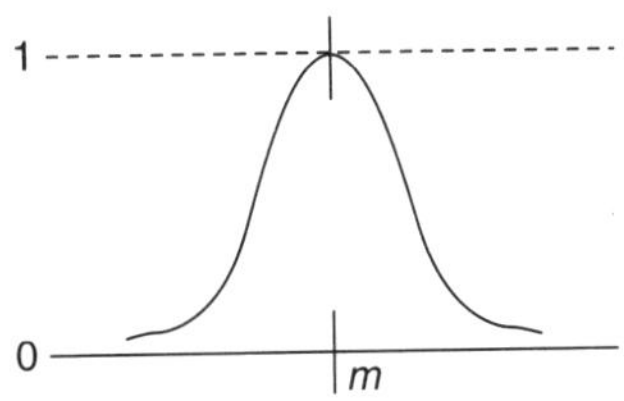

Fig. 2.11. *Gaussian function*

(d) S-function The S-function, defined by Equation 2.14 and shown in Fig. 2.12, is also differentiable everywhere. Moreover, the step function can be approximated by the S-function as closely as required by adjusting the parameters *a* and *b*.

$$\mu(x)=\begin{cases}0, & if \quad x\leq a\\ 2\left(\dfrac{x-a}{b-a}\right)^2, & if \quad a\leq x\leq m\\ 1-2\left(\dfrac{x-b}{b-a}\right)^2, & if \quad m\leq x\leq b\\ 1, & if \quad x\geq b\end{cases} \tag{2.14}$$

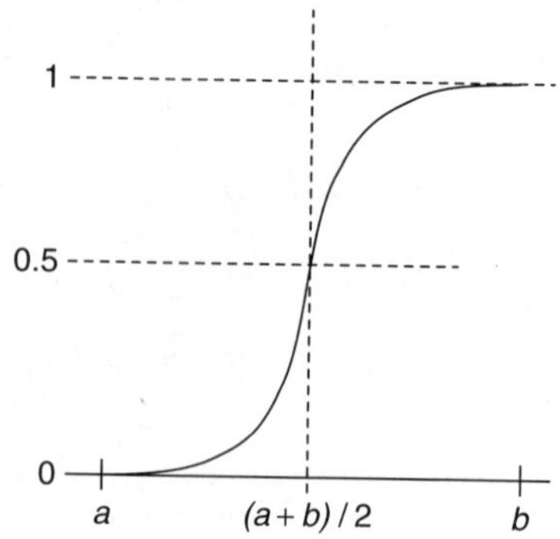

Fig. 2.12. *The S - function*

The point $m = (a + b) / 2$ is known as the crossover point of the S-function.

2.3.2 Transformations

There are a few simple but useful transformations often applied to fuzzy membership functions. The so called *normalization, dilation, concentration, contrast intensification* and *fuzzification* are widely used. These transformations are briefly discussed in this subsection. The effects of these transformations on Gaussian functions are shown graphically.

(*a*) **Normalization:** The normalization operation converts a subnormal fuzzy set F to a normal fuzzy set. It is obtained by dividing each membership value by the height of the fuzzy set (See Eqn. 2.15 and Fig. 2.13).

$$NORM(F,x) = \frac{\mu_F(x)}{height(F)} \tag{2.15}$$

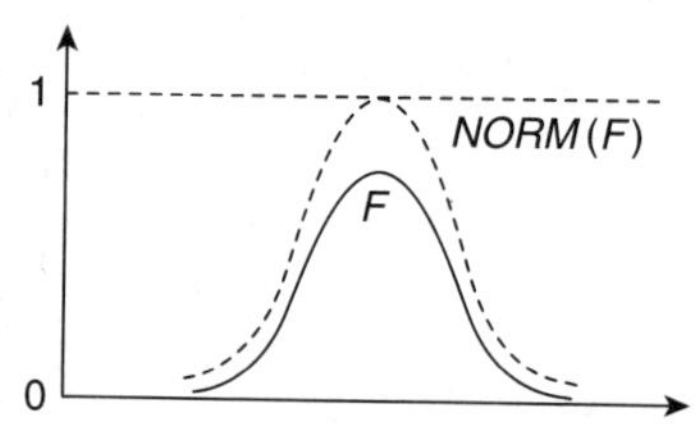

Fig. 2.13. *Normalization*

(*b*) **Dilation:** This operation 'flattens' the membership function so that it attains relatively higher values and consequently the overall shape of the membership function gets dilated. In other words, the resultant function is less pointed around the higher membership values. The effect is shown in Fig. 2.14 with respect to the Gaussian function.

$$DIL(F,x) = [\mu_F(x)]^{1/2} \tag{2.16}$$

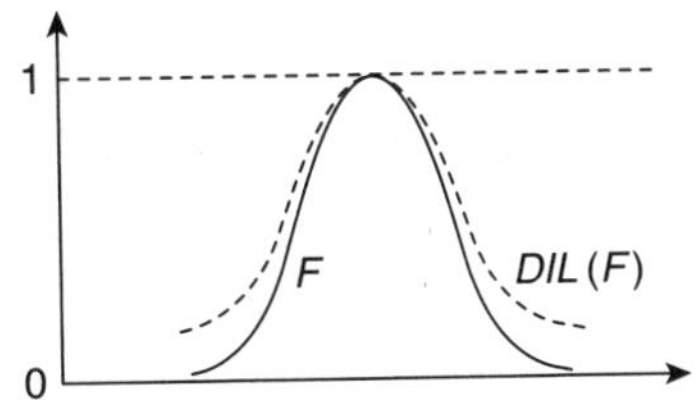

Fig. 2.14. *Dilation*

(*c*) **Concentration:** Concentration has the reverse effect of dilation. Here the function attains relatively lower values and consequently it gets more pointed around the higher membership values. The formula for concentration is given by Eqn. 2.17 and Fig. 2.15 shows the effect on Gaussian function.

$$CON(F,x)=[\mu_F(x)]^2 \tag{2.17}$$

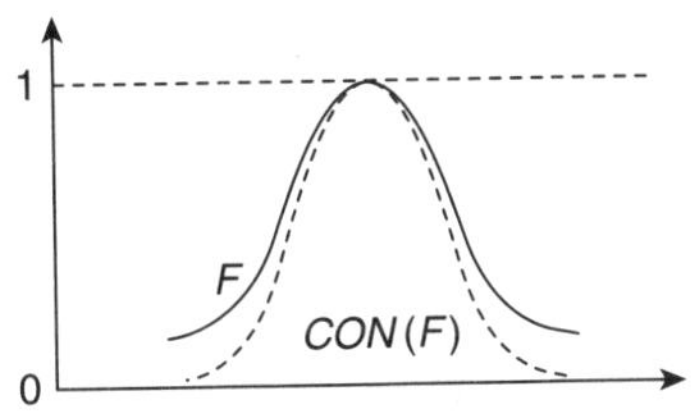

Fig. 2.15. *Concentration*

(*d*) **Contrast Intensification:** Contrast intensification is achieved by reducing the membership values that are less than 0.5 and elevating those with values higher that 0.5 (see Eqn. 2.18 and Fig. 2.16).

$$INF\,(F,x)=\begin{cases}2[\mu_F(x)]^2, & if\ 0\le\mu_F(x)\le 0.5\\ 1-2[1-\mu_F(x)]^2, & otherwise\end{cases} \tag{2.18}$$

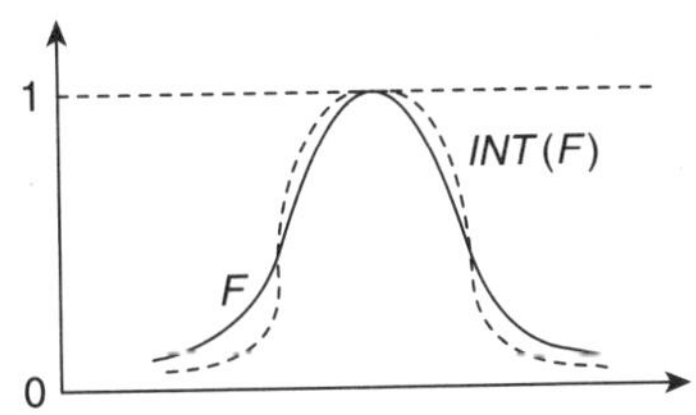

Fig. 2.16. *Contrast intensification*

(*e*) **Fuzzification:** Fuzzification produces the reverse effect of contrast intensification. Here the membership values that are less than 0.5 are elevated while those with a value more than 0.5 are reduced. The mathematical formula for fuzzification is given in Eqn. 2.19 and its effect on Gaussian function is shown in Fig. 2.17.

$$FUZZ\,(F,x)=\begin{cases}[\mu_F(x)/2]^{1/2}, & if\ 0\le\mu_F(x)\le 0.5\\ 1-\sqrt{(1-\mu_F(x))/2}, & otherwise\end{cases} \tag{2.19}$$

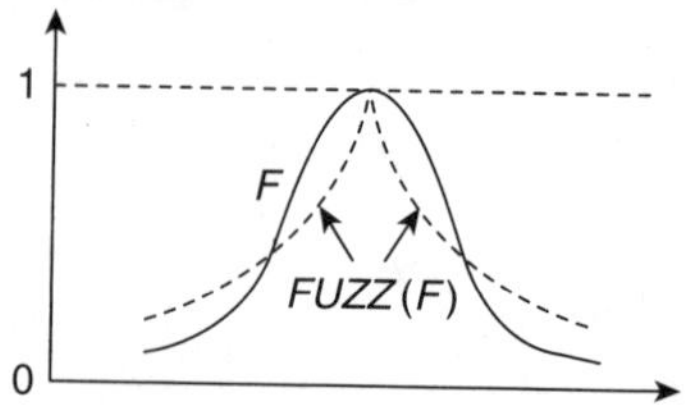

Fig. 2.17. *Fuzzification*

2.3.3 Linguistic Variables

The transformations presented above are useful while dealing with the so called **linguistic variables.** Conventional variables usually have numeric or alphanumeric string values. In contrast, a linguistic variable may have one of a number of allowable words, or phrases, as its value. Each of these legitimate linguistic values corresponds to a fuzzy set. For instance, consider the variable *Height*. As a conventional variable it may have any real number as its value. But as a linguistic variable it's value is allowed to be one of a few predefined words, say {*short, average, tall*}. We may define a fuzzy set for each of the words *short, average*, and *tall*. Now, consider the attribute *very tall*. Here the word *very* may be viewed as a transformation applied to the fuzzy meaning of *tall*. One can reasonably implement *very* with the help of the concentration operation. The reason is *concentration* reduces the magnitude of the membership value. What is *tall* to some extent might be thought of *very tall* to a lesser extent. Therefore, the membership function for *very tall* should always be less than that of *tall* and moreover, the transition from low *very tall* to high *very tall* should be steeper than the transition from low *tall* to high *tall*. Fig. 2.18 gives an idea about the relationship described above.

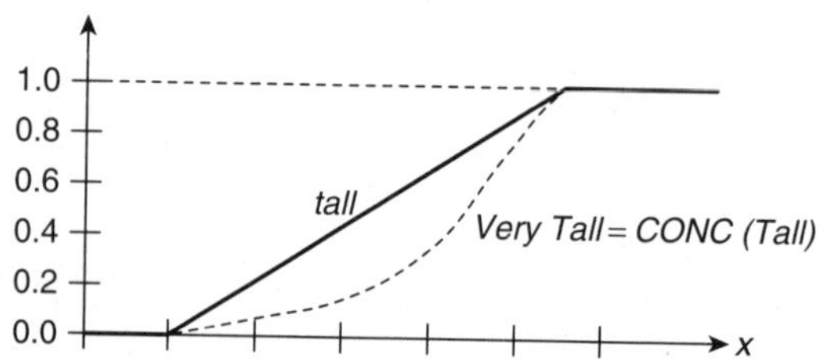

Fig. 2.18. *Transformation on linguistic variable fuzzy set*

Example 2.11 (*Transformations on fuzzy membership functions*)

Consider the fuzzy set F with a triangular membership function defined on the interval $[-2, +2]$.

$$\mu_F(x) = \begin{cases} 0, & \text{if } -2 \le x \le -1 \\ x+1, & \text{if } -1 \le x \le 0 \\ 1-x, & \text{if } 0 \le x \le 1 \\ 0, & \text{if } 1 \le x \le 2 \end{cases} \tag{2.20}$$

Fig. 2.19 presents the shape of the triangular function defined above. Now let us apply the transformations normalization, dilation, concentration, contrast intensification and fuzzification on this membership function and see the resultant functional forms.

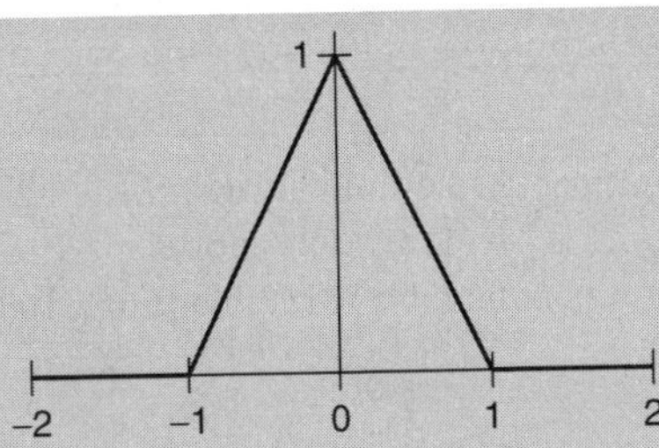

Fig. 2.19. *Triangular membership function given by Eqn. 2.20*

Since the height of the given membership function is 1, normalization has no effect on it. The forms of the resultant memberships due to the other operations, *viz.*, dilation, concentration, contrast intensification, and fuzzification are shown in Figs 2.20 to 2.23.

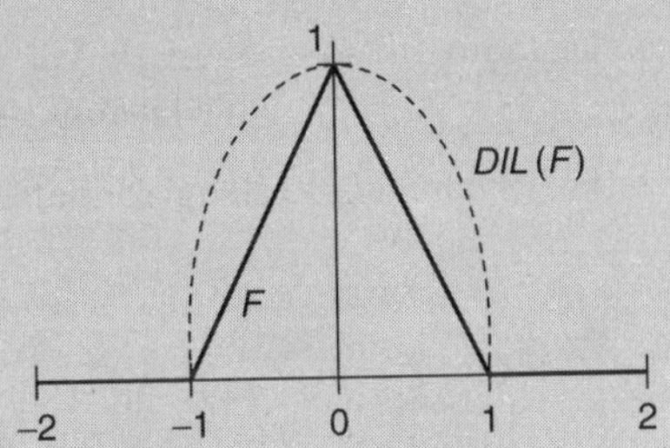

Fig. 2.20. *Dilation*

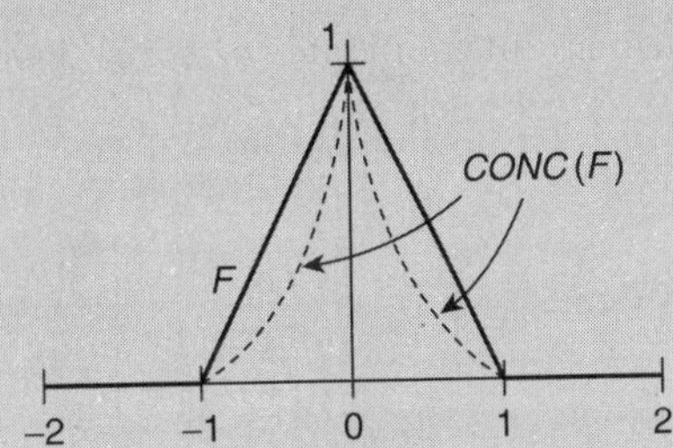

Fig. 2.21. *Concentration*

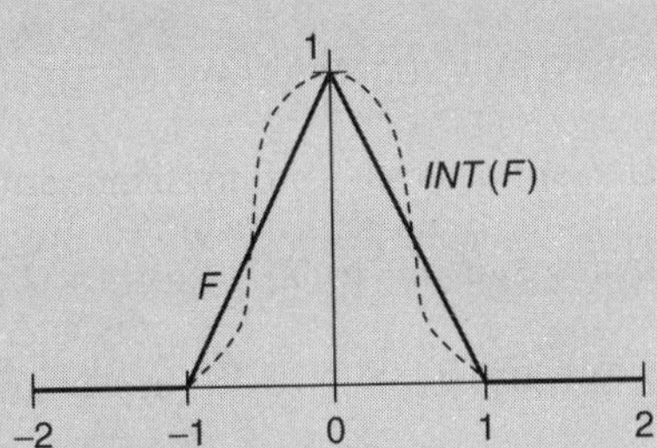

Fig. 2.22. *Contrast intensification*

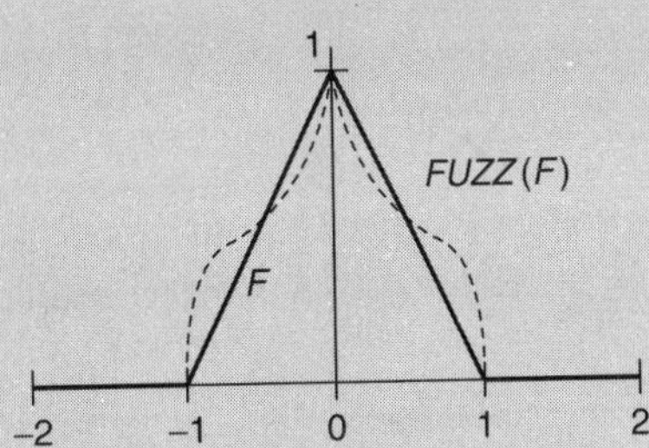

Fig. 2.23. *Fuzzification*

2.4 OPERATIONS ON FUZZY SETS

Most of the usual set theoretic operations e.g., union, intersection, complementation etc. are readily extended to fuzzy sets. A list of such operators along with their definitions is shown in Table 2.3.

Table 2.3. *Operations on fuzzy sets*

#	Operation/Relation	Description
1	Union ($P \cup Q$)	$\mu_{P \cup Q}(x) = max\ \{\mu_P(x), \mu_Q(x)\}, \forall x \in U$
2	Intersection ($P \cap Q$)	$\mu_{P \cap Q}(x) = min\ \{\mu_P(x), \mu_Q(x)\}, \forall x \in U$
3	Complementation (P')	$\mu_{P'}(x) = 1 - \mu_P(x), \forall x \in U$

(Continued)

Table 2.3. *Continued*

#	Operation/Relation	Description
4	Equality ($P = Q$)	Two fuzzy sets P and Q are equal if and only if $\forall x \in U$, $\mu_P(x) = \mu_Q(x)$
5	Inclusion ($P \subseteq Q$)	P is included in Q, i.e., P is a subset of Q, written as $P \subseteq Q$, if and only if $\forall x \in U$, $\mu_P(x) \le \mu_Q(x)$
6	Product ($P \cdot Q$)	$\mu_{P.Q}(x) = \mu_P(x) \times \mu_Q(x)$, $\forall x \in U$
7	Difference ($P - Q$)	$P - Q = P \cap Q'$
8	Disjunctive sum ($P \oplus Q$)	$P \oplus Q = (P \cap Q') \cup (P' \cap Q)$

Obviously the union of two fuzzy sets is the *smallest* fuzzy set containing both and their intersection is the *largest* fuzzy set contained by both the given sets.

Example 2.12 (*Fuzzy set operations*)

Let us recall the reference set of the family members presented in Table 2.1 and the fuzzy set A of senior persons which is repeated here A = {(*Grand-pa*, 1.0), (*Grand-ma*, 0.825), (*Dad*, 0.275), (*Mom*, 0.2), (*Aunty*, 0.55)}, or, in the other notation

$$A = \frac{1.0}{Grand\text{-}pa} + \frac{0.825}{Grand\text{-}ma} + \frac{0.275}{Dad} + \frac{0.2}{Mom} + \frac{0.55}{Aunty}$$

The membership function for A is as follows

$$\mu_A(x) = \begin{cases} 0, & if \;\; age(x) \le 30 \\ \frac{x-30}{40}, & if \;\; 30 \le age(x) \le 70 \\ 1, & if \;\; age(x) \ge 70 \end{cases} \tag{2.21}$$

We now introduce another fuzzy set B of *active* persons on the same reference set. The degree of activeness is assumed to be a function of the concerned person's age. Here is the membership function.

$$\mu_B(x) = \begin{cases} 0, & if \;\; age(x) \le 10 \\ \frac{x-10}{15}, & if \;\; 10 \le age(x) \le 25 \\ 1, & if \;\; 25 \le age(x) \le 50 \\ \frac{80-x}{30}, & if \;\; 50 \le age(x) \le 80 \\ 0, & if \;\; age(x) \ge 80 \end{cases} \tag{2.22}$$

Fig. 2.24 presents the graphical view of the two membership functions. Computing the values of $\mu_B(x)$ for each x in U using the membership function defined in formula 2.22 we get B = {(*Grand-pa*, 0.267), (*Grand-ma*, 0.567), (*Dad*, 1.0), (*Mom*, 1.0), (*Daughter*, 0.333), (*Son*, 0.2), (*Aunty*, 0.933)}, or using the summation notation,

$$B = \frac{0.267}{Grand\text{-}pa} + \frac{0.567}{Grand\text{-}ma} + \frac{1.0}{Dad} + \frac{1.0}{Mom} + \frac{0.333}{Daughter} + \frac{0.2}{Son} + \frac{0.933}{Aunty}$$

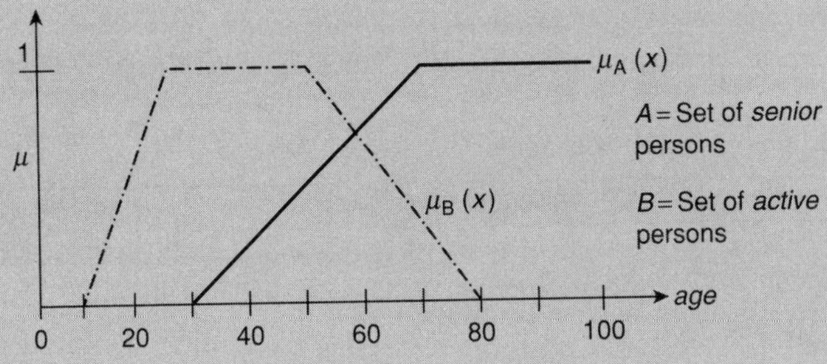

Fig. 2.24. *Membership profiles of aged persons and active persons*

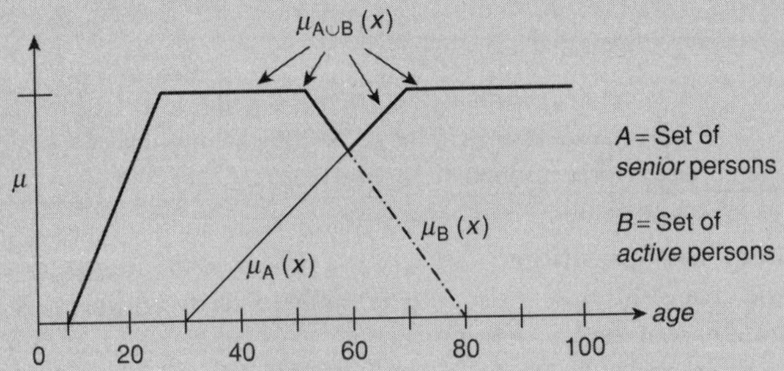

Fig. 2.25. *Membership profile of senior OR active persons.*

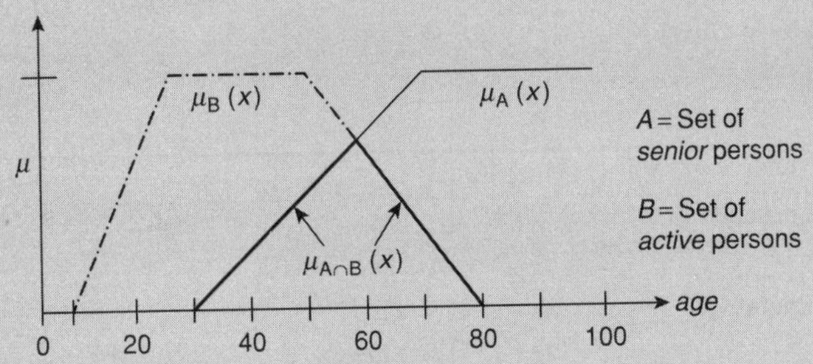

Fig. 2.26. *Membership profiles of senior AND active persons.*

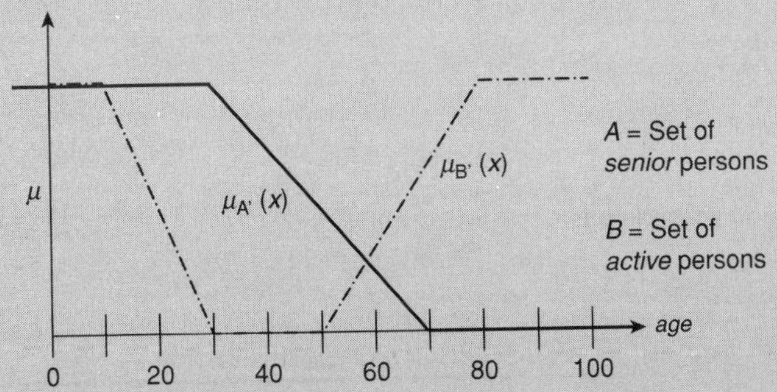

Fig. 2.27. *Membership profiles of NOT senior persons and NOT active persons.*

Table 2.4 shows the fuzzy sets $A \cup B$, $A \cap B$, A', and B' obtained using definitions listed in Table 2.3. The profiles of the membership functions of the resultant fuzzy sets are depicted in Figs. 2.25 to 2.27.

Table 2.4. *Operations on Fuzzy Sets Senior and Active Persons*

#	Operation		Resultant fuzzy set
1.	$A \cup B$	*senior* OR *active*	{(*Grand-pa*, 1.0), (*Grand-ma*, 0.825), (*Dad*, 1.0), (*Mom*, 1.0), (*Daughter*, 0.333), (*Son*, 0.2), (*Aunty*, 0.933)}
2.	$A \cap B$	*senior* AND *Active*	{(*Grand-pa*, 0.267), (*Grand-ma*, 0.567), (*Dad*, 0.275), (*Mom*, 0.2), (*Aunty*, 0.55)}
3.	A', B'	NOT *senior*, NOT *active*	A′ = {(*Grand-ma*, 0.175), (*Dad*, 0.725), (*Mom*, 0.8), (*Sister*, 1.0), (*Brother*, 1.0), (*Aunty*, 0.45)} B′ = {(*Grand-pa*, 0.733), (*Grand-ma*, 0.433), (*Daughter*, 0.667), (*Son*, 0.8), (*Aunty*, 0.067)}

Properties of fuzzy set operations Most of the properties of crisp sets, with the exception of a few, hold good in the area of fuzzy sets also. It is possible to verify on the basis of the definitions of various fuzzy set operations that the laws listed in Table 2.5 are satisfied by arbitrary fuzzy sets *P*, *Q*, and *R* on some universe of discourse *U*. However, the relations $P \cup P' = U$, and $P \cap P' = \Phi$ obeyed by crisp sets are no longer valid for fuzzy sets. For an arbitrary fuzzy set *P*, we have in general $P \cup P' \neq U$, and $P \cap P' \neq \Phi$ because $\mu_P(x) \in [0, 1]$, and $\mu_{P \cup P'}(x) = max\{\mu_P(x), 1 - \mu_P(x)\} \neq 1$, and $\mu_{P \cap P'}(x) = min\{\mu_P(x), 1 - \mu_P(x)\} \neq 0$, unless either $\mu_P(x) = 0$, or $\mu_P(x) = 1$.

Table 2.5. *Fuzzy Set Identities*

#	Law	Description
1	Associativity	(a) $(P \cup Q) \cup R = P \cup (Q \cup R)$ (b) $(P \cap Q) \cap R = P \cap (Q \cap R)$
2	Commutativity	(a) $P \cup Q = Q \cup P$ (b) $P \cap Q = Q \cap P$
3	Distributivity	(a) $P \cup (Q \cap R) = (P \cup Q) \cap (P \cup R)$ (b) $P \cap (Q \cup R) = (P \cap Q) \cup (P \cap R)$
4	Idempotency	(a) $P \cup P = P$ (b) $P \cap P = P$
5	De Morgan's law	(a) $(P \cup Q)' = P' \cap Q'$ (b) $(P \cap Q)' = P' \cup Q'$
6	Boundary Conditions	(a) $P \cup \Phi = P$, $P \cup U = U$ (b) $P \cap \Phi = \Phi$, $P \cap U = P$
7	Involution	$(P')' = P$
8	Transitivity	If $P \subseteq Q$ and $Q \subseteq R$ then $P \subseteq R$

2.5 FUZZY RELATIONS

We have treated fuzzy sets as generalization of crisp sets where the degree of inclusiveness of an element may be anything from 0 to 1, and not just 0, or 1 as it is in case of crisp sets. In a similar fashion, the concept of a relation between two, or more, sets can be generalized to fuzzy relation. This section provides a review of the fundamentals of crisp relations, followed by a discussion on fuzzy relations.

2.5.1 Crisp Relations

In case of crisp relation R between two crisp sets A and B, two elements, x from A and y from B, are either related, or not. There is no scope of being partially related to each other. Therefore a crisp relation is defined simply as a subset of the Cartesian product of sets concerned.

Definition 2.19 (*Cartesian product*) Let A and B be two sets. Then the Cartesian product of A and B, denoted by $A \times B$, is the set of all ordered pairs (a, b) such that $a \in A$, and $b \in B$.

$$A \times B = \{(a, b) \mid a \in A, \text{ and } b \in B\}$$

Since $(a, b) \neq (b, a)$ we have in general $A \times B \neq B \times A$. Hence the operation of Cartesian product is not commutative.

Example 2.13 (*Cartesian product*)

Let $A = \{p, q, r\}$, and $B = \{1, 2, 3\}$. Then $A \times B = \{(p, 1), (p, 2), (p, 3), (q, 1), (q, 2), (q, 3), (r, 1), (r, 2), (r, 3)\}$, and $B \times A = \{(1, p), (1, q), (1, r), (2, p), (2, q), (2, r), (3, p), (3, q), (3, r)\}$.

Example 2.14 (*Cartesian product*)

Let $P = \{Math, Phy, Chem\}$, and $Q = \{O, E, A, B, C\}$ is the set of possible grades, e.g., *outstanding* (O), *excellent* (E), *very good* (A), *good* (B), and *fair* (C). Then $P \times Q = \{(Math, O), (Math, E), \ldots, (Math, C), (Phy, O), \ldots, (Chem, C)\}$.

Obviously, there are as many elements in $A \times B$ as the product of the number of elements of A and B.

$$|A \times B| = |A| \times |B|$$

Definition 2.20 (*Crisp relation*) Given two crisp sets A and B, a crisp relation R between A and B is a subset of $A \times B$.

$$R \subseteq A \times B$$

Example 2.15 (*Crisp relation*)

Consider the sets $A = \{1, 2, 3\}$, $B = \{1, 2, 3, 4\}$ and the relation $R = \{(a, b) \mid b = a + 1, a \in A, \text{ and } b \in B\}$. Then $R = \{(1, 2), (2, 3), (3, 4)\}$. Obviously, here $R \subset A \times B$.

A crisp relation between sets A and B is conveniently expressed with the help of a *relation matrix* T. The rows and the columns of the relation matrix T correspond to the members of A and B respectively. The entries of T are defined as

$$T_{ij} = \begin{cases} 1, & if \quad (a_i, b_j) \in R \\ 0, & \quad otherwise \end{cases} \tag{2.22}$$

Example 2.16 *(Relation matrix for crisp relation)*

Let us, once again, consider the sets $A = \{1, 2, 3\}$, $B = \{1, 2, 3, 4\}$and the relation $R = \{(a, b) \mid b = a + 1, a \in A, \text{and } b \in B\}$ cited in the previous example. The relation matrix for R is given below.

$$\begin{array}{c} \quad\ \ 1 \ \ 2 \ \ 3 \ \ 4 \quad B \\ T_R = \begin{array}{c} 1 \\ 2 \\ 3 \end{array} \begin{bmatrix} 0 & 1 & 0 & 0 \\ 0 & 0 & 1 & 0 \\ 0 & 0 & 0 & 1 \end{bmatrix} \\ A \end{array}$$

Example 2.17 *(Relation matrix for crisp relation)*

Let $P = \{Tony, Bobby, Mike\}$ be a set of three students and $Q = \{Math, Phy, Chem\}$ be a set of three subjects in which *Tony*, *Bobby*, and *Mike* have taken a test. Table 2.6 shows the grades obtained by these students in these subjects.

Table 2.6. *Grades obtained by three students*

	Math	Phy	Chem
Tony	C	B	A
Bobby	A	A	B
Mike	C	A	A

We define a relation R between a student and a subject in which they have secured A grade as $R = \{(x, y) \mid x \in P, y \in Q, \text{and } x \text{ has secured grade } A \text{ in subject } y\}$. Then $R = \{(Tony, Chem), (Bobby, Math), (Bobby, Phy), (Mike, Phy), (Mike, Chem)\}$. The corresponding relation matrix is shown below.

$$\begin{array}{c} \quad\quad Math \quad Phy \quad Chem \\ T_R = \begin{array}{c} T \\ B \\ M \end{array} \begin{bmatrix} 0 & 0 & 1 \\ 1 & 1 & 0 \\ 0 & 1 & 1 \end{bmatrix} \end{array}$$

Operations on relations Certain operations, e.g., *union, intersection, complementation, composition etc.*, are occasionally applied on relations. Table 2.7 provides the description of these operations with respect to relations R and S.

The **Composition** ($R \circ S$) operation is also known as **max–min composition** because it can be equivalently defined, in terms of the corresponding relation matrices, as $R \circ S = \{(a, c) \mid (a, c) \in A \times C$, and $(R \circ S)(a, c) = max\ [\ min\ \{R(a, b), S(b, c)\}]$.

Table 2.7. *Operations on crisp relations*

#	Operation	Description
1	Union (R ∪ S)	Let *R* and *S* are relations defined on $A \times B$. Then $R \cup S = \{(a, b) \mid (a, b) \in R$, or $(a, b) \in S$, or both$\}$. In terms of the relation matrices, this can be equivalently stated as $(R \cup S)(a, b) = max\,\{R(a, b), S(a, b)\}$, where $R(a, b)$, $S(a, b)$, or $(R \cup S)(a, b)$ are the (a, b) th element of the relations *R*, *S*, or $R \cup S$ respectively.
2	Intersection (R ∩ S)	$R \cap S = \{(a, b) \mid (a, b) \in R$, and $(a, b) \in S\}$. In other words, $(R \cap S)(a, b) = min\,\{R(a, b), S(a, b)\}$.
3	Complementation (R′)	$R' = \{(a, b) \mid (a, b) \notin R\}$, i.e., $R'(a, b) = 1 - R(a, b)$.
4	Composition (R ° S)	Let *R* and *S* are relations defined on $A \times B$ and $B \times C$ respectively. Then $R \circ S = \{(a, c) \mid (a, c) \in A \times C$, and there exists $b \in B$ such that $(a, b) \in R$, and $(b, c) \in S\}$.

Example 2.18 *(Composition)*

Let $A = B = C = \{0, 1, 2, 3\}$ and the relations *R*, *S*, and *T* defined as follows :

$R \subseteq A \times B$, $R = \{(a, b) \mid a + b$ is an even number$\}\}$
$S \subseteq A \times B$, $S = \{(a, b) \mid b = (a + 2)$ MOD $3\}$
$T \subseteq B \times C$, $T = \{(b, c) \mid |b - c| = 1\}$

These relations can be explicitly written as

$R = \{(0, 0), (0, 2), (1, 1), (1, 3), (2, 0), (2, 2), (3, 1), (3, 3)\}\}$
$S = \{(0, 2), (1, 0), (2, 1), (3, 2)\}$, and
$T = \{(0, 1), (1, 0), (1, 2), (2, 1), (2, 3), (3, 2)\}$.

The relation matrices T_R, T_S, T_T for *R*, *S*, and *T* are given below.

$$T_R = \begin{array}{c} \\ 0 \\ 1 \\ 2 \\ 3 \end{array}\!\!\begin{array}{c} \begin{matrix} 0 & 1 & 2 & 3 \end{matrix} \\ \begin{bmatrix} 1 & 0 & 1 & 0 \\ 0 & 1 & 0 & 1 \\ 1 & 0 & 1 & 0 \\ 0 & 1 & 0 & 1 \end{bmatrix} \end{array} \quad T_S = \begin{array}{c} \\ 0 \\ 1 \\ 2 \\ 3 \end{array}\!\!\begin{array}{c} \begin{matrix} 0 & 1 & 2 & 3 \end{matrix} \\ \begin{bmatrix} 0 & 0 & 1 & 0 \\ 1 & 0 & 0 & 0 \\ 0 & 1 & 0 & 0 \\ 0 & 0 & 1 & 0 \end{bmatrix} \end{array} \quad T_T = \begin{array}{c} \\ 0 \\ 1 \\ 2 \\ 3 \end{array}\!\!\begin{array}{c} \begin{matrix} 0 & 1 & 2 & 3 \end{matrix} \\ \begin{bmatrix} 0 & 1 & 0 & 0 \\ 1 & 0 & 1 & 0 \\ 0 & 1 & 0 & 1 \\ 0 & 0 & 1 & 0 \end{bmatrix} \end{array}$$

Relations $R \cup S$, $R \cap S$, and R' can be easily obtained directly through the definitions of union, intersection and complementation given above. Their relation matrices $T_{R \cup S}$, $T_{R \cap S}$, and $T_{R'}$ are given below.

$$T_{R \cup S} = \begin{array}{c} \\ 0 \\ 1 \\ 2 \\ 3 \end{array}\!\!\begin{array}{c} \begin{matrix} 0 & 1 & 2 & 3 \end{matrix} \\ \begin{bmatrix} 1 & 0 & 1 & 0 \\ 1 & 1 & 0 & 1 \\ 1 & 1 & 1 & 0 \\ 0 & 1 & 1 & 1 \end{bmatrix} \end{array} \quad T_{R \cap S} = \begin{array}{c} \\ 0 \\ 1 \\ 2 \\ 3 \end{array}\!\!\begin{array}{c} \begin{matrix} 0 & 1 & 2 & 3 \end{matrix} \\ \begin{bmatrix} 0 & 0 & 1 & 0 \\ 0 & 0 & 0 & 0 \\ 0 & 0 & 0 & 0 \\ 0 & 0 & 0 & 0 \end{bmatrix} \end{array} \quad T_{R'} = \begin{array}{c} \\ 0 \\ 1 \\ 2 \\ 3 \end{array}\!\!\begin{array}{c} \begin{matrix} 0 & 1 & 2 & 3 \end{matrix} \\ \begin{bmatrix} 0 & 1 & 0 & 1 \\ 1 & 0 & 1 & 0 \\ 0 & 1 & 0 & 1 \\ 1 & 0 & 1 & 0 \end{bmatrix} \end{array}$$

Let us now compute the composite relation $R \circ T$. By definition of $R \circ T$, the ordered pair (0, 0) is in $R \circ T$ if and only if there exists an $x \in B$ such that $(0, x) \in R$, and $(x, 0) \in T$. From the relation matrix T_R of R we see that there are two ordered pairs, (0, 0) and (0, 2) in R with 0 as the first element. The corresponding second elements are 0, and 2 respectively. Therefore if any of the pairs (0, 0) and (2, 0) appears in T, then (0, 0) is in $R \circ T$. However, a look into the relation matrix of T, *i.e.*, T_T, reveals that neither (0, 0), nor (2, 0) belongs to the relation T. Hence $(0, 0) \notin R \circ T$, and $T_{R \circ T}(0, 0) = 0$. On the other hand $(0, 1) \in R \circ T$ because $(0, 2) \in R$ and $(2, 1) \in T$. Computations of other elements of $R \circ T$ are shown below.

$$\begin{array}{llll}
(0, 2) \in R & \text{and} & (2, 1) \in T, & \therefore \ (0, 1) \in R \circ T \\
(0, 2) \in R & \text{and} & (2, 3) \in T, & \therefore \ (0, 3) \in R \circ T \\
(1, 1) \in R & \text{and} & (1, 0) \in T, & \therefore \ (1, 0) \in R \circ T \\
(1, 1) \in R & \text{and} & (1, 2) \in T, & \therefore \ (1, 2) \in R \circ T \\
(2, 0) \in R & \text{and} & (0, 1) \in T, & \therefore \ (2, 1) \in R \circ T \\
(2, 2) \in R & \text{and} & (2, 3) \in T, & \therefore \ (2, 3) \in R \circ T \\
(3, 1) \in R & \text{and} & (1, 0) \in T, & \therefore \ (3, 0) \in R \circ T \\
(3, 1) \in R & \text{and} & (1, 2) \in T, & \therefore \ (3, 2) \in R \circ T
\end{array}$$

Hence the relation matrix $T_{R \circ T}$ for $R \circ T$ looks like

$$T_{R \circ T} = \begin{array}{c} \\ 0 \\ 1 \\ 2 \\ 3 \end{array} \begin{array}{c} \begin{array}{cccc} 0 & 1 & 2 & 3 \end{array} \\ \begin{bmatrix} 0 & 1 & 0 & 1 \\ 1 & 0 & 1 & 0 \\ 0 & 1 & 0 & 1 \\ 1 & 0 & 1 & 0 \end{bmatrix} \end{array}$$

It should be noted that for crisp relations R and T their composition $R \circ T$ as defined above and their *max–min* composition, to be defined in the next subsection in the context of fuzzy relations, are equivalent. In fact crisp composition is a special case of max–min composition and the later is a generalized concept which is applicable to the realm of fuzzy relations too.

2.5.2 Fuzzy Relations

As stated earlier the concept of crisp relations can be generalized to that of *fuzzy relations*. All we have to do is to allow the pairs of elements to be partially related, i.e., the entries of the relation matrix would be anything between 0 and 1. Let us consider some simple instances before the formal definition of fuzzy relations is presented.

Example 2.19 (*Fuzzy relation*)

Let $P = \{money, fame, power\}$ and $Q = \{politics, showbiz, academics\}$ be two crisp sets. Then R might be an imaginary relation between P and Q expressed by the relation matrix

$$T_R = \begin{array}{c} \\ m \\ f \\ p \end{array} \begin{array}{c} \begin{array}{ccc} ps & sz & as \end{array} \\ \begin{bmatrix} 0.7 & 0.9 & 0.6 \\ 0.8 & 0.9 & 0.5 \\ 1.0 & 0.7 & 0.3 \end{bmatrix} \end{array} \qquad \begin{array}{ll} m : money & ps : politics \\ f : fame & sz : showbiz \\ p : power & as : academics \end{array}$$

Example 2.20 (*Fuzzy relation*)

Let us consider the set of all real numbers in the interval $P = [\,0, 1\,] = \{x \mid 0 \le x \le 1\}$. A relation R, say *a close to b*, on P^2 (i.e. $P \times P$) may be defined in the following way

$$R\,(a, b) = 1 - |\,a - b\,|,\ \forall\ a, b \text{ in } [\,0, 1\,]$$

It should be noted that fuzzy relations defined on discrete sets can be expressed with the help of relation matrices. Relations defined on continuous domains as exemplified in Example 2.20 cannot be expressed with any relation matrix. Moreover, in the foregoing discussions we have considered fuzzy relations on crisp sets. It is also possible to define a fuzzy relation on fuzzy sets. This is dependent on the concept of *fuzzy Cartesian product.*

Definition 2.21 (*Fuzzy Cartesian product*) Let A and B be two fuzzy sets on reference sets X and Y respectively. The fuzzy Cartesian product of A and B, denoted by $A \times B$, is defined as $A \times B \subseteq X \times Y$, and $\mu_{A \times B}(a, b) = min\ \{\mu_A(a), \mu_B(b)\} \forall a \in X, \forall b \in Y$.

Example 2.21 (*Fuzzy Cartesian product*)

Let us consider the reference sets $X = \{m, n\}$ and $Y = \{p, q, r\}$ and the fuzzy sets A and B defined on them.

$$A = \frac{0.3}{m} + \frac{0.7}{n}, \qquad B = \frac{0.5}{p} + \frac{0.1}{q} + \frac{0.8}{r}$$

Now $\mu_{A \times B}(m, p) = min\ \{\mu_A(m), \mu_B(p)\} = min\ \{0.3, 0.5\} = 0.3$. But $\mu_{A \times B}(m, q) = min\ \{\mu_A(m), \mu_B(q)\} = min\ \{0.3, 0.1\} = 0.1$. The membership values of the other elements of the fuzzy Cartesian product $A \times B$ can also be found in similar fashion. The Cartesian product itself can be looked upon as a fuzzy relation between the fuzzy sets A and B. It can be expressed with the help of the relation matrix

$$A \times B = \begin{array}{c} \\ m \\ n \end{array} \begin{array}{c} \begin{array}{ccc} p & q & r \end{array} \\ \begin{bmatrix} 0.3 & 0.1 & 0.3 \\ 0.5 & 0.1 & 0.7 \end{bmatrix} \end{array}$$

A **fuzzy relation** R between two fuzzy sets A and B is a subset of the fuzzy Cartesian product $A \times B$. Hence $R \subseteq A \times B$ where $A \times B$ is the fuzzy Cartesian product of the fuzzy sets A and B.

Example 2.22 (*Fuzzy relation*)

We consider the fuzzy sets A and B cited in Example 2.21 and their Cartesian product. The relation matrix given below presents a subset of $A \times B$ because for all $x \in X$ and $y \in Y$, $\mu_R(x, y) \le \mu_{A \times B}(x, y)$. Therefore R is a fuzzy relation between the fuzzy sets A and B.

$$R = \begin{array}{c} \\ m \\ n \end{array} \begin{array}{c} \begin{array}{ccc} p & q & r \end{array} \\ \begin{bmatrix} 0.2 & 0.1 & 0.1 \\ 0.3 & 0.0 & 0.5 \end{bmatrix} \end{array}$$

Now let us consider the matrix R' given below.

$$R' = \begin{array}{c} \\ m \\ n \end{array} \begin{array}{c} \begin{array}{ccc} p & q & r \end{array} \\ \begin{bmatrix} 0.2 & 0.3 & 0.1 \\ 0.3 & 0.0 & 0.5 \end{bmatrix} \end{array}$$

Here $R'(m, q) = 0.3 > A \times B\ (m, q) = 0.1$. Hence R' is not a fuzzy relation between the fuzzy sets A and B.

2.5.3 Operations on Fuzzy Relations

The familiar set theoretic operations, e.g., union, intersection, complementation etc. are applicable to fuzzy relations also.

Union	$(R \cup S)\ (x, y) = max\ \{R\ (x, y), S\ (x, y)\}$
Intersection	$(R \cap S)\ (x, y) = min\ \{R\ (x, y), S\ (x, y)\}$
Complementation	$R'\ (x, y) = 1 - R\ (x, y)$

Moreover, the common relations of inclusion, dominance, and equality also hold good for fuzzy relations.

Inclusion	$R \subseteq S$	if $\forall x, y, R\ (x, y) \leq S\ (x, y)$
Dominance	$R \supseteq S$	if $\forall x, y, R\ (x, y) \geq S\ (x, y)$
Equality	$R = S$	if $\forall x, y, R\ (x, y) = S\ (x, y)$

Apart from the operations and properties stated above the crisp relational operation of composition of two relations is generalized to the so-called *max–min composition* of fuzzy relations.

Definition 2.22 (*max–min composition*) Let A, B, and C be three crisp sets. R and S are fuzzy relations over $A \times B$ and $B \times C$ respectively. The max–min composition of R and S, denoted by $R \circ S$, is a relation over $A \times C$ such that

$$(R \circ S)(x,z) = \max_{y \in B} \{\min\{R(x,y), S(y,z)\}\}$$

Example 2.23 (*max–min composition*)

Suppose $A = \{a, b, c\}$, $B = \{x, y\}$, and $C = \{p, q, r\}$ be three crisp sets. There are two fuzzy relations R and S defined over $A \times B$ and $B \times C$, respectively. The relation matrices of R and S are

$$R = \begin{array}{c} \\ a \\ b \\ c \end{array} \begin{array}{c} \begin{array}{cc} x & y \end{array} \\ \begin{bmatrix} 0.3 & 0.7 \\ 0.9 & 0.4 \\ 0.2 & 0.5 \end{bmatrix} \end{array}, \quad S = \begin{array}{c} \\ x \\ y \end{array} \begin{array}{c} \begin{array}{ccc} p & q & r \end{array} \\ \begin{bmatrix} 0.4 & 0.1 & 0.8 \\ 0.3 & 0.7 & 0.6 \end{bmatrix} \end{array}$$

The max–min composition $R \circ S$ is defined on the Cartesian product $A \times C$. Let us consider the computation of the first element $(R \circ S)\ (a, p)$.

$$(R \circ S)(a,p) = \max_{i \in B} \{\min(R(a,i), S(i,p))\}$$
$$= \max \{\min (R (a, x), S (x, p)), \min (R (a, y), S (y, p))\}$$
$$= \max \{\min (0.3, 0.4), \min (0.7, 0.3)\}$$
$$= \max \{0.3, 0.3\}$$
$$= 0.3$$

Similarly, the next element is computed as follows.

$$(R \circ S)(a,q) = \max_{i \in B} \{\min(R(a,i), S(i,q))\}$$
$$= \max \{\min (R (a, x), S (x, q)), \min (R (a, y), S (y, q))\}$$
$$= \max \{\min (0.3, 0.1), \min (0.7, 0.7)\}$$
$$= \max \{0.1, 0.7\}$$
$$= 0.7$$

Computation of the rest of the elements is left as an exercise. Finally $R \circ S$ looks like

$$R \circ S = \begin{array}{c} \\ a \\ b \\ c \end{array} \begin{array}{c} \begin{array}{ccc} p & q & r \end{array} \\ \begin{bmatrix} 0.3 & 0.7 & 0.6 \\ 0.4 & 0.7 & 0.8 \\ 0.3 & 0.5 & 0.5 \end{bmatrix} \end{array}$$

Example 2.24 (*max–min composition*)

Let us consider two kinds of troubles a PC may suffer from, viz., the *system hangs while running*, and *the system does not boot*. We symbolize the former by h and the later by b and define the set $A = \{h, b\}$ of PC troubles. Two possible causes of these troubles are *computer virus* (v) and *disc crash* (c) and they form the set $B = \{c, v\}$ of PC trouble makers. And finally, let the sources of the causes mentioned above are *internet* (i) and *obsolescence* (o) and $C = \{i, o\}$ is the set of PC trouble causes. The relation between PC troubles and their causes is expressed by R, a fuzzy relation over $A \times B$. Similarly, S is the fuzzy relation over $B \times C$, i.e., the relation between the causes of troubles and the sources of those causes. The relations R and S in terms of their relation matrices are shown below.

$$R = \begin{array}{c} \\ h \\ b \end{array} \begin{array}{c} \begin{array}{cc} v & c \end{array} \\ \begin{bmatrix} 0.7 & 0.2 \\ 0.5 & 0.8 \end{bmatrix} \end{array}, \qquad S = \begin{array}{c} \\ v \\ c \end{array} \begin{array}{c} \begin{array}{cc} i & o \end{array} \\ \begin{bmatrix} 0.9 & 0.7 \\ 0.1 & 0.2 \end{bmatrix} \end{array}$$

The relation between PC troubles and their ultimate sources, *i.e.*, between A and C, can be computed on the basis of R and S above as the max–min composition $R \circ S$. The first element of $R \circ S$, expressed as $(R \circ S)$ (h, i) is computed as follows.

$$(R \circ S)(h, i) = max \{min (R (h, v), S (v, i)), min (R (h, c), S (c, i))\}$$
$$= max \{min (0.7, 0.9), min (0.2, 0.1)\}$$
$$= max \{0.7, 0.1\}$$
$$= 0.7$$

The rest of the elements of $R \circ S$ can be found in a similar fashion.

$$(R \circ S)(h, o) = 0.7$$
$$(R \circ S)(b, i) = 0.5$$
$$(R \circ S)(b, o) = 0.5$$

And finally we get,

$$R \circ S = \begin{array}{c} \\ h \\ b \end{array} \begin{array}{c} \begin{array}{cc} i & o \end{array} \\ \begin{bmatrix} 0.7 & 0.7 \\ 0.5 & 0.5 \end{bmatrix} \end{array}$$

2.6 FUZZY EXTENSION PRINCIPLE

This section presents a discussion on the fuzzy extension principle which provides a way to map certain mathematical concepts of crisp set theory to their fuzzy counterparts.

2.6.1 Preliminaries

Before we present the fuzzy extension principle, it is necessary to understand a few concepts that form the basis of the said principle. This subsection provides the groundwork for this purpose.

(a) **Level set:** Corresponding to every fuzzy set there is a crisp set consisting of the membership values of its singletons. This is known as the *level set* of the fuzzy set. Its members are real values between 0 and 1, including 1 but excluding 0.

Definition 2.23 (*Level set*) Let F be a fuzzy set on the universe U. The level set of F, denoted as $L(F)$, is a crisp set of real values $x \in (0, 1]$ such that for each $x \in L(F)$ there is a singleton $(y, x) \in F$.

$$L(F) = \{x \mid 0 < x \leq 1 \text{ and } \exists\, y \in U \text{ such that } \mu_F(y) = x\}$$

Example 2.25 (*Level set*)

Let F be a fuzzy set on the universe $U = \{a, b, c, d, e\}$.

$$F = \frac{0.3}{a} + \frac{0.8}{b} + \frac{0.0}{c} + \frac{0.5}{d} + \frac{0.7}{e}$$

The corresponding level set is $L(F) = \{0.3, 0.5, 0.7, 0.8\}$. It may be noted that the membership value 0.0 of the element c is not included in $L(F)$.

Example 2.26 (*Level set*)

Let F be a fuzzy set on the universe $U = \{a, b, c, d, e\}$.

$$F = \frac{0.3}{a} + \frac{0.8}{b} + \frac{0.0}{c} + \frac{0.3}{d} + \frac{0.7}{e}$$

The corresponding level set is $L(F) = \{0.3, 0.7, 0.8\}$. The membership value 0.3 is repeated twice in F so that there are only three distinct non-zero membership values included in $L(F)$.

Example 2.27 *(Level set)*

Let us consider the following membership function for a fuzzy set F.

$$\mu_F(x) = 1 - e^{-x}, \quad \text{if } x \geq 0$$
$$= 0, \quad \text{otherwise.}$$

If the universe of discourse is the entire real line extending from $-\infty$ to $+\infty$ then the membership function will attain values within the range [0, 1). Hence $L(F) = (0, 1)$.

(b) **α-cut:** Occasionally we are interested in the elements whose degrees of membership to a given fuzzy set lie above a given level. This is provided with the help of the *α-cut*.

Definition 2.24 *(α-cut)* Let F be a fuzzy set on the universe U and α be a number such that $0 < \alpha \leq 1$. The α-cut of F, denoted as F_α, is a crisp set containing those elements of U whose membership value with respect to the fuzzy set F is greater than, or equal to, α.

$$F_\alpha = \{x \in U \mid \mu_F(x) \geq \alpha\}$$

Example 2.28 *(α-cut)*

Let $U = \{a, b, c, d\}$ be a universe and F be a fuzzy set on U.

$$F = \frac{0.6}{a} + \frac{0.3}{b} + \frac{0.7}{c} + \frac{1.0}{d}$$

The α-cuts for various α are : $F_{1.0} = \{d\}$, $F_{0.7} = \{c, d\}$, $F_{0.6} = \{a, c, d\}$, $F_{0.3} = \{a, b, c, d\}$. Moreover, it is obvious from the example that

$$\text{For all } \alpha, 0 < \alpha \leq 0.3, F_\alpha = F_{0.3}$$
$$\text{For all } \alpha, 0.3 < \alpha \leq 0.6, F_\alpha = F_{0.6}$$
$$\text{For all } \alpha, 0.6 < \alpha \leq 0.7, F_\alpha = F_{0.7}$$
$$\text{For all } \alpha, 0.7 < \alpha \leq 1.0, F_\alpha = F_{1.0}$$

Example 2.29 *(α-cut)*

Let F be a fuzzy set defined on $U = [0, 1]$. The membership function μ_F is graphically shown in Fig. 2.28. Fig. 2.29 shows the profile of the α-cut of F for $\alpha = 0.7$.

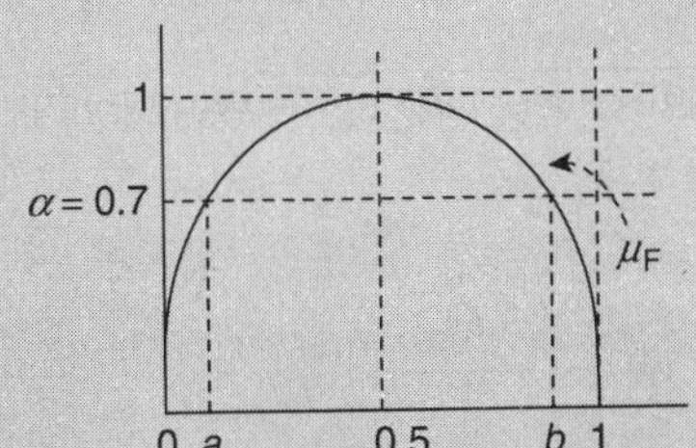

Fig. 2.28

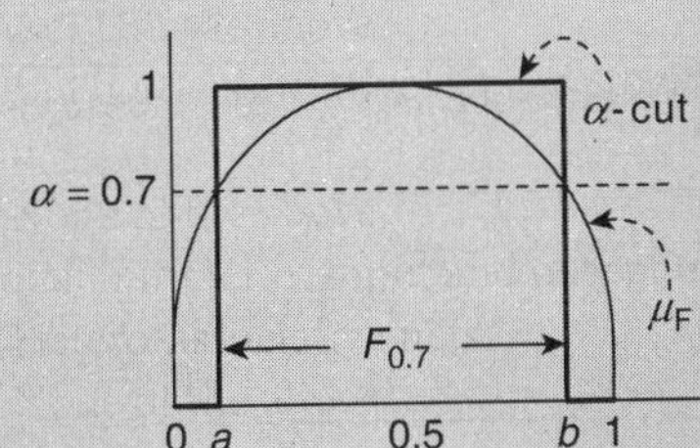

Fig. 2.29

It may be noted that as α increases from 0 to 1, the size of the corresponding α-cuts decreases, i.e., given two real values α and β, $0 < \alpha \leq \beta \leq 1$, we must have $F_\alpha \supseteq F_\beta$.

(c) **The α-cut decomposition theorem:** Before introducing the α-cut decomposition theorem we need to get acquainted with a new notation. Given a crisp set A, and a real number x, $0 \le x \le 1$, $x.A$ is a fuzzy set consisting of all members of A with membership value x. For example, if $A = \{p, q, r\}$ and x is 0.4, then $x.A = \{(p, 0.4), (q, 0.4), (r, 0.4)\}$.

The **α-cut decomposition theorem** states that any fuzzy set F can be decomposed into a number of the α-cuts, say F_αs, such that

$$F = \bigcup_{\alpha} \alpha.F_\alpha$$

Example 2.30 *(α-cut decomposition theorem)*

Let $F = \frac{0.6}{a} + \frac{0.3}{b} + \frac{0.7}{c} + \frac{1.0}{d}$ be a fuzzy set on the universe $U = \{a, b, c, d\}$. We see

$F_{0.3} = \{a, b, c, d\}$, and $0.3.F_{0.3} = \frac{0.3}{a} + \frac{0.3}{b} + \frac{0.3}{c} + \frac{0.3}{d}$

$F_{0.6} = \{a, c, d\}$, and $0.6.F_{0.6} = \frac{0.6}{a} + \frac{0.6}{c} + \frac{0.6}{d}$

$F_{0.7} = \{c, d\}$, and $0.7.F_{0.7} = \frac{0.7}{c} + \frac{0.7}{d}$

$F_{1.0} = \{d\}$, and $1.0.F_{1.0} = \frac{1.0}{d}$

Therefore $(0.3.F_{0.3}) \cup (0.6.F_{0.6}) \cup (0.7.F_{0.7}) \cup (1.0.F_{1.0}) = \frac{0.6}{a} + \frac{0.3}{b} + \frac{0.7}{c} + \frac{1.0}{d} = F$

(d) **Restricted scalar multiplication (*RSM*)**: Restricted scalar multiplication (*RSM*) is a way of relating two fuzzy sets. Given a fuzzy set F on the universe U, and a real number α, $0 \le \alpha \le 1$, **restricted scalar multiplication** (*RSM*) of F by α is the process of creating another set, denoted by αF on the same universe whose memberships are obtained as

$$\mu_{\alpha F}(x) = \alpha \,.\, \mu_F(x),\ \forall x \in U$$

RSM is a kind of fuzzification procedure because it produces a fuzzy set out of a given set, crisp, or fuzzy.

Example 2.31 *(Restricted scalar multiplication)*

Consider the fuzzy set $F = \frac{0.6}{a} + \frac{0.3}{b} + \frac{0.7}{c} + \frac{1.0}{d}$ on the universe $U = \{a, b, c, d\}$ cited in Example 2.30. If $\alpha = 0.1$. Then *RSM* of F by α produces the set $\alpha F = \frac{0.06}{a} + \frac{0.03}{b} + \frac{0.07}{c} + \frac{0.1}{d}$.

Like other operations on fuzzy sets *RSM* too satisfies certain properties. Given the fuzzy sets F and G on the universe U, and two real numbers α, β, $0 < \alpha, \beta \le 1$, the following properties hold good.

(i) $\alpha(F \cup G) = \alpha F \cup \alpha G$
(ii) $\alpha(F \cap G) = \alpha F \cap \alpha G$
(iii) $(\alpha\beta) F = \alpha(\beta F)$
(iv) $1 . F = F$
(v) $\alpha F \subseteq F$

Definition 2.25 (*Fuzzy cardinality*) Let F be a fuzzy set on the universe U. $L(F)$ is the level set of F and for all $\alpha \in L(F)$, F_α is the α-cut of F. The fuzzy cardinality of F, denoted by $f_c(F)$, is defined as the fuzzy set

$$f_c(F) = \sum_{\alpha \in L(F)} \frac{\alpha}{|F_\alpha|}$$

$|F_\alpha|$ is the cardinality of F_α which is a natural number. Therefore, fuzzy cardinality of any fuzzy set is another fuzzy set defined on natural numbers. The following example illustrates the concept of fuzzy cardinality.

Example 2.32 (*Fuzzy cardinality*)

Let us consider the fuzzy set H of four happy persons.

$$H = \frac{0.3}{mita} + \frac{0.7}{neeta} + \frac{0.4}{jeet} + \frac{0.8}{joy}$$

We have the level set $L(H) = \{0.3, 0.4, 0.7, 0.8\}\}$and the following cardinalities

$$|H_{0.3}| = |\{mita, neeta, jeet, joy\}| = 4,$$
$$|H_{0.4}| = |\{neeta, jeet, joy\}| = 3,$$
$$|H_{0.7}| = |\{neeta, joy\}| = 2,$$
$$|H_{0.8}| = |\{joy\}| = 1.$$

Hence the fuzzy cardinality of H is given by

$$f_c(H) = \sum_{\alpha \in L(H)} \frac{\alpha}{|H_\alpha|} = \frac{0.3}{4} + \frac{0.4}{3} + \frac{0.7}{2} + \frac{0.8}{1}$$

2.6.2 The Extension Principle

The extension principle provides a way to map certain mathematical concepts pertaining to crisp sets to their fuzzy counterparts.

Consider a function $f: U_1 \times U_2 \times \cdots \times U_n \to V$ where the U_is and V are crisp sets and $U_1 \times U_2 \times \cdots \times U_n$ is the Cartesian product of $U_1, U_2, \ldots, U_n$. If there is a point $(u_1, u_2, \ldots, u_n)$ in the n-dimensional space $U_1 \times U_2 \times \cdots \times U_n$ and there is a $v \in V$ such that $f(u_1, u_2, \ldots, u_n) = v$ then v is said to be the *image* of the point $(u_1, u_2, \ldots, u_n)$. Equivalently, the point $(u_1, u_2, \ldots, u_n)$ is referred to as the *pre-image* of v, (see Fig. 2.30) and is indicated by the expression

$$(u_1, u_2, \ldots, u_n) = f^{-1}(v)$$

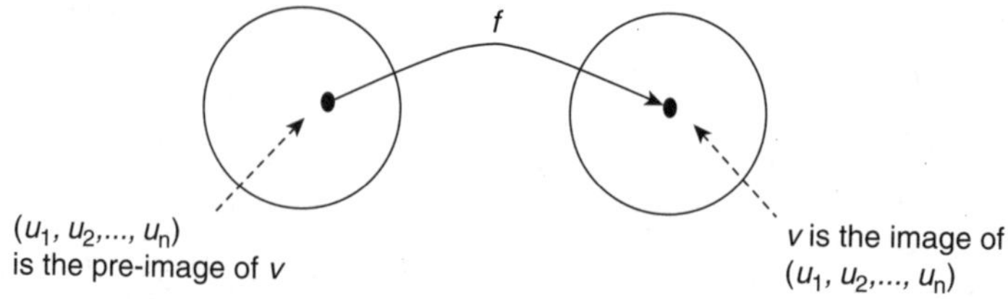

Fig. 2.30. *An image and its pre-image under function f*

Now, let us consider fuzzy sets $A_1, A_2, \ldots, A_n$ on the universes $U_1, U_2, \ldots, U_n$ respectively. Given the function f as mentioned above it is possible to construct a fuzzy set B on V in the following manner: for each $v \in V$ we define

$$\mu_B(v) = 0, \text{ if } f^{-1}(v) = \phi, \text{ i.e., there is no pre-image of } v \text{ in } U_1 \times U_2 \times \cdots \times U_n$$
$$= max \quad \{min\,(\mu_{A1}(u_1), \mu_{A2}(u_2), \ldots, \mu_{An}(u_n))\} \text{ otherwise.}$$
$$\forall\,(u_1, u_2, \ldots, u_n), \text{ where } (u_1, u_2, \ldots, u_n) = f^{-1}(v)$$

If we define a fuzzy set A on $A_1 \times A_2 \times \cdots \times A_n$ where $\mu_A(u_1, u_2, \ldots, u_n) = min\,\{\mu_{A1}(u_1), \mu_{A2}(u_2), \ldots, \mu_{An}(u_n)\}$ then the procedure described above to obtain the fuzzy set B can be considered to be an extension of the crisp function $f: U_1 \times U_2 \times \cdots \times U_n \rightarrow V$ to the corresponding fuzzy domain $f: A_1 \times A_2 \times \cdots \times A_n \rightarrow B$. Here the fuzzy set B is termed as the image of A under f, and is denoted as $B = f(A)$. The subsequent two examples illustrate the extension principle described above.

Example 2.33 (*Fuzzy extension principle*)

Let us consider the crisp domains $P = \{3, 4, 5\}$, $Q = \{6, 7, 8\}$, and $R = \{0, 1, 2\}$. Table 2.8 shows the function $f: P \times Q \rightarrow R$ where f is defined as *addition modulo 3*. Fig. 2.31 depicts the function graphically.

We see that $f(3, 6) = f(5, 7) = f(4, 8) = 0$ so that 0 has three pre-images, (3, 6), (5, 7), and (4, 8). Therefore $f^{1}(0) = \{(3, 6), (5, 7), (4, 8)\}$. Similarly, $f^{1}(1) = \{(4, 6), (3, 7), (5, 8)\}\}$and $f^{1}(2) = \{(5, 6), (4, 7), (3, 8)\}$.

Table 2.8. *The function f ≡ Addition modulo 3*

↑ P ↓ \ ← Q →	6	7	8
3	0	1	2
4	1	2	0
5	2	0	1

Now consider the fuzzy sets A and B on P and Q respectively as described below.

$$A = \frac{0.1}{3} + \frac{0.8}{4} + \frac{0.5}{5}, \qquad B = \frac{0.6}{6} + \frac{0.2}{7} + \frac{0.7}{8}$$

Applying the procedure of extension principle, it is possible to *extend* the function $f \equiv$ *Addition modulo 3* as *Fuzzy addition modulo 3* from $A \times B$ to C, where C is a fuzzy set defined on R. The membership values of various $x \in R$ in the fuzzy set C are obtained as described below

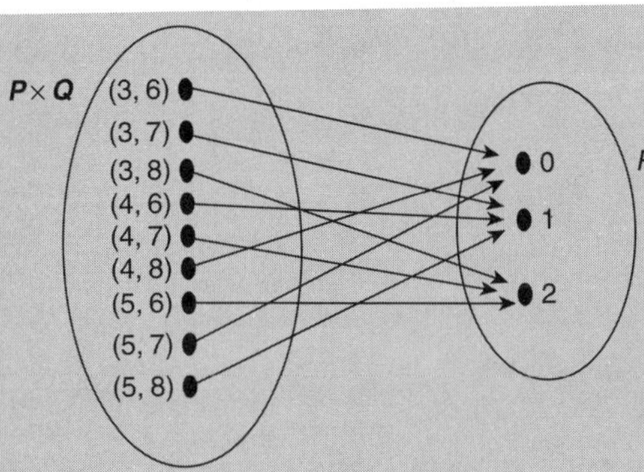

Fig. 2.31. *Addition modulo 3 over P Q.*

(a) For $0 \in R$

$f^{-1}(0) = \{(3, 6), (5, 7), (4, 8)\}$

$\therefore \mu_C(0) = max\ \{min\ (\mu_A(3), \mu_B(6)), min\ (\mu_A(5), \mu_B(7)), min\ (\mu_A(4), \mu_B(8))\}$

$= max\ \{min\ (0.1, 0.6), min\ (0.5, 0.2), min\ (0.8, 0.7)\}$

$= max\ \{0.1, 0.2, 0.7\}$

$= 0.7.$

(b) For $1 \in R$

$f^{-1}(1) = \{(4, 6), (3, 7), (5, 8)\}$

$\therefore \mu_C(1) = max\ \{min\ (\mu_A(4), \mu_B(6)), min\ (\mu_A(3), \mu_B(7)), min\ (\mu_A(5), \mu_B(8))\}$

$= max\ \{min\ (0.8, 0.6), min\ (0.1, 0.2), min\ (0.5, 0.7)\}$

$= max\ \{0.6, 0.1, 0.5\}$

$= 0.6.$

(c) For $2 \in R$

$f^{-1}(2) = \{(5, 6), (4, 7), (3, 8)\}$

$\therefore \mu_C(2) = max\ \{min\ (\mu_A(5), \mu_B(6)), min\ (\mu_A(4), \mu_B(7)), min\ (\mu_A(3), \mu_B(8))\}$

$= max\ \{min\ (0.5, 0.6), min\ (0.8, 0.2), min\ (0.1, 0.7)\}$

$= max\ \{0.5, 0.2, 0.1\}$

$= 0.5.$

Hence the image of $A \times B$ under f is given by $C = \{(0, 0.7), (1, 0.6), (2, 0.5)\}$, or

$$C = \frac{0.7}{0} + \frac{0.6}{1} + \frac{0.5}{2}$$

Example 2.34 (*Fuzzy extension principle*)

Let $P = \{a, b, c\}$, $Q = \{d, e, f\}$, and $R = \{g, h, i, j, k\}\}$ be three crisp sets, and $f : P \times Q \rightarrow R$ be a function defined as $f(x, y) = x + y + 2$, where '+' is to be interpreted as the addition of the sequence number of x and y in the English alphabet. For example, the letter a has the sequence number 1 as it is the first letter of the English alphabet, and that of the letter d is 4. Therefore the expression $a + d$ produces the letter with sequence number $1 + 4 = 5$, the letter e. Similarly, $a + d + 2 = g$. Table 2.9 shows the function table for the function $f : P \times Q \rightarrow R$. Fig. 2.32 shows the same function graphically.

Table 2.9. *Function Table of f (x, y) = x + y + 2*

P \ Q	d	e	f
a	g	h	i
b	h	i	j
c	i	j	k

Now, let us consider the fuzzy sets A and B on P and Q as described below.

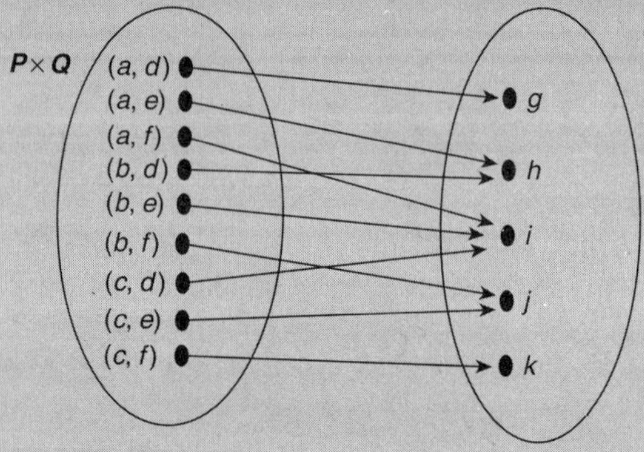

Fig. 2.32. $f(x, y) = x + y + 2$ over $P \times Q$

$$A = \frac{0.4}{a} + \frac{0.3}{b} + \frac{0.8}{c}, \qquad B = \frac{0.7}{d} + \frac{0.5}{e} + \frac{0.8}{f}$$

Computation of the fuzzy set C on R as the image of $A \times B$ with the extension principle is detailed below.

(a) For $g \in R$

$f^{-1}(g) = \{(a, d)\}$

$$\begin{aligned}\therefore \mu_C(g) &= max\ \{min\ (\mu_A(a), \mu_B(d))\} \\ &= max\ \{min\ (0.4, 0.7)\} \\ &= max\ \{0.4\} \\ &= 0.4.\end{aligned}$$

(b) For $h \in R$

$f^{-1}(h) = \{(a, e), (b, d)\}$

$$\begin{aligned}\therefore \mu_C(h) &= max\ \{min\ (\mu_A(a), \mu_B(e)), min\ (\mu_A(b), \mu_B(d))\} \\ &= max\ \{min\ (0.4, 0.5), min\ (0.3, 0.7)\} \\ &= max\ \{0.4, 0.3\} \\ &= 0.4.\end{aligned}$$

(c) For $i \in R$

$f^{-1}(i) = \{(a, f), (b, e), (c, d)\}$

$$\begin{aligned}\therefore \mu_C(i) &= max\ \{min\ (\mu_A(a), \mu_B(f)), min\ (\mu_A(b), \mu_B(e)), min\ (\mu_A(c), \mu_B(d))\} \\ &= max\ \{min\ (0.4, 0.8), min\ (0.3, 0.5), min\ (0.8, 0.7)\} \\ &= max\ \{0.4, 0.3, 0.7\} \\ &= 0.7.\end{aligned}$$

(d) For $j \in R$

$f^{-1}(j) = \{(b, f), (c, e)\}$

$\therefore \mu_C(j) = max\ \{min\ (\mu_A(b), \mu_B(f)), min\ (\mu_A(c), \mu_B(e))\}$

$= max\ \{min\ (0.3, 0.8), min\ (0.8, 0.5)\}$

$= max\ \{0.3, 0.5\}$

$= 0.5.$

(e) For $k \in R$

$f^{-1}(k) = \{(c, f)\}$

$\therefore \mu_C(k) = max\ \{min\ (\mu_A(c), \mu_B(f))\}$

$= max\ \{min\ (0.8, 0.8)\}$

$= max\ \{0.8\}$

$= 0.8.$

Hence the image of $A \times B$ under f is given by $C = f(A \times B) = \{(g, 0.4), (h, 0.4), (i, 0.7), (j, 0.5), (k, 0.8)\}$, *i.e.*,

$$C = \frac{0.4}{g} + \frac{0.4}{h} + \frac{0.7}{i} + \frac{0.5}{j} + \frac{0.8}{k}.$$

CHAPTER SUMMARY

A summary of the matters discussed in this chapter is provided below.

- Traditional set theory is not adequately equipped to model the vagueness/inexactness that we are used to tackle in our everyday life.
- Fuzzy set theory is an extension, or generalization, of crisp set theory that takes into account the vagueness mentioned above by allowing partial membership to set. Hence, the degree of membership of an element to a fuzzy set is any real value between 0 and 1, both inclusive.
- The membership profile of a fuzzy set is customarily expressed with the help of a membership function $\mu : U \to [0, 1]$. Popular membership functions are the triangular function, trapezoidal function, Gaussian function, *S*-function etc.
- Fuzzy sets are characterized with the help of certain parameters, e.g., normality, height, support, core, cardinality etc.
- Fuzzy sets are occasionally transformed through operations like normalization, dilation, concentration, contrast intensification, and fuzzyfication. These transformations help to deal with linguistic variables.
- Familiar crisp set operations, e.g., union, intersection, complementation, equality, inclusion, difference, disjunctive sum etc., are extended to fuzzy domain.
- Most of the properties of crisp sets, e.g., associativity, commutativity, distributivity, idempotency, De Morgan's law, transitivity etc., are also satisfied by fuzzy set operations. However, unlike crisp sets, in the fuzzy domain we have $P \cup P' \neq U$, and $P \cap P' \neq \Phi$ because $\mu_P(x) \in [\,0, 1\,]$, and $\mu_{P \cup P'}(x) = max\ \{\mu_P(x), 1 - \mu_P(x)\} \neq 1$, and $\mu_{P \cap P'}(x) = min\ \{\mu_P(x), 1 - \mu_P(x)\} \neq 0$.
- The concept of a crisp relation is generalized to fuzzy relation. A fuzzy relation may exist between two crisp sets, or two fuzzy sets. A fuzzy relation between two fuzzy sets is a subset of their fuzzy Cartesian product.
- A fuzzy relation between two crisp sets consists of ordered pairs of the elements of the sets and a membership value for each ordered pair that ranges from 0 to 1.

- Common operations on fuzzy relations are union, intersection, complementation, and max–min composition.
- The fuzzy extension principle provides a way to map certain mathematical concepts pertaining to crisp sets to their fuzzy counterparts.

SOLVED PROBLEMS

Problem 2.1 Which of the following sets are identical to each other?

$A = \{x \mid x \text{ is even and } 0 \le x \le 10\}$
$B = \{0, 2, 4, 6, 8\ 10\}$
$C = \{10, 0\ 8, 2, 6, 4\}$
$D = \{6, 8, 6, 0, 0, 4, 10, 10, 2\}$

Solution 2.1 All of the sets *A*, *B*, *C* and *D* have the same members, irrespective of their descriptions, ordering, or repetition. Hence all of them are identical. $A = B = C = D$.

Problem 2.2 Describe the following sets by citing a property shared by all its members.

A = {Helium, Neon, Argon, Krypton, Xenon, Radon}
$B = \{2, 3, 5, 7, 11, 13, 17, 19, 23\}$
$C = \{0, 3, 8, 15, 24, 35, 48, 63, \ldots\}$

Solution 2.2 The required descriptions are given below.

$A = \{x \mid x \text{ is an inert gas}\}$
$B = \{x \mid x \text{ is a prime number and } 2 \le x < 25\}$
$C = \{x^2 - 1 \mid x \text{ is a natural number}\}$

Problem 2.3 Let *A* be the set of all non-negative integers, *B* be that of the non-positive integers inclusive of 0 and *I* be the set of all integers, the universal set. Find $A \cup B$, $A \cap B$, A', B', $A - B$, $B - A$, and $A \oplus B$.

Solution 2.3 According to the problem statement, $A = \{0, 1, 2, 3, \ldots\}$, $B = \{0, -1, -2, -3, \ldots\}$, and $I = \{\ldots, -3, -2, -1, 0, 1, 2, 3, \ldots\}$. Therefore

$A \cup B = \{\ldots, -3, -2, -1, 0, 1, 2, 3, \ldots\} = I$
$A \cap B = \{0\}$
$A' = \{-1, -2, -3, \ldots\}$
$B' = \{1, 2, 3, \ldots\}$
$A - B = \{1, 2, 3, \ldots\} = B'$
$B - A = \{-1, -2, -3, \ldots\} = A'$
$A \oplus B = \{\ldots, -3, -2, -1, 1, 2, 3, \ldots\} = I - \{0\}$

Problem 2.4 For arbitrary sets *P* and *Q*, under what condition $P \times Q = Q \times P$?

Solution 2.4 By definition, $P \times Q = \{(x, y) \mid x \in P, \text{ and } y \in Q\}$ and $Q \times P = \{(x, y) \mid x \in Q, \text{ and } y \in P\}$. Hence $P \times Q = Q \times P$ if and only if $P = Q$.

Problem 2.5 Prove De Morgan's theorem with the help of Venn diagrams.

Solution 2.5 Fig. 2.33 (a) – (f) depict the process of constructing the sets $(P \cup Q)'$ and $P' \cap Q'$. It is seen that the Venn diagrams for $(P \cup Q)'$ and $P' \cap Q'$ are identical. Hence $(P \cup Q)' = P' \cap Q'$, as stated by De Morgan's theorem. The other part of the theorem, i.e., $(P \cap Q)' = P' \cup Q'$ can be proved similarly.

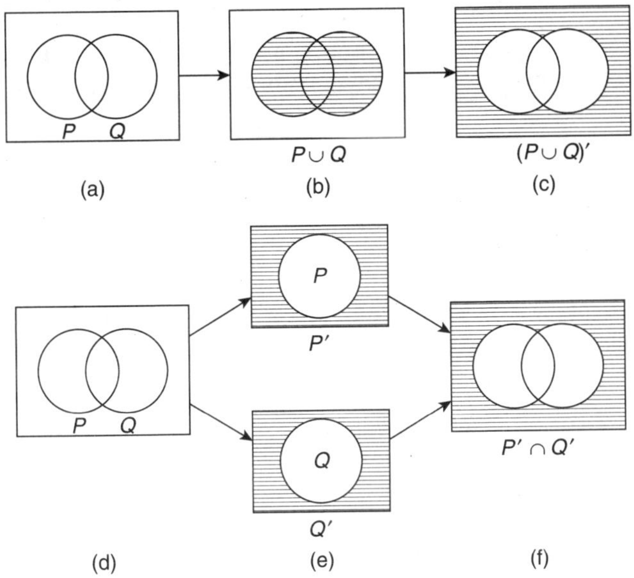

Fig. 2.33. *Proof of De Morgan's theorem.*

Problem 2.6 Prove that for any set S, $S \oplus S = \varnothing$.

Solution 2.6 $S \oplus S = (S \cap S') \cup (S' \cap S) = (\varnothing \cup \varnothing) = \varnothing$

Problem 2.7 Prove that $A - (A - B) = A \cap B$

Solution 2.7 L.H.S

$$
\begin{aligned}
&= A - (A - B) \\
&= A - (A \cap B') \\
&= A \cap (A \cap B')' \\
&= A \cap (A' \cup B) \\
&= (A \cap A') \cup (A \cap B) \\
&= \varnothing \cup (A \cap B) \\
&= A \cap B \\
&= \text{R.H.S}
\end{aligned}
$$

Problem 2.8 Prove that if $A \cup C = B \cup C$, and $A \cap C = B \cap C$, then $A = B$. However, $A \cup C = B \cup C$ does not imply that $A = B$. Nor $A \cap C = B \cap C$ implies that $A = B$.

Solution 2.8 $A = A \cup (A \cap C)$

$$
\begin{aligned}
&= A \cup (B \cap C) && \text{: Since } A \cap C = B \cap C \text{ (given)} \\
&= (A \cup B) \cap (A \cup C) \\
&= (A \cup B) \cap (B \cup C) && \text{: Since } A \cup C = B \cup C \text{ (given)} \\
&= (B \cup A) \cap (B \cup C)
\end{aligned}
$$

$$= B \cup (A \cap C)$$
$$= B \cup (B \cap C) \qquad : \text{Since } A \cap C = B \cap C \text{ (given)}$$
$$= B$$

The fact the $A \cup C = B \cup C \not\Rightarrow A = B$ can be proved by setting $A = \emptyset$, and $B = C \neq \emptyset$.

Problem 2.9 Let *F* be a fuzzy set of *matured* persons where the maturity is measured in terms of age in years. The fuzzy membership function followed is given below

$$\mu_F(x) = \begin{cases} 0, & if \quad x \leq 5 \\ \left(\dfrac{x-5}{20}\right)^2, & if \quad 5 \leq x \leq 25 \\ 1, & if \quad x \geq 25 \end{cases}$$

The universe consists of the individuals Sunny, Moon, Pikoo, Gina, Osho, Chang, Paul, Lalu, Lila, and Poly whose ages are 15, 20, 10, 27, 32, 12, 18, 24, 3, and 8 years respectively. Find the *normalcy* of the set as well as *Height* (*F*), *Support* (*F*), *Core* (*F*), and *Cardinality* (*F*).

Solution 2.9 We calculate the membership values of each individual with the help of the membership function to obtain the following fuzzy set

$$F = \frac{0.25}{Sunny} + \frac{0.5625}{Moon} + \frac{0.0625}{Pikoo} + \frac{1.0}{Gina} + \frac{1.0}{Osho} + \frac{0.1225}{Chang} + \frac{0.4225}{Paul} + \frac{0.9025}{Lalu} + \frac{0}{Lila} + \frac{0.0225}{Poly}$$

The set is normal because there are two members, Gina and Osho, who attain full memberships. Obviously, *Height* (*F*) = 1.0. *Support* (*F*) = {*Sunny, Moon, Pikoo, Gina, Osho, Chang, Paul, Lalu, Poly*}, *Core* (*F*) = {*Gina, Osho*}, and *Cardinality* (*F*) = 0.25 + 0.5625 + 0.0625 + 1.0 + 1.0 + 0.1225 + 0.4225 + 0.9025 + 0 + 0.0225 = 4.345.

Problem 2.10 Fig. 2.34 shows a membership profile in the form of a reverse triangle. It is defined as follows:

$$\mu_F(x) = \begin{cases} -x, & if \quad -1 \leq x \leq 0 \\ x, & if \quad 0 \leq x \leq 1 \\ 1, & \quad elsewhere \end{cases}$$

Apply the transforms of normalization, dilation, concentration, contrast intensification, and fuzzification on the membership function and show the resultant profiles.

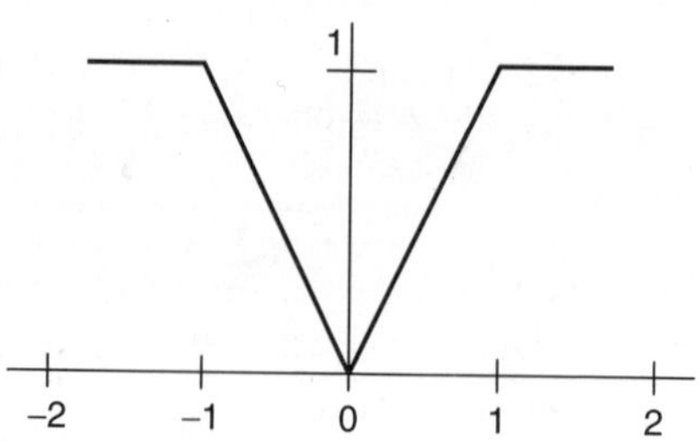

Fig. 2.34. *A reverse triangular membership function*

Solution 2.10 The given membership function is already normal and therefore normalization leaves the function unaltered. To obtain the shape of a transformed membership function, membership values at individual points are calculated. Then these values are mapped to the transformed membership values. For example, let us take the point $x = -0.5$ so that $\mu_F(x) = 0.5$. Under dilation, $DIL(\mu_F(x) = 0.5) = (0.5)^{0.5} = 0.71$ (approximate). On the other hand, under concentration, contrast intensification or fuzzification, this membership value maps to CON $(\mu_F(x) = 0.5) = (0.5)^2 = 0.25$, INT $(\mu_F(x) = 0.5) = 2 \times (0.5)^2 = 0.5$, and FUZZ $(\mu_F(x) = 0.5) = (0.5 / 2)^{0.5} = 0.5$ respectively. The approximate shapes of the transformed functions are shown with dotted line in Fig. 2.35 (*a*), Fig. 2.35 (*b*), Fig. 2.35 (*c*), and Fig. 2.35 (*d*).

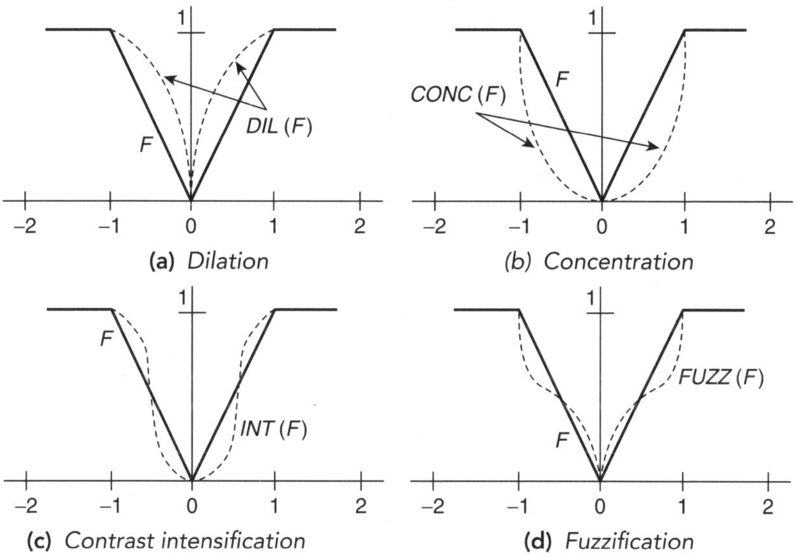

Fig. 2.35. *Transformations on the reverse triangular function.*

Problem 2.11 Let U = *Flowers* = {*Jasmine, Rose, Lotus, Daffodil, Sunflower, Hibiscus, Chrysanthemum*} be a universe on which two fuzzy sets, one of *Beautiful flowers* and the other one of *Fragrant flowers* are defined as shown below.

$$P = Beautiful\ flowers = \frac{0.3}{Jasmine} + \frac{0.9}{Rose} + \frac{1.0}{Lotus} + \frac{0.7}{Daffodil} + \frac{0.5}{Sunflower} + \frac{0.4}{Hibiscus} + \frac{0.6}{Chrysanthemum}$$

$$Q = Fragrant\ flowers = \frac{1.0}{Jasmine} + \frac{1.0}{Rose} + \frac{0.5}{Lotus} + \frac{0.2}{Daffodil} + \frac{0.2}{Sunflower} + \frac{0.1}{Hibiscus} + \frac{0.4}{Chrysanthemum}$$

Compute the fuzzy sets $P \cup Q$, $P \cap Q$, P', Q', $P - Q$, $P \oplus Q$. Also, verify that $P \cup P' \neq U$, $P \cap P' \neq \phi$.

Solution 2.11 The results are obtained directly from the definitions of the respective operations.

$$P \cup Q = \frac{1.0}{Jasmine} + \frac{1.0}{Rose} + \frac{1.0}{Lotus} + \frac{0.7}{Daffodil} + \frac{0.5}{Sunflower} + \frac{0.4}{Hibiscus} + \frac{0.6}{Chrysanthemum}$$

$$P \cap Q = \frac{0.3}{Jasmine} + \frac{0.9}{Rose} + \frac{0.5}{Lotus} + \frac{0.2}{Daffodil} + \frac{0.2}{Sunflower} + \frac{0.1}{Hibiscus} + \frac{0.4}{Chrysanthemum}$$

$$P' = \frac{0.7}{Jasmine} + \frac{0.1}{Rose} + \frac{0}{Lotus} + \frac{0.3}{Daffodil} + \frac{0.5}{Sunflower} + \frac{0.6}{Hibiscus} + \frac{0.4}{Chrysanthemum}$$

$$= \frac{0.7}{Jasmine} + \frac{0.1}{Rose} + \frac{0.3}{Daffodil} + \frac{0.5}{Sunflower} + \frac{0.6}{Hibiscus} + \frac{0.4}{Chrysanthemum}$$

$$Q' = \frac{0}{Jasmine} + \frac{0}{Rose} + \frac{0.5}{Lotus} + \frac{0.8}{Daffodil} + \frac{0.8}{Sunflower} + \frac{0.9}{Hibiscus} + \frac{0.6}{Chrysanthemum}$$

$$= \frac{0.5}{Lotus} + \frac{0.8}{Daffodil} + \frac{0.8}{Sunflower} + \frac{0.9}{Hibiscus} + \frac{0.6}{Chrysanthemum}$$

$$P - Q = P \cap Q'$$

$$= \frac{0}{Jasmine} + \frac{0}{Rose} + \frac{0.5}{Lotus} + \frac{0.7}{Daffodil} + \frac{0.5}{Sunflower} + \frac{0.4}{Hibiscus} + \frac{0.6}{Chrysanthemum}$$

$$P \oplus Q = (P \cap Q') \cup (P' \cap Q)$$

$$= \left(\frac{0}{Jasmine} + \frac{0}{Rose} + \frac{0.5}{Lotus} + \frac{0.7}{Daffodil} + \frac{0.5}{Sunflower} + \frac{0.4}{Hibiscus} + \frac{0.6}{Chrysanthemum}\right) \cup$$
$$\left(\frac{0.7}{Jasmine} + \frac{0.1}{Rose} + \frac{0}{Lotus} + \frac{0.2}{Daffodil} + \frac{0.2}{Sunflower} + \frac{0.1}{Hibiscus} + \frac{0.4}{Chrysanthemum}\right)$$

$$= \frac{0.7}{Jasmine} + \frac{0.1}{Rose} + \frac{0.5}{Lotus} + \frac{0.7}{Daffodil} + \frac{0.5}{Sunflower} + \frac{0.4}{Hibiscus} + \frac{0.6}{Chrysanthemum}$$

$$P \cup P'$$

$$= \frac{0.7}{Jasmine} + \frac{0.9}{Rose} + \frac{1.0}{Lotus} + \frac{0.7}{Daffodil} + \frac{0.5}{Sunflower} + \frac{0.6}{Hibiscus} + \frac{0.6}{Chrysanthemum} \neq U$$

$$P \cap P'$$

$$= \frac{0.3}{Jasmine} + \frac{0.1}{Rose} + \frac{0}{Lotus} + \frac{0.3}{Daffodil} + \frac{0.5}{Sunflower} + \frac{0.4}{Hibiscus} + \frac{0.4}{Chrysanthemum} \neq \varphi$$

Problem 2.12 Let A = {*Gogo, Didi, Pozzo, Lucky*} be a set of individuals and B = {*Colour, Game, Flower, Pet*}. Table 2.10 presents the liking data of these individuals with respect to the listed aspects. We define a relation R on $A \times A$ such that $x\,R\,y$ if there is z which both x and y likes. Show the relation matrix for R.

Table 2.10. *Liking data of Gogo, Didi, Pozzo and Lucky*

	Likes			
	Colour	**Game**	**Flower**	**Pet**
Gogo	Blue	Tennis	Rose	Parrot
Didi	Red	Baseball	Lotus	Parrot
Pozzo	Green	Soccer	Lotus	Dog
Lucky	Red	Tennis	Rose	Cat

Solution 2.12 The relation matrix is given in Table 2.11.

Table 2.11. *Relation matrix for R*

	R			
	Gogo	**Didi**	**Pozzo**	**Lucky**
Gogo	1	1	0	1
Didi	1	1	1	1
Pozzo	0	1	1	0
Lucky	1	1	0	1

Problem 2.13 Along with relation *R* of Problem 2.12, consider one more relation among Gogo, Didi, Pozzo, Lucky regarding who is fond of whom, as shown in Table 2.12. We define a relation *S* such that $x\ S\ y$ if there exists z for which x is fond of z and z is fond of y. Show the relation matrix of *S* and then find $R \cup S$, $R \cap S$, $R \circ S$.

Table 2.12. *Who is fond of whom*

	is fond of			
	Gogo	**Didi**	**Pozzo**	**Lucky**
Gogo	1	0	1	1
Didi	0	0	0	1
Pozzo	0	0	1	0
Lucky	1	1	0	0

Solution 2.13 The relation matrix of *S* is shown in Table 2.13. Table 2.14 and Table 2.15 present the relation matrices for $R \cup S$ and $R \cap S$.

Table 2.13. *Relation matrix for S*

	S			
	Gogo	**Didi**	**Pozzo**	**Lucky**
Gogo	1	1	1	1
Didi	1	1	0	0
Pozzo	0	0	1	0
Lucky	1	0	1	1

Table 2.14. *Relation matrix for* $R \cup S$

	$R \cup S$			
	Gogo	**Didi**	**Pozzo**	**Lucky**
Gogo	1	1	1	1
Didi	1	1	1	1
Pozzo	0	1	1	0
Lucky	1	1	1	1

Table 2.15. *Relation matrix for $R \cap S$*

	$R \cap S$			
	Gogo	**Didi**	**Pozzo**	**Lucky**
Gogo	1	1	0	1
Didi	1	1	0	0
Pozzo	0	0	1	0
Lucky	1	0	0	1

Now let us compute $R \circ S$. Does (Gogo, Gogo) $\in R \circ S$? We see, (Gogo, Gogo) $\in R$ and (Gogo, Gogo) $\in S$. Moreover, (Gogo, Didi) $\in R$ and (Didi, Gogo) $\in S$. Hence (Gogo, Gogo) $\in R \circ S$. However there is no x such that (Pozzo, x) $\in R$ and (x, Lucky) $\in S$. Other members of $R \circ S$ are found in similar fashion (see Table 2.16).

Table 2.16. *Relation matrix for $R \circ S$*

	$R \circ S$			
	Gogo	**Didi**	**Pozzo**	**Lucky**
Gogo	1	1	1	1
Didi	1	1	1	1
Pozzo	1	1	1	0
Lucky	1	1	1	1

Problem 2.14 Show that Cartesian product of crisp sets is a special case of fuzzy Cartesian product.

Solution 2.14 Let A and B be two fuzzy sets on reference sets X and Y respectively. As per definition of fuzzy Cartesian product $\mu_{A\times B}(a, b) = min\{\mu_A(a), \mu_B(b)\}[\forall a \in X, \forall b \in Y$. Now, if A and B are crisp sets, then $\mu_A(a) = \mu_B(b) = 1, \forall a \in X, \forall b \in Y$. Therefore, $\mu_{A\times B}(a, b) = min\{\mu_A(a), \mu_B(b)\} = 1$. Hence Cartesian product of crisp sets is a special case of fuzzy Cartesian product.

Problem 2.15 A = {Jack, Lucy, Harry}, B = {Flute, Drum, Violin, Piano}, C = {String, Wind, Percussion} on which the relation R = *Plays* $\subseteq P \times Q$ and S = *instrument type* $\subseteq Q \times R$ is defined (Table 2.17 and 2.18). Find $R \circ S$.

Table 2.17. *Relation matrix for R = Plays*

	R			
	Flute	**Drum**	**Violin**	**Piano**
Jack	0	1	0	1
Lucy	1	0	1	1
Harry	1	1	1	0

Table 2.18. *Relation matrix for S = instrument type*

	S		
	String	**Wind**	**Percussion**
Flute	0	1	0
Drum	0	0	1
Violin	1	0	0
Piano	1	0	0

Solution 2.15 Table 2.19 shows the relation matrix for $R \circ S$.

Table 2.19. *Relation matrix for R ° S*

	S		
	String	Wind	Percussion
Jack	1	0	1
Lucy	1	1	0
Harry	1	1	1

Problem 2.16 Let A = {Mimi, Bob, Kitty, Jina} be a set of four children, B = {Tintin, Asterix, Phantom, Mickey} be a set of four comic characters, and C = {funny, cute, dreamy} be a set of three attributes. The fuzzy relations $R = x$ Likes y is defined on $A \times B$ and $S = x$ IS y is defined on $B \times C$ as shown in Table 2.20 and Table 2.21. Find R ° S.

Table 2.20. *Relation matrix for R = x Likes y*

	R ≡ Likes			
	Tintin	Asterix	Phantom	Mickey
Mimi	0.8	0.5	0.7	0.8
Bob	0.4	0.9	0.3	0.3
Kitty	0.6	0.7	0.4	0.9
Jina	0.3	0.8	0.2	0.5

Table 2.21. *Relation matrix for S = x IS y*

	S ≡ IS		
	funny	cute	dreamy
Tintin	0.6	0.7	0.3
Asterix	0.8	0.4	0.2
Phantom	0.1	0.2	0.1
Mickey	0.9	0.8	0.3

Table 2.22. *Relation matrix for R ° S*

	R°S		
	funny	cute	dreamy
Mimi	0.8	0.8	0.3
Bob	0.8	0.4	0.3
Kitty	0.9	0.8	0.3
Jina	0.8	0.5	0.3

Solution 2.16 Let us recall the definition of composition of fuzzy relations. If A, B and C are three crisp sets and R and S are fuzzy relations over $A \times B$ and $B \times C$, then the composition of R and S, $R \circ S$, is a relation over $A \times C$ such that

$$(R \circ S)(x, R) = \max_{y \in B} \{\min(R(x, y), S(y, z))\}$$

Now, $R \circ S$ (Mimi, funny) = max {min (R (Mimi, Tintin), S (Tintin, funny)), min (R (Mimi, Asterix), S (Asterix, funny)), min (R (Mimi, Phantom), S (Phantom, funny)), min (R (Mimi, Mickey), S (Mickey, funny))}= max {min (0.8, 0.6), min (0.5, 0.8), min (0.7, 0.1), min (0.8, 0.9)}= max {0.6, 0.5, 0.1, 0.8}= 0.8. The membership values for the rest of the ordered pairs can be computed similarly. The resultant relation matrix is shown in Table 2.22.

Problem 2.17 A fuzzy set *N* of naughty children is given below. Find the level set of *N*.

$$N = \frac{0.3}{Piku} + \frac{0.8}{Mini} + \frac{1.0}{Lotus} + \frac{0.3}{Jojo} + \frac{0.5}{Nina} + \frac{0.5}{Joy} + \frac{0.8}{Lila}$$

Solution 2.17 The level set of *N*, *L* (*N*), is the crisp set of real values $x \in (0, 1]$ such that for each $x \in L\,(F)$ there is a singleton $(y, x) \in F$. Symbolically, $L\,(N) = \{x \mid 0 < x \leq 1 \text{ and } \exists\, y \in U \text{ such that } \mu_N(y) = x\}$. Hence

$$L\,(N) = \{0.3, 0.5, 0.8, 1.0\}.$$

Problem 2.18 A fuzzy set *F* has the membership profile given below. What is the level set of *F*?

$$\mu_F(x) = \frac{1}{1+e^{-x}}, \quad -\infty \leq x \leq \infty$$

Solution 2.18 The level set is $L\,(N) = (0, 1)$.

Problem 2.19 For the naughty children of Problem 2.17, find N_α for $\alpha = 0.4$ and 0.2.

Solution 2.19 The α-cut of *N*, N_α, is the crisp set containing those elements whose membership values with respect to *N* are greater than, or equal to, α. Symbolically, $N_\alpha = \{x \mid \mu_N(x) \geq \alpha\}$. Accordingly we find,

$N_{0.4} = \{x \mid \mu_N(x) \geq 0.4\}\}$= {Mini, Lotus, Nina, Joy, Lila}, and
$N_{0.2} = \{x \mid \mu_N(x) \geq 0.2\}\}$= {Piku, Mini, Lotus, Jojo, Nina, Joy, Lila}

Problem 2.20 For *F* of Problem 2.18, find F_α for $\alpha = 0.5$ and 0.

Solution 2.20 $F_{0.5} = [\,0, \infty)$ and $F_0 = (-\infty, \infty)$.

Problem 2.21 Find the fuzzy cardinality of a fuzzy set *LC* of low calorie food. The fuzzy set is given below.

$$LC = \frac{1}{Cucumber} + \frac{1}{Watermelon} + \frac{0.5}{Chicken} + \frac{0.1}{Ice\text{-}cream} + \frac{0.1}{Chocolate} + \frac{0.3}{Rice} + \frac{0.8}{Egg}$$

Solution 2.21 Let *F* be a fuzzy set and *L* (*F*) is the level set of *F* and for all $\alpha \in L\,(F)$, F_α is the α-cut of *F*. The fuzzy cardinality of *F*, $f_c(F)$, is the fuzzy set

$$f_c(F) = \sum_{\alpha \in L(F)} \frac{\alpha}{|F_\alpha|}$$

In the present instance, $L\,(LC) = \{0.1, 0.3, 0.5, 0.8, 1.0\}$. The α-cuts of *LC* for $\alpha = 0.1, 0.3, 0.5, 0.8$ and 1.0 are

$LC_{0.1}$ = {Ice-cream, Chocolate, Rice, Chicken, Egg, Cucumber, Watermelon}, and $|LC_{0.1}| = 7$, $LC_{0.3}$ = {Rice, Chicken, Egg, Cucumber, Watermelon}, and $|LC_{0.3}| = 5$, $LC_{0.5}$ = {Chicken, Egg, Cucumber, Watermelon}, and $|LC_{0.5}| = 4$, $LC_{0.8}$ = {Egg, Cucumber, Watermelon}, and $|LC_{0.8}| = 3$, $LC_{1.0}$ = {Cucumber, Watermelon}, and $|LC_{1.0}| = 2$. Therefore the fuzzy cardinality of LC is given by

$$f_c(LC) = \sum_{\alpha \in L(F)} \frac{\alpha}{|LC_\alpha|} = \frac{0.1}{7} + \frac{0.3}{5} + \frac{0.5}{4} + \frac{0.8}{3} + \frac{1.0}{2}$$

Problem 2.22 Consider two sets of colours C-1 = {Red, Blue, Green} and C-2= {Red, Blue, Green, Yellow, Cyan, Magenta}. A function $f: C\text{-}1 \times C\text{-}1 \rightarrow C\text{-}2$ is defined as shown in the matrix below.

	Red	**Blue**	**Green**
Red	Red	Magenta	Yellow
Blue	Magenta	Blue	Cyan
Green	Yellow	Cyan	Green

We define two shades of the colours in {Red, Blue, Green} as fuzzy sets S-1 and S-2.

$$S\text{-}1 = \frac{0.3}{red} + \frac{0.5}{blue} + \frac{0.7}{green} \qquad S\text{-}2 = \frac{0.8}{red} + \frac{0.2}{blue} + \frac{0.4}{green}$$

Extend the function f to the domain $S\text{-}1 \times S\text{-}2$ by applying the fuzzy extension principle.

Solution 2.22 Let us denote the fuzzy equivalent of f as ff. The pre-images of the elements of C-2 under f are

$f^{-1}(R) = \{(R, R)\}$
$f^{-1}(G) = \{(G, G)\}$
$f^{-1}(B) = \{(B, B)\}$
$f^{-1}(M) = \{(R, B), (B, R)\}$
$f^{-1}(Y) = \{(R, G), (G, R)\}$
$f^{-1}(C) = \{(B, G), (G, B)\}$

Computations of the fuzzy memberships of the elements of C-2 under ff are shown below.

$ff^{-1}(R) = \{(R, R)\}$
$\therefore \mu_{C2}(R) = max\ \{min\ (\mu_{s\text{-}1}(R), \mu_{s\text{-}2}(R))\}$
$= max\ \{min\ (0.3, 0.8)\}$
$= max\ \{0.3\}\} = 0.3$

$ff^{-1}(B) = \{(B, B)\}$
$\therefore \mu_{C\text{-}2}(B) = max\ \{min\ (\mu_{s\text{-}1}(B`), \mu_{s\text{-}2}(B))\}$
$= max\ \{min\ (0.5, 0.2)\}$
$= max\ \{0.2\}\} = 0.2$

$ff^{-1}(G) = \{(G, G)\}$
$\therefore \mu_{C\text{-}2}(G) = max\ \{min\ (\mu_{s\text{-}1}(G), \mu_{s\text{-}2}(G))\}$
$= max\ \{min\ (0.7, 0.4)\}$
$= max\ \{0.4\}\} = 0.4$

$ff^{-1}(M) = \{(R, B), (B, R)\}$
$\therefore \mu_{C\text{-}2}(M) = max\ \{min\ (\mu_{s\text{-}1}(R), \mu_{s\text{-}2}(B)),\ min\ (\mu_{s\text{-}1}(B), \mu_{s\text{-}2}(R))\}$
$= max\ \{min\ (0.3, 0.2), min\ (0.5, 0.8)\}$
$= max\ \{0.2, 0.5\}\} = 0.5$

$ff^{-1}(Y) = \{(R, G), (G, R)\}$
$\therefore \mu_{C\text{-}2}(Y) = max\ \{min\ (\mu_{s\text{-}1}(R), \mu_{s\text{-}2}(G)),\ min\ (\mu_{s\text{-}1}(G), \mu_{s\text{-}2}(R))\}$
$= max\ \{min\ (0.3, 0.4), min\ (0.7, 0.8)\}$
$= max\ \{0.3, 0.7\}\} = 0.7$

$ff^{-1}(C) = \{(B, G), (G, B)\}$
$\therefore \mu_{C\text{-}2}(C) = max\ \{min\ (\mu_{s\text{-}1}(B), \mu_{s\text{-}2}(G)),\ min\ (\mu_{s\text{-}1}(G), \mu_{s\text{-}2}(B))\}$
$= max\ \{min\ (0.5, 0.4), min\ (0.7, 0.2)\}$
$= max\ \{0.4, 0.2\}\} = 0.4$

✓ TEST YOUR KNOWLEDGE

2.1 Which of the following phenomena is modeled by fuzzy set theory?
   a) Randomness
   b) Vagueness
   c) Uncertainty
   d) None of the above

2.2 Which of the following relations hold good for fuzzy sets?
   a) $\mu(x) \in [0, 1]$
   b) $\mu(x) \notin [0, 1]$
   c) $\mu(x) = 0$, or 1
   d) None of the above

2.3 Which of the following relations hold good for crisp sets?
   a) $\mu(x) \in [0, 1]$
   b) $\mu(x) \notin [0, 1]$
   c) $\mu(x) = 0$, or 1
   d) None of the above

2.4 Let $U = \{a, b, c\}$, and $P = \frac{0.5}{a} + \frac{0.5}{c}$ be a fuzzy set on U. Then which of the following is true?
   a) P is normal
   b) P is sub-normal
   c) Both (*a*) and (*b*)
   d) None of the above

2.5 Let $U = \{a, b, c\}$, and $P = \frac{0.5}{a} + \frac{0.75}{c}$ be a fuzzy set on U. Then what is the *height* of P?
   a) 0.5
   b) 0.75
   c) 1.25
   d) 1.0

2.6 What is the *support* of the fuzzy set P cited in item 2.5?
   a) $\{a, c\}$
   b) $\{b\}$
   c) $\{a, b, c\}$
   d) Φ

2.7 What is the *core* of the fuzzy set P cited in item 2.5?
   a) $\{a, c\}$
   b) $\{b\}$
   c) $\{a, b, c\}$
   d) Φ

2.8 What is the *cardinality* of the fuzzy set P cited in item 2.4?
   a) 0.0
   b) 0.5
   c) 1.0
   d) None of the above

2.9 Which of the following membership functions must have a *height* of 1.0?
   a) Triangular function
   b) Trapezoidal function
   c) Gaussian function
   d) None of the above

2.10 Which of the following transformations on membership functions of fuzzy sets *enhances* the membership values?

a) Dilation
b) Concentration
c) Contrast intensification
d) Fuzzification

2.11 Which of the following transformations on membership functions of fuzzy sets *reduces* the membership values?

a) Dilation
b) Concentration
c) Contrast intensification
d) Fuzzification

2.12 Which of the following transformations on membership functions of fuzzy sets *reduces* as well as *enhances* the membership values selectively?

a) Contrast intensification
b) Fuzzification
c) Both (*a*) and (*b*)
d) None of the above

2.13 Which of the following properties is not satisfied by fuzzy sets *P*, *Q*, *R*?

a) $(P \cup Q) \cup R = P \cup (Q \cup R)$
b) $(P \cup Q)' = P' \cap Q'$
c) $(P')' = P$
d) $P \cup P' = U$

2.14 Which of the following properties is not satisfied by arbitrary fuzzy set *P*?

a) $P \cup P' = U$
b) $P \cap P' = \Phi$
c) Both (*a*) and (*b*)
d) None of the above

2.15 Which of the following properties is true for arbitrary fuzzy set *P*?

a) $P \cup P' \neq U$
b) $P \cap P' \neq \Phi$
c) Both (*a*) and (*b*)
d) None of the above

2.16 Which of the following properties does not hold good for Cartesian product of sets?

a) Commutativity
b) Associativity
c) Both (*a*) and (*b*)
d) None of the above

2.17 Let $F = \frac{0}{0} + \frac{1}{1}$ be a fuzzy set on the universe $U = \{0, 1\}$. Which of the following is $L(F)$, *i.e.*, the level set of *F*?

a) $L(F) = \{0\}$
b) $L(F) = \{1\}$
c) $L(F) = \{0, 1\}$
d) None of the above

2.18 Which of the following is true regarding variation of the size of *C* of a fuzzy set as α increases from 0 to 1?

a) Size of the α-*cut* increases
b) Size of the α-*cut* decreases
c) They are not related
d) None of the above

2.19 Let F_α, F_β be the α-cuts of a fuzzy set *F* such that $0 \leq \alpha \leq \beta \leq 1$. Then which of the following is true?

a) $F_\alpha \subseteq F_\beta$
b) $F_\alpha \supseteq F_\beta$
c) $F_\alpha = F_\beta$
d) None of the above

2.20 Let $F = \frac{0.1}{a} + \frac{0.5}{b} + \frac{1.0}{c}$ be a fuzzy set on the universe $U = \{a, b, c\}$. *F* can be decomposed into a number of α-cuts such that $F = \bigcup_{\alpha} \alpha . F_\alpha$. How many such α-cut decompositions exist?

a) One
b) Three
c) Infinite
d) None of the above

2.21 Which of the following is a *fuzzyfication* process?

a) Restricted scalar multiplication
b) α-cut decomposition
c) Both (*a*) and (*b*)
d) None of the above

2.22 Let αF denotes the fuzzy set obtained through restricted scalar multiplication of F by α, $0 \le \alpha \le 1$. Then given $0 \le \alpha \le \beta \le 1$, and two fuzzy sets F and G, which of the following is not true?
   a) $\alpha(F \cup G) = \alpha F \cup \alpha G$
   b) $(\alpha\beta) F = \alpha(\beta F)$
   c) $\alpha F \subseteq F$
   d) None of the above

2.23 Let $F = \frac{0.5}{a} + \frac{0.5}{b}$ be a fuzzy set. Then the fuzzy cardinality of F is
   a) $\frac{0.5}{1}$
   b) $\frac{0.5}{2}$
   c) $\frac{1.0}{2}$
   d) None of the above

2.24 Let (a, b) and (c, d) be the pre-images of an element p under a function f. The fuzzy membership values of a, b, c, and d in a fuzzy set are 0.5, 0.4, 0.7 and 0.2 respectively. What is the fuzzy membership of p when f is extended to its fuzzy domain?
   a) 0.5
   b) 0.4
   c) 0.7
   d) 0.2

2.25 Which of the following statements is true about a linguistic variable?
   a) A linguistic variable has linguistic values
   b) The values of a linguistic variable are fuzzy sets
   c) Both (*a*) and (*b*)
   d) None of the above

Answers

2.1 (b)	2.2 (a)	2.3 (c)	2.4 (b)	2.5 (b)
2.6 (a)	2.7 (d)	2.8 (c)	2.9 (d)	2.10 (a)
2.11 (b)	2.12 (c)	2.13 (d)	2.14 (c)	2.15 (c)
2.16 (c)	2.17 (b)	2.18 (b)	2.19 (b)	2.20 (c)
2.21 (a)	2.22 (d)	2.23 (b)	2.24 (b)	2.25 (c)

EXERCISES

2.1 Show that set difference operation is not associative, i.e., $A - (B - C) \neq (A - B) - C$.

2.2 Prove with the help of Venn Diagrams that for arbitrary sets A and B, $A - B = A \cap B'$.

2.3 Fig. 2.36 shows a trapezoidal membership function with $a = 0$, $m = 1$, $n = 2$, $b = 4$. Show the effect of normalization, dilation, concentration, contrast intensification and fuzzification on this membership function.

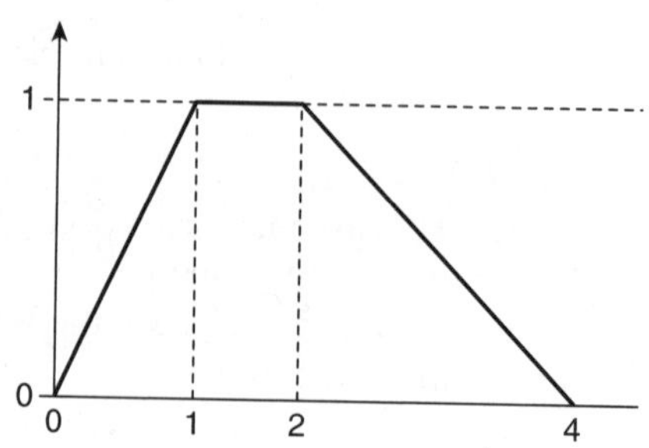

Fig. 2.36. *Trapezoidal function* $\mu_T(x, 0, 1, 2, 4)$

2.4 Fig. 2.37 shows the profile of a membership function defined below. Show the effect of normalization, dilation, concentration, contrast intensification and fuzzification on this membership function.

$$\mu_F(x) = +\sqrt{1-x^2}, \qquad -1 \leq x \leq +1$$

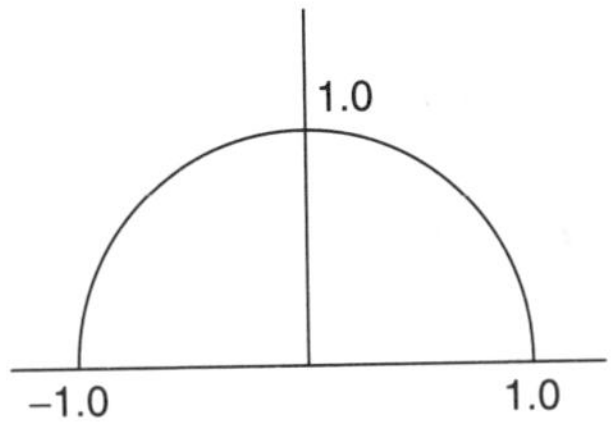

Fig. 2.37. *Semicircular membership profile*

2.5 Let P and Q be two fuzzy sets defined on the interval $[0, \pi]$ with the help of the following membership functions:

$$\mu_P(x) = \sin x, \quad x \in [0, \pi]$$

$$\mu_Q(x) = \begin{cases} \dfrac{\pi - 2x}{\pi}, & if \quad 0 \leq x \leq \pi/2 \\ \dfrac{2x - \pi}{\pi}, & if \quad \pi/2 \leq x \leq \pi \end{cases}$$

Show the membership function for the fuzzy sets P', Q', $P \cup Q$, $P \cap Q$, $P - Q$, and $P \oplus Q$.

2.6 Verify the fuzzy *De Morgan*'s law with the fuzzy sets A and B cited in Example 2.12.

2.7 Let $A = \{0, 1, 2, 3\}$, $B = \{2, 3, 5\}$, and $C = \{0, 2, 4\}\}$be three sets. R, S, and T are three relations defined on $A \times B$, $A \times B$, and $B \times C$ respectively. These relations are described below.

$$R = \{(a, b) \mid (a + b) \text{ is a prime number}\}, R \subseteq A \times B$$
$$S = \{(a, b) \mid |a - b| \text{ is a prime number}\}, S \subseteq A \times B$$
$$T = \{(b, c) \mid (b + c) \text{ is a prime number}\}, T \subseteq B \times C$$

Find $R \cup S$, $R \cap S$, R', S', T', $R \circ T$, and $S \circ T$.

2.8 Let $V = \{A, B, C, D\}$ be the set of four kinds of vitamins, $F = \{f_1, f_2, f_3\}$ be three kinds of fruits containing the said vitamins to various extents, and $D = \{d_1, d_2, d_3\}$ be the set of three diseases that are caused by deficiency of the vitamins. Vitamin contents of the fruits are expressed with the help of the fuzzy relation R over $F \times V$, and the extent to which the diseases are caused by the deficiency of these vitamins is given by the fuzzy relation S over $V \times D$. Relations R and S are given below.

$$R = \begin{array}{c} \\ f_1 \\ f_2 \\ f_3 \end{array} \begin{array}{c} \begin{array}{cccc} A & B & C & D \end{array} \\ \begin{bmatrix} 0.5 & 0.2 & 0.1 & 0.1 \\ 0.2 & 0.7 & 0.4 & 0.3 \\ 0.4 & 0.4 & 0.8 & 0.1 \end{bmatrix} \end{array}, \qquad S = \begin{array}{c} \\ A \\ B \\ C \\ D \end{array} \begin{array}{c} \begin{array}{ccc} d_1 & d_2 & d_3 \end{array} \\ \begin{bmatrix} 0.3 & 0.5 & 0.7 \\ 0.1 & 0.8 & 0.4 \\ 0.9 & 0.1 & 0.2 \\ 0.5 & 0.5 & 0.3 \end{bmatrix} \end{array}$$

Assuming that the max–min composition $R \circ S$ represents, in some way, the correlation between the amount of a certain fruit that should be taken while suffering from a disease, find $R \circ S$.

2.9 According to the *α-cut* decomposition theorem, any fuzzy set F can be decomposed into a number of α-cuts, F_α, such that $F = \bigcup_\alpha \alpha . F_\alpha$. Usually the αs are taken from the level set $L(F)$ of F. Prove that there exists sets of α s, other than $L(F)$, which satisfies the α-cut decomposition theorem.

2.10 Let $F = \frac{0.6}{a} + \frac{0.2}{b} + \frac{0.3}{c} + \frac{0.9}{d}$ be a fuzzy set. Find a set of α-cuts such that $F = \bigcup_\alpha \alpha . F_\alpha$. How many such sets of α-cuts are there? Justify your answer.

2.11 The membership function of a fuzzy set *HIG*, where *HIG* stands for *high income group*, is defined as follows:

$$\mu_{HIG}(i) = \begin{cases} 0, & \text{if } i \le 3 \\ \dfrac{i-3}{3}, & \text{if } 3 \le i \le 6 \\ 1, & \text{if } 6 \le i \end{cases}$$

The income i is given in lakh of Rupees per annum. Let $U = \{Joy, Jeev, Nina, Simi\}$ be a universe of four persons. Yearly income of *Joy*, *Jeev*, *Nina*, and *Simi* are Rs. 5 lakh, Rs. 8 lakh, Rs. 4 lakh, and Rs. 3.5 lakh respectively. Construct a fuzzy set *Rich* on U where the richness of a person is given by the membership value of his / her income with respect to the fuzzy set *HIG*. Compute the fuzzy cardinality of *Rich*.

2.12 Let us consider the crisp sets $P = Q = R = \{0, 1, 2\}$. A function $f: P \times Q \rightarrow R$ is defined as $f(x, y) = |x - y|$, for all $x \in P$, $y \in Q$. Show the function table for f.
Now consider the fuzzy sets A and B on the reference sets P and Q respectively as given below.

$$A = \frac{1}{0} + \frac{0.5}{1} + \frac{0}{2}, \qquad B = \frac{0}{0} + \frac{0.5}{1} + \frac{1}{2}$$

Apply the extension principle to obtain the fuzzy equivalent of the function f with respect to the fuzzy sets A and B, $f: A \times B \rightarrow C$, where C is the image of $A \times B$, defined on the universe R.

2.13 Let $P = Q = \{0, 1, 2\}$ and $R = \{0, 0.5, 1, 1.5, 2\}$ be crisp sets and $f: P \times Q \rightarrow R$ be a function signifying the mean of two numbers, $f(x, y) = (x + y)/2$, for all $x \in P$, $y \in Q$. Construct the function table for f.

Now consider the fuzzy set A representing the closeness of a number x to 1 and B representing its distance from 1. A and B are defined on the reference sets P and Q respectively. The sets A and B may look like

$$A = \frac{0.5}{0} + \frac{1}{1} + \frac{0.5}{2}, \qquad B = \frac{1}{0} + \frac{0}{1} + \frac{1}{2}$$

Extend the function $f: P \times Q \rightarrow R$ to $f: A \times B \rightarrow C$ with the help of the extension principle where C is the image of $A \times B$, defined on the universe R.

BIBLIOGRAPHY AND HISTORICAL NOTES

Fuzzy Sets, as we know them today was developed by the noted Iranian scientist Lotfi Akser Zadeh and presented through his celebrated work "Fuzzy Sets" in Information and Control (8) 1965, pp. 338 –353, as an extension of the classical set theory, henceforth known as crisp sets. However, the concept of fuzziness dates back to 500 B.C. when first references are found in teachings of Gautam Buddha, who believed that almost everything in this universe contains a set of opposites. The same was argued by

Greek philosopher Heraclitus who believed that things can be simultaneously 'true' and 'not true'. The Greeks toyed with such ideas until Aristotle and his two valued logic gained ground. Around the same time as Zadeh, Dieter Klaua also proposed a similar concept (Klaua, D. (1965) Über einen Ansatz zur mehrwertigen Mengenlehre. Monatsb. Deutsch. Akad. Wiss. Berlin 7, 859–867). Like all revolutionary notions, the concept of fuzzy sets too was viewed initially with lot of skepticism and many rated it merely as an extension of probability theory. It wasn't until the early 1980's that it gained popular ground, and it was around this time that the use of fuzzy controllers in consumer electronic goods started and the word fuzzy became popular among scientists and non-scientists alike. Numerous brilliant works are reported on fuzzy set theory in the past few decades. Only a few of these are cited below.

Dubois, D. and Prade, H. (1980). *Fuzzy sets and systems: theory and applications.* New York: Academic Press.

Dubois, D. and Prade, H. (1988). *Fuzzy sets and systems.* New York: Academic Press.

Kandal, A. and Lee, S. C. (1979). *Fuzzy switching and automata.* Crane, Russak and Co.

Kauffmann, A. (1975). *Introduction to the theory of Fuzzy subsets.* New York: Academic Press.

Kickert, W. J. M. (1978). *Fuzzy theories on decision making.* Martinus-Nijhoff.

Klir, G. J. and Yuan, B. (1997). *Fuzzy sets and fuzzy logic: theory and applications PHI.*

Pedrycz, W. and Gomide, F. (1998). *An introduction to fuzzy sets: analysis and design.* Cambridge, MA: MIT Press.

Yager, R. R. (1982). *Fuzzy sets and probability theory*. Oxford: Pergamon Press.

Zadeh, L. A. (1965). Fuzzy sets. *Information and Control*, Vol. 8, pp. 338–353.

Zadeh, L. A. (1968). Probability measures of Fuzzy events. *Journal of Mathematical Analysis and Applications*, Vol. 10, pp. 421–427.

Zadeh, L. A. (1975). The concept of a linguistic variable and its application to approximate reasoning. *Information Sciences*, Vol. 8, pp. 199–249, 301–357, Vol. 9, pp. 43–80.

Zadeh, L. A. (1978). Fuzzy sets as a basis for a theory of possibility. *Fuzzy Sets and Systems*, Vol. 1, pp. 3–28.

3

Fuzzy Logic

Key Concepts

Abduction, Induction and Analogy, Addition, Chain rule, Consistency, Contradiction, Existential quantifier, First order predicate logic (FOPL), Fuzzy if-then, Fuzzy if-then-else, Fuzzy logic operations, Fuzzy proposition, Fuzzy quantifier, Fuzzy reasoning, Fuzzy rules, Fuzzy truth value, Generalized modus ponens, Generalized modus tolens, Interpretation, Linguistic variable, Logical equivalence, Modus Ponens, Modus Tollens/Indirect Reasoning/Law of Contraposition, Non-deductive rules of inference, Propositional logic, Resolution, Rules of inference, Simplification, Tautology, Universal quantifier, Universal specialization, Validity of argument, Well-formed formulae (wwf)

Chapter Outline

Various features of the fuzzy set theory are discussed in Chapter 2. This chapter presents the fundamentals of fuzzy logic. It starts with a review of the classical crisp logic and then presents fuzzy logic as an extension, or generalization of crisp logic. Logic is the study of the structure and principles of reasoning and sound argument. The universe of discourse of logic is the set of all statements, or, propositions. A statement, or proposition, is a sentence that has a truth value, either True or False, in crisp logic. Logic is not concerned about the content or meaning of a statement, but only with their possible truth values. Symbolic logic is logic using symbols that represent actual statements. Crisp logic asserts that a statement can be either true or false. It does not accept a third possibility. However, in real life we come across situations where such sharp distinction between truth and falsehood do not exist. On the contrary, there are infinite shades of truths between black and white absolute truth and absolute falsehood. Fuzzy logic accepts this state of affair and builds a system of reasoning on the basis of the possibility of infinite number of truth values. Over the last few decades fuzzy logic has been successfully applied to solve numerous practical problems of engineering, science and business.

3.1 CRISP LOGIC: A REVIEW

Classical logic is based on the Aristotlian 'Law of excluded middle' which states that a statement is either true or false and nothing else. In contrast, fuzzy logic accepts the point of view that there are infinitely many shades of truth (or falsehood) between the absolutely false and the absolutely true. The logical system that allows only two truth-values is called crisp logic. This section presents a review of the essential features of crisp logic. We start with propositional logic, followed by the more powerful system called the predicate logic. A brief discussion on rules of inferences is provided at the end of this section.

3.1.1 Propositional Logic

Propositional logic is concerned about the properties and laws governing the universe of propositions. A proposition is a statement that is either true or false and nothing else. A few propositions are cited below.

1. This rose is red.
2. Mona Lisa was painted by Leonardo de Vinci.
3. Tiger is a domestic animal.
4. The smallest prime number is 5.
5. Every action has an equal and opposite reaction.

As far as logic is concerned it does not matter whether a proposition is empirically true or false, or not known at all whether true or false. This is an empirical problem and logic is not concerned about it. The only matter of logical concern is that the statement has a definite truth-value, known or unknown. Here are a few sentences that are not valid propositions.

1. Is this a red rose? (Interrogation)
2. What a great artist was Leonardo de Vinci! (Exclamation)
3. The blue ideas are sleeping furiously. (Meaningless)

In symbolic logic, propositions are expressed with symbols or symbolic expressions that are combinations of symbols.

Propositional calculus deals with the symbolic expressions of propositional logic and their manipulation. The valid symbolic expressions of propositional logic are known as well-formed formulae (wff). These wffs are composed of

- The logical constants 'True' (represented by T or 1) and 'False' (F or 0)
- Propositions (usually symbolically represented by a, b, p, q etc.)
- Parenthesis (, and)
- Logical operators or connectives, e.g.,

AND	(Conjunction, denoted as $\wedge$ or '$\cdot$')
OR	(Disjunction, denoted as $\vee$ or '+')
NOT	(Negation, denoted as $\neg$ or '′')
Implication	(Conditional, If … Then …, denoted as $\rightarrow$)

The behaviour of logical operators are described with the help of truth tables. The truth tables for the logical operators NOT, AND, OR are shown in Table 3.1 and Table 3.2.

Table 3.1. *Truth table for logical NOT operation*

a	a′
0	1
1	0

Table 3.2. *Truth table for logical AND, OR, IMPLICATION*

a	b	a • b	a + b	a → b
0	0	0	0	1
0	1	0	1	1
1	0	0	1	0
1	1	1	1	1

Definition 3.1 (*Propositional logic well-formed-formula*) A propositional logic well-formed formula (wff) is recursively defined as follows.

(i) The logical constants T and F are wffs.
(ii) A propositional symbol (e.g. a, b, p, q etc.) is a wff.
(iii) Given two wffs W_1 and W_2, the following are also wffs
- $(W_1) \cdot (W_2)$ (Conjunction of two wffs is a wff)
- $(W_1) + (W_2)$ (Disjunction of two wffs is a wff)
- $(\neg W_1)$ (Negation of a wffs is a wff)
- $(W_1) \rightarrow (W_2)$ (Implication of two wffs is a wff)
- $(W_1) \leftrightarrow (W_2)$ (Equivalence of two wffs is a wff)

(iv) Nothing else is a propositional logic well-formed formula (wff).

The symbol ↔ stands for logical equivalence (implies and implied by, or bicondition) and is defined as $(a \rightarrow b) \bullet (b \rightarrow a)$. The truth table for ↔ is shown in Table 3.3. In practice, while writing a wff, the number of parentheses is usually minimized by obeying a set of precedence rules among the operators.

Table 3.3. *Truth table of logical equivalence*

a	b	a ↔ b
0	0	1
0	1	0
1	0	0
1	1	1

Example 3.1 (*Propositional logic well-formed-formulae*)

Some valid and invalid propositional logic wffs are given below in Table 3.4. For the sake of simplicity the parentheses are used sparingly. Moreover the conjunction operation is not explicitly used where its existence is obvious from the context.

Table 3.4. *Examples of valid and invalid wffs*

#	wff	Validity	Remark
1	1	Valid	
2	0	Valid	
3	$a + b$	Valid	
4	$(a + b)\ c \rightarrow a'b'c'$	Valid	
5	$((a \rightarrow b)\ (c' \rightarrow a')) \rightarrow b'$	Valid	
6	$a + \bullet\ b$	Invalid	A binary operator must be immediately preceded and succeeded by its operands
7	$a \bullet (b + c'$	Invalid	Matching parenthesis is absent
8	$)\ a + b\ ($	Invalid	Wrong pair of parentheses

Table 3.5. *Properties of propositional logic wffs*

#	Relation	Remarks
1	$(A \bullet B) \bullet C \equiv A \bullet (B \bullet C)$	Associativity
	$(A + B) + C \equiv A + (B + C)$	
2	$A \bullet B \equiv B \bullet A$	Commutativity
	$A + B \equiv B + A$	
3	$A \bullet (B + C) \equiv (A \bullet B) + (A \bullet C)$	Distributivity
	$A + (B \bullet C) \equiv (A + B) \bullet (A + C)$	
4	$(A \bullet B)' \equiv A' + B'$	De Morgan's law
	$(A + B)' \equiv A' \bullet B'$	
5	$A \rightarrow B \equiv B' \rightarrow A'$	Contrapositive law
6	$A + A' \equiv 1$	Law of excluded middle
7	$A \bullet A' \equiv 0$	Law of Contradiction
8	$A + A \equiv A$	Idempotency
	$A \bullet A \equiv A$	
9	$A \bullet (A + B) \equiv A$	Absorption
	$A + (A \bullet B) \equiv A$	

Properties of Propositional Logic wffs Propositional logic statements in the form of wffs obey certain properties. Some of these are listed in Table 3.5.

Definition 3.2 (*Interpretation of a logical expression*) Let $e\ (x_1, x_2, \ldots, x_n)$ be a logical expression involving n propositions $x_1, x_2, \ldots, x_n$. An interpretation of the expression $e\ (x_1, x_2, \ldots, x_n)$ is a combination of truth values for the constituent individual propositions $x_1, x_2, \ldots, x_n$.

Obviously, an expression $e\ (x_1, x_2, \ldots, x_n)$ involving n propositions have exactly 2^n interpretations. For example, if $e\ (a, b, c)) = a + b + a \bullet b'$ be the logical expression then $a = 1, b = 0, c = 0$ is one of its interpretations. For this interpretation the expression attains the truth value $e\ (a, b, c) = a + b + a \bullet b' = 1$.

Definition 3.3 (*Logical equivalence of two wffs*) Two wffs are said to be equivalent if they attain the same truth value for all possible interpretations.

The logical equivalence of two expressions can be easily checked with the help of their truth tables. For example Table 3.6 shows that the expression $a \rightarrow b$ is equivalent to $a' + b$.

Table 3.6. *Equivalence of a → b and a′+ b*

a	b	a → b	a′+ b
0	0	1	1
0	1	1	1
1	0	0	0
1	1	1	1

Definition 3.4 (*Tautology*) A tautology is a proposition which is true for all possible interpretations.

Definition 3.5 (*Contradiction*) A contradiction is a proposition which is false for all possible interpretations.

Definition 3.6 (*Consistency*) A collection of statements is said to be consistent if they can all be true simultaneously.

Example 3.2 (*Tautology, Contradiction, Consistency*)

The most obvious examples of a tautology and a contradiction are $a' + a$ and $a' \bullet a$ respectively. A few more tautologies and contradictions are cited below in Table 3.7. Table 3.8 presents a number of consistent and a few inconsistent pairs of propositional logic expressions. Verification of the tautologies, contradictions, consistencies and inconsistencies using the truth table method is left as an exercise.

Table 3.7. *Tautologies and contradictions*

#	wff	Category
1	1	Tautology
2	ab + a′+ b′	Tautology

(*Continued*)

Table 3.7. *Continued*

#	wff	Category
3	a + b + a′b′	Tautology
4	a′b′+ a′b + ab′+ ab	Tautology
5	(1 + a) (1 + b)	Tautology
6	0	Contradiction
7	a′b′ (a + b)	Contradiction
8	(a + b) (a′+ b) (a + b′) (a′+ b′)	Contradiction
9	a′b (a + b′)	Contradiction

Table 3.8. *Consistent and inconsistent expressions*

#	wff pairs	Remark
1	{a, b}	Consistent. Both are true when a = 1, b = 1
2	{a′, b′}	Consistent. Both are true when a = 0, b = 0
3	{a′+ b, a + b′}	Consistent. Both are true when a = 1, b = 1
4	{a + b′c′, ab + b}	Consistent. Both are true when a = 1, b = 1, c = 0
5	{a, a′}	Inconsistent. Complimentary wffs.
6	{a + b, a′b′}	Inconsistent. Complimentary wffs.
7	{(a + b) c, a′b′+ c′}	Inconsistent. Complimentary wffs.

Definition 3.7 (*Validity of an argument*) An argument is said to be valid if the conclusion is true whenever the premises are true.

Example 3.3 (*Validity of an argument*)

As an example, let us consider the following argument: *If Basant Kumar plays the role of the hero's, then the film will be a hit if Basanti Devi is the heroine. If Basant Kumar plays the hero's role, then Basanti Devi will be the heroine. Therefore, if Basant Kumar plays the hero's role, the film will be a hit.* Is the argument valid? This can be easily answered by constructing the corresponding truth table and checking if the conclusion is True whenever the premises are True. Let us denote

Statement 'Basant Kumar plays the hero's part' as a
Statement 'The film will be a hit' as b
Statement 'Basanti Devi is the heroine' as c

Then the argument is symbolically presented as

Premise No. 1.		$a \rightarrow (c \rightarrow b)$
Premise No. 2.		$a \rightarrow c$
Conclusion.	Therefore,	$a \rightarrow b$

The corresponding truth table is shown in Table 3.9. The two premises of the argument, $a \rightarrow (c \rightarrow b)$ and $a \rightarrow c$, are arranged in Columns 5 and 6, respectively. The conclusion $a \rightarrow b$ is shown in Column 7. In Rows 1, 2, 3, 4 and 8, both the premises are true. The corresponding truth-values of the conclusion, noted in Column 7 are also true. Hence the argument is valid

Table 3.9. *Consistency checking*

	(1)	(2)	(3)	(4)	(5)	(6)	(7)
	a	b	c	$c \rightarrow b$	$a \rightarrow (c \rightarrow b)$	$a \rightarrow c$	$a \rightarrow b$
(1)	0	0	0	1	1	1	1
(2)	0	0	1	0	1	1	1
(3)	0	1	0	1	1	1	1
(4)	0	1	1	1	1	1	1
(5)	1	0	0	1	1	0	0
(6)	1	0	1	0	0	1	0
(7)	1	1	0	1	1	0	1
(8)	1	1	1	1	1	1	1

3.1.2 Predicate Logic

The propositional logic described above suffers from certain limitations. These limitations motivated the logicians to extend it to a more powerful formalism called the Predicate Logic. It provides mechanisms to capture the inner structure of propositions such as the subject–predicate relation, or quantifiers like 'for all' or 'there exists'. Natural language statements can be expressed as predicate logic wffs, so that they could be processed by automated tools of intelligent systems according to the rules of sound reasoning. This subsection provides a discussion on the basic features of First Order Predicate Logic (FOPL). We start with an exposure to the limitations of propositional logic. The features of FOPL are presented subsequently.

Limitations of propositional logic Let us consider the argument: *If monkeys have hair on their bodies then they are mammals. Monkeys have hairs on their bodies. Therefore, monkeys are mammals.* This argument can be symbolically presented as

Premise No. 1.		$p \rightarrow q$
Premise No. 2.		p
Conclusion.	*Therefore,*	q

where p denotes the proposition *Monkeys have hairs on their bodies* and q denotes the proposition *Monkeys are mammals.* Validity of this argument can be easily verified using the truth table method. This is shown in Table 3.10, which shows that the conclusion q is true whenever both the premises are true (Row 4).

Table 3.10

	(1)	(2)	(3)
	p	q	$p \to q$
(1)	0	0	1
(2)	0	1	1
(3)	1	0	0
(4)	1	1	1

Now, consider another argument leading to the same conclusion as before: *All animals having hairs on their bodies are mammals. Monkeys have hairs on their bodies. Therefore monkeys are mammals.* This argument has the form

Premise No. 1.		a
Premise No. 2.		b
Conclusion.	*Therefore,*	c

where a denotes the statement *All animals having hairs on their bodies are mammals*, b denotes the statement *Monkeys have hairs on their bodies* and c denotes the statement *Monkeys are mammals.* This is not a valid argument because given the two propositions a and b as premises we cannot conclude a third proposition c that is independent of the premises. Applying the truth table method we obtain the combinations of truth values of a, b and c as shown in Table 3.11.

Table 3.11

	a	b	c
(1)	0	0	0
(2)	0	0	1
(3)	0	1	0
(4)	0	1	1
(5)	1	0	0
(6)	1	0	1
(7)	1	1	0
(8)	1	1	1

The 7th row of the table shows that the conclusion c is false even though both the premises a, b are true. We know that an argument is valid if and only if the conclusion is true whenever the premises are true. Therefore, according to the formalism of propositional calculus, the second argument is invalid. However, intuitively we feel that the second argument is as valid as the first argument.

The weakness of propositional logic is, it is inadequate to express the inner meaning of a statement like 'All animals having hairs on their bodies are mammals'. A more powerful logical system is required to overcome this limitation. Predicate logic offers the solution. In predicate logic, the aforementioned argument will be represented as:

Premise No. 1.	For all x, if x is a hairy animal, then x is a mammal.
Premise No. 2.	Monkey is a hairy animal.
Conclusion.	*Therefore*, Monkey is a mammal.

Using predicate logic expressions, the argument looks like

$$(\forall x)\ H(x) \rightarrow M(x)$$

$$H(Monkey)$$

$$\therefore \quad M(Monkey)$$

where, the symbols have the following meanings

$\forall x$	: for all x
$H(x)$	: x is a hairy animal.
$M(x)$	: x is a mammal.
$H(Monkey)$	: Monkey is a hairy animal.
$M(Monkey)$	: Monkey is a mammal.

H and M are two predicate symbols used in this argument. The validity of such argument will be proved later in this subsection.

Table 3.12. *Constituents of predicate logic wffs*

#	Element type	Symbols commonly used
1	Non-predicate constants	a, b, c, …
2	Variables	x, y, z, …
3	Predicate constants	P, Q, R, …
4	Function Constants	f, g, h, …
5	Universal quantifier	∀ (for all)
6	Existential quantifier	∃ (there exists)
7	Logical connectives	¬,′ (NOT), • (AND), + (OR), → (implication), ↔ (equivalence)
8	Parentheses	(,)

Syntax As in propositional logic, statements of predicate logic are also expressed as well-formed formulae (wffs). However, predicate logic wffs are extensions of propositional logic wffs. The structural elements of these wffs are listed in Table 3.12. These elements are briefly described below.

Non-predicate constants Non-predicate constants are symbolic or numeric non-predicate values that do not change over time. Examples of non-predicate constants are *Socrates, X-123, 007, -63, India* etc.

Variables Variables are symbolic expressions that can assume different non-predicate values over a certain domain. For example, if x is a variable denoting the name of a month, then x may assume any value from *January* to *December*.

Predicate constants Predicate constants are symbols that denote the predicate part of a proposition. They are relations or mappings from the elements of a certain domain D to a truth value. For example, let *MAN* be a predicate constant and *MAN* (x) means 'x is a man'. Then *MAN* (John) is true as John is a man but *MAN* (Mary) is false because Mary is not a man. Similarly, if *SON* is a predicate constant such that *SON* (x, y) means x is the son of y, then *SON* (*John*, *Smith*) is True if *John* is the son of *Smith*, otherwise it returns false. The argument(s) of a predicate constant are non-predicate constants, variables, or functions.

Function constant A predicate logic function is syntactically similar to a predicate constant except that instead of a truth value, it may return a value from any domain. As an instance of a function, consider *age* (*person*) which returns the age of a person. If we substitute *Sam* for the variable *person* whose age is 30 years, then *age* (*Sam*) would return 30. Similarly, *owner* (*phone-number*) might be a function that returns the name of the owner of a given phone-number.

Quantifiers There are two quantifiers, the universal quantifier (denoted by $\forall$ and pronounced as *for all*) and the existential quantifier (denoted by $\exists$ and pronounced as *there exists*). The universal quantifier $\forall$ is employed when a statement applies to all members of a domain. For example, the statement '*All integers are real numbers*' is universally quantified. On the other hand, the *existential quantifier* is used when a statement holds good for at least one element of the concerned domain. Consider, for example, the statement, *There is an employee who is a doctorate.* It does not state that all employees are doctorates (though that possibility is not negated by the given statement) but it ensures that there are some, at least one, employee who is a doctorate.

Logical connectives The five logical connectives frequently used in predicate logic wffs are $\neg$, or (*NOT*), $\bullet$ (*AND*), + (*OR*), $\rightarrow$ (*implication*), $\leftrightarrow$ (*equivalence*). They have the same semantics as in propositional logic.

Parentheses Parentheses are used as delimiters. Braces and square brackets are also used as delimiters for the sake of better readability.

Apart from the elements mentioned above, there are a few terms used frequently in first order predicate logic. These are defined below.

Definition 3.8 (*Term*) In predicate logic, a term is a non-predicate constant symbol, or a variable symbol, or a function symbol.

Examples of terms are *A*, *min*, $f(a, b)$ etc.

Definition 3.9 (*Atom*) A predicate expression, consisting of a predicate symbol followed by the list of parameters within a pair of parentheses, is said to be an atom, or atomic formula.

Examples of atoms are *MAN* (x), *LESS-THAN* (x, y) etc.

Definition 3.10 (*Literal*) A literal is either an atom, or the negation of an atom.

So if *MAN* (x) is an atom, both *MAN* (x) and *MAN* (x)′ are literals.

Example 3.4 (*wff expression for a predicate logic proposition*)

Let us consider the proposition *The probability of any event is a real number between 0 and 1, both inclusive.* Logically, this is equivalent to the statement: *For all n, if n is an event then probability of n is a real number, and probability of n is greater than or equal to 0, and probability of n is less than or equal to 1.* The *wff* for the statement is

$$(\forall n)\ EVENT\ (n) \rightarrow REAL\ (p\ (n)) \bullet GE\ (p\ (n), 0) \bullet LE\ (p\ (n), 1)$$

The symbols used in this *wff* have meanings and categories as listed in Table 3.13.

Table 3.13

#	Symbol	Meaning	Category
1	*n*	An unknown entity	Variable
2	0	The number zero	Non-predicate constant
3	1	The number one	Non-predicate constant
4	*E* (x)	x is an event	Predicate atom
5	*R* (x)	x is a real number	Predicate atom
6	*GE* (x, *y*)	x is greater than or equals to *y*	Predicate atom
7	*LE* (x, *y*)	x is less than or equals to *y*	Predicate atom
8	p (x)	Probability of event x	Function atom
9	∀	For all	Universal quantifier
10	→, •	Implication, AND	Logical connectives
11	(,)	Delimiters	Parentheses

It must be understood that a predicate and a function, though syntactically similar, are actually different. When evaluated a predicate term returns a truth value, true or false, whereas a function term may return any value from the related domain. In the present example, given real numbers x and y, $GE\ (x, y)$ is either true, or false. However, given an event x, $p\ (x)$ is a real number within the range [0, 1].

The predicate logic discussed here is of first order in the sense that only constants over predicates and functions are allowed and no variables over predicates or functions are allowed. The first order predicate logic wffs are recursively defined as follows.

Definition 3.11 (*First order predicate logic well-formed formula*) The first order predicate logic well formed formula can be recursively defined as follows:

1. If P is a predicate constant with k arguments and $\alpha_1, \ldots, \alpha_k$ are terms, i.e., variables, constants, or functions, then $P\ (\alpha_1, \ldots, \alpha_k)$ is a wff.
2. If W is a wff then $(\neg W)$ is a wff.

3. If W_1 and W_2 are wffs, then the following are wffs.
   (i) $(W_1 \bullet W_2)$
   (ii) $(W_1 + W_2)$
   (iii) $(W_1 \rightarrow W_2)$
   (iv) $(W_1 \leftrightarrow W_2)$
4. If $W(x)$ is a wff containing a free variable x (x is free if it is not already quantified by either $\forall$, or $\exists$ in $W(x)$) then $(\forall x)\ W(x)$and $(\exists x)\ W(x)$ are also wffs.
5. Only those which are obtained using the rules 1 to 4 cited above are wffs.

It is obvious from the recursive definition given above that all FOPL wffs are composed of atomic formulae with appropriate logical connectives, quantifiers and the parentheses. A few valid propositions and corresponding FOPL wffs are given below.

	Proposition	FOPL wff
(i)	The earth is a planet.	*PLANET* (earth)
(ii)	The sky is blue and forst is green	*BLUE* (*sky*) • *GREEN* (*forest*)
(iii)	If x is greater than y and y is greater than z then x is greater than z.	$(\forall x, y, z)$ [*GE* (x, y) • *GE* (y, z)] $\rightarrow$ *GE* (x, z)
(iv)	For every x there is a y such that $y = x^2$.	$(\forall x)$ $(\exists y)$ EQ (y, *square-of* (x))
(v)	Every man has a father and a mother.	$(\forall x)$ *MAN* $(x) \rightarrow$ [$(\exists y, z)$ *FATHER* (y, x) • *MOTHER* (z, x)]
(vi)	If x is irrational then x is not an integer.	$(\forall x)$ *IRRATIONAL* $(x) \rightarrow \neg$ *INTEGER* (x)

However, the following expressions are not valid FOPL wffs due to the reasons specified on the right.

PLANET (*Sun′*)	A constant term cannot be negated.
$(\forall P)\ (\exists Q)\ P(x) \rightarrow \neg\, Q(x)$	Predicate cannot be quantified.
LESS-THAN (*NEG* (x), *POS* (y))	A predicate cannot be an argument of a function.
score-of (*Sam*)	A function is not a wff.

Semantics of FOPL wffs The semantics of FOPL is an extension of the semantics of propositional logic. The logical connectives ′, •, +, →, ↔, have the same truth tables in both systems. However, unlike propositional logic, an FOPL wff is always understood in the context of some domain, or universe of discourse. For example, let *Family* = {*Sam*, *Mita*, *Bilu*, *Milu*} be a domain. We may define predicates like *HUSBAND* (x), *WIFE* (y), *CHILD* (x), *MARRIED-TO* (x, y) etc. and functions like *son-of* (x), or *spouse-of* (y) etc. on this domain. It is tacitly assumed that all variables and constants take values from the corresponding domain.

An *interpretation* is a set of values assigned to various terms and atomic formulae of an FOPL wff. An atomic formula, which is nothing but a predicate expression, evaluates to a truth value. Since a wff is composed of literals, i.e., atomic formulae in negated or non-negated forms, the truth value of a wff should be computable with the help of the truth table method. Just as in propositional logic, if two wffs evaluate to the same truth value under any interpretation, they are said to be *equivalent*. Moreover, a predicate that has no variables is called a *ground atom*. For example, *MAN* (*Socrates*) is a ground atom, but $(\forall x)$ *MAN* $(x) \rightarrow$ *MORTAL* (x) is not a ground atom.

Table 3.14. *ODD (x) and EVEN (x) OVER U = {0, 1}*

x	ODD (x)	EVEN (x)	ODD (x) + EVEN (x)
0	False	True	True
1	True	False	True

Table 3.15. *SUM (x, y)*

x	y	Sum (x, y)
0	0	0
0	1	1
1	0	1
1	1	0

Evaluation of a wff containing variable arguments needs special attention. This is because the wff $(\forall x)$ $P[x]$, where $P[x]$ is a wff containing the free variable x, is true if and only if $P[x]$ is true for all values of x within its domain. Therefore, to determine whether the statement $(\forall x)$ $P[x]$ is true or false one must evaluate $P[x]$ for every possible value of x within its domain. On the other hand, $(\exists x)$ $P[x]$ is true if and only if there exists at least one value of x for which $P[x]$ is true. Moreover, to determine the truth of the statement $(\exists x)$ $P[x]$ one has to go on evaluating $P[x]$ for various possible values of x until either $P[x]$ is true for some x or all possible values of x have been tried. Evaluation of an FOPL wff containing quantified variables is illustrated in Example 3.5.

Example 3.5 *(Interpretation of Predicate Logic wff)*

Let $U = \{0, 1\}$ be the universe of discourse. There are two predicates *ODD* (x) and *EVEN* (x) and a function *sum* (x, y) that returns addition modulo two of its arguments x and y, i.e., *sum* $(x, y) = (x + y)$ % 2. The values of the predicates and the functions for various combinations of their arguments are given in Table 3.14 and Table 3.15.

Now consider the statements

(i) $(\forall x)$ *ODD* (x) + *EVEN* (x)
(ii) $(\forall x)$ *ODD* $(x) \rightarrow (\exists y)$ *EVEN* (*sum* (x, y))

The first statement can be evaluated by checking whether *ODD* (x) + *EVEN* (x) is true for all possible values of x. Table 3.14 shows that the statement *ODD* (x) + *EVEN* (x) is true for all possible values of x in its domain, i.e., for both $x = 0$, and $x = 1$. Hence statement $(\forall x)$ *ODD* (x) + *EVEN* (x) is true. The truth table for the second statement is shown in Table 3.16.

There is only one odd value of x, 1, and so *ODD* (x) is True for $x = 1$. Now, to evaluate the expression $(\forall x)$ *ODD* $(x) \rightarrow (\exists y)$ *EVEN* (*sum* (x, y)) is true, we have to set $x = 1$ and then look for a value of y such that *sum* (x, y) is even, or 0. Table 3.16 shows that there does exist a y that satisfies the condition stated above. We see that for $x = 1$, and $y = 1$, *ODD* (x) is True and *EVEN* (*sum* (x, y)) is also true so that *ODD* $(x) \rightarrow (\exists y)$ *EVEN* (*sum* (x, y)) is true which in turn makes the given wff true.

Table 3.16

x	y	ODD (x)	Sum (x, y)	EVEN (sum (x, y))
0	0	False	0	True
0	1	False	1	False
1	0	True	1	False
1	1	True	0	True

In contrast, consider the statement $(\forall x)$ $(\forall y)$ *ODD* (*sum* $(x, y)) \rightarrow$ *ODD* (y). This is not true because at $x = 1$ and $y = 0$ we find that *ODD* (*sum* (x, y)) is true but *ODD* (y) is false

Properties of FOPL well-formed formulae As in propositional logic, the concepts of validity, consistency, satisfiability, logical consequence etc. applies to FOPL too.

An FOPL wff is valid if it is true for every interpretation. A wff is inconsistent (or unsatisfiable) if it is false for every interpretation. An invalid wff is one that is not valid. In other words, if a wff evaluates to False for some interpretation then it is invalid. Similarly, a consistent (or satisfiable) wff is one that is not inconsistent, and hence, is True for some interpretation. Moreover, a wff W is a logical consequence of certain wffs, say W_1, W_2, …, W_k, if and only if whenever W_1, …, W_k are true for some interpretation, W is also true for the same interpretation.

Table 3.17. *Some important FOPL identities*

#	Identity	
1.	$P \bullet Q \equiv Q \bullet P$	Commutative law
	$P + Q \equiv Q + P$	
2.	$P \bullet (Q \bullet R) \equiv (P \bullet Q) \bullet R$	Associative law
	$P + (Q + R) \equiv (P + Q) + R$	
3.	$P + (Q \bullet R) \equiv (P + Q) \bullet (P + Q)$	Distributive law
	$P \bullet (Q + R) \equiv (P \bullet Q) + (P \bullet R)$	
4.	$\neg(P + Q) \equiv (\neg P) \bullet (\neg Q)$	De Morgan's law
	$\neg(P \bullet Q) \equiv (\neg P) + (\neg Q)$	
5.	$\neg((\forall x)\ P[x]) \equiv (\exists x)\ (\neg P[x])$	
	$\neg((\exists x)\ P[x]) \equiv (\forall x)\ (\neg P[x])$	
6.	$(\forall x)\ P[x] \bullet (\forall y)\ Q[y] \equiv (\forall z)\ (P[z] \bullet Q[z])$	
	$(\exists x)\ P[x] + (\exists y)\ Q[y] \equiv (\exists z)\ (P[z] + Q[z])$	

The concepts of free and bound variables in FOPL wffs are important. A variable that exists within the scope of a quantifier is called a bound variable. For example, in the formula $(\forall x)$ $(\exists y)$ $P(x) \rightarrow Q(y)$, both x and y are bound variables. However, in $(\forall x)$ $P(x, y) \rightarrow (\exists z)$ $Q(x, z)$ x and z are bound variables but y is free. It should be noted that an FOPL wff can be evaluated only when all variables in it are bound. Such wffs are also referred to as sentences.

Two FOPL wffs are said to be *equivalent* if for all interpretations, both of them evaluate to the same truth value. Table 3.17 presents some important logical identities involving FOPL wffs. Here P and Q are arbitrary wffs and $P[x]$ represents a wff P that involves the variable x.

The identities in Row 6 should be considered carefully. First of all, we must appreciate that all variables are essentially 'dummy' variables in the sense that any symbol can be used for them, so long as they do not 'collide' with one another. For example, $(\forall x)\ P\ [x]$ is equivalent to $(\forall y)\ P\ [y]$. Similarly, $(\forall x)\ P\ [x] \bullet (\forall y)\ Q\ [y]$ is equivalent to $(\forall x)\ P\ [x] \bullet (\forall x)\ Q\ [x]$ because in the later expression the scope of the first x is $P\ [x]$, while the scope of the latter x is $Q\ [x]$. So, though the same symbol x is used in both cases actually they represent two unrelated variables.

Now let us consider the equivalence $(\forall x)\ P\ [x] \bullet (\forall y)\ Q\ [y] \equiv (\forall z)\ (P\ [z] \bullet Q\ [z])$. As a supporting example, let $P\ [x]$ means '*x is a rational number*', and $Q\ [y]$ means '*y is a real number*'. Obviously, for the aforementioned identity hold good the variables x, y and z must belong to the same universe of discourse. Let us suppose that the universe here is the set of all integers. Now the left hand side and the right hand side of the identity $(\forall x)\ P\ [x] \bullet (\forall y)\ Q\ [y] \equiv (\forall z)\ (P\ [z] \bullet Q\ [z])$ can be stated as :

L.H.S.: $(\forall x)\ P\ [x] \bullet (\forall y)\ Q\ [y]$ *All integers are rational numbers and all integers are real numbers.*
R.H.S.: $(\forall z)\ (P\ [z] \bullet Q\ [z])$ *All integers are rational numbers as well as real numbers.*

Both the statements are true. However, if we replace conjunction with disjunction, the identity no longer holds good.

$$(\forall x)\ P\ [x] + (\forall y)\ Q\ [y] \neq (\forall z)\ (P\ [z] + Q\ [z])$$

To convince ourselves about the non-equivalence of the L.H.S and the R.H.S, let us suppose $P\ [x]$ represents the statement '*x is an even number*' and $Q\ [y]$ represents '*y is an odd number*'. Then the statements on the L.H.S. and R.H.S. correspond to

L.H.S.: $(\forall x)\ P\ [x] + (\forall y)\ Q\ [y]$ *All integers are odd or all integers are even.*
R.H.S.: $(\forall z)\ (P\ [z] + Q\ [z])$ *All integers are either odd, or even.*

Here the second statement is true but the first is not. Hence they are not equivalent.

To appreciate the equivalence $(\exists x)\ P\ [x] + (\exists y)\ Q\ [y] \equiv (\exists z)\ (P\ [z] + Q\ [z])$ and the non-equivalence $(\exists x)\ P\ [x] \bullet (\exists y)\ Q\ [y] \neq (\exists z)\ (P\ [z] \bullet Q\ [z])$ we may consider the propositions $P\ [x]$ = '*x is alive*' and $Q\ [x]$ = '*x is dead*' with the assumption that nothing can be simultaneously alive and dead. Here the universe of discourse may be the set of all human beings, dead or alive.

3.1.3 Rules of Inference

Rules of inference are rules with which new propositions are obtained from a set of given statements. There are two kinds of rules of inference, deductive and non-deductive. Some important deductive rules of inference are Modus Ponens, Universal Specialization, Chain Rule, Resolution, Modus Tollens (also called Indirect Reasoning, or Law of Contraposition), Simplification, Addition, etc. Examples of non-deductive rules of inference are Abduction, Induction, and Analogy. These are briefly described in this Subsection.

Deductive rules of inference An inference rule consists of two parts, the premise(s) and the conclusion. For instance, Modus Ponens has two premises, $P \rightarrow Q$, and P. And the conclusion is Q.

(a)

Modus Ponens

Premise No. 1.	$P \rightarrow Q$
Premise No.2.	P
Conclusion	*Therefore, Q*

Example 3.6 (*Modus Ponens*)

Premise No. 1.	*If the car is expensive then it is comfortable.*
Premise No. 2.	*The car is expensive.*
Conclusion	*Therefore, the car is comfortable.*

The other inference rules are described below with illustrative examples.

(b)

Universal Specialization

Premise No. 1.	$(\forall x)\ W[x]$
Conclusion.	*Therefore,* $W[A]$

A is a constant belonging to the universe of discourse.

Example 3.7 (*Universal Specialization*)

Premise No. 1.	*All natural numbers are integers.*
Conclusion.	*Therefore, 3 is an integer.*

(c)

Chain Rule

Premise No. 1.	$P \rightarrow Q$
Premise No. 2.	$Q \rightarrow R$
Conclusion.	*Therefore,* $P \rightarrow R$

Example 3.8 (*Chain Rule*)

Premise No. 1.	*If the day is sunny then there will be a large crowd.*
Premise No. 2.	*If there is a large crowd then the sell is high.*
Conclusion.	*Therefore, If the day is sunny then the sell is high.*

(d)

Simplification

Premise No. 1.	$P \bullet Q$
Conclusion.	*Therefore,* P *(or* Q*).*

Example 3.9 *(Simplification)*

Premise No. 1.	*The sky is blue and 2 is a prime number.*
Conclusion	*Therefore, The sky is blue. (or, 2 is a prime number)*

(e) *Resolution*

Premise No. 1.	$P_1 + \cdots + P_m$
Premise No. 2.	$\neg P_1 + Q_2 + \cdots + Q_n$
Conclusion.	*Therefore,* $P_2 + \cdots + P_m + Q_2 + \cdots + Q_n$

Example 3.10 *(Resolution)*

Premise No. 1.	*It is a rainy day, or I have a raincoat.*
Premise No. 2.	*It is not a rainy day, or dog is a faithful animal.*
Conclusion.	*Therefore, I have a raincoat, or dog is a faithful animal.*

(f) *Modus Tollens*

Premise No. 1.	$P \rightarrow Q$
Premise No. 2.	$\neg Q$
Conclusion.	*Therefore,* $\neg P$

Example 3.11 *(Modus Tollens)*

Premise No. 1.	*If the shirt is cheap then there is life on Mars.*
Premise No. 2.	*There is no life on Mars.*
Conclusion.	*Therefore, The shirt is not cheap.*

(g) *Addition*

Premise No. 1.	P
Conclusion.	*Therefore,* $P + Q$

Example 3.12 *(Addition)*

Premise No. 1.	*The Earth is round.*
Conclusion.	*Therefore, Earth is round, or Man is mortal.*

Non-deductive Rules of Inference Non-deductive inference rules are important because they represent the common sense reasoning process that we employ in everyday life to tackle practical problems. These rules are followed to arrive at a conclusion or take a decision which is most likely to be valid or correct though not guaranteed to be so. The three non-deductive inference rules, viz. Abduction, Induction and Analogy, are briefly explained below.

Abduction Let $P \xrightarrow{c} Q$ be the expression for a possible cause and effect relationship between the statements *P* and *Q* where *P* is the cause and *Q* is its possible effect. In abduction, given $P \xrightarrow{c} Q$ and Q, we can conclude *P*. Hence

(a)

Abduction

Premise No. 1.	$P \xrightarrow{c} Q$
Premise No. 2.	Q
Conclusion.	*Therefore, P*

Example 3.13 (*Abduction*)

Premise No. 1.	*If you work hard then you will be successful.*
Premise No. 2.	*You are successful.*
Conclusion.	*Therefore, You have worked hard.*

Induction In practical life, if we find a statement to be true for a number of cases, we tend to assume that it is true in general. This is expressed by the inductive rule of inference.

(b)

Induction

Premise No. 1.	$P[A_1]$
Premise No. 2.	$P[A_2]$
:	:
:	:
Premise No. *k*.	$P[A_k]$
Conclusion.	*Therefore*, $(\forall x)\, P[x]$

Example 3.14 (*Induction*)

Premise No. 1.	*Mr Ghosh is a businessman and he is rich.*
Premise No. 2.	*Mr Rao is a businessman and he is rich.*
Premise No. 3.	*Mr Smith is a businessman and he is rich.*
Premise No. 4.	*Mr Ansari is a businessman and he is rich.*
Premise No. 5.	*Mr Fujiwara is a businessman and he is rich.*
Conclusion.	*Therefore, all businessmen are rich.*

Analogy Our everyday experience tells us that if a situation, or object, or entity is similar to another situation, or object, or entity in some aspect, then they are likely to be similar in other aspects too. If we represent the fact that P is related to Q as $P \xrightarrow{r} Q$, and P is similar to P_1 as $P \approx P_1$, then, the analogical rule of inference can be stated as

(c) *Analogy*

Premise No. 1.	$P \xrightarrow{r} Q$
Premise No. 2.	$P \approx P_1$
Premise No. 3.	$Q \approx Q_1$
Conclusion.	*Therefore,* $P_1 \xrightarrow{r} Q_1$

Example 3.15 *(Analogy)*

Premise No. 1.	*Gentle people are generally soft spoken.*
Premise No. 2.	*Gorillas are much like people.*
Premise No. 3.	*Soft spoken creatures seem to be humble.*
Conclusion.	*Therefore, Gentle gorillas are generally humble.*

3.2 FUZZY LOGIC BASICS

The propositional logic and the predicate logic discussed so far are crisp. These are *two-valued* logic because they are based on the law of excluded middle according to which a statement can be either true or false, and nothing else. Fuzzy logic extends crisp logic by accepting the possibility of the infinite shades truths between absolute falsehood and absolute truth. This section presents the fundamental concepts of fuzzy logic.

Table 3.18. *Fuzzy truth values*

Linguistic	Numeric (tentative)
Absolutely False	0.00
Partly False	0.25
Neither False nor True	0.50
Both False and True	0.50
Partly True	0.75
Absolutely True	1.00

3.2.1 Fuzzy Truth Values

In classical (or crisp) logic there are only two possible truth values, true and false, numerically expressed as 1 and 0 respectively. Unlike crisp truth values, there are various fuzzy truth values including the crisp truth values. Certain common linguistic fuzzy truth values and their tentative numeric values are shown in Table 3.18. The numeric truth values indicated above are not absolute. They may vary depending on requirement of context and interpretation. There may be other linguistic truth values such as *more-or-less false*, *very true*, *almost true* etc.

Fuzzy propositions A proposition that can have a fuzzy truth value is known as a fuzzy proposition. Let p be a fuzzy proposition. Then the truth value of p is denoted by $\tau(p)$ where $0 \le \tau(p) \le 1$. A few examples of fuzzy propositions are cited in Table 3.19 along with their possible fuzzy truth values – both linguistic and numeric.

Table 3.19. *Fuzzy proposition and their possible truth values*

#	Proposition (p)	Fuzzy Truth Value, $\tau(p)$	
		Lingustic	Numeric
1.	√2 is a rational number.	Absolutely False	0.00
2.	She is very emotional.	Partly True	0.70
3.	The book is quite costly.	Partly False	0.30
4.	He is rich.	Partly False	0.40
5.	Humble people are usually polite.	Mostly True	0.80
6.	The Earth is round.	Almost Absolutely True	0.97
7.	The only even prime number is 2.	Absolutely True	1.00

Obviously, the numeric truth values against their linguistic counterparts are tentative. They may vary depending on requirement of context and interpretation.

Fuzzy logic operations Various operations of crisp logic, e.g., disjunction (+), conjunction (•), negation (′), implication (→) etc., have their fuzzy counterparts. The basic fuzzy operations are given in Table 3.20.

Table 3.20. *Fuzzy logic operations*

#	Operation	Symbol	Usage	Definition
1	*disjunction*	+	$P + Q$	$\tau(P + Q) = max\{\tau(P), \tau(Q)\}$
2	*conjunction*	•	$P \bullet Q$	$\tau(P \bullet Q) = min\{\tau(P), \tau(Q)\}$
3	*negation*	¬	$\neg P$	$\tau(\neg P) = 1 - \tau(P)$
4	*implication*	→	$P \to Q$	$\tau(P \to Q) = max\{1 - \tau(P), \tau(Q)\}$

There are various interpretations of fuzzy implication such as

$$\begin{aligned}\tau(P \to Q) &= 1 \text{ if } \tau(P) \le \tau(Q),\\ &= 0, \text{ otherwise}\\ \tau(P \to Q) &= 1 \text{ if } \tau(P) \le \tau(Q),\\ &= \tau(Q), \text{ otherwise}\\ \tau(P \to Q) &= \min\{1, \tau(Q)/\tau(P)\}\\ \tau(P \to Q) &= \min\{1, [\tau(Q)(1-\tau(P)] / [\tau(P)(1 - \tau(Q)]\}\end{aligned}$$

$\tau(P \rightarrow Q) = \min\{1, 1 - \tau(P) + \tau(Q)\}$
$\tau(P \rightarrow Q) = \max\{\min(\tau(P), \tau(Q)), 1 - \tau(P)\}$

The last one was proposed by Zadeh. Depending on the context and application, user has to identify and select the appropriate interpretation of fuzzy implication.

Example 3.16 *(Fuzzy logic operations)*

Let us consider the following two fuzzy propositions along with their fuzzy truth values

p = Mr. Bakshi is handsome. $\tau(p) = 0.7$
q = Mr. Bakshi is tall. $\tau(q) = 0.4$

Various fuzzy operations on these fuzzy operations are shown below.

Fuzzy AND. $\tau(p \bullet q) = min\{\tau(p), \tau(q)\} = min\{0.7, 0.4\} = 0.4$
Fuzzy OR. $\tau(p + q) = max\{\tau(p), \tau(q)\} = max\{0.7, 0.4\} = 0.7$
Fuzzy NOT. $\tau(p') = 1 - \tau(p) = 1 - 0.7 = 0.3,$
$\tau(q') = 1 - \tau(q) = 1 - 0.4 = 0.6$
Fuzzy implication $\tau(p \rightarrow q) = max\{1 - \tau(p), \tau(q)\} = max\{1\text{-}0.7, 0.4\} = 0.4$

3.3 FUZZY TRUTH IN TERMS OF FUZZY SETS

Fuzzy logic can be related to fuzzy sets by equating fuzzy truth values to the degrees membership to fuzzy sets. Let F be a fuzzy set over the universe U and $x \in U$. Then what is the truth value of the statement p = 'x is a member of F'? Obviously, it should be nothing but the extent to which x is a member of F. Hence $\tau(p) = \mu_F(x)$. This association between fuzzy set membership and fuzzy logic truth value is illustrated in Example 3.17.

Example 3.17 *(Fuzzy truth values in terms of fuzzy membership)*

Let a = *warm-colour*, and b = *cool-colour* be fuzzy sets on the universe of *colour* = {*violet, mauve, magenta, blue, green, brown, yellow, orange, pink*}.

$$a = warm\text{-}colour = \frac{0.2}{mauve} + \frac{0.4}{brown} + \frac{0.6}{yellow} + \frac{0.8}{orange} + \frac{1.0}{pink}$$

$$b = cool\text{-}colour = \frac{0.3}{mauve} + \frac{0.5}{brown} + \frac{0.2}{yellow} + \frac{0.8}{blue} + \frac{1.0}{green}$$

Then the truth values of the fuzzy proposition p = '*yellow is a warm-colour*,' and q = '*blue is a cool-colour*' would be

$\tau(p) = \mu_{\text{warm-colour}}(yellow) = 0.6$
$\tau(q) = \mu_{\text{cool-colour}}(blue) = 0.8.$

Let a and b be two fuzzy sets on the universe U and p = 'x is a member of a,' q = 'x is a member of b' are two fuzzy propositions. Then $\tau(p + q) = max\{\tau(p), \tau(q)\} = \max\{\mu_A(x), \mu_B(x)\} = \mu_{A \cup B}(x)$. Similarly $\tau(p \bullet q) = \mu_{A \cap B}(x)$, and $\tau(p') = \mu_{A'}(x)$. Therefore fuzzy logic and fuzzy set theory are isomorphic systems.

Fuzzy truth and linguistic variables An atomic fuzzy proposition has the form '*x* is *P*' where *P* is a predicate and a linguistic fuzzy value of a linguistic variable, say *L*. Moreover, *L* must be measurable and must have a crisp value corresponding to *x*. How to find the truth value of a fuzzy proposition *s* = '*x* is *P*'? The truth value of *s*, $\tau(s)$, can be obtained in the following way

1. Evaluate *L* for *x*. This is possible because *L* is measurable.
2. Find the membership of $L(x)$ in *P*, *i.e.*, find $\mu_P(L(x))$.
3. $\tau(s) = \mu_P(L(x))$.

Hence, *s* is true to the extent $L(x)$ is a member of *P*. This is illustrated in Example 3.18.

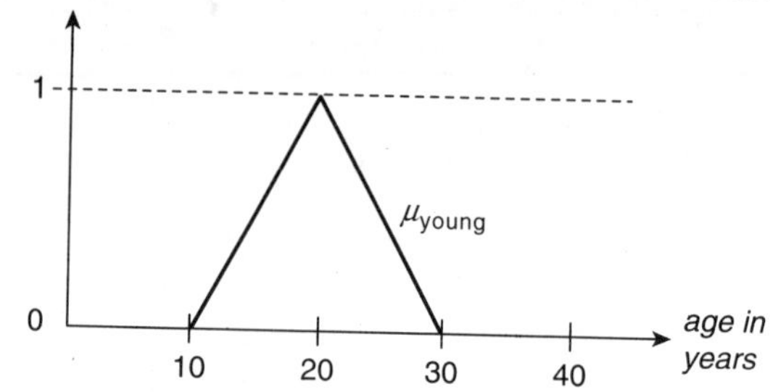

Fig. 3.1. *Membership profile of young*

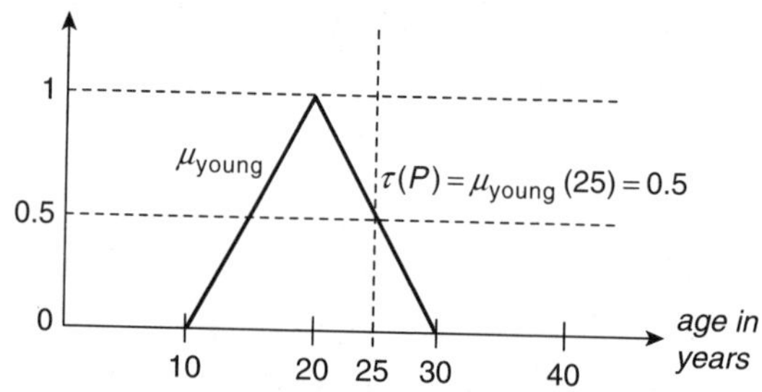

Fig. 3.2. *Finding fuzzy truth value from degree of membership*

Example 3.18 (*Fuzzy truth-value in terms of fuzzy membership*)

Consider the fuzzy proposition *p* = '*Anita is young*'. Here the predicate *young* is a linguistic value of the linguistic variable *age*. Other possible linguistic values of *age* are *very young, middle-aged, aged, old, very old*, and so on. Each of these linguistic values corresponds to a fuzzy set on the universe of *age*. Let the membership profile of *young* be as shown in Fig. 3.1. As *age* is a measurable quantity it is possible to find the value of *age* of Anita. If Anita's age is 25 years then we have *age* (*Anita*) = 25. From the membership profile of *young* we see that $\mu_{young}(age\ (Anita)) = \mu_{young}(25) = 0.5$ (Fig. 3.2). Hence the fuzzy truth value of the proposition *p* = '*Anita is young*' is $\tau(p) = 0.5$.

3.4 FUZZY RULES

Fuzzy rules are of special interest because they constitute an integral part of the so called fuzzy inference systems, or fuzzy inference mechanisms. The core of fuzzy inference system is the *fuzzy rule base*, which consists of a set of fuzzy rules. In real life, the concept of fuzzy inference system is used to construct fuzzy controllers. These topics are discussed in greater details in the next chapter.

3.4.1 Fuzzy If-Then

An elementary fuzzy rule R is a statement of the form

$$\text{If } p \text{ Then } q \tag{3.1}$$

where p and q are atomic fuzzy propositions known as the antecedent and the consequent respectively. They have the form of an atomic propositions 'x is A'.

We have seen that the truth value of a fuzzy statement p = 'x is A' is given by the membership value of the fuzzy set A. Moreover, A is the predicate of the statement p = 'x is A' so that using the formalism of predicate logic p is denoted as A (x). Therefore the fuzzy rule

$$R : \text{If '}x \text{ is } A\text{' Then '}y \text{ is } B\text{'} \tag{3.2}$$

is symbolically expressed as

$$R : A\,(x) \rightarrow B\,(y) \tag{3.3}$$

Hence, the fuzzy rule *If* 'x is A' *Then* 'y is B' can be expressed as a fuzzy relation between A and B where

$$R\,(x, y) = \tau\ [A\,(x) \rightarrow B\,(y)] \tag{3.4}$$

There are various interpretations of fuzzy rule. Among these, interpretations proposed by Mamdani and Zadeh are the most popular. These are

a) *Mamdani's interpretation of fuzzy rule*:

$$\begin{aligned} R\,(x, y) &= \tau\ [A\,(x) \rightarrow B\,(y)] \\ &= min\ [\tau\ (A\,(x)), \tau\ (B\,(y))] = min\ [\mu_A(x), \mu_B(y)] \end{aligned} \tag{3.5}$$

b) *Zadeh's interpretation of fuzzy rule*:

$$\begin{aligned} R\,(x, y) &= \tau\ [A\,(x) \rightarrow B\,(y)] \\ &= max\ [min\ \{\mu_A(x), \mu_B(y)\}, 1 - \mu_A(x)] \end{aligned} \tag{3.6}$$

Assuming U and V to be the universes for the fuzzy sets A and B respectively, Zadeh's interpretation of fuzzy rule is equivalent to the relation

$$R = (A \times B) \cup (A' \times V) \tag{3.7}$$

where V is used as a fuzzy set in which all the members have membership value 1.

Example 3.19 *(Zadeh's interpretation of fuzzy rules)*

Let R : If '*job is risky*' Then '*compensation is high*' be a fuzzy rule. There are four jobs job_1, job_2, job_3 and job_4, constituting the universe $job = \{job_1, job_2, job_3, job_4\}$. Also, there are four categories of compensation c_1, c_2, c_3, and c_4 in ascending order. Hence the universe for compensations is *compensation* = $\{c_1, c_2, c_3, c_4\}$. The fuzzy sets *risky-job* and *high-compensation* are defined on the universes *job* and *compensation* respectively as given below.

$$risky\text{-}job = \frac{0.3}{job_1} + \frac{0.8}{job_2} + \frac{0.7}{job_3} + \frac{0.9}{job_4}$$

$$high\text{-}compensation = \frac{0.2}{c_1} + \frac{0.4}{c_2} + \frac{0.6}{c_3} + \frac{0.8}{c_4}$$

Using Zadeh's interpretation, the truth value of rule R is expressed by the relation

$$R = (\textit{risky-job} \times \textit{high-compensation}) \cup (\overline{\textit{risky} - \textit{job}} \times \textit{compensation})$$

Now,

$$\textit{risky-job} \times \textit{high-compensation} = \begin{array}{c|cccc} & C_1 & C_2 & C_3 & C_4 \\ \hline job_1 & 0.2 & 0.3 & 0.3 & 0.3 \\ job_2 & 0.2 & 0.4 & 0.6 & 0.8 \\ job_3 & 0.2 & 0.4 & 0.6 & 0.7 \\ job_4 & 0.2 & 0.4 & 0.6 & 0.8 \end{array},$$

$$\text{and, } \overline{\textit{risky} - \textit{job}} \times \textit{compensation} = \begin{array}{c|cccc} & C_1 & C_2 & C_3 & C_4 \\ \hline job_1 & 0.7 & 0.7 & 0.7 & 0.7 \\ job_2 & 0.2 & 0.2 & 0.2 & 0.2 \\ job_3 & 0.3 & 0.3 & 0.3 & 0.3 \\ job_4 & 0.1 & 0.1 & 0.1 & 0.1 \end{array},$$

and finally, $R = (\textit{risky-job} \times \textit{high-compensation}) \cup (\overline{\textit{risky} - \textit{job}} \times \textit{compensation})$

$$= \begin{array}{c|cccc} job_1 & 0.7 & 0.7 & 0.7 & 0.7 \\ job_2 & 0.2 & 0.4 & 0.6 & 0.8 \\ job_3 & 0.3 & 0.4 & 0.6 & 0.7 \\ job_4 & 0.2 & 0.4 & 0.6 & 0.8 \end{array}$$

Hence the matrix R obtained above embodies the information in the fuzzy implication IF *job is risky* THEN *compensation is high* on the basis of the fuzzy concepts *risky-job* and *high-compensation* as defined above.

3.4.2 Fuzzy If-Then-Else

A fuzzy If-Then-Else rule R has the form

$$\text{If '}x \text{ is } A\text{' Then '}y \text{ is } B\text{' Else '}y \text{ is } C\text{'} \tag{3.8}$$

where A is a fuzzy set on some universe U and B and C are fuzzy sets on the universe V. The truth value of R, in terms of the membership values of the fuzzy sets is given by

$$\begin{aligned} \tau(R(x, y)) &= \mu_R(x, y) \\ &= \max\,[\min\,\{\mu_A(x), \mu_B(y)\}, \min\,\{1 - \mu_A(x), \mu_C(y)\}] \end{aligned} \tag{3.9}$$

This is nothing but the fuzzy relation

$$R = (A \times B) \cup (A' \times C) \tag{3.10}$$

Example 3.20 illustrates the fuzzy If-Then-Else rule.

Example 3.20 (*Fuzzy If-Then-Else rule*)

The fuzzy If-Then-Else rule under consideration is R : If '*distance is long*' Then '*drive at high speed*' Else '*drive at moderate speed*'. To match with the form given in Expression 3.8, this rule can be restated as R : If '*distance is long*' Then '*speed is high*' Else '*speed is moderate*'. The relevant sets (crisp and fuzzy) are, *distance* = {100, 500, 1000, 5000} is the universe of the fuzzy set *long-distance*, *speed* = {30, 50, 70, 90, 120} is the universe of the fuzzy sets *high-speed* as well as *moderate-speed*, and

$$long\text{-}distance = \frac{0.1}{100} + \frac{0.3}{500} + \frac{0.7}{1000} + \frac{1.0}{5000}$$

$$high\text{-}speed = \frac{0.1}{30} + \frac{0.3}{50} + \frac{0.5}{70} + \frac{0.7}{90} + \frac{0.9}{120}$$

$$moderate\text{-}speed = \frac{0.3}{30} + \frac{0.8}{50} + \frac{0.6}{70} + \frac{0.4}{90} + \frac{0.1}{120}$$

Applying Expression 3.10 we get

$$R = (A \times B) \cup (A' \times C)$$
$$= (long\text{-}distance \times high\text{-}speed) \cup (\overline{long\text{-}distance} \times moderate\text{-}speed).$$

The relation matrix R is computed as follows.

$$long\text{-}distance \times high\text{-}speed = \begin{array}{c} \\ 100 \\ 500 \\ 1000 \\ 5000 \end{array} \begin{array}{c} \begin{array}{ccccc} 30 & 50 & 70 & 90 & 120 \end{array} \\ \begin{bmatrix} 0.1 & 0.1 & 0.1 & 0.1 & 0.1 \\ 0.1 & 0.3 & 0.3 & 0.3 & 0.3 \\ 0.1 & 0.3 & 0.5 & 0.7 & 0.7 \\ 0.1 & 0.3 & 0.5 & 0.7 & 0.9 \end{bmatrix} \end{array}$$

$$\overline{long\text{-}distance} \times moderate\text{-}speed = \begin{array}{c} \\ 100 \\ 500 \\ 1000 \\ 5000 \end{array} \begin{array}{c} \begin{array}{ccccc} 30 & 50 & 70 & 90 & 120 \end{array} \\ \begin{bmatrix} 0.3 & 0.8 & 0.6 & 0.4 & 0.1 \\ 0.3 & 0.7 & 0.6 & 0.4 & 0.1 \\ 0.3 & 0.3 & 0.3 & 0.3 & 0.1 \\ 0.0 & 0.0 & 0.0 & 0.0 & 0.0 \end{bmatrix} \end{array}$$

$$\therefore R = (A \times B) \cup (A' \times C)$$
$$= (\text{long distance} \times \text{high-speed}) \cup (\overline{long\text{-}distance} \times \text{normal-speed})$$

$$= \begin{array}{c} \\ 100 \\ 500 \\ 1000 \\ 5000 \end{array} \begin{array}{c} \begin{array}{ccccc} 30 & 50 & 70 & 90 & 120 \end{array} \\ \begin{bmatrix} 0.3 & 0.8 & 0.6 & 0.4 & 0.1 \\ 0.3 & 0.7 & 0.6 & 0.4 & 0.3 \\ 0.3 & 0.3 & 0.5 & 0.7 & 0.7 \\ 0.1 & 0.3 & 0.5 & 0.7 & 0.9 \end{bmatrix} \end{array}$$

So far we have discussed the simplest kind of fuzzy rules. They can be generalized to accommodate several fuzzy propositions into the antecedent part. The Generalized Fuzzy Rule is expressed as

$$\text{If '}x_1 \text{ is } A_1\text{'} \bullet \ldots \bullet \text{'}x_m \text{ is } A_m\text{' Then '}y_1 \text{ is } B_1\text{'} \bullet \ldots \bullet \text{'}y_n \text{ is } B_n\text{'} \tag{3.11}$$

Fuzzy rules are the foundation of reasoning in fuzzy logic. Fuzzy reasoning is discussed in the next Section.

3.5 FUZZY REASONING

Reasoning is the process of finding new propositions from old propositions. It is accomplished by applying the rules of inference on propositions already known to be true. In subsection 3.1.3, the rules of inference of crisp logic, e.g., *modus ponens, universal specialization, chain rule, resolution* etc. have been discussed. Fuzzy reasoning refers to reasoning involving fuzzy propositions, applying fuzzy rules of inference, producing new fuzzy propositions. The fundamentals of fuzzy reasoning are presented in the subsequent parts of this section.

3.5.1 Fuzzy Quantifiers

Recall that predicate logic had two quantifiers, the universal quantifier $\forall$, and the existential quantifier $\exists$. Fuzzy propositions too may contain quantifiers and these quantifiers are usually referred to as fuzzy quantifiers. There are two kinds of fuzzy quantifiers, absolute and relative. A fuzzy quantifier that refers to some specific value is known as absolute fuzzy quantifier. A relative fuzzy quantifier, however, do not refer to any specific value. A few instances of both types of fuzzy quantifiers are cited below.

Fuzzy Quantifiers

Absolute	Relative
Nearly 100	Almost
Far below 0	Most
Much greater than 50	About
Somewhere around 300	Few
Round about 1000	Nearly

3.5.2 Generalized Modus Ponens

As the name suggests, generalized modus ponens is the generalization of crisp modus ponens but differs in two aspects. First, it applies to statements that are fuzzy, and second, the conclusion need not be exactly the same as the consequent. A typical fuzzy reasoning employing generalized modus ponens may look like

Premise No. 1.	If *this car is expensive* Then *it is comfortable.*
Premise No. 2.	This car is more or less expensive.
Conclusion.	*Therefore*, This car is more or less comfortable.

Therefore, the generalized modus ponens rule of inference may be presented as follows :

Generalized Modus Ponens

Premise No. 1.	If 'x *is* A' Then 'y *is* B'.
Premise No. 2.	x is A_1.
Conclusion.	*Therefore*, y is B_1.

where A, A_1, B, B_1 are fuzzy statements and A_1 and B_1 are modified versions of A and B respectively.

The generalized modus ponens described above is also known as fuzzy inference. Zadeh interpreted fuzzy inference in terms of max–min composition of relations on fuzzy sets. Let A and A_1 be fuzzy sets on the universe U, and B, B_1 are fuzzy sets on the universe V. Then the truth value of the conclusion 'y is B_1' in terms of membership functions of the related fuzzy sets is obtained as

$$\tau(y \text{ is } B_1) = \mu_{B_1}(y) = \max_{x \in U}[\min\{\mu_{A_1}(x), \mu_R(x, y)\}] \tag{3.12}$$

where R represents the relation corresponding to the rule 'If '*x is A*' Then '*y is B*'. The formula stated above actually computes the fuzzy set B_1 as the max-min composition of A and R.

$$B_1 = A_1 \circ R \tag{3.13}$$

Example 3.21 (*Fuzzy reasoning with the help of generalized modus ponens*)

Let us reconsider the implication 'If *service is good* Then *customer is satisfied*'. The associated universes of discourse are

$$U = \textit{service-rating} = \{a, b, c, d, e\}$$
$$V = \textit{satisfaction-grade} = \{1, 2, 3, 4, 5\}$$

The sequences a, b, c, d, e and 1, 2, 3, 4, 5 are in descending and ascending order respectively. The fuzzy sets *good-service* and *satisfied* are given below.

$$\textit{good-service} = \frac{1.0}{a} + \frac{0.8}{b} + \frac{0.6}{c} + \frac{0.4}{d} + \frac{0.2}{e}$$

$$\textit{satisfied} = \frac{0.2}{1} + \frac{0.4}{2} + \frac{0.6}{3} + \frac{0.8}{4} + \frac{1.0}{5}$$

The information contained in the implication stated above is expressed by the relation

$$R = (\textit{good-service} \times \textit{satisfied}) \cup (\overline{\textit{good-service}} \times \textit{satisfaction-grade})$$

The relation R is found to be

$$R = \begin{array}{c} \\ a \\ b \\ c \\ d \\ e \end{array} \begin{array}{c} \begin{array}{ccccc} 5 & 4 & 3 & 2 & 1 \end{array} \\ \begin{bmatrix} 1.0 & 0.8 & 0.6 & 0.4 & 0.2 \\ 0.8 & 0.8 & 0.6 & 0.4 & 0.2 \\ 0.6 & 0.6 & 0.6 & 0.4 & 0.4 \\ 0.6 & 0.6 & 0.6 & 0.6 & 0.6 \\ 0.8 & 0.8 & 0.8 & 0.8 & 0.8 \end{bmatrix} \end{array}$$

Let us now consider *very-good-service*, a modified version of *good-service* as given below.

$$\textit{very-good-service} = \frac{0.8}{a} + \frac{0.6}{b} + \frac{0.4}{c} + \frac{0.0}{d} + \frac{0.0}{e}$$

The reasoning process may now be expressed as

Premise No. 1.	If *service is good* Then *customer is satisfied*.
Premise No. 2.	Service is very good.
Conclusion.	*Therefore*, Customer is very satisfied.

The fuzzy information content of the conclusion is obtained by applying generalized modus ponens in the form of the relation

$$very\text{-}satisfied = very\text{-}good\text{-}service \circ R$$

Computation of the individual elements of the fuzzy set *very-satisfied* is illustrated subsequently.

$$\begin{aligned}
\mu_{very\text{-}satisfied}(1) &= \max_{x \in U}[\min\{\mu_{very\text{-}good\text{-}service}(x), \mu_R(x,1)\}] \\
&= \max[\min\{\mu_{very\text{-}good\text{-}service}(a), \mu_R(a,1)\}, \min\{\mu_{very\text{-}good\text{-}service}(b), \mu_R(b,1)\}, \\
&\quad \min\{\mu_{very\text{-}good\text{-}service}(c), \mu_R(c,1)\}, \min\{\mu_{very\text{-}good\text{-}service}(d), \mu_R(d,1)\}, \\
&\quad \min\{\mu_{very\text{-}good\text{-}service}(e), \mu_R(e,1)\}] \\
&= \max[\min(0.8, 0.2), \min(0.6, 0.2), \min(0.4, 0.4), \\
&\quad \min(0.0, 0.6), \min(0.0, 0.8)] \\
&= \max[0.2, 0.2, 0.4, 0.0, 0.0] \\
&= 0.4
\end{aligned}$$

Similarly,

$$\begin{aligned}
\mu_{very\text{-}satisfied}(2) &= \max[\min(0.8, 0.4), \min(0.6, 0.4), \min(0.4, 0.4), \\
&\quad \min(0.0, 0.6), \min(0.0, 0.8)] \\
&= \max[0.4, 0.4, 0.4, 0.0, 0.0] \\
&= 0.4.
\end{aligned}$$

$$\begin{aligned}
\mu_{very\text{-}satisfied}(3) &= \max[\min(0.8, 0.6), \min(0.6, 0.6), \min(0.4, 0.6), \\
&\quad \min(0.0, 0.6), \min(0.0, 0.8)] \\
&= \max[0.6, 0.6, 0.4, 0.0, 0.0] \\
&= 0.6.
\end{aligned}$$

$$\begin{aligned}
\mu_{very\text{-}satisfied}(4) &= \max[\min(0.8, 0.8), \min(0.6, 0.8), \min(0.4, 0.6), \\
&\quad \min(0.0, 0.6), \min(0.0, 0.8)] \\
&= \max[0.8, 0.6, 0.4, 0.0, 0.0] \\
&= 0.8.
\end{aligned}$$

$$\begin{aligned}
\mu_{very\text{-}satisfied}(5) &= \max[\min(0.8, 1.0), \min(0.6, 0.8), \min(0.4, 0.6), \\
&\quad \min(0.0, 0.6), \min(0.0, 0.8)] \\
&= \max[0.8, 0.6, 0.4, 0.0, 0.0] \\
&= 0.8.
\end{aligned}$$

Hence the conclusion '*Customer is very-satisfied*' is defined by the fuzzy set

$$very\text{-}satisfied_1 = \frac{0.4}{1} + \frac{0.4}{2} + \frac{0.6}{3} + \frac{0.8}{4} + \frac{0.8}{5}$$

3.5.3 Generalized Modus Tollens

As in case of generalized modus ponens, generalized modus tollens is the generalization of crisp modus tollens. A typical fuzzy reasoning employing generalized modus tollens has the form

Premise No. 1.	If *this car is expensive* Then *it is comfortable.*
Premise No. 2.	This car is more or less comfortable.
Conclusion.	*Therefore*, This car is more or less expensive.

Hence, the generalized modus tollens rule of inference may be presented as follows :

Generalized Modus Tollens

Premise No. 1.	If '*x is A*' Then '*y is B*'.
Premise No. 2.	y is B_1.
Conclusion.	*Therefore*, x is A_1.

where A, A_1, B, B_1 are fuzzy statements and A_1 and B_1 are modified versions of A and B respectively. The formula to compute the fuzzy set A_1 as the max-min composition of B_1 and R.

$$A_1 = B_1 \circ R \tag{3.14}$$

This can be computed by applying the formula

$$\tau(x \text{ is } A_1) = \mu_A(x) = \max_{x \in U}[\min\{\mu_{B1}(y), \mu_R(x,y)\}] \tag{3.15}$$

where R represents the relation corresponding to the rule 'If '*x is A*' Then '*y is B*'.

Example 3.22 (*Fuzzy reasoning with the help of Generalized Modus Tollens*)

Premise No. 1.	If *a man is honest* Then *he is happy.*
Premise No. 2.	This man is most probably happy.
Conclusion.	*Therefore*, This man is most probably honest.

CHAPTER SUMMARY

The main points of the foregoing discussion are given below.

- In classical, or crisp, logic a proposition is either true or false. It does not allow more than these two truth values. Fuzzy logic accepts infinite number of truth values between false and true. Numerically a fuzzy truth value is any real number between 0 and 1, both inclusive.
- In propositional logic an interpretation of a logical expression is a combination of truth values for the constituent individual propositions.
- Symbolic expressions of propositional logic and predicate logic are known as well-formed formulae (wffs). Two wffs are said to be logically equivalent if they attain the same truth value for all possible interpretations. A proposition which is true for all possible interpretations is said to be a

tautology. A contradiction is a proposition which is false for all possible interpretations. A number of statements is said to be consistent if they can all be true simultaneously. An argument is said to be valid if the conclusion is true whenever the premises are true.

- Predicate logic is an extension of propositional logic. It captures the inner structure of a statement by introducing symbolic representation of the predicate part of a statement, and also by including the two quantifiers, viz., the universal quantifier ($\forall$), and the existential quantifier ($\exists$) into its formalism.
- Unlike propositional logic, a predicate logic statement is always interpreted in the context of some domain called the universe of discourse.
- An FOPL wff is valid if it is true for every interpretation. It is inconsistent (or unsatisfiable) if it is false for every interpretation. An FOPL wff W is a logical consequence of certain wffs, say W_1, W_2, ..., W_k, if and only if whenever W_1, ..., W_k are true for some interpretation, W is also true for the same interpretation.
- An FOPL wff of the form $(\forall x)\ P[x]$ is true if and only if it is true for all values of x within its domain. And the wff $(\exists x)\ P[x]$ is true if and only if there exists at least one value of x for which $P[x]$ is true.
- Rules of Inference are rules with which new propositions are obtained from a set of given statements. There are two kinds of rules of inference, deductive and non-deductive. Some important deductive rules of inference are Modus Ponens, Universal Specialization, Chain Rule, Resolution, Modus Tollens (also called Indirect Reasoning, or Law of Contraposition), Simplification, Addition, etc. The most useful non-deductive rules of inference are Abduction, Induction, and Analogy.
- An atomic fuzzy proposition has the form '*x* is *P*' where *P* is a predicate that corresponds to a fuzzy set. The truth value of the fuzzy statement '*x* is *P*' is evaluated in terms of the membership function of the fuzzy set for the predicate *P*.
- A fuzzy rule has the form If '*x* is *A*' Then '*y* is *B*'. It can be interpreted as a fuzzy relation. According to Zadeh's interpretation, a fuzzy rule may be expressed as the relation

$$R = (A \times B) \cup (A' \times V)$$

where V is the universe of B and is used here as a fuzzy set in which all the members have membership value 1.

- Two widely used fuzzy inference rules are the generalized modus ponens (GMP) and the generalized modus tollens (GMT). These two rules of inference are stated below.

Generalized Modus Ponens (*GMP*)

Premise No. 1.	If '*x* is *A*' Then '*y* is *B*'.
Premise No. 2.	*x* is A_1.
Conclusion.	Therefore, *y* is B_1.

Generalized Modus Tollens (*GMT*)

Premise No. 1.	If '*x* is *A*' Then '*y* is *B*'.
Premise No. 2.	*y* is B_1.
Conclusion.	Therefore, *x* is A_1.

A, A_1, B, B_1 are fuzzy statements. A_1 and B_1 are modified versions of A and B respectively. The reasoning process using GMP is also referred to as fuzzy inference.

- In fuzzy inference, the truth value of the conclusion '*y* is B_1' in terms of membership functions of the related fuzzy sets is obtained as

$$\tau(y \text{ is } B_1) = \mu_{B_1}(y) = \max_{x \in U}[\min\{\mu_{A1}(x), \mu_R(x, y)\}]$$

This corresponds to the max-min composition of *A* and *R*.

$$B_1 = A_1 \circ R$$

Here *R* denotes the relation corresponding to the rule If '*x is A*' Then '*y is B*'.

- In case of GMT, the fuzzy set A_1 is computed as the max-min composition of B_1 and *R*.

$$A_1 = B_1 \circ R$$

Or,

$$\tau(x \text{ is } A_1) = \mu_A(x) = \max_{x \in U}[\min\{\mu_{B1}(y), \mu_R(x, y)\}]$$

As usual, *R* denotes the relation corresponding to the rule If '*x is A*' Then '*y is B*'.

SOLVED PROBLEMS

Problem 3.1. Determine whether the following propositional logic formulae are tautologies.

(i) $(a \rightarrow b) \rightarrow ((a \rightarrow b') \rightarrow a')$
(ii) $(a \rightarrow b) \rightarrow ((a+c) \rightarrow (b+c))$

Solution 3.1. (i) The truth table for $\Psi = (a \rightarrow b) \rightarrow ((a \rightarrow b') \rightarrow a') = X \rightarrow Y$ where $X = a \rightarrow b$, and $Y = (a \rightarrow b') \rightarrow a'$ is shown in Table 3.21. Column 8 of Table 3.21 tabulates the truth values of $\Psi = (a \rightarrow b) \rightarrow ((a \rightarrow b') \rightarrow a') = X \rightarrow Y$ corresponding to different combinations of truth values of *a*, *b*, and *c*. As all entries of column 8, which represents the given expression, are true, the expression is a tautology.

Table 3.21. *Truth Table for* $\Psi = (a \rightarrow b) \rightarrow ((a \rightarrow b') \rightarrow a')$

	(1)	(2)	(3)	(4)	(5)	(6)	(7)	(8)
	a	b	a′	b′	a→b (X)	a→b′	(a→b′) →a′ (Y)	X→Y (Ψ)
(1)	0	0	1	1	1	1	1	1
(2)	0	1	1	0	1	1	1	1
(3)	1	0	0	1	0	1	0	1
(4)	1	1	0	0	1	0	1	1

(ii) Let $X = (a \rightarrow b)$, $Y = (a+c)$, $Z = (b+c)$. Then the expression $\Psi = (a \rightarrow b) \rightarrow ((a+c) \rightarrow (b+c))$ is represented as $X \rightarrow (Y \rightarrow Z)$. The corresponding truth table is shown in Table 3.22. Column 8 of Table 3.22, which tabulates the truth values of the given expression under different interpretations, contains true value in all its entries. Therefore, the given expression is a tautology.

Table 3.22. *Truth Table for $\Psi = (a \rightarrow b) \rightarrow ((a+c) \rightarrow (b+c))$*

	(1)	(2)	(3)	(4)	(5)	(6)	(7)	(8)
	a	b	c	a→b (X)	a+c (Y)	b+c (Z)	Y→Z	X→(Y→Z)
(1)	0	0	0	1	0	0	1	1
(2)	0	0	1	1	1	1	1	1
(3)	0	1	0	1	0	1	1	1
(4)	0	1	1	1	1	1	1	1
(5)	1	0	0	0	1	0	0	1
(6)	1	0	1	0	1	1	1	1
(7)	1	1	0	1	1	1	1	1
(8)	1	1	1	1	1	1	1	1

Problem 3.2. Find out whether the following formulae are equivalent.

(i) $a \rightarrow (b+c)$ and $a'+b+c$
(ii) $a + (b' \rightarrow c)$ and $a + (b \rightarrow c)'$
(iii) $(a \rightarrow b) \rightarrow c$ and $a \rightarrow (b \rightarrow c)$

Solution 3.2 (i) The Truth Table for $a \rightarrow (b+c)$ and $a'+b+c$ is shown in Table 3.23. Column 5 and Column 7, representing the formulae $a'+b+c$ and $a \rightarrow (b+c)$ respectively, are identical. Therefore they attain the same truth value for all possible interpretations. Hence, these two expressions are equivalent.

Table 3.23. *Truth Tables for $a \rightarrow (b+c)$ and $a'+b+c$*

	(1)	(2)	(3)	(4)	(5)	(6)	(7)
	a	b	c	a′	a′+b +c	b+c	a→ (b+c)
(1)	0	0	0	1	1	0	1
(2)	0	0	1	1	1	1	1
(3)	0	1	0	1	1	1	1
(4)	0	1	1	1	1	1	1
(5)	1	0	0	0	0	0	0
(6)	1	0	1	0	1	1	1
(7)	1	1	0	0	1	1	1
(8)	1	1	1	0	1	1	1

(ii) The truth table for $a+(b' \rightarrow c)$ and $a+(b \rightarrow c)'$ is shown in Table 3.24. Column 6 and column 8 of Table 3.24 represent the formulae $a+(b' \rightarrow c)$ and $a+(b \rightarrow c)'$ respectively. The truth values in the entries of row 2 and row 4 for these columns are complementary. Hence, these two expressions are not equivalent.

Table 3.24. *Truth Tables for a+(b′→c) and a+(b→c)′*

	(1)	(2)	(3)	(4)	(5)	(6)	(7)	(8)
	a	b	c	b′	b′→c	a+(b′→c)	b→c	a+(b→c)′
(1)	0	0	0	1	0	0	1	0
(2)	0	0	1	1	1	1	1	0
(3)	0	1	0	0	1	1	0	1
(4)	0	1	1	0	1	1	1	0
(5)	1	0	0	1	0	1	1	1
(6)	1	0	1	1	1	1	1	1
(7)	1	1	0	0	1	1	0	1
(8)	1	1	1	0	1	1	1	1

(iii) Table 3.25 shows the truth table for $(a \rightarrow b) \rightarrow c$ and $a \rightarrow (b \rightarrow c)$. Column 6 and column 7 of Table 3.25 represent the formulae $(a \rightarrow b) \rightarrow c$ and $a \rightarrow (b \rightarrow c)$, respectively. The truth values in the entries of row 1 and row 3 for these columns are complementary. Hence, these two expressions are not equivalent.

Table 3.25. *Truth Tables for (a→b)→c and a→(b →c)*

	(1)	(2)	(3)	(4)	(5)	(6)	(7)
	a	b	c	a→b	b→c	(a→b)→c	a→(b→c)
(1)	0	0	0	1	1	0	1
(2)	0	0	1	1	1	1	1
(3)	0	1	0	1	0	0	1
(4)	0	1	1	1	1	1	1
(5)	1	0	0	0	1	1	1
(6)	1	0	1	0	1	1	1
(7)	1	1	0	1	0	0	0
(8)	1	1	1	1	1	1	1

Problem 3.3. Determine whether the following argument is valid or not. *'If today is a holiday and the weather is sunny then we shall go for shopping. Today is a holiday. Today's weather is sunny. Therefore we shall go for shopping.'*

Table 3.26

	(1)	(2)	(3)	(4)	(5)
	a	b	c	a • b	(a • b)→c
(1)	F	F	F	F	T
(2)	F	F	T	F	T
(3)	F	T	F	F	T
(4)	F	T	T	F	T
(5)	T	F	F	F	T
(6)	T	F	T	F	T

(Continued)

Table 3.26 *Continued*

	(1)	(2)	(3)	(4)	(5)
	a	b	c	a • b	(a•b)→c
(7)	T	T	F	T	F
(8)	T	T	T	T	T

Solution 3.3. Let us denote '*Today is a holiday*' as *a*, '*The weather is sunny*' as *b*, and '*We shall go for shopping*' as *c*. Then the argument can be represented by the following sequence of expressions.

	Proposition	Expression
Premise No. 1.	If *today is a holiday* and *the weather is sunny* Then *we shall go for shopping.*	$(a \wedge b) \rightarrow c$
Premise No. 2.	Today is a holiday.	a
Premise No. 3.	Today's weather is sunny.	b
Conclusion.	Therefore, we shall go for shopping	$\therefore c$

Table 3.26 presents the various combinations of truth values for these expressions. An argument is said to be valid if the conclusion is true whenever the premises are true. It may be noted that the only case where all the premises, i.e., $(a \bullet b) \rightarrow c$, a, and b, are simultaneously true corresponds to Row 8 of the table. And the conclusion c is also true for this row. Therefore the given argument is valid.

Problem 3.4. Determine whether the following sets of formulae are consistent or not.

(i) $\{a+b, b \bullet c, (a+b) \rightarrow (b \bullet c)\}$
(ii) $\{a \rightarrow c', (a \rightarrow b)', a \rightarrow (c' \rightarrow b)\}$

Solution. 3.4 (i) A set of propositions is consistent if they all can be true simultaneously. Table 3.27 shows the truth table for the set of propositional formulae $\{a+b, b \bullet c, (a+b) \rightarrow (b \bullet c)\}$. The truth values of $a+b$, $b \bullet c$, and $(a+b) \rightarrow (b \bullet c)$ for various interpretations are noted in columns 4, 5, and 6 respectively. A careful scrutiny of the table reveals that there are truth value combinations for a, b, and c which renders all three propositions true (Rows 4 and 8). Hence the propositions are consistent.

Table 3.27. *Truth Table for a+b, b•c, and (a+b)→(b•c)*

	(1)	(2)	(3)	(4)	(5)	(6)
	a	b	c	a + b	b • c	(a + b)→(b • c)
(1)	0	0	0	0	0	1
(2)	0	0	1	0	0	1
(3)	0	1	0	1	0	0
(4)	0	1	1	1	1	1
(5)	1	0	0	1	0	0
(6)	1	0	1	1	0	0
(7)	1	1	0	1	0	0
(8)	1	1	1	1	1	1

Table 3.28. *Truth Table for a→c′, (a→b)′, a →(c′→b)*

	(1)	(2)	(3)	(4)	(5)	(6)	(7)	(8)
	a	b	c	c′	a→c′	(a →b)′	c′→b	a →(c′→b)
(1)	0	0	0	1	1	0	0	1
(2)	0	0	1	0	1	0	1	1
(3)	0	1	0	1	1	0	1	1
(4)	0	1	1	0	1	0	1	1
(5)	1	0	0	1	1	1	0	0
(6)	1	0	1	0	0	1	1	1
(7)	1	1	0	1	1	0	1	1
(8)	1	1	1	0	0	0	1	1

(ii) Table 3.28 presents the Truth Tables for the propositional formulae $a \rightarrow c'$, $(a \rightarrow b)'$, $a \rightarrow (c' \rightarrow b)$. The truth values of $a \rightarrow c'$, $(a \rightarrow b)'$, $a \rightarrow (c' \rightarrow b)$ for various interpretations are noted in Columns 5, 6, and 8 respectively. It is seen that these formulae are never true simultaneously. Since a set of propositions is consistent only when they all can be true simultaneously, the given formulae are not consistent.

Problem 3.5. Consider the following statements: '*I may fall sick if I smoke. I am not happy if I fall sick. I smoke. I am happy*.' Are they consistent?

Solution 3.5. Let denote the statement '*I may fall sick*' by *a*, '*I smoke*' by *b*, and '*I am happy*' by *c*. Then, the given statements are represented by a sequence of Propositional Logic formulae as shown below:

#	Proposition	Formula
1.	I may fall sick if I smoke.	$b \rightarrow a$
2.	I am not happy if I fall sick.	$a \rightarrow c'$
3.	I smoke.	b
4.	I am happy.	c

From the Truth Table shown in Table 3.29 it is evident that these formulae are never simultaneously true. Hence the statements are not consistent.

Table 3.29. *Truth table for b→a and a→c′*

	(1)	(2)	(3)	(4)	(5)	(6)
	a	b	c	c′	b→a	a→c′
(1)	0	0	0	1	1	1
(2)	0	0	1	0	1	1
(3)	0	1	0	1	0	1
(4)	0	1	1	0	0	1
(5)	1	0	0	1	1	1
(6)	1	0	1	0	1	0
(7)	1	1	0	1	1	1
(8)	1	1	1	0	1	0

Problem 3.6. Determine whether the following argument is valid or not.

	Proposition
Premise No. 1.	$a \rightarrow (b \bullet c')$
Premise No. 2.	$a \bullet (b \rightarrow c)$
Conclusion.	$\therefore a$

Solution 3.6. Table 3.30 shows the truth tables for the propositions of the given argument. An argument is valid if the conclusion is true whenever the premises are true. However, there is no interpretation for which both the premises (Column 6 and Column 8) are true simultaneously. Therefore the condition for validity of an argument is not violated in this case. Hence the argument is valid.

Table 3.30. *Truth table for* $a \rightarrow (b \bullet c')$ *and* $a \bullet (b \rightarrow c)$

	(1)	(2)	(3)	(4)	(5)	(6)	(7)	(8)
	a	b	c	c'	$b \bullet c'$	$a \rightarrow (b \bullet c')$	$b \rightarrow c$	$a \bullet (b \rightarrow c)$
(1)	0	0	0	1	0	1	1	0
(2)	0	0	1	0	0	1	1	0
(3)	0	1	0	1	1	1	0	0
(4)	0	1	1	0	0	1	1	0
(5)	1	0	0	1	0	0	1	1
(6)	1	0	1	0	0	0	1	1
(7)	1	1	0	1	1	1	0	0
(8)	1	1	1	0	0	0	1	1

Problem 3.7. Illustrate the following inference rules with an example for each: Modus Ponens, Universal Specialization, Chain Rule, Resolution, Modus Tollens, Simplification, Addition, Abduction, Induction, and Analogy.

Solution 3.7. The illustrative examples are cited below.

(i) *Modus Ponens*

Premise No. 1.	If *Anand is good* Then *Anand is popular.*
Premise No. 2.	*Anand is good.*
Conclusion.	Therefore, *Anand is popular.*

(ii) *Universal Specialization*

Premise No. 1.	*All men are mortal.*
Conclusion.	Therefore, *Anand is mortal.*

(iii) *Chain Rule*

Premise No. 1.	If *x is a natural number* Then *x is an integer.*
Premise No. 2.	If *x* is *an integer* Then *x is a real number.*
Conclusion.	Therefore, *If x is a natural number* Then *x is a real number.*

(iv) *Resolution*

Premise No. 1.	*Man is rational* or *God is divine.*
Premise No. 2.	*Man is not rational* or *The universe is expanding.*
Conclusion.	Therefore, *Gods is divine* or *The universe is expanding.*

(v) *Modus tollens*

Premise No. 1.	If *man is rational* Then *man is good.*
Premise No.2.	*Man is not good.*
Conclusion.	Therefore, *Man is not rational.*

(vi) *Simplification*

Premise No. 1.	*Anand is a man* and *Anand plays chess.*
Conclusion.	Therefore, *Anand is a man* (*or Anand plays chess*)

(vii) *Addition*

Premise No. 1.	*Anand is a man.*
Conclusion.	Therefore, *Anand is a man* or *2 is a prime number.*

(viii) *Abduction*

Premise No. 1.	If *it rains* Then *the grass is wet.*
Premise No.2.	*The grass is wet.*
Conclusion.	Therefore, *it has rained.*

(ix) *Induction*

Premise No. 1.	The *prime number 29 is odd.*
Premise No. 2.	The *prime number 53 is odd.*
Premise No. 3.	The *prime number 41 is odd.*
Premise No. 4.	The *prime number 211 is odd.*
Conclusion.	Therefore, *All prime numbers are odd.*

(x) *Analogy* Consider the fact that man can stand on two legs and therefore, they can use their two free hands for various purposes which the four legged animals generally cannot. Now, gorillas also occasionally stand on two legs. Hence, by virtue of the analogical reasoning we may conclude that gorillas can also employ their hands to perform various activities similar to human beings.

Problem 3.8. Apply the resolution rule of inference to prove statement 4 from statements 1, 2, and 3 as given below.

(i)			(ii)		
	1.	$p \rightarrow q$		1.	$p \rightarrow q$
	2.	$r \rightarrow s$		2.	$r \rightarrow s$
	3.	$p + r$		3.	$q' + s'$
	4.	$\therefore q + s$		4.	$\therefore p' + r'$

Solution 3.8 The proofs are given below, with brief explanation of each step on the right.

(i)	1.	$p' + q$	[1, since $p \rightarrow q \equiv p'+q$]
	2.	$r' + s$	[2, since $r \rightarrow s \equiv r'+s$]
	3.	$p + r$	[3]
	4.	$q + r$	[1 and 3, Resolution]
	5.	$q + s$	[2 and 4, Resolution]
(ii)	1.	$p' + q$	[1, since $p \rightarrow q \equiv p'+q$]
	2.	$r' + s$	[2, since $r \rightarrow s \equiv r'+s$]
	3.	$q' + s'$	[3]
	4.	$p' + s'$	[1 and 3, Resolution]
	5.	$p' + r'$	[2 and 4, Resolution]

Problem 3.9 Prove that any statement can be derived from a contradiction.

Solution 3.9. Given, $a + a'$ as the premise, we have to derive b, where b is an arbitrary statement. The proof is given below.

1.	$a + a'$	[1]
2.	a	[1, Simplification]
3.	a'	[1, Simplification]
4.	$a' + b$	[3, Addition]
5.	b	[2 and 4, Resolution]

Problem 3.10. Given $p \rightarrow q$, prove that $p \rightarrow (p \bullet q)$. This is called Absoption.

Solution 3.10. The proof is given below.

1.	$p'+q$	[1, since $p \rightarrow q \equiv p' + q$]
2.	True $\bullet$ $(p'+q)$	[1, since X = True $\bullet$ X]
3.	$(p'+p) \bullet (p'+q)$	[2, since $T = p'+p$]
4.	$p'+(p\bullet q)$	[3, Distributive law]
5.	$p\rightarrow(p\bullet q)$	[4, since $a \rightarrow b \equiv a' + b$]

Problem 3.11. Prove the validity of the following argument.

1.	$p \rightarrow (q+r')$
2.	$s \rightarrow r$
3.	p
4.	q'
5.	$\therefore s'$

Solution 3.11. Validity of the argument is given below.

1.	$p \rightarrow (q+r')$	[1]
2.	$s \rightarrow r$	[2]
3.	p	[3]
4.	q'	[4]
5.	$q+r'$	[1 and 3, Modus Ponens]
6.	$r \rightarrow q$	[5, since $r \rightarrow q \equiv r'+q$]
7.	$s \rightarrow q$	[2 and 6, Chain Rule]
8.	s'	[4 and 7, Modus Tollens]

Problem 3.12. Consider the fuzzy rule R : If *service is good* Then *customer is satisfied*. Related universes are *service-rating* = {*a*, *b*, *c*, *d*, *e*}, and *satisfaction-grade* = {1, 2, 3, 4, 5} where the service-ratings *a*, *b*, *c*, *d*, *e* are in descending order and the satisfaction-grades 1, 2, 3, 4, 5 are in the ascending order. The fuzzy sets *good-service* and *satisfied* are defined as follows:

$$good\text{-}service = \frac{1.0}{a} + \frac{0.8}{b} + \frac{0.6}{c} + \frac{0.4}{d} + \frac{0.2}{e}$$

$$satisfied = \frac{0.2}{1} + \frac{0.4}{2} + \frac{0.6}{3} + \frac{0.8}{4} + \frac{1.0}{5}.$$

Find the relation matrix for this rule according to Jadeh's interpretation.

Solution 3.12. According to Zadeh's interpretation, the rule R is expressed by the relation

$$R = (good\text{-}service \times satisfied) \cup (\overline{good\text{-}service} \times satisfaction\text{-}grade)$$

The computation of the relation R representing the information contained in the fuzzy rule stated above is given below.

$$good\text{-}service \times satisfied = \begin{array}{c} \\ a \\ b \\ c \\ d \\ e \end{array} \begin{array}{c} \begin{array}{ccccc} 5 & 4 & 3 & 2 & 1 \end{array} \\ \begin{bmatrix} 1.0 & 0.8 & 0.6 & 0.4 & 0.2 \\ 0.8 & 0.8 & 0.6 & 0.4 & 0.2 \\ 0.6 & 0.6 & 0.6 & 0.4 & 0.2 \\ 0.4 & 0.4 & 0.4 & 0.4 & 0.2 \\ 0.2 & 0.2 & 0.2 & 0.2 & 0.2 \end{bmatrix} \end{array},$$

$$\overline{good\text{-}service} \times satisfaction\text{-}grade = \begin{array}{c} \\ a \\ b \\ c \\ d \\ e \end{array}\begin{array}{c} \begin{array}{ccccc} 5 & 4 & 3 & 2 & 1 \end{array} \\ \begin{bmatrix} 0.0 & 0.0 & 0.0 & 0.0 & 0.0 \\ 0.2 & 0.2 & 0.2 & 0.2 & 0.2 \\ 0.4 & 0.4 & 0.4 & 0.4 & 0.4 \\ 0.6 & 0.6 & 0.6 & 0.6 & 0.6 \\ 0.8 & 0.8 & 0.8 & 0.8 & 0.8 \end{bmatrix} \end{array},$$

Therefore, $R = (good\text{-}service \times satisfied) \cup (\overline{good\text{-}service} \times satisfaction\text{-}grade)$

$$= \begin{array}{c} \\ a \\ b \\ c \\ d \\ e \end{array}\begin{array}{c} \begin{array}{ccccc} 5 & 4 & 3 & 2 & 1 \end{array} \\ \begin{bmatrix} 1.0 & 0.8 & 0.6 & 0.4 & 0.2 \\ 0.8 & 0.8 & 0.6 & 0.4 & 0.2 \\ 0.6 & 0.6 & 0.6 & 0.4 & 0.4 \\ 0.6 & 0.6 & 0.6 & 0.6 & 0.6 \\ 0.8 & 0.8 & 0.8 & 0.8 & 0.8 \end{bmatrix} \end{array}$$

Problem 3.13. Recall the rule If *job is risky* Then *compensation is high*' discussed in Example 3.19. The related fuzzy sets are

$$risky\text{-}job = \frac{0.3}{job_1} + \frac{0.8}{job_2} + \frac{0.7}{job_3} + \frac{0.9}{job_4}$$

$$high\text{-}compensation = \frac{0.2}{c_1} + \frac{0.4}{c_2} + \frac{0.6}{c_3} + \frac{0.8}{c_4}$$

on the universes $job = \{job_1, job_2, job_3, job_4\}$ and $compensation = \{c_1, c_2, c_3, c_4\}$. Now, let the premise be '*job is risky*$_1$' where the predicate *risky*$_1$ is represented by the fuzzy set

$$risky_1\text{-}job = \frac{0.3}{job_1} + \frac{1.0}{job_2} + \frac{1.0}{job_3} + \frac{0.2}{job_4}$$

Employing Generalized Modus Ponens, we reach the conclusion '*compensation is high*$_1$'. Compute *high*$_1$-*compensation.*

Solution 3.13. The rule R : If *job is risky* Then *compensation is high*' is represented by the fuzzy relation

$$R = (risky\text{-}job \times high\text{-}compensation) \cup (\overline{risky\text{-}job} \times compensation)$$

Which, on necessary calculations, is expressed by the fuzzy relation

$$R = \begin{array}{c} \\ job_1 \\ job_2 \\ job_3 \\ job_4 \end{array}\begin{array}{c} \begin{array}{cccc} C_1 & C_2 & C_3 & C_4 \end{array} \\ \begin{bmatrix} 0.7 & 0.7 & 0.7 & 0.7 \\ 0.2 & 0.4 & 0.6 & 0.8 \\ 0.3 & 0.4 & 0.6 & 0.7 \\ 0.2 & 0.4 & 0.6 & 0.8 \end{bmatrix} \end{array}.$$

Now, the fuzzy set *high$_1$-compensation* = *risky$_1$-job*°*R* is obtained as

$$[0.3\ 1.0\ 1.0\ 0.2] \circ \begin{bmatrix} 0.7 & 0.7 & 0.7 & 0.7 \\ 0.2 & 0.4 & 0.6 & 0.8 \\ 0.3 & 0.4 & 0.6 & 0.7 \\ 0.2 & 0.4 & 0.6 & 0.8 \end{bmatrix}$$

$$= [0.3\ 0.4\ 0.6\ 0.8]$$

Hence,

$$high_1\text{-}compensation = \frac{0.3}{c_1} + \frac{0.4}{c_2} + \frac{0.6}{c_3} + \frac{0.8}{c_4}$$

Problem 3.14. Let $U = V = \{0, 1, 2, 3, 4\}$ be the universe of discourse on which the fuzzy set $small = \frac{1.0}{0} + \frac{0.5}{1} + \frac{0.2}{2} + \frac{0.1}{3} + \frac{0.0}{4}$ is defined. Again, let R be the fuzzy relation '*more or less the same*' which is defined by the relation matrix shown below.

$$R = \begin{array}{c} \\ 0 \\ 1 \\ 2 \\ 3 \\ 4 \end{array} \begin{array}{c} \begin{array}{ccccc} 0 & 1 & 2 & 3 & 4 \end{array} \\ \begin{bmatrix} 1.0 & 0.5 & 0.1 & 0.0 & 0.0 \\ 0.5 & 1.0 & 0.5 & 0.1 & 0.0 \\ 0.1 & 0.5 & 1.0 & 0.5 & 0.1 \\ 0.0 & 0.1 & 0.5 & 1.0 & 0.5 \\ 0.0 & 0.0 & 0.1 & 0.5 & 1.0 \end{bmatrix} \end{array}$$

If the premise and the rule are stated as

Premise: *x is small.*
Rule: *x is more or less the same as y*

then apply a suitable fuzzy rule of inference to obtain the conclusion and express it suitably as a relation.

Solution 3.14. The conclusion *C* is given by the fuzzy set obtained by the *max-min* composition of the fuzzy set *small* and the relation *R*, *i.e.*, *C* = *small* °*R*. Therefore,

$$C = small \circ R = [1.0\ 0.5\ 0.2\ 0.1\ 0.0] \circ \begin{bmatrix} 1.0 & 0.5 & 0.1 & 0.0 & 0.0 \\ 0.5 & 1.0 & 0.5 & 0.1 & 0.0 \\ 0.1 & 0.5 & 1.0 & 0.5 & 0.1 \\ 0.0 & 0.1 & 0.5 & 1.0 & 0.5 \\ 0.0 & 0.0 & 0.1 & 0.5 & 1.0 \end{bmatrix}.$$

According to the definition of max-min composition

$$\mu_C(y) = \max_{x \in U}[\min\{\mu_{small}(x), \mu_R(x,y)\}].$$

Therefore,

$$\begin{aligned} \mu_C(0) &= \max[\min\{\mu_{small}(0), \mu_R(0,0)\}, \min\{\mu_{small}(1), \mu_R(1,0)\}, \min\{\mu_{small}(2), \mu_R(2,0)\}, \min\{\mu_{small}(3), \mu_R(3,0)\}, \\ &\quad \min\{\mu_{small}(4), \mu_R(4,0)\}] \\ &= \max[\min\{1, 1\}, \min\{.5, .5\}, \min\{.2, .1\}, \min\{.1, 0\}, \min\{0, 0\}] \\ &= \max[1, .5, .1, 0, 0] \\ &= 1. \end{aligned}$$

Similarly,

$$\begin{aligned}
\mu_C(1) &= \max\,[\min\{1, .5\}, \min\{.5, 1\}, \min\{.2, .5\}, \min\{.1, .1\}, \min\,\{0, 0\}] \\
&= \max\,[.5, .5, .2, .1, 0] \\
&= .5. \\
\mu_C(2) &= \max\,[\min\{1, .1\}, \min\{.5, .5\}, \min\{.2, 1\}, \min\{.1, .5\}, \min\,\{0, .1\}] \\
&= \max\,[.1, .5, .2, .1, 0] \\
&= .5. \\
\mu_C(3) &= \max\,[\min\{1, 0\}, \min\{.5, .1\}, \min\{.2, .5\}, \min\{.1, 1\}, \min\,\{0, .5\}] \\
&= \max\,[0, .1, .2, .1, 0] \\
&= .2. \\
\mu_C(4) &= \max\,[\min\{1, 0\}, \min\{.5, 0\}, \min\{.2, .1\}, \min\{.1, .5\}, \min\,\{0, 1\}] \\
&= \max\,[0, 0, .1, .1, 0] \\
&= .1.
\end{aligned}$$

Therefore, the conclusion is $C = \frac{1.0}{0} + \frac{0.5}{1} + \frac{0.5}{2} + \frac{0.2}{3} + \frac{0.1}{4}$. This can be fairly interpreted as '*more or less small*'. Hence the conclusion can be stated as '*y is more or less small*.'

✓ TEST YOUR KNOWLEDGE

3.1 Which of the following is a logical constant?
a) True b) False
c) Both (*a*) and (*b*) d) None of the above

3.2 Which of the following sets of logical operations is not functionally complete?
a) {•, ′} b) {+, ′}
c) {→, ′} d) None of the above

3.3 Which of the following expressions is not equivalent to the others?
a) $p \rightarrow q$ b) $p' \rightarrow q'$
c) $q' \rightarrow p'$ d) None of the above

3.4 Which of the following is a tautology?
a) $p \rightarrow q$ b) $p + q$
c) $p \bullet p'$ d) True

3.5 Which of the following is a contradiction?
a) $p \rightarrow p'$ b) $p' \rightarrow p$
c) $p \bullet (p \rightarrow p')$ d) $p \bullet (p' \rightarrow p)$

3.6 Given a set of propositional logic expressions, if there is an interpretation for which the expressions are all False, then the set of expressions
a) Must be consistent b) Must be inconsistent
c) Can be consistent or inconsistent d) Can neither be consistent nor inconsistent

3.7 Consider the following argument.

Premise No. 1.	*The universe is expanding.*
Premise No. 2.	*The universe is not expanding.*
Conclusion.	*Therefore, this is a red rose.*

The argument is
a) Valid b) Invalid
c) Both (*a*) and (*b*) d) Neither (*a*) nor (*b*)

3.8 Which of the following equivalences is incorrect?
a) $a \bullet (a + b) \equiv a$
b) $a \rightarrow b \equiv b' \rightarrow a'$
c) $a + (b \bullet c) \equiv (a+b) \bullet (a+c)$
d) None of the above

3.9 What is the truth-value of the statement "2+3 = 7 or 7 is a prime number"?
a) False
b) True
c) Both (*a*) and (*b*)
d) Neither (*a*) nor (*b*)

3.10 Which of the following is true for the proposition $p \bullet (p' + q)$?
a) It's a tautology
b) It's a contradiction
c) Both (*a*) and (*b*)
d) Neither (*a*) nor (*b*)

3.11 Which of the following logic systems support universal and existential quantification of variables?
a) Propositional Logic
b) Predicate Logic
c) Both (*a*) and (*b*)
d) None of the above

3.12 Which of the following is not an atomic formula of First Order Predicate Logic?
a) P(A)
b) $[(\forall x)\ P(x)]'$
c) $[(\forall x)\ (\exists y) P(x) \wedge Q(y)]'$
d) None of the above

3.13 First Order Predicate Logic is called '*first order*' because
(a) It does not allow predicate variables
b) It does not allow function variables
c) Both (*a*) and (*b*)
d) None of the above

3.14 Which of the following is a ground atom?
a) $P\ (f(A, B))$
b) $P(x)$
c) $P(x, y)$
d) None of the above

3.15 Which of the following wffs contain a free variable?
a) $(\forall x)P[x]$
b) $(\forall x)\ (\exists \underline{y})\ Q\ [x, y]$
c) $(\exists y)R\ [A, y]$
d) None of the above

3.16 Which of the following identities is not valid?
a) $(\forall x)\ P[x] + (\forall y)\ Q[y] = (\forall z)\ (P[z] + Q[z])$
b) $(\exists x)\ P[x] \bullet (\exists y)\ Q[y] = (\exists z)\ (P[z] \bullet Q[z])$
c) Both (*a*) and (*b*)
d) None of the above

3.17 Which of the following identities is valid?
a) $\neg(\forall x)P[x] = (\exists x)(\neg P[x])$
b) $\neg(\exists x)P[x] = (\forall x)\ (\neg P[x])$
c) Both (*a*) and (*b*)
d) None of the above

3.18 Which of the following is true with respect to the expression $(\forall x)P[x] \bullet (\exists y)(P[y])$?
a) Variable *x* is inside the scope of variable *y*
b) Variable *y* is inside the scope of variable *x*
c) None of the variables *x* and *y* is inside the scope of the other
d) None of the above

3.19 Which of the following wffs is equivalent to $(\forall x)P[x] \bullet (\exists y)(Q[y])$?
a) $(\exists x)P[x] \bullet (\forall y)(Q[y])$
b) $(\forall y)P[y] \bullet (\exists x)(Q[x])$
c) $(\exists y)P[y] \bullet (\forall x)(Q[x])$
d) None of the above

3.20 Which of the following identities is valid?
a) $(\forall x)\ P[x] \bullet (\forall y)\ Q[y] = (\forall z)\ (P[z] \bullet Q[z])$
b) $(\exists x)\ P[x] + (\exists y)\ Q[y] = (\exists z)\ (P[z] + Q[z])$
c) Both (*a*) and (*b*)
d) None of the above

3.21 Which of the following inference rules does not follow deductive logic?
a) Modus Ponens
b) Abduction
c) Modus Tollens
d) Simplification.

3.22 Which of the following inference rules follow deductive logic?
a) Analogy
b) Induction
c) Abduction
d) None of the above

3.23 Applying the Resolution rule of inference on the clauses p and p', we get -
a) False
b) True
c) p
d) p'

3.24 I meet three Englishmen consecutively, each of whom have blue eyes. I conclude that all Englishmen have blue eyes. Which rule of inference I apply?
a) Abduction
b) Induction
c) Analogy
d) None of the above

3.25 A pair of simultaneous equations under two variables x, y can be solved through the method of elimination. When I am asked to solve three simultaneous equations under three variables x, y, z, I assume that the same method applies here too. What rule of inference I am employing here?
(a) Abduction
b) Induction
(c) Analogy
d) None of the above

3.26 If one is bitten by a honeybee on his nose, his nose swells up. You see a person with swollen nose and conclude that he must have been bitten by some honeybee. What rule of inference you are following while making this conclusion?
a) Abduction
b) Induction
c) Analogy
d) None of the above

3.27 Which of the following rules of inference cannot be obtained using resolution?
a) Modus Ponens
b) Modus Tollens
c) Chain Rule
d) Universal specialization

3.28 Which of the following rules of inference relates to our commonsense reasoning?
a) Analogy
b) Abduction
c) Both (*a*) and (*b*)
d) Neither (*a*) nor (*b*)

3.29 In order to apply the resolution rules of inference, the prepositions must be in the form of
a) Well formed formulae
b) Clauses
c) Conjunctive normal form
d) Disjunctive normal form

3.30 Which of the following is *not* a fuzzy linguistic truth value?
a) True
b) Almost true
c) Very much true
d) None of the above

3.31 Which of the following can be regarded as a fuzzy linguistic truth value?
a) Nearly false
b) Absolutely false
c) Both (*a*) and (*b*)
d) None of the above

3.32 If $\tau(a)$ and $\tau(b)$ be the fuzzy truth values of propositions a and b, then which of the following is not an interpretation of $\tau(a \rightarrow b)$?
a) $max\,\{(1-\tau(a)), \tau(b)\}$
b) $min\,\{1, 1-\tau(a)+\tau(b)\}$
c) $max\,\{min(\tau(a),\tau(b)),1-\tau(a)\}$
d) None of the above

3.33 Let R be the fuzzy rule If 'x is A' Then 'y is B', where A, B are fuzzy predicates corresponding to the fuzzy sets A, B defined on the universes U and V respectively. Then which of the following is Zadeh's interpretation?
a) $R = A \times B$
b) $R = (A \times B) \cup (A' \times V)$
c) $R = (A' \times B)$
d) None of the above

3.34 Let R be the fuzzy rule If 'x is A' Then 'y is B' Else 'y is C'. Then

a) $R = (A{\times}B)\cup(A'{\times}C)$
b) $R = (A'{\times}B)\cup(A{\times}C)$
c) $R = (A{\times}B)\cup(A{\times}C)$
d) None of the above

3.35 Which of the following represents the most generalized form of a fuzzy rule?

a) If 'x_1 is A_1' • ...• 'x_k is A_k' Then 'y is B'
b) If 'x is A' Then 'y_1 is B_1' • ...• 'y_k is B_k'
c) If 'x_1 is A_1' • ...• 'x_k is A_k' Then 'y_1 is B_1' • ...• 'y_k is B_k'
d) None of the above

3.36 Which of the following is involved in a reasoning process using *Generalized Modus Ponens*?

a) Fuzzy propositions
b) A set of clauses
c) Universal quantifier
d) None of the above

3.37 Let R : If 'x is A' Then 'y is B' be a fuzzy rule. In a fuzzy reasoning process employing Generalized Modus Ponens, A_1, a modified version of A, is used as the premise. Moreover, let B_1 be the conclusion where B_1 is probably a modified version of B. If $B_1 = A_1$ *op* R, then according to Zadeh's interpretation, *op* is :

a) Fuzzy Cartesian product
b) Max-min composition
c) Fuzzy implication
d) None of the above

3.38 Which of the following is known as Fuzzy Inference?

a) Generalized Modus Ponens
b) Generalized Modus Tollens
c) Both (*a*) and (*b*)
d) None of the above

3.39 Which of the following is an 'absolute' fuzzy quantifier?

a) Most
b) nearly 1000
c) Few
d) None of the above

3.40 Which of the following cannot be a linguistic variable?

a) Age
b) Speed
c) Price
d) None of the above

Answers

3.1 (c)	3.2 (d)	3.3 (b)	3.4 (d)	3.5 (c)
3.6 (c)	3.7 (a)	3.8 (d)	3.9 (b)	3.10 (d)
3.11 (b)	3.12 (c)	3.13 (a)	3.14 (a)	3.15 (d)
3.16 (c)	3.17 (c)	3.18 (c)	3.19 (b)	3.20 (c)
3.21 (b)	3.22 (d)	3.23 (a)	3.24 (b)	3.25 (c)
3.26 (a)	3.27 (d)	3.28 (c)	3.29 (b)	3.30 (d)
3.31 (c)	3.32 (d)	3.33 (b)	3.34 (a)	3.35 (c)
3.36 (a)	3.37 (b)	3.38 (a)	3.39 (b)	3.40 (d)

EXERCISES

3.1 Show that the set of logical operators $\{\rightarrow, '\}$ is functionally complete.

3.2 Prove that the proposition $a + (a \bullet b)'$ is a tautology.

3.3 Determine the validity of the argument given below.

Premise No. 1.	$a \rightarrow b'$
Premise No. 2.	$c \rightarrow b$
Premise No. 3.	c
Conclusion.	$\therefore a'$

3.4 Determine the validity of the argument given below.

Premise No. 1.	If *Hari works hard* Then *he will be successful.*
Premise No. 2.	If *Hari is not sick* Then *he works hard.*
Premise No. 3.	*Hari is not successful.*
Conclusion.	*Therefore, Hari is sick.*

3.5 Find whether the following propositions are consistent.

1. If *rose is red* Then *ice is white.*
2. If *ice is not white* Then *the earth is a tetrahedron.*
3. *Rose is not red* And *ice is not white.*

3.6 Show that Modus Ponens, Modus Tollens, and Chain rules are special cases of Resolution.

3.7 Derive the conclusion p' from the premises $p \to q$, $p \to r$, and $q' + r'$ using the resolution rule of inference. Also, derive the conclusion $p \to r$ from the premises $p \to (q \to r)$ and q using the resolution rule of inference.

3.8 Let us consider the universe of discourse U = {*John, Jane, Smith, Monica*} of four persons. *Jane* is married to *John*, and *Monica* is married to *Smith*. Three predicates, *MLE*(x), *FML*(y), *MRD*(x, y) are defined on U meaning 'x is a male', 'y is a female', and 'x and y are married' respectively. They have the following combinations truth values.

x	*MLE* (x)
John	*True*
Jane	*False*
Smith	*True*
Monica	*False*

x	*FML* (x)
John	*False*
Jane	*True*
Smith	*False*
Monica	*True*

x	y	*MRD* (x, y)
John	*John*	*False*
John	*Jane*	*True*
John	*Smith*	*False*
John	*Monica*	*False*
Jane	*John*	*True*
Jane	*Jane*	*False*
Jane	*Smith*	*False*
Jane	*Monica*	*False*
Smith	*John*	*False*
Smith	*Jane*	*False*
Smith	*Smith*	*False*
Smith	*Monica*	*True*
Monica	*John*	*False*
Monica	*Jane*	*False*
Monica	*Smith*	*True*
Monica	*Monica*	*False*

In this context determine if the following statements are true.

i) $(\forall x)(\forall y)\ MRD\ (x, y) \rightarrow MRD\ (y, x)$
ii) $(\forall x)(\forall y)\ MRD\ (x, y) \rightarrow \{MLE(x) \bullet FML(y)\}$
iii) $(\forall x)\ MLE\ (x) \rightarrow (\exists y)\{FML(y) \bullet MRD\ (x, y)\}$

3.9 Given the statements '*All men are mortal*' and '*Anand is a man*' prove that '*Anand is mortal*'. Indicate the rules of inference you apply at each step of the proof.

3.10 Consider the fuzzy rule R : If *the car is expensive* Then *it is comfortable*. The related universes are *cars* = {*a*, *b*, *c*, *d*}, and *comfort-levels* = {1, 2, 3, 4, 5}. The fuzzy sets *expensive-cars* and *comfortable* are defined on the universes *cars* and *comfort-levels* respectively. These sets are as given below.

$$expensive\text{-}cars = \frac{0.2}{a} + \frac{0.6}{b} + \frac{0.7}{c} + \frac{1.0}{d}$$

$$comfortable = \frac{0.1}{1} + \frac{0.2}{2} + \frac{0.5}{3} + \frac{0.8}{4} + \frac{1.0}{5}$$

Express the rule R : 'If *the car is expensive* Then *it is comfortable*' as a fuzzy relation using Zadeh's interpretation.

3.11 Let $U = V = \{0, 1, 2, 3, 4\}$ be two universes. The fuzzy set $small = \frac{1.0}{0} + \frac{0.5}{1} + \frac{0.2}{2} + \frac{0}{3} + \frac{0}{4}$ is defined on U. Moreover, R is the relation '*much less than*', symbolized as '<<' and is defined by the relation matrix

$$R = \begin{array}{c} \\ 0 \\ 1 \\ 2 \\ 3 \\ 4 \end{array}\begin{array}{c} \begin{array}{ccccc} 0 & 1 & 2 & 3 & 4 \end{array} \\ \begin{bmatrix} 0.0 & 0.1 & 0.2 & 0.8 & 1.0 \\ 0.0 & 0.0 & 0.1 & 0.2 & 0.8 \\ 0.0 & 0.0 & 0.0 & 0.1 & 0.2 \\ 0.0 & 0.0 & 0.0 & 0.0 & 0.1 \\ 0.0 & 0.0 & 0.0 & 0.0 & 0.0 \end{bmatrix} \end{array}$$

Now given the propositions 'x is small' and '$x << y$' find the conclusion. How can you describe the conclusion in language?

3.12 Let $low = \frac{1.0}{0} + \frac{0.5}{1} + \frac{0.2}{2} + \frac{0}{3} + \frac{0}{4}$ and $high = \frac{0}{0} + \frac{0}{1} + \frac{0.2}{2} + \frac{0.5}{3} + \frac{1.0}{4}$ be fuzzy sets defined on the universes $U = V = \{0, 1, 2, 3, 4\}$. If R : If 'x is low' Then 'y is high' be the fuzzy If-Then rule and the premise is 'x is very low', then what is the conclusion? The fuzzy predicate '*very low*' is to be interpreted as the set

$$very\text{-}low = \frac{1.0}{0} + \frac{0.3}{1} + \frac{0}{2} + \frac{0}{3} + \frac{0}{4}.$$

BIBLIOGRAPHY AND HISTORICAL NOTES

Numerous papers, books etc. have been published on fuzzy logic since its inception by A. Zadeh. A list of selected articles and books are cited below.

Hájek, P. (1995). Fuzzy Logic and Arithmetical Hierarchy. *Fuzzy Sets and Systems*, Vol. 3, No. 8, pp. 359–363.

Hájek, P. (1998). *Metamathematics of Fuzzy Logic*. Kluwer.

Klir, G. and Folger, T. (1987). *Fuzzy Sets, Uncertainty, and Information*. Englewood Cliffs, NJ: Prentice Hall.

Kosko, B. (1993). *Fuzzy Thinking: The New Science of Fuzzy Logic*. New York: Hyperion.

Kosko, B. and Isaka, S. (1993). Fuzzy Logic. *Scientific American*, Vol. 269, No. 1, pp. 76–81.

McNeill, D. and Freiberger, P. (1992). *Fuzzy Logic: The Discovery of a Revolutionary Computer Technology*. Simon and Schuster.

McNeill F. M. and Thro, E. (1994). *Fuzzy Logic: A Practical Approach*. Academic Press.

Novák, V., Perfilieva, I., and Močkoř, J. (1999). *Mathematical Principles of Fuzzy Logic*. Kluwer Academic.

Zadeh, Lotfi A. (1974). Fuzzy logic and its application to approximate reasoning. *Information Processing, Proc. IFIP Congr.*, pp. 591–594.

Zadeh., Lotfi A. (2002). From Computing with Numbers to Computing with Words — From Manipulation of Measurements to Manipulation of Perceptions. *International Journal of Applied Mathematics and Computer Science*, Vol. 12, No. 3, pp. 307–324.

4

FUZZY INFERENCE SYSTEMS

Key Concepts

Aggregation, Centre-of-sums (CoS) method, Centroid/Centre-of-gravity method, Defuzzification, Fuzzification, Fuzzy air-conditioner controller, Fuzzy associative memory (FAM), Fuzzy controller, Fuzzy cruise controller, Fuzzy rule base, Mean-of-maxima (MoM) method, Rule implication

Chapter Outline

The previous chapter provides the basic concepts of fuzzy logic. This chapter includes a discussion on fuzzy inference system, which is a kind of input–output mapping that exploits the concepts and principles of fuzzy logic. Such systems are widely used in machine control, popularly known as fuzzy control systems. The advantage of fuzzy inference systems is that here the solution to the problem can be cast in terms of familiar human operators. Hence, the human experience can be used in the design of the controller. Engineers developed a variety of fuzzy controllers for both industrial and consumer applications. These include vacuum cleaners, autofocusing camera, air conditioner, low-power refrigerators, dish washer etc. Fuzzy inference systems have been successfully applied to various areas including automatic control, computer vision, expert systems, decision analysis, data classification, and so on. Moreover, these systems are associated with such diverse entities as rule based systems, expert systems, modeling, associative memory etc. These versatile application areas show the multidisciplinary nature of fuzzy inference systems.

4.1 INTRODUCTION

A fuzzy inference system (FIS) is a system that transforms a given input to an output with the help of fuzzy logic. The input-output mapping provided by the fuzzy inference system creates a basis for decision-making process. The procedure followed by a fuzzy inference system is known as fuzzy inference mechanism, or simply fuzzy inference. It makes use of various aspects of fuzzy logic, viz., membership function, fuzzy logical operation, fuzzy IF-THEN rules etc. There are various kinds of fuzzy inference systems. In this chapter we describe the principles of fuzzy inference systems proposed by Ebrahim Mamdani in 1975. It is the most common fuzzy inference methodology and moreover, it is employed in the earliest control system built using fuzzy logic. The fundamental concepts of a fuzzy inference system are explained subsequently along with illustrative examples.

Let us consider a person trying to cross a road while a car is approaching towards him. At what pace should he proceed? It depends on the distance of the approaching car from the person, and its speed. If the car is far away and is running slowly then the person can walk across the road quite leisurely. If the car is far away but approaching fast then he should not try to cross the road leisurely, but a bit faster, say, unhurriedly. However, in case the car is nearby, or is running fast, then he has to cross the road quickly. All these constitute the rule base that guides the pace of the person's movement across the road.

The sequence of steps followed by a fuzzy inference system for the problem stated above is shown in Fig. 4.1. It presents the basic structure of any fuzzy inference system. The entire fuzzy inference process comprises five steps

(i) Fuzzification of the input variables
(ii) Application of fuzzy operators on the antecedent parts of the rules
(iii) Evaluation of the fuzzy rules
(iv) Aggregation of fuzzy sets across the rules
(v) Defuzzification of the resultant fuzzy set

The following sections explain these steps briefly.

4.2. FUZZIFICATION OF THE INPUT VARIABLES

The inputs to a fuzzy inference system are a number of crisp values corresponding to some parameters. For each input, we have to determine the degree to which it belongs to the appropriate fuzzy set through membership function. This is known as fuzzification, the first step of the entire fuzzy inference process.

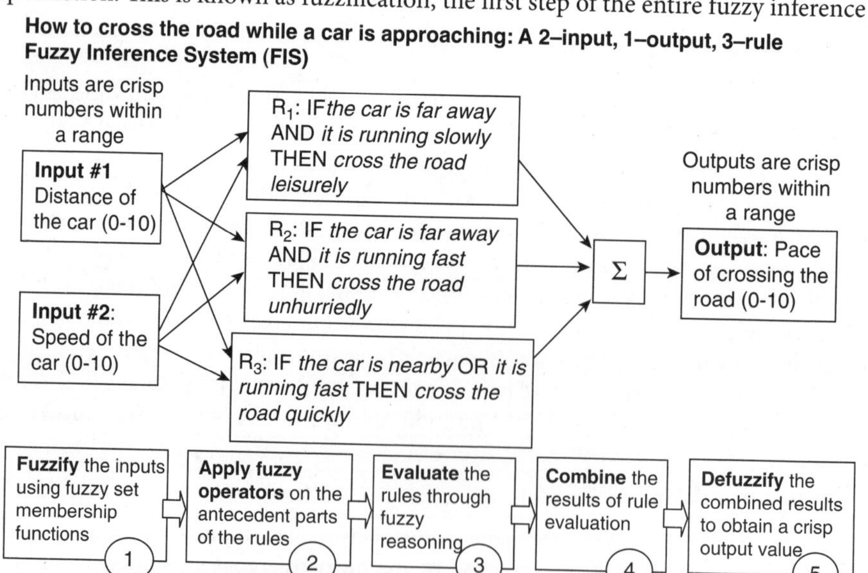

Fig. 4.1. *Structure of a fuzzy inference system.*

In the present example there are two inputs, the distance of the car from the man, and its speed, both scaled to the range 0–10. There are three rules, and each of them requires that the inputs should be resolved into certain fuzzy linguistic sets. The concerned linguistic values related to the antecedent parts here are, far away ('the car is far away'), nearby ('the car is nearby'), running slowly ('it is running slowly'), and running fast ('it is running fast').

Fig. 4.2 shows fuzzification of the car's distance with respect to the fuzzy set *far away*. Assuming the distance to be 7 (in the range 0–10) the fuzzy membership is seen to be 0.5 here. The third row in Fig. 4.6 shows the profile of the fuzzy set *nearby* where the fuzzy membership for distance = 7 is 0.2. Figs. 4.3, 4.4, and 4.6 depict the fuzzification of the other input variable speed = 3 with respect to the fuzzy sets *slowly* and *fast*.

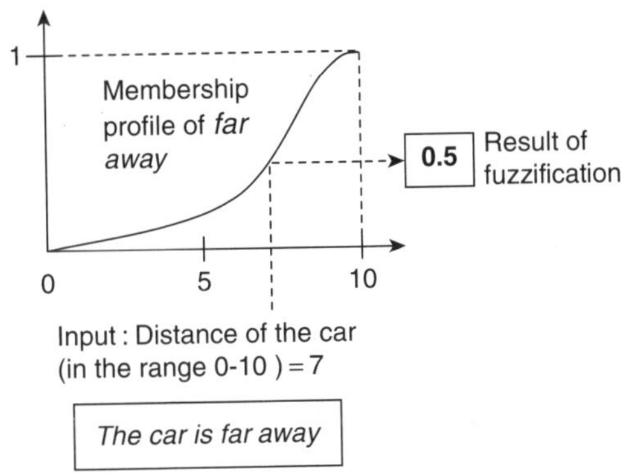

Fig. 4.2. *Fuzzification of input variables.*

4.3 APPLICATION OF FUZZY OPERATORS ON THE ANTECEDENT PARTS OF THE RULES

The antecedent of a fuzzy rule may consist of a single part or more than one parts joined together with AND, or OR, operators. In this example, each rule has antecedents with two parts. In rules R_1 and R_2 the parts are joined together with the AND operator, and in R_3 they are joined with the OR operator. If, however, we had a rule like 'IF *the car is very close* THEN *cross the road very quickly*', then, obviously, the antecedent would have been composed of a single part. Fuzzification of inputs determines the degree to which each part of the antecedent (or, just the antecedent, in case it consists of a single part) is satisfied.

When the antecedent of a given rule has more than one parts, we need to apply the appropriate fuzzy operator so that a single number representing the result of the entire antecedent is obtained. The input to the fuzzy operator is two, or more, membership values from the fuzzified input variables and the output is a single truth value. This single truth value is applied to the consequent part of the fuzzy rule to obtain the resultant fuzzy set corresponding to that rule.

Table 4.1. *Common fuzzy AND, OR methods*

#	Operator	Method	
1	AND	(min)	$\tau(P.AND.Q) = min[\tau(P), \tau(Q)]$
		(product)	$\tau(P.AND.Q) = \tau(P) \times \tau(Q)$
2	OR	(max)	$\tau(P.OR.Q) = max[\tau(P), \tau(Q)]$
		(probabilistic OR)	$\tau(P.OR.Q) = \tau(P) + \tau(Q) - \tau(P) \times \tau(Q)$

There are various methods of implementing the fuzzy AND and OR operators. The most popular among these, two for each of AND and OR, are summarized in Table 4.1. In the present example the *min* method of AND, and *max* method of OR are followed. Fig. 4.3 illustrates the process of applying fuzzy operator on the antecedent part of rule R_1. The first part and the second part of the antecedent produces the membership values 0.5 and 0.6, respectively. The resultant truth value of the entire antecedent is therefore *min* (0.5, 0.6) = 0.5. A similar process carried out on the rules R_2 and R_3 is shown in Fig. 4.6.

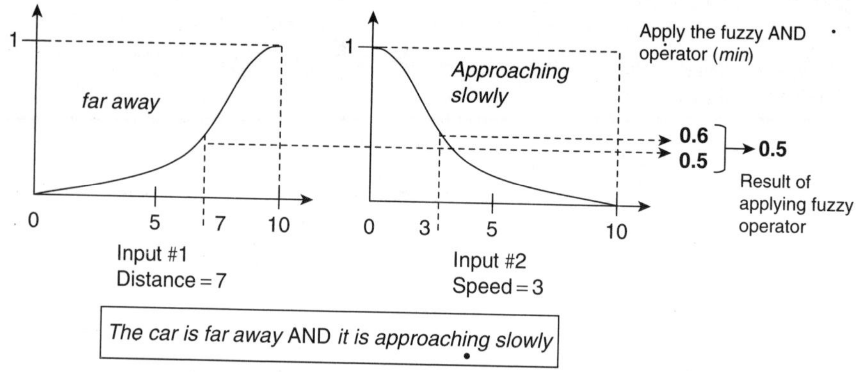

Fig. 4.3. *Applying fuzzy operators on the antecedent parts of the rules.*

4.4 EVALUATION OF THE FUZZY RULES

Fuzzy rules are evaluated by employing some implication process. The input to the implication process is the number provided by the antecedent and its output is a fuzzy set. This output fuzzy set is obtained by reshaping the fuzzy set corresponding to the consequent part of the rule with the help of the number given by the antecedent.

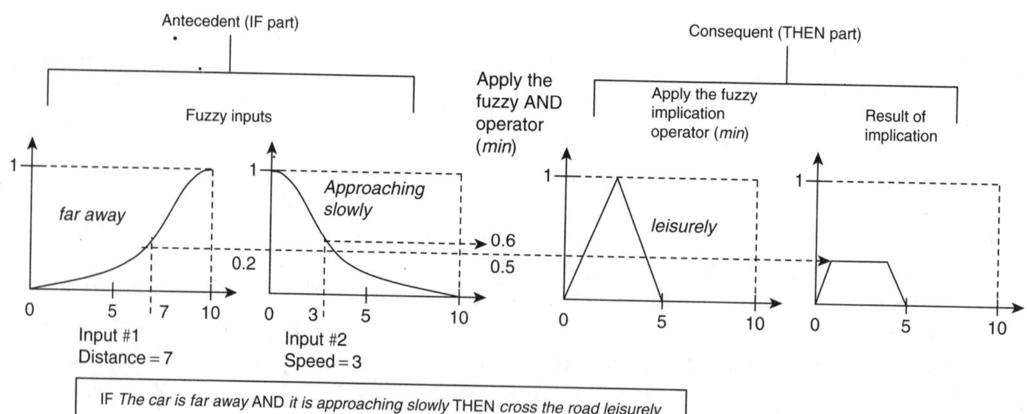

Fig. 4.4. *Evaluation of fuzzy rule during fuzzy inference process.*

The implication process is illustrated in Fig. 4.4. The fuzzy set for the consequent of the rule R_1, i.e., cross the road leisurely, has a triangular membership profile as shown in the figure. As a result of applying fuzzy AND operator as the minimum of its operands, the antecedent returns the value 0.5, which is subsequently passed on to the consequent to complete the implication process. The implication process reshapes the membership function of the fuzzy set *leisurely* by taking the minimum between 0.5, and the membership value of *leisurely* at any point. The result is a trapezoidal membership function as depicted in the figure. As in the case of fuzzy logic operators there are several implication methods. Among these the *min* method proposed by Mamdani is followed here. It effectively truncates the fuzzy membership profile of the consequent with the value returned by the antecedent.

It should be noted that the rules of an FIS may have various weights attached to them ranging from 0 to 1. In the present case all rules are assigned the same weight 1. In case a rule has a non-zero but less-than-one weight, it has to be applied on the number given by the antecedent prior to realization of the implication process.

4.5 AGGREGATION OF OUTPUT FUZZY SETS ACROSS THE RULES

Decision-making through a fuzzy inference system has to take into account the contribution of each rule in the system. Therefore the individual fuzzy sets obtained by evaluating the rules must be combined in some manner into a single resultant fuzzy set. This aggregation process takes the truncated membership profiles returned by the implication process as its input, and produces one fuzzy set for each output variable as the output.

Various aggregation methods are used in practice. Taking the maximum among all inputs (*max*), or taking the algebraic sum of all inputs (*sum*) are two methods widely employed by the professionals. Fig. 4.5 illustrates the principle of these two methods. In Fig. 4.6, all three rules R_1, R_2, and R_3 are placed together to show how the outputs of all the rules are combined into a single fuzzy set using the *max* aggregation method.

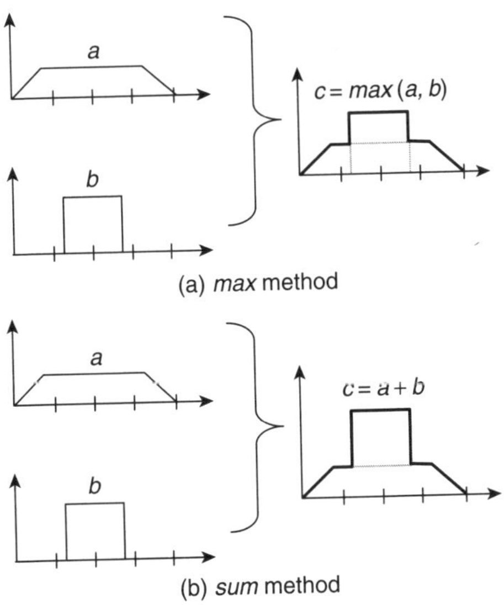

Fig. 4.5. *Two popular aggregation methods – max and sum.*

4.6 DEFUZZIFICATION OF THE RESULTANT AGGREGATE FUZZY SET

Defuzzification is the process of converting the aggregate output sets into one crisp value for each output variable. This is the last step of a fuzzy inference process. The final desired output for each variable is generally a single number because like the inputs, the outputs too are usually variables signifying physical parameters, e.g., voltage, pressure etc., under control. Since the aggregate of a number of fuzzy sets is itself a fuzzy set and encompass a range of output values, it is not suitable to drive a physical system. It has to be defuzzified in order to resolve into a single output value for the related output variable. There are several defuzzification methods in vogue, viz., centroid method, centre-of-sums (CoS) method, mean-of-maxima (MoM) method etc. These are briefly explained in subsections 4.6.1, 4.6.2 and 4.6.3.

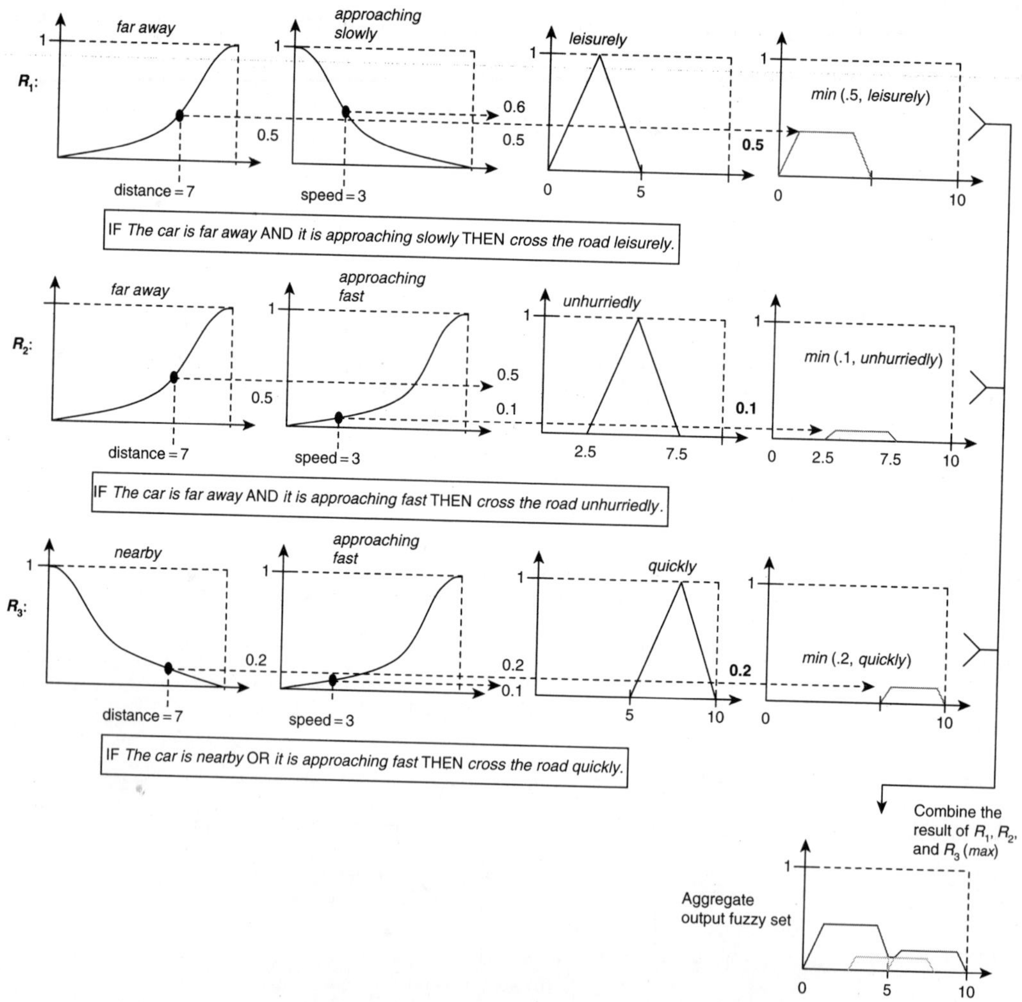

Fig. 4.6. *Aggregation of fuzzy sets across the rules.*

4.6.1 Centroid Method

The centroid method is also referred to as centre-of-gravity or centre-of-area method. In this method the individual output fuzzy sets are superimposed into a single aggregate fuzzy set (the max method) and then the centroid, or centre-of-gravity, or centre-of-area of the resultant membership profile is taken as the defuzzified output. Fig. 4.7 illustrates the method graphically.

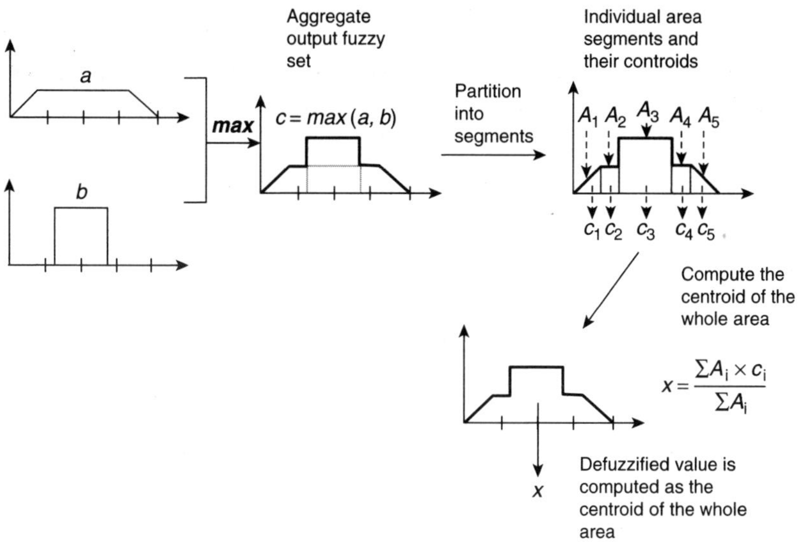

Fig. 4.7. *The centroid method of defuzzification.*

If the total area under the aggregate output fuzzy set is partitioned into disjoint segments $A_1, \ldots, A_k$, and the corresponding centroids are $c_1, \ldots, c_k$, then the centroid of the whole area is obtained as

$$x_{centroid} = \frac{\sum_{i=1}^{k} A_i \times c_i}{\sum_{i=1}^{k} A_i} \tag{4.1}$$

For discrete membership function, the formula is

$$x_{centroid} = \frac{\sum_{i=1}^{n} x_i \times \mu(x_i)}{\sum_{i=1}^{n} \mu(x_i)} \tag{4.2}$$

whereas the expression for the centroid in case of continuous membership function is given by

$$x_{centroid} = \frac{\int_a^b x\mu(x)dx}{\int_a^b \mu(x)dx} \tag{4.3}$$

where $[a, b]$ is the domain of x.

4.6.2 Centre-of-Sums (CoS) Method

The CoS method works almost in the same way as that of the centroid method described earlier. The only difference is, here the aggregate output set is obtained by the sum method rather than the max method. Effectively, this boils down to counting the overlapping areas twice instead of once. Therefore, in CoS method, the areas and the centroids of individual fuzzy sets (obtained as a result of evaluating the fuzzy rules) are computed, and then the defuzzified value of x is obtained as

$$x_{COS} = \frac{\sum_{i=1}^{m} A_i \times c_i}{\sum_{i=1}^{m} A_i} \tag{4.4}$$

where $A_1, \ldots, A_m$, are the areas corresponding to the m number of individual output fuzzy sets and $c_1, \ldots, c_m$ are respective centroids. The technique of CoS aggregation method is illustrated in Fig. 4.8.

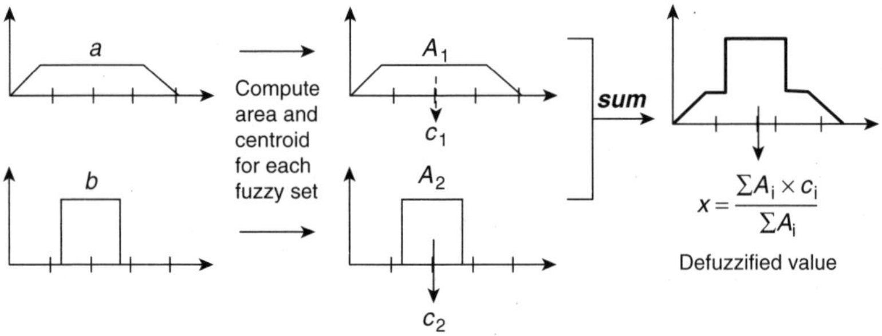

Fig. 4.8. *The centre-of-sum (CoS) method of defuzzification*

Now consider the situation where the fuzzy sets are discrete. Let the number of sets be m and $x_1, \ldots, x_n$ be the n number of members. For each member x_i let $\mu_1(x_i), \ldots, \mu_m(x_i)$ be the degrees of membership of x_i to the respective fuzzy sets. Then according to the *CoS* method of defuzzification, the defuzzified value is computed as

$$x_{COS} = \frac{\sum_{i=1}^{n} x_i \left(\sum_{j=1}^{m} \mu_j(x_i) \right)}{\sum_{i=1}^{n} \sum_{j=1}^{m} \mu_j(x_i)} \tag{4.5}$$

4.6.3 Mean-of-Maxima (MoM) Method

MoM is a simple defuzzification method where the highest degree of membership among all fuzzy sets is taken as the output defuzzified value. In case there are more than one elements, say $x_1, \ldots, x_k$, having the same highest degree of membership, then the mean of those points is taken as the defuzzified value.

$$x_{MOM} = \frac{\sum_{i=1}^{k} x_i}{k} \quad (\textit{for discrete fuzzy sets}) \tag{4.6}$$

$$x_{MOM} = \frac{\int_a^b x dx}{(b-a)} \quad (for\ continuous\ fuzzy\ sets) \tag{4.7}$$

Fig. 4.9 illustrates the MoM method of defuzzification.

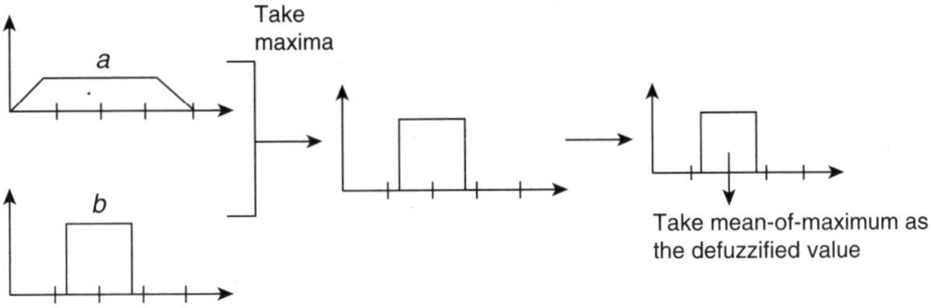

Fig. 4.9. *The mean-of-maxima (MoM) method of defuzzification.*

In the present example defuzzification is carried out using the CoS method as detailed in Table 4.2. The defuzzified value is computed as

$$x = \frac{A_1 \times c_1 + A_2 \times c_2 + A_3 \times c_3}{A_1 + A_2 + A_3} = 4.25.$$

This implies that if the distance of the car is 7 (in the scale of 0–10) and it is approaching with a speed 3 (again in the scale 0–10) then according to the FIS exemplified here the person should cross the road with a pace of 4.25 (in the scale 0–10). The entire fuzzy inference process is schematically depicted in Fig. 4.10.

Table 4.2. *Computation of areas and centroids*

#	Rule	Output fuzzy set	Area	Centroid
1.	R_1	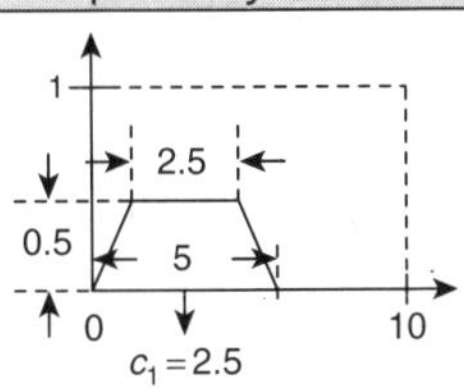	A_1 = 1/2 (5 + 2.5) × 0.5 = 15/8	c_1 = 2.5
2.	R_2	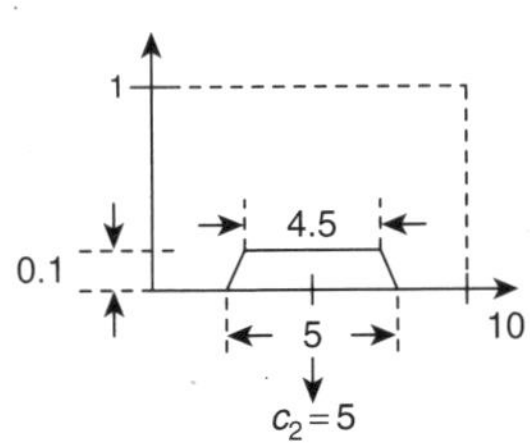	A_2 = 1/2 (5 + 4.5) × 0.1 = 189/40	c_2 = 5
3.	R_3	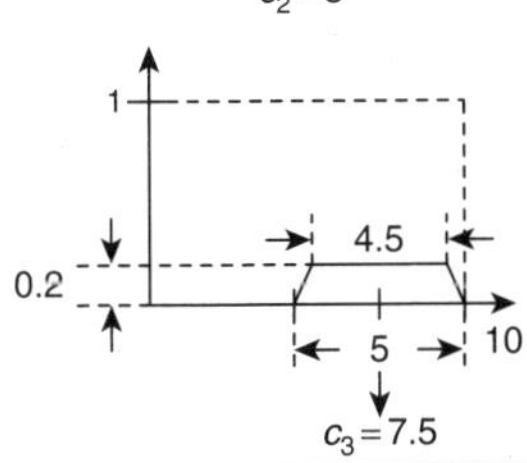	A_3 = 1/2 (5 + 4) × 0.2 = 9/10	c_3 = 7.5

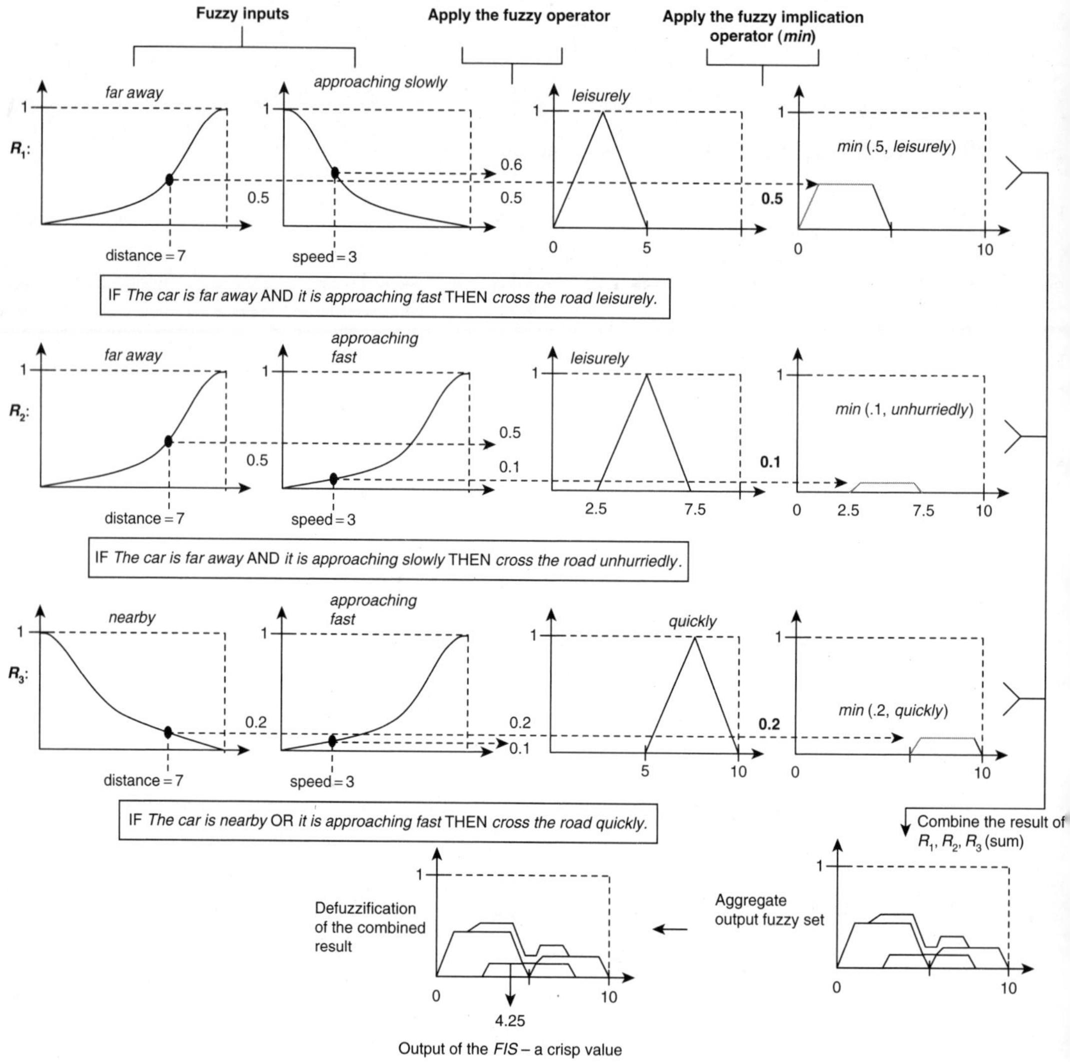

Fig. 4.10. *Fuzzy inference process using centre of sums (CoS) method.*

4.7 FUZZY CONTROLLERS

Most obvious examples of fuzzy inference systems are the so called fuzzy controllers. These are controlling and decision-making systems that exploit rules involving fuzzy linguistic descriptions for the purpose of controlling a physical process. They employ fuzzy inference process as their functional principle. E. H. Mamdani and S. Assilian have shown in 1974 that a model steam engine could be regulated with the help of a set of fuzzy IF-THEN rules. Since then innumerable fuzzy controllers have been developed for such diverse applications areas as blast furnace, mobile robots, cement kilns, unmanned helicopters, subway trains and so on. As a result of the advent of fuzzy microprocessors, the realm of fuzzy controllers have been extended to consumer electronics and home appliances, e.g., washing machine, vacuum cleaner, camera, air conditioner.

The basic structure of a fuzzy controller is rather simple. It consists of three stages, *viz.*, the input stage, the processing stage, and the output stage (Fig. 4.11).

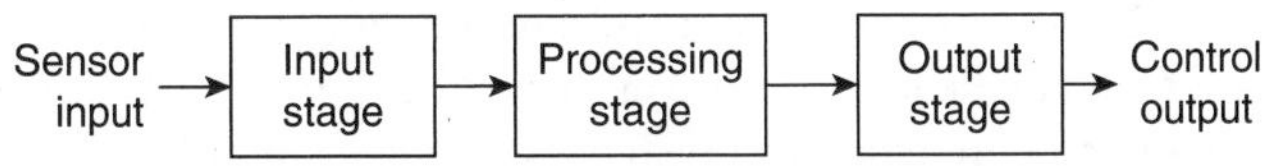

Fig. 4.11. *Basic structure of a fuzzy controller.*

Sensor or any other inputs are fed to the controller through the input values and mapped to membership values of appropriate fuzzy sets. This is the fuzzification step. The processing stage utilizes a fuzzy rule base that consists of a number of fuzzy rules. The basic form of a fuzzy rule, as mentioned earlier, is

$$R: \text{IF } x \text{ is } A \text{ THEN } y \text{ is } B$$

where x and y are the input and the output parameters, and A and B are linguistic values. A typical fuzzy rule may look like 'IF *room temperature is cool* THEN *heater is high*'. The 'IF' part of a fuzzy rule is known as the 'antecedent' and the 'THEN' part is called the 'consequent'. In case of the rule 'IF *room temperature is cool* THEN *heater is high*' the antecedent is '*room temperature is cool*' while '*heater is high*' is the consequent. However, the antecedent of a practical fuzzy rule may consist of several statements of the form 'x is A'. The general form of a rule in the rule base is

$$R: \text{IF } (x_1 \text{ is } A_1) \text{ and } (x_2 \text{ is } A_2) \text{ and } \ldots \text{ and } (x_k \text{ is } A_k) \text{ THEN } y \text{ is } B$$

The fuzzification step produces the truth values of various statements 'x_1 is A_1', 'x_2 is A_2', … , 'x_k is A_k' and depending on these values certain rules of the rule base are *fired*. The processing stage carries some manipulations on the basis of the fired rules to obtain fuzzy sets relating to the consequent parts of the fired rules. Finally, the outcome of the processing stage on each rule are combined together to arrive at a crisp value for each control parameter. This is carried out during the output stage and is termed as defuzzification. The block diagram shown in Fig. 4.12 gives a bit more detailed picture of a fuzzy controller than provided in Fig. 4.11.

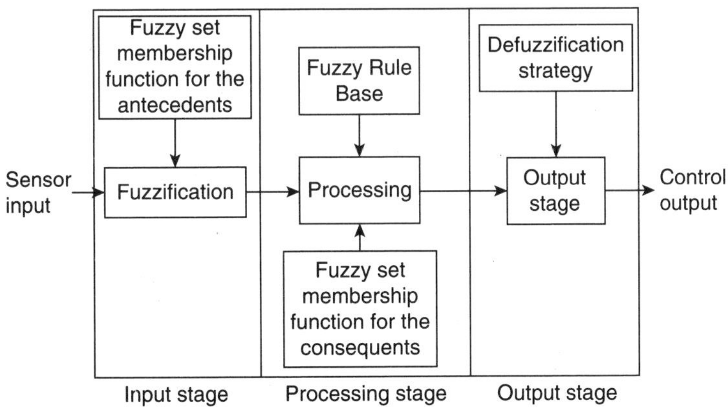

Fig. 4.12. *Block diagram of a fuzzy controller.*

As discussed earlier in the context of fuzzy inference systems, there are various defuzzification techniques, e.g., centroid, CoS, MoM etc. The designer is to choose the technique most appropriate for his application. In the subsequent parts of this section we present the essential features of two model fuzzy controllers, *viz.*, a fuzzy air-conditioner controller, and a fuzzy cruise controller.

4.7.1 Fuzzy Air Conditioner Controller

Let us consider a highly simplified version of an air-conditioner (AC). Its function is to keep track of the room temperature and regulate the temperature of the air flown into the room. The purpose is to maintain the room temperature at a predefined value. For the sake of simplicity we assume that the AC does not regulate the flow of air into the room, but only the temperature of the air to be flown.

Let T_0 be the desired room temperature. The air conditioner has a thermometer to measure the current room temperature T. The difference $\Delta T = T - T_0$ is the input to the controller. When $\Delta T > 0$, the room is hotter than desired temperature and the AC has to blow cool air into the room so that the room-temperature comes down to T_0. If, on the other hand, $\Delta T < 0$, the room needs to be warmed up and so, the AC is to blow hot air into the room. In order to achieve the required temperature of the air to be blown into the room, a 'dial' is turned at the appropriate position within the range $[-1, +1]$. The scheme is shown in Fig. 4.13.

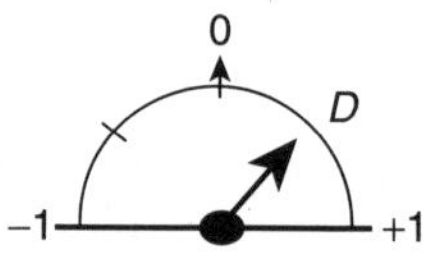

Fig. 4.13. *Air-conditioning dial*

A positive value of the dial means hot air will be blown, and a negative value means cold air will be blown. The degree of hotness, or coldness, is determined by the magnitude of the dial position. No air is blown when the dial is at 0. The input to the fuzzy controller is $\Delta T = T - T_0$, and the output is D, i.e., the position to which the AC dial is to be turned. Both ΔT and D are crisp values, but the mapping of ΔT to D takes place with the help of fuzzy logic. Various features of the controller are briefly described below.

(a) **Fuzzy sets:** Occasionally, for fuzzy control systems, it is convenient to categorize the strength of the input and the output parameters with the help of certain fuzzy sets referred to as Large Negative (*LN*), Medium Negative (*MN*), Small Negative (*SN*), Zero (*ZE*), Small Positive (*SP*), Medium Positive (*MP*), Large Positive (*LP*) etc. These are indicative of the magnitude of the respective parameters in the context of the given application. For the system under consideration, the fuzzy sets defined on the input parameter ΔT and D are *LN*, *MN*, *ZE*, *MP*, and *LP*. Fig. 4.14 and Fig. 4.15 show the membership profiles of these fuzzy sets. For example, membership of ΔT to Medium Positive (*MP*) is zero for $\Delta T \le 0$, and $\Delta T \ge 6$. The said membership increases uniformly as ΔT increases from 0 to 3, becomes 1 at 3, and then uniformly diminishes to 0 as ΔT approaches 6 from 3 (Fig. 1.14).

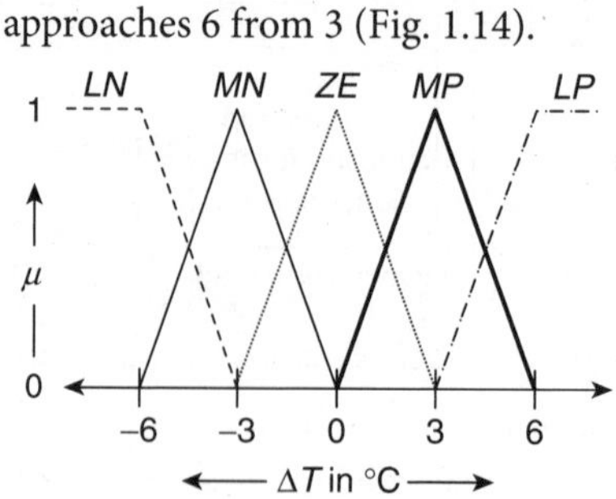

Fig. 4.14. *Fuzzy membership functions on ΔT*

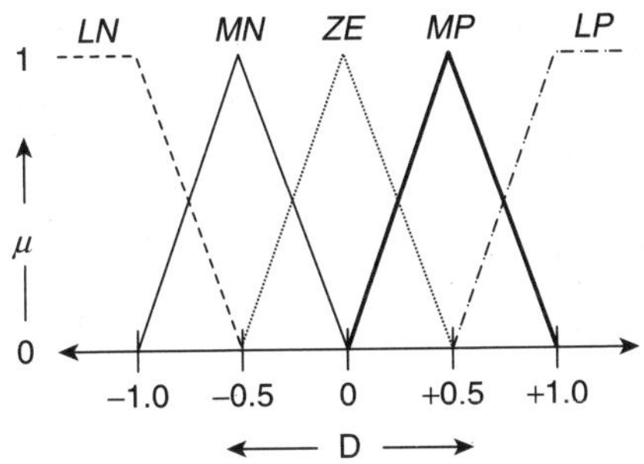

Fig. 4.15. *Fuzzy membership functions on D.*

All membership functions stated above are of a triangular type, which is widely used in fuzzy controllers. If required, other kinds of membership functions can also be employed.

(b) **Fuzzy rule base:** The system under consideration has a simple rule base consisting of five fuzzy rules. These are listed below.

R_1 : IF ΔT *is LN* THEN *D is LP.*

R_2 : IF ΔT *is MN* THEN *D is MP.*

R_3 : IF ΔT *is ZE* THEN *D is ZE.*

R_4 : IF ΔT *is MP* THEN *D is MN.*

R_5 : IF ΔT *is LP* THEN *D is LN.*

The block diagram of the fuzzy inference process for this controller is shown in Fig. 4.16. The input to the system is ΔT, which is first fuzzified with the help of the fuzzy sets membership functions *LN, MN, ZE, MP, LP* for ΔT. Depending on the result of this fuzzification, some of the rules among $R_1, \ldots, R_5$ are *fired.* As a result of this firing of rules, certain fuzzy sets are obtained out of the specification of *LN, MN, ZE, MP, LP* for *D*. These are combined and defuzzified to obtain the crisp value of *D* as the output.

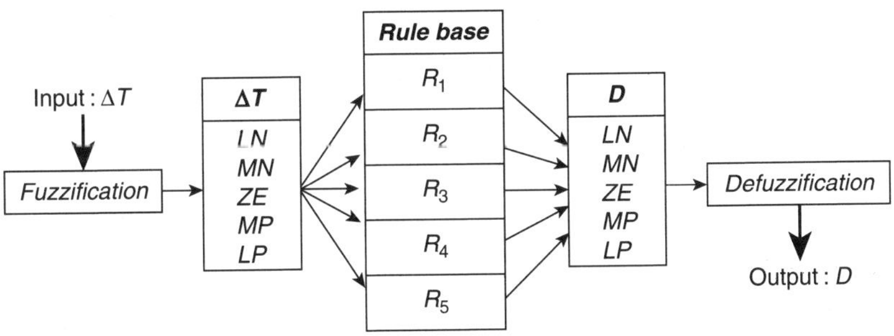

Fig. 4.16. *Inference process of the simplified fuzzy air-conditioner controller.*

We shall now work out the functionality of the system for the crisp input $\Delta T = -2$.

(a) **Fuzzification:** Given $\Delta T = -2$, we compute the degree of membership of ΔT with respect to the fuzzy sets *LN, MN, ZE, MP, LP* using the respective membership profiles (Fig. 4.17) as follows.

$$\mu_{LN}^{\Delta T}(-2) = 0,\ \mu_{MN}^{\Delta T}(-2) = \frac{2}{3} = 0.67,\quad \mu_{ZE}^{\Delta T}(-2) = \frac{1}{3} = 0.33,\quad \mu_{MP}^{\Delta T}(-2) = 0,\quad \mu_{LP}^{\Delta T}(-2) = 0$$

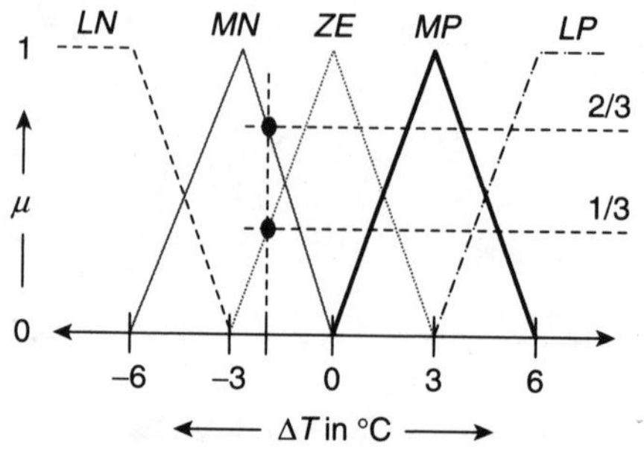

Fig. 4.17. *Fuzzy memberships for $\Delta T = -2$*

Since only *MN* and *ZE* attain non-zero values, rules R_2, and R_3 are fired. Hence, we have to map these membership values of the antecedents of rules R_2, and R_3 to the corresponding *D* values in the respective consequents. This is done in the implication phase. Moreover, as the antecedents of all the rules consist of only single parts, the phase of applying fuzzy operators is not relevant here.

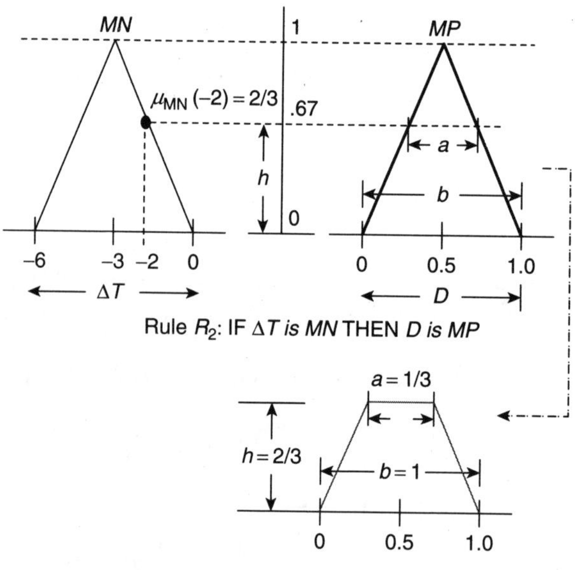

Fig. 4.18. *Evaluation of rule R_2*

(b) **Rule implication:** The rule implication process is illustrated in Fig. 4.18 and Fig. 4.19. Fig. 4.18 shows the implication process of Rule R_2 and Fig. 4.19 depicts that for Rule R_3. In case of R_2 the fuzzy membership of input $\Delta T = -2$ with respect to the fuzzy set *MN*, *i.e.*, $\mu_{MN}(-2) = 2/3$, is used to reshape the fuzzy set *MP* of the consequent part. The result is a fuzzy set with trapezoidal membership function which is shown in the lower region in Fig. 4.18. The area and the centroid (i.e., centre-of-area) this trapezoidal region are computed as $area_1 = 4/9$, $centroid_1 = 0.5$. Similarly, $area_2 = 5/18$, and $centroid_2 = 0$ are obtained as a result of the implication process carried out on Rule R_3.

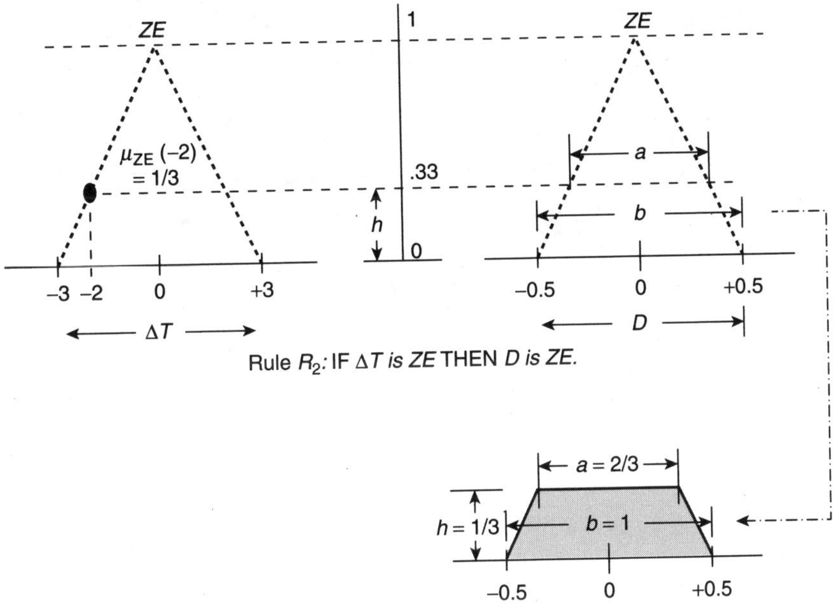

Fig. 4.19. *Evaluation of rule* R_3

(c) **Aggregation and defuzzification:** The aggregation and defuzzification process according to the CoS method, centroid method, and MoM method are described below.

(i) *Centre-of-sums*: Here the defuzzified output is obtained as

$$D_{COS} = \frac{\sum_i area_i \times centroid_i}{\sum_i area_i} = \frac{area_1 \times centroid_1 + area_2 \times centroid_2}{area_1 + area_2}$$

$$= \frac{\frac{4}{9}\times 0.5 + \frac{5}{18}\times 0.0}{\frac{4}{9}+\frac{5}{18}} = \frac{4}{13} \approx 0.308$$

Therefore, when the room temperature is below the set temperature T_0 by 2 degrees ($\Delta T = -2$) the fuzzy AC controller under consideration will set the AC dial at + 0.308 so that air, hot to the extent indicated by the value just mentioned, is blown into the room to bring the room temperature back to T_0.

(ii) *Centroid*: The first step in this method is to superimpose the outputs of the rule implication process. Accordingly, the trapezoidal regions of Fig. 4.18 and Fig. 4.19 are superimposed to obtain the polygon *ABCDEF* shown in Fig. 4.20. The polygon *ABCDEF* is then partitioned into six regions, ΔABJ (A_1), *BCIJ* (A_2), *CKHI* (A_3), ΔCDK (A_4), *DEGH* (A_5), and ΔEFG (A_6). These regions are either rectangles or right-angled triangles. It is easily seen that when the membership functions of the fuzzy sets related to the rules are triangular in shape, the aggregated polygonal region can be partitioned into a numbers of rectangles and right-angled triangles.

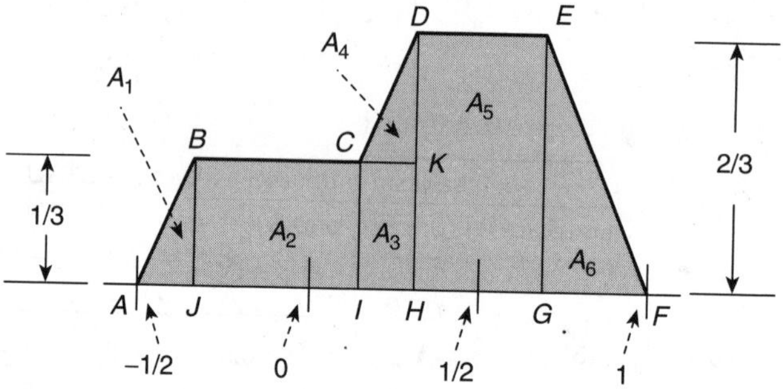

Fig. 4.20. *Aggregate region obtained in centroid method of defuzzification.*

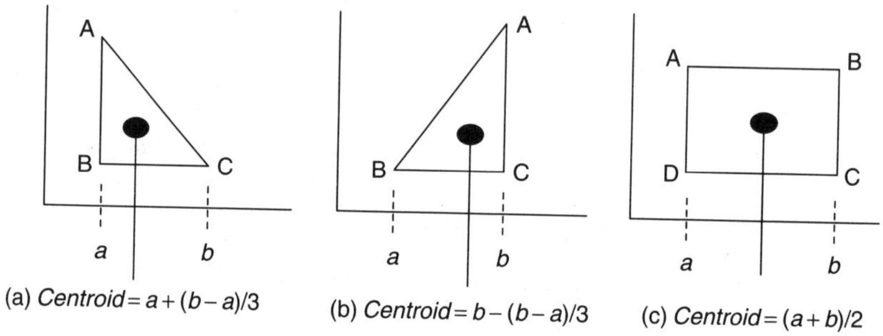

Fig. 4.21. *Computing the centroids of rectangular and right-angled triangular regions.*

Computation of centroids, i.e., centre-of-areas, of rectangular and right-angled triangular regions is illustrated in Fig. 4.21 (a), (b) and (c). Table 4.3 shows the details of computation of the areas and the centroids of various segments of Fig. 4.20. The crisp output of the fuzzy controller obtained through the centroid method is

$$D_{centroid} = \frac{A_1 \times c_1 + A_2 \times c_2 + A_3 \times c_3 + A_4 \times c_4 + A_5 \times c_5 + A_6 \times c_6}{A_1 + A_2 + A_3 + A_4 + A_5 + A_6}$$

$$= \frac{\frac{1}{36}\times\left(-\frac{7}{18}\right)+\frac{1}{6}\times\left(-\frac{1}{12}\right)+\frac{1}{18}\times\frac{1}{4}+\frac{1}{36}\times\frac{5}{18}+\frac{2}{9}\times\frac{1}{2}+\frac{1}{9}\times\frac{7}{9}}{\frac{1}{36}+\frac{1}{6}+\frac{1}{18}+\frac{1}{36}+\frac{2}{9}+\frac{1}{9}} = \frac{5}{22} = 0.227$$

Table 4.3. *Computation of areas and centroids of various regions*

Region	Areas	Centroids
Δ *ABJ* (A_1)	1/2 × (1/2 −1/3) × 1/3 = 1/36	−7/18 (c_1)
BCIJ (A_2)	1/3 × (1/3 + 1/6) = 1/6	−1/12 (c_2)
CKHI (A_3)	1/3 × (1/3 −1/6) = 1/18	1/4 (c_3)
Δ *CDK* (A_4)	1/2 × (1/3 −1/6) ×1/3 = 1/36	5/18 (c_4)
DEGH (A_5)	2/3 ×1/3 = 2/9	1/2 (c_5)
Δ *EFG* (A_6)	1/2 ×1/3 × 2/3 = 1/9	7/9 (c_6)

Hence according to the centroid method, the AC dial is to be set at $D = +0.227$.

(iii) *Mean of Maxima:* As it is seen from Fig. 4.20, the maximal membership is $2/3 = 0.667$, and this maxima is attained from point H to point G along the D-axis. Distances of H and G from the origin are $+ 1/3$, and $+ 2/3$ respectively. Therefore the value of D in MoM method is obtained as below:

$$D_{MoM} = \frac{OG + OH}{2} = \frac{\frac{1}{3}+\frac{2}{3}}{2} = \frac{1}{2} = 0.5$$

Therefore, the AC dial D should be set at 0.5 as per MoM method of defuzzification.

4.7.2 Fuzzy Cruise Controller

This fuzzy controller was proposed by Greg Viot in 1993. Its purpose is to maintain a vehicle at a desired speed. Fig 4.22 shows the high level block diagram of the system. There are two inputs, *viz.*, speed difference (Δu) and acceleration (a). The only output is the Throttle control (T).

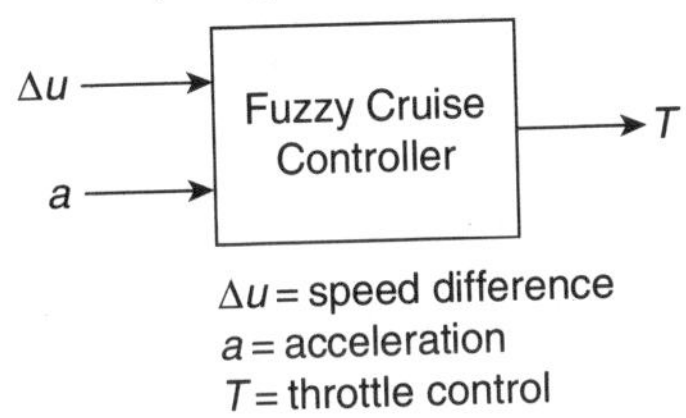

Fig. 4.22. *Block diagram of fuzzy cruise controller.*

The speed difference is computed as $\Delta u = u - u_0$, where u_0 is the desired speed and u is the current speed. For the sake of simplicity all the parameters, Δu, a, T, are normalized here to the range 0–63 and all of them are categorized by the fuzzy sets *LN, MN, SN, ZE, SP, MP, LP.* Under normalization, the membership profiles of these sets for various parameters are identical and appear as shown in Fig. 4.23.

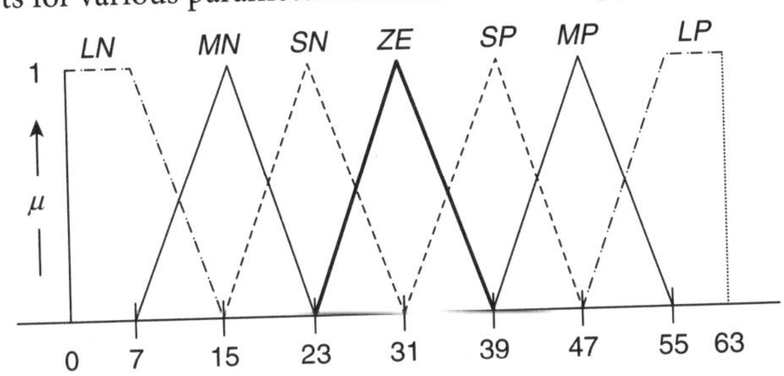

Fig. 4.23. *Membership profiles of fuzzy sets on speed difference (Δu), acceleration (a) and throttle control (T).*

The rule base can be constituted with various sets of rules corresponding to combinations of fuzzy sets on Δu and a. In this example we consider the exhaustive set of rules obtained by taking all possible combinations of fuzzy sets on Δu and a. This is depicted in Table 4.4. This way of tabular representation of a fuzzy rule base is often referred to as a *fuzzy associative memory* (*FAM*) table. The entries in the table can be interpreted in the following way: consider the cell at the intersection of row 3 and column 4. Row 3 corresponds to the fuzzy set Small Negative (*SN*) of Δu and Column 4 corresponds to *ZE* of acceleration a. The entry in their intersecting cell is *SP*. Therefore, this entry represents the rule

$$R_{34}: \text{IF } (\Delta u \text{ is } SN) \text{ AND } (a \text{ is } ZE) \text{ THEN } (T \text{ is } SP)$$

Table 4.4. *Fuzzy associative memory (FAM) table*

(Δu) \ (a)	(1) **LN**	(2) **MN**	(3) **SN**	(4) **ZE**	(5) **SP**	(6) **MP**	(7) **LP**
(1) **LN**	LP	LP	LP	LP	MP	SP	ZE
(2) **MN**	LP	LP	LP	MP	SP	ZE	ZE
(3) **SN**	LP	LP	MP	SP	ZE	SN	MN
(4) **ZE**	LP	MP	SP	ZE	SN	MN	LN
(5) **SP**	MP	MP	SP	SN	SN	MN	LN
(6) **MP**	SP	ZE	SN	MN	MN	LN	LN
(7) **LP**	ZE	SN	SN	LN	LN	LN	LN

Usually the FAM table may contain some empty cells. An empty cell in the *FAM* table, if there exists one, indicates the absence of the corresponding rule in the rule base.

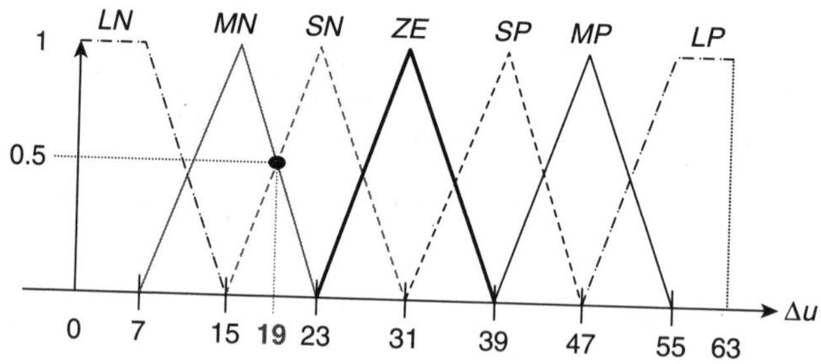

Fig. 4.24. $\mu_{MN}^{\Delta u}(\Delta u = 19) = 0.5$ *and* $\mu_{SN}^{\Delta u}(\Delta u = 19) = 0.5.$

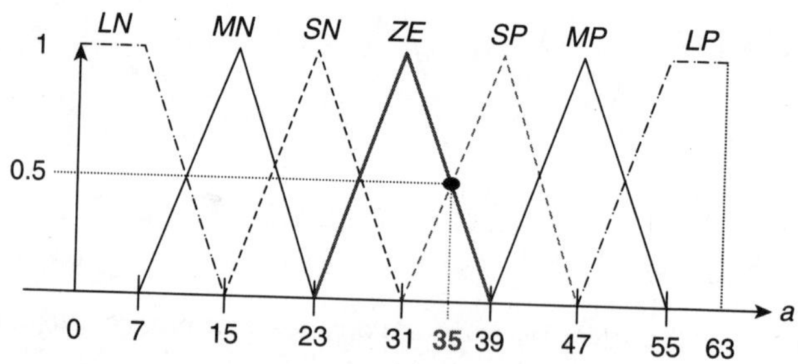

Fig. 4.25. $\mu_{ZE}^{a}(a = 35) = 0.5$ *and* $\mu_{ZE}^{a}(a = 35) = 0.5$

Let us now work out the output of the controller when the normalized speed difference (Δu) and acceleration (a) are 19 and 35 respectively. It is apparent from Fig. 4.24 that for $\Delta u = 19$, all fuzzy sets except *MN* and *SN* have zero membership. Similarly, for $a = 35$ only the fuzzy sets *ZE* and *SP* have non-zero memberships. Moreover, it is observed from Fig. 4.24 that at $\Delta u = 19$ membership to *MN* is 0.5, $\mu_{MN}^{\Delta u}(\Delta u = 19) = 0.5$. Similarly $\mu_{SN}^{\Delta u}(\Delta u = 19) = 0.5$. Also, from Fig. 4.25 we get, $\mu_{ZE}^{a}(a = 35) = 0.5$ and

$\mu_{SP}^{a}(a = 35) = 0.5$. Therefore the rules corresponding to cells (*MN*, *ZE*), (*MN*, *SP*), (*SN*, *ZE*), and (*SN*, *SP*), cells (2, 4), (2, 5), (3, 4) and (3, 5) of the *FAM* table, R_{24}, R_{25}, R_{34}, R_{35} are fired. These rules are

R_{24} : IF (Δu is *MN*) AND (a is *ZE*) THEN (T is *MP*)
R_{25} : IF (Δu is *MN*) AND (a is *SP*) THEN (T is *SP*)
R_{34} : IF (Δu is *SN*) AND (a is *ZE*) THEN (T is *SP*)
R_{35} : IF (Δu is *SN*) AND (a is *SP*) THEN (T is *ZE*)

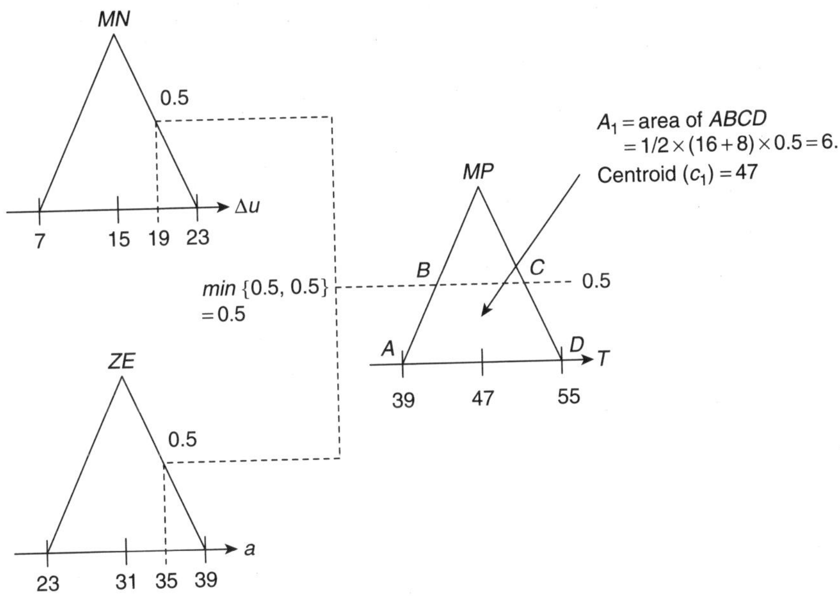

Fig. 4.26. *Processing of Rule* R_{24}.

Let us employ *min* function to implement the 'AND' operation in the antecedent part of a rule. Accordingly, the processing of R_{24} is shown in Fig. 4.26. Table 4.5 shows the complete set of areas and their centroids obtained through processing the rules R_{24}, R_{25}, R_{34}, R_{35}.

Table 4.5. *Areas and centroids*

Rule	Area	Centroid
R_{24}	$A_1 = 6$	$c_1 = 47$
R_{25}	$A_2 = 6$	$c_2 = 39$
R_{34}	$A_3 = 6$	$c_3 = 39$
R_{35}	$A_4 = 6$	$c_4 = 31$

The defuzzified output, according to the CoS method is computed as shown below.

$$T_{COS} = \frac{A_1 \times c_1 + A_2 \times c_2 + A_3 \times c_3 + A_4 \times c_4}{A_1 + A_2 + A_3 + A_4} = \frac{6 \times 47 + 6 \times 39 + 6 \times 39 + 6 \times 31}{6 + 6 + 6 + 6} = 39.$$

However, to compute $T_{centroid}$, the defuzzified output value of throttle control, we have to consider the superimposed region *ABCD* shown in Fig. 4.27.

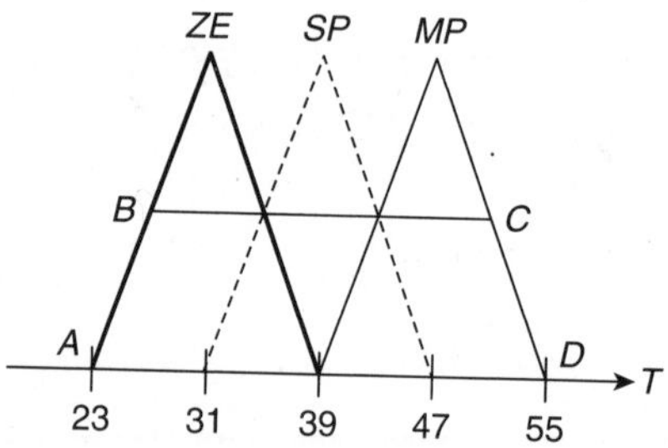

Fig. 4.27. *Region for computation of* $T_{centroid}$.

It is evident from Fig. 4.27 that the region *ABCD* is a trapezium. The centroid of a trapezium passes through the middle of its parallel sides. Hence, centroid of *ABCD* is 39. Moreover,

$$\text{area of } ABCD = 1/2 \times (\text{sum of the lengths of the parallel sides}) \times \text{height}$$
$$= 1/2 \times (32+24) \times 0.5 = 14.$$

Therefore,

$$T_{centroid} = \frac{(area\,of\ ABCD)\times(centroid\,of\ ABCD)}{area\,of\ ABCD} = \frac{14\times 39}{14} = 39$$

Hence, the value of the throttle control, when computed through the centroid method, too is 39. It may be verified that the defuzzified output, obtained by employing the MoM is also 39. Hence, for this instance of the fuzzy cruise controller we have $T_{cos} = T_{centroid} = T_{MoM} = 39$.

CHAPTER SUMMARY

The main points of foregoing discussions on fuzzy inference systems are summarized below.

- A fuzzy inference system (*FIS*) is a system that transforms a given input to an output with the help of fuzzy logic. The procedure followed by a fuzzy inference system is known as fuzzy inference mechanism, or simply fuzzy inference.
- The entire fuzzy inference process comprises five steps, fuzzification of the input variables, application of fuzzy operators on the antecedent parts of the rules, evaluation of the fuzzy rules, aggregation of fuzzy sets across the rules, and defuzzification of the resultant aggregate fuzzy set.
- The first step, fuzzification, determines the degree to which each input belongs to various fuzzy sets through the respective membership functions.
- When the antecedent of a given rule has more than one parts, the appropriate fuzzy operator is applied to obtain a single number representing the result of the entire antecedent. This constitutes the second step of fuzzy inference process.
- In the third step fuzzy rules are evaluated through some implication process. The output fuzzy set is obtained by reshaping the fuzzy set corresponding to the consequent part of the rule with the help of the number given by the antecedent.

- The aggregation process takes the truncated membership profiles returned by the implication process as its input, and produces one fuzzy set for each output variable as the output. This constitutes the fourth step of the fuzzy inference process.
- Defuzzification is the process of converting the aggregate output sets into one crisp number per output variable. This is the fifth, and last, step in a fuzzy inference process.
- There are various defuzzification methods. The most popular among them are the centroid method, CoS method and the MoM method.

SOLVED PROBLEMS

Problem 4.1 (*Fuzzy air conditioner*) Consider the fuzzy air conditioner controller discussed in subsection 4.7.1. What is the dial position for $\Delta T = +0.5$?

Solution 4.1 The step by step computational process is described below.

(i) *Fuzzification* Given $\Delta T = +0.5$, we compute the degree of membership of ΔT with respect to the fuzzy sets *LN, MN, ZE, MP, LP* using the respective membership profiles depicted in Fig. 4.14. All memberships, except *ZE* and *MP* are 0 (Fig. 4.28). For *ZE* and *MP* the membership values are 5/6 and 1/6, respectively.

$$\mu_{LN}^{\Delta T}(+0.5) = \mu_{MN}^{\Delta T}(+0.5) = \mu_{LP}^{\Delta T}(+0.5) = 0$$

$$\mu_{ZE}^{\Delta T}(+0.5) = \frac{5}{6}, \quad \mu_{MP}^{\Delta T}(+0.5) = \frac{1}{6}$$

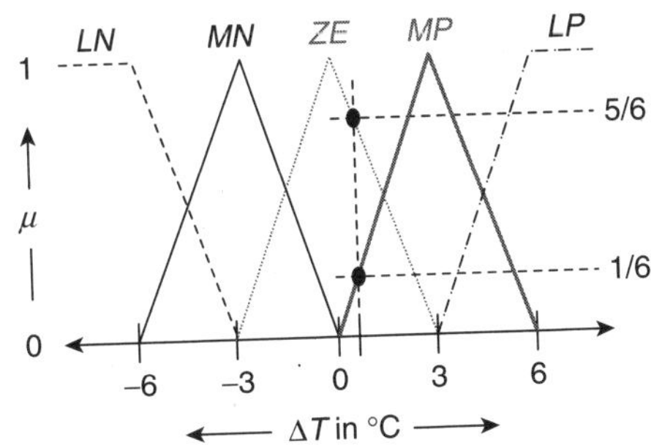

Fig. 4.28. Fuzzy memberships for $\Delta T = +0.5$

(ii) *Rule implication* The fuzzy rule base employed is given by

R_1 : IF ΔT *is LN* THEN *D is LP.*

R_2 : IF ΔT *is MN* THEN *D is MP.*

R_3 : IF ΔT *is ZE* THEN *D is ZE.*

R_4 : IF ΔT *is MP* THEN *D is MN.*

R_5 : IF ΔT *is LP* THEN *D is LN.*

As *ZE* and *MP* are the only fuzzy sets having non-zero membership values for $\Delta T = +0.5$, the fired rules are R_3 and R_4. The rule implication processes are shown in Fig. 4.29 and Fig. 4.30.

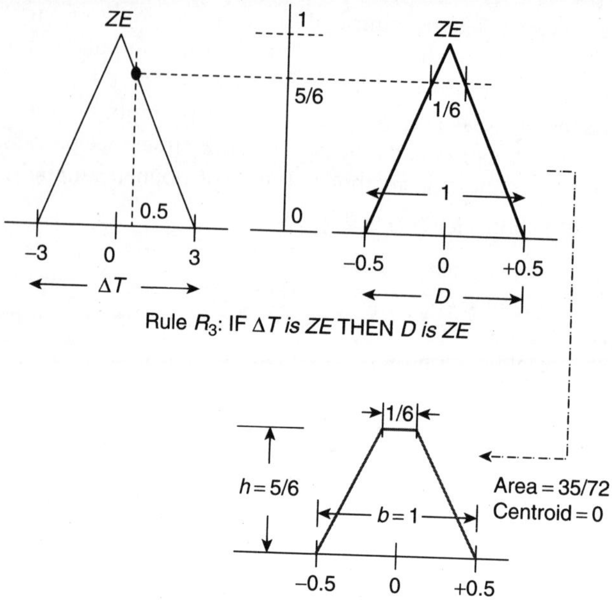

Fig. 4.29. *Evaluation of rule R_3.*

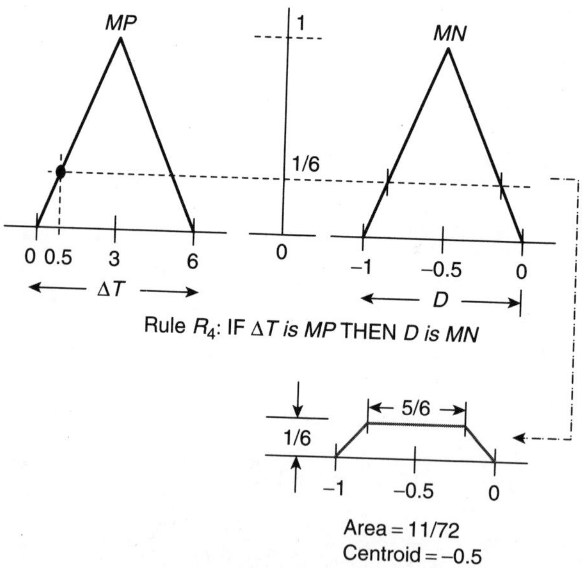

Fig. 4.30. *Evaluation of rule R_4.*

The implication of the rules R_3 and R_4 results in two regions of areas 35/72 and 11/72 respectively. The corresponding centroids are 0 and – 0.5.

(iii) *Aggregation* Calculation of the dial value in the CoS method is as follows

$$D_{COS} = \frac{A_1 \times C_1 + A_2 \times C_2}{A_1 + A_2} = \frac{\frac{35}{72} \times 0 + \frac{11}{72} \times (-0.5)}{\frac{35}{72} + \frac{11}{72}} = \frac{-\frac{0.5 \times 11}{72}}{\frac{46}{72}} = -\frac{11}{72}$$

Hence, the output of the fuzzy controller is D = – 11/72.

Problem 4.2 (*Fuzzy cruise controller*) Consider the fuzzy cruise controller discussed in subsection 4.7.2. What will be the value of the throttle control for normalized speed difference (Δu) = 41, and acceleration (a) = 15?

Solution 4.2 The step by step computational process is given below.

(i) *Fuzzification* Since there are two input parameters, Δu and a, we need to fuzzify both. Considering Δu, we see that the non-zero memberships are $\mu_{SP}^{\Delta u}(\Delta u = 41) = \frac{3}{4}$ and $\mu_{MP}^{\Delta u}(\Delta u = 41) = \frac{1}{4}$ and rest of the membership values are all zeros (see Fig. 4.31). Therefore,

$$\mu_{LN}^{\Delta u}(\Delta u = 41) = \mu_{MN}^{\Delta u}(\Delta u = 41) = \mu_{SN}^{\Delta u}(\Delta u = 41) = \mu_{ZE}^{\Delta u}(\Delta u = 41) = \mu_{LP}^{\Delta u}(\Delta u = 41) = 0$$

$$\mu_{SP}^{\Delta u}(\Delta u = 41) = \frac{6}{8} = \frac{3}{4}, \mu_{MP}^{\Delta u}(\Delta u = 41) = \frac{2}{8} = \frac{1}{4}.$$

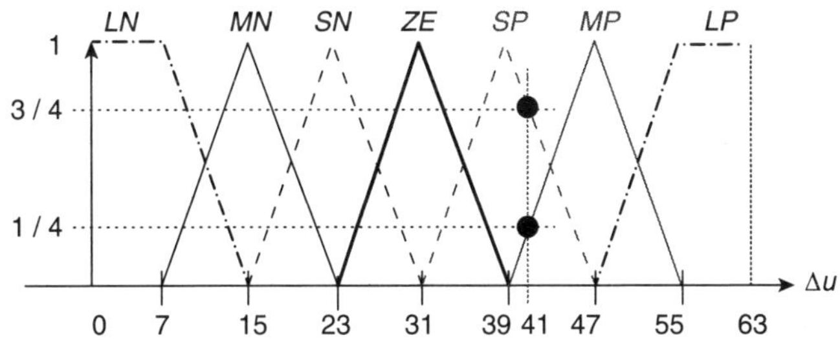

Fig. 4.31. $\mu_{SP}^{\Delta u}(\Delta u = 41) = \frac{3}{4}$ and $\mu_{MP}^{\Delta u}(\Delta u = 41) = \frac{1}{4}$

Similarly, for a, all membership values except *MN* are zeros (Fig. 4.32), so that

$$\mu_{LN}^{a}(a = 15) = \mu_{SN}^{a}(a = 15) = \mu_{ZE}^{a}(a = 15) = \mu_{SP}^{a}(a = 15) = \mu_{MP}^{a}(a = 15) = \mu_{LP}^{a}(a = 15) = 0$$

$$\mu_{MN}^{a}(a = 15) = 1$$

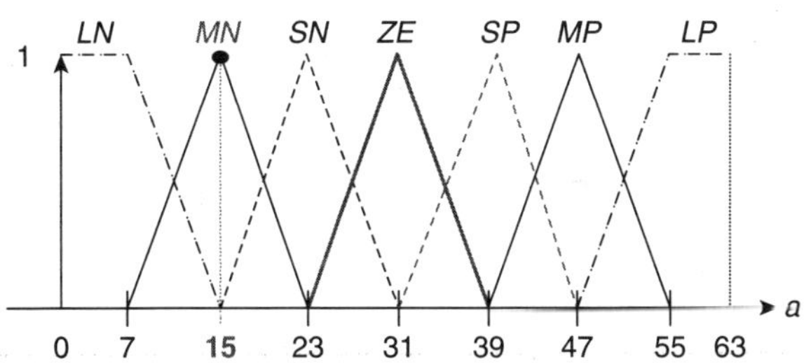

Fig. 4.32. $\mu_{MN}^{a}(a = 15) = 1$

(ii) *Rule implication* The results of the fuzzification phase imply that rules R_{52} and R_{62} are fired (see Table 4.6 which is a repetition of Table 4.4 with relevant portions highlighted). Hence we need to process the following fuzzy rules:

R_{52} : IF (Δu is *SP*) AND (a is *MN*) THEN (T is *MP*)

R_{62} : IF (Δu is *MP*) AND (a is *MN*) THEN (T is *ZE*)

Table 4.6. *Fired Rules in the FAM Table*

(a) / (Δu)	(1) **LN**	(2) **MN**	(3) **SN**	(4) **ZE**	(5) **SP**	(6) **MP**	(7) **LP**
(1) **LN**	*LP*	*LP*	*LP*	*LP*	*MP*	*SP*	*ZE*
(2) **MN**	*LP*	*LP*	*LP*	*MP*	*SP*	*ZE*	*ZE*
(3) **SN**	*LP*	*LP*	*MP*	*SP*	*ZE*	*SN*	*MN*
(4) **ZE**	*LP*	*MP*	*SP*	*ZE*	*SN*	*MN*	*LN*
(5) **SP**	*MP*	***MP***	*SP*	*SN*	*SN*	*MN*	*LN*
(6) **MP**	*SP*	***ZE***	*SN*	*MN*	*MN*	*LN*	*LN*
(7) **LP**	*ZE*	*SN*	*SN*	*LN*	*LN*	*LN*	*LN*

The rule implication process is graphically shown in Fig. 4.33 and Fig. 4.34.

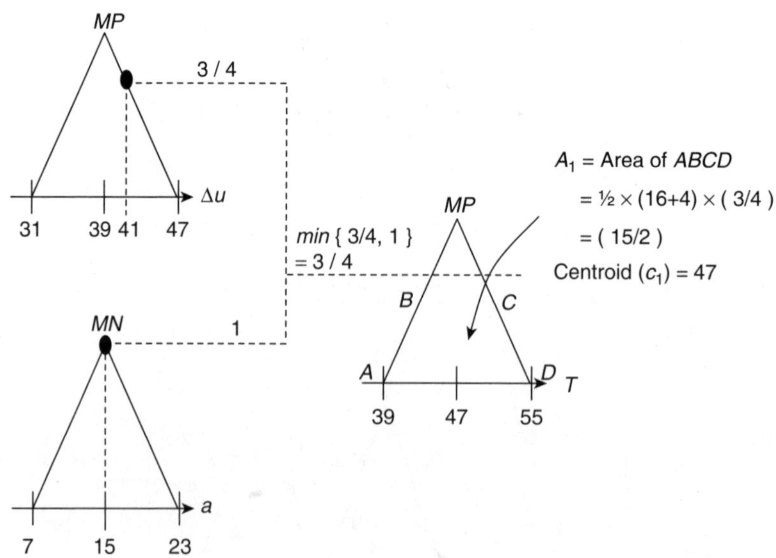

Fig. 4.33. *Processing of Rule R_{52}.*

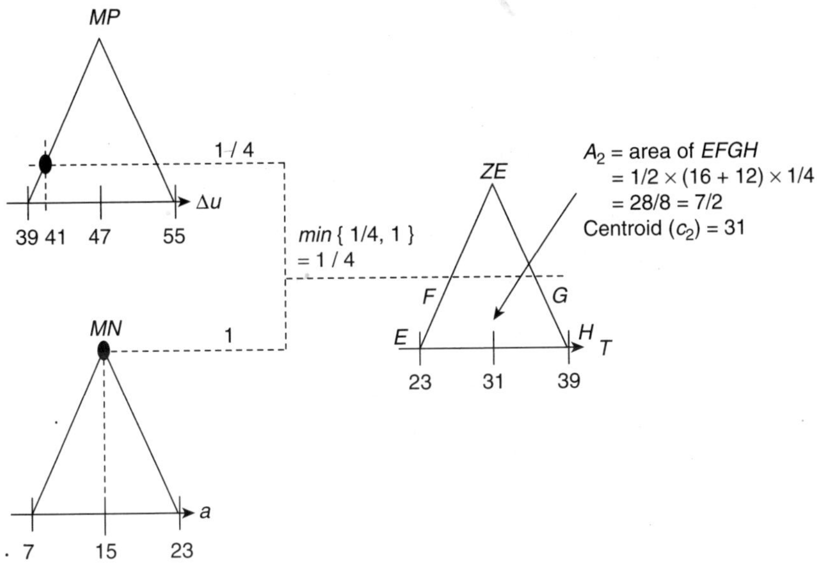

Fig. 4.34. *Processing of Rule R_{62}.*

The rule implication process yields two trapeziums ABCD and EFGH with areas $A_1 = 15/2$ and $A_2 = 7/2$, and centroids $c_1 = 47$ and $c_2 = 31$ respectively.

(iii) *Aggregation* For aggregation, we consider the CoS method only. The calculations are given below.

$$T = \frac{A_1 \times c_1 + A_2 \times c_2}{A_1 + A_2} = \frac{\frac{15}{2} \times 47 + \frac{7}{2} \times 31}{\frac{15}{2} + \frac{7}{2}} = \frac{15 \times 47 + 7 \times 31}{15 + 7} \approx 42$$

Hence, the throttle control value will be approximately 42 for normalized speed difference $(\Delta u) = 41$, and acceleration $(a) = 15$.

Problem 4.3 (*Fuzzy tipper*) This problem, popularly known as the tipping problem, concerns the amount of tip to be given to a waiter at a restaurant. It is a typical situation where the principles of fuzzy inference system may be applied successfully. Given a number between 0 and 10 that represents the quality of service at a restaurant (where 10 is excellent), and another number between 0 and 10 that represents the quality of the food at that restaurant (again, 10 is excellent), what should the tip be?

Solution 4.3 The starting point is to write down the three golden rules of tipping as given below.

1. If the service is poor or the food is rancid, then tip is cheap.
2. If the service is good, then tip is average.
3. If the service is excellent or the food is delicious, then tip is generous.

The procedure to solve the problem using the relevant MatLab toolbox is being described as a sequence of steps, along with MatLab snapshots.

Step 1. Open Toolboxes → Fuzzy Logic → FIS Editor GUI (Fuzzy).(Fig. 4.35)

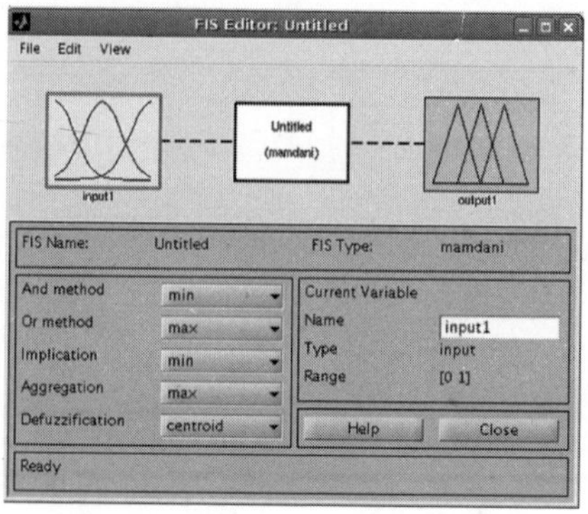

Fig. 4.35. *Step 1 of Fuzzy tipper*

Step 2. Open Edit → Add variable → Input. (Normally there is one input and one output available, but we would need two inputs here) (Fig. 4.36)

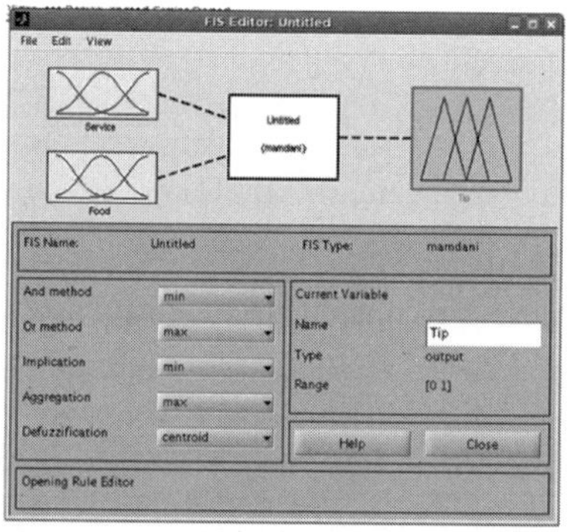

Fig. 4.36

Step 3. Double click on one of the yellow boxes to go to the Membership Function Editor.

Step 4. Select Input1 (Service), Input2 (Food) and Output(Tip) to change the variables of the membership functions to suitable values. (Fig. 4.37–4.44)

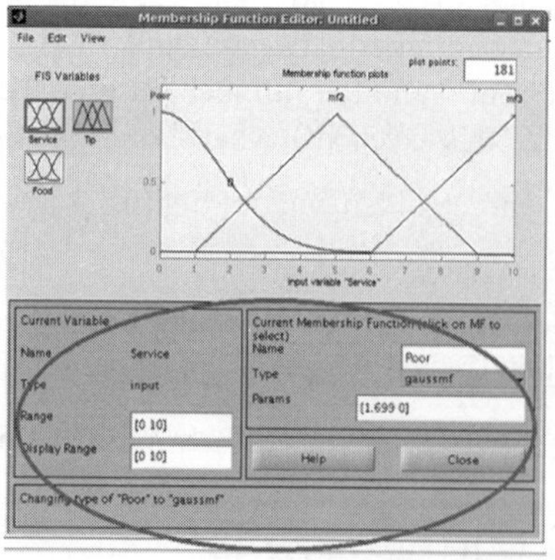

Fig. 4.37

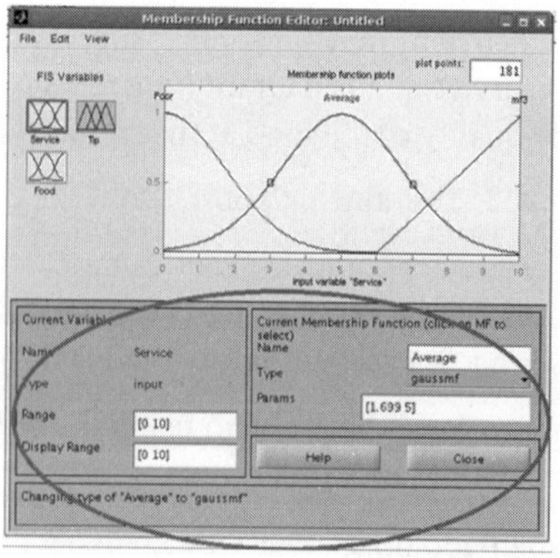

Fig. 4.38

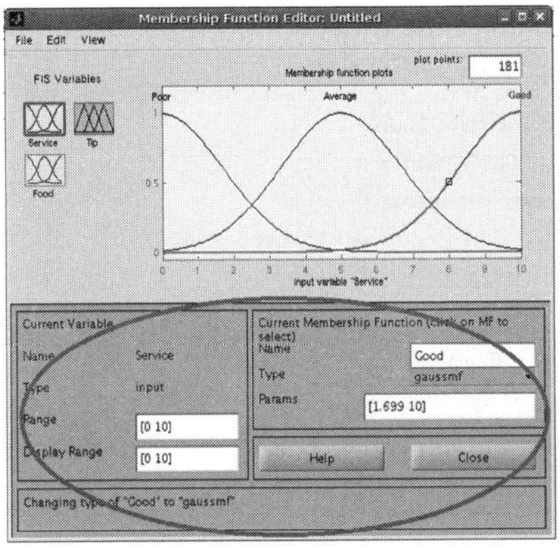

Fig. 4.39

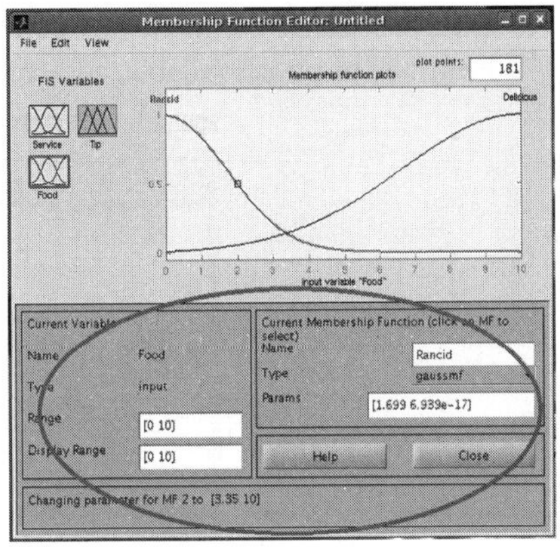

Fig. 4.40

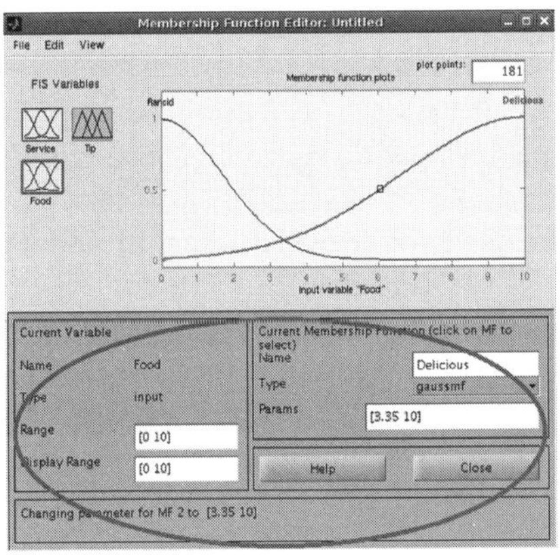

Fig. 4.41

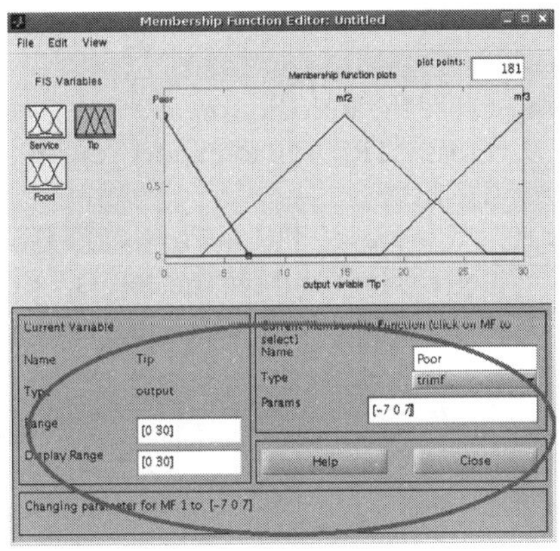

Fig. 4.42

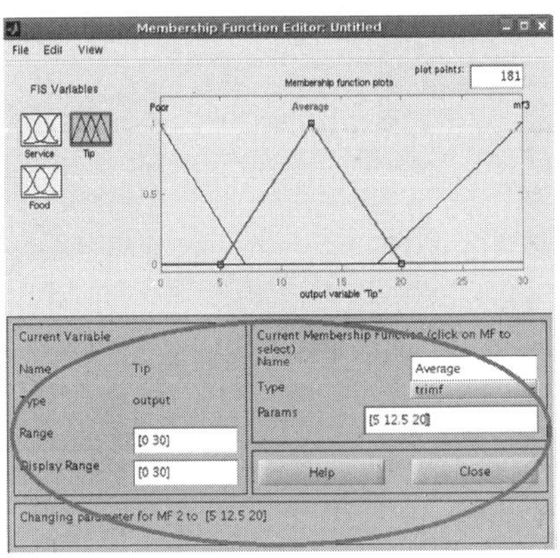

Fig. 4.43

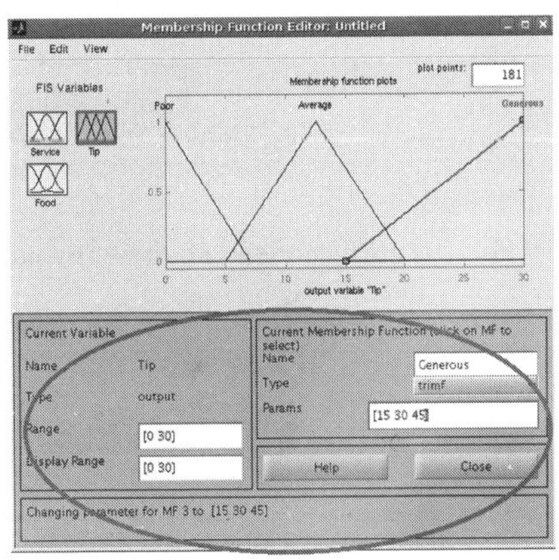

Fig. 4.44

Step 5. Close the Membership Function Editor to return to FIS Editor.

Step 6. Double click on the white box in the middle to go to the Rule Editor.

Step 7. From the options available, add rules as above. (Fig. 4.45)

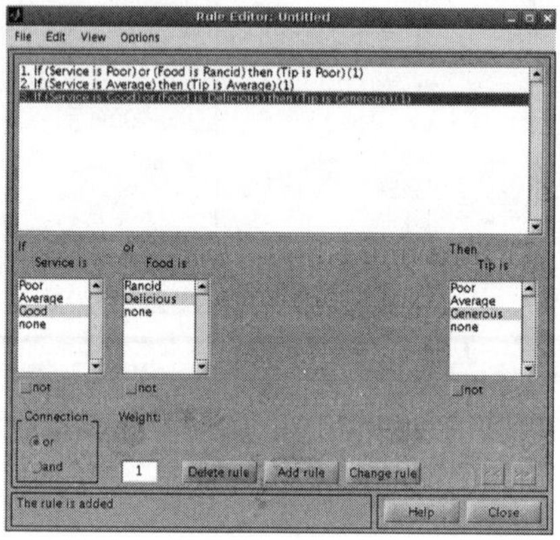

Fig. 4.45

Step 8. Close the Rule Editor.

Step 9. Press CTRL + T to export your FIS to Workspace/File or do so from FILE → EXPORT → TO FILE

Step 10. Now press CTRL + 5 to see the Graphical Rule Viewer where you can vary the input parameter values and see the corresponding output values. (Fig. 4.46)

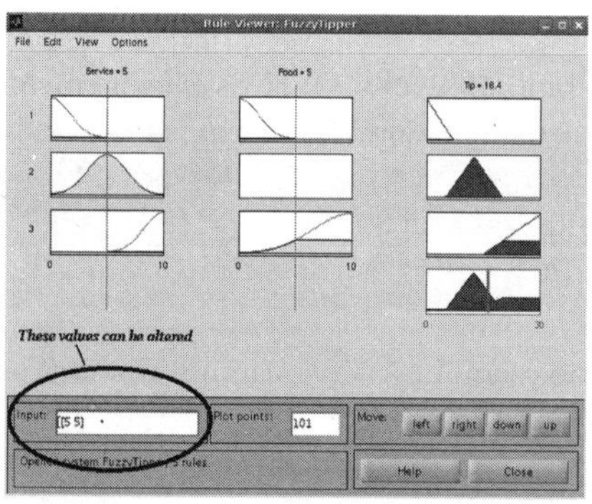

Fig. 4.46

Step 11. The surface viewer can be invoked by CTRL+6. (Fig. 4.47)

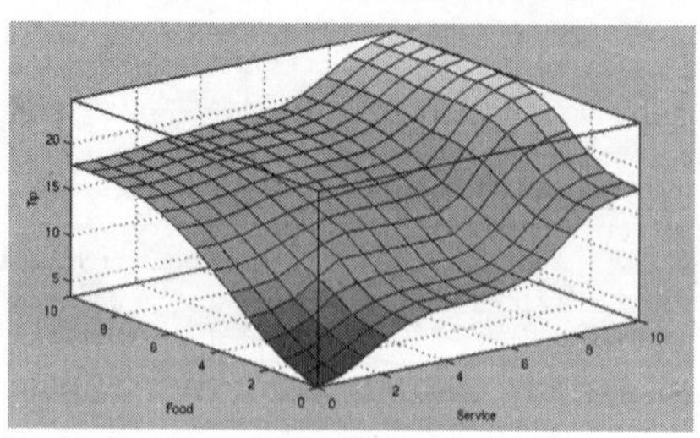

Fig. 4.47

Problem 4.4 (*Fuzzy controlled camera*) Present day digital cameras have fuzzy controllers to control the aperture and shutter speed of the camera based upon light conditions and the state of motion of the object. Table 4.7 shows the behavior pattern of such a camera. Design a fuzzy inference system to control the aperture and the shutter speed on the basis of light and object motion.

Table 4.7. *Camera adjustments*

#	Inputs		Outputs	
	Light	Object motion	Aperture	Shutter Speed
1	Low	Static	High	Low
2	Moderate	Static	Moderate	Moderate
3	High	Static	Low	High
4	Low	Mobile	High	Moderate
5	Moderate	Mobile	Moderate	High
6	High	Highly Mobile	Low	High
7	Low	Highly Mobile	High	Moderate
8	Low	Mobile	High	Moderate
9	High	Mobile	Low	Moderate

Solution 4.4 The MatLab implementation of the fuzzy inference system is described below in a stepwise manner.

Step 1. Open Toolboxes → Fuzzy Logic → FIS Editor GUI (Fuzzy). (Fig. 4.48)

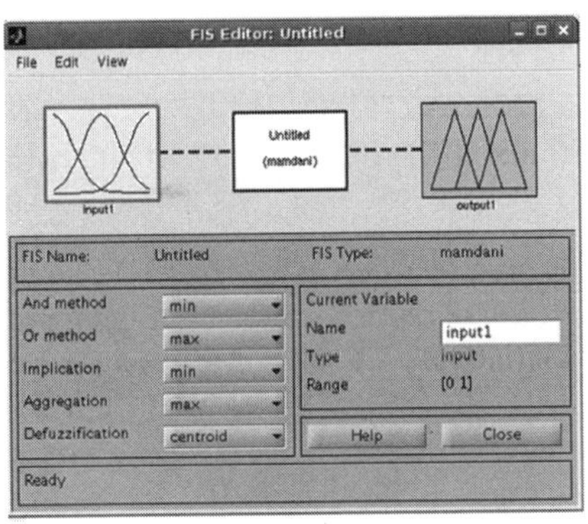

Fig. 4.48

Step 2. Open Edit → Add variable → Input (Normally there is one input and one output available, but we would need two each here.)

Step 3. Open Edit → Add variable → Output (To add the second output variable)

Step 4. Double click on one of the yellow boxes to go to the Membership Function Editor.

Step 5. Select Input 1 (Light) and change the variables of the membership functions to suitable values. (Fig. 4.49, 4.50, 4.51)

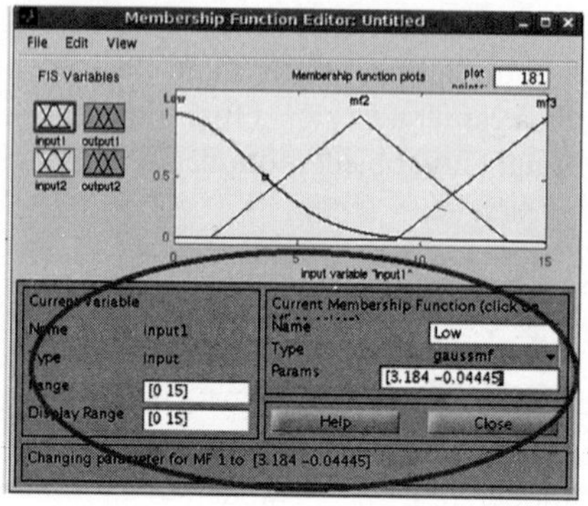

Fig. 4.49

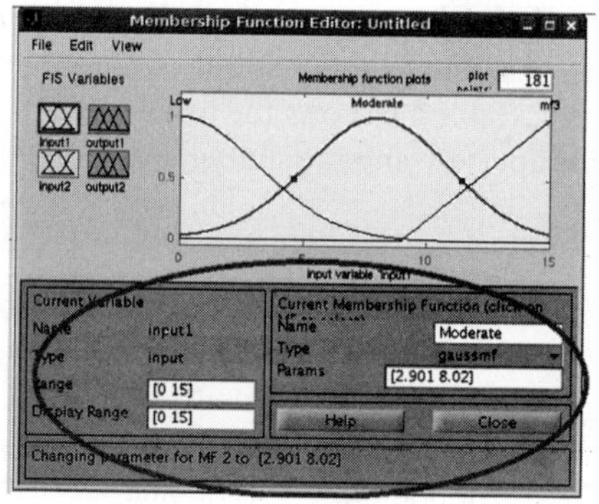

Fig. 4.50

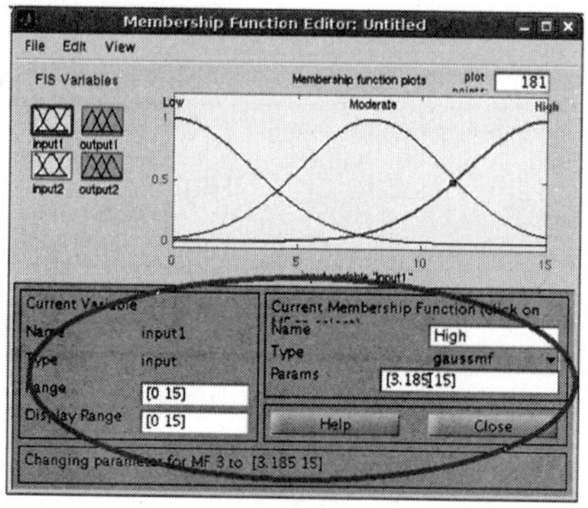

Fig. 4.51

Step 6. Repeat steps for Input 2 (Object Motion)

```
mf1 -
NAME: Static
RANGE: [0 1]
DISPLAY RANGE: [0 1]
TYPE: trapmf
PARAMS:[-0.36 -0.04 0.24 0.36]
mf2 -
NAME: Mobile
RANGE: [0 1]
DISPLAY RANGE: [0 1]
TYPE: trimf
PARAMS:[0.23 0.5 0.8]
mf3-
NAME: HighlyMobile
RANGE: [0 1]
DISPLAY RANGE: [0 1]
TYPE: trimf
PARAMS:[0.75 1 3.4]
```

Step 7. Repeat steps for Output 1 (Aperture)

```
mf1 -
NAME: High
RANGE: [0 16]
DISPLAY RANGE: [0 16]
TYPE: trimf
PARAMS:[-6.4 1.11e-16 6.4]

mf2 -
NAME: Moderate
RANGE: [0 16]
DISPLAY RANGE: [0 16]
TYPE: trimf
PARAMS:[1.6 8 14.4]

mf3 -
NAME: Low
RANGE: [0 16]
DISPLAY RANGE: [0 16]
TYPE: trimf
PARAMS:[9.6 16 22.4]
```

Step 8. Repeat steps for Output 2 (ShutterSpeed)

```
mf1 -
NAME: Low
RANGE: [0 250]
DISPLAY RANGE: [0 250]
TYPE: trimf
PARAMS:[-100 -1.776e-15 100]

mf2 -
NAME: Moderate
RANGE: [0 250]
DISPLAY RANGE: [0 250]
TYPE: trimf
PARAMS:[24.99 125 225]

mf3 -
NAME: High
RANGE: [0 250]
DISPLAY RANGE: [0 250]
TYPE: trimf
PARAMS:[150 250 350]
```

Step 9. Close the Membership Function Editor to return to FIS Editor.
Step 10. Double click on the white box in the middle to go to the Rule Editor.

Step 11. From the options available, add rules that appear in the table above.

Step 12. Close the Rule Editor.

Step 13. Press CTRL + T to export your FIS to Workspace/File or do so from FILE → EXPORT → TO FILE.

Step 14. Now press CTRL + 5 to see the Graphical Rule Viewer where you can vary the input parameter values and see the corresponding output values. (Fig. 4.52)

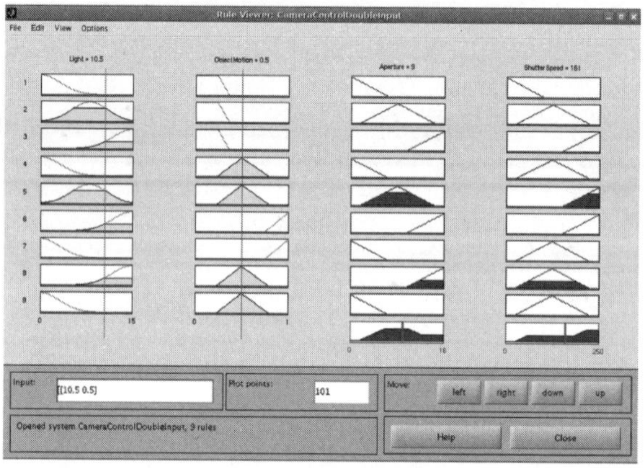

Fig. 4.52

Step 15. The Surface Viewer can be invoked by CTRL + 6. (Fig. 4.53 and 4.54)

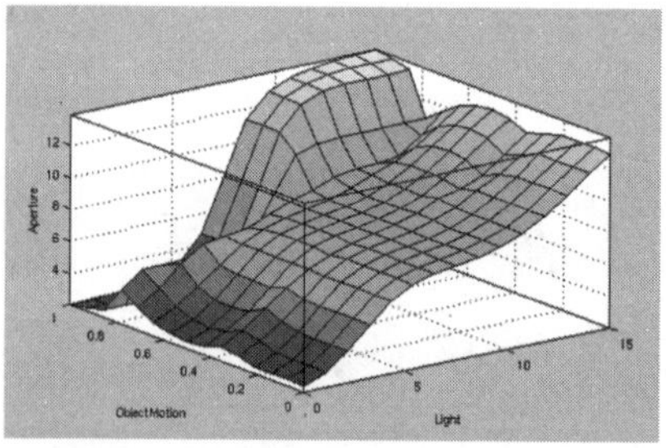

Fig. 4.53

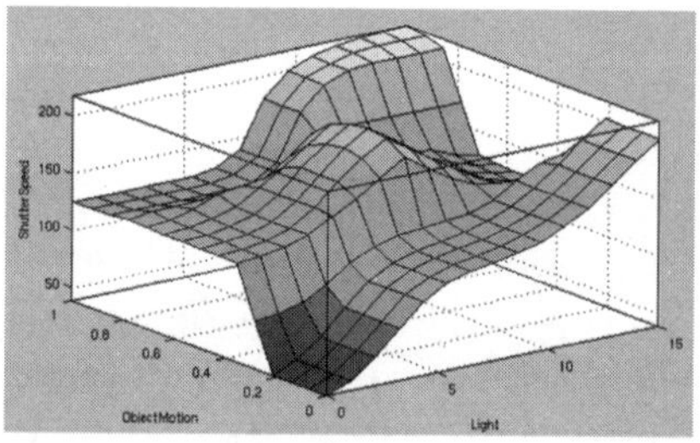

Fig. 4.54

✓ TEST YOUR KNOWLEDGE

4.1 Which of the following is the first step of a fuzzy inference process ?
   a) Fuzzification   b) Defuzzification
   c) Either (*a*) or (*b*)   d) None of the above

4.2 Which of the following is the last step of a fuzzy inference process ?
   a) Fuzzification   b) Defuzzification
   c) Either (*a*) or (*b*)   d) None of the above

4.3 An input to a fuzzy inference system is a
   a) A crisp value   b) A linguistic variable
   c) A fuzzy set   d) None of the above

4.4 An output of a fuzzy inference system is a
a) A crisp value
b) A linguistic variable
c) A fuzzy set
d) None of the above

4.5 Which of the following is not a defuzzification method?
a) Centroid
b) Centre-of-sums (CoS)
c) Mean-of-maxima (MoM)
d) None of the above

4.6 Fuzzy controllers are built on the basis of
a) Fuzzy Inference Systems
b) Fuzzy Extension Principle
c) Both (*a*) or (*b*)
d) None of the above

4.7 Which of the following is used to store a fuzzy rule base of a fuzzy controller?
a) Fuzzy Relation Matrix
b) Fuzzy Associative Memory table
c) Both (*a*) or (*b*)
d) None of the above

4.8 Which of the following defuzzification methods is never used in a fuzzy controller?
a) Centroid
b) Center-of-sums (CoS)
c) Mean-of-Maxima (MoM)
d) None of the above

4.9 An empty cell in a Fuzzy Associative Memory (FAM) table indicates
a) An error in the FAM specification
b) A rule that is absent in the rule base
c) Both (*a*) and (*b*)
d) None of the above

4.10 Which of the following phases of a fuzzy controller uses the fuzzy rule base?
a) Fuzzification
b) Rule implication
c) Both (*a*) and (*b*)
d) None of the above

Answers

4.1 (a)	4.2 (b)	4.3 (a)	4.4 (a)	4.5 (d)
4.6 (a)	4.7 (b)	4.8 (d)	4.9 (b)	4.10 (b)

EXERCISES

4.1. A test is being conducted to ascertain the creative and logical ability of a person. The test has two parts, *viz.*, a reasoning part, and a design part. The score of each part is normalized to the scale of 0–10. There are two output indices, *viz.*, the creative index, and the logical index, both are within the range [0, 1]. The scores of the tests, as well as the outputs, *i.e.*, the creative index, and the logical index, are categorized by the linguistic variables *low*, *medium*, and *high*.

Propose suitable fuzzy set membership functions for each linguistic variable described above. Also propose a fuzzy rule base involving the input and output parameters mentioned above. Design a fuzzy inference system, structurally similar to a fuzzy controller, to find the values of the two indices when the normalized score of the test is given. Find the values of the creative and logical indices for the following sets scores:

Reasoning = 7, and Design = 4
Reasoning = 3, and Design = 8

4.2 In Solved Problem No. 4.1 and 4.2, calculate the outputs through centroid method and mean of maxima method.

BIBLIOGRAPHY AND HISTORICAL NOTES

Zadeh introduced the idea of a linguistic variable defined as a fuzzy set in 1973. In 1975 Ebrahim Mamdani proposed a fuzzy control system for a steam engine combined with a boiler by employing a set of linguistic control rules provided by human operators from their past experience. In 1987 Takeshi Yamakawa applied fuzzy control, with the help of a set of fuzzy logic chips, in the famous inverted pendulum experiment. In this control problem, a vehicle tries to keep a pole mounted on its top by a hinge upright by moving back and forth. Numerous fuzzy controllers built upon the concepts of fuzzy inference systems were developed for both industrial and consumer applications such as vacuum cleaners, autofocusing camera, air conditioner, low-power refrigerators, dish washer etc. Fuzzy inference systems have been successfully applied to various areas including automatic control, computer vision, expert systems, decision analysis, data classification, and so on. A brief list of the literature in this area is given below.

Hirota, K. (ed.) (1993). *Industrial Applications of Fuzzy Technology*. Springer, Tokyo,

Holmblad L.P. and Ostergaard J.-J. (1982). *Control of a cement kiln by fuzzy logic*. In *Fuzzy Information and Decision Processes*, Gupta, M.M. and Sanchez, E. (ed.), pp. 389–399. North-Holland.

Jantzen, J. (2007). *Foundations of Fuzzy Control*. Wiley.

Mamdani E.H. and Assilian S. (1975). An experiment in linguistic synthesis with a fuzzy logic controller. *International Journal of Man-Machine Studies*, Vol. 7, pp. 1–13.

Passino, K. M. and Yurkovich, S. (1998). *Fuzzy Control*. Addison Wesley Longman, Menlo Park, CA.

Santhanam S. and Langari R. (1994). Supervisory fuzzy adaptive control of a binary distillation column. *In Proceedings of the 3rd IEEE International Conference on Fuzzy Systems*, Vol. 2, pp. 1063–1068, Orlando, FL.

Tanaka, K. and Wang, H. O. (2001). *Fuzzy Control Systems Design and Analysis: a Linear Matrix Inequality Approach*. John Wiley and Sons, New York.

Terano, T., Asai, K., and Sugeno, M. (1994). *Applied Fuzzy Systems*. Academic Press, Boston.

Vadiee, N. (1993). *Fuzzy rule based expert systems*. In *Fuzzy Logic and Control*. Prentice-Hall.

Yager, R. and Filev, D. (1994). *Essentials of Fuzzy Modeling and Control*. John Wiley and Sons, New York.

Yasunobu, S. and Miyamoto, S. (1985). *Automatic train operation system by predictive fuzzy control*. In *Industrial Applications of Fuzzy Control*, M. Sugeno (ed.), pp. 1–18. North-Holland.

5

ROUGH SETS

Key Concepts

Boundary region, Data clustering, Decision systems, Discernibility function, Discernibility matrix, Indiscernibility, Inexactness, Information systems, Lower approximation, Minimal reduct, Reduct, Rough membership, Rule extraction, Upper approximation, Vagueness

Chapter Outline

An important feature of intelligent behaviour is the ease with which it deals with vagueness, or inexactness. Vagueness, or inexactness, is the result of inadequate knowledge. In the realm of Computer Science, more particularly in Soft Computing, two models of vagueness have been proposed. The concept of a fuzzy set, proposed by Lotfi Zadeh, models vagueness with the help of partial membership, in contrast with crisp membership used in the classical definition of a set. Fuzzy set theory and related topics are discussed in Chapter 2 (Fuzzy set theory), Chapter 3 (Fuzzy logic), and Chapter 4 (Fuzzy inference systems) of this book. This chapter introduces the other model known as the *Rough* set theory. The concept of rough sets, proposed by Zdzisław Pawlak, considers vagueness from a different point of view. In *Rough* set theory, vagueness is not expressed by means of set membership but in terms of *boundary regions* of a set of *objects*. There are situations related to large reservoir of multidimensional data when it is not possible to decide with certainty whether a given object belongs to a set or not. These objects are said to form a *boundary region* for the set. If the boundary region is empty, then the set is crisp, otherwise it is *rough*, or inexact. The existence of a non-empty boundary region implies our lack of sufficient knowledge to define the set precisely, with certainty. There are many interesting applications of the rough set theory. This approach appears to be of fundamental importance to AI and cognitive sciences, especially in the areas of machine learning, knowledge acquisition, decision analysis, knowledge discovery from databases, expert systems, inductive reasoning and pattern recognition. Rest of this chapter provides an introductory discussion on the fundamentals of the Rough set theory.

5.1 INFORMATION SYSTEMS AND DECISION SYSTEMS

A datum (singular form of the word 'data') is usually presented either as a number, or a name. 'Information' is processed or structured data that may convey some meaning. Data in itself do not carry any meaning, and therefore useless for practical purposes. However, when interpreted in a particular context, it becomes meaningful and useful for taking decisions. For example, the word 'John' and the number '30' are two data. They are meaningless and useless in this raw form. But if these two data are interpreted as 'John is 30 years old,' or 'John owes \$30 to Sheela,' or 'John lives 30 km to the North of London,' they convey meaning and become useful.

The simplest way to associate meaning to data is to present them in a structured form, like, in a table. Every column of such a table represents an attribute or property and every row represents an *object*. By 'object' we mean an ordered n-tuple of attribute values. An instance of rendering sense to a set of data by virtue of their arrangement in tabular form is cited in Example 5.1.

Example 5.1 *(Information presented as structured data)*

Let us consider the set of numerical data $D = \{1, 2, 3, 4, 5, 6, 7, 59, 73, 12, 18, 33, 94, 61\}$. Table 5.1 shows the data arranged in tabular form. Columns 2 and 3 of Table 5.1 present the attributes *Roll Number* and *Score* respectively. There are seven objects corresponding to the seven rows of the table. Each object is a 2-tuple. The objects here are (1, 59), (2, 73), (3, 12), (4, 18), (5, 33), (6, 94), and (7, 61).

Table 5.1. *Information presented as structured data*

#	Roll No.	Score
1	1	59
2	2	73
3	3	12
4	4	18
5	5	33
6	6	94
7	7	61

A number of data arranged in a tabular format is often termed as an *information system*. An information system can be formally defined in the following way.

Definition 5.1 *(Information System)* Let $A = (A_1, A_2, A_3, \ldots, A_k)$ be a non-empty finite set of attributes and $U = \{(a_1, a_2, \ldots, a_k)\}$ be a non-empty finite set of k-tuples, termed as the objects. $V(A_i)$ denote the set of values for the attributes A_i. Then an **information system** is defined as an ordered pair $I(U, A)$ such that for all $i = 1, 2, \ldots, k$ there is a function f_i

$$f_i : U \rightarrow V(A_i)$$

This means, every object in the set U has an attribute value for every element in the set A. The set U is called the *universe* of the information system.

Example 5.2 (*Information system*)

Table 5.2 shows an information system regarding the scores of seven students in three subjects. The information system consists of seven objects, each corresponding to a student. Here U includes the objects (1, 82, 90, 98), ..., (7, 10, 12, 0) and the set A consists four attributes *Roll No.*, *Physics*, *Chemistry* and *Mathematics*. V (*Roll No.*) = {1, 2, 3, 4, 5, 6, 7} and V (*Physics*) = V (*Chemistry*) = V (*Mathematics*) = {0, 1, 2, ..., 100}, assuming that the score of a subject is given as whole numbers.

Table 5.2. *An information system*

#	Roll No.	Physics	Chemistry	Mathematics
1	1	82	90	98
2	2	80	96	100
3	3	63	62	68
4	4	70	92	100
5	5	54	51	36
6	6	92	94	90
7	7	10	12	0

Quite often, an information system includes a special attribute that presents a decision. For example, the information system shown in Table 5.2 may be augmented with a special attribute *Admitted* as in Table 5.3. This attribute will indicate whether the student concerned is admitted to a certain course on the basis of the marks scored in Physics, Chemistry and Mathematics. Such systems which show the outcome of a classification are known as *decision systems*. The attribute presenting the decision is called the *decision attribute*. Values of the decision attribute depend on the combination of the other attribute values.

Example 5.3 (*Decision system*)

Table 5.3 presents a decision system obtained by augmenting the information system depicted in Table 5.2 by a decision attribute *Admitted*.

Table 5.3. *An information system augmented with a decision attribute*

Roll No.	Physics	Chemistry	Mathematics	PCM %age	Admitted
1	82	90	98	90	Yes
2	80	96	100	92	Yes
3	63	62	68	64.3	No
4	70	92	100	87.3	Yes
5	54	51	36	47	No
6	92	94	90	92	Yes
7	10	12	0	7.3	No

Definition 5.2 (*Decision System*) A **decision system** $D(U, A, d)$ is an information system $I(U, A)$ augmented with a special attribute $d \notin A$, known as the decision attribute.

The decision system shown in Table 5.3 has the decision attribute *Admitted* that has binary values 'Yes' or 'No'. These values are based on certain rules which guide the decision. On a closer scrutiny into Table 5.3, this rule maybe identified as *If PCM %age is greater than or equal to 87.3 then Admitted = Yes, else Admitted = No.*

5.2 INDISCERNIBILITY

Decision systems have the capacity to express knowledge about the underlying information system. However, a decision table may contain redundancies such as indistinguishable states or superfluous attributes. In Table 5.3, the attributes *Physics, Chemistry* and *Mathematics* are unnecessary to take decision about admittance so long as the aggregate percentage is available. The decision attributes in decision systems are generated from the conditional attributes. These conditional attributes share common properties as clarified in the subsequent examples. However, before we go on to discuss these issues, we need to review the concept of equivalence relation.

Definition 5.3 (*Equivalence Relation*) A binary relation $R \subseteq A \times A$ is an **equivalence relation** if it is

(i) Reflexive $(\forall x \in A, xRx)$,
(ii) Symmetric $(\forall x, y \in A, xRy \Rightarrow yRx)$, and
(iii) Transitive $(\forall x, y, z \in A, xRy \wedge yRz \Rightarrow xRz)$.

Informally, two objects or cases are equivalent if they share some common properties. Equivalence is however, limited only to those common properties which these elements share.

Example 5.4 (*Equivalence relation*)

As a rather trivial case, let us consider *similarity* (~) of triangles. Two triangles ΔABC and ΔPQR are similar (written as $\Delta ABC \sim \Delta PQR$) if they have the same set of angles, say $\angle A = \angle P$, $\angle B = \angle Q$, and $\angle C = \angle R$. This is an equivalence relation because

(i) ~ is reflexive $(\Delta ABC \sim \Delta ABC)$,
(ii) ~ is symmetric $(\Delta ABC \sim \Delta PQR \Rightarrow \Delta PQR \sim \Delta ABC)$, and
(iii) ~ is transitive $(\Delta ABC \sim \Delta PQR \wedge \Delta PQR \sim \Delta KLM \Rightarrow \Delta ABC \sim \Delta KLM)$.

Example 5.5 (*Equivalence relation*)

Let us consider a case of hostel accommodation. Let S be a set of students and R be a relation on S defined as follows : $\forall x, y \in S$, *xRy if and only if x and y are in the same hostel.* R is an equivalence relation because

(i) R is reflexive (A student stays in the same hostel as himself.)
(ii) R is symmetric (If x stays in the same hostel as y, then y stays in the same hostel as x), and
(iii) R is transitive (If x stays in the same hostel as y, and y stays in the same hostel as z, then x stays in the same hostel as z).

Example 5.6 *(Equivalence Relation)*

Let I be the set of all integers and let R be a relation on I, such that two integers x and y are related, xRy, if and only if x and y are prime to each other. This relation is symmetric but neither reflexive nor transitive. Therefore it is not an equivalence relation.

Example 5.7 *(Equivalence Relation)*

Let us consider matrix algebra and multipliability of matrices. Two matrices A and B are related if $A \times B$ is defined. This relation is neither reflexive, nor symmetric, nor transitive. Hence it is not an equivalence relation.

Definition 5.4 *(Equivalence Class)* An equivalence class of an element $x \in U$, U being the universe, is the set of all elements $y \in U$ such that xRy, i.e., x and y are related. Hence, if $E \subseteq U$, be an equivalence class, then $\forall\ a, b \in E$, aRb holds good.

Example 5.8 *(Equivalence Class)*

Let $U = \{0, 1, 2, 3, 4, 5, 6, 7, 8, 9\}$ and $\forall\ a, b \in U$, aRb if and only if a MOD 3 = b MOD 3. This relation partitions U into three equivalence classes corresponding to the x MOD 3 = 0, 1, and 2. These equivalence classes are $\{0, 3, 6, 9\}$, $\{1, 4, 7\}$, and $\{2, 5, 8\}$ respectively.

Definition 5.5 *(Indiscernibility)* Let $I = (U, A)$ be an information system where $U = \{(a_1, \ldots, a_k)\}$ is the non-empty finite set of k-tuples known as the objects and $A = \{A_1, \ldots, A_k\}$ is a non-empty finite set of attributes. Let $P \subseteq A$ be a subset of the attributes. Then the set of *P-indiscernible* objects is defined as the set of objects having the same set of attribute values.

$$IND_I(P) = \{(x, y),\ x, y \in U \mid \forall a \in P, x(a) = y(a)\} \tag{5.1}$$

The concept of indiscernibility is illustrated in Example 5.9.

Table 5.4. *Personnel profiles*

Name	Gender	Nationality	Complexion	Mother-tongue	Profession
Amit	M	Indian	Dark	Hindi	Lawyer
Bao	M	Chinese	Fair	Chinese	Teacher
Catherine	F	German	Fair	German	Journalist
Dipika	F	Indian	Fair	Hindi	Journalist
Lee	M	Chinese	Dark	Chinese	Lawyer

Example 5.9 *(Indiscernibility)*

Consider the profiles of a set of persons as shown Table 5.4. Let P = {*Gender*, *Complexion*, *Profession*} $\subseteq A$ = {*Gender*, *Nationality*, *Complexion*, *Mother-tongue*, *Profession*}. From the information system shown in Table 5.4 Catherine and Dipika are *P*-indiscernible as both are fair complexioned lady journalists. Similarly, Amit and Lee are also *P*-indiscernible. Hence, $IND_I(P)$ = {{Catherine, Dipika}, {Bao}, {Amit, Lee}}. On the other hand, the set of *P*-indiscernible objects with respect to *P* = {*Gender, Complexion*} happens to be $IND_I(P)$ = {{Amit, Lee}, {Bao}, {Catherine, Dipika}}.

Example 5.10 (*Indiscernibility*)

Table 5.5 presents an information system regarding various features of three types of cars, viz., Car *A*, *B* and *C*. Unlike the other tables, the attributes are arranged here in rows while the objects are along the columns.

Table 5.5. *Car features*

Features	Car A	Car B	Car C
Power Door Locks	Yes	Yes	No
Folding Rear Seats	No	Yes	No
Rear Wash Wiper	Yes	Yes	Yes
Tubeless Tyres	Yes	Yes	Yes
Remote Boot	Yes	No	Yes
Steering Adjustment	No	No	Yes
Rear Defroster	Yes	No	Yes
Seating Capacity	4	5	4
Mileage (in km/litre)	18	18	16
Max. Speed (in km/h)	160	160	180

Here, *A* = {*Power Door Locks, Folding Rear Seat, Rear Wash Wiper, Tubeless Tyres, Remote Boot, Steering Adjustment, Rear Defroster, Seating Capacity, Mileage, Max. Speed*}, *U* = {*Car A, Car B, Car C*}. Let us consider the three subsets of attributes *M* = {*Mileage, Max. Speed*}, *R* = {*Rear Wash Wiper, Remote Boot, Rear Defroster*} and *L* = {*Power Door Locks, Steering Adjustment*}. Then $IND_I(M)$ = {{*Car A, Car B*}, {*Car C*}}, $IND_I(R)$ = {{*Car A, Car C*}, {*Car B*}}, $IND_I(L)$ = {{*Car A, Car B*}, {*Car C*}}.

Indiscernibility is an equivalence relation and an indiscernibility relation partitions the set of objects in an information system into a number of equivalence classes. The set of objects *B*-indiscernible from *x* is denoted as $[x]_B$. For example, if *B* = {*Folding Rear Seats, Rear Wash Wiper, Tubeless Tyres, Remote Boot, Rear Defroster*}, then $[Car\ A]_B$ = {*Car A, Car C*}. However, if *F* = {*Power Door Locks, Steering Adjustments, Mileage, Max. Speed*}, then $[Car\ A]_F$ = {*Car A, Car B*}.

5.3 SET APPROXIMATIONS

In a decision system, the indiscernibility equivalence relation partitions the universe *U* into a number of subsets based on identical values of the outcome attribute. Such partitions are crisp and have clear boundaries demarcating the area of each subset. However, such crisp boundaries might not always be possible. For example consider the decision system presented in Table 5.6. It consists of age and activity information of eight children aged between 10 to 14 months. The outcome attribute 'Walk' has the possible values of YES or NO depending on whether the child can walk or not. A closer observation reveals that it is not possible to crisply group the pairs (Age, Can Walk) based on the outcome into YES / NO categories. The problem arises in case of entries 1 and 5 where the ages of the children are same but the outcomes differ. Therefore, it is not possible to decisively infer whether a child can walk or not on the basis of its age information only.

Table 5.6. *Child activity information*

#	Age (in months)	Can Walk
1	12	No
2	14	Yes
3	14	Yes
4	13	Yes
5	12	Yes
6	10	No
7	10	No
8	13	Yes

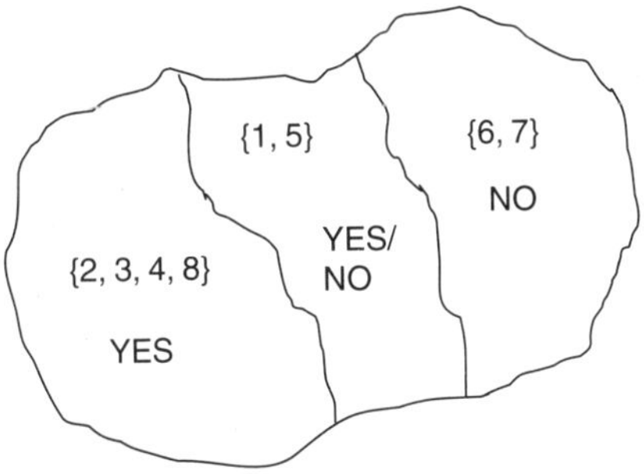

Fig. 5.1. *Roughness in a decision system*

The situation is depicted in Fig. 5.1. Objects 2, 3, 4 and 8 belong to the class that can be described by the statement 'If age is 13 or 14 months then the child *can* walk'. Similarly, objects 6 and 7 define a class corresponding to the rule 'If age is 10 months then the child *can not* walk'. However, objects 1 and 5 are on the boundary region in the sense that though both of them correspond to children of age 12 years, their 'Can Walk' information is NO in case of object 1 and YES in case of object 5. It is under such circumstances that the concept of rough sets comes into the picture and informally we may say that 'Sets which consist objects of an information system whose membership cannot be ascertained with certainty or any measure of it are called rough sets. Formally, rough sets are defined in terms of lower and upper approximations. These are described below.

Definition 5.6 (*Lower and Upper Approximations*) Let $I = (U, A)$ be an information system and $B \subseteq A$ is a subset of attributes and $X \subseteq U$ is a set of objects. Then

$$B\text{-lower approximation of } X = \underline{B}(X) = \{x \mid [x]_B \subseteq X\} \tag{5.2}$$

$$B\text{-upper approximation of } X = \overline{B}(X) = \{x \mid [x]_B \cap X \neq \emptyset\} \tag{5.3}$$

The objects that comply with the condition 5.2 and fall in $\underline{B}(X)$ are classified with certainty as members of set X, while, those objects that comply with 5.3 and therefore belong to $\overline{B}(X)$ are classified as *possible* members.

Definition 5.7 (*Boundary Region*) The set $BN_B(X) = \overline{B}(X) - \underline{B}(X)$ is called the *B-boundary region* of X. The B-boundary region of X consists of those objects which we cannot decisively classify as inside or outside the set X on the basis of the knowledge of their values of attributes in B. If a set has a non-empty boundary region, it is said to be a rough set.

Definition 5.8 (*Outside Region*) The set $U - \overline{B}X$ is called the *B-outside region* of X. The *B-outside region* of X consists of elements that are classified with certainty as not belonging to X on the basis of knowledge in B.

Example 5.11 (*Set approximations*)

With reference to the information system presented in Table 5.6, let $W = \{y \mid \textit{Can Walk}(y) = \textit{Yes}\} = \{2, 3, 4, 5, 8\}$. Now, the set of *Age*-indiscernible objects of U, $IND_{Age}(U) = \{\{1, 5\}, \{2, 3\}, \{4, 8\}, \{6, 7\}\}$. Hence the sets of the *Age*-indiscernible objects for various objects are $[1]_{Age} = [5]_{Age} = \{1, 5\}$, $[2]_{Age} = [3]_{Age} = \{2, 3\}$, $[4]_{Age} = [8]_{Age} = \{4, 8\}$, $[6]_{Age} = [7]_{Age} = \{6, 7\}$. Thus, assuming $B = \{Age\}$ we have

B-lower approximation of W: $\underline{B}W = \{2, 3, 4, 8\}$
B-upper approximation of W: $\overline{B}W = \{1, 2, 3, 4, 5, 8\}$
B-boundary region of W: $BN_B(W) = \{1, 5\}$
B-outside region of W: $U - \overline{B}W = \{6, 7\}$

As $BN_B(W) = \{1, 5\} \neq \emptyset$, W is a rough set with respect to knowledge about walking.

5.4 PROPERTIES OF ROUGH SETS

Rough sets, defined as above in terms of the lower and upper approximations, satisfy certain properties. Some of these properties are cited below. These properties are either obvious or easily provable from the definitions presented above.

1. $\underline{B}(X) \subseteq X \subseteq \overline{B}(X)$ (5.4)
2. $\underline{B}(\emptyset) = \overline{B}(\emptyset) = \emptyset$; $\underline{B}(U) = \overline{B}(U) = U$ (5.5)
3. $\overline{B}(X \cup Y) = \overline{B}(X) \cup \overline{B}(Y)$ (5.6)
4. $\underline{B}(X \cap Y) = \underline{B}(X) \cap \underline{B}(Y)$ (5.7)
5. $\underline{B}(X \cup Y) \supseteq \underline{B}(X) \cup \underline{B}(Y)$ (5.8)
6. $\overline{B}(X \cap Y) \subseteq \overline{B}(X) \cap \overline{B}(Y)$ (5.9)
7. $X \subseteq Y \Rightarrow \underline{B}(X) \subseteq \underline{B}(Y)$ and $\overline{B}(X) \subseteq \overline{B}(Y)$ (5.10)
8. $\underline{B}(U - X) = U - \overline{B}(X)$ (5.11)

9. $\overline{B}(U-X)=U-\underline{B}(X)$ (5.12)

10. $\underline{B}\underline{B}(X)=\overline{B}\underline{B}(X)=\underline{B}(X)$ (5.13)

11. $\overline{B}\overline{B}(X)=\underline{B}\overline{B}(X)=\overline{B}(X)$ (5.14)

5.5 ROUGH MEMBERSHIP

Rough sets are also described with the help of rough membership of individual elements. The membership of an object x to a rough set X with respect to knowledge in B is expressed as $\mu_X^B(x)$. Rough membership is similar, but not identical, to fuzzy membership. It is defined as

$$\mu_X^B(x)=\frac{|[x]_B \cap X|}{|[x]_B|} \quad (5.15)$$

Obviously, rough membership values lie within the range 0 to 1, like fuzzy membership values.

$$\mu_X^B : U \rightarrow [0,1]$$

The rough membership function may as well be interpreted as the conditional probability that x belongs to X given B. It is the degree to which x belongs to X in view of information about x expressed by B. The lower and upper approximations, as well as the boundary regions, can be defined in terms of rough membership function.

$$\underline{B}(X)=\{x \in U \mid \mu_X^B(x)=1\} \quad (5.16)$$

$$\overline{B}(X)=\{x \in U \mid \mu_X^B(x)>0\} \quad (5.17)$$

$$BN_B(X)=\{x \in U \mid 0<\mu_X^B(x)<1\} \quad (5.18)$$

Example 5.12 (*Rough membership*)

Let us again consider the information system presented in Table 5.6. $W = \{y \mid Can\ Walk\ (y) = Yes\} = \{2, 3, 4, 5, 8\}$ and $B = \{Age\}$. In Example 5.11 we have found $IND_{Age}(U) = \{\{1, 5\}, \{2, 3\}, \{4, 8\}, \{6, 7\}\}$, $\underline{B}W = \{2, 3, 4, 8\}$, $\overline{B}W = \{1, 2, 3, 4, 5, 8\}$, $BN_B(W) = \{1, 5\}$, and $U - \overline{B}W = \{6, 7\}$. Moreover, $[1]_{Age} = [5]_{Age} = \{1, 5\}$, $[2]_{Age} = [3]_{Age} = \{2, 3\}$, $[4]_{Age} = [8]_{Age} = \{4, 8\}$, $[6]_{Age} - [7]_{Age} - \{6, 7\}$. Now

$$\mu_W^B(1)=\frac{|[1]_B \cap W|}{|[1]_B|}=\frac{|\{1,5\} \cap \{2,3,4,5,8\}|}{|\{1,5\}|}=\frac{1}{2}$$

Similarly, $\mu_W^B(5)=\frac{1}{2}, \mu_W^B(2)=\mu_W^B(3)=\mu_W^B(4)=\mu_W^B(8)=1, \mu_W^B(6)=\mu_W^B(7)=0.$

The properties listed below are satisfied by rough membership functions. These properties either follow from the definition or are easily provable.

1. $\mu_X^B(x)=1 \ iff \ x \in \underline{B}(X)$ (5.19)

2. $\mu_X^B(x) = 0$ *iff* $x \in U - \overline{B}(X)$ (5.20)

3. $0 < \mu^B(x) < 1$ *iff* $x \in BN_B(X)$ (5.21)

4. $\mu_{U-X}^B(x) = 1 - \mu_X^B(x)$ (5.22)

5. $\mu_{X \cup Y}^B(x) \geq \max\ (\mu_X^B(x), \mu_Y^B(x))$ (5.23)

6. $\mu_{X \cap Y}^B(x) \leq \min\ (\mu_X^B(x), \mu_Y^B(x))$ (5.24)

We are now in a position to define rough sets from two different perspectives, the first using approximations and the second using membership functions. Both definitions are given below.

Definition 5.9 (*Rough Sets*) Given an information system $I = (U, A)$, $X \subseteq U$ and $B \subseteq A$, roughness of X is defined as follows.

(i) Set X is *rough* with respect to B if $\underline{B}(X) \neq \overline{B}(X)$ or $\overline{B}(X) - \underline{B}(X) \neq \phi$

(ii) Set X is *rough* with respect to B if there exist $x \in U$ such that $0 < \mu_X^B(x) < 1$.

Based on the properties of set approximations and the definition of indiscernibility, four basic classes of rough sets are defined. These are mentioned in Table 5.7.

Table 5.7. *Categories of vagueness*

#	Category	Condition
1	X is roughly B-definable	$\underline{B}(X) \neq \varnothing$ and $\overline{B}(X) \neq U$
2	X is internally B-definable	$\underline{B}(X) = \varnothing$ and $\overline{B}(X) \neq U$
3	X is externally B-definable	$\underline{B}(X) \neq \varnothing$ and $\overline{B}(X) = U$
4	X is totally B-indefinable	$\underline{B}(X) = \varnothing$ and $\overline{B}(X) = U$

We can further characterize rough sets in terms of the accuracy of approximation, defined as

$$\alpha_B(X) = \frac{\underline{B}(X)}{\overline{B}(X)} \tag{5.25}$$

It is obvious that $0 \leq \alpha_B(X) \leq 1$. If $\alpha_B(X) = 1$, the set X is *crisp* with respect to B, otherwise, if $\alpha_B(X) < 1$, then X is rough with respect to B.

Definition 5.10 (*Dependency*) Let $I = (U, A)$ be an information system and $B_1, B_2 \in A$ are sets of attributes. B_1 is said to be totally dependent on attribute B_2 if all values of attribute B_1 are uniquely determined by the values in B_2. This is denoted as $B_2 \Rightarrow B_1$.

5.6 REDUCTS

An indiscernibility relation partitions the objects of an information system into a set of equivalence classes. However, the entire set of attributes, A, may not be necessary to preserve the indiscernibility among a set of indiscernible objects. In other words, there may exist a subset $B \subseteq A$, which is sufficient to maintain the classification based on indiscernibility. A minimal set of attributes required to preserve the indiscernibility relation among the objects of an information system is called a *reduct*.

Definition 5.11 (*Reduct*) Given an information system $I = (U, A)$, a *reduct* is a minimal set of attributes $B \subseteq A$ such that $IND_I(B) = IND_I(A)$.

Definition 5.12 (*Minimal Reduct*) A Reduct with minimal cardinality is called a *minimal reduct*.

Table 5.8. *Dog breed comparison*

	1	2	3	4	5
Breed	**Rottweiler**	**Saint Bernard**	**Saluki**	**German Shepherd**	**Golden Retriever**
Weight	Heavy	Heavy	Medium	Heavy	Heavy
Grooming	Low	Medium	Low	Medium	Medium
Exercise	Heavy	Heavy	Heavy	Heavy	Heavy
Living space	Large	Average	Large	Average	Average
Training	Medium	Medium	High	High	High
Child tolerance	Low	Very High	Low	Very High	Very High
Stranger tolerance	Low	Low	Low	High	High
Recommendation	No	No	No	Yes	Yes

Example 5.13 (*Reduct*)

Let us consider the information system $I = (U, \{Weight, Grooming, Exercise, Living\ Space, Training, Child\ Tolerance, Stranger\ Tolerance\}, \{Recommendation\})$, concerning comparative study of dog breed, as shown in Table 5.8. For convenience, the attributes are arranged rowwise and the individual objects are presented columnwise.

Here $IND_I(A) = \{\{Rottweile\ r\}, \{Saint\ Bernard\}, \{Saluki\}, \{German\ Shepard, Golden\ Retriever\}\}$. The same equivalence classes are obtained if we consider only two of the attributes $B = \{Training, Child\ Tolerance\}$. However, the classification is different if we remove any of the attributes from the set $B = \{Training, Child\ Tolerance\}$. Therefore, B is a minimal set of attributes. Thus $B = \{Training, Child\ Tolerance\}$ is a reduct of the given information system. Moreover, let us consider the set $C = \{Weight, Grooming, Living\ Space\}$. We see that $IND_I(C) = IND_I(B) = IND_I(A)$, however the same set of equivalence classes is obtained for the set $C' = \{Weight, Grooming\} \subseteq C = \{Weight, Grooming, Living\ Space\}$. As C is not a minimal set of attributes to maintain the $IND_I(A)$ classification, it is not a reduct. Again, the set of attributes $D = \{Grooming, Living\ Space\}$ produces the D-indiscernible classes $IND_I(D) = \{\{Rottweiler, Saluki\}, \{Saint\ Bernard, German\ Shepard, Golden\ Retriever\}\} \neq IND_I(A)$. Hence D is not a reduct. Moreover, as there is no reduct of size less than 2 for this information system, the set $B = \{Training, Child\ Tolerance\}$ is a minimum reduct.

For practical information systems with a large number of attributes, the process of finding a minimum reduct is highly computation intensive. A method based on *discernibility* matrix is presented below.

Definition 5.13 (*Discernibility Matrix*) Given an information system $I = (U, A)$ with n objects, the *discernibility matrix D* is a symmetric $n \times n$ matrix where the $(i, j)^{th}$ element d_{ij} is given by $d_{ij} = \{a \in A \mid a(x_i) \neq a(x_j)\}$

Each entry of a discernibility matrix is one or more attributes for which the objects x_i and x_j differ.

Example 5.14 (*Discernibility Matrix*)

The discernibility matrix for the information system depicted in Table 5.8 on dog breed comparison is shown in Table 5.9. Here $d_{12} = \{G, L, C\}$, which means that object #1 and #2, i.e., the breeds Rottweiler and Saint Bernard differ in the attributes *Grooming, Living Space*, and *Child Tolerance*. They match in the rest of the attributes of the information system.

Table 5.9. *Discernibility matrix for dog breed information system*

	1	2	3	4	5
1	∅	G, L, C	W, T	G, L, T, C, S	G, L, T, C, S
2	-	∅	W, G, L, T, C	T, S	T, S
3	-	-	∅	W, G, L, C, S	W, G, L, C, S
4	-	-	-	∅	∅

Definition 5.14 (*Discernibility Function*) A *discernibility function* f_I for an information system $I = (U, A)$ is a Boolean function of n Boolean variables $a_1, a_2, \ldots, a_n$ corresponding to the n number of attributes $A_1, \ldots, A_n$ such that

$$f_I(a_1, a_2, \ldots, a_n) = \wedge\{\vee d_{ij} \mid 1 \leq i \leq n, d_{ij} \neq \Phi\} \tag{5.26}$$

where d_{ij} is the $(i, j)^{th}$ entry of the discernibility matrix.

The set of all prime implicants corresponds to the set of all reducts of I. Hence, our aim is to find the prime implicants of f_I.

Example 5.15 (*Discernibility Function*)

The discernibility function for the discernibility matrix shown in Table 5.9 is given by

$f_1(B, W, G, E, L, T, C, S)$

$$\begin{aligned}
&= (G \vee L \vee C) \wedge (W \vee T) \wedge (G \vee L \vee T \vee C \vee S) \wedge \\
&\quad (G \vee L \vee T \vee C \vee S) \wedge (W \vee G \vee L \vee T \vee C) \wedge \\
&\quad (T \vee S) \wedge (T \vee S) \wedge (W \vee G \vee L \vee C \vee S) \wedge \\
&\quad (W \vee G \vee L \vee C \vee S) \\
&= (G \vee L \vee C) \wedge (W \vee T) \wedge (G \vee L \vee T \vee C \vee S) \wedge \\
&\quad (W \vee G \vee L \vee T \vee C) \wedge (T \vee S) \wedge (W \vee G \vee L \vee C \vee S) \\
&= (G \vee L \vee C) \wedge (W \vee T) \wedge (T \vee S)
\end{aligned}$$

$$= (G \wedge W \wedge T) \vee (G \wedge W \wedge S) \vee (G \wedge T) \vee (G \wedge T \wedge S) \vee$$
$$(L \wedge W \wedge T) \vee (L \wedge W \wedge S) \vee (L \wedge T) \vee (L \wedge T \wedge S) \vee$$
$$(C \wedge W \wedge T) \vee (C \wedge W \wedge S) \vee (C \wedge T) \vee (C \wedge T \wedge S)$$
$$= (G \wedge W \wedge S) \vee (G \wedge T) \vee (L \wedge W \wedge S) \vee (L \wedge T) \vee (C \wedge W \wedge S) \vee (C \wedge T)$$
$$= (G \wedge W \wedge S) \vee (L \wedge W \wedge S) \vee (C \wedge W \wedge S) \vee (G \wedge T) \vee (L \wedge T) \vee (C \wedge T)$$

The prime implecants are $(G \wedge W \wedge S)$, $(L \wedge W \wedge S)$, $(C \wedge W \wedge S)$, $(G \wedge T)$, $(L \wedge T)$, and $(C \wedge T)$. Each of the sets $\{G, W, S\}$, $\{L, W, S\}$, $\{C, W, S\}$, $\{G, T\}$, $\{L, T\}$, and $\{C, T\}$ is a minimal set of attributes that preserves the classification $IND_I(A)$. Hence each of them is a reduct. Moreover, each of the sets $\{G, T\}$, $\{L, T\}$, and $\{C, T\}$ is a minimal reduct because they are of size 2, and there is no reduct of size smaller than 2 for the present information system.

5.7 APPLICATION

The theory of rough sets is fast emerging as an intelligent tool to tackle vagueness in various application areas. It provides an effective granular approach for handling uncertainties through set approximations. Several software systems have been developed to implement rough set operations and apply them to solve practical problems. Rough set theory is successfully employed in image segmentation, classification of data and data mining in the fields of medicine, telecommunication, and conflict analysis to name a few.

Example 5.16 illustrates the process of rule generation from a given information system / decision system. Subsequently, Example 5.17 presents a case study to show how the concepts of rough set theory can be used for the purpose of data clustering.

Table 5.10. *Decision system relating to scholarship information*

#	Degree	CGPA	Backlog	Recommendation	Decision
1	B.Tech.	Average	No	High	Granted
2	B.Tech.	Fresher	No	None	Not Granted
3	BS	Low	No	Moderate	Not Granted
4	MS	High	No	None	Granted
5	MS	Average	No	None	Not Granted
6	MS	High	No	High	Granted
7	B.Tech.	High	Yes	Moderate	Granted
8	BS	Low	Yes	High	Not Granted

Example 5.16 (*Rule generation*)

Let us consider a decision system $D = (U, \{Degree, CGPA, Backlog, Recommendation\}, \{Decision\})$ concerning scholarship granting information at an educational institution, as shown in Table 5.10. Table 5.11 presents the corresponding discernibility matrix.

Table 5.11. *Discernibility matrix for information system of Table 5.10*

	2	3	4	5	6	7	8
1	C, R	D, C, R	D, C, R	D, R	D, C	C, B, R	D, C, B
2	Ø	D, C, R	D, C	D, C	D, C, R	C, B, R	D, C, B, R
3	-	Ø	D, C, R	D, C, R	D, C, R	D, C, B	B, R
4	-	-	Ø	C	R	D, B, R	D, C, B, R
5	-	-	-	Ø	C, R	D, C, B, R	D, C, B, R
6	-	-	-	-	Ø	D, B, R	D, C, B
7	-	-	-	-	-	Ø	D, C, R

The discernibility function obtained from the discernibility table is as follows (using '+' for the logical operator ∨ and '·' for ∧).

$f_I(D, C, B, R) =$

$$[(C+R)(D+C+R)(D+C+R)(D+R)(D+C)(C+B+R)(D+C+B)]$$
$$[(D+C+R)(D+C)(D+C)(D+C+R)(C+B+R)(D+C+B+R)]\cdot$$
$$[(D+C+R)(D+C+R)(D+C+R)(D+C+B)(B+R)]\cdot$$
$$[(C)(R)(D+B+R)(D+C+B+R)]\cdot$$
$$[(C+R)(D+C+B+R)(D+C+B+R)]\cdot$$
$$[(D+B+R)(D+C+B)]$$
$$[(D+C+R)] = (C)\cdot(R)$$

Hence the system has a unique minimum reduct {*CGPA*, *Recommendation*}. The sample space after attribute reduction is shown in Table 5.12. The rules extracted using the minimal reduct obtained above are given in Table 5.13.

Table 5.12. *Sample space after attribute reduction*

#	CGPA	Departmental Recommendation	Decision
1	Average	High	Granted
2	Fresher	None	Not Granted
3	Low	Moderate	Not Granted
4	High	None	Granted
5	Average	None	Not Granted
6	High	High	Granted
7	High	Moderate	Granted
8	Low	High	Not Granted

Table 5.13. *Extracted rules*

Rule #		Antecedent		Consequent
1	**IF**	(CGPA = Average) and (Recommendation = High)	**THEN**	Decision = Granted
2	**IF**	(CGPA = Low) and {(Recommendation = Moderate) Or (Recommendation = High)}	**THEN**	Decision = Not Granted
3	**IF**	(CGPA = High) and {(Recommendation = None) Or (Recommendation = Moderate) Or (Recommendation = High)}	**THEN**	Decision = Granted
4	**IF**	(CGPA = Average) and (Recommendation = None)	**THEN**	Decision = Not Granted
5	**IF**	(CGPA = Fresher) and (Recommendation = None)	**THEN**	Decision = Not Granted

Example 5.17 *(Data Clustering)*

In this example, we consider an animal world dataset based on an example cited by T. Herawan, *et. al.* in the paper entitled '*Rough Set Approach for Categorical Data Clustering*,' in International Journal of Database Theory and Application, Vol. 3, No.1. March 2010. We illustrate the process of data clustering using the concepts of rough set theory.

Table 5.14. *Animal world dataset*

#	Animal	Hair	Teeth	Eye	Feather	Feet	Eat	Milk	Fly	Swim
1	Lion	Yes	Pointed	Forward	No	Claw	Meat	Yes	No	Yes
2	Dolphin	No	No	Sideway	No	No	Fish	No	No	Yes
3	Cow	Yes	Blunt	Sideway	No	Hoof	Grass	Yes	No	No
4	Tiger	Yes	Pointed	Forward	No	Claw	Meat	Yes	No	Yes
5	Cheetah	Yes	Pointed	Forward	No	Claw	Meat	Yes	No	Yes
6	Giraffe	Yes	Blunt	Sideway	No	Hoof	Grass	Yes	No	No
7	Zebra	Yes	Blunt	Sideway	No	Hoof	Grass	Yes	No	No
8	Ostrich	No	No	Sideway	Yes	Claw	Grain	No	No	No
9	Penguin	No	No	Sideway	Yes	Web	Fish	No	No	Yes
10	Albatross	No	No	Sideway	Yes	Claw	Grain	No	Yes	Yes
11	Eagle	No	No	Forward	Yes	Claw	Meat	No	Yes	No
12	Viper	No	Pointed	Forward	No	No	Meat	No	No	No

Table 5.14 presents data related to twelve animals, *viz.*, Lion, Dolphin, Cow, Tiger, Cheetah, Giraffe, Zebra, Ostrich, Penguin, Albatross, Eagle, and Viper. The attributes are *Hair* (whether the animal has hair or not), *Teeth*, *Eye* (whether the eyes are directed forward or sideways), *Feather*, *Feet* (the options are clawed, hoofed, webbed, or no feet), *Eat* (*i.e*, eating habit, options are meat, grass, fish, grain), *Milk*, *Fly*, and *Swim*. The sets of attribute values are, V_{Hair} = {Yes, No}, V_{Teeth} = {Pointed, Blunt, No}, V_{Eye} = {Forward, Sideway}, $V_{Feather}$ = {Yes, No}, V_{Feet} = {Claw, Hoof, Web, No}, V_{Eat} = {Meat, Grass, Grain, Fish}, V_{Milk} = {Yes, No}, V_{Fly} = {Yes, No}, V_{Swim} = {Yes, No}.

The partitions using singleton attributes are as given below.

1. X (Hair = yes) = {1, 3, 4, 5, 6, 7}, X (Hair = no) = {2, 8, 9, 10, 11, 12}.
   $\therefore IND_I$ (Hair) = {{1, 3, 4, 5, 6, 7}, {2, 8, 9, 10, 11, 12}}.
2. X (Teeth = pointed) = {1, 4, 5, 12}, X (Teeth = Blunt) = {3, 6, 7}, X (Teeth = no) = {2, 8, 9, 10, 11}.
   $\therefore IND_I$ (Teeth) = {{1, 4, 5, 12}, {3, 6, 7}, {2, 8, 9, 10, 11}}.
3. X (Eye = Forward) = {1, 4, 5, 11, 12}, X (Eye = Sideway) = {2, 3, 6, 7, 8, 9, 10}.
   $\therefore IND_I$ (Eye) = {{1, 4, 5, 11, 12}, {2, 3, 6, 7, 8, 9, 10}}.
4. X (Feather = yes) = {8, 9, 10, 11}, X (Feather = no) = {1, 2, 3, 4, 5, 6, 7, 12}.
   $\therefore IND_I$ (Feather) = {{8, 9, 10, 11}, {1, 2, 3, 4, 5, 6, 7, 12}}.
5. X (Feet = claw) = {1, 4, 5, 8, 10, 11}, X (Feet = hoof) = {3, 6, 7}, X (Feet = Web) = {9}, X (Feet = No) = {2, 12}.
   $\therefore IND_I$ (Feet) = {{1, 4, 5, 8, 10, 11}, {3, 6, 7}, {9}, {2, 12}}.
6. X (Eat = Meat) = {1, 4, 5, 11, 12}, X (Eat = Grass) = {3, 6, 7}, X (Eat = Grain) = {8, 10}, X (Eat = Fish) = {2, 9}.
   $\therefore IND_I$ (Eat) = {{1, 4, 5, 11, 12}, {3, 6, 7}, {8, 10}, {2, 9}}.
7. X (Milk = Yes) = {1, 3, 4, 5, 6, 7}, X (Milk = No) = {2, 8, 9, 10, 11, 12}.
   $\therefore IND_I$ (Milk) = {{1, 3, 4, 5, 6, 7}, {2, 8, 9, 10, 11, 12}}.
8. X (Fly = Yes) = {10, 11}, X (Fly = no) = {1, 2, 3, 4, 5, 6, 7, 8, 9, 12}.
   $\therefore IND_I$ (Fly) = {{10, 11}, {1, 2, 3, 4, 5, 6, 7, 8, 9, 12}}.
9. X (Swim = Yes) = {1, 2, 4, 5, 9, 10}, X (Swim = No) = {3, 6, 7, ,8, 11, 12}.
   $\therefore IND_I$ (Swim) = {{1, 2, 4, 5, 9, 10}, {3, 6, 7, 8, 11, 12}}.

Now, let us focus on the dependency between the attributes *Teeth* and *Hair*. We already have IND_I (Teeth) = {{1, 4, 5, 12}, {3, 6, 7}, {2, 8, 9, 10, 11}} and IND_I (Hair) = {{1, 3, 4, 5, 6, 7}, {2, 8, 9, 10, 11, 12}}. Since {3, 6, 7} ⊆ {1, 3, 4, 5, 6, 7} and {2, 8, 9, 10, 11} ⊆ {2, 8, 9, 10, 11, 12}, but {1, 4, 5, 12} ⊄ {1, 3, 4, 5, 6, 7} and {1, 4, 5, 12} ⊄ {2, 8, 9, 10, 11, 12}, the attribute dependency of Hair on Teeth is computed as follows

$$\frac{|\{3,6,7\}|+|\{2,8,9,10,11\}|}{|U|}=\frac{3+5}{12}=\frac{2}{3}\text{, hence } Teeth \Rightarrow_{2/3} Hair$$

This implies that the attribute *Hair* is partially dependent on the attribute *Teeth*. The other attribute dependencies for *Hair* are found similarly.

$$Eye \Rightarrow_0 Hair, \text{ because } k=\frac{|\Phi|}{|U|}=0.$$

$$Feather \Rightarrow_{1/3} Hair, \text{ because } k=\frac{|\{8,9,10,11\}|}{|U|}=\frac{4}{12}=\frac{1}{3}.$$

$$Feet \Rightarrow_{1/2} Hair, \text{ because } k=\frac{|\{3,6,7\}|+|\{9\}|+|\{2,12\}|}{|U|}=\frac{6}{12}=\frac{1}{2}.$$

$$Eat \Rightarrow_{7/12} Hair, \text{ because } k=\frac{|\{3,6,7\}|+|\{8,10\}|+|\{2,9\}|}{|U|}=\frac{7}{12}.$$

$$Milk \Rightarrow_1 Hair,\ because\ k = \frac{|\{1,3,4,5,6,7\}| + |\{2,8,9,10,11,12\}|}{|U|} = \frac{12}{12} = 1.$$

$$Fly \Rightarrow_{1/6} Hair,\ because\ k = \frac{|\{10,11\}|}{|U|} = \frac{2}{12} = \frac{1}{6}.$$

$$Swim \Rightarrow_0 Hair,\ because\ k = \frac{|\Phi|}{|U|} = 0.$$

It is found from these calculations that there is complete dependency between the attributes *Milk* and *Hair*. Therefore the animal world depicted in the information system Table 5.14 can be partitioned into two clusters on the basis of these two attributes. The resultant clusters are shown in Fig. 5.2.

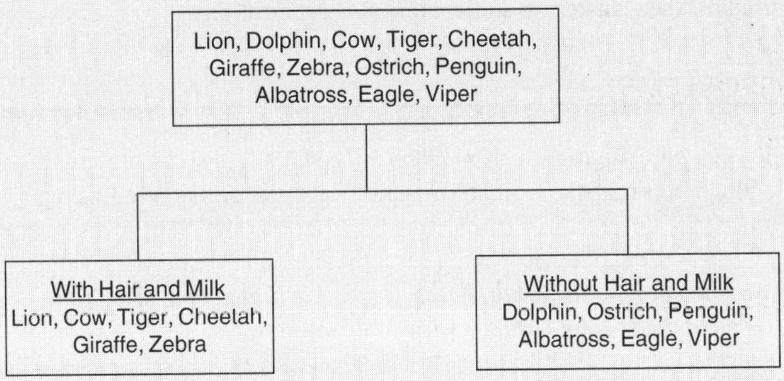

Fig. 5.2. *Clusters in the animal world*

CHAPTER SUMMARY

The main points of the topics discussed in this chapter are summarized below.

- Theory of **rough sets** provides a formalism to tackle *vagueness* in real life relating to information systems.
- An **information system** is a set of data presented in structured, tabular form. It consists of a universe of **objects** and a number of **attributes**. Each object is an ordered *n*-tuple. The ith element of an object is a possible value of the ith attribute.
- A **decision system** is an information system with a special attribute called the *decision attribute*.
- Two objects of an information system are said to be ***P*-indiscernible**, where *P* is a set of attributes of the system, if they have the same set of values of the attributes of *P*. The *P*-indiscernibility is an equivalence relation.
- Given an information system $I = (U, A)$, a set of objects $X \subseteq U$ and a set of attributes $B \subseteq A$, roughness, or otherwise, of *X* with respect to knowledge in *B* is defined in terms of the sets ***B*-lower approximation** of *X* and ***B*-upper approximation** of *X*. The *B*-lower approximation of *X* is the set of objects that are *certainly* in *X*. On the other hand, the set of objects that are *possibly* in *X* constitute the *B*-upper approximation of *X*. The set *X* is said to be rough with respect to our knowledge in *B* if the difference between the *B*-upper approximation of *X* and *B*-lower approximation of *X* is non-empty.

- The membership of an object x to a rough set X with respect to knowledge in B is expressed as $\mu_X^B(x)$ where $\mu_X^B(x) = \frac{|[x]_B \cap X|}{|[x]_B|}$. Like fuzzy membership, rough membership values lie within the range 0 to 1.
- A minimal set of attributes that preserves the indiscernibility relation among the objects of an information system is called a **reduct**. A **minimal reduct** is a reduct with minimal size among all reducts.
- A **discernibility matrix** contains information about pairs of discernibile objects and the attributes in which they differ. A **discernibility function** presents the same information as a Boolean function in the form of conjunction of disjunctions. The discernibility matrix and the discernibility function are used to find the reducts as well as the minimal reducts of an information system.
- The theory of rough set is applied to extract hidden rules underlying an information system. It is also used for data clustering and data mining applications.

SOLVED PROBLEMS

Problem 5.1 (*Set approximations and rough membership*) Table 5.14 presents a decision system for a number of individuals seeking loan from a bank and the bank's decision in this regard. The conditional attributes are *Gender, Age, Income, Car* (indicating whether the applicant owns a car or not), *Defaulter* (whether the applicant is a defaulter in paying off a previous loan) and their valid attribute values are {*Male, Female*}, {*Middle-aged, Young-adult, Aged*}, {*High, Medium, Low*}, {*Yes, No*}, and {*Yes, No*} respectively. The decision attribute is *Loan Granted* with value set {*Yes, No*}.

Let $B = \{Age, Income, Car\} \subset A = \{Gender, Age, Income, Car, Defaulter\}$ be a set of attributes. Then

(i) Compute $IND_B(I)$

(ii) If $X = \{x \in U \mid Loan\ Granted\ (x) = Yes\}$ then compute B-lower and B-upper approximations of X and determine if X is rough in terms of knowledge in B.

(iii) Calculate $\mu_X^B(x)$ for each $x \in U$.

Table 5.14. *Loan applicants' data set*

#	Name	Gender (G)	Age (A)	Income (*I*)	Car (*C*)	Defaulter (*D*)	Loan Granted
1	Tony	M	Middle-aged	High	Yes	Yes	No
2	Vinod	M	Middle-aged	High	No	No	Yes
3	Sheela	F	Young-adult	High	Yes	No	Yes
4	Kete	F	Aged	Low	No	No	No
5	Nina	F	Middle-aged	Middle	Yes	No	Yes
6	Sandip	M	Aged	High	No	No	No
7	Mita	F	Young-adult	High	No	No	Yes
8	Bob	M	Young-adult	High	Yes	Yes	No

#	Name	Gender (G)	Age (A)	Income (I)	Car (C)	Defaulter (D)	Loan Granted
9	Bill	M	Middle-aged	Middle	No	No	Yes
10	Martha	F	Middle-aged	Middle	No	No	Yes
11	Bruce	M	Middle-aged	High	Yes	No	Yes
12	Gogo	M	Aged	Low	No	No	No

Solution 5.1 The computations are shown below.

(i) $IND_B(I) = \{\{1, 11\}, \{2\}, \{3, 8\}, \{4, 12\}, \{5\}, \{6\}, \{7\}, \{9, 10\}\}$

(ii) $X = \{x \in U \mid Loan\ Granted\ (x) = Yes\} = \{2, 3, 5, 7, 9, 10, 11\}$

$\underline{B}(X) = \{2, 5, 7, 9, 10\}$, $\overline{B}(X) = \{1, 2, 3, 5, 7, 8, 9, 10, 11\}$ and $BN_B(X) = \{1, 8\} \neq \phi$.

$\therefore$ X is rough with respect to knowledge of the attributes {*Age*, *Income*, *Car*} (Fig. 5.3).

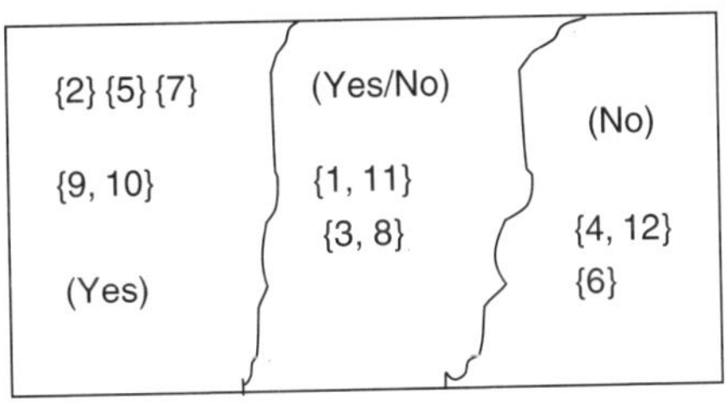

Fig. 5.3 *Set approximations*

(iii) Computations of the rough membership values for individual elements are shown below.

$$\mu_X^B(1) = \mu_X^B(11) = \frac{|\{1,11\} \cap \{2,3,5,7,9,10,11\}|}{|\{1,11\}|} = \frac{1}{2}$$

Similarly,

$$\mu_X^B(3) = \mu_X^B(8) = \frac{|\{3,8\} \cap \{2,3,5,7,9,10,11\}|}{|\{3,8\}|} = \frac{1}{2}$$

$$\mu_X^B(2) = \mu_X^B(5) = \mu_X^B(7) = \mu_X^B(9) = \mu_X^B(10) = 1, \text{ and}$$

$$\mu_X^B(4) = \mu_X^B(6) = \mu_X^B(12) = 0.$$

Problem 5.2 (*Minimum reduct*) We know that the discernibility matrix is constructed to find the reducts of an information system, and thereby the minimal reduct. Each cell of a discernibility matrix correspond to a pair of objects. It contains the attributes in which the pair of objects differ. The discernibility function is a conjunction of terms where each term is constituted from the entries of the discernibility matrix. A term is a disjunction of attributes in a cell of the discernibility matrix.

Propose a technique to simplify the discernibility matrix, or discernibility function, so that the set of reducts and thereby the minimal reducts of the system could be found efficiently. Apply this technique to the information system depicted in Table 5.14 and find it's minimal reduct.

Solution 5.2 The discernibility function is a conjunction of disjunctions. This function can be simplified by repeated application of the boolean identy

$$A \cdot (A + B) = A \tag{5.27}$$

The technique consists of identifying a pair of non-empty cells, say α and β such that all attributes in α are contained in β. We can ignore the set of attributes in β on the basis of the identity 5.27. This way the 'dependent' cells are eliminated resulting in a reduced discernibility matrix. The discernibility function is constructed from the reduced matrix and is transformed to a disjunction of conjunction, i.e., sum of products, form. The entire procedure is presented in **Procedure** *Find-Min-Reduct* (*U*, *A*), shown as Fig. 5.4.

Execution of **Procedure** *Find-Min-Reduct* (*U*, *A*) for the given information system is described below.

Procedure *Find-Min-Reduct* (*U*, *A*)

/* Given an information system $I = (U, A)$ where U is a non-empty set of objects and A is a non-empty set of attributes, to find the set of reducts of I, and thereby the minimal reducts of I. */

0. **Begin**
1. Construct the discernibility matrix D of I. Let $c_1, c_2, \ldots, c_r$ be the sets of attributes corresponding to the non-empty cells of D.
2. Arrange $c_1, c_2, \ldots, c_r$ in non-decreasing order of their sizes. Let $C_1, C_2, \ldots, C_r$ be the rearranged sets of attributes such that
$$|C_1| \le |C_2| \le \ldots \le |C_r|$$
3. Let $T = \{\}$ and $S = \{C_1, C_2, \ldots, C_r\}$
4. **Repeat** Steps 5, 6, 7 and 8 **While** $S \neq \phi$
5. Let c be a minimal member of S, i.e., $|c| \le |C_i|\ \forall C_i \in S$
6. $T = T \cup \{c\}$
7. $\forall C_i \in S$, **If** $c \subseteq C_i$, **Then** remove C_i from S, $S = S - \{C_i\}$
8. Let $t_1, t_2, \ldots, t_k$ be the members of T constructed through Steps 4-7 above. For each $t_i \in T$ form a Boolean clause T_i as the disjunction of the attributes in t_i. Construct the discernibility function f_D as the conjunction of all T_i's.
9. Simplify f_D to sum-of-products form. Each product term corresponds to a reduct of the information system I. Any one of the product terms with minimal cardinality is a minimal reduct of I.
10. **END-*Find-Min-Reduct***

Fig. 5.4 *Procedure Find-Min-Reduct (U, A)*

Step 1. Construct the discernibility matrix D of I. Let $c_1, c_2, \ldots, c_r$ be the sets of attributes corresponding to the non-empty cells of D.

We construct the discernibility matrix for the given information system as shown in Table 5.15. The sets of attributes are {*C*, *D*}, {*G*, *A*, *D*}, {*G*, *A*, *I*, *C*, *D*}, {*G*, *I*, *D*}, …, {*A*, *I*, *C*}. There are 66 such sets altogether.

Step 2. Arrange $c_1, c_2, \ldots, c_r$ in non-decreasing order of their sizes. Let $C_1, C_2, \ldots, C_r$ be the rearranged sets of attributes such that $|C_1| \le |C_2| \le \ldots \le |C_r|$.
The arrangement is : {*A*}, {*D*}, {*A*}, {*I*}, {*C*}, {*C*}, {*G*}, {*C*}, {*I*}, {*G*}, {*C, D*}, {*G, A*}, …, {*G, A, I, C, D*}.

Table 5.15. *Discernibility matrix*

	2	3	4	5	6	7	8	9	10	11	12
1	C,D	G,A,D	G,A,I,C,D	G,I,D	A,C,D	G,A,C,D	A	I,C,D	G,I,C,D	D	A,I,C,D
2		G,A,C	G,A,I	G,I,C	A	G,A	A,C,D	I	G,I	C	A,I
3			A,I,C	A,I	G,A,C	C	G,D	G,A,I,C	A,I,C	G,A	G,A,I,C
4				A,I,C	G,I	A,I	G,A,I,C,D	G,A,I	A,I	G,A,I,C	G
5					G,A,I,C	A,I,C	G,A,I,D	G,C	C	G,I	G,A,I,C
6						G,A	A,C,D	A,C	G,A,I	A,C	I
7							G,C,D	G,A,I	A,I	G,A,C	G,A,I
8								A,I,C,D	G,A,I,C,D	A,D	A,I,C,D
9									G	I,C	A,I
10										G,I,C	G,A,I
11											A,I,C

Step 3-7. Let $T = \{\}$ and $S = \{C_1, C_2, \ldots, C_r\}$

Repeat **While** $S \neq \phi$

Let c be a minimal member of S, i.e., $|c| \le |C_i|\ \forall\ C_i \in S$

$T = T \cup \{c\}$

$\forall C_i \in S$, **If** $c \subseteq C_i$, **Then** remove C_i from S, $S = S - \{C_i\}$

All sets of attributes except {*A*}, {*D*}, {*I*}, {*C*}, {*G*} are removed in the process described above. Hence, *T* = {{*A*}, {*D*}, {*I*}, {*C*}, {*G*}}.

Step 8. Let $t_1, t_2, \ldots, t_k$ be the members of T constructed through Steps 3-7 above. For each $t_i \in T$ form a Boolean clause T_i as the disjunction of the attributes in t_i. Construct the discernibility function f_D as the conjunction of all T_i's.

Here the discernibility function is $f_I(G, A, I, C, D) = G \wedge A \wedge I \wedge C \wedge D$.

Step 9. Simplify f_D to sum-of-products form. Each product term corresponds to a reduct of the information system I. Any one of the product terms with minimal cardinality is a minimal reduct of I.

In the present case the discernibility function $f_I(G, A, I, C, D) = G \wedge A \wedge I \wedge C \wedge D$ contains a single product term and is already in simplified form. Therefore, the minimum reduct for the given information system is unique and consists of all the attributes *A* = {*Gender, Age, Income, Car, Defaulter*}.

Problem 5.3 (*Minimum reduct*) Table 5.16 presents data related to the shopping habits of a number of customers to a shopping mall. Four kinds of items, viz., *Food* (*F*), *Garment* (*GM*), *Cosmetics* (*C*), and *Toys* (*T*) are considered. If a customer buys a certain kind of item, the corresponding entry in the table is *Yes*, otherwise *No*. The attribute *Amount* (*A*) express the amount paid by the customer which is either *High*, or *Medium*, or *Low*. There are two *modes of payment* (*P*), *Cash* and *Credit Card* (*CC*). Find the reducts of the information system presented in Table 5.16 as well as the minimal reducts from the set of reducts obtained. Also, extract the rules on the basis of one of the minimal reducts and assuming *P* to be the decision attribute.

Table 5.16. *Shopping habit data set*

#	Customer Name	Gender (GD)	Food (F)	Garment (GM)	Cosmetics (C)	Toys (T)	Amount (A)	Payment Mode (P)
1	Mili	F	Yes	Yes	Yes	Yes	High	CC
2	Bill	M	Yes	No	No	No	Low	Cash
3	Rita	F	Yes	Yes	Yes	Yes	High	CC
4	Pam	F	Yes	Yes	Yes	Yes	High	CC
5	Maya	F	No	No	Yes	No	Medium	Cash
6	Bob	M	Yes	No	No	No	Medium	CC
7	Tony	M	Yes	No	No	No	Low	Cash
8	Gaga	F	Yes	Yes	Yes	Yes	High	CC
9	Sam	M	Yes	No	No	No	Low	Cash
10	Abu	M	Yes	No	No	No	Low	Cash

Solution 5.3 The step-by-step process for finding the reducts and the minimal reducts is given below.

Step 1. Construct the discernibility matrix D of I. Let c_1, c_2, …, c_r be the sets of attributes corresponding to the non-empty cells of D.

The discernibility matrix constructed is shown in Table 5.17. The blank cells indicate the indiscernible pairs of objects. For example, cell (1, 3) is blank, as the objects 1 and 3 are indescernible. Similarly, null entries at cells (1, 4) and (1, 8) indicate indiscernibility of the objects 1, 4, and 8. As indiscernibility is an equivalence relation, we find that the set {1, 3, 4, 8} forms a class of indiscernible objects. Table 5.17 reveals that indiscernible classes are {1, 3, 4, 8}, {2, 7, 9, 10}, {5}, and {6}. In order to further simplify the process of finding the reducts of the given information system, we reduce the discernibility matrix by taking one object from each of the equivalence classes. The reduced discernibility matrix is shown in Table 5.18. The objects 1, 2, 5 and 6 are considered as representatives of the classes {1, 3, 4, 8}, {2, 7, 9, 10}, {5}, and {6} respectively.

Step 2. Arrange c_1, c_2, …, c_r in non-decreasing order of their sizes. Let C_1, C_2, …, C_r be the rearranged sets of attributes such that $|C_1| \leq |C_2| \leq \ldots \leq |C_r|$.

The arrangement is : {*A*, *P*}, {*GD*, *F*, *C*, *A*}, {*GD*, *F*, *C*, *P*}, {*F*, *GM*, *T*, *A*, *P*}, {*GD*, *GM*, *C*, *T*, *A*}, {*GD*, *GM*, *C*, *T*, *A*, *P*}.

Table 5.17. *Discernibility matrix for shopping habit data set*

	2	3	4	5	6	7	8	9	10
1	GD,GM, C,T,A,PM			F,GM,T, A,PM	GD,GM, C,T,A	GD,GM, C,T,A,P		GD,GM, C,T,A,P	GD,GM,C,T,A,P
2		GD,GM, C,T,A,P	GD,GM, C,T,A,P	GD,F, C,A	A,P		GD,GM, C,T,A,P		
3				F,GM,T, A,PM	GD,GM, C,T,A,P	GD,GM, C,T,A,P		GD,GM, C,T,A,P	GD,GM,C,T,A,P
4				F,GM,T, A,P	GD,GM, C,T,A	GD,GM, C,T,A,P		GD,GM, C,T,A,P	GD,GM,C,T,A,P
5					GD,F,C, P	GD,F,C,A	F,GM,T, A,P	F,GM,T, A,P	F,GM,T, A,P
6						A,P	GD,GM, C,T,A	A,P	A,P
7							GD,GM, C,T,A,P		
8								GD,GM, C,T,A,P	GD,GM,C,T,A,P
9									

Table 5.18. *The reduced discernibility matrix*

	2	5	6
1	GD, GM, C, T, A, P	F, GM, T, A, P	GD, GM, C, T, A
2		GD, F, C, A	A, P
5			GD, F, C, P

Step 3-7. Let $T = \{\}$ and $S = \{C_1, C_2, \ldots, C_r\}$

Repeat **While** $S \neq \phi$

Let c be a minimal member of S, i.e., $|c| \leq |C_i| \; \forall C_i \in S$

$T = T \cup \{c\}$

$\forall C_i \in S$, **If** $c \subseteq C_i$, **Then** remove C_i from S, $S = S - \{C_i\}$

We find $T = \{\{A, P\}, \{GD, F, C, A\}, \{GD, F, C, P\}, \{GD, GM, C, T, A\}\}$.

Step 8. Let t_1, t_2, ..., t_k be the members of T constructed through Steps 3-7 above. For each $t_i \in T$ form a Boolean clause T_i as the disjunction of the attributes in t_i. Construct the discernibility function f_D as the conjunction of all T_i's.

The discernibility function is $f_I(GD, F, GM, C, T, A, P) = (A + P)\cdot(GD + F + C + A)\cdot(GD + F + C + P)\cdot(GD + GM + C + T + A)$

Step 9. Simplify f_D to sum-of-products form. Each product term corresponds to a reduct of the information system I. Any one of the product terms with minimal cardinality is a minimal reduct of I.

After further simplification the discernibility function in sum-of-products form is given by

$$f_I(GD, F, GM, C, T, A, P)$$
$$= GD\cdot P + A\cdot GD + A\cdot P + A\cdot F + A\cdot C + C\cdot P + F\cdot T\cdot P + F\cdot GM\cdot P$$
$$= A\cdot(C + F + P + GD) + P\cdot(GD + C + F\cdot T + F\cdot GM)$$

Therefore, the given information system has eight reducts $\{GD, P\}$, $\{A, GD\}$, $\{A, P\}$, $\{A, F\}$, $\{A, C\}$, $\{C, P\}$, $\{F, T, P\}$and $\{F, GM, P\}$. Each of the reducts $\{GD, P\}$, $\{A, GD\}$, $\{A, P\}$, $\{A, F\}$, $\{A, C\}$ and $\{C, P\}$ is a minimal reduct.

Rules extracted On the basis of the reduct $\{A, C\}$ and taking P as the decision attribute we get the following rules as shown in Table 5.19.

Table 5.19. *Extracted rules*

R #		Antecedent		Consequent
1	IF	(Cosmetics = Yes) and (Amount = High)	THEN	Payment Mode = Credit Card
2	IF	(Cosmetics = No) and (Amount = Low)	THEN	Payment Mode = Cash
3	IF	(Cosmetics = Yes) and (Amount = Medium)	THEN	Payment Mode = Cash
4	IF	(Cosmetics = No) and (Amount = Medium)	THEN	Payment Mode = Credit Card

✓ TEST YOUR KNOWLEDGE

5.1 Which of the following is not a part of an information system?
a) A non-empty set of objects
b) A non-empty set of attributes
c) Both (*a*) and (*b*)
d) None of the above

5.2 Which of the following contains a decision attribute?
a) An information system
b) A decision system
c) Both (*a*) and (*b*)
d) None of the above

5.3 Two objects of a decision system are said to be indiscernible if
a) They have the same decision attribute value
b) They have the same conditional attributes value
c) Both (*a*) and (*b*)
d) None of these

5.4 The indiscernibility relation over a given information system is
a) Reflexive
b) Symmetric
c) Transitive
d) All of the above

5.5 Let $I = (U, A)$ be an information system and $P \subset Q \subset A$ and $x, y \in U$ be objects of I. Then which of the following statements is true?
a) If x and y are P-indiscernible then they are Q-indiscernible
b) If x and y are Q-indiscernible then they are P-indiscernible
c) The P and Q-indiscernibility of x and y are unrelated
d) None of these

5.6 Let $I = (U, A)$ be an information system and $B \subset A$ and $X \subset U$. Then which of the following relations holds good for a rough set?
a) $\underline{B}(X) \subseteq \overline{B}(X)$
b) $\underline{B}(X) \supseteq \overline{B}(X)$
c) $\underline{B}(X) = \overline{B}(X)$
d) None of the above

5.7 Let $I = (U, A)$ be an information system and $B \subset A$ and $X \subset U$. Then which of the following is defined as the B-boundary region of X?
a) $\underline{B}(X) - \overline{B}(X)$
b) $\overline{B}(X) - \underline{B}(X)$
c) $\underline{B}(X) \cup \overline{B}(X)$
d) $\underline{B}(X) \cap \overline{B}(X)$

5.8 Let $I = (U, A)$ be an information system and $B \subset A$ and $X \subset U$. Then which of the following is defined as the B-outside region of X?
a) $U - \underline{B}(X)$
b) $U - \overline{B}(X)$
c) $\overline{B}(X) - \underline{B}(X)$
d) None of the above

5.9 Let $I = (U, A)$ be an information system and $B \subset A$ and $X \subset U$. Then which of the following relations is not valid?
a) $\underline{B}(X \cap Y) = \underline{B}(X) \cap \underline{B}(Y)$
b) $\underline{B}(X \cup Y) \supseteq \underline{B}(X) \cup \underline{B}(Y)$
c) Both (a) and (b)
d) None of the above

5.10 Let $I = (U, A)$ be an information system and $B \subset A$ and $X \subset U$. Then which of the following relations is not valid?
a) $\overline{B}(X \cup Y) = \overline{B}(X) \cup \overline{B}(Y)$
b) $\overline{B}(X \cap Y) \subseteq \overline{B}(X) \cap \overline{B}(Y)$
c) Both (a) and (b)
d) None of the above

5.11 Which of the following is not true?
a) $x \in \underline{B}(X) \rightarrow \mu_X^B(x) - 1$
b) $x \in U - \overline{B}(X) \Rightarrow \mu_X^B(x) = 0$
c) $x \in BN_B(X) \Rightarrow 0 < \mu_X^B(x) < 1$
d) None of the above

5.12 Which of the following is the value of $\mu_X^B(x) + \mu_{U-X}^B(x)$?
a) 0
b) 1
c) Between 0 and 1
d) None of the above

5.13 Which of the following relations is true?
a) $\mu_{XUY}^B(x) \geq \max(\mu_X^B(x), \mu_Y^B(x))$
b) $\mu_{X \cap Y}^B(x) \leq \min(\mu_X^B(x), \mu_Y^B(x))$
c) Both (a) and (b)
d) None of the above

5.14 If $\underline{B}(X) \neq \Phi$ and $\overline{B}(X) = U$, then
a) X is totally B-indefinable
b) X is externally B-definable
c) X is internally B-definable
d) X is roughly B-definable

5.15 Let $P \subset Q \subset A$ be sets of attributes of an information system $I = (U, A)$ such that $IND_A(P) = IND_A(Q)$. Then which of the following is certainly not true?
a) P is not a reduct of U
b) Q is not a reduct of U
c) Q-P is not a reduct of U
d) None of the above

5.16 Let D be the discernity matrix of an information system $I = (U, A)$ with n objects. If the $(i, j)^{th}$ element of D contains an attribute $p \in A$, and x_i and x_j denote the ith and the jth objects of U, then which of the following is true?
a) $p(x_i) = p(x_j)$
b) $p(x_i) \neq p(x_j)$
c) $p(x_i)$ and $p(x_j)$ are not related
d) None of the above

5.17 Which of the following helps us to find the minimum reduct of an information system?
a) Discernibility Matrix
b) Discernibility function
c) Both (*a*) and (*b*)
d) None of the above

5.18 The entries of discernibility matrix consists of
a) A set of objects
b) A set of attributes
c) A rough membership value
d) None of the above

5.19 Which of the following is not an application area of the rough set theory?
a) Rule extraction
b) Data clustering
c) Both (*a*) and (*b*)
d) None of the above

5.20 Which of the following is an appropriate condition for applying rough set theory?
a) Non-determinism
b) Uncertainty
c) Vagueness
d) None of the above

Answers

5.1 (d)	5.2 (b)	5.3 (b)	5.4 (d)	5.5 (b)
5.6 (a)	5.7 (b)	5.8 (b)	5.9 (d)	5.10 (d)
5.11 (d)	5.12 (b)	5.13 (c)	5.14 (a)	5.15 (b)
5.16 (b)	5.17 (c)	5.18 (b)	5.19 (d)	5.20 (c)

EXERCISES

5.1. Prove that indiscernibility is an equivalence relation.

5.2 Prove the following identities for an information system $I = (U, A)$ and $B \subseteq A$.
i) $\underline{\underline{B}}(U - X) = U - \overline{B}(X)$
ii) $\overline{B}(U - X) = U - \underline{B}(X)$

5.3 Consider the information system presented in Table 5.14 showing the loan applicants' data set. We want to investigate if there is any correlation between the attributes {*Age*, *Income*} and possession of a car. If B = {*Age*, *Income*}, then
i) Find IND_B (*I*)
ii) Let $X = \{x \in U \mid x\,(Car) = Yes\}$. Find if X is rough in terms of knowledge in B.

5.4 Let $I = (U, A)$ be an information system and $C \subseteq B \subseteq A$. Then prove that $\forall x \in U$, $[x]_B \subseteq [x]_C$.

5.5 Consider the information system presented in Table 5.16 on the shopping habit of a number of customers. As shown in solved problem no. 3, {*A*, *GD*} is a minimal reduct of the system. Find the rules underlying the system on the basis of the reduct {*A*, *GD*} and taking *P* as the decision attribute.

5.6 Table 5.8 present an information system on *Dog Breed Comparison*. Compute the attribute dependencies $X \rightarrow Grooming$ for all attributes X other than Grooming, i.e. $X \in$ {*Weight, Exercise, Living Space, Training, Child Tolerance, Stranger Tolerance*}.

Is it possible to partition the cited dog breeds into clusters on the basis of these attribute dependencies? If yes, then show the clusters with the help of a tree structure.

Can you further partition the clusters thus formed into sub-clusters on the basis of knowledge of other attributes?

Do you identify any other attribute dependency on the basis of which the given dog breeds could be partitioned into yet another set of clusters?

5.7 The information system on the shopping habits of a number of customers is given in Table 5.16. Cluster the objects on the basis of the attribute dependencies $X \rightarrow Toys$, X being any of the attributes *Gender* (*GD*), *Food* (*F*), *Garment* (*GM*), *Cosmetics* (*C*), and *modes of payment* (*P*)

5.8 The Solved Problem No. 5.2 proposes a technique to compute the minimal reducts of a given information system. However, there are other methods to find the minimal reducts. Can you devise your own method to solve the problem?

BIBLIOGRAPHY AND HISTORICAL NOTES

After the introduction and initiation of rough sets in 1981-1982, there were a few interesting works on rough set theory by Pawlak himself, Iwinski, Banerjee and so on. In 1991, Pawlak threw some light on the utility of rough sets. Next year Skowron and Rauszer published their works on intelligent decision support using the concept of discernibility matrices. By 1992, Rough Set Theory had gained much ground and as suggested from the compilation '*Intelligent Decision Support - Handbook of Applications and Advances of the Rough Sets Theory*,' significant work were being carried out in the field of intelligent decision support systems using rough sets. In 1994, Pawlak and Andrez Skowron proposed an extension through rough membership functions. In 1997, Pawlak published on the applicability of rough set theory on data analysis and in the same year E. Orlowska applied the principles on incomplete information systems. First notable application of rough sets on data mining was published by T.Y. Lin and N.Cercone where they dealt with the analysis of imperfect data. Thereafter, a number of applications have come up and rough sets have been used in various areas including data mining and knowledge discovery, pattern classification, incomplete information systems, fault diagnosis, software safety analysis etc. to name a few. Rough sets have also been used in pairs with other soft computing techniques giving birth to such hybrid systems as rough-fuzzy, rough-neural and rough-GA systems. A few important references in this area are given below.

Banerjee, M. and Chakraborty, M. K. (1987). Rough algebra. *Bulletin of the Polish Academy of Sciences, Mathematics*, 41, 293–287.

Iwinski, T. B. (1987). Algebraic approach to rough sets. *Bulletin of the Polish Academy of Sciences, Mathematics*, 35, 673–683.

Iwinski, T. B. (1988). Rough orders and rough concepts. *Bulletin of the Polish Academy of Sciences, Mathematics*, 36, 187–192.

Lin, T.Y. and Cercone, N. (1997). *Rough Sets and Data Mining – Analysis of Imperfect Data*. Boston: Kluwer Academic Publishers.

Orlowska, E. (1997). *Incomplete Information: Rough Set Analysis*. Physica-Verlag, Heidelberg.

Pawlak, Z. (1981). Information Systems, Theoretical Foundations. *Information Systems*, 6, 205-218.

Pawlak, Z. (1982). Rough sets. *International Journal of Computer and Information Sciences,* 11, 341–356.

Pawlak, Z. (1984). Rough classification. *International Journal of Man-Machine Studies*, 20, 469–483.

Pawlak, Z., Wong, S. K. M., and Ziarko, W. (1988). Rough sets: Probabilistic versus deterministic approach. *International Journal of Man-Machine Studies*, 29, 81–95.

Pawlak, Z. (1991). *Rough sets: Theoretical aspects of reasoning with data.* Kluwer Academic Publishers, Boston.

Pawlak, Z. and Skowron, A. (1994). *Rough membership functions.* In *'dvances in the Dempster--Schafer Theory of Evidence,'* R. R., Fedrizzi, M., and Kacprzyk, J. (eds.), New York: Wiley, 251-271.

Pawlak, Z. (1997). *Rough Sets: Theoretical Aspects of Reasoning about Data.* Dordrecht: Kluwer.

Skowron, A. and Rauszer, C. (1992). *The discernibility matrices and functions in information systems.* In *Intelligent Decision Support – Handbook of Applications and Advances of the Rough Sets Theory*, R. Slowiński (ed.), Dordrecht: Kluwer, 331–362.

Ziarko, W. P. (ed.) (1994). *Rough sets, fuzzy sets and knowledge discovery.* Springer–Verlag, London.

Ziarko, W. P. (2002). *Rough set approaches for discovery of rules and attribute dependencies.* In *Handbook of Data Mining and Knowledge Discovery*, Klösgen, W. and Zytkow, J. M. (ed.), Oxford, 328–339.

6

Artificial Neural Networks: Basic Concepts

Key Concepts

Activation, Activation function, Artificial neural network (ANN), Artificial neuron, Axon, Binary sigmoid, Code-book vector, Competitive ANN, Correlation learning, Decision plane, Decision surface, Delta learning, Dendrite, Epoch of learning, Euclidean distance, Exemplar, Extended delta rule, Heaviside function, Heb learning, Hebb rule, Hidden layer, Hopfield network, Hyperbolic tangent function, Identity function, Learning rate, Least-mean square (LMS) learning, Linear separability, Logistic sigmoid, McCulloch–Pitts neural model, Multi-layer feed forward, Neuron, Outstar learning, Parallel relaxation, Pattern, Pattern association, Pattern classification, Perceptron, Perceptron convergence theorem, Perceptron learning, Processing element (PE), Recurrent network, Sigmoid function, Single layer feed forward, Soma, Steepness parameter, Step function, Supervised learning, Synapse, Threshold function, Training vector, Unsupervised learning, Widrow–Hoff rule, Winner takes all, XOR problem

Chapter Outline

Artificial neural networks (ANNs) follow a computational paradigm that is inspired by the structure and functionality of the brain. The brain is composed of nearly 100 billion neurons each of which is locally connected to its neighbouring neurons. The biological neuron possesses very elementary signal processing capabilities like summing up the incoming signals and then propagating to its neighbours depending on certain conditions. However the sum total of the parallel and concurrent activities of these 100 billion neurons gives rise to the highly sophisticated, complex, and mysterious phenomenon that we call 'consciousness'. This chapter provides an overview of the basic concepts of ANNs. Unlike mainstream computation where information is stored as localized bits, an ANN preserves information as weights of interconnections among its processing units. Thus, as in the brain, information in ANNs too resides in a distributed manner, resulting in greater fault tolerance. Moreover, multiple information may be superimposed on the same ANN for storage purpose. We will see that like the human brain, ANNs also perform computation in terms of patterns rather than data. This chapter presents the major artificial neural models, as well as the various ANN architectures and activation functions. The basic learning strategies are also discussed in this chapter.

6.1 INTRODUCTION

Computation is generally perceived as a sequence of operations that processes a set of input data to yield a desired result. The agent that carries out the computation is either an intelligent human being or a typical Von Neumann computer consisting of a processor and a memory, along with the input and the output units (Fig. 6.1). The memory contains both instruction and data. Computation is accomplished by the CPU through a sequence of fetch and execute cycles.

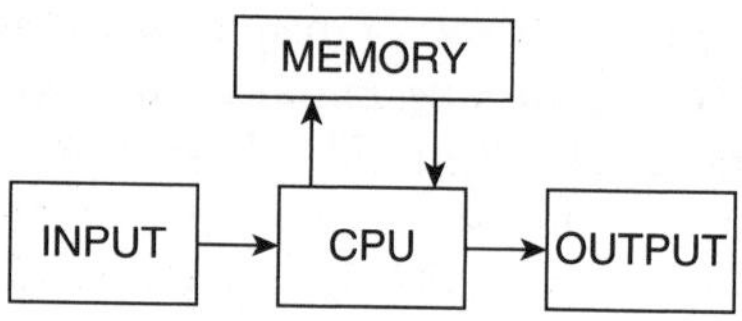

Fig. 6.1. *Block diagram of a stored program computer*

The sequential fetch and execute model of computation, based on a single-processor stored program digital computer as the hardware platform, has been immensely successful in the history of computers. Its notorious member-crunching and symbol-manipulating capacity has rendered it an indispensable tool for the civilized world. Innumerable applications in everyday activities and other enterprises, *e.g.* commerce, industry, communication, management, governance, research, entertainment, healthcare, and so on, were developed, are being developed, and shall be developed on the basis of the this model.

However, the power of such a computational model is not unchallenged. There are activities that a normal human being may require a fraction of a second to perform while it would take ages by even the fastest computer. Take, for example, the simple task of recognizing the face of a known person. We do it effortlessly, in spite of the infinite variations due to distance, angle of vision, lighting, posture, distortion due to mood, or emotion of the person concerned, and so on. Occasionally, we recognize a face after a gap of, say, twenty years, even though the face has changed a lot through aging, and has little semblance to its appearance of twenty year ago. This is still very difficult, if not impossible, to achieve for a present day computer.

Where does the power of a human brain, vis-à-vis a stored program digital computer, lie? Perhaps it lies in the fact that we, the human beings, do not *think* in terms of *data* as a computer does, but in terms of *patterns*. When we look at a face, we never think in terms of the pixel values, but perceive the face as a whole, as a pattern. Moreover, the structure of the human brain is drastically different from the Von-Neuman architecture. Instead of one, or a few, processors, the brain consists of 100 billion interconnected cells called the neurons. Individually, a neuron can do no more than some primitive tasks like collecting stimuli from the neighboring neurons and then passing them on to other neighbouring neurons after some elementary processing. But the *sum* of these simultaneous activities of 100 billion neurons is what we call the human consciousness. Artificial neural network, occasionally abbreviated as ANN, is an alternative model of computation that is inspired by the structure and functionality of the human brain.

6.1.1 The Biological Neuron

The building block of a human brain is the biological neuron. The main parts of the cross-section of a common biological neuron and their functions are shown in Fig. 6.2.

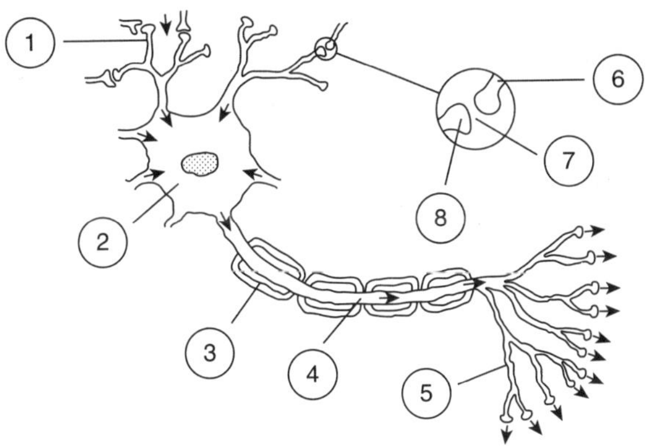

1. Dendrite (receives signals from neighbouring neurons)
2. Soma (accumulates the signals received through the dendrites)
3. Insulating fatty layer
4. Axon (transmits signal from soma to the axon terminals)
5. Axon terminal (propagates stimulus to neighbouring neurons)
6. Axon of a neighbouring neuron
7. Synapse (scales the signals by a weight)
8. Dendrite of the neuron

Fig. 6.2. *Structure of a biological neuron*

It consists of three primary parts, *viz.*, the *dendrites*, *soma*, and the *axon*. The dendrites collect stimuli from the neighbouring neurons and pass it on to soma which is the main body of the cell. The soma accumulates the stimuli received through the dendrites. It 'fires' when sufficient stimuli is obtained. When a neuron fires it transmits its own stimulus through the axon. Eventually, this stimulus passes on to the neighboring neurons through the axon terminals. There is a small gap between the end of an axon terminal and the adjacent dendrite of the neighbouring neuron. This gap is called the *synapse*. A nervous stimulus is an electric impulse. It is transmitted across a synaptic gap by means of electrochemical process.

The synaptic gap has an important role to play in the activities of the nervous system. It scales the input signal by a weight. If the input signal is x, and the synaptic weight is w, then the stimulus that finally reaches the soma due to input x is the product $x \times w$. The significance of the weight w provided by the synaptic gap lies in the fact that this weight, together with other synaptic weights, embody the knowledge stored in the network of neurons. This is in contrast with digital computers where the knowledge is stored as a program in the memory. The salient features of biological neurons are summarized in Table 6.1.

Table 6.1. *Salient features of a biological neuron*

#	Feature
1	The body of the neuron is called the *soma* that acts as a processing element to receive numerous signals through the dendrites simultaneously.
2	The strengths of the incoming signals are modified by the synaptic gaps.
3	The role of the soma, i.e., the processing element of a neuron, is simple. It sums up the weighted input signals and if the sum is sufficiently high, it transmits an output signal through the axon. The output signal reaches the receiving neurons in the neighbourhood through the axon terminals.
4	The weight factors provided by the synaptic gaps are modified over time and experience. This phenomenon, perhaps, accounts for development of skills through practice, or loss of memory due to infrequent recall of stored information.

6.1.2 The Artificial Neuron

An artificial neuron is a computational model based on the structure and functionality of a biological neuron. It consists of a processing element, a number of inputs and weighted edges connecting each input to the processing element (Fig. 6.3). A processing unit is usually represented by a circle, as indicated by the unit Y in Fig. 6.3. However, the input units are shown with boxes to distinguish them from the processing units of the neuron. This convention is followed throughout this book. An artificial neuron may consist of m number of input units $X_1, X_2, \ldots, X_m$. In Fig. 6.3 the corresponding input signals are shown as $x_1, x_2, \ldots, x_m$, and y_out is the output signal of the processing unit Y.

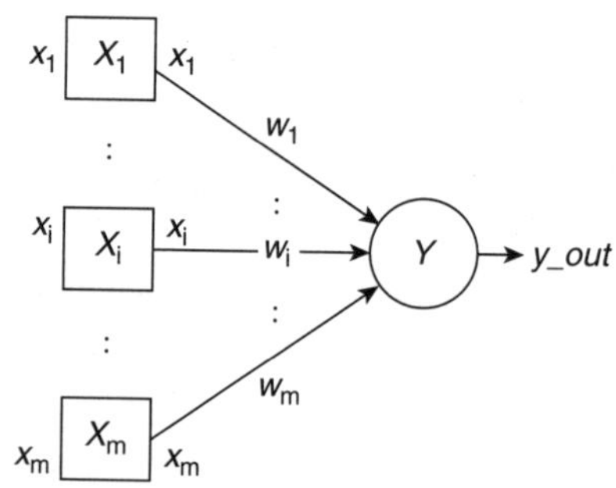

Fig. 6.3 *Structure of an artificial neuron*

The notations used in Fig. 6.3 are summarized in Table 6.2. These notational conventions are followed throughout this text unless otherwise stated.

Table 6.2. *Notational convention*

Symbol Used	Description
X_i	The *i*th input unit.
Y	The output unit. In case there are more than one output units, the *j*th output unit is denoted as Y_j.
x_i	Signal to the input unit X_i. This signal is transmitted to the output unit Y scaled by the weight w_i.

(*Continued*)

Table 6.2. *Continued*

Symbol Used	Description
w_i	The weight associated with the interconnection between input unit X_i and the output unit Y. In case there are more than one output units, w_{ij} denotes the weight between input unit X_i and the jth output unit Y_j.
y_in	The total (or net) input to the output unit Y. It is the algebraic sum of all weighted inputs to Y.
y_out	Signal transmitted by the output unit Y. It is known as the activation of Y.

The net input *y_in* to the processing element Y is obtained as

$$y\_in = x_1 w_1 + x_2 w_2 + \cdots + x_m w_m = \sum_{i=1}^{m} x_i w_i \tag{6.1}$$

If there are more than one output units, then the net input to the jth output unit Y_j, denoted as y_in_j, is given by

$$y\_in_j = x_1 w_{1j} + x_2 w_{2j} + \cdots + x_{mj} w_{mj} = \sum_{i=1}^{m} x_i w_{ij} \tag{6.2}$$

The weight w_i associated with the input X_i may be positive, or negative. A positive weight w_i means the corresponding input X_i has an excitatory effect on Y. If, however, w_i is negative then the input X_i is said to have an inhibitory effect on Y. The output signal transmitted by Y is a function of the net input *y_in*. Hence,

$$y\_out = f(y\_in) \tag{6.3}$$

In its simplest form *f*(.) is a *step function*. A *binary step function* for the output unit is defined as

$$y\_out = f(y\_in) = \begin{cases} 1, & \text{if } y\_in > 0, \\ 0, & \text{if } y\_in \le 0. \end{cases} \tag{6.4}$$

Taking Equation 6.1 into consideration we get

$$y\_out = f(y\_in) = \begin{cases} 1, & \text{if } \sum_{i=1}^{m} x_i w_i > 0, \\ 0, & \text{if } \sum_{i=1}^{m} x_i w_i \le 0. \end{cases} \tag{6.5}$$

When a non-zero threshold θ is used Equations 6.4 and 6.5 take the forms

$$y\_out = f(y\_in) = \begin{cases} 1, & \text{if } y\_in > \theta, \\ 0, & \text{if } y\_in \le \theta. \end{cases} \tag{6.6}$$

Or,

$$y\_out = f(y\_in) = \begin{cases} 1, & \text{if } \sum_{i=1}^{m} x_i w_i > \theta, \\ 0, & \text{if } \sum_{i=1}^{m} x_i w_i \le \theta. \end{cases} \tag{6.7}$$

The function *f*(.) is known as the *activation function* of the neuron, and the output *y_out* is referred to as the *activation* of *Y*. Various activation functions are discussed in later parts of this chapter.

The structure of an artificial neuron is simple, like its biological counterpart. It's processing power is also very limited. However, a network of artificial neurons, popularly known as ANN has wonderful capacities. The computational power of ANNs is explored in the subsequent chapters with greater details.

6.1.3 Characteristics of the Brain

Since brain is the source of inspiration, as well as the model that ANNs like to follow and achieve, it is worthwhile to ponder over the characteristics of a brain as a computing agent. The most striking feature of a brain is its extremely parallel and decentralized architecture. It consists of more or less 100 billion neurons interconnected among them. The interconnections are local in the sense that each neuron is connected to its neighbours but not to a neuron far away. There is practically no centralized control in a brain. The neurons act on the basis of local information. These neurons function in parallel mode and concurrently. Apparently the brain is very slow compared to the present day computers. This is due to the fact that neurons operate at milliseconds range while the modern VLSI microchip process signals at nanosecond scale of time. The power of the brain lies not in the signal processing speed of its neuron but in the parallel and concurrent activities of 100 billion neurons. Another fascinating fact about the brain is its fault tolerance capability. As the knowledge is stored inside the brain in a distributed manner it can restore knowledge even when a portion of the brain is damaged. A summary of the essential features of a brain is presented in Table 6.3.

Table 6.3. *Essential features of a brain*

#	Aspect	Description
1	Architecture	The average human brain consists of about 100 billion neurons. There are nearly 10^{15} number of interconnections among these neurons. Hence the brain's architecture is highly connected.
2	Mode of operation	The brain operates in extreme parallel mode. This is in sharp contrast with the present day computers which are essentially single-processor machines. The power of the brain lies in the simultaneous activities of 100 billion neurons and their interactions.
3	Speed	Very slow, and also very fast. Very slow in the sense that neurons operate at milliseconds range which is miserably slow compared to the speed of present day VLSI chips that operate at nanoseconds range. So computers are tremendously fast and flawless in number crunching and data processing tasks compared to human beings. Still the brain can perform activities in split-seconds (*e.g.*, converse in natural language, carry out common sense reasoning, interpret a visual scenery, *etc.*) which a modern supercomputer may take ages to carryout.
4	Fault tolerance	The brain is highly fault tolerant. Knowledge is stored within the brain in a distributed manner. Consequently, if a portion of the brain is damaged, it can still go on functioning by retrieving or regenerating the lost knowledge from the remaining neurons.

(Continued)

Table 6.3. *Continued*

#	Aspect	Description
5	Storage mechanism	The brain stores information as strengths of the interconnections among the neurons. This accounts for the adaptability of the brain. New information can be added by adjusting the weights without destroying the already stored information.
6	Control	There is no global control in the brain. A neuron acts on local information available with its neighbouring neurons. The neurons pass on the results of processing only to the neurons adjacent to them.

6.2 COMPUTATION IN TERMS OF PATTERNS

It was observed earlier in this chapter that the brain perceives the physical world in terms of *patterns*, rather than *data*. Since ANNs are inspired by the brain, both structurally and behaviourally, it is worthwhile to consider the nature of pattern-oriented computation *vis-a-vis* computation on the basis of stored program. Two fundamental operations relating to patterns, pattern classification and pattern association, are explained in this subsection with the help of simple illustrative examples.

6.2.1 Pattern Classification

Classification is the process of identifying the class to which a given pattern belongs. For example, let us consider the set S of all 3-bit patterns. We may divide the patterns of S into two classes A and B where A is the class of all patterns having more 0s than 1s and B the converse. Therefore

$$S = \{000, 001, 010, 011, 100, 101, 110, 111\}$$
$$A = \{000, 001, 010, 100\}$$
$$B = \{011, 101, 110, 111\}$$

Now, given an arbitrary 3-bit pattern, the classification problem here is to decide whether it belongs to the class A, or class B. In other words, we have to establish the mapping shown in Fig. 6.4.

The simplest way to achieve this is to execute a table look-up procedure, as shown in Fig. 6.5(a). All we have to do is to find the appropriate row in the table corresponding to the given pattern and read the class name to which it belongs. However, creation and storage of the table becomes impractical as the volume of stored patterns increases. In practice, we may have to deal with billions of multidimensional patterns.

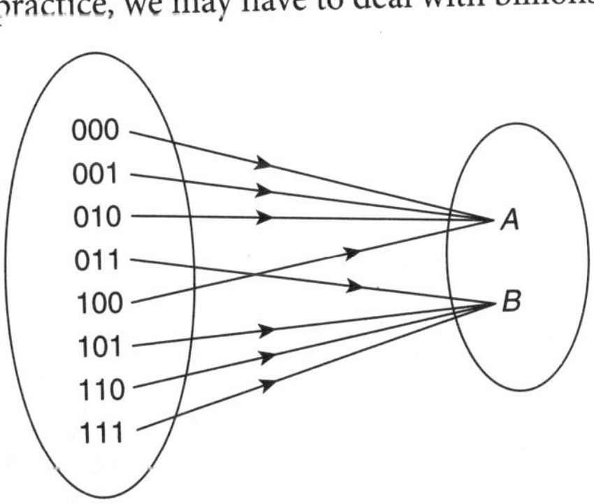

Fig. 6.4. *Classification of 3-bit patterns based on the number of 0s and 1s.*

Fig. 6.5(b) presents a conventional computer program to perform this task. The program is written in a pseudo-language. The technique is to count the number of 0s and 1s in the given patterns and store them in the local variables n_0 and n_1. Then depending on whether $n_0 > n_1$ or $n_0 < n_1$ the program returns the class name *A* or *B* respectively. The algorithm has a time complexity of $O(n_b)$ where n_b is the number of bits in the given pattern.

Row #	Pattern			Class
0	0	0	0	A
1	0	0	1	A
2	0	1	0	A
3	0	1	1	B
4	1	0	0	A
5	1	0	1	B
6	1	1	0	B
7	1	1	1	B

(a) Classification as a table look-up procedure

```
Procedure Classify (x, A, B)
Begin
   n0 = n1 = 0;    /* initialize
   counts */
   /* count 0s and 1s in x */
   For i ← 1 to 3 do
     If the ith bit is 0 Then
       n0 ++;    Else n1 ++;
     End-if
   End-for
   If n0 > n1   Then Return A;
               Else Return B;
   End-if
End-procedure
```

(b) A procedure for classification of 3-bit patterns

Fig. 6.5. *Two methods for classification of 3-bit patterns*

Is it possible to solve the problem in a different way? Fig. 6.6 shows an artificial neuron with three inputs x_1, x_2, x_3 connected to a processing element *Y* through the weight factors as shown in the figure. It is a simplified version of a neural model called perception, proposed by Rosenblatt in 1962.

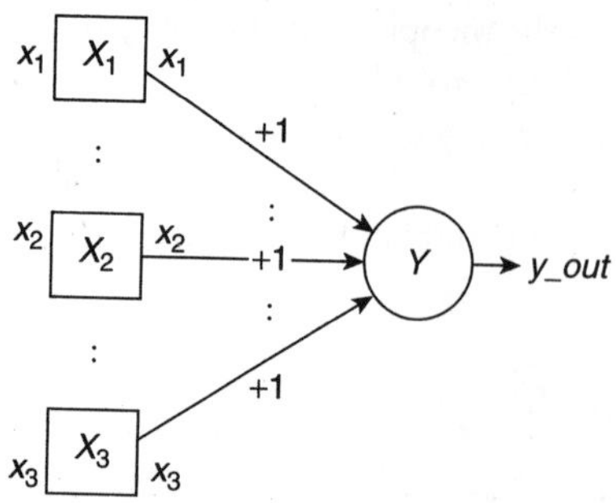

$$y\_in = \sum_{i=1}^{3} x_i w_i = x_1 w_1 + x_2 w_2 + x_3 w_3$$
$$= x_1 + x_2 + x_3$$

$$y\_out = f(y\_in) = \begin{cases} 1, & \text{if } y\_in \geq 2, \\ 0, & \text{otherwise.} \end{cases}$$

Fig. 6.6 *An artificial neuron to classify 3-bit binary patterns based on the number of 0s and 1s*

The weights w_1, w_2, w_3 associated with the interconnection paths from the inputs x_1, x_2, x_3 to *Y* are chosen in a way that the net input *y_in* to *Y* is greater than or equal to 2 when there are two or more 1s among x_1, x_2, x_3. The activation *y_out* then becomes 1, indicating that the patterns belongs to the class *B*. On the other hand, when there are more 0s than 1s, the net (total) input $y\_in = \sum_{i=1}^{3} w_i x_i \leq 1 < 2$, so that the output signal, the *activation*, is $y\_out = 0$. This implies that the given pattern belongs to the class A. Time complexity of this method is $O(1)$ because the inputs are fed to the processing element parallely.

An alternative arrangement of two output nodes Y_1 and Y_2 to solve the same classification problem is shown in Fig. 6.7. Here both the units Y_1 and Y_2 are connected to the same inputs x_1, x_2, x_3 and these units explicitly correspond to the classes A and B respectively. If the input pattern belongs to the class A then Y_1 fires (i.e., computes the activation as $y\_out_1 = 1$), otherwise, unit Y_2 fires. Y_1 and Y_2 never fire simultaneously.

It should be noted that Fig. 6.5(a) and 6.5(b) presents the classification knowledge in the form of an algorithm. On the other hand, the ANN counterpart of the concerned classification task embodies the same knowledge in the form of certain interconnection weights and the activation functions. If we change the weights, or the activation functions $f(y\_in)$, the capability of the ANN changes accordingly.

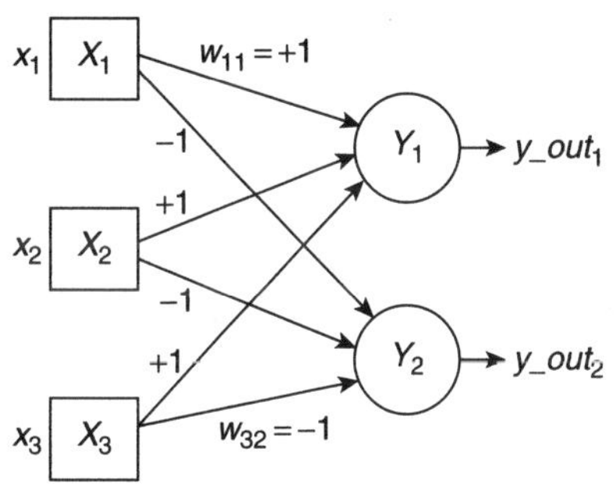

$$y\_in_1 = \sum_{i=1}^{3} x_i w_{i1} = x_1 w_{11} + x_2 w_{21} + x_3 w_{31}$$

$$= x_1 + x_2 + x_3$$

$$y\_out_1 = f(y\_in_1) = \begin{cases} 1, & \text{if } y\_in_1 \geq 2, \\ 0, & \text{otherwise.} \end{cases}$$

$$y\_in_2 = \sum_{i=1}^{3} x_i w_{i2} = x_1 w_{12} + x_2 w_{22} + x_3 w_{32}$$

$$= -x_1 - x_2 - x_3$$

$$y\_out_2 = f(y\_in_2) = \begin{cases} 1, & \text{if } y\_in_2 \geq -1, \\ 0, & \text{otherwise.} \end{cases}$$

Fig. 6.7. *Classification of 3-bit patterns with two output units*

6.2.2 Pattern Association

Associating an input pattern with one among several patterns already stored in memory, in case such a mapping exists, is an act that we, the human beings, carry out effortlessly in our daily life. A person, with his eyes closed, can visualize a rose by its fragrance. How does it happen? It seems that various odours are already stored in our memory. When we smell an odour, our brain tries to map this sensation to its stored source. It returns the nearest match and this correspond to recognizing the odour, or the sensation in general. However, in case there is no match between the input sensation and any of the stored patterns – we fail to associate the input, or, to be more precise, we conclude that the input is unknown to us.

Given an input pattern, and a set of patterns already stored in the memory, finding the closest match of the input pattern among the stored patterns and returning it as the output, is known as pattern association. The basic concept of pattern association is explained below with the help of a simple illustrative example. The example is inspired by Hopfield network [1982] which is discussed later in greater details.

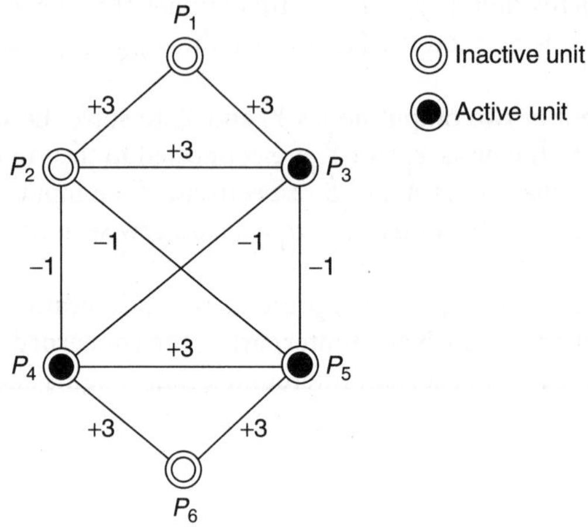

Fig. 6.8. *A network for pattern recognition*

Let us consider a network of six processing elements (*PEs*) or units as shown in Fig. 6.8. The essential features of the network are described below.

i) *PE states* At any instant, a unit may either be in an *active* or an *inactive* state. Moreover, depending on the circumstances, the state of a unit may change from active to inactive, and vice versa. In Fig. 6.8 an active unit is shown with a black circle and an inactive unit is indicated by a hollow circle.
ii) *Interconnections* All interconnections are bidirectional. Magnitude of the weight associated with an interconnection gives the strength of influence the connected units play on each other.
iii) *Signed weights* A negative weight implies that the corresponding units tend to inhibit, or deactivate, each other. Similarly, positively interconnected units tend to activate each other.
iv) *Initialization* The network is initialized by making certain units active and keeping others inactive. The initial combination of active and inactive units is considered as the input pattern. After initialization, the network passes through a number of transformations. The transformations take place according to the rules described below.
v) *Transformations* At each stage during the sequence of transformations, the next state of every unit P_i, $i = 1, \ldots, 6$, is determined. The next state of a unit P_i is obtained by considering all *active* neighbours of P_i and taking the algebraic sum of the weights of the paths between P_i and the neighbouring active units. If the sum is greater than 0, then P_i becomes active for the next phase. Otherwise it becomes inactive. The state of a unit without any active unit in its neighbourhood remains unaltered. This process is known as *parallel relaxation.*

For example, let the network be initialized with the pattern shown in Fig. 6.9(a). Initially, all units except P_2 and P_5 are inactive. To find the state of P_1 in the next instant, we look for the active neighbours of P_1 and find that P_2 is the only active unit connected to P_1 through an interconnection link of weight +3. Hence P_1 becomes active in the next instant. Similarly, for P_3, both P_2 and P_5 are active units in its neighbourhood. The sum of the corresponding weights is $w_{23} + w_{35} = +3 - 1 = +2$. Hence P_3 also becomes active. However P_2 itself becomes inactive because the only active unit in its vicinity, P_5, is connected to it through a negatively weighted link. Table 6.4 shows the details of computations for transformation of the network from Fig. 6.9(a) to Fig. 6.9(b). The configuration of Fig. 6.9(b) is not stable. The network further transforms itself from Fig. 6.9(b) to Fig. 6.9(c), which is a stable state. Therefore, we can say that the given network associates the pattern shown in Fig. 6.9(a) to that shown in Fig. 6.9(c).

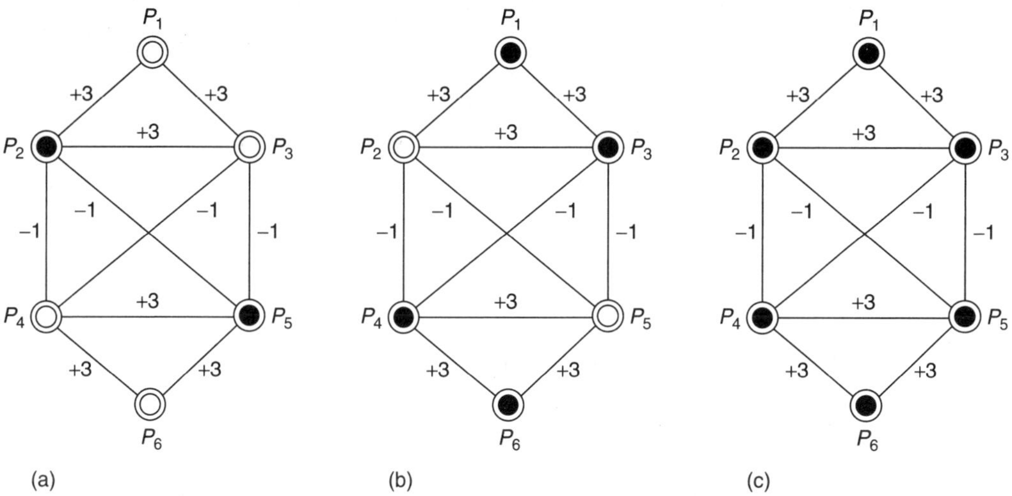

Fig. 6.9. *Pattern association through parallel relaxation*

A little investigation reveals that the given network has three non-trivial stable states as shown in Fig. 6.10(a)-(c). The trivial state is that where all units are inactive. It can be easily verified that if one or more of the units P_1, P_2, P_3 is/are active initially while the rest, P_4, P_5, P_6 are inactive, the network converges to the pattern shown in Fig. 6.10(a). Similarly, the pattern of Fig. 6.10(b) is associated with any input pattern where at least one unit of the group $\{P_4, P_5, P_6\}$ is/are active. Finally, an input pattern having active units from both the groups $\{P_1, P_2, P_3\}$ and $\{P_4, P_5, P_6\}$ would associate to with the patterned depicted in Fig. 6.10(c). Hence, the given network may be thought of as storing three non-trivial patterns as discussed above. Such networks are also referred to as *associative memories*, or *content-addressable memories*.

Table 6.4. *Computation of parallel relaxation on Fig. 6.9 (a)*

Unit	Present state	Active neighbouring unit(s)	Sum	Next state
P_1	Inactive	P_2	+3	Active
P_2	Active	P_5	−1	Inactive
P_3	Inactive	P_2, P_5	+3 − 1 = +2	Active
P_4	Inactive	P_2, P_5	−1 + 3 = +2	Active
P_5	Active	P_2	−1	Inactive
P_6	Inactive	P_5	+3	Active

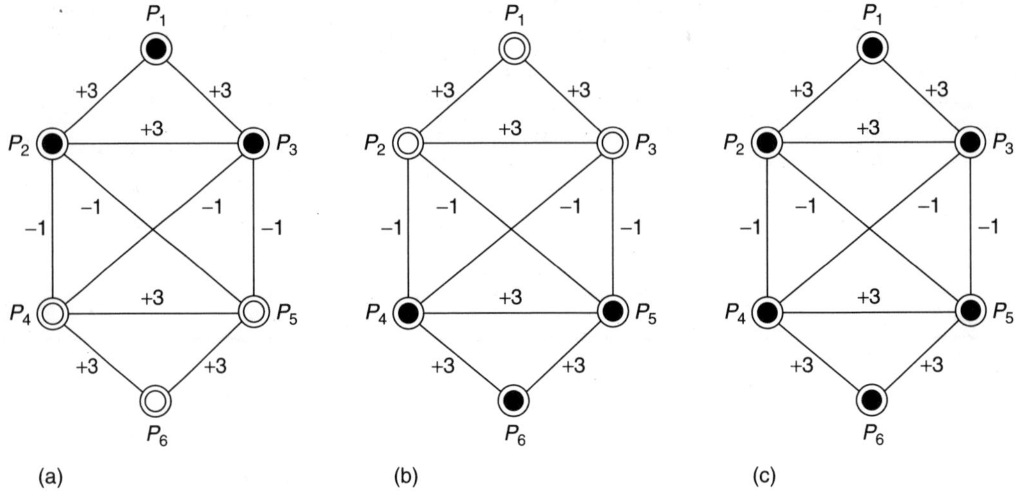

Fig. 6.10. *Non-trivial patterns stored in a Hopfield network*

6.3 THE McCULLOCH–PITTS NEURAL MODEL

The earliest artificial neural model was proposed by McCulloch and Pitts in 1943. Fig. 6.11 depicts its structure. It consists of a number of input units connected to a single output unit. The interconnecting links are unidirectional. There are two kinds of inputs, namely, excitatory inputs and inhibitory inputs. The salient features of a McCulloch and Pitts neural net are summarized in Table 6.5.

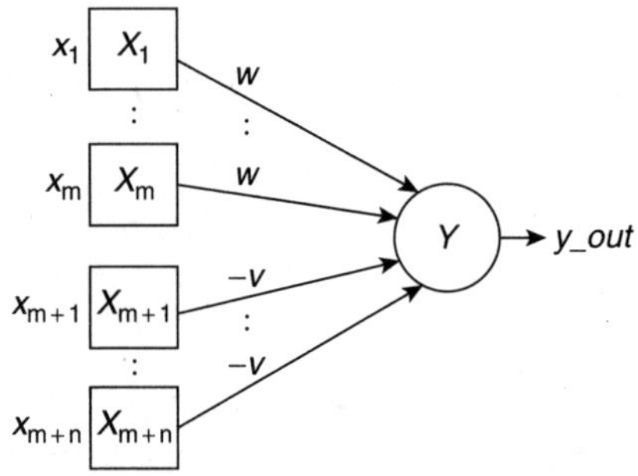

Fig. 6.11. *Structure of a McCulloch-Pitts neuron*

Table 6.5. *Salient features of McCulloch-Pitts artificial neuron*

1	There are two kinds of input units, *excitatory*, and *inhibitory*. In Fig. 6.11 the excitatory inputs are shown as inputs $X_1, \ldots, X_m$ and the inhibitory inputs are $X_{m+1}, \ldots, X_{m+n}$. The excitatory inputs are connected to the output unit through positively weighted links. Inhibitory inputs have negative weights on their connecting paths to the output unit.
2	All excitatory weights have the same positive magnitude w and all inhibitory weights have the same negative magnitude $-v$.

(Continued)

Table 6.5. *Continued*

3	The activation $y\_out = f(y\_in)$ is binary, i.e., either 1 (in case the neuron fires), or 0 (in case the neuron does not fire).
4	The activation function is a binary step function. It is 1 if the net input y_in is greater than or equal to a given threshold value θ, and 0 otherwise.
5	The inhibition is absolute. A single inhibitory input should prevent the neuron from firing irrespective of the number of active excitatory inputs.

The net input y_in to the neuron Y is given by

$$y\_in = \sum_{i=1}^{m} x_i \times w + \sum_{j=m+1}^{n} x_j \times (-v) = w\sum_{i=1}^{m} x_i - v\sum_{i=m+1}^{n} x_j \tag{6.8}$$

If θ be the threshold value, then the activation of Y, i.e., y_out, is obtained as

$$y\_out = f(y\_in) = \begin{cases} 1, & if\ y\_in \geq \theta, \\ 0, & otherwise. \end{cases} \tag{6.9}$$

To ensure absolute inhibition, y_in should be less than the threshold even when a single inhibitory input is on while none of the excitatory inputs are off. Assuming that the inputs are binary, i.e., 0 or 1, the criterion of absolute inhibition requires

$$y\_in = w\sum_{i=1}^{m} x_i - v < \theta \tag{6.10}$$

$$\therefore w \times m - v < \theta. \tag{6.11}$$

Simple McCulloch-Pitts neutrons can be designed to perform conventional logical operations. For this purpose one has to select the appropriate number of inputs, the inter connection weights and the appropriate activation function. A number of such logic-performing McCulloch-Pitts neural nets are presented below as illustrative examples.

(a) Truth Table

x_1	x_2	x_1 AND x_2
0	0	0
0	1	0
1	0	0
1	1	1

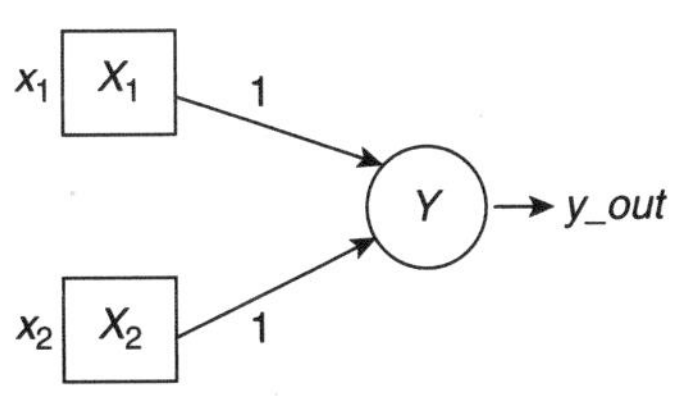

(b) Neural structure

$$y\_in = x_1 + x_2$$

$$y\_out = f(y\_in) = \begin{cases} 1, & if\ y\_in \geq 2, \\ 0, & otherwise. \end{cases}$$

(c) Activation function

Fig. 6.12. *A McCulloch-Pitts neuron to implement logical AND operation*

Example 6.1 *(Implementation of logical AND with McCulloch-Pitts neural model)*

Fig. 6.12 shows a McCulloch-Pitts neuron to perform the logical *AND* operation. It should be noted that all inputs in Fig. 6.12(b) are excitatory. No inhibitory input is required to implement the logical *AND* operation. The interconnection weights and the activation functions are so chosen that the output is 1 if and only if both the inputs are 1, otherwise it is 0.

Example 6.2 *(Implementation of logical OR with McCulloch-Pitts neural model)*

The McCulloch-Pitts neuron to perform logical *OR* operation is shown in Fig. 6.13. It is obvious from the figure that the neuron outputs a 1 whenever there is at least one 1 at its inputs. The neuron is structurally identical to the *AND*-performing neuron. Only the activation function is changed appropriately so that the desired functionality is ensured.

(a) Truth Table

x_1	x_2	x_1 OR x_2
0	0	0
0	1	1
1	0	1
1	1	1

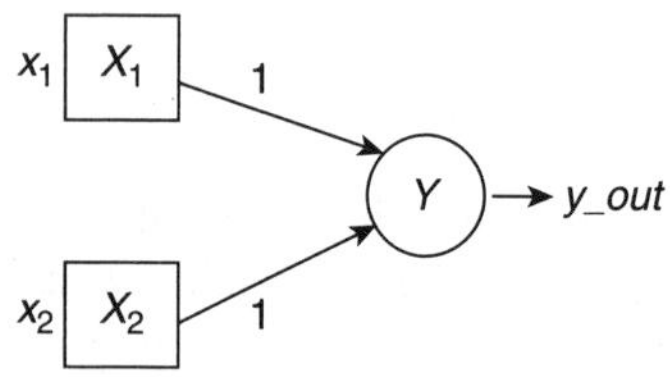

(b) Neural structure

$$y\_in = x_1 + x_2$$

$$y\_out = f(y\_in) = \begin{cases} 1, & if\ y\_in \geq 1, \\ 0, & otherwise. \end{cases}$$

(c) Activation function

Fig. 6.13. *A McCulloch-Pitts Neuron to implement logical OR operation*

Example 6.3 *(Implementation of logical AND-NOT with McCulloch-Pitts neural model)*

The logical *AND-NOT* operation is symbolically expressed as $x_1 . x_2'$, or x_1 *AND* (*NOT* x_2). It produces a 1 at the output only when x_1 is 1 and x_2 is 0. The McCulloch-Pitts neuron to perform this operation is shown in Fig. 6.14. The inhibitory effect of x_2 is implemented by attaching a negative weight to the path between x_2 and Y. The arrangement ensures that the output is 1 only when $x_1 = 1$ and $x_2 = 0$. For all other combinations of x_1 and x_2 the output is 0.

Example 6.4 *(Implementation of logical XOR with McCulloch-Pitts neural model)*

As in digital logic design, simple McCulloch-Pitts neurons performing basic logical operations can be combined together to implement complex logic functions. As an example, Fig. 6.15 shows the implementation of the *XOR* function with two *AND-NOT* operations. Unlike the previous examples, here we had to implement the function with the help of a network of neurons, rather them a single neuron. Moreover, the neurons are placed at various levels so that the outputs from a lower level are fed as inputs to the next level of neurons. All the three processing elements, Y_1, Y_2, and Z, have the same activation function as described in Fig. 6.15 (c). The *net_in* is the net input to a processing element. For example, *net-in* for Y_1, is $y\_in_1 = x_1 - x_2$. The same for the units Y_2 and Z are $y\_in_2 = -x_1 + x_2$, and $z\_in = y\_out_1 + y\_out_2$ respectively, where y_out_1 and y_out_2 are the respective activations of the units Y_1 and Y_2.

(a) Truth Table

x_1	x_2	x_1 AND (NOT x_2)
0	0	0
0	1	0
1	0	1
1	1	0

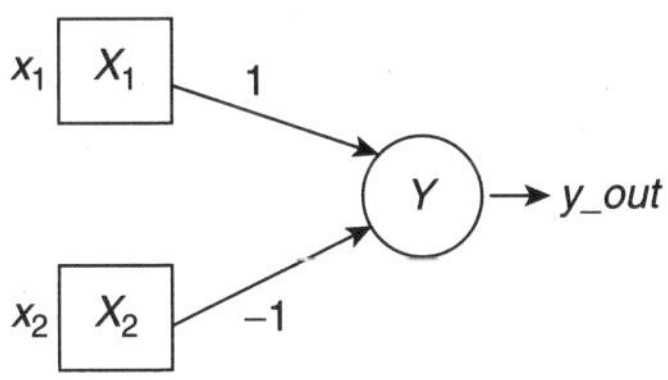

$$y\_in = x_1 - x_2$$

$$y\_out = f(y\_in) = \begin{cases} 1, & \text{if } y\_in \geq 1, \\ 0, & \text{otherwise.} \end{cases}$$

(b) Neural structure (c) Activation function

Fig. 6.14. *Logical AND-NOT operation with a McCulloch-Pitts neuron*

(a) Truth Table

x_1	x_2	x_1 XOR x_2
0	0	0
0	1	1
1	0	1
1	1	0

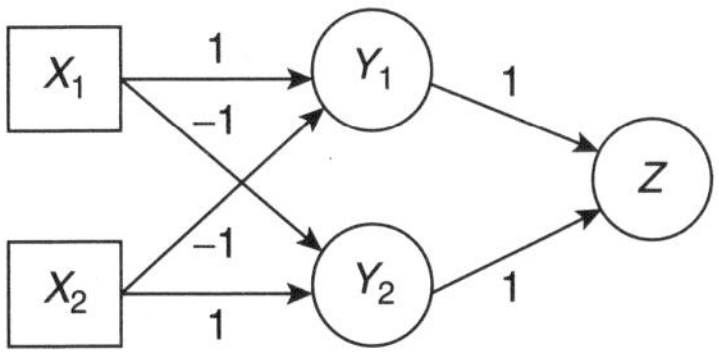

$$f(net\_in) = \begin{cases} 1, & \text{if } net\_in \geq 1, \\ 0, & \text{otherwise.} \end{cases}$$

(b) Neural structure (c) Activation function

Fig. 6.15. *McCulloch-Pitts neural network to implement logical XOR operation*

Example 6.5 *(Finding the function of a given McCulloch-Pitts net)*

Consider the McCulloch-Pitts neural network shown in Fig. 6.16. All the units, except those at the input level, have the activation function

$$f(x) = \begin{cases} 1, & \text{if } x \geq 2, \\ 0, & \text{otherwise.} \end{cases}$$

What are the responses of the output unit *Z* with respect to various input combinations? We assume the inputs are binary. What logical function the whole network realizes?

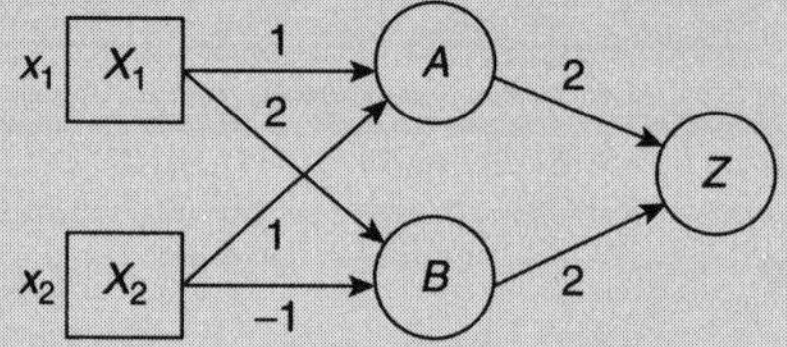

Fig. 6.16. *A McCulloch-Pitts neural network*

Let us first compute the responses of the intermediate units *A* and *B*. The responses of the output unit *Z* will be determined subsequently.

a) Responses of unit *A*

Inputs		Net input to *A* ($A\_in = x_1 + x_2$)	Activation of *A* (A_out)	Logic function realized
x_1	x_2			
0	0	0	0	
0	1	1	0	AND
1	0	1	0	
1	1	2	1	

b) Responses of unit *B*

Inputs		Net input to *B* ($B\_in = 2x_1 - x_2$)	Activation of *B* (B_out)	Logic function realized
x_1	x_2			
0	0	0	0	
0	1	−1	0	AND NOT
1	0	2	1	
1	1	1	0	

c) Responses of unit Z

Inputs x_1	Inputs x_2	A_out	B_out	Net input to Z (Z_in = 2A_out + 2B_out)	Z_out	Logic function realized
0	0	0	0	0	0	x_1
0	1	0	0	0	0	
1	0	0	1	2	1	
1	1	1	0	2	1	

Hence the logic function realized by the whole network is $f(x_1, x_2) = x_1$.

6.4 THE PERCEPTRON

The perceptron is one of the earliest neural network models proposed by Rosenblatt in 1962. Early neural network enthusiasts were very fond of the perceptron due to its simple structure, pattern classifying behaviour, and learning ability. As far as the study of neural networks is concerned the perceptron is a very good starting point. This section provides the fundamental features of perceptron, namely, its structure, capability, limitations, and clues to overcome the limitations.

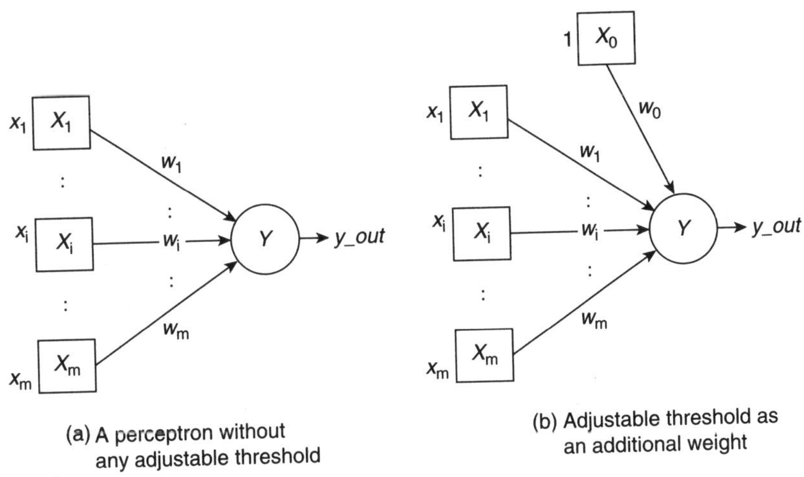

Fig. 6.17. *Structure of a perceptron*

6.4.1 The Structure

The structure of a perceptron is essentially same as that presented in subsection 6.1.2 and is shown here as Fig. 6.17(a). It consists of a number of input units $X_1, \ldots, X_m$ and a processing unit Y. The connecting path from input X_i to Y is unidirectional and has a weight w_i. The weight w_i is positive if x_i is an excitatory input and is negative if it is inhibitive. The net input y_in of the perceptron to Y is the algebraic sum of the weighted inputs.

$$y\_in = \sum_{i=1}^{m} x_i w_i \tag{6.12}$$

Equation 6.12 can be expressed concisely in matrix notation as given in Equations 6.13(a) and 6.13(b).

$$y\_in = \sum_{i=1}^{m} x_i w_i = [x_1 x_2 \ldots x_m] \times \begin{bmatrix} w_1 \\ w_2 \\ \vdots \\ w_m \end{bmatrix} \tag{6.13a}$$

$$\therefore y\_in = X \times W^T \tag{6.13b}$$

Here $X = [x_1, \ldots, x_m]$ and $W = [w_1, \ldots, w_m]$ are the input and the weight vectors.

The perceptron sends an output 1 if the net input *y_in* is greater than a predefined adjustable threshold value θ, otherwise it sends output 0. Hence, the activation function of a perceptron is given by Equation 6.6, repeated below.

$$y\_out = f(y\_in) = \begin{cases} 1, & \text{if } y\_in > \theta, \\ 0, & \text{if } y\_in \leq \theta. \end{cases} \tag{6.14}$$

Therefore, in matrix notation,

$$y\_out = \begin{cases} 1, & \text{if } X \times W^T > \theta, \\ 0, & \text{Otherwise.} \end{cases} \tag{6.15}$$

It is customary to include the adjustable threshold θ as an additional weight w_0. This additional weight w_0 is attached to an input X_0 which is permanently maintained as 1. The modified structure inclusive of the adjustable weight w_0 and the additional input unit X_0 replacing the threshold θ is shown in Fig. 6.17(b). The expressions for the net input *y_in* and the activation *y_out* of the perceptron now take the forms

$$y\_in = x_0 w_0 + x_1 w_1 + \cdots + x_m w_m = \sum_{i=0}^{m} x_i w_i \tag{6.16}$$

and

$$y\_out = f(y\_in) = \begin{cases} 1, & \text{if } \sum_{i=0}^{m} x_i w_i > 0, \\ 0, & \text{otherwise.} \end{cases} \tag{6.17}$$

The following points should be noted regarding the structure of a perceptron.

i) The inputs to a perceptron $x_0, \ldots, x_m$ are real values.
ii) The output is binary (0, or 1).
iii) The perceptron itself is the totality of the input units, the weights, the summation processor, activation function, and the adjustable threshold value.

The perceptron acts as the basic ANN structure for pattern classification. The next subsection describes the capabilities of a perceptron as a pattern classifier.

6.4.2 Linear Separability

As mentioned earlier, perceptrons have the capacity to classify patterns. However, this pattern-classifying capacity is not unconditional. In this subsection, we investigate the criteria for a perceptron to act properly as a pattern classifier.

Let us consider, for example, two sets of points on a two-dimensional Cartesian plane $A = \{a, b, c\} = \{(-1, 3), (1, 2), (3, 3)\}$, and $B = \{p, q, r\} = \{(0, -1), (2, 1), (3, 0)\}$. These points are shown in Fig. 6.18. The points belonging to the set *A*, or *B* are indicated with white, and black dots respectively.

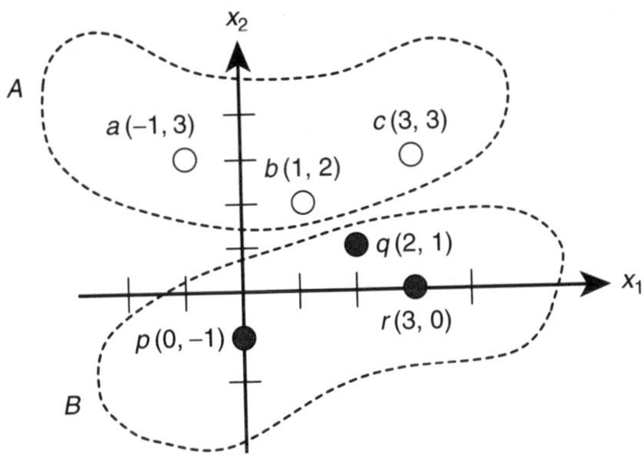

Fig. 6.18. *A classification problem consisting for two sets of patterns A, and B.*

We look for a classifier that can take an input pattern of the form (x_1, x_2) and decide to which class, *A* or *B*, the pattern belongs. A perceptron that carries out this job is shown in Fig. 6.19. The weights of the perceptron are carefully chosen so that the desired behaviour is achieved. However, we shall see that the weights need not to be *chosen*, but be *learnt* by the perceptron. The activation $y\_out = 1$ if the input pattern belongs to class *A*, and $y\_out = 0$ if it belongs to class *B*. Table 6.6 verifies that the perceptron shown in Fig. 6.19 can solve the classification problem posed in Fig. 6.18.

In fact, the pattern classifying capability of a perceptron is determined by the equations

$$y\_in = 0, \tag{6.18}$$

$$or, \sum_{i=0}^{m} x_i w_i = 0, \tag{6.19}$$

$$or,\ x_0 w_0 + x_1 w_1 + \ldots + x_m w_m = 0 \tag{6.20}$$

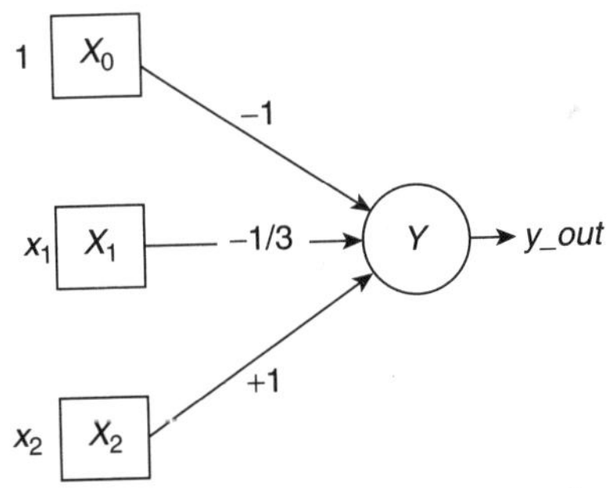

$$y\_in = \sum_{i=0}^{2} x_i w_i = -1 - \frac{x_1}{3} + x_2$$

$$y\_out = \begin{cases} 1, & if\ y\_in > 0, \\ 0, & otherwise \end{cases}$$

Fig. 6.19. *A perceptron to solve the classification problem shown in Fig. 6.18.*

Table 6.6. *Details of classification of patterns between sets A and B*

#	Input pattern	x_1	x_2	Net input (y_in)	Activation (y_out)	Class
1	a	−1	3	$2\frac{1}{3}$	1	A
2	b	1	2	2/3	1	A
3	c	3	3	1	1	A
4	p	0	−1	−2	0	B
5	q	2	1	− 2/3	0	B
6	r	3	0	− 2	0	B

Applying Equations 6.18–6.20 for the perceptron under consideration we get

$$y\_in = -1 - \frac{x_1}{3} + x_2 = 0$$

$$or, x_2 = \frac{x_1}{3} + 1 \tag{6.21}$$

Equation 6.21 represents a straight line that separates the given sets of patterns *A* and *B* (Fig. 6.20). For two dimensional patterns of the form (x_1, x_2) the equation in terms of the weights looks like

$$x_2 = -\frac{w_1}{w_2}x_1 - \frac{w_0}{w_2} \tag{6.22}$$

Similarly, when the patterns are 3-dimensional and of the form (x_1, x_2, x_3), Equation 6.20 would be

$$x_3 = -\frac{w_2}{w_3}x_2 - \frac{w_1}{w_3}x_1 - \frac{w_0}{w_3} \tag{6.23}$$

which represents a plane surface. In general, for *n*-dimensional patterns, Equation 6.20 represents a hyperplane in the corresponding *n*-dimensional hyperspace. Such a plane for a given perceptron capable of solving certain classification problem is known as a *decision plane*, or more generally, the *decision surface.*

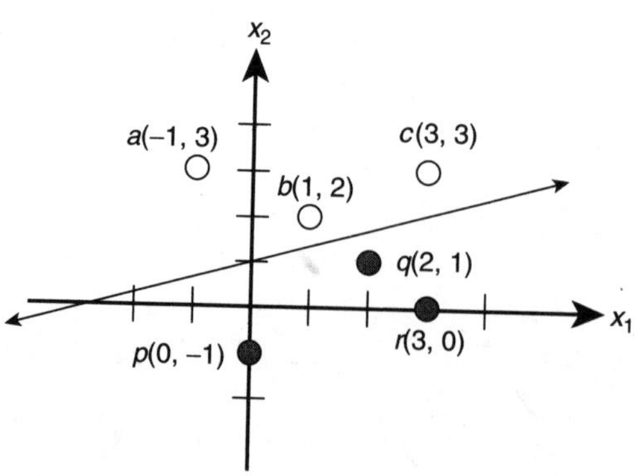

Fig. 6.20. *Linearly separable set of patterns*

A *linearly separable* set of patterns is one that can be completely partitioned by a decision plane into two classes. The nice thing about the perceptrons is, for a given set of linearly separable patterns, it is always possible to find a perceptron that solves the corresponding classification problem. The only thing we have to ensure is to find the appropriate combination of values for the weights $w_0, w_1, \ldots, w_m$. This is achieved through a process called learning by or training a perceptron. The famous *perceptron convergence theorem* (Rosenblatt [1962]) states that a perceptron is guaranteed to learn the appropriate values of the weights $w_0, w_1, \ldots, w_m$ so that the given a set of linearly separable patterns are properly classified by the perceptron. There are various techniques for training neural networks. A brief overview of these techniques is presented in the later parts of this chapter.

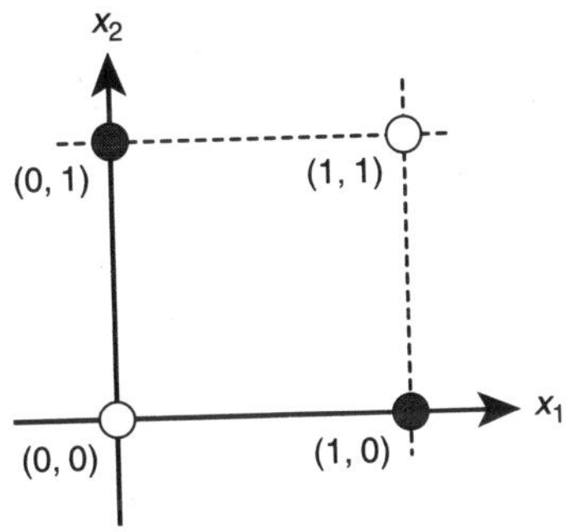

Fig. 6.21. *The XOR problem offers patterns that are not linearly separable*

6.4.3 The *XOR* Problem

Real life classification problems, however, rarely offer such well-behaved linearly separable data as required by a perceptron. Minsky and Papert [1969] showed that no perceptron can learn to compute even a trivial function like a two bit *XOR*. The reason is, there is no single straight line that may separate the 1-producing patterns {(0, 1), (1, 0)} from the patterns 0-producing patterns {(0, 0), (1, 1)}. This is illustrated in Fig. 6.21. Is it possible to overcome this limitation? If yes, then how? There are two ways. One of them is to draw a curved decision surface between the two sets of patterns as shown in Fig. 6.22(a) or 6.22(b). However, perceptron cannot model any curved surface.

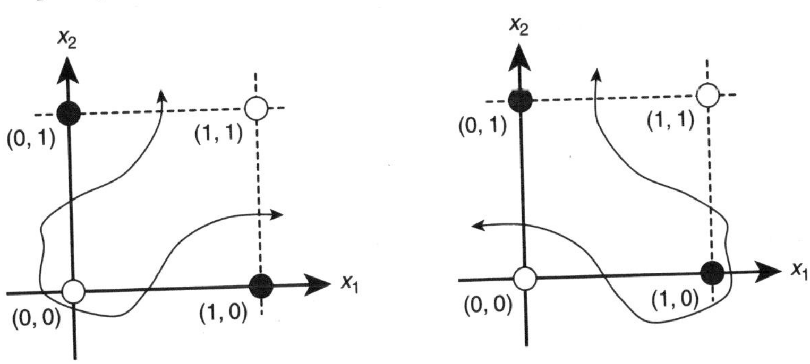

Fig. 6.22. *Solving the XOR problem with curved decision surface*

The other way is to employ two, instead of one, decision lines. The first line isolates the point (1, 1) from the other three points, *viz.*, (0, 0), (0, 1), and (1, 0). The second line partitions {(0, 0), (0, 1), (1, 0)} into the classes {(0, 1), (1, 0)} and {(0, 0)}. The technique is shown is Fig. 6.23. Fig. 6.23(b) shows another pair of lines that solve the problem in a different way.

Using this idea, it is possible design a multi-layered perceptron to solve the *XOR* problem. Such a multilayered perceptron is shown in Fig. 6.24. Here the first perceptron *Y* fires only when the input is (1, 1). But this sends a large inhibitive signal of magnitude –2.0 to the second perceptron *Z* so that the excitatory signals from x_1 and x_2 to *Z* are overpowered. As a result the net input to *Z* attains a negative value and the perceptron fails to fire. On the other hand, the remaining three input patterns, (0, 0), (0, 1), and (1, 0), for which perceptron *Y* does not influence *Z*, are processed by *Z* in the desired way.

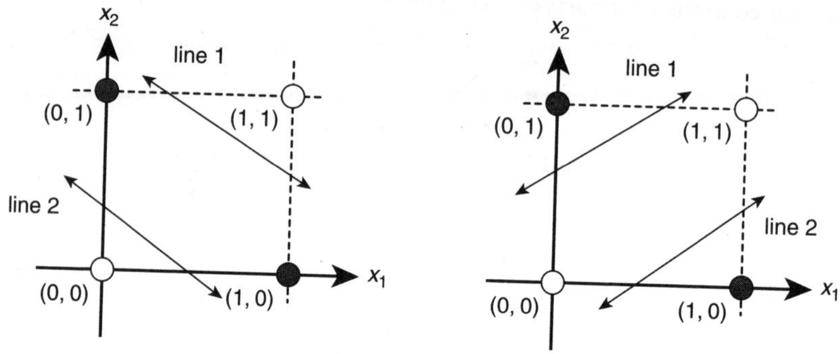

Fig. 6.23. *Solving the XOR problem with two decision lines*

Hence, the arrangement of perceptrons shown in Fig. 6.24 successfully classifies the patterns posed by the *XOR* problem. The critical point is, the perceptron convergence theorem is no longer applicable to multilayer perceptrons. The perceptron learning algorithm can adjust the weights of the interconnections between the inputs and the processing element, but not between the processing elements of two different perceptrons. The weight –2.0 in Fig. 6.24 is decided through observation and analysis, not by training.

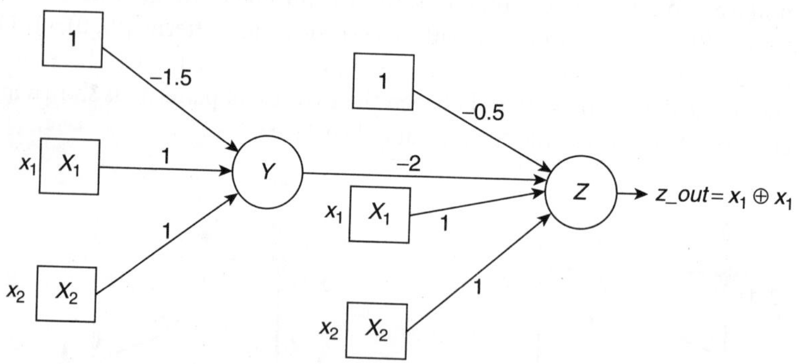

Fig. 6.24. *A multi-layer perceptron to solve the XOR problem*

6.5 NEURAL NETWORK ARCHITECTURES

An ANN consists of a number of artificial neurons connected among themselves in certain ways. Sometime these neurons are arranged in layers, with interconnections across the layers. The network may, or may not, be fully connected. Moreover, the nature of the interconnection paths also varies. They are either unidirectional, or bidirectional. The topology of an ANN, together with the nature of its interconnection paths, is generally referred to as its architecture. This section presents an overview of the major ANN architectures.

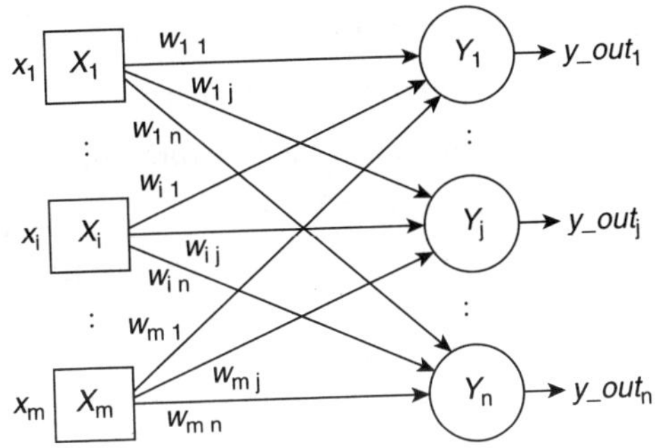

Fig. 6.25. *Structure of a single-layer feed forward ANN*

6.5.1 Single Layer Feed Forward ANNs

Single layer feed forward is perhaps the simplest ANN architecture. As shown in Fig. 6.25, it consists of an array of input neurons connected to an array of output neurons. Since the input neurons do not exercise any processing power, but simply forward the input signals to the subsequent neurons, they are not considered to constitute a layer. Hence, the only layer in the ANN shown in Fig. 6.25 is composed of the output neurons $Y_1, \ldots, Y_n$.

The ANN shown in Fig. 6.25 consists of m inputs $X_1, \ldots, X_m$ and n outputs $Y_1, \ldots, Y_n$. The signal transmitted by input X_i is denoted as x_i. Each input X_i is connected to each output Y_j. The weight associated with the path between X_i and Y_j is denoted as w_{ij}. The interconnection paths are unidirectional and are directed from the input units to the output units.

The net input y_in_1 to the output unit Y_1 is given by

$$y\_in_1 = x_1w_{11} + x_2w_{21} + \cdots + x_mw_{m1} = \sum_{i=1}^{m} x_iw_{i1} \tag{6.24}$$

In vector notation, Equation 6.24 can be expressed as

$$y\_in_1 = [x_1 \ldots x_m] \times \begin{bmatrix} w_{11} \\ \vdots \\ w_{m1} \end{bmatrix} = X \times W_{*1} \tag{6.25}$$

where $X = [x_1 \ldots x_m]$ is the input vector of the input signals and W_{*1} is the first column of the weight matrix

$$W = \begin{bmatrix} w_{11} & w_{12} & \cdots & w_{1n} \\ w_{21} & w_{22} & \cdots & w_{2n} \\ \vdots & \vdots & \cdots & \vdots \\ w_{m1} & w_{m2} & \cdots & w_{mn} \end{bmatrix} \tag{6.26}$$

In general, the net input y_in_j to the output unit Y_j is given by

$$y\_in_j = [x_1 \ldots x_m] \times \begin{bmatrix} w_{1j} \\ \vdots \\ w_{mj} \end{bmatrix} = X \times W_{*_j} \tag{6.27}$$

If Y_in denotes the vector for the net inputs to the array of output units

$$Y\_in = [y\_in_1 \ldots y\_in_n]$$

then the net input to the entire array of output units can be expressed concisely in matrix notation as

$$Y\_in = X \times W \tag{6.28}$$

The signals transmitted by the output units, of course, depend on the nature of the activation functions. There are various kinds of activation functions and these are discussed in greater details in the next subsection. The basic single layer feed forward network architecture presented in this section has its own variations. For example, in some cases the network may allow interconnections among the input or output units themselves. These will be discussed later in greater details.

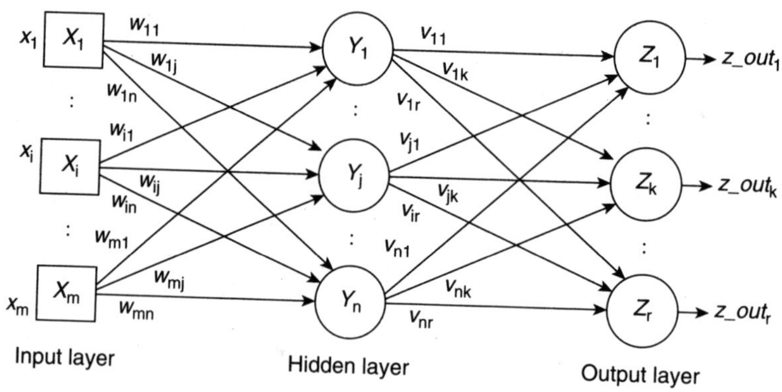

Fig. 6.26. *A multi-layer feed forward network with one hidden layer*

6.5.2 Multilayer Feed Forward ANNs

A multilayer feed forward net is similar to single layer feed forward net except that there is (are) one or more additional layer(s) of processing units between the input and the output layers. Such additional layers are called the *hidden* layers of the network. Fig. 6.26 shows the architecture of a multi-layer feed forward neural net with one hidden layer.

The expressions for the net inputs to the hidden layer units and the output units are obtained as

$$Y\_in = X \times W \tag{6.29}$$

$$Z\_in = Y\_out \times V \tag{6.30}$$

where

$X = [x_1, x_2, \cdots, x_m]$, X is the input vector,

$Y\_in = [y\_in_1, y\_in_2, \cdots, y\_in_n]$, is the net input vector to the hidden layer,

$Z\_in = [z\_in_1, z\_in_2, \cdots, z\_in_r]$, is the net input vector to the output layer,

$Y\_out = [y\_out_1, y\_out_2, \cdots, y\_out_n]$, is the output vector from the hidden layer,

W and V are the weight matrices for the interconnections between the input layer, hidden layer, and output layer respectively.

$$W = \begin{bmatrix} w_{11} & w_{12} & \cdots & w_{1n} \\ w_{21} & w_{22} & \cdots & w_{2n} \\ \vdots & \vdots & \cdots & \vdots \\ w_{m1} & w_{m2} & \cdots & w_{mn} \end{bmatrix} \text{ and } V = \begin{bmatrix} v_{11} & v_{12} & \cdots & v_{1r} \\ v_{21} & v_{22} & \cdots & v_{2r} \\ \vdots & \vdots & \cdots & \vdots \\ v_{n1} & v_{n2} & \cdots & v_{nr} \end{bmatrix}$$

Fig. 6.26 shows the structure of a multi-layered feed forward net with one hidden layer. Obviously, it is possible to include more than one hidden layers in such networks.

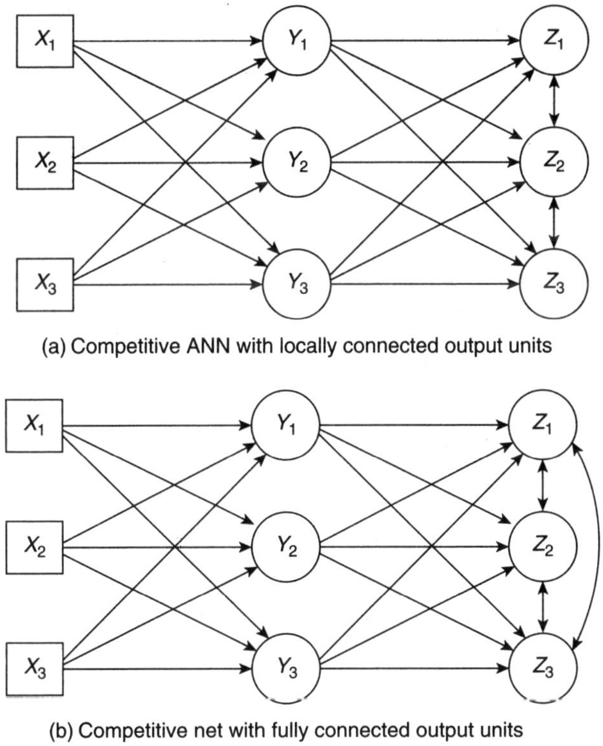

Fig. 6.27. *Competitive ANN architectures*

6.5.3 Competitive Network

Competitive networks are structurally similar to single layer feed forward nets. However, the output units of a competitive neural net are connected among themselves, usually through negative weights. Fig. 6.27(a) and 6.27(b) show two kinds of competitive networks. In Fig. 6.27(a), the output units are connected only to their respective neighbours, whereas the network of Fig. 6.27(b) shows a competitive network whose output units are fully connected. For a given input pattern, the output units of a competitive network tend to compete among themselves to represent that input. Thus the name competitive network.

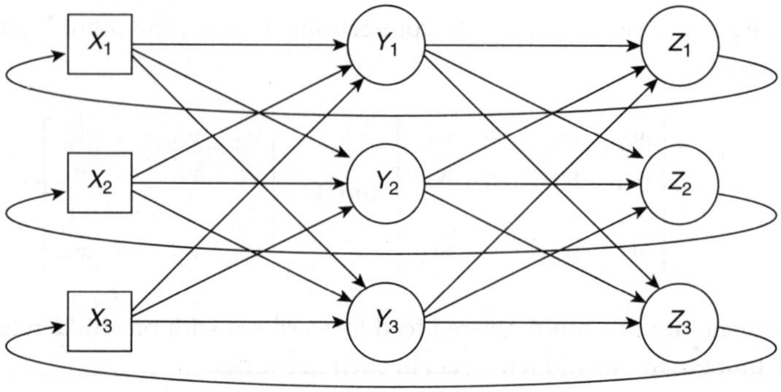

Fig. 6.28 *A recurrent network with feedback paths from the output layer to the input layer*

6.5.4 Recurrent Networks

In a feed forward network signals flow in one direction only and that is from the input layer towards the output layer through the hidden layers, if any. Such networks do not have any feedback loop. In contrast, a recurrent network allows feedback loops. A typical recurrent network architecture is shown in Fig. 6.28. Fig. 6.29(a) shows a fully connected recurrent network. Such networks contain a bidirectional path between every pair of processing elements. Moreover, a recurrent network may contain self loops, as shown in Fig. 6.29(b).

6.6 ACTIVATION FUNCTIONS

The output from a processing unit is termed as its activation. Activation of a processing unit is a function of the net input to the processing unit. The function that maps the net input value to the output signal value, i.e., the activation, is known as the activation function of the unit. Some common activation functions are presented below.

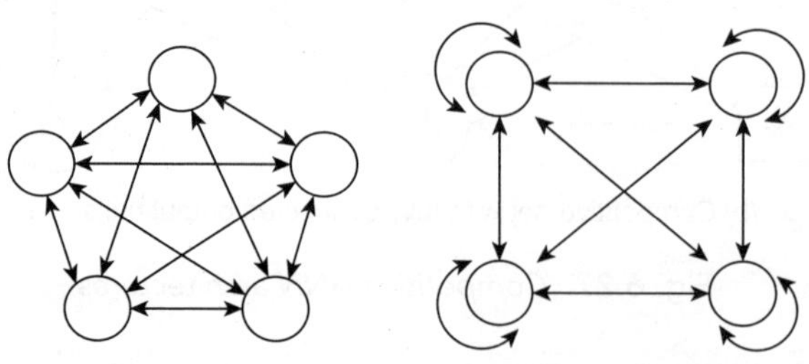

(a) A fully connected recurrent network

(b) A recurrent network with self loops

Fig. 6.29. *Recurrent network architectures*

6.6.1 Identity Function

The simplest activation function is the identity function that passes on the incoming signal as the outgoing signal without any change. Therefore, the identity activation function $g(x)$ is defined as

$$g(x) = x \tag{6.31}$$

Fig. 6.30 shows the form of the identity function graphically. Usually, the units of the input layer employ the identity function for their activation. This is because in ANN, the role of an input unit is to forward the incoming signal as it is to the units in the next layer through the respective weighted paths.

6.6.2 Step Function

Another frequently used activation function is the step function. The basic step function produces a 1 or 0 depending on whether the net input is greater than 0 or otherwise. This is the only activation function we have used so far in this text. Mathematically the step function is defined as follows.

$$g(x) = \begin{cases} 1, & \text{if } x > 0, \\ 0, & \text{otherwise.} \end{cases} \tag{6.32}$$

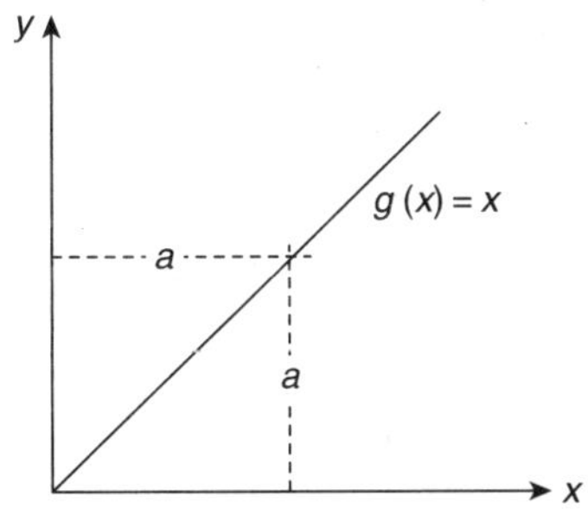

Fig. 6.30. *The identity activation function*

Fig. 6.31(a) shows the shape of the basic step function graphically. Occasionally, instead of 0 a non-zero threshold value θ is used. This is known as the threshold function and is defined as

$$g(x) = \begin{cases} 1, & \text{if } x > \theta, \\ 0, & \text{otherwise.} \end{cases} \tag{6.33}$$

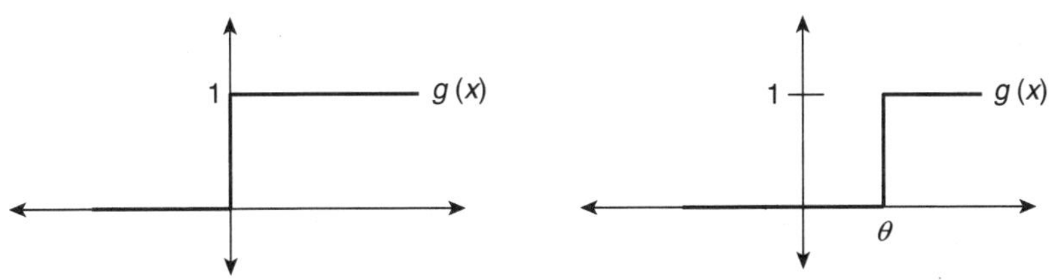

(a) Basic step function

(b) Threshold function function

Fig. 6.31. *Step functions*

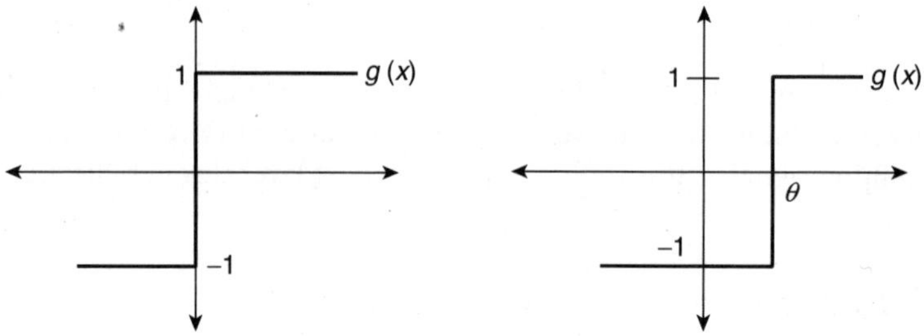

(c) Bipolar step function function

(d) Bipolar threshold function function

Fig. 6.31. *(Continued)*

The shape of the threshold function is shown in Fig. 6.31(b). The step function is also known as the *heaviside* function. The step functions discussed so far are binary step functions since they always evaluates to 0 or 1.

Occasionally, it is more convenient to work with bipolar data, −1 and +1, than the binary data. If a signal of value 0 is sent through a weighted path, the information contained in the interconnection weight is lost as it is multiplied by 0. To overcome this problem, the binary input is converted to bipolar form and then a suitable bipolar activation function is employed. Accordingly, binary step functions have their bipolar versions. The output of a bipolar step function is −1, or +1, not 0, or 1. The bipolar step function and threshold function are shown in Fig. 1.31(c) and (d) respectively. They are defined as follows.

Bipolar step function:

$$g(x) = \begin{cases} +1, & \text{if } x > 0, \\ -1, & \text{otherwise.} \end{cases} \quad (6.34)$$

Bipolar threshold function:

$$g(x) = \begin{cases} +1, & \text{if } x > \theta, \\ -1, & \text{otherwise.} \end{cases} \quad (6.35)$$

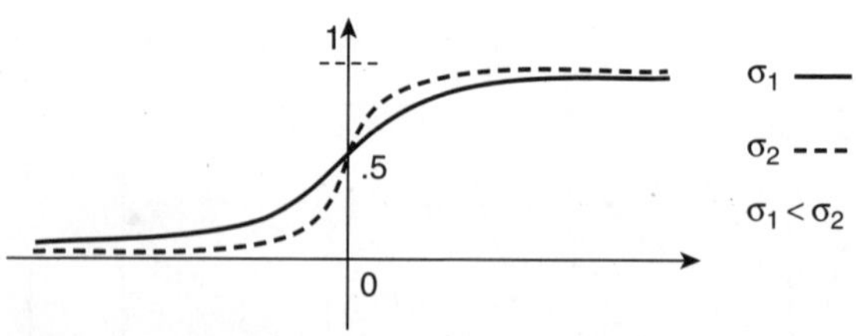

Fig. 6.32. *Binary Sigmoid function*

6.6.3 The Sigmoid Function

As the step function is not continuous it is not differentiable. Some ANN training algorithm requires that the activation function be continuous and differentiable. The step function is not suitable for such cases. Sigmoid functions have the nice property that they can approximate the step function to the desired extent without losing its differentiability. Binary *sigmoid*, also referred to as the *logistic* sigmoid, is defined by Equation 6.36.

$$g(x) = \frac{1}{1+e^{-\sigma x}} \tag{6.36}$$

The parameter σ in Equation 6.36 is known as the *steepness parameter*. The shape of the sigmoid function is shown in Fig. 6.32. The transition from 0 to 1 could be made as steep as desired by increasing the value of σ to appropriate extent.

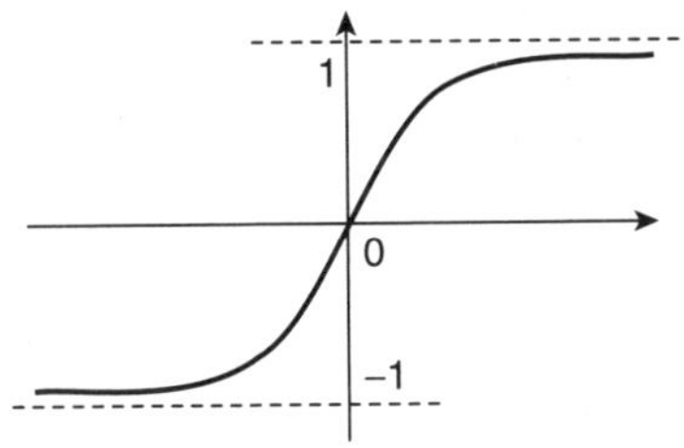

Fig. 6.33. *Bipolar Sigmoid function*

The first derivative of $g(x)$, denoted by $g'(x)$ is expressed as

$$g'(x) = \sigma g(x)(1 - g(x)) \tag{6.37}$$

Depending on the requirement, the binary sigmoid function can be scaled to any range of values appropriate for a given application. The most widely used range is from −1 to +1, and the corresponding sigmoid function is referred to as the bipolar sigmoid function. The formulae for the bipolar sigmoid function and its first derivative are given below as Equations 6.38 and 6.39 respectively. Fig. 6.33 presents its form graphically.

$$g(x) = \frac{1-e^{-\sigma x}}{1+e^{-\sigma x}} \tag{6.38}$$

$$g'(x) = \frac{\sigma}{2}(1+g(x))(1-g(x)) \tag{6.39}$$

6.6.4 Hyperbolic Tangent Function

Another bipolar activation function that is widely employed in ANN applications is the *hyperbolic tangent function*. The function, as well as its first derivative, are expressed by Equations 6.40 and 6.41 respectively.

$$h(x) = \frac{e^{x} - e^{-x}}{e^{x} + e^{-x}} \tag{6.40}$$

$$h'(x) = (1+h(x))(1-h(x)) \tag{6.41}$$

The hyperbolic tangent function is closely related to the bipolar sigmoid function. When the input data is binary and not continuously valued in the range from 0 to 1, they are generally converted to bipolar form and then a bipolar sigmoid or hyperbolic tangent activation function is applied on them by the processing units.

6.7 LEARNING BY NEURAL NETS

An ANN is characterized by three entities, it's architecture, activation function, and the learning technique. Learning by an ANN refers to the process of finding the appropriate set of weights of the interconnections so that the ANN attains the ability to perform the designated task. The process is also referred to as training the ANN.

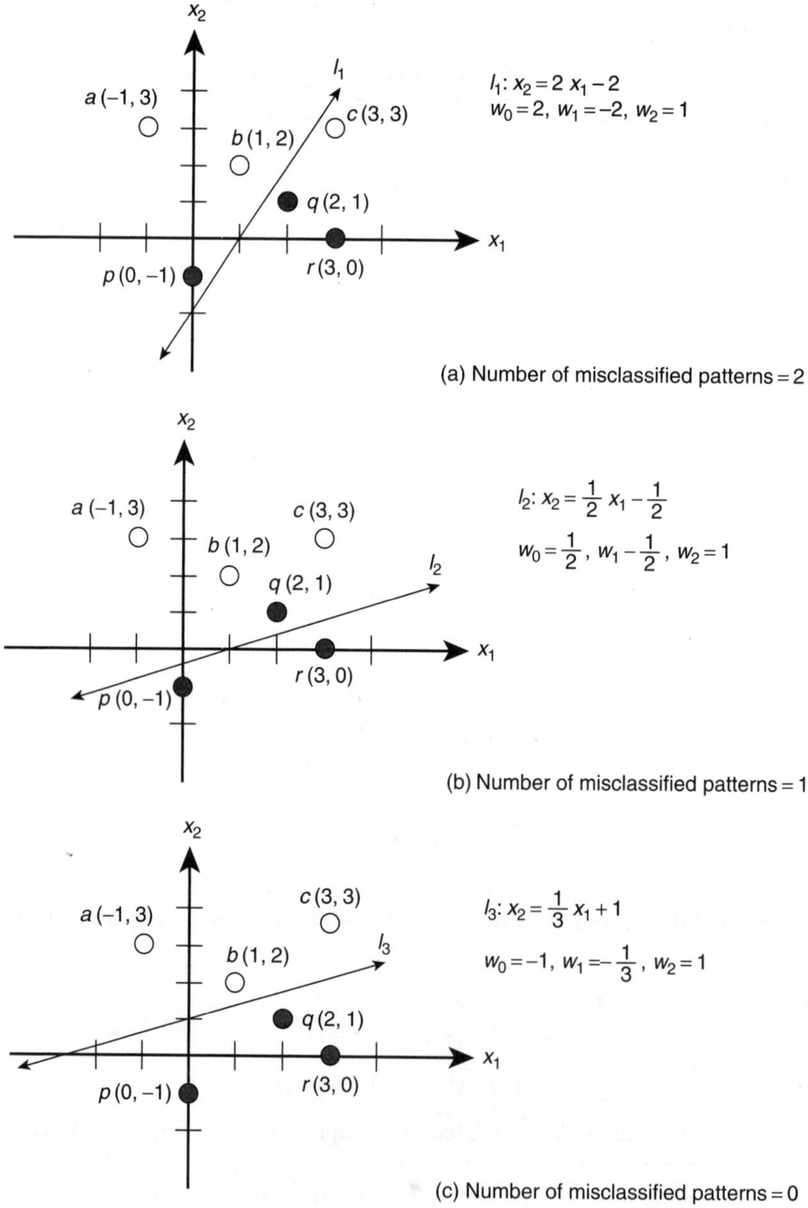

(a) Number of misclassified patterns = 2

(b) Number of misclassified patterns = 1

(c) Number of misclassified patterns = 0

Fig. 6.34. *Learning a pattern classification task by a perceptron*

Let us, once again, consider the classification problem posed in Section 6.4.2 (Fig. 6.18). A perceptron is presented (Fig. 6.19) to solve the problem. It has the following combination of interconnection weights : $w_0 = -1$, $w_1 = -1/3$, $w_2 = 1$. It is easy to verify that an arbitrary set of weights may not be able to solve the given classification problem. The question is, how to find the appropriate set of weights for an ANN so that the ANN is able to solve a given problem? One way is to start with a set of weights and then gradually modify them to arrive at the final set of weights. This is illustrated in Fig. 6.34(a), (b), (c). Suppose we start with a set of randomly chosen values, say $w_0 = 2$, $w_1 = -2$, $w_2 = 1$. The corresponding decision line is l_1 (Fig. 6.34(a)) which is algebraically expressed by the equation $x_2 = 2\,x_1 - 2$. As Fig. 6.34(a) shows, line l_1 classifies the points *a* (−1, 3), *b* (1, 2), *q* (2, 1), and *r* (3, 0) correctly. But it misclassifies the points c (3, 3) (wrongly put in the class *B*) and the point p (0, −1) (wrongly put in the class *A*). In the next step the weights are modified to $w_0 = 1/2$, $w_1 = -1/2$, $w_2 = 1$, so that the new decision line $l_2 : x_2 = 1/2\,x_1 - 1/2$ reduces the number of misclassified data to 1, only the point *q* (2, 1). This is shown in Fig. 6.34(b). Then the weights are further modified to obtain the decision line $l_3 : x_2 = 1/3\,x_1 + 1$, that leaves no pattern misclassified (Fig. 6.34(c)).

This learning instance illustrates the basic concept of *supervised learning*, i.e., learning assisted by a teacher. However, quite a number of issues are yet to be addressed. For example, given a set of interconnection weights, how to determine the adjustments required to compute the next set of weights? Moreover, how do we ensure that the process converges, i.e., the number of misclassified patterns are progressively reduced and eventually made 0? The subsequent parts of this section briefly introduce the popular learning algorithms employed in ANN systems.

The basic principle of ANN learning is rather simple. It starts with an initial distribution of interconnection weights and then goes on adjusting the weights iteratively until some predefined stopping criterion is satisfied. Therefore, if $w(k)$ be the weight of a certain interconnection path at the kth iteration, then $w(k+1)$, the same at the $(k+1)$th iteration, is obtained by

$$w(k+1) = w(k) + \Delta w(k) \tag{6.42}$$

where $\Delta w(k)$ is the kth adjustment to weight w. A learning algorithm is characterized by the method undertaken by it to compute $\Delta w(k)$.

6.7.1 Supervised Learning

A neural network is trained with the help of a set of patterns known as the training vectors. The outputs for these vectors might be, or might not be, known beforehand. When these are known, and that knowledge is employed in the training process, the training is termed as *supervised* learning. Otherwise, the learning is said to be unsupervised. Some popular supervised learning methods are perceptron learning, delta learning, least-mean-square (LMS) learning, correlation learning, outstar learning etc. These are briefly introduced below.

(a) Hebb Rule

The Hebb rule is one of the earliest learning rules for ANNs. According to this rule the weight adjustment is computed as

$$\Delta w_i = x_i \times t \tag{6.43}$$

where t is the target activation.

There are certain points to be kept in mind regarding the Hebb learning rule. First, Hebb rule cannot learn when the target is 0. This is because the weight adjustment Δw_i becomes zero when $t = 0$, irrespective of the value of x_i. Hence, obviously, the Hebb rule results in better learning if the input / output both are in bipolar form. The most striking limitation of the Hebb rule is it does not guarantee to learn a classification instance even if the classes are linearly separable. This is illustrated in Chapter 7. The Example 6.6 below gives an instance of Hebb Learning.

Example 6.6 *(Realizing the logical AND function through Hebb learning)*

To realize a two input *AND* function we need a net with two input units and one output unit. A bias is also needed. Hence the structure of the required neural net should be as shown in Fig. 6.35. Moreover, the input and output signals must be in *bipolar* form, rather than the *binary* form, so that the net may be trained properly. The advantage of bipolar signals over binary signals is discussed in greater detail in Chap. 7. Considering the truth table of *AND* operation, and the fact that the bias is permanently set to 1, we get the training set depicted in Table 6.7.

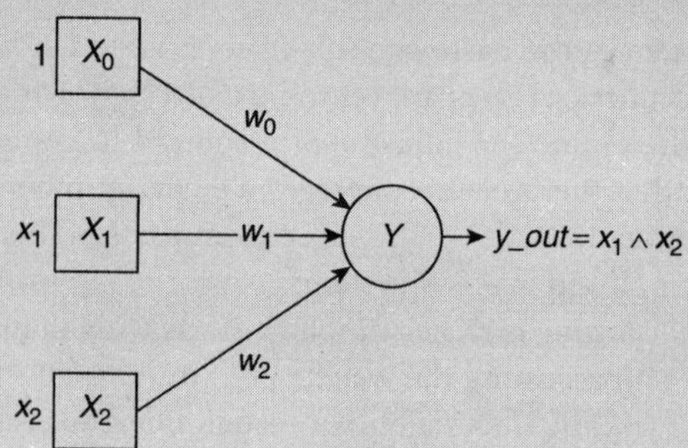

Fig. 6.35. *Structure of a neural net to realize the AND function*

Table 6.7 *Training set for AND function*

Input Patterns			Output
x_0	x_1	x_2	t
+1	1	1	1
+1	1	−1	−1
+1	−1	1	−1
+1	−1	−1	−1

During the training process, all weights are initialized to 0. Therefore initially

$$w_0 = w_1 = w_2 = 0$$

At each training instance, the weights are changed according to the formula

$$w_i(new) = w_i(old) + \Delta w_i$$

where Δw_i, the increment in w_i, is computed as $\Delta w_i = x_i . \times t$. After initialization, the progress of the learning process by the network is shown in Table 6.8.

Table 6.8. *Hebbian learning of AND function*

#	Training Pattern			Target output	Weight Adjustments			Weights		
	x_0	x_1	x_2	t	Δw_0	Δw_1	Δw_2	w_0	w_1	w_2
0								0	0	0
1	1	1	1	1	1	1	1	1	1	1
2	1	1	−1	−1	−1	−1	1	0	0	2
3	1	−1	1	−1	−1	1	−1	−1	1	1
4	1	−1	−1	−1	−1	1	1	−2	2	2

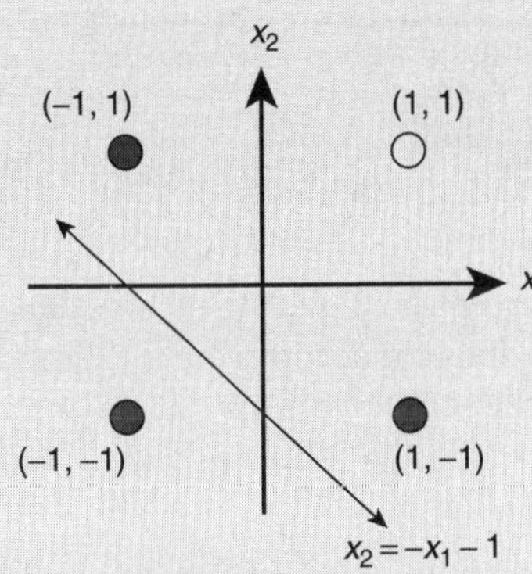

(a) After 1st pattern (1, 1)

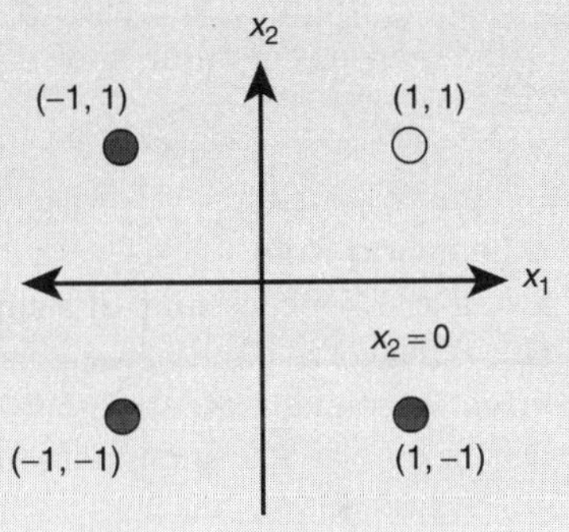

(b) After 2nd pattern (1, −1)

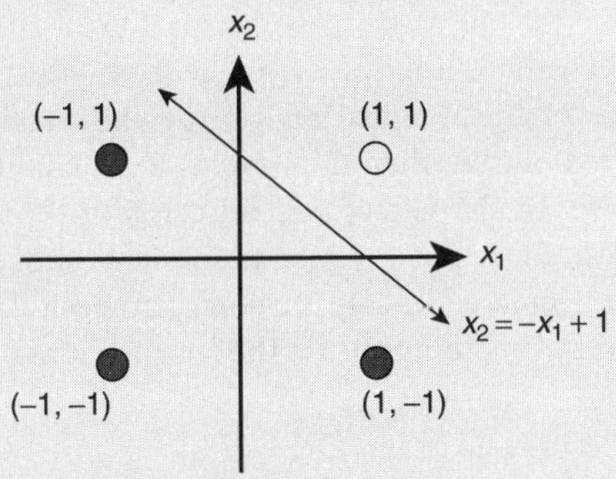

(c) After 3rd pattern (−1, 1)

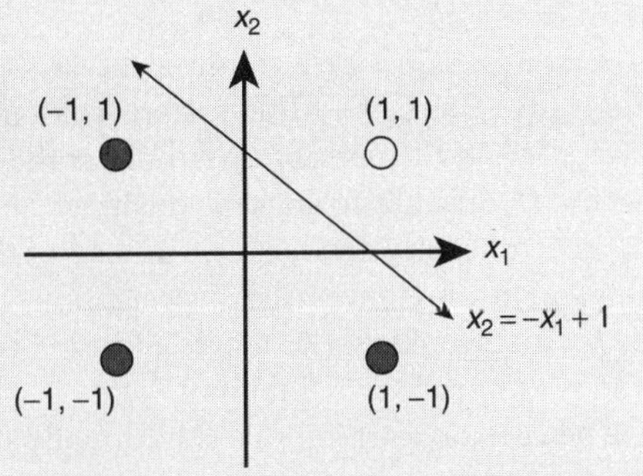

(d) After 4th pattern (−1, −1)

Fig. 6.36. *Hebbian training to learn AND function*

Hence, on completion of one epoch of training, the weight vector is $W = [w_0, w_1, w_2] = [-2, 2, 2]$. The progress in learning by the net can be visualized by observing the orientation of the decision line after each training instance. Putting the values of the interconnection weights in the equation

$$x_2 = -\frac{w_1}{w_2}x_1 - \frac{w_0}{w_2}$$

we get (*i*) $x_2 = -x_1 - 1$, after the 1st training instance,
(*ii*) $x_2 = 0$, after the 2nd training instance,
(*iii*) $x_2 = -x_1 + 1$, after the 3rd training instance, and finally,
(*iv*) $x_2 = -x_1 + 1$, after the 4th training instance.

This progress in the learning process is depicted in Fig. 6.36(a)-(d). We see that after training with the first pattern $[x_0, x_1, x_2] = [1, 1, 1]$, the ANN learns to classify two patterns (−1, −1) and (1, 1) successfully. But it fails to classify correctly the other two patterns (−1, 1) and (1, −1). After learning with the second pattern (1, −1) the situation is better. Only (−1, 1) is still misclassified. This is corrected after training with the third pattern (−1, 1). Now all the −1 producing patterns are, i.e., (1, −1), (−1, 1) and (−1, −1) are in the same class and the remaining pattern (1, 1) constitutes the other class.

(b) Perceptron Learning Rule

Let us consider a simple ANN consisting of a single perceptron Y with m+1 input units $X_0, \ldots, X_m$ as shown in Fig. 6.17(b). The corresponding weights of the interconnections are $w_0, \ldots, w_m$. The bias is introduced as the weight w_0 connected to the input X_0 whose activation is fixed at 1. For the output unit, it is convenient to use the bipolar activation function :

$$y\_out = \begin{cases} 1, & if\ y\_in > 0 \\ 0, & if\ y\_in = 0 \\ -1 & if\ y\_in < 1 \end{cases} \tag{6.44}$$

Now, let $X = (x_0, \ldots, x_m)$ be a training vector for which the output of the perceptron is expected to be t, where t = 1, 0, or −1. The current combination of the weights is given by the weight vector $W = (w_0, \ldots, w_m)$. If the perceptron produces the desired output, then the weights $w_0, \ldots, w_m$ need not be changed and they are to be kept unaltered. If, however, the perceptron misclassifies X negatively (meaning, it erroneously produces −1 instead of the desired output +1) then the weights should be appropriately increased. Conversely, the weights are to be decreased in case the perceptron misclassifies X positively (i.e., it erroneously produces +1 instead of the desired output −1). The learning strategy of the perceptron is summarized in Table 6.9.

Hence the perceptron learning rule is informally stated as

IF *the output is erroneous* THEN *adjust the interconnection weights*
ELSE *leave the interconnection weights unchanged.*

In more precise terms,

IF $y\_out \neq t$ THEN

FOR $i = 0$ TO m DO $w_i(new) = w_i(old) + \eta \times t \times x_i$

ELSE

FOR $i = 0$ TO m DO $w_i(new) = w_i(old)$.

Table 6.9. *Perceptron learning rules*

#	Condition	Action
1	The perceptron classifies the input pattern correctly ($y\_out = t$)	No change in the current set of weights $w_0, w_1, \ldots, w_m$.
2	The perceptron misclassifies the input pattern negatively ($y\_out = -1$, but $t = +1$)	Increase each w_i by Δw_i, where Δw_i is proportional to x_i, for all $i = 0, 1, \ldots, m$.
3	The perceptron misclassifies the input pattern positively ($y\_out = +1$, but $t = -1$)	Decrease each w_i by Δw_i, where Δw_i is proportional to x_i, for all $i = 0, 1, \ldots, m$.

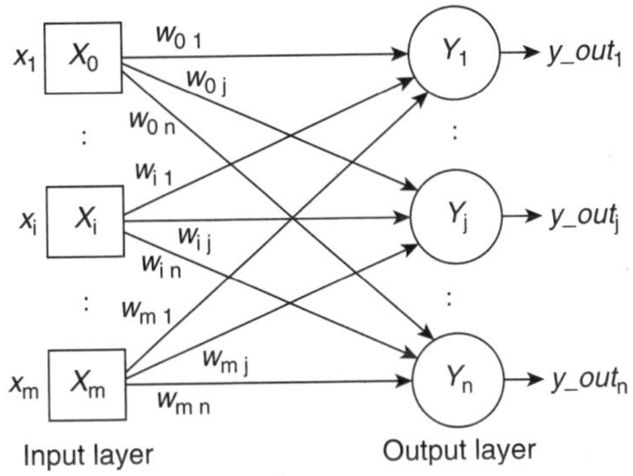

Fig. 6.37. *Structure of an ANN with several perceptrons*

Thus the perceptron learning rule can be formulated as

$$\Delta w_i = \eta \times (t - y\_out) \times x_i, \text{ for } i = 0, 1, \ldots, m \tag{6.45}$$

Here η is a constant known as the *learning rate*. It should be noticed that when a training vector is correctly classified then $y\_out = t$, and the weight adjustment $\Delta w_i = 0$. When $y\_out = -1$ but $t = +1$, i.e., the pattern is misclassified negatively, then $t - y\_out = +2$ so that Δw_i is incremental and is proportional to x_i. If, however, the input pattern is misclassified positively, the adjustment is decremental, and obviously, proportional to x_i. Using matrix notation, the perceptron learning rule may now be written as

$$\Delta W = \eta \times (t - y\_out) \times X \tag{6.46}$$

where, ΔW and X are the vectors corresponding to the interconnection weights and the inputs.

$$\Delta W = [\Delta w_0, \ldots, \Delta w_m], \text{ and}$$

$$X = [x_0, x, \ldots, x_m].$$

Equation 6.45 can be easily extended to a network of several perceptrons at the output layer. Such architecture is shown in Fig. 6.37. The net inputs to the perceptrons are

$$\begin{bmatrix} y\_in_1 \\ \vdots \\ y\_in_j \\ \vdots \\ y\_in_n \end{bmatrix} = \begin{bmatrix} w_{01} & \cdots & w_{i1} & \cdots & w_{m1} \\ \vdots & & \vdots & & \vdots \\ w_{0j} & \cdots & w_{ij} & \cdots & w_{mj} \\ \vdots & & \vdots & & \vdots \\ w_{0n} & \cdots & w_{in} & \cdots & w_{mn} \end{bmatrix} \times \begin{bmatrix} x_0 \\ \vdots \\ x_i \\ \vdots \\ x_m \end{bmatrix}$$

or,
$$Y\_in^{T} = W^{T} \times X^{T} \tag{6.47}$$

For such an ANN, the adjustment Δw_{ij} of the weight w_{ij} is given by

$$\Delta w_{ij} = \eta \times (t_j - y\_out_j) \times x_i \tag{6.48}$$

Let us assume the following matrix notations :

$$\Delta W = \begin{bmatrix} \Delta w_{01} & \Delta w_{02} & \cdots & \Delta w_{0n} \\ \Delta w_{11} & \Delta w_{12} & \cdots & \Delta w_{1n} \\ \vdots & \vdots & \vdots & \vdots \\ \Delta w_{m1} & \Delta w_{m2} & \cdots & \Delta w_{mn} \end{bmatrix},\ T = \begin{bmatrix} t_1 & \cdots & t_n \end{bmatrix},$$
$$X = \begin{bmatrix} x_0, & ..., & x_m \end{bmatrix}, and\ Y\_out = \begin{bmatrix} y\_out_1, & ..., & y\_out_n \end{bmatrix}.$$

Then the expression of the perceptron learning rule for the architecture shown in Fig. 6.34 becomes

$$[\Delta W]^{T} = \eta \times [T - Y\_out]^{T} \times X \tag{6.49}$$

Example 6.7 *(Learning the logical AND function by a perceptron)*

Let us train a perceptron to realize the logical AND function. The training patterns and the corresponding target outputs for *AND* operation where the input and outputs are in bipolar form are given in Table 6.7. The structure of the perceptron is same as shown in Fig. 6.35. Activation function for the output unit is :

$$y\_out = g(y\_in) = \begin{cases} 1, & if\ y\_in > 0 \\ 0, & if\ y\_in = 0 \\ -1, & if\ y\_in < 0 \end{cases}$$

The successive steps of computation with the first training pair are given below.

i) Initialize weights : $w_0 = w_1 = w_2 = 0$, and the learning rate $\eta = 1$.

ii) For the training pair $s : t = (1, 1, 1) : (1)$, compute the net input *y_in* and the activation *y_out* :

$$\begin{aligned} y\_in &= w_0 \times x_0 + w_1 \times x_1 + w_2 \times x_2 \\ &= 0 \times 1 + 0 \times 1 + 0 \times 1 \\ &= 0 \\ \therefore\ y\_out &= 0. \end{aligned}$$

iii) Apply the perceptron learning rule to find the weight adjustments. The rule is :
If $y\_out = t$, then the weights are not changed, otherwise change the weights according to the formula $w_i\,(new) = w_i\,(old) + \Delta w_i$ where $\Delta w_i = \eta t\, x_i$. In the present case, $y\_out = 0$, and $t = 1$, and $y\_out \neq t$. Therefore the weights are to be adjusted.

$$\begin{aligned} w_0\,(new) &= w_0\,(old) + \Delta w_0 \\ &= w_0\,(old) + \eta t x_0 \\ &= 0 + 1 \times 1 \times 1 \\ &= 1. \end{aligned}$$

Similarly, $w_1(new) = w_1(old) + \Delta w_1$

$$= w_1(old) + \eta t x_1$$
$$= 0 + 1 \times 1 \times 1$$
$$= 1.$$

And, $w_2(new) = 1.$

Putting these values of the weights in the formula

$$x_2 = -\frac{w_1}{w_2}x_1 - \frac{w_0}{w_2}$$

we get the separating line as $x_2 = -x_1 - 1$, which classifies the patterns (1, 1) and (−1, −1) correctly but misclassifies the patterns (−1, 1) and (1, −1) (Fig. 6.36(a)). A trace of the remaining steps of the first *epoch* of training (an *epoch* of training consists of successive application of each and every training pair of the training set for once) are noted in Table 6.10.

Hence, the set of weights obtained at the end of the first epoch of training is (−1, 1, 1) which represents to the decision line

$$x_2 = -x_1 + 1$$

It can be easily verified that this line (and the corresponding set of weights) successfully realizes the AND function for all possible input combinations. Hence, there is no need of further training.

Table 6.10. *Perceptron learning of AND function*

#	Input pattern			Net input	Activation	Target output	Weight Adjustments			Weights		
	x_0	x_1	x_2	y_in	y_out	t	Δw_0	Δw_1	Δw_2	w_0	w_1	w_2
0										0	0	0
1	1	1	1	0	0	1	1	1	1	1	1	1
2	1	1	−1	1	1	−1	−1	−1	1	0	0	2
3	1	−1	1	2	1	−1	−1	1	−1	−1	1	1
4	1	−1	−1	−3	−1	−1	0	0	0	−1	1	1

(c) Delta / LMS (Least Mean Square), or, Widrow-Hoff Rule

Least Mean Square (*LMS*), also referred to as the Delta, or Widrow-Hoff Rule, is another widely used learning rule in ANN literature. Here the weight adjustment is computed as

$$\Delta w_i = \eta \times (t - y\_in) \times x_i \tag{6.50}$$

where the symbols have their usual meanings. In *LMS* learning, the identity function is used as the activation function during the training phase. The learning rule minimizes mean squared error between the activation and the target value. The output of *LMS* learning is in binary form. Example 6.8 illustrates LMS learning of the AND function.

Example 6.8 *(Realize the logical AND function through LMS learning rule)*

The training patterns and the corresponding target outputs for *AND* operation where the input and outputs are in bipolar form are given in Table 6.7. The structure of the perceptron is same as shown in Fig. 6.35. The successive steps of computation for the first epoch are given below.

(i) Initialize weights : $w_0 = w_1 = w_2 = .3$, and the learning rate $\eta = .2$ (These values are randomly chosen)

(ii) For the training pair $s : t = (1, 1, 1) : (1)$, compute the net input y_in as

$$y\_in = w_0 \times x_0 + w_1 \times x_1 + w_2 \times x_2$$
$$= .3 \times 1 + .3 \times 1 + .3 \times 1$$
$$= .9$$

(iii) Apply the *LMS* learning rule to find the weight adjustments. The rule is, $w_i\,(new) = w_i\,(old) + \Delta w_i$, where $\Delta w_i = \eta(t - y\_in)\, x_i$. Hence

$$w_i\,(new) = w_i\,(old) + \eta(t - y\_in)\, x_i,$$

In the present case, $y\_in = .9$, and $t = 1$. Therefore

$$w_0\,(new) = w_0\,(old) + \Delta w_0$$
$$= w_0\,(old) + \eta(t - y\_in)\, x_0$$
$$= .3 + .2 \times (1 - .9) \times 1$$
$$= .3 + .02$$
$$= .32$$

Similarly, $\qquad w_1\,(new) = w_2\,(new) = .32$

Second iteration is to be carried out with the training pair $s : t = (1, 1, -1) : (-1)$. The net input y_in is now

$$y\_in = w_0 \times x_0 + w_1 \times x_1 + w_2 \times x_2$$
$$= .32 \times 1 + .32 \times 1 + .32 \times (-1)$$
$$= .32$$

The new weights are computed as follows :

$$w_0\,(new) = w_0\,(old) + \Delta w_0$$
$$= w_0\,(old) + \eta(t - y\_in)\, x_0$$
$$= .32 + .2 \times (-1 - .32) \times 1$$
$$= .32 - .264$$
$$= .056$$

Similarly, $$w_1(new) = .056$$

However, $$w_2(new) = .32 + .2 \times (-1 - .32) \times (-1)$$

$$= .32 + .264$$

$$= .584$$

Hence, at the end of the second iteration, we get $w_0 = .056$, $w_1 = .056$, and $w_2 = .584$. The details of the computation for the first epoch are recorded in Table 6.11. We see that the weights arrived at the end of the first epoch are $w_0 = -.281$, $w_1 = .393$, and $w_2 = .287$. Table 6.12 shows that this set of weights is appropriate to realize the *AND* function. Hence there is no need to iterate further.

Table 6.11. *LMS Learning of AND function*

#	Input Pattern			Net input	Target output	Error	Weight Adjustments			Weights		
	x_0	x_1	x_2	y_in	t	$t - y\_in$	Δw_0	Δw_1	Δw_2	w_0	w_1	w_2
0										.3	.3	.3
1	1	1	1	.9	1	.1	.02	.02	.02	.32	.32	.32
2	1	1	−1	.32	−1	−1.32	−.264	−.264	.264	.056	.056	.584
3	1	−1	1	.584	−1	−1.584	−.317	.317	−.317	−.261	.373	.267
4	1	−1	−1	−.901	−1	−.099	−.02	.02	.02	−.281	.393	.287

Table 6.12. *Performance of the net after LMS learning*

#	Input Pattern			Net input	Output	Target Output
	x_0	x_1	x_2	$y\_in = \Sigma w_i x_i$	y_out	t
1	1	1	1	.399 > 0	1	1
2	1	1	−1	−.175 < 0	−1	−1
3	1	−1	1	−.387 < 0	−1	−1
4	1	−1	−1	−.961 < 0	−1	−1

(d) Extended Delta Rule

The Extended Delta Rule removes the restriction of the output activation function being the identity function only. Any differentiable function can be used for this purpose. Here the weight adjustment is given by

$$\Delta w_{ij} = \eta \times (t_j - y\_out_j) \times x_1 \times g'(y\_in_j) \tag{6.51}$$

where $g(.)$ is the output activation function and $g'(.)$ is its first derivative.

6.7.2 Unsupervised Learning

So far we have considered only supervised learning where the training patterns are provided with the target outputs. However, the target output may not be available during the learning phase.

Typically, such a situation is posed by a pattern *clustering* problem, rather than a classification or association problem.

Let us, for instance, consider a set of points on a Cartesian plane as shown in Fig. 6.38 (*a*). The problem is to divide the given patterns into two clusters so that when the neural net is presented with one of these patterns, its output indicates the cluster to which the pattern belongs. Intuitively, the patterns those are *close* to each other should form a cluster. Of course we must have a suitable measure of *closeness*. Fig. 6.38(b) shows the situation after the neural net learns to form the clusters, so that it 'knows' the cluster to which each of the given pattern belongs.

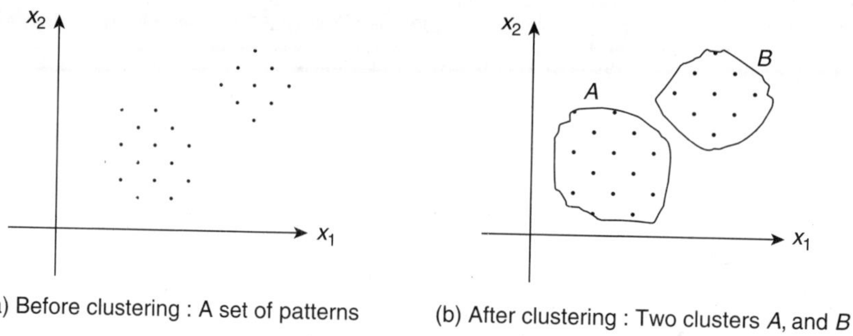

Fig. 6.38. *Clustering a given set of patterns*

Clustering is an instance of unsupervised learning because it is not assisted by any *teacher*, or, any target output. The network itself has to *understand* the patterns and put them into appropriate clusters. The only clue is the given number of clusters. Let us suppose that the network output layer has one unit for each cluster. In response to a given input pattern, exactly one among the output units has to fire. To ensure this, additional features need to be included in the network so that the network is compelled to make a decision as to which unit should fire due to certain input pattern. This is achieved through a mechanism called *competition*. The most commonly used competitive learning mechanism is the so called *winner-takes-all* learning. The basic principle of winner-take-it-all is discussed below.

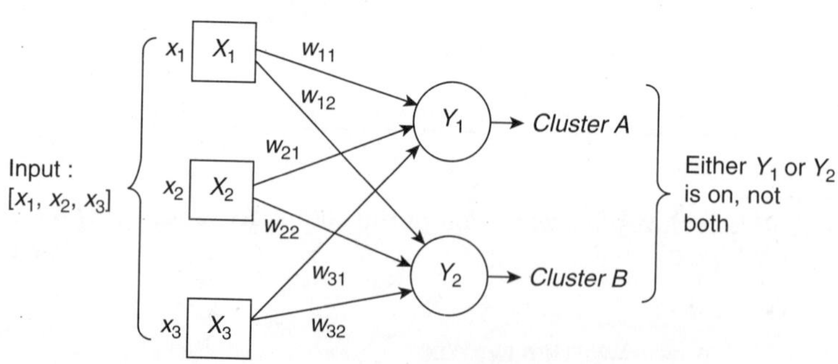

Fig. 6.39. *A 3 input 2 output clustering network*

Winner-takes-all Let us consider a simple ANN consisting of three input units and two output units as shown in Fig. 6.39. As each input unit of a clustering network corresponds to a component of the input vector, this network accepts input vectors of the form $[x_1, x_2, x_3]$. Each output unit of a clustering network represents a cluster. Therefore the present network will divide the set of input patterns into two clusters. The weight vector for an output unit in a clustering network is known as the *exemplar* or *code-book vector* for the vectors of the cluster represented by the corresponding output unit. Hence, for the net in Fig. 6.39, the weight vector $[w_{11}, w_{21}, w_{31}]$ is an exemplar (or code-book vector) for the patterns of cluster *A*. Similarly, $[w_{12}, w_{22}, w_{32}]$ is the exemplar for the patterns of cluster *B*.

In the winner-takes-all strategy, the network finds the output unit that matches best for the current input vector and makes it the winner. The weight vector for the winner is then updated according to the learning algorithm. One way of deciding the winner is to employ the square of the Euclidean distance between the input vector and the exemplar. The unit that has the smallest Euclidean distance between its weight vector and the input vector is chosen as the winner. The algorithmic steps for an *m*-input *n*-output clustering network are given below:

1. For each output unit Y_j, $j = 1$ to n, compute the squared Euclidean distance as

$$D(j) = \sum_{i=1}^{m} (w_{ij} - x_i)^2.$$

2. Let Y_J be the output unit with the smallest squared Euclidean distance $D(J)$.
3. For all output units within a specified neighbourhood of Y_J, update the weights as follows :

$$w_{ij}(new) = w_{ij}(old) + \eta \times [x_i - w_{ij}(old)]$$

The concepts of neighbourhood, and winner-takes-all, in general, will be discussed in greater detail in the chapter on competitive neural nets. Example 6.9 illustrates the winner-takes-all strategy more explicitly.

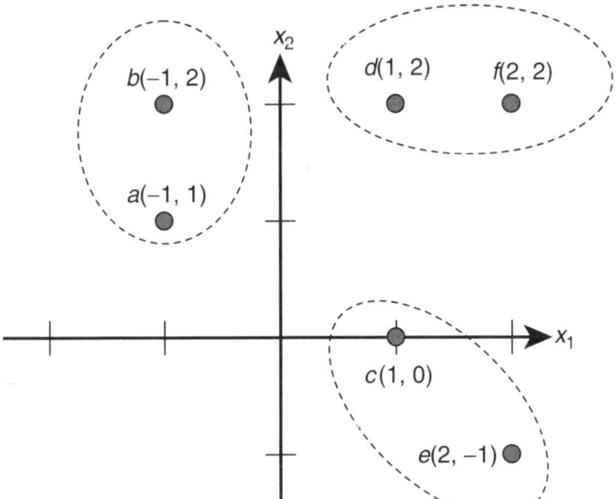

Fig. 6.40. *A clustering problem showing the expected clusters*

Example 6.9 *(Competitive learning through Winner-takes-all strategy)*

Let us consider a set of six patterns $S = \{a\,(-1, 1), b\,(-1, 2), c\,(1, 0), d\,(1, 2), e\,(2, -1), f\,(2, 2)\}$. The positions of these points on a two dimensional Eucledian plane are shown in Fig. 6.40. Intuitively, the six points form three clusters $\{a, b\}$, $\{d, f\}$, and $\{c, e\}$. Given the number of clusters to be formed as 3, how should a neural net learn the clusters by applying the winner-takes-all as its learning strategy? Let us see.

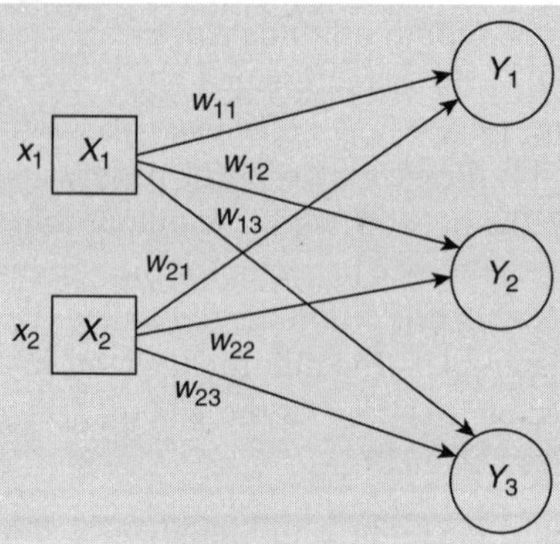

Fig. 6.41. *A 2 input 3 output ANN to solve the clustering problem of Example 6.9*

The input patterns are of the form (x_1, x_2) and the whole data set is to be partitioned into three clusters. So the target ANN should have two input units and three output units (Fig. 6.41). Let the initial distribution of (randomly chosen) weights be

$$W = \begin{bmatrix} w_{11} & w_{12} & w_{13} \\ w_{21} & w_{22} & w_{23} \end{bmatrix} = \begin{bmatrix} 0 & -1 & 2 \\ 2 & 0 & 1 \end{bmatrix}$$

This means that the exemplars, or code vectors, are initially $C_1 = (w_{11}, w_{21}) = (0, 2)$, $C_2 = (w_{12}, w_{22}) = (-1, 0)$, and $C_3 = (w_{13}, w_{23}) = (2, 1)$. The positions of the code vectors as well as the patterns to be clustered are shown in Fig. 6.42.

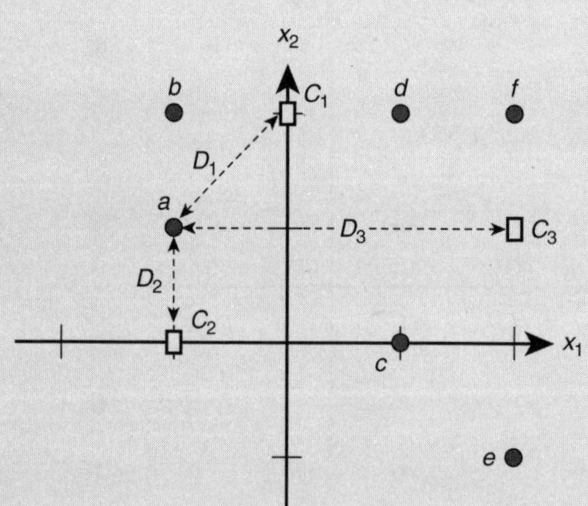

Fig. 6.42. *Initial positions of the code vectors*

Clusters are formed on the basis of the distances between a pattern and a code vector. For example, to determine the cluster for the pattern a $(-1, 1)$ we need to compute the Euclidean distance between the point a and each code vector C_1, C_2, C_3. The pattern is then clustered with nearest among the three code vectors. Let D_1, D_2, D_3 be the squares of the Euclidean distances between a pattern and C_1, C_2, C_3 respectively. For a $(-1, 1)$ the computations of D_1, D_2, D_3 are as follows.

$$D_1 = (w_{11} - x_1)^2 + (w_{21} - x_2)^2 = (0 + 1)^2 + (2 - 1)^2 = 2$$
$$D_2 = (w_{12} - x_1)^2 + (w_{22} - x_2)^2 = (-1 + 1)^2 + (0 - 1)^2 = 1$$
$$D_3 = (w_{13} - x_1)^2 + (w_{23} - x_2)^2 = (2 + 1)^2 + (1 - 1)^2 = 9$$

Since D_2 is the minimum among these distances the corresponding exemplar C_2 is declared the winner and the pattern is clustered around the code vector C_2. Similar computations for the pattern b (−1, 2) are given below.

$$D_1 = (w_{11} - x_1)^2 + (w_{21} - x_2)^2 = (0 + 1)^2 + (2 - 2)^2 = 1$$
$$D_2 = (w_{12} - x_1)^2 + (w_{22} - x_2)^2 = (-1 + 1)^2 + (0 - 2)^2 = 4$$
$$D_3 = (w_{13} - x_1)^2 + (w_{23} - x_2)^2 = (2 + 1)^2 + (1 - 2)^2 = 10$$

In this case D_1 is the minimum making C_1 the winner. Table 6.13 summarizes the initial clustering process yielding the clusters $C_1 = \{b, d\}$, $C_2 = \{a\}$ and $C_3 = \{c, e, f\}$ (Fig. 6.43). The minimum distance is indicated by a pair of parentheses.

Table 6.13. *Initial cluster formation*

#	Pattern	Squared Euclidean distance			Minimum of D_1, D_2, D_3	Winner / Cluster
		D_1	D_2	D_3		
1	a (−1, 1)	2	(1)	9	D_2	C_2
2	b (−1, 2)	(1)	4	10	D_1	C_1
3	c (1, 0)	5	4	(2)	D_3	C_3
4	d (1, 2)	(1)	8	2	D_1	C_1
5	e (2, −1)	13	10	(4)	D_3	C_3
6	f (2, 2)	4	13	(1)	D_3	C_3

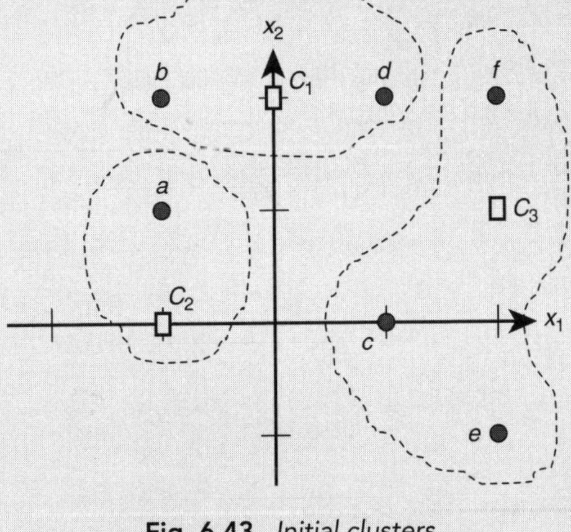

Fig. 6.43. *Initial clusters*

The initial clustering depicted in Fig. 6.43 is neither perfect, nor final. This will change as the learning proceeds through a number of epochs. This is explained below.

We take the value of the learning rate $\eta = 0.5$ and follow the steps of winner-takes-all strategy to modify the positions of the exemplars so that they represent the respective clusters better. The process is described below.

(a) 1st Epoch

(i) Find the winner for the pattern a (−1, 1) and adjust the corresponding code-vector

$$D_1 = (w_{11} - x_1)^2 + (w_{21} - x_2)^2 = (0 + 1)^2 + (2 - 1)^2 = 2$$
$$D_2 = (w_{12} - x_1)^2 + (w_{22} - x_2)^2 = (-1 + 1)^2 + (0 - 1)^2 = 1$$
$$D_3 = (w_{13} - x_1)^2 + (w_{23} - x_2)^2 = (2 + 1)^2 + (1 - 1)^2 = 9$$

Since D_2 is the minimum among these, the winner is C_2. Hence the weights w_{12} and w_{22} are to be changed. The new weights are obtained as

$$w_{12}(new) = w_{12}(old) + \eta\,(x_1 - w_{12}(old)) = -1 + .5 \times (-1 + 1) = -1$$

$$w_{22}(new) = w_{22}(old) + \eta\,(x_2 - w_{22}(old)) = 0 + .5 \times (1 - 0) = .5$$

The new code vector C_2 is (−1, .5). It is closer to the training vector a (−1, 1) than the old code vector (−1, 0) (Fig. 6.44(b)). The weight matrix now changes to

$$W = \begin{bmatrix} w_{11} & w_{12} & w_{13} \\ w_{21} & w_{22} & w_{32} \end{bmatrix} = \begin{bmatrix} 0 & -1 & 2 \\ 2 & .5 & 1 \end{bmatrix}$$

(ii) Find the winner for the pattern b (−1, 2) and adjust the corresponding code-vector

$$D_1 = (w_{11} - x_1)^2 + (w_{21} - x_2)^2 = (0 + 1)^2 + (2 - 2)^2 = 1$$
$$D_2 = (w_{12} - x_1)^2 + (w_{22} - x_2)^2 = (-1 + 1)^2 + (.5 - 2)^2 = 2.25$$
$$D_3 = (w_{13} - x_1)^2 + (w_{23} - x_2)^2 = (2 + 1)^2 + (1 - 2)^2 = 10$$

Since D_1 is the minimum among these, the winner is C_1. Hence the weights w_{11} and w_{21} are to be changed. The new weights are obtained as

$$w_{11}(new) = w_{11}(old) + \eta\,(x_1 - w_{11}(old)) = 0 + .5 \times (-1 - 0) = -.5$$

$$w_{21}(new) = w_{21}(old) + \eta\,(x_2 - w_{21}(old)) = 2 + .5 \times (2 - 2) = 2$$

The new code vector C_1 is (−.5, 2). It is closer to the training vector b (−1, 2) than the old code vector (0, 2) (Fig. 6.44(c)). The new weight matrix is

$$W = \begin{bmatrix} w_{11} & w_{12} & w_{13} \\ w_{21} & w_{22} & w_{23} \end{bmatrix} = \begin{bmatrix} -.5 & -1 & 2 \\ 2 & .5 & 1 \end{bmatrix}$$

The successive iterations of the 1st epoch with the rest of the training vector are carried out in a similar fashion and are summarized in Table 6.14. The corresponding changes in the positions of the code vectors are depicted in Fig. 6.44(b)-(g).

Table 6.14. *Clustering process during the 1st epoch*

#	Training Patterns	Squared Euclidean Distance			Winner	New Code Vectors		
		D_1	D_2	D_3		C_1 (w_{11}, w_{21})	C_2 (w_{12}, w_{22})	C_3 (w_{13}, w_{23})
0						(0, 2)	(−1, 0)	(2, 1)
1	a (−1, 1)	2	(1)	9	C_2	(0, 2)	(−1, .5)	(2, 1)
2	b (−1, 2)	(1)	2.25	10	C_1	(−.5, 2)	(−1, .5)	(2, 1)
3	c (1, 0)	6.25	4.25	(2)	C_3	(−.5, 2)	(−1, .5)	(1.5, .5)
4	d (1, 2)	(2.25)	6.25	2.5	C_1	(.25, 2)	(−1, .5)	(1.5, .5)
5	e (2, −1)	12.06	11.25	(2.5)	C_3	(.25, 2)	(−1, .5)	(1.75, −.25)
6	f (2, 2)	(3.06)	11.25	5.13	C_1	(1.13, 2)	(−1, .5)	(1.75, −.25)

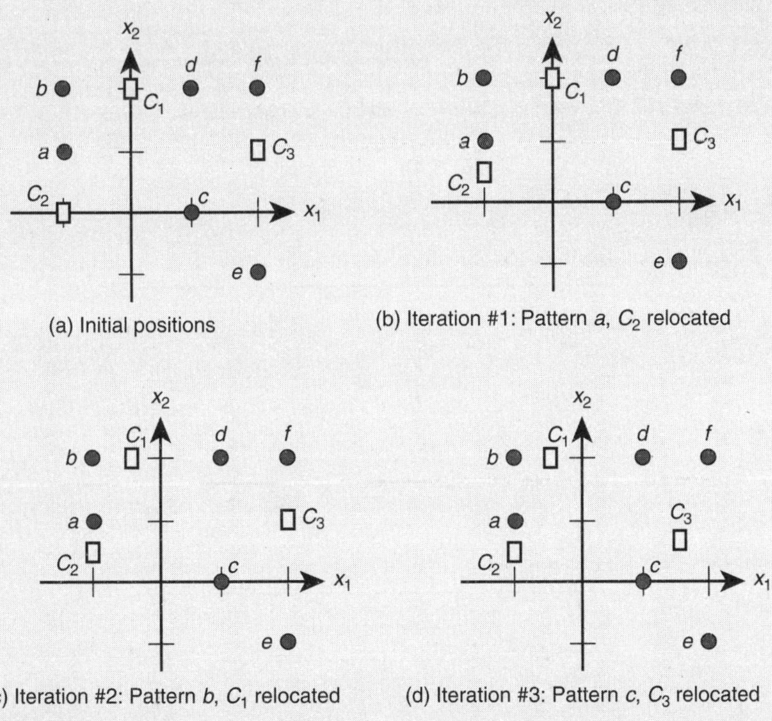

(a) Initial positions

(b) Iteration #1: Pattern *a*, C_2 relocated

(c) Iteration #2: Pattern *b*, C_1 relocated

(d) Iteration #3: Pattern *c*, C_3 relocated

Fig. 6.44. *Successive positions of the code vectors during the 1st epoch of the clustering process*

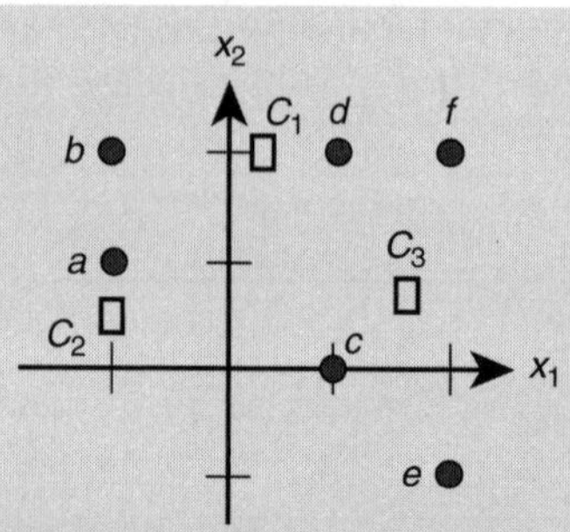

(e) Iteration #4: Pattern *d*, C_1 relocated

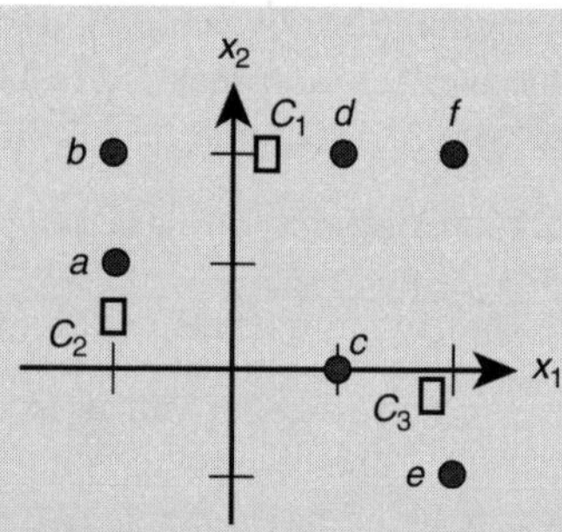

(f) Iteration #5: Pattern *e*, C_3 relocated

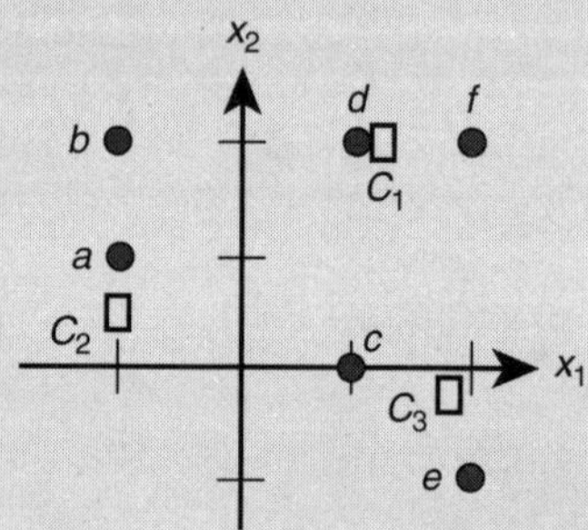

(g) Iteration #6: Pattern *e*, C_1 relocated

Fig. 6.44. *(Continued)*

Table 6.15. *Clusters after the 1st epoch*

#	Training Vector	Cluster
1	a (−1, 1)	C_2
2	b (−1, 2)	C_2
3	c (1, 0)	C_3
4	d (1, 2)	C_1
5	e (2, −1)	C_3
6	f (2, 2)	C_1

Clusters formed

C_1	:	{d, f}
C_2	:	{a, b}
C_3	:	{c, e}

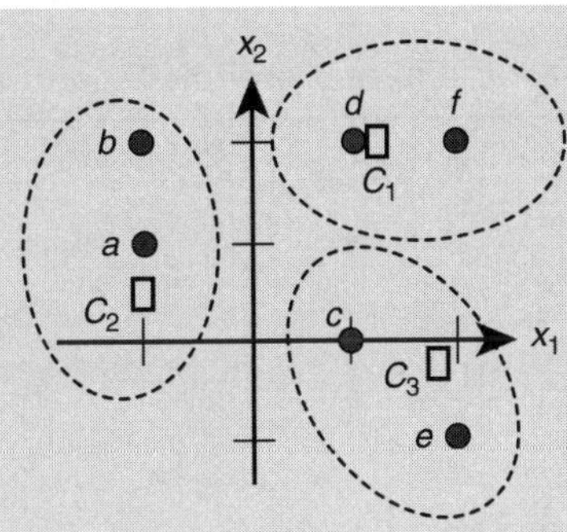

Fig. 6.45. *Clusters formed after the 1st epoch*

Therefore, the weight matrix at the end of the first epoch is obtained as

$$W = \begin{bmatrix} w_{11} & w_{12} & w_{13} \\ w_{21} & w_{22} & w_{23} \end{bmatrix} = \begin{bmatrix} 1.13 & -1 & 1.75 \\ 2 & .5 & -.25 \end{bmatrix}$$

The corresponding clusters can be easily found by computing the distance of each training vector from the three code vectors and attaching it to the cluster represented by the nearest code vector. Table 6.15 summarizes these results and Fig. 6.45 shows the clusters formed at the end of the 1st epoch. It is obvious from Fig. 6.45 that the clusters formed conform to our intuitive expectation. However, this should be further consolidated by a second epoch of training.

(b) 2nd Epoch

Table 6.16. *Clustering process during the 2nd epoch*

#	Training Patterns	Squared Euclidean Distance			Winner	New Code Vectors		
		D_1	D_2	D_3		C_1 (w_{11}, w_{21})	C_2 (w_{12}, w_{22})	C_3 (w_{13}, w_{23})
0						(1.13, 2)	(−1, .5)	(1.75, −.25)
1	a (−1, 1)	5.54	(.25)	9.13	C_2	(1.13, 2)	(−1, 1.5)	(1.75, −.25)
2	b (−1, 2)	4.54	(.25)	12.63	C_2	(1.13, 2)	(−1, 1.75)	(1.75, −.25)
3	c (1, 0)	4.02	7.06	(.63)	C_3	(1.13, 2)	(−1, 1.75)	(1.38, −.13)
4	d (1, 2)	(.02)	4.06	4.68	C_1	(1.07, 2)	(−1, 1.75)	(1.38, −.13)
5	e (2, −1)	9.86	16.63	(1.14)	C_3	(1.07, 2)	(−1, 1.75)	(1.69, −.57)
6	f (2, 2)	(.86)	9.06	6.7	C_1	(1.56, 2)	(−1, 1.75)	(1.69, −.57)

The summary of the second epoch of training is given in Table 6.16. Table 6.17 shows the clusters formed at the end of this epoch and Fig. 6.46 depicts the location of the code vectors as well as the corresponding clusters. It should be noted that though the clusters has not changed from the first epoch, the positions of the exemplars has changed. In fact, these have moved towards the 'centre' of the respective clusters. This is expected, because the exemplar is the representative of a cluster.

Table 6.17. *Clusters after the 2nd epoch*

#	Training Vector	Cluster
1	a (−1, 1)	C_2
2	b (−1, 2)	C_2
3	c (1, 0)	C_3
4	d (1, 2)	C_1
5	e (2, −1)	C_3
6	f (2, 2)	C_1

Clusters formed

C_1	:	{d, f}
C_2	:	{a, b}
C_3	:	{c, e}

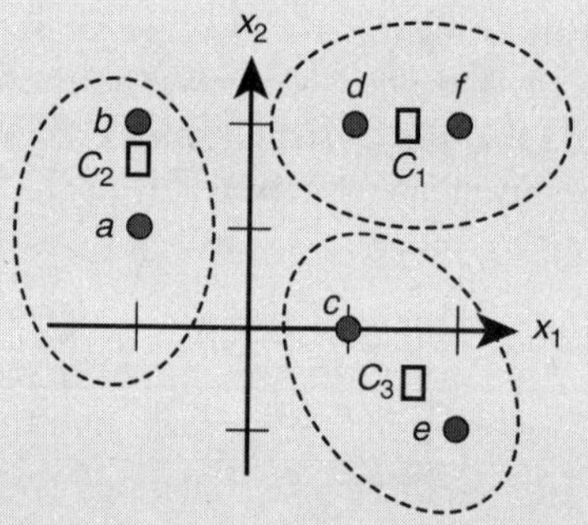

Fig. 6.46. *Clusters formed after the 2nd epoch*

CHAPTER SUMMARY

Certain fundamental concepts of artificial neural networks have been presented in this chapter. The main points of the foregoing text are summerized below.

- ANNs are inspired by the biological brain that processes data in terms of patterns rather than sequential fetch and execute cycle of instruction execution by a classical Von Neuman digital computer.
- Information is stored in brain as strengths of the synaptic gaps between the neurons. Similarly, knowledge is stored in an ANN as weights of interconnection between neural processing units. Thus both the brain and the ANN stores information in a distributed manner.
- ANNs are suitable for problems related to pattern classification and pattern association.
- The earliest artificial neural model was proposed by McCulloch and Pitts in 1943.
- The perceptron model was proposed by Rosenblatt in 1962. It has the nice property of being able to learn to classify a linearly separable set of patterns.
- ANNs have various architectures, such as, single-layer feed forward, multy-layer feed forward, competitive networks, recurrent networks etc.

- Certain functions such as the identity function, the step function, the sigmoid function, the hyperbolic tangent function etc. are widely used as activation functions in an ANN.
- There are two kinds of learning methods for an ANN, supervised and unsupervised. Learning takes place with the help of a set of training patterns. Under supervised learning each training pattern is accompanied by its target output. These target outputs are not available during unsupervised learning.
- The formulae for interconnection weight adjustment Δw_i for different learning rules are shown in Table 6.18.

Table 6.18. *Summary of ANN learning rules*

#	Learning Rule	Formula for Δw_i
1	Hebb	$\Delta w_i = x_i \times t$
2	Perceptron	$\Delta w_i = \eta \times (t - y\_out) \times x_i,$
3	Delta/LMS/Widrow-Hoff	$\Delta w_i = \eta \times (t - y\_in) \times x_i$
4	Extended delta	$\Delta w_{ij} = \eta \times (t_j - y\_out_j) \times x_1 \times g'(y\_in_j)$
5	Winner-takes-all	$\Delta w_{ij} = \eta \times [x_i - w_{ij}(old)]$

- The weight vector associated with an output of a clustering ANN is called the exemplar or the code-book vector. It represents the cluster corresponding to the output unit of the clustering ANN.

SOLVED PROBLEMS

Problem 6.1 Write MATLAB Code to realize the logical AND function with a neural net that learns the desired function through Hebb learning.

Solution 6.1 The MATLAB code and the output are given below as Fig. 6.47 and Fig. 6.48.

```
%MATLAB Code to realize the logical AND function with a neural net that
%learns the desired function through Hebb learning.
clear;
clc;
Inp1=[1 1 1];
Inp2=[1 1 -1];
Inp3=[1 -1 1];
Inp4=[1 -1 -1];
Mat(1,1:3)=Inp1;
Mat(2,1:3)=Inp2;
Mat(3,1:3)=Inp3;
Mat(4,1:3)=Inp4;
wt(1:3)=0;
Tar_Act=[1 -1 -1 -1];
bias=1;
for i=1:4
  wt=wt+Mat(i,1:3)*Tar_Act(i);
  bias=bias+Tar_Act(i);
  disp('Weight Matrix');
  disp(wt);
```

```
    disp('Bias');
    disp(bias);
end
disp('***********Final Weight Matrix************');
disp(wt);
disp('****************Bias********************');
disp(bias);
```

Fig.6.47. *MATLAB code for Hebb learning of AND function by an ANN*

Results

```
Weight Matrix
      1     1     1
Bias
      2
Weight Matrix
      0     0     2
Bias
      1
Weight Matrix
     -1     1     1
Bias
      0
Weight Matrix
     -2     2     2
Bias
     -1
***********Final Weight Matrix************
     -2     2     2
****************Bias********************
     -1
```

Fig. 6.48. *MATLAB results for Hebb learning of AND function*

Problem 6.2 Write MATLAB Code to realize the logical AND function with a neural net that learns the desired function through Perceptron learning.

Solution 6.2 The MATLAB code for the purpose is given below in Fig. 6.49. Fig. 6.50 presents the corresponding screenshot.

```
% Example 1.7: Design a perceptron and train it to realize the logical AND
function.
P = [0 0 1 1; 0 1 0 1];            % Possible values of 2 variables in a ma-
                                     trix format
T = [0 0 0 1];                     % Expected outputs for above dataset
```

```
net = newp([0 1; 0 1],1);           % Creates network with two inputs and 1
                                      output with ranges of values
net.trainParam.epochs = 20;          % Sets the number of maximum iterations
net = train(net,P,T);                % Trains the network
simulation = sim(net,P)              % Simulates neural network
plotpv(P,T)                          % Plot input/target vectors
plotpc(net.iw{1,1},net.b{1})         % Plot classification line
```

Fig. 6.49. *MATLAB code for perceptron learning of AND function*

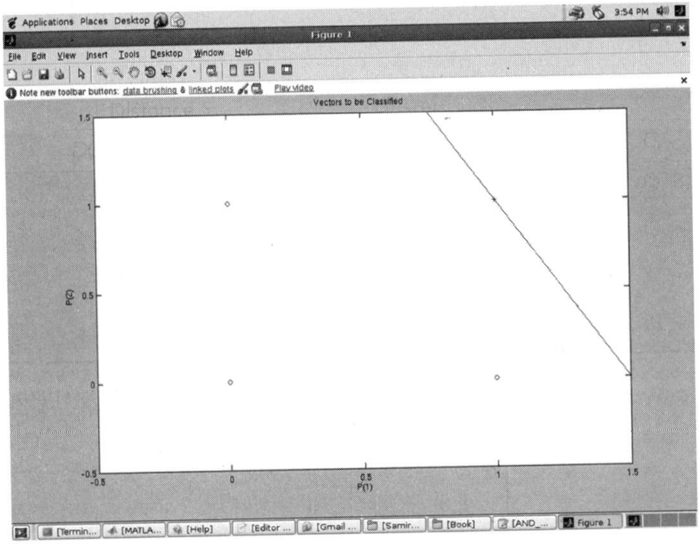

Fig. 6.50. *MATLAB output for perceptron implementing AND function*

Problem 6.3 Write MATLAB Code to realize the logical AND function with a neural net that learns the desired function through LMS learning.

Solution 6.3 The MATLAB code for the purpose is given in Fig. 6.51. Fig. 6.52 shows the results and screenshot is shown in Fig. 6.53.

```
%Matlab Code to implement LMS learning
clear;
clc;
Inp1=[1 1 1];
Inp2=[1 1 -1];
Inp3=[1 -1 1];
Inp4=[1 -1 -1];
Mat(1,1:3)=Inp1;
Mat(2,1:3)=Inp2;
Mat(3,1:3)=Inp3;
Mat(4,1:3)=Inp4;
```

```
wt(1:3)=0.3;
wt_new(1:3)=0;
y_in(1:4)=0;
Tar_Act=[1 -1 -1 -1];
bias=1;
Learn_Rate=0.2;
for j=1:4
y_in(j)=wt(1)*Mat(j,1)+wt(2)*Mat(j,2)+wt(3)*Mat(j,3);
  for i=1:3
     wt_new(i)=wt(i)+ (Learn_Rate*(Tar_Act(j)-y_in(j))*Mat(j,i));
     wt(i)=wt_new(i);
     disp('Weight Matrix');
     disp(wt);
     end
end
disp('**********Final Weight Matrix***********');
disp(wt);
```

Fig. 6.51. *MATLAB code for LMS learning of AND function by an ANN*

```
Weight Matrix
    0.3200    0.3000    0.3000
Weight Matrix
    0.3200    0.3200    0.3000
Weight Matrix
    0.3200    0.3200    0.3200
Weight Matrix
    0.0560    0.3200    0.3200
Weight Matrix
    0.0560    0.0560    0.3200
Weight Matrix
    0.0560    0.0560    0.5840
Weight Matrix
   -0.2608    0.0560    0.5840
Weight Matrix
   -0.2608    0.3728    0.5840
Weight Matrix
   -0.2608    0.3728    0.2672
Weight Matrix
   -0.2806    0.3728    0.2672
Weight Matrix
   -0.2806    0.3926    0.2672
Weight Matrix
   -0.2806    0.3926    0.2870
**********Final Weight Matrix***********
   -0.2806    0.3926    0.2870
```

Fig. 6.52. *MATLAB results for LMS learning of AND function*

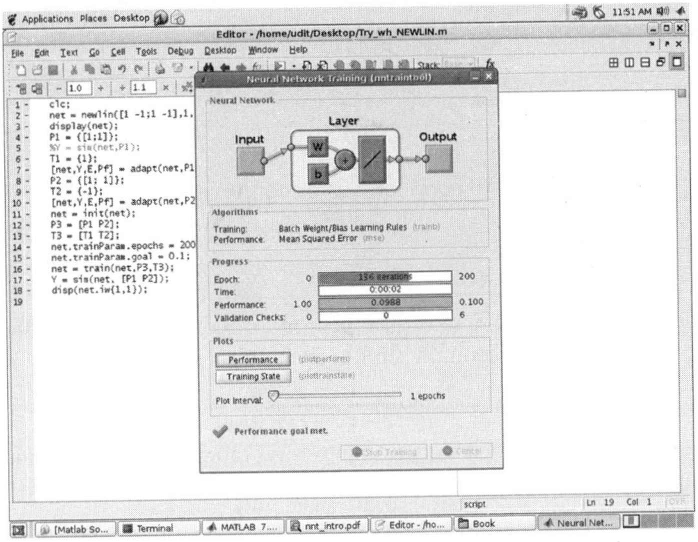

Fig. 6.53. *MATLAB screen showing results of LMS learning of AND function*

Problem 6.4 Write MATLAB Code to implement the Winner-takes-all strategy of pattern clustering.

Solution 6.4 The MATLAB code is shown in Fig. 6.54. The data set is taken from Example 6.9.

```
clear;
clc;
lr = 0.5;
  Inp = [-1 -1 1 1 2 2; 1 2 0 2 -1 2];
  wt = [-1 0 0; 1 -1 1];
[rowInp, colInp] = size(Inp);
[rowwt, colwt] = size(wt);
Res = 0;
High_Indx = 0;
for i = 1:colInp
  Inp(:,i) = Inp(:,i)/norm(Inp(:,i));
  for j = 1:colwt
     wt(:,j) = wt(:,j)/norm(wt(:,j));
     matrx_mult = dot(wt(:,j),Inp(:,i));
     if matrx_mult > Res
       Res = matrx_mult;
       High_Indx = j;
       disp (wt(:,j))
     end
  end
  wt(:,High_Indx) = wt(:,High_Indx) + lr*(Inp(:,i) - wt(:,High_Indx));
disp('********************Weights********************');
  wt(:,High_Indx) = wt(:,High_Indx)/norm(wt(:,High_Indx));
end
```

```
figure
plot(Inp(1,:), Inp(2,:),  wt(1,:), wt(2,:))
axis([-max(max(abs(Inp)))-0.5max(max(abs(Inp))) + 0.5-
max(max(abs(Inp)))-0.5 max(max(abs(Inp)))+0.5])
```

Fig. 6.54. *MATLAB code for clustering through winner-takes-all*

✓ TEST YOUR KNOWLEDGE

6.1 Which of the following parts of a biological neuron is modeled by the weighted interconnections between the input units and the output unit of an artificial neural model?
a) Dendrite b) Axon
c) Soma d) Synapse

6.2 The effect of the synaptic gap in a biological neuron is modeled in artificial neuron model as
a) The weights of the interconnections
b) The activation function
c) The net input to the processing element
d) None of the above

6.3 In an artificial neural model, the activation function of the input unit is
a) The step function b) The identity function
c) The sigmoid function d) None of the above

6.4 Which of the following is not true about Perceptrons ?
a) It can classify linearly separable patterns
b) It does not have any hidden layer
c) It has only one output unit
d) None of the above

6.5 Recognition of hand written characters is an act of
a) Pattern classification b) Pattern association
c) Both (*a*) and (*b*) d) None the above

6.6 Identification of an object, *e.g.*, a chair, a tree, or a human being, from the visual image of our surroundings, is an act of
a) Pattern classification b) Pattern association
c) Both (*a*) and (*b*) d) None the above

6.7 The interconnections of a Hopfield network are
a) Unidirectional b) Bidirectional
c) Both (*a*) and (*b*) d) None the above

6.8 The interconnections of a perception are
a) Unidirectional b) Bidirectional
c) Both (*a*) and (*b*) d) None the above

6.9 Parallel relaxation is a process related to the functionality of
a) Perceptrons b) McCulloch-Pitts neurons
c) Hopfield networks d) None the above

6.10 In which of the following ANN models the inhibition is absolute, i.e., a single inhibitive input can prevent the output to fire, irrespective of the number of excitatory inputs?

a) Perceptrons
b) Hopfield network
c) McCulloch-Pitts neurons
d) None the above

6.11 Which of the following is not true about McCulloch-Pitts neurons?
a) The interconnections are unidirectional
b) All excitatory interconnections have the same weight
c) All inhibitory interconnections have the same weight
d) The activation is bipolar

6.12 Which of the following operations can be realized by a network of McCulloch-Pitts neurons, but not a network of perceptions?
a) Logical *AND*
b) Logical *OR*
c) Logical *XOR*
d) None the above

6.13 Which of the following kinds of classification problems can be solved by a perception?
a) Linearly separable
b) Non-linearly separable
c) Both (*a*) and (*b*)
d) None the above

6.14 Which of the following entities is guaranteed by the Perceptron Convergence Theorem to converge during the learning process?
a) The output activation
b) The interconnection weights
c) Both (*a*) and (*b*)
d) None the above

6.15 The *XOR* function cannot be realized by a Perceptron because the input patterns are
a) Not bipolar
b) Not linearly separable
c) Discrete
d) None the above

6.16 The *XOR* function can be realized by
a) A Perceptron
b) A network of Perceptrons
c) A Hopfield network
d) None the above

6.17 Which of the following ANN architectures contains bidirectional interconnections?
a) Single-layered feed forward
b) Multi-layered feed forward
c) Competitive networks
d) None the above

6.18 Which of the following activation functions is not differentiable?
a) Identity function
b) Heaviside function
c) Sigmoid function
d) None the above

6.19 Which of the following ANN learning algorithms is not a supervised learning?
a) Perceptron learning
b) Widrow-Hoff learning
c) Winner-takes-all
d) None the above

6.20 During learning, if a Perceptron misclassifies a training data negatively, i.e., erroneously yields an output -1 instead of $+1$, the interconnection weights are to be
a) Increased
b) Decreased
c) Kept unaltered
d) None the above

6.21 During learning, if a Perceptron misclassifies a training data positively, i.e., erroneously yields an output $+1$ instead of -1, the interconnection weights are
a) Increased
b) Decreased
c) Kept unaltered
d) None the above

6.22 Which of the following learning rules does not guarantee to learn a classification instance even if the classes are linearly separable ?
a) Perceptron learning rule
b) Hebb rule
c) Both (*a*) and (*b*)
d) None of the above

6.23 Which of the following is a competitive learning method?
 a) Winner-takes-all b) Least-Mean-square
 c) Extended delta d) None the above

6.24 The weight vector attached to an output unit of a clustering network is known as
 a) an exemplar b) a code vector
 c) Both (*a*) and (*b*) d) None of the above

6.25 Which of the following ANN learning methods use Euclidean distance between the weight vector and the input vector to compute the output ?
 a) Perceptron learning b) Widrow-Hoff learning
 c) Winner-takes-all learning d) None of the above

Answers

6.1 (d)	6.2 (a)	6.3 (b)	6.4 (d)	6.5 (b)
6.6 (a)	6.7 (b)	6.8 (a)	6.9 (c)	6.10 (c)
6.11 (d)	6.12 (d)	6.13 (a)	6.14 (b)	6.15 (b)
6.16 (b)	6.17 (c)	6.18 (b)	6.19 (c)	6.20 (a)
6.21 (b)	6.22 (b)	6.23 (a)	6.24 (c)	6.25 (c)

EXERCISES

6.1 There are two ways to interpret the role of the brain while considering the human body as a computational agent. One of them is to view the entire brain as a single unit that acts as the CPU for the whole body. The other is to consider the brain as a huge network of billions of processing units called neurons. Compare and contrast between these two views from computational perspective.

6.2 The majority function outputs a 0 if there are more 0s in the inputs than 1s, and outputs a 1 if there are more 1s in the inputs than 0s. In short, it returns the majority input to the output. The truth table for a 3 input majority function is given as Table 6.19. Design a McCulloch-Pitts neural net to realize the 3-input majority function.

Table 6.19. *Three input majority function*

#	Inputs			Output
	x_1	x_2	x_3	$M(x_1, x_2, x_3)$
0	0	0	0	0
1	0	0	1	0
2	0	1	0	0
3	0	1	1	1
4	1	0	0	0
5	1	0	1	1
6	1	1	0	1
7	1	1	1	1

6.3 Consider the sets of points A and B shown in Fig. 6.54 where $A = \{a\ (-1, 1), b\ (-1, 0), c\ (-1, -1), e\ (0, 0), f\ (0, -1)\}$ and $B = \{d\ (0, 2), g\ (1, 2), h\ (1, 1), i\ (2, 2), j\ (2, 1)\}$. Propose two different Perceptrons to classify these sets of patterns by observation, analysis, and understanding only (and not by learning).

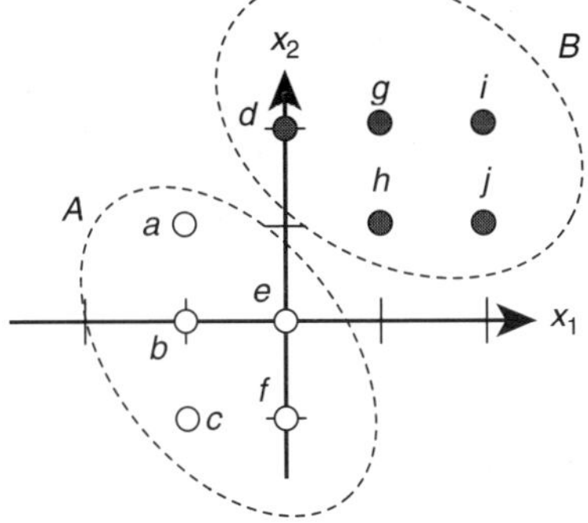

Fig. 6.54. *A classification problem instance*

6.4. Consider the 3-input majority function cited in Exercise No. 6.2. Fig. 6.55 shows the positions of the input patterns in a 3-dimensional space, classified on the basis of the corresponding output values. Are these patterns linearly separable? If so, propose a perceptron to realize this function.

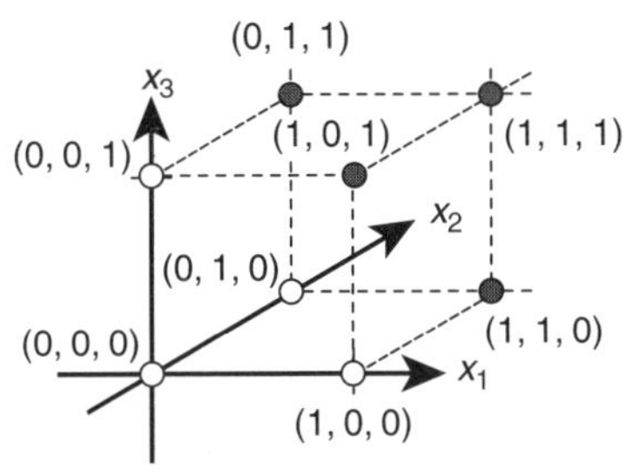

Fig. 6.55. *Three input majority function*

6.5 Draw the structure of a 3-3-2 multi-layered feed forward neural net. Also, present the matrix algebraic expression for the net inputs and the outputs of each layer.

6.6 Train a neural net through the Hebb rule to realize the logical OR function.

6.7 Realize the 3-input majority function through the Perceptron learning rule.

6.8 Train a neural net through the LMS rule to realize the logical OR function.

6.9 Let S be a set of six points on an Euclidean plane where S = $\{a\ (0, -1), b\ (0, -2), c\ (1, 2), d\ (1, 1), e\ (1, -1), f\ (2, 1)\}$ (Fig. 6.56). Taking the initial code vectors as $C_1 = (0, 0)$, and $C_2 = (-1, -2)$ find i) the initial clusters, and ii) final cluster with the help of winner-takes-all strategy.

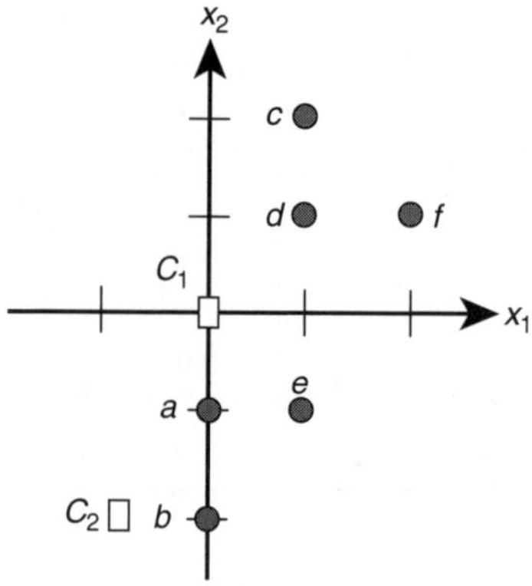

Fig. 6.56. *A clustering problem with initial code vectors*

BIBLIOGRAPHY AND HISTORICAL NOTES

Research in the area of ANNs started in early 40s, when neuro-physiologist, Warren McCulloch and mathematician Walter Pitts proposed their celebrated McCulloch-Pitts Theory of Formal Neural Networks. They even designed and developed a primitive ANN using simple electric circuits. The theories of McCulloch and Pitts on the nature and functionalities of neurons were further supported by Donald Hebb in his 1949 book 'The organization of behaviour'. In 1954 Marvin Minsky wrote his Ph.D. thesis entitled 'Theory of Neural-Analog Reinforcement Systems and its Application to the Brain-Model Problem', which is widely acclaimed as an important early research into neural networks. Then in 1958 Frank Rosenblatt, a neuro-biologist at Cornell University, proposed the Perceptron, the first 'practical' ANN. However, Marvin Minsky and Seymour Papert proved in their book of 1969 entitled 'Perceptrons' that the capabilities of perceptrons are very limited. As a consequence, enthusiasm declined over the subsequent few years. The first neural networks that could be applied to real problems, ADALINE (ADAptive LINear Elements) and MADALINE (Multiple ADAptive LINear Elements), were developed by Bernard Wildrow and Marcian Hoff of Stanford University between 1959 and 1960. In 1982 John Hopfield of Caltech presented some new ideas in neural networks that eventually came to be known as Hopfield networks. A new era in neural networks started in 1986 when Rumelhart, Hinton and Williams proposed the back-propagation algorithm to overcome the limitations of perceptron. Many more developments took place in the last few decades in the field of ANNs. A few seminal works in this area are referred below.

Anderson, J. A. and Rosenfield, E., (eds). (1988). *Neurocomputing: Foundations of research.* Cambridge, MA, MIT Press.

Angeniol, B., Vaubois, G., and Le Texier, J.-Y. (1988). Self-organizing feature maps and the traveling salesman problem. *Neural Networks*, 1(4), pp. 289–293.

Block, H. D. (1962). The perceptron: A model for brain functioning. *Reviews for modern physics.* Vol. 34, pp. 123–135.

Cohen, M. A. and Grossberg, S. (1983). Absolute stability of global pattern formation and parallel memory storage by competitive neural networks. *IEEE transactions on Systems, Man and Cybernetics*, SMC-13, pp. 815–826.

Hopfield, J. J. (1982). Neural networks and physical systems with emergent collective computational properties. *Proc. of the National Academy of Sciences of the USA*, 79, pp. 2554–2588.

Hopfield, J. J. and Tank, D. W. (1985). Neural computation of decisions in optimization problems. *Biological cybernetics*, 52(3), pp. 141–152.

Hopfield, J. J. and Tank, D.W. (1986). Computing with neural circuits. *Science*, 233, pp. 625–633.

Grossberg, S. (1973). Contour enhancement, short-term memory, and constancies in reverberating neural networks. *Studies in Applied Mathematics*, 52.

Grossberg, S. (1982). *Studies of mind and brain.* Boston, Reidel.

Hebb, D. O. (1949). *The organization of behaviour.* New York, John Wiley and Sons.

Kohonen, T. (1982). Self-organized formation of topologically correct feature maps. *Biological cybernetics*, 43, pp. 59–69.

McCulloch, W. and Pitts, W. (1943). A logical calculus of the ideas immanent in nervous activity. *Bulletin of Mathematical Biophysics*, 7, pp.115–133.

Minsky, M. and Papert, S. (1969). *Perceptrons.* MIT Press.

Rosenblatt, F. (1959). Two theorems of statistical separability in the perceptron. *Mechanization of thought process: proceedings of the symposium at National Physical Laboratory*, London, pp. 421–456.

Rosenblatt, F. (1962). *Principles of Neurodynamics.* Spartan Books.

Rumelhart, D. E., Hinton, G. E. and Williams, R. J. (1986). Learning representations by back-propagating errors. *Nature*, 323, pp. 533–536.

Tank, D. W., and Hopfield, J. J. (1987). Collective computation in neuronlike circuits. *Scientific American*, 257, pp. 104–114.

Von Neumann, J. (1958). *The computer and the brain.* New Haven : Yale University Press.

Widrow, B. and Hoff, M. E. (1960). Adaptive switching circuits. *IRE WESCON convention record*, part 4, pp. 96–104.

7

PATTERN CLASSIFIERS

Key Concepts

ADALINE (Adaptive Linear Neuron), Hebb Learning, Hebb Nets, Learning Rate, Least Mean Square, MADALINE (Many Adaptive Linear Neurons), MR-I Algorithm, MR-II Algorithm, Perceptrons, Perceptron Learning, Widrow-Hoff Learning

Chapter Outline

Chapter 6 provides an overview of various aspects of artificial neural nets including their architecture, activation functions, training rules, etc. This chapter presents discussions on certain elementary patterns classifying neural nets. Four kinds of nets, *viz.*, *Hebb net*, *Perceptron*, *ADALINE*, and *MADALINE*, are included here. Among these, the first three are single layer, single output nets, and the last one, *MADALINE*, is a single-output net with one hidden layer. White Hebb network and Perceptron are trained by their respective training rules, both *ADALINE* and *MADALINE* employ the least mean square (*LMS*), or delta rule. More general multi-layer networks, especially the feed-forward networks, are dealt with later in a separate chapter.

7.1 HEBB NETS

A single-layer feedforward neural net trained through the Hebb learning rule is known as a Hebb net. The Hebb learning rule is introduced in Chapter 6. Example 6.6 illustrates the training procedure for a Hebb net where a net is trained to implement the logical AND function. The detailed algorithm is presented here as **Procedure** *Hebb-Learning* (Fig. 7.1). Fig. 7.2 shows the architecture of the Hebb net.

Procedure *Hebb-Learning*

Step 1. Initialize all weights to 0.

$$w_i = 0, \text{ for all } i = 0 \text{ to } m.$$

Step 2. For each training vector and target output pair, ***s*** : ***t***, do steps 3-5.

Step 3. Assign the input vectors to the input layer.

$$x_0 = 1, \text{ and } x_i = s_i \text{ for all } i = 1 \text{ to } m$$

Step 4. Activate the output unit with the target output ***y_out*** = ***t***.

Step 5. Adjust the weights

$$w_i \text{ (new)} = w_i \text{ (old)} + x_i \times y\_out$$

Step 6. Stop

Fig. 7.1 *Procedure Hebb-learning*

It should be noted that the input unit X_0 and the associated weight w_0 play the role of the bias. The activation of X_0 is always kept at 1. Hence, the expression for adjustment of w_0 becomes

$$w_0 \text{ (new)} = w_0 \text{ (old)} + 1 \times y\_out = w_0 \text{ (old)} + y\_out \tag{7.1}$$

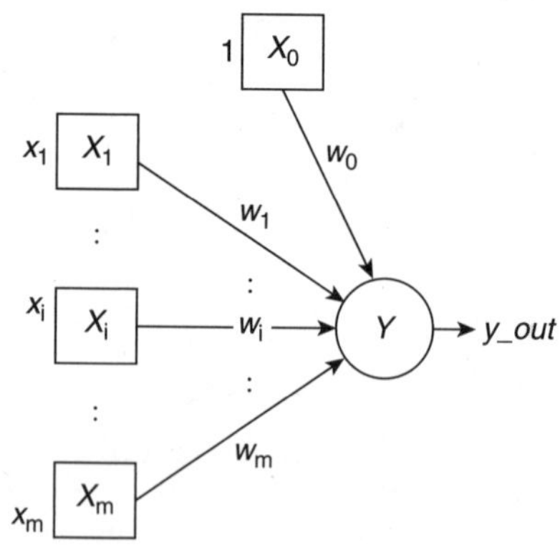

Fig. 7.2. *Structure of a Hebb net*

Procedure *Hebb-Learning* requires only one pass through the training set. There are other equivalent methods of applying Hebb learning in different contexts, say, pattern association. Example 6.6 illustrates the training procedure of a Hebb net to realize the *AND* function. In this example, both the input and output of the function were expressed in bipolar form. Example 7.1 illustrates the limitation of binary representation of data for training a neural net through Hebb learning. Example 7.2 shows that Hebb net may not learn a classification task even if the patterns concerned are linearly separable.

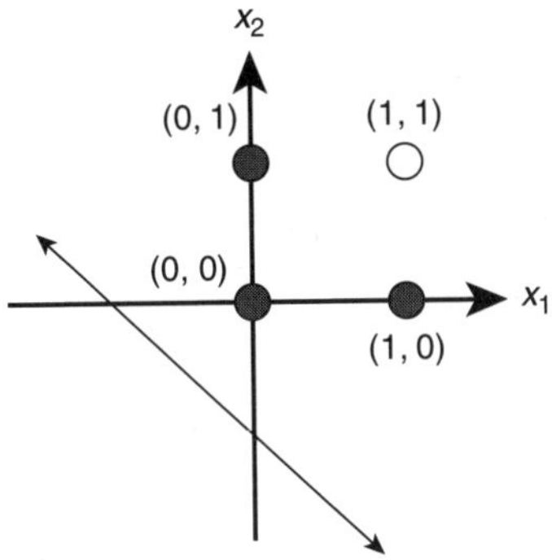

Fig. 7.3. *Decision line of Hebb net to realize the AND function when both the input and the output are expressed in binary form*

Example 7.1 *(Disadvantage of input data in binary form)*

In this example, we apply the Hebb learning rule to train a neural net for the *AND* function with binary inputs. Can the net learn the designated task? We will observe and draw appropriate conclusions from our observation.

Two cases need to be considered. First, the target output is presented in binary, then, in bipolar. The input is in binary form in both cases.

Table 7.1 shows the details of the computation when both the input patterns and the target outputs are presented in binary from. We see that as the target output is 0 for the first three patterns, and as the adjustments $\Delta w_i = x_i \times y\_out = x_i \times 0 = 0$, no learning takes place. The final set of weights is $(w_0, w_1, w_2) = (1, 1, 1)$. It can be easily verified that this net fails to classify the patterns $(x_1, x_2) = (0, 0)$, $(0, 1)$, or $(1, 0)$. Fig. 7.3 shows the decision line for this net. We assume the activation function:

$$g(x) = \begin{cases} 1, & \text{if } x > 0 \\ 0, & \text{otherwise} \end{cases}$$

This shows that a Hebb net fails to learn the *AND* function if both the inputs and the target outputs are expressed in binary. What happens when the output is in bipolar form?

Table 7.2 shows the details of the training process when the output is expressed in bipolar form. As the 0s in the column for 'Target output (t)' are replaced by −1, learning takes place for all training pairs from (0, 0) : (−1) to (1, 1) : (1). The final set of weights are $w_0 = -2$, $w_1 = 0$, $w_2 = 0$. Therefore, the activation of the net is permanently at −1, irrespective of input pattern. It is obvious that though this net classifies the patterns (0, 0), (0, 1), (1, 0) correctly, it is unable to do so for the pattern (1, 1).

Table 7.1 *Hebb learning of AND function with Binary Target Output*

#	Training Inputs			Target output (t)	Weight changes			Weights		
	X_0	X_1	X_2		Δw_0	Δw_1	Δw_2	w_0	w_1	w_2
0								0	0	0
1	1	0	0	0	0	0	0	0	0	0

(Continued)

Table 7.1 *Continued*

#	Training Inputs			Target output (t)	Weight changes			Weights		
	X_0	X_1	X_2		Δw_0	Δw_1	Δw_2	w_0	w_1	w_2
2	1	0	1	0	0	0	0	0	0	0
3	1	1	0	0	0	0	0	0	0	0
4	1	1	1	1	1	1	1	1	1	1

$$\Delta w_i = x_i \times y\_out = x_i \times t$$

Table 7.2 *Hebb learning for AND function (binary input and bipolar output)*

#	Training Inputs			Target output (t)	Weight changes			Weights		
	X_0	X_1	X_2		Δw_0	Δw_1	Δw_2	w_0	w_1	w_2
0								0	0	0
1	1	0	0	−1	−1	0	0	−1	0	0
2	1	0	1	−1	−1	0	−1	−2	0	−1
3	1	1	0	−1	−1	−1	0	−3	−1	−1
4	1	1	1	1	1	1	1	−2	0	0

$$\Delta w_i = x_i \times y\_out = x_i \times t$$

The foregoing discussion shows that if the training patterns and the target outputs are presented in binary form, there is no guarantee that a Hebb net may learn the corresponding classification task.

Example 7.2 *(Limitation of Hebb net)*

This example shows, with the help of a suitable problem instance, that a Hebb net may not be able learn to classify a set of patterns even though they are linearly separable.

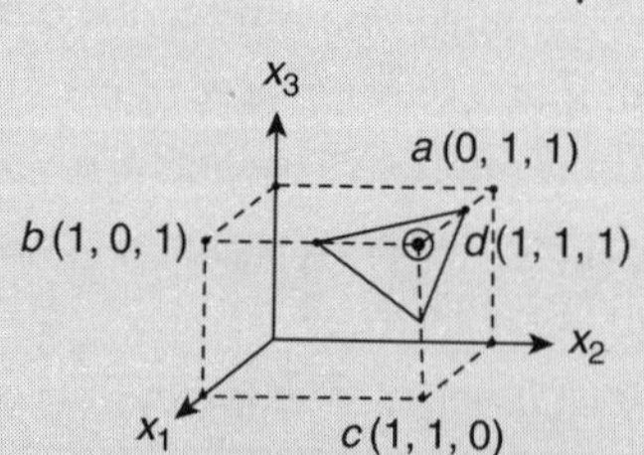

Fig. 7.4. *A linearly separable set of points that a Hebb net fails to learn to classify*

Let us consider four points a (0, 1, 1), b (1, 0, 1), c (1, 1, 0) and d (1, 1, 1) and the corresponding outputs as 0, 0, 0, and 1, respectively. Fig. 7.4 shows these patterns on a 3-dimensional space, and Table 7.3 and Table 7.4 present the training sets expressed in binary and bipolar forms.

Table 7.3. *Training pairs in binary form*

Input pattern			Target output
x_1	x_2	x_3	(t)
0	1	1	0
1	0	1	0
1	1	0	0
1	1	1	1

Table 7.4. *Training pairs in bipolar form*

Input pattern			Target output
x_1	x_2	x_3	(t)
−1	1	1	−1
1	−1	1	−1
1	1	−1	−1
1	1	1	1

It is obvious from Fig. 7.4 that the given set of patterns is linearly separable. Any plane that cuts the cube diagonally to isolate the point d (1, 1, 1) from the rest of the three points serves the purpose. In Fig. 7.4, the triangle around the point d represents such a plane. If we present the inputs and the outputs in bipolar form, then a single layer single output net with the interconnection weights $w_0 = -2$, $w_1 = 1$, $w_2 = 1$, and $w_3 = 1$ can solve the classification problem readily (Fig. 7.5).

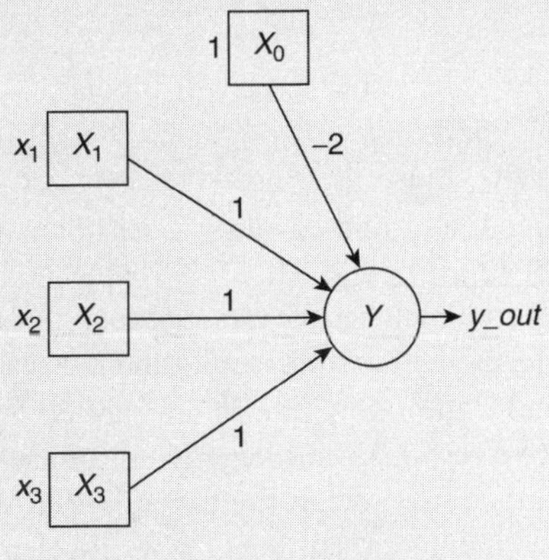

Fig. 7.5. *A net to solve the classification problem posed in Table 7.4*

Can we make a net learn this, or any other suitable set of weights, through Hebb learning rule so that it acquires the capacity to solve the concerned classification problem? Table 7.5 shows the calculations for such an effort. As the table shows, the weight vector arrived at the end of the process is $(w_0, w_1, w_2, w_3) = (-2, 0, 0, 0)$. Now, this set of weights fails to distinguish the pattern (1, 1, 1) from the rest. Hence, the resultant net has not learnt to solve this classification problem.

Table 7.5. *Hebb training of classification problem posed in Table 7.4*

#	Training Input				Target output (t)	Weight changes				Weights			
	x_0	x_1	x_2	x_3		Δw_0	Δw_1	Δw_2	Δw_3	w_0	w_1	w_2	w_3
										0	0	0	0
	1	−1	1	1	−1	−1	1	−1	−1	−1	1	−1	−1
	1	1	−1	1	−1	−1	−1	1	−1	−2	0	0	−2
	1	1	1	−1	−1	−1	−1	−1	1	−3	−1	−1	−1
	1	1	1	1	1	1	1	1	1	−2	0	0	0

As this network cannot distinguish (1, 1, 1) from the rest, it fails to learn to classify the given patterns even though they are linearly separable.

Hebb net is one of the earliest neural net meant for classification tasks. However, it has very limited capacity. A more powerful ANN is the famous perceptron. These are discussed in the next section.

7.2 PERCEPTRONS

An overview of perceptrons including their structure, learning rule, etc., is provided in Chapter 6. This section presents the detailed learning algorithm and an example to illustrate the superiority of the perceptron learning rule over the Hebb learning rule. Perceptron learning process is presented as Procedure Perceptron Learning (Fig. 7.6). The notable points regarding **Procedure** Perceptron-Learning are given below:

1. The input vectors are allowed to be either binary or bipolar. However, the outputs must be in bipolar form.
2. The bias w_0 is adjustable but the threshold θ used in the activation function is fixed.
3. Learning takes place only when the computed output does not match the target output. Moreover, as $\Delta w_i = \eta \times t \times x_i$ the weight adjustment is 0 if $x_i = 0$. Hence, no learning takes place if either the input is 0, or the computed output matches the target output. Consequently, as training proceeds, more and more training patterns yield correct results and less learning is required by the net.
4. The threshold θ of the activation function may be interpreted as a separating band of width 2θ between the region of positive response and negative response. The band itself is 'undecided' in the sense that if the net input falls within the range $[-\theta, \theta]$, the activation is neither positive, nor negative. Moreover, changing the value of θ would change the width of the undecided region, along with the position of the separating lines. Therefore, for Perceptrons, the bias and the threshold are no longer interchangeable.
5. The band separating the regions of positive response from that of the negative response is defined by the pair of lines

$$w_0x_0 + w_1x_1 + w_2x_2 = \theta$$
$$w_0x_0 + w_1x_1 + w_2x_2 = -\theta \quad (7.2)$$

```
Procedure Perceptron-Learning

Step 1.  Initialize all weights, w0, ...., wm.
Step 2.  Set learning rate η such that 0 < η ≤ 1, and threshold θ.
Step 3.  For each training pair s : t do Steps 4-8.
Step 4.  Activate the input units, xi = si, for i = 0, ...., m.
Step 5.  Compute the net input to the output unit
```

$$y\_in = \sum_{i=0}^{m} w_i x_i$$

```
Step 6.  Compute the activation of the output unit using the function
```

$$y\_out = \begin{cases} 1, & \text{if } y\_in > \theta \\ 0, & \text{if } -\theta \le y\_in \le \theta \\ -1, & \text{if } y\_in < -\theta \end{cases}$$

```
Step 7.  If there is an error, i.e., y_out ≠ t, then adjust the weights as
         follows
```

$$w_i \text{ (new)} = w_i \text{ (old)} + \eta \times t \times x_i$$

```
         If, however, no error has occurred, the weights are kept unchanged.
Step 8.  If there were no error, i.e., y_out = t, for the entire set of
         training pairs, then stop.  Otherwise go to Step 3.
```

Fig. 7.6. *Procedure perceptron learning*

Example 7.3 (*Power of the perceptron learning rule*)

This example intends to show that the perceptron learning rule is more powerful than the Hebb learning rule.

Let us consider the classification problem mentioned in Example 7.2. We have seen that the Hebb learning rule is not powerful enough to train a neural net to realize this classification task even though the concerned patterns are linearly separable. Is it possible to achieve this ability through the perceptron learning rule?

Table 7.6 shows the details of perceptron learning process of the function presented in Table 7.4. For the sake of simplicity, the initial weights are all kept at 0 and the learning rate is set to $\eta = 1$. Both the inputs and the outputs are presented in bipolar form. It is seen that five epochs of training are required by the perceptron to learn the appropriate interconnection weights. Calculations at the 6th epoch show that the net successfully produces the expected outputs and no weight adjustments are further required. The final set of the interconnection weights are found to be $w_0 = -4$, $w_1 = w_2 = w_3 = 2$.

Table 7.6. *Perceptron learning of function shown in Table 7.4*

#	Input				Net input	Output	Target	Weight adjustments				Weights			
	x_0	x_1	x_2	x_3	*y_in*	*y_out*	*t*	Δw_0	Δw_1	Δw_2	Δw_3	w_0	w_1	w_2	w_3
0												0	0	0	0
1	1	1	1	1	0	0	1	1	1	1	1	1	1	1	1
2	1	−1	1	1	2	1	−1	−1	1	−1	−1	0	2	0	0
3	1	1	−1	1	2	1	−1	−1	−1	1	−1	−1	1	1	−1
4	1	1	1	−1	2	1	−1	−1	−1	−1	1	−2	0	0	0
							Epoch #1								
0												−2	0	0	0
1	1	1	1	1	−2	−1	1	1	1	1	1	−1	1	1	1
2	1	−1	1	1	0	0	−1	−1	1	−1	−1	−2	2	0	0
3	1	1	−1	1	0	0	−1	−1	−1	1	−1	−3	1	1	−1
4	1	1	1	−1	0	0	−1	−1	−1	−1	1	−4	0	0	0
							Epoch #2								
0												−4	0	0	0
1	1	1	1	1	−4	−1	1	1	1	1	1	−3	1	1	1
2	1	−1	1	1	−2	−1	−1	0	0	0	0	−3	1	1	1
3	1	1	−1	1	−2	−1	−1	0	0	0	0	−3	1	1	1
4	1	1	1	−1	−2	−1	−1	0	0	0	0	−3	1	1	1
							Epoch #3								
0												−3	1	1	1
1	1	1	1	1	0	0	1	1	1	1	1	−2	2	2	2
2	1	−1	1	1	0	0	−1	−1	1	−1	−1	−3	3	1	1
3	1	1	−1	1	0	0	−1	−1	−1	1	−1	−4	2	2	0
4	1	1	1	−1	0	0	−1	−1	−1	−1	1	−5	1	1	1
							Epoch #4								

(*Continued*)

Table 7.6. *Continued*

#	Input				Net input	Out-put	Tar-get	Weight adjustments				Weights			
	x_0	x_1	x_2	x_3	y_in	y_out	t	Δw_0	Δw_1	Δw_2	Δw_3	w_0	w_1	w_2	w_3
0												−5	1	1	1
1	1	1	1	1	−2	−1	1	1	1	1	1	−4	2	2	2
2	1	−1	1	1	−2	−1	−1	−1	1	−1	−1	−4	2	2	2
3	1	1	−1	1	−2	−1	−1	−1	−1	1	−1	−4	2	2	2
4	1	1	1	−1	−2	−1	−1	−1	−1	−1	1	−4	2	2	2

Epoch #5

#	x_0	x_1	x_2	x_3	y_in	y_out	t	Δw_0	Δw_1	Δw_2	Δw_3	w_0	w_1	w_2	w_3
0												−4	2	2	2
1	1	1	1	1	2	1	1	0	0	0	0	−4	2	2	2
2	1	−1	1	1	−2	−1	−1	0	0	0	0	−4	2	2	2
3	1	1	−1	1	−2	−1	−1	0	0	0	0	−4	2	2	2
4	1	1	1	−1	−2	−1	−1	0	0	0	0	−4	2	2	2

Epoch #6

7.3 ADALINE

The *ADALINE* (*Adaptive Linear Neuron*), introduced by Widrow and Hoff in 1960, is a single output unit neural net with several input units. One of the input units acts as the bias and is permanently fixed at 1. An *ADALINE* is trained with the help of the delta, or LMS (Least Mean Square), or Widrow-Hoff learning rule. The learning process is presented here as **Procedure** *ADALINE-Learning* (Fig. 7.7).

The salient features of *ADALINE* are

- Both the inputs and the outputs are presented in bipolar form.
- The net is trained through the delta, or LMS, or Widrow-Hoff rule. This rule tries to minimize the mean-squared error between activation and the target value.
- *ADALINE* employs the identity activation function at the output unit *during training*. This implies that during training $y\_out = y\_in$.
- During application the following bipolar step function is used for activation.

$$y = \begin{cases} 1, & if\ y\_in \geq 0 \\ -1, & if\ y\_in < 0 \end{cases}$$

- Learning by an *ADALINE* net is sensitive to the value of the learning rate. A too large learning rate may prevent the learning process to converge. On the other hand, if the learning rate is too low, the learning process is extremely slow. Usually, the learning rate is set on the basis of the inequality $.1 \leq m \times \eta \leq 1.0$, where m is the number of input units.

Procedure *ADALINE-Learning*

Step 1. Initialize weights with small random values ($0 < w_i < 1$).

Step 2. Set the learning rate η, usually on the basis of the inequality $0.1 \leq m \times \eta \leq 1.0$, where m is the number of input units.

Step 3. Do Step 4 to Step 7 white stopping criteria is not fulfilled.

Step 4. For each bipolar training pair $s : t$, do Steps 5 to 7.

Step 5. Set activation for the input units.

$$x_0 = 1,$$

$$x_i = s_i \quad \text{for } i = 1, \ldots, m$$

Step 6. Compute the net input to the output unit, $y\_in = \sum_{i=0}^{m} x_i w_i$

Step 7. Adjust the weights using the following formula.

$$w_i\ (\text{new}) = w_i\ (\text{old}) + \eta \times (t - y\_in) \times x_i\ , \quad i = 0, \ldots, m$$

Fig. 7.7. *Procedure ADALINE-Learning*

Procedure *ADALINE-Learning* (Fig. 7.7) presents the step by step algorithm for the *ADALINE* learning process. Learning through the delta rule is illustrated in Chapter 6. Since *ADALINE* employs the delta learning rule, the training process is practically the same. Example 7.4 illustrates the process of training on *ADALINE* through the delta rule.

Example 7.4 (*ADALINE training for the AND-NOT function*)

In this example, we train an *ADALINE* to realize the *AND-NOT* function.

The *AND-NOT* function is presented in Example 6.3. It is a 2-input logic function that produces an output 1 only when $x_1 = 1$, and $x_2 = 0$. For all other input combinations the output is 0. The computations for the learning of an *ADALINE* to realize the *AND-NOT* function are shown in Table 7.7. Columns 2, 3, and 4 contain the input patterns expressed in bipolar form. The column x_0 stands for the bias which is permanently set to 1. The initial weights are taken as $w_0 = w_1 = w_2 = .25$, and the learning rate is set to $\eta = .2$. As Table 7.8 indicates, the net learns the designated task after the first two epochs.

Table 7.7. *ADALINE Learning of AND NOT Function*

$$w_i\,(\text{new}) = w_i\,(\text{old}) + \eta \times (t - y\_in) \times x_i,\ \eta = .2$$

#	Input pattern			Net input	Target output	Error	Weight adjustments			Weights		
	x_0	x_1	x_2	*y_in*	t	*t − y_in*	Δw_0	Δw_1	Δw_2	w_0	w_1	w_2
0										.25	.25	.25
1	1	1	1	.75	−1	−1.75	−.35	−.35	−.35	−.10	−.10	−.10
2	1	1	−1	−.10	1	1.10	.22	.22	−.22	.12	.12	−.32
3	1	−1	1	−.32	−1	−.68	−.14	.14	−.14	−.02	.26	−.46
4	1	−1	−1	.18	−1	−1.18	−.24	.24	.24	−.26	.50	−.22
						Epoch #1						
0										−.26	.50	−.22
1	1	1	1	.02	−1	−1.02	−.20	−.20	−.20	−.46	.30	−.42
2	1	1	−1	.26	1	.74	.15	.15	−.15	−.31	.45	−.57
3	1	−1	1	−1.33	−1	.33	.07	−.07	.07	−.24	.38	−.50
4	1	−1	−1	−.12	−1	−.88	−.18	.18	.18	−.42	.56	−.32
						Epoch #2						

Table 7.8. *Performance of the ADALINE after two epochs of learning*

#	Input pattern			Net input	Output	Target output
	x_0	x_1	x_2	$y\_in = \Sigma w_i x_i$	*y_out*	t
1	1	1	1	−.18 < 0	−1	−1
2	1	1	−1	.46 > 0	1	1
3	1	−1	1	−1.30 < 0	−1	−1
4	1	−1	−1	−.66 < 0	−1	−1

7.4 MADALINE

Several *ADALINEs* arranged in a multilayer net is known as *Many ADALINES*, or *Many Adaptive Linear Neurons*, or *MADALINE* in short. The architecture of a two input, one output, one hidden layer consisting of two hidden *MADALINE* is shown in Fig. 7.8. *MADALINE* is computationally more powerful than *ADALINE*. The enhanced computational power of the *MADALINE* is due to the hidden *ADALINE* units. Salient features of *MADALINE* are mentioned below.

- All units, except the inputs, employ the same activation function as in *ADALINE*, *i.e.*,

$$f(x)=\begin{cases}1, & if\ x\geq 0,\\ -1, & if\ x<0.\end{cases}$$

As mentioned earlier, the enhanced computational power of the *MADALINE* is due to the hidden *ADALINE* units. However, existence of the hidden units makes the training process more complicated.

- There are two training algorithms for *MADALINE*, *viz.*, *MR-I* and *MR-II*.

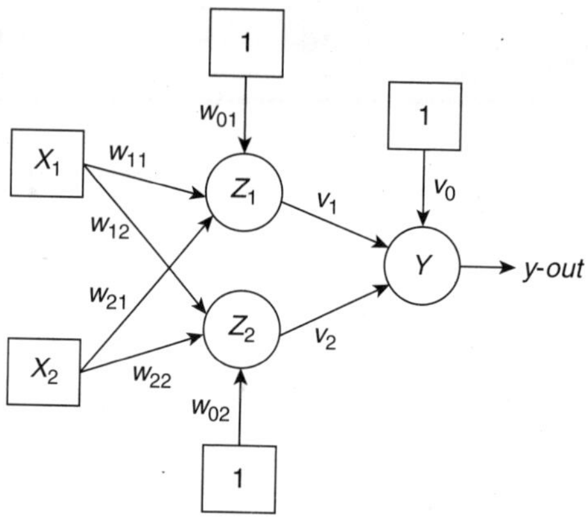

Fig. 7.8. *A two input, one output, one hidden layer with two hidden units MADALINE*

Procedure *MADALINE-MR-I-Learning*

Step 1. Initialize v_0, v_1, v_2 with 0.5 and other weights w_{01}, w_{11}, w_{12}, w_{02}, w_{12} and w_{22} by small random values. All bias inputs are set to 1.

Step 2. Set the learning rate η to a suitable value.

Step 3. For each bipolar training pair $s : t$, do Steps 4-6

Step 4. Activate the input units: $x_1 = s_1$, $x_2 = s_2$, all biases are set to 1 permanently.

Step 5. Propagate the input signals through the net to the output unit Y.
5.1 Compute net inputs to the hidden units.

$$z\_in_1 = 1 \times w_{01} + x_1 \times w_{11} + x_2 \times w_{21}$$

$$z\_in_2 = 1 \times w_{02} + x_1 \times w_{12} + x_2 \times w_{22}$$

5.2 Compute activations of the hidden units z_out_1 and z_out_2 using the bipolar step function

$$z\_out = \begin{cases}1, & \text{if } z\_in \geq 0\\ -1, & \text{if } z\_in < 0.\end{cases}$$

5.3 Compute net input to the output unit

$$y\_in = 1 \times v_0 + z\_out_1 \times v_1 + z\_out_2 \times v_2$$

5.4 Find the activation of the output unit *y-out* using the same activation function as in Step 5.2, *i.e.*,

$$y\_out = \begin{cases} 1, & \text{if } y\_in \geq 0 \\ -1, & \text{if } y\_in < 0. \end{cases}$$

Step 6. Adjust the weights of the hidden units, if required, according to the following rules:

i) If ($y\_out = t$) then the net yields the expected result. Weights need not be updated.

ii) If ($y\_out \neq t$) then apply one of the following rules whichever is applicable.

Case I: $t = 1$
Find the hidden unit z_j whose net input z_in_j is closest to 0. Adjust the weights attached to z_j according to the formula

$$w_{ij}\text{ (new)} = w_{ij}\text{ (old)} + \eta \times (1 - z\_in_j) \times x_i, \text{ for all } i.$$

Case II: $t = -1$
Adjust the weights attached to those hidden units z_j that have positive net input.

$$w_{ij}\text{ (new)} = w_{ij}\text{ (old)} + \eta \times (-1 - z\_in_j) \times x_i, \text{ for all } i.$$

Step 7. Test for stopping condition. It can be any one of the following:

i) No change of weight occurs in Step 6.
ii) The weight adjustments have reached an acceptable level.
iii) A predefined number of iterations have been carried out.

If the stopping condition is satisfied then stop. Otherwise go to Step 3.

Fig. 7.9. *Procedure MADALINE-MRI-Learning*

- In *MR-I* algorithm, only the weights of the hidden units are modified during the training and the weights for the inter-connections from the hidden units to the output unit are kept unaltered. However, in case of *MR-II*, all weights are adjusted, if required.

The *MR-I* algorithm (Widrow and Hoff, 1960)

As mentioned earlier, in *MR-I* training algorithm, the weights associated with the output unit *Y*, *i.e.*, v_0, v_1, v_2 are fixed and are not altered during the training process. Effectively the output unit *Y* implements a logical *OR* operation such that if either of z_out_1 or z_out_2 is 1 then *Y* will yield an activation of 1. Hence, v_0, v_1, v_2 are fixed at 0.5. Keeping $v_0 = v_1 = v_2 = 0.5$ adjustments are done only on w_{01}, w_{11}, w_{21}, w_{02}, w_{12} and w_{22} during training. The stepwise training process is given in **Procedure** *MADALINE-MR-I-Learning* (Fig. 7.9).

Step 6 of **Procedure** *MADALINE-MRI-Learning* is based on two observations:

1. The weights should be adjusted only when there is a mismatch between the actual output *y_out* and the target output t.
2. The adjustments of the weights are to be done in a manner so that the possibility of producing the target output is enhanced.

On the basis of these observations, let us analyze the two cases mentioned in Step 6.

Case I: $t = 1$, and *y_out* $= -1$.
As *y_out* is -1, both z_out_1 and z_out_2 are -1. To make *y_out* $= 1 = t$, we must ensure that at least one of the activations of the hidden units is 1. The unit whose net input is closest to 0 is the suitable unit for this purpose, and the corresponding weights are adjusted as described in Step 6.

Case II: $t = -1$, and *y_out* $= 1$.
In this case, since *y_out* $= 1$, at least one of z_out_1 and z_out_2 must be 1. In order to make *y_out* $= -1 = t$, both z_out_1 and z_out_2 are to be made -1. This implies that all hidden units having positive net inputs are to be adjusted so that these are reduced under the new weights.

Example 7.5 (*MADALINE training for the XOR function*)

Let us train a *MADALINE* net through the *MR-I* algorithm to realize the two-input *XOR* function. The architecture of the net is same as shown in Fig. 7.8. The bipolar training set, including the bias input x_0 which is permanently fixed at 1 is given in Table 7.9. Table 7.10 presents the randomly chosen initial weights, as well as the learning rate.

The details of the calculations for the first training pair $s : t = (1, 1) : -1$ of the first epoch of training are described below.

Steps 1–4 are already taken care of. Calculations of Steps (5.1) and (5.2) are given below.

Table 7.9. *Bipolar training set for XOR function*

x_0	x_1	x_2	t
1	1	1	−1
1	1	−1	1
1	−1	1	1
1	−1	−1	−1

Table 7.10. *Initial weights and the fixed learning rate*

w_{01}	w_{11}	w_{21}	w_{02}	w_{12}	w_{22}	η
.2	.3	.2	.3	.2	.1	.5

```
Step 5.1 Compute net inputs z_in1 and z_in2 to the hidden units z1 and z2.
Step 5.2 Compute activations of the hidden units z_out1 and z_out2 using
         the bipolar step function.
```

$$z\_in_1 = 1 \times w_{01} + x_1 \times w_{11} + x_2 \times w_{21}$$
$$= 1 \times .2 + 1 \times .3 + 1 \times .2 = .7$$
$$z\_out_1 = 1$$
$$z\_in_2 = 1 \times w_{02} + x_1 \times w_{12} + x_2 \times w_{22}$$
$$= 1 \times .3 + 1 \times .2 + 1 \times .1 = .6$$
$$\therefore z\_out_2 = 1$$

```
Step 5.3 Compute net inputs y_in to the output units.
Step 5.4 Find the activation of the output unit y-out using the same ac-
         tivation function as in Step 5.2, i.e.,
```

$$y\_in = 1 \times v_0 + z\_out_1 \times v_1 + z\_out_2 \times v_2$$
$$= 1 \times .5 + 1 \times .5 + 1 \times .5 = 1.5$$
$$\therefore y\_out = 1$$

```
Step 6 Adjust the weights of the hidden units, if required.
```

Since $t = -1$, $y\_out = 1 \neq t$. Moreover, since $t = -1$, CASE II of Step 6 is applicable here. Therefore, we have to update weights on all units that have positive net inputs. Hence in this case we need to update the values of w_{01}, w_{11}, w_{21} as well as those of w_{02}, w_{12}, w_{22}. The computations for the said adjustments are shown below.

$$w_{01}(new) = w_{01}(old) + \eta \times (-1 - z\_in_1)$$
$$= .2 + .5 \times (-1 - .7)$$
$$= .2 - .85$$
$$= -.65$$
$$w_{11}(new) = w_{11}(old) + \eta \times (-1 - z\_in_1)$$
$$= .3 - .85$$
$$= -.55$$
$$w_{21}(new) = w_{21}(old) + \eta \times (-1 - z\_in_1)$$
$$= .2 - .85$$
$$= -.65$$
$$w_{02}(new) = w_{02}(old) + \eta \times (-1 - z\_in_2)$$
$$= .3 + .5 \times (-1 - .6)$$
$$= .3 - .8$$
$$= -.5$$

$$w_{12}(new) = w_{12}(old) + \eta \times (-1 - z\_in_2)$$
$$= .2 - .8$$
$$= -.6$$
$$w_{22}(new) = w_{22}(old) + \eta \times (-1 - z\_in_2)$$
$$= .1 - .8$$
$$= -.7$$

Hence the new set of weights after training with the first training pair (1, 1) : −1 in the first epoch is obtained as

$$W = \begin{bmatrix} w_{01} & w_{02} \\ w_{11} & w_{12} \\ w_{21} & w_{22} \end{bmatrix} = \begin{bmatrix} -.65 & -.5 \\ -.55 & -.6 \\ -.65 & -.7 \end{bmatrix}$$

Table 7.11 gives the details of the training process until the *MADALINE* learns the required function. It is found that four epochs of training are required to arrive at the appropriate weights for realizing the XOR function.

The empty fields in the table indicate no change in the weights. The entries in the Epoch #4 portion of the table show that all the training inputs produce the expected target outputs and consequently, the weights at the beginning of this epoch have remained unchanged. Hence the weights finally arrived at by the *MADALINE* net are given by

$$W = \begin{bmatrix} w_{01} & w_{02} \\ w_{11} & w_{12} \\ w_{21} & w_{22} \end{bmatrix} = \begin{bmatrix} -.88 & -.84 \\ -1.54 & 1.56 \\ .88 & -1.52 \end{bmatrix}$$

Table 7.11. *MADALINE Learning of XOR Function through MR-I algorithm*

#	x_0	x_1	x_2	t	z_in_1	z_in_2	z_out_1	z_out_2	y_in	y_out	w_{01}	w_{11}	w_{21}	w_{02}	w_{12}	w_{22}
0											.2	.3	.2	.3	.2	.1
1	1	1	1	−1	.7	.6	1	1	1.5	1	−.65	−.55	−.65	−.5	−.6	−.7
2	1	1	−1	1	−.55	−.4	−1	−1	−.5	−1	−.65	−.55	−.65	.2	.1	−1.4
3	1	−1	1	1	−.75	−1.3	−1	−1	−.5	−1	.23	−1.43	.13	.2	.1	−1.4
4	1	−1	−1	−1	1.56	1.5	1	1	1.5	1	−1.05	−.15	1.41	−1.05	1.35	−.15
								Epoch #1								
0											−1.05	−.15	1.41	−1.05	1.35	−.15
1	1	1	1	−1	.21	.15	1	1	1.5	1	−1.66	−.76	.8	−1.63	.77	−.73
2	1	1	−1	1	−3.22	−.13	−1	−1	−.5	−1	−1.66	−.76	.8	−2.07	.33	−.29
3	1	−1	1	1	−.1	−1.45	−1	−1	−.5	−1	−2.11	−.31	.35	−2.07	.33	−.29
4	1	−1	−1	−1	−2.15	−2.11	−1	−1	−.5	−1					-	
								Epoch #2								
0											−2.11	−.31	.35	−2.07	.33	−.29
1	1	1	1	−1	−2.07	−2.03	−1	−1	−.5	−1						
2	1	1	−1	1	−2.77	−1.45	−1	−1	−.5	−1	−2.11	−.31	.35	−.84	1.56	−1.52
3	1	−1	1	1	−1.45	−3.92	−1	−1	−.5	−1	−.88	−1.54	.88	−.84	1.56	−1.52
4	1	−1	−1	−1	−.22	−.88	−1	−1	−.5	−1						
								Epoch #3								

(continued)

Table 7.11. *Continued*

#	x_0	x_1	x_2	t	z_in_1	z_in_2	z_out_1	z_out_2	y_in	y_out	w_{01}	w_{11}	w_{21}	w_{02}	w_{12}	w_{22}
0											−.88	−1.54	.88	−.84	1.56	−1.52
1	1	1	1	−1	−1.54	−.8	−1	−1	−.5	−1						
2	1	1	−1	1	−3.3	2.24	−1	1	.5	1						
3	1	−1	1	1	1.54	−3.92	1	−1	.5	1						
4	1	−1	−1	−1	−.22	−.88	−1	−1	−.5	−1						

Epoch #4

CHAPTER SUMMARY

An overview of the elementary pattern classifying ANNs, e.g., Hebb nets, Perceptrons, MADALINE and ADALINE have been presented in this chapter. The main points of the foregoing discussion are given below.

- A single-layer feedforward neural net trained through the Hebb learning rule is known as a Hebb net.
- It is possible for a Hebb net not to learn a classification task even if the patterns concerned are linearly separable.
- Perceptrons are more powerful than the Hebb nets. Formula for weight adjustment in perceptron learning is $\Delta w_i = \eta \times t \times x_i$ where η is the learning rate.
- The *ADALINE* (*Adaptive Linear Neuron*) is a single output unit neural net with several input units. One of the input units acts as the bias and is permanently fixed at 1.
- *ADALINE* is trained with the help of the delta, or LMS (Least Mean Square), or Widrow-Hoff learning rule.
- Several *ADALINE*s arranged in a multilayer net is known as *Many ADALINES*, or *Many Adaptive Linear Neurons*, or *MADALINE* in short. *MADALINE* is computationally more powerful than *ADALINE*.
- There are two training algorithms for *MADALINE*, *viz.*, *MR-I* and *MR-II*. In *MR-I* algorithm, only the weights of the hidden units are modified during the training and the weights for the inter-connections from the hidden units to the output unit are kept unaltered. However, in case of *MR-II*, all weights are adjusted, if required.

SOLVED PROBLEMS

Problem 7.1 (*Hebb net to realize OR function*) Design a Hebb net to realize the logical *OR* function.

Solution 7.1 It is observed earlier that a Hebb net may not learn the designated task if the training pairs are presented in binary form. Hence, we first present the truth table of *OR* function in bipolar form, as given in Table 7.12. Table 7.13 presents the details of the training process. The interconnection weights we finally arrive at are $w_0 = 2$, $w_1 = 2$, and $w_2 = 2$, and the corresponding separating line is given by

$$1 + x_1 + x_2 = 0$$

$$\therefore x_2 = - x_1 - 1$$

Table 7.12 *Truth table of OR function in bipolar form*

Input		Output
x_1	x_2	x_1 *OR* x_2
−1	−1	−1
−1	1	1
1	−1	1
1	1	1

Fig. 7.10 shows the location and orientation of this line. The Hebb net, thus, is able to learn the designated *OR* function.

Table 7.13 *Hebb learning of OR function*

#	Training Inputs			Target output	Weight changes			Weights		
	x_0	x_1	x_2	(*t*)	Δw_0	Δw_1	Δw_2	w_0	w_1	w_2
0								0	0	0
1	1	−1	−1	−1	−1	1	1	−1	1	1
2	1	−1	1	1	1	−1	1	0	0	2
3	1	1	−1	1	1	1	−1	1	1	1
4	1	1	1	1	1	1	1	2	2	2

$$\Delta w_i = x_i \times y\_out = x_i \times t$$

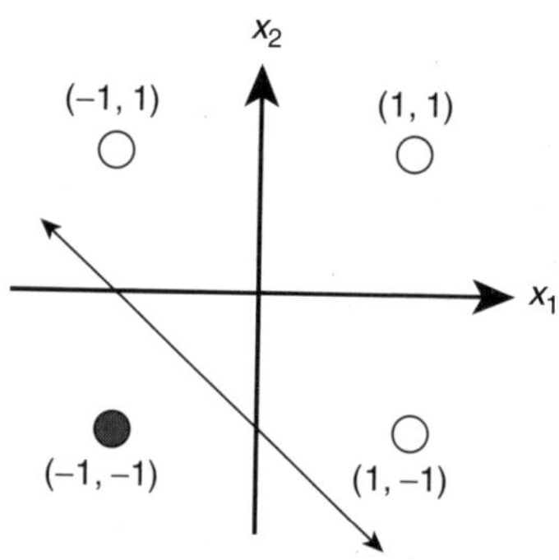

Fig. 7.10. *Decision line of Hebb net realizing the OR function*

Problem 7.2 (*A perceptron and a Hebb net as a traffic controller*) A busy town crossing has two signal posts with the usual three-colour light signal system. The post with the rectangular light frame is meant for vehicles plying on the road, while the post with the oval frame is meant for pedestrians trying to cross the road over the zebra. When the traffic light is green, the pedestrian light is red and vice versa while they share a common yellow state. In spite of this arrangement, unruly traffic caused accidents regularly by ignoring the signal. To overcome this problem, the town administration decided to install an automatic gate across the road that will come down across when the traffic light is red and the pedestrian light is green. The state table is as shown in Table 7.14. Design the gate controller with a perceptron, as well as with a Hebb net.

Table 7.14 *State table for the traffic controller*

Traffic signal	Pedestrian signal	Gate
Green	Red	Up
Yellow	Yellow	Up
Red	Green	Down

Solution 7.2 If we decide to design the gate controller based on a perceptron model, we may encode the light colours as described in Table 7.15.

Table 7.15. *Traffic controller state table translated to numbers*

Traffic signal	Pedestrian signal	Gate
2 (Green)	0 (Red)	0 (Up)
1 (Yellow)	1 (Yellow)	0 (Up)
0 (Red)	2 (Green)	1 (Down)

The controller can now be designed as a perceptron on MatLab. The MatLab code for this purpose is shown in Fig. 7.11. Fig. 7.12 depicts the resultant classifier.

```
P = [0 1 2 ; 2 1 0];                % Possible values of 2 variables in a ma-
                                      trix format
T = [1 0 0];                        % Expected outputs for above dataset
net = newp([0 2; 0 2],1);           % Creates network with two inputs with
                                      ranges of values and 1 output
net.trainParam.epochs = 20;         % Sets the number of maximum iterations
net = train(net,P,T);               % Trains the network
simulation = sim(net,P)             % Simulates neural network
plotpv(P,T)                         % Plot input/target vectors
plotpc(net.iw{1,1},net.b{1})        % Plot classification line
```

Fig. 7.11. *MatLab code for traffic controller perceptron*

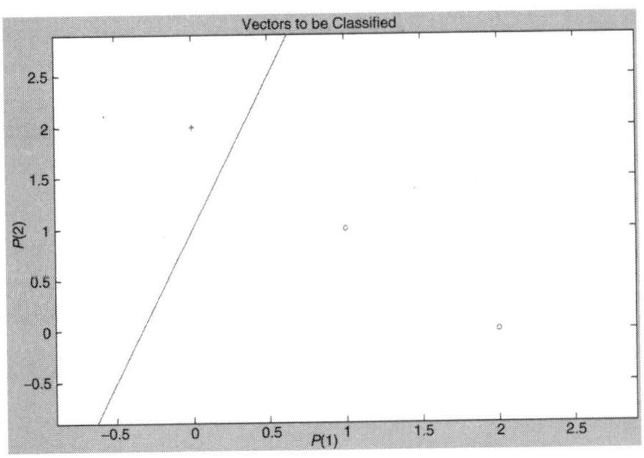

Fig. 7.12. *Output plot for traffic controller perceptron*

This problem can also be solved using Hebb learning. The corresponding MatLab code is given in Fig. 7.13. Fig. 7.14 (a) and (b) shows the resultant classifier after 20 and 150 epochs of training, respectively. Interestingly, the classification is not satisfactory after only 20 epochs of training. Performance is improved by increasing the number of epochs to 150.

```
clear;
clc;
P = [0 1 2 ; 2 1 0];              % Possible values of 2 variables in a ma-
                                    trix format
T = [1 0 0];                      % Expected outputs for above dataset
net = newp([0 2; 0 2],1);         % Creates network with two inputs with
                                    ranges of values and 1 output
net.trainFcn = 'trainr';
net.adaptFcn = 'trains';
net.inputWeights{1,1}.learnFcn = 'learnh';
net.layerWeights{1,1}.learnFcn = 'learnh';
net.trainParam.epochs = 20;       % Sets the number of maximum iterations
net = train(net,P,T);             % Trains the network
simulation = sim(net,P);          % Simulates neural network
plotpv(P,T)                       % Plot input/target vectors
plotpc(net.iw{1,1},net.b{1})      % Plot classification line
```

Fig. 7.13. *MatLab code for traffic controller Hebb net*

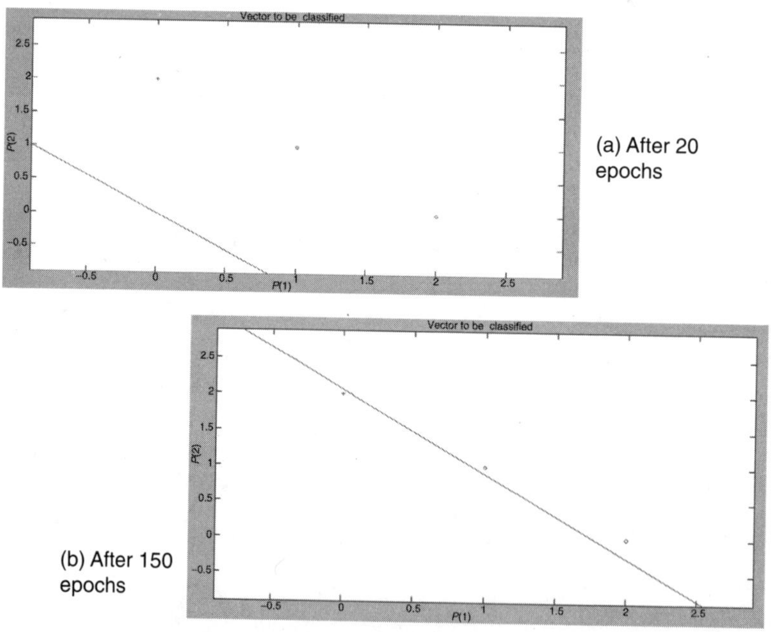

Fig. 7.14. *Output plots for Hebbian traffic controller*

Problem 7.3 (*Classification of two-dimensional patterns with Hebb net*) Consider the following patterns to represent the digits 0 and 1 (Fig. 7.15).

Using Matlab design a Hebb net to classify these two input patterns.

Pattern 1 (for 0)						Pattern 2 (for 1)				
–	#	#	#	–		–	–	#	–	–
#	–	–	–	#		–	#	#	–	–
#	–	–	–	#		–	–	#	–	–
#	–	–	–	#		–	–	#	–	–
–	#	#	#	–		–	#	#	#	–

Pattern 1 (for 0) Pattern 2 (for 1)

Fig. 7.15. *Two 2-dimensional patterns for 0 and 1.*

Solution 7.3 For simplicity, let us consider the target class to correspond to the pattern for '1'. The patterns not classified as '1' will be treated as '0'. Then we convert the patterns into bipolar input vectors by replacing every '#' by '1' and every '–' by '–1' and represent each two dimensional pattern as an input vector by taking the rows and concatenating them one after the other. Fig. 7.16 explains the technique.

Pattern 1 (for 0)						Pattern 2 (for 1)				
–1	1	1	1	–1		–1	–1	1	–1	–1
1	–1	–1	–1	1		–1	1	1	–1	–1
1	–1	–1	–1	1		–1	–1	1	–1	–1
1	–1	–1	–1	1		–1	–1	1	–1	–1
–1	1	1	1	–1		–1	1	1	1	–1

Pattern 1 (for 0) Pattern 2 (for 1)

–1 1 1 1 –1 1 –1 –1 –1 1 1 –1 –1 –1 1 1 –1 –1 –1 1 –1 1 1 1 –1

Input vector for pattern 1 (for 0)

–1 –1 1 –1 –1 –1 1 1 –1 –1 –1 –1 1 –1 –1 –1 –1 1 –1 –1 –1 1 1 1 –1

Input vector for pattern 2 (for 1)

Fig. 7.16. *Encoding the input patterns*

The MatLab code for the Hebb net to solve the classification problem is given in Fig. 7.17.

```
%MATLAB Implementation of Hebb Net to classify 2D Input Patterns
clear;
clc;
Pat1 = [-1 1 1 1 -1 1 -1 -1 -1 1 1 -1 -1 -1 1 1 -1 -1 -1 1 -1 1 1 1 -1];
Pat2 = [-1 -1 1 -1 -1 -1 1 1 -1 -1 -1 -1 1 -1 -1 -1 -1 1 -1 -1 -1 1 1
     1 -1];
```

```
Mat(1,1:25) = Pat1;
Mat(2,1:25) = Pat2;
wt(1:25) = 0;
Tar_Act = [-1 1];
bias = 0;
   for i = 1:2
      wt=wt+Mat(i,1:25)*Tar_Act(i);
      bias=bias+Tar_Act(i);
      disp('Weight Matrix');
      disp(wt);
      disp('Bias');
      disp(bias);
   end
disp('**********Final Weight Matrix***********');
disp(wt);
disp('***************Bias********************');
disp(bias);
disp('*************************DotPat1*******************');
Mat_Out(1,1:1) = dot(Pat1,wt);
disp(Mat_Out(1,1:1))
disp('*************************DotPat2*******************');
Mat_Out(2,1:1)=dot(Pat2,wt);
disp(Mat_Out(2,1:1))
```

Fig. 7.17. *Matlab code for Hebb net of problem 7.3*

The output of the training process is given below.

```
Weight Matrix
Columns 1 through 22
1 -1 -1 -1 1 -1 1 1 1 -1 -1 1 1 1 -1 -1 1 1 1 -1 1 -1
Columns 23 through 25
-1 -1 1
Bias
-1
Weight Matrix
Columns 1 through 22
0 -2 0 -2 0 -2 2 2 0 -2 -2 0 2 0 -2 -2 0 2 0 -2 0 0
Columns 23 through 25
0 0 0
Bias
  0
**********Final Weight Matrix***********
Columns 1 through 22
 0 -2 0 -2 0 -2  2 2 0 -2 -2 0 2 0 -2 -2 0 2 0 -2 0 0
 Columns 23 through 25
```

```
  0    0    0
****************Bias*******************

 0
*****************DotPat1*****************

-24
*****************DotPat1*****************

24
```

✓ TEST YOUR KNOWLEDGE

7.1 How many passes are required by Hebb learning algorithm ?

a) One b) Two
c) No fixed number of passes d) None of the above

7.2 In which of the following cases Hebb learning does not guarantee that the net will learn the classification task even if it was possible for a Hebb net to learn the task under suitable conditions ?

a) The training set is bipolar b) The training set is binary
c) Both (*a*) and (*b*) d) None of the above

7.3 The statement that a Hebb net may fail to learn a classification task consisting of a linearly separable set of patterns is

a) True b) False
c) Uncertain d) None of the above

7.4 For Perceptron learning, the bias and the threshold are

a) Interchangable b) Not interchangable
c) Conditionally interchangable d) None of the above

7.5 Which of the following functions is used for activation of the output unit of the *ADALINE* during training ?

a) Identity b) Binary
c) Bipolar step function d) None of the above

7.6 Which of the following functions is used for activation of the output unit of the *ADALINE* during application ?

a) Identity b) Binary
c) Bipolar step function d) None of the above

7.7 Which of the following learning rule is used in *ADALINE* training ?

a) Hebb learning b) Perceptron learning
c) Delta learning d) None of the above

7.8 Which of the following nets is more powerful than *MADALINE* ?

a) *ADALINE* b) Hebb
c) Both (*a*) and (*b*) d) None of the above

7.9 Which of the following is not a pattern classifying net ?

a) *ADALINE* b) *MADALINE*
c) Both (*a*) and (*b*) d) None of the above

7.10 Which of the following is a pattern classifying net ?

a) *ADALINE* b) *MADALINE*
c) Both (*a*) and (*b*) d) None of the above

Answers

7.1 (a)	7.2 (b)	7.3 (a)	7.4 (b)	7.5 (a)
7.6 (c)	7.7 (c)	7.8 (d)	7.9 (d)	7.10 (c)

EXERCISES

7.1 Design a Hebb net to realize the NAND function.
7.2 Design a Perceptron to realize the NOR function.
7.3 Design an ADALINE to realize the NAND function.
7.4 Design a MADALINE to realize the X-NOR (the complement of XOR) function.

BIBLIOGRAPHY AND HISTORICAL NOTES

The first learning law in the field of artificial neural networks was introduced by Donald Hebb in 1949. Frank Rosenblatt proposed and developed the much celebrated class of ANN called Perceptrons during late fifties and early sixties. ADALINE was proposed by Bernerd Widrow and his student, Mercian Hoff, in 1960. This was closely followed by MADALINE by them. Some milestone works relating to ANN classifiers are here.

Block, H. D. (1962). The Perceptron : A model for brain functioning. *Reviews of Modern Physics*, Vol. 34, pp. 123–135.

Hebb, D.O. (1961). *Distinctive features of learning in the higher animal.* In J. F. Delafresnaye (Ed.). *Brain Mechanisms and Learning.* London: Oxford University Press.

Hebb, D.O. (1949). *The Organization of Behavior.* New York: Wiley and Sons.

Minsky, M. and Papert, P. (1969). *Perceptrons : An Introduction to Computational Geometry.* MIT Press.

Rosenblatt, F. (1958). The Perceptron: A Probabilistic Model for Information Storage and Organization in the Brain, Cornell Aeronautical Laboratory. *Psychological Review*, Vol. 65, No. 6, pp. 386–408.

Rosenblatt, F. (1962). *Principles of Neurodynamics.* New York: Spartan.

Widrow, B. and Lehr, M. A. (1990). 30 Years of Adaptive Neural Networks : Perceptron, MADALINE and Backpropagation. *Proceedings of IEEE*, Vol. 78, No. 9, pp. 1415–1442.

Widrow, B. and Stearns, S. D. (1985). *Adaptive Signal Processing.* Englewood Cliffs, NJ: Prentice-Hall.

8

PATTERN ASSOCIATORS

Key Concepts

Associative Memory, Auto-associative Nets, Bidirectional Associative Memory (BAM), Content-addressable Memory, Delta Learning, Feedforward Nets, Hebb Learning, Hetero-associative Nets, Hopfield Networks, Inner product, Orthogonal Vectors, Recurrent (iterative) Nets, Self-connection

Chapter Outline

Relating a given pattern to one already stored in memory is known as pattern association. It is a task that we, the human beings, perform regularly in course of our daily life almost without any conscious effort. Recognition of a known face from an image (either distorted or undistorted) or visualization of a rose from its fragrance are instances of pattern association.

The phenomenon of pattern association may be formally stated as follows. Let $\mathbf{s}_1 : \mathbf{t}_1, \mathbf{s}_2 : \mathbf{t}_2, \ldots, \mathbf{s}_k : \mathbf{t}_k$ be a number of pairs of patterns. If there is a system that yields the pattern t_i when presented as input with the pattern $\mathbf{s}_i$, $i = 1, \ldots, k$, then we say that the system is an *associative* or *content addressable memory* storing the pattern pairs $\mathbf{s}_1 : \mathbf{t}_1, \ldots, \mathbf{s}_k : \mathbf{t}_k$. The act of relating a given pattern $\mathbf{s}_i$ to its corresponding stored pattern $\mathbf{t}_i$ is known as pattern association. One important property of an associative memory is its capacity to correctly associate a noisy input pattern to the desired output pattern. However, there is a limit to the extent of noise tolerable to a given associative memory network.

Associative memory neural nets are those which store a set of pattern associations. There are two kinds of associative memory neural nets. These are *auto-associative* and *hetero-associative*. In auto-associative neural nets, the input and output patterns are identical. In hetero-associative neural nets, the inputs and the outputs are different.

Regarding architecture, an associative memory neural net may be either *feedforward* type or *recurrent* (*iterative*) type. In feedforward nets, signals are unidirectional. They flow from input to output and not in the reverse direction. In recurrent (or iterative) nets, signals flow back and forth between the input and the output until the net reaches an equilibrium state.

In the subsequent parts of this chapter, four kinds of associative neural nets are described, *viz., auto-associative* nets, *hetero-associative* nets, *Hopfield* nets, and *Bidirectional Associative Memory* (*BAM*). While the auto-associative and hetero-associative nets are feedforward type of nets, the Hopfield nets and BAM are recurrent networks. There are various representation schemes for the input and output patterns to associative networks. Here we consider, unless otherwise stated, only bipolar input and output patterns.

8.1 AUTO-ASSOCIATIVE NETS

The input and output patterns of an auto-associative net are the same. Presented with an input pattern, perhaps noisy to some extent, an auto-associative net returns the same pattern (this time without any noise) in case the input matches one of the stored patterns. The architecture of an auto-associative net is shown in Fig. 8.1. It has the same number of input and output units.

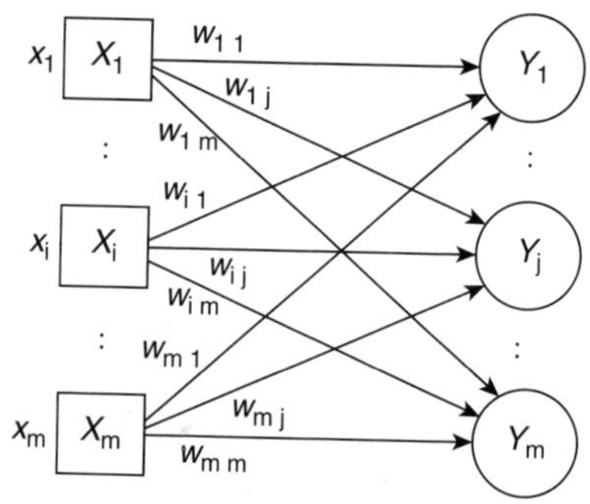

Fig. 8.1. *Architecture of a feed-forward auto-associative net*

8.1.1 Training

An auto-associative network can be trained with Hebb, delta, or extended delta rule. However, for the sake of simplicity, here we apply only the Hebb rule for training an associative net. Let us first consider the case of storing a single pattern $\mathbf{s} = [s_1, s_2, \ldots, s_m]$ on an auto-associative net. The weight matrix W of the net is obtained as

$$W = \mathbf{s}^{\mathrm{T}} \times \mathbf{s} = \begin{pmatrix} s_1 \\ \vdots \\ s_i \\ \vdots \\ s_m \end{pmatrix} \times \left(s_1 \cdots s_j \cdots s_m\right) = \begin{pmatrix} s_1 \times s_1 & \cdots & s_1 \times s_j & \cdots & s_1 \times s_m \\ \vdots & & & & \\ s_i \times s_1 & \cdots & s_i \times s_j & \cdots & s_i \times s_j \\ \vdots & & & & \\ s_m \times s_1 & \cdots & s_m \times s_j & \cdots & s_m \times s_m \end{pmatrix} \tag{8.1}$$

Example 8.1 illustrates the training process of an auto-associative net to store a single pattern.

Example 8.1 *(Training an auto-associative net to store a single pattern)*

Let us find the weight matrix of an auto-associative net to store and recognize the vector $\mathbf{s} = [1, -1, -1, 1]$. Applying Equation 8.1 we get the following weight matrix.

$$W = \mathbf{s}^T \times \mathbf{s} = \begin{pmatrix} 1 \\ -1 \\ -1 \\ 1 \end{pmatrix} \times (1\ -1\ -1\ 1) = \begin{pmatrix} 1 & -1 & -1 & 1 \\ -1 & 1 & 1 & -1 \\ -1 & 1 & 1 & -1 \\ 1 & -1 & -1 & 1 \end{pmatrix}$$

8.1.2 Application

Once the weight matrix is obtained through the appropriate training method, it is ready for application. Let $\boldsymbol{x} = [x_1, \ldots, x_i, \ldots, x_m]$ be an arbitrary input pattern of length m. To recognize the input pattern $\boldsymbol{x}$, we have to determine whether the given pattern matches with the stored pattern. The following steps are carried out to achieve this.

1. For each output unit Y_j, $j = 1, \ldots, m$, compute the net input y_in_j to Y_j.

$$y\_in_j = \sum_{i=1}^{m} x_i . w_{ij}$$

In matrix notation, $\boldsymbol{Y\_in} = \boldsymbol{x} \times W$, where $\boldsymbol{Y\_in} = [y\_in_1, \ldots, y\_in_m]$, $\boldsymbol{x} = [x_1, \ldots, x_m]$, and W is the weight matrix.

2. For each output unit Y_j, $j = 1, \ldots, m$, find the activation using the function

$$y\_out = \begin{cases} 1, & \text{if } y\_in > 0, \\ -1, & \text{otherwise} \end{cases}$$

If the output vector thus found is identical to the stored pattern, i.e., $\boldsymbol{Y\_out} = [y\_out_1, \ldots, y\_out_m] = [s_1, \ldots, s_m] = \mathbf{s}$ then the input is recognized, otherwise not.

Example 8.2 *(Pattern association by auto-associative net)*

Refer to the auto-associative net built in Example 8.1. To see if the resultant net can recognize the stored pattern $\boldsymbol{x} = [1, -1, -1, 1]$, we follow the steps described above.

1. Compute the vector **Y_in** for net inputs to the output units.

$$\boldsymbol{Y\_in} = [y\_in_1, y\_in_2, y\_in_3, y\_in_4]$$

$$= [1\ -1\ -1\ 1] \times \begin{pmatrix} 1 & -1 & -1 & 1 \\ -1 & 1 & 1 & -1 \\ -1 & 1 & 1 & -1 \\ 1 & -1 & -1 & 1 \end{pmatrix}$$

$$= [4, -4, -4, 4]$$

2. Find the output vector employing the activation function.

$$\boldsymbol{Y\_out} = [y\_out_1, y\_out_2, y\_out_3, y\_out_4]$$

$$= [1, -1, -1, 1]$$

Hence, the net has acquired the ability to recognize the stored pattern.

8.1.3 Elimination of Self-connection

It is convenient to set the diagonal elements of the weight matrix W to 0 to indicate that the net does not have any self-connection. This is more useful for nets that store several patterns. For such nets, the diagonal elements are set to 0s to ensure that these elements do not dominate during application of the net. Otherwise, the net has a tendency to reproduce the input pattern rather than the stored pattern.

Example 8.3 *(Performance of associative net with diagonal elements set to 0s)*

The weight matrix of the net cited in Example 8.1 becomes, with all diagonal elements set to 0,

$$W = \begin{bmatrix} 0 & -1 & -1 & 1 \\ -1 & 0 & 1 & -1 \\ -1 & 1 & 0 & -1 \\ 1 & -1 & -1 & 0 \end{bmatrix}$$

Therefore, the net input to the output units are computed as

$$\boldsymbol{Y\_in} = [y\_in_1, y\_in_2, y\_in_3, y\_in_4]$$

$$= [1\ -1\ -1\ 1] \times \begin{pmatrix} 0 & -1 & -1 & 1 \\ -1 & 0 & 1 & -1 \\ -1 & 1 & 0 & -1 \\ 1 & -1 & -1 & 0 \end{pmatrix}$$

$$= [3, -3, -3, 3]$$

And the output vector is obtained as

$$\boldsymbol{Y\_out} = [y\_out_1, y\_out_2, y\_out_3, y\_out_4]$$

$$= [1, -1, -1, 1]$$

Hence, the net retains the ability to recognize the stored pattern.

8.1.4 Recognition of Noisy Patterns

Mere recognition of the pattern already stored in the net is not sufficient because this could as well be achieved with a diagonal weight matrix. The strength of a neural net lies in it tolerance of noisy input pattern, provided the input is sufficiently close to the stored pattern in spite of it being noisy.

Two kinds of noises may appear in the input pattern. These are (a) missing elements and (b) erroneous elements. A missing element is represented by 0, instead of a 1 or −1, in the appropriate place. An erroneous element presents the complement of the correct value, i.e., 1 (−1) in place of −1 (1). The following example illustrates the capacity of auto-associative nets to recognize noisy patterns.

Example 8.4 *(Recognition of noisy input with one missing element)*

Let us consider a noisy input pattern where the leftmost element of the input vector is missing. Thus, the input pattern appears as $[0\ {-1}\ {-1}\ 1]$ instead of $[1\ {-1}\ {-1}\ 1]$. Computation of the net input and subsequently the output vector is done in the usual way.

$$\boldsymbol{Y\_in} = [y\_in_1, y\_in_2, y\_in_3, y\_in_4]$$

$$= [0\ {-1}\ {-1}\ 1] \times \begin{pmatrix} 0 & -1 & -1 & 1 \\ -1 & 0 & 1 & -1 \\ -1 & 1 & 0 & -1 \\ 1 & -1 & -1 & 0 \end{pmatrix}$$

$$= [3, -2, -2, 2]$$

$$\boldsymbol{Y\_out} = [y\_out_1, y\_out_2, y\_out_3, y\_out_4]$$

$$= [1, -1, -1, 1]$$

Hence the net recognizes the noisy input pattern with the first element missing. Similar computations with other single missing entries reveal that the net is able to recognize input patterns with a single missing element. These computations are summarized in Table 8.1.

Table 8.1. *Recognition of noisy input with one missing element*

#	Input pattern (noisy)	Net input to the output layer ($Y\_in = s \times W$)	Output pattern
i	[1, 0, −1, 1]	[2, −3, −2, 2]	[1, −1, −1, 1]
ii	[1, −1, 0, 1]	[2, −2, −3, 2]	[1, −1, −1, 1]
iii	[1, −1, −1, 0]	[2, −2, −2, 3]	[1, −1, −1, 1]

We see that the net has the capacity to recognize an input pattern with a single missing element. Is the net able to withstand two or more missing inputs? What if there are erroneous inputs, not just missing inputs? Problems 8.1 and 8.2 in the section 'Solved Problems' deal with these issues.

8.1.5 Storage of Multiple Patterns in an Auto-associative Net

More than one patterns can be stored in an auto-associative neural net. The *capacity* of such a net is defined as the number of patterns that can be stored in it and be recalled by the net. If one tries to store more patterns than its capacity, then the net tends to *forget* the stored patterns. The important points regarding storage of several patterns in an auto-associative net are stated below.

1. The stored patterns must be mutually orthogonal. Two vectors $\boldsymbol{x} = [x_1, x_2, \ldots, x_n]$ and $\boldsymbol{y} = [y_1, y_2, \ldots, y_n]$ are said to be orthogonal if their inner product is zero, i.e.,

$$x \cdot y = \sum_{i=1}^{n} x_i y_i = 0 \tag{8.2}$$

2. The weight matrix of the net storing several patterns is the sum of the individual weight matrices. Let $\boldsymbol{s}_1, \boldsymbol{s}_2, \ldots, \boldsymbol{s}_k$ be k mutually orthogonal vectors and $W_1, W_2, \ldots, W_k$ be the weight matrices for the auto-associative nets recognizing the vectors $\boldsymbol{s}_1, \boldsymbol{s}_2, \ldots, \boldsymbol{s}_k$, respectively. The diagonal elements of all the weight matrices are all set to zeros. Then the weight matrix W of the auto-associative net recognizing the given patterns is obtained by adding the individual weight matrices $W_1, W_2, \ldots, W_k$.

$$W = W_1 + W_2 + \cdots + W_k = \sum_{i=1}^{k} W_i \tag{8.3}$$

3. An n-input auto-associative net can store at most $n-1$ number of mutually orthogonal vectors, each of which consists of n components. An attempt to store more than $n-1$ mutually orthogonal n-component vectors in a manner described in point 2 above will result in a singular weight matrix. Hence an auto-associative net with n input nodes cannot store n patterns.
4. The diagonal elements of the weight matrix W are set to zero. This is to ensure that the diagonal terms do not dominate during application of the net and prevent the net from reproducing an input pattern rather than a stored pattern.

The above points are illustrated below with the help of simple illustrative examples.

Example 8.5 (*Storage of multiple bipolar patterns in auto-associative neural net*)

We consider an auto-associative neural net with four input units. At most three orthogonal vectors can be stored in it in a recognizable form. Let $\boldsymbol{s}_1 = [1, 1, 1, 1]$, $\boldsymbol{s}_2 = [-1, 1, -1, 1]$, and $\boldsymbol{s}_3 = [-1, -1, 1, 1]$ be three vectors to be stored. These vectors are mutually orthogonal.

$$\boldsymbol{s}_1 \cdot \boldsymbol{s}_2 = [1, 1, 1, 1] \cdot [-1, 1, -1, 1] = 0$$

$$\boldsymbol{s}_1 \cdot \boldsymbol{s}_3 = [1, 1, 1, 1] \cdot [-1, -1, 1, 1] = 0$$

$$\boldsymbol{s}_2 \cdot \boldsymbol{s}_3 = [-1, 1, -1, 1] \cdot [-1, -1, 1, 1] = 0$$

The weight matrices W_1, W_2, and W_k of the nets storing the given patterns individually are given below. All the diagonal elements of the matrices are set to zero.

$$W_1 = \begin{bmatrix} 0 & 1 & 1 & 1 \\ 1 & 0 & 1 & 1 \\ 1 & 1 & 0 & 1 \\ 1 & 1 & 1 & 0 \end{bmatrix}, \ W_2 = \begin{bmatrix} 0 & -1 & 1 & -1 \\ -1 & 0 & -1 & 1 \\ 1 & -1 & 0 & -1 \\ -1 & 1 & -1 & 0 \end{bmatrix}, \text{ and } W_3 = \begin{bmatrix} 0 & 1 & -1 & -1 \\ 1 & 0 & -1 & -1 \\ -1 & -1 & 0 & 1 \\ -1 & -1 & 1 & 0 \end{bmatrix}$$

Therefore, the weight matrix of the desired net for storing the three patterns s_1, s_2, s_3 is

$$W = W_1 + W_2 + W_3 = \begin{bmatrix} 0 & 1 & 1 & -1 \\ 1 & 0 & -1 & 1 \\ 1 & -1 & 0 & 1 \\ -1 & 1 & 1 & 0 \end{bmatrix}$$

The calculations in the next example, Example 8.6, show that the resultant net indeed has the capacity to recognize the stored patterns.

Example 8.6 *(Recognizing patterns by auto-associative nets storing multiple patterns)*

We consider the net constructed in Example 8.5 above. The output vector for the input pattern s_1 = [1, 1, 1, 1] is calculated as follows.

Input pattern: s_1 = [1, 1, 1, 1]
Net input to the output layer: $Y\_in = s_1 \times W$ = [1, 1, 1, 1] × W = [1, 1, 1, 1]
Activation at the output layer: Y_out = [1, 1, 1, 1] = s_1

Hence, the net can recognize the pattern s_1 = [1, 1, 1, 1]. Table 8.2 shows the details of the calculations of the outputs for all the stored patterns. Entries in the last column (Output pattern) of Table 8.2 clearly show that the net recognizes all the stored patterns.

Table 8.2. *Recognition of multiple patterns by auto-associative net*

#	Input pattern	Net input to the output layer ($Y\_in = s_i \times W$)	Output pattern
i	s_1 = [1, 1, 1, 1]	[1, 1, 1, 1]	[1, 1, 1, 1]
ii	s_2 = [−1, 1, −1, 1]	[−1, 1, −1, 1]	[−1, 1, −1, 1]
iii	s_3 = [−1, −1, 1, 1]	[−1, −1, 1, 1]	[−1, −1, 1, 1]

Problems 8.3 and 8.4 in the section 'Solved problems' illustrate the inability of auto-associative nets to store/recognize non-orthogonal patterns, or more than $n-1$ number of patterns.

8.2 HETERO-ASSOCIATIVE NETS

An auto-associative net stores the association between identical patterns so that given an input pattern, it can recall whether it is one of the stored patterns or not. In contrast, a hetero-associative net is used to store the associations between pairs of patterns that are not identical. This means, if **s** : **t** be a pair of associated patterns and this association is stored in a hetero-associative net, then **s** ≠ **t**.

The structure of a hetero-associative net is shown in Fig. 8.2. It is almost identical to the structure of an auto-associative net depicted in Fig. 8.1 except that in case of hetero-associative networks the number of input units (m) is not necessarily equal to the number of the output units (n). Other aspects of this network, e.g., training and application, are discussed below.

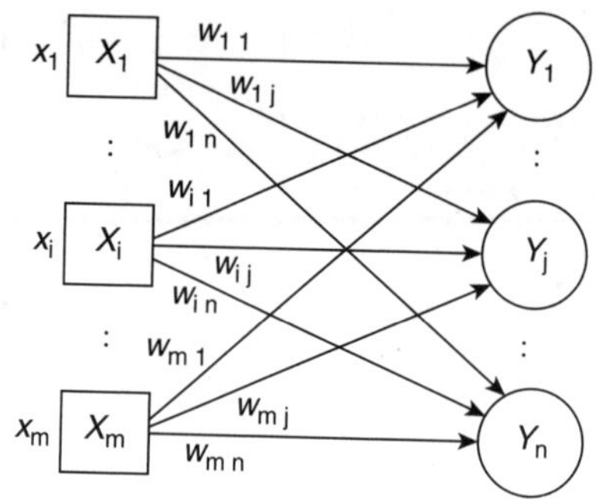

Fig. 8.2. *Architecture of a feed-forward hetero-associative net*

8.2.1 Training

Let **s** : **t** be an association of two patterns where **s** = $[s_1, s_2, \ldots, s_m]$ and **t** = $[t_1, t_2, \ldots, t_n]$. Let W be the weight matrix of the hetero-associative net storing the association $s : t$.

$$W = \begin{bmatrix} w_{11} & w_{12} & \cdots & w_{1n} \\ \vdots & \ddots & & \\ w_{m1} & w_{m2} & \cdots & w_{mn} \end{bmatrix}$$

Then W is obtained using the Hebb rule as described below.

$$w_{ij} = s_i \times t_j, \quad (i = 1, \ldots, m \text{ and } j = 1, \ldots, n) \tag{8.4}$$

Using matrix notation, the relation becomes

$$W = \mathbf{s}^{\mathrm{T}} \times \mathbf{t} = \begin{pmatrix} s_1 \\ \vdots \\ s_i \\ \vdots \\ s_m \end{pmatrix} \times (t_1 \cdots t_j \cdots t_n) = \begin{pmatrix} s_1 \times t_1 & \cdots & s_1 \times t_j & \cdots & s_1 \times t_n \\ \vdots & & & & \\ s_i \times t_1 & \cdots & s_i \times t_j & \cdots & s_i \times t_n \\ \vdots & & & & \\ s_m \times t_1 & \cdots & s_m \times t_j & \cdots & s_m \times t_n \end{pmatrix} \tag{8.5}$$

As usual, multiple associations are stored by adding up the individual weight matrices. If **s** (k) : **t** (k), $k = 1, \ldots, P$, and $W_1, W_2, \ldots, W_P$ be the weight matrices for storing the associations **s** (1) : **t** (1), **s** (2) : **t** (2), …, **s** (P) : **t** (P), respectively, then the weight matrix of the resultant net is obtained as follows.

$$W = W_1 + W_2 + \cdots + W_P = \sum_{i=1}^{P} W_i \tag{8.6}$$

Example 8.7 *(Hetero-associative net for single association)*

Consider a pair $s : t$ of patterns where $s = [1, -1, 1, -1]$ and $t = [-1, 1, -1]$. The weight matrix of the net storing this association is calculated below.

$$W = s^{\mathrm{T}} \times t = \begin{pmatrix} 1 \\ -1 \\ 1 \\ -1 \end{pmatrix} \times (-1\ 1\ -1) = \begin{pmatrix} -1 & 1 & -1 \\ 1 & -1 & 1 \\ -1 & 1 & -1 \\ 1 & -1 & 1 \end{pmatrix}$$

8.2.2 Application

Application of a hetero-associative net is the same as that for auto-associative nets described in Section 8.1.2. Example 8.8 illustrates the application process with respect to the net cited in Example 8.7.

Example 8.8 *(Application of hetero-associative net for single association)*

To verify if the net developed in Example 8.7 is able to behave in the expected manner, we need to find the output vector for the input pattern $x = [1, -1, 1, -1]$.

Input pattern: $x = [1, -1, 1, -1]$
Net input to the output layer: $Y\_in = x \times W = [1, -1, 1, -1] \times W = [-4, 4, -4]$
Activation at the output layer: $Y\_out = [-1, 1, -1] = t$
Hence the net associates the input $[1, -1, 1, -1]$ to the stored pattern $[-1, 1, -1]$.

Example 8.9 *(Recognition of noisy input by hetero-associative net)*

Consider again the net developed in Example 8.7. Suppose the input to the net is $x = [1, -1, 0, -1]$ where the third element is missing. Performance of the net for such an input is described below.

Input pattern: $x = [1, -1, 0, -1]$
Net input to the output layer: $Y\_in = x \times W = [1, -1, 0, -1] \times W = [-3, 3, -3]$
Activation at the output layer: $Y\_out = [-1, 1, -1] = t$

Hence, the net correctly associates the noisy input pattern $[1, -1, 0, -1]$ to the stored pattern $[-1, 1, -1]$. Verification of the performance of the net with other kinds of noisy inputs is left as an exercise.

A hetero-associative net may store multiple pattern associations. This capacity is illustrated in Problem 8.5 in the section 'Solved Problems'.

8.3 HOPFIELD NETWORKS

Associative networks that do not respond immediately to an input pattern but take several steps to converge to a stable output are called iterative, or recurrent, networks. Hopfield networks, proposed by John Hopfield (1982, 1984, 1988), is one of the earliest and popular iterative auto-associative networks. The basic features of discrete Hopfield networks are presented in this section.

8.3.1 Architecture

A Hopfield net is a fully interconnected net with symmetric weights and without any self-loop. This means that for a Hopfield net, $w_{ij} = w_{ji}$, for all $i \neq j$, and $w_{ii} = 0$, for all i. As the net is fully connected, the idea of various layers of processing units is no longer meaningful here. Each unit gets input from each of the remaining units, as well as the corresponding element of the input pattern. Hence, for an m-unit Hopfield net, the net input to unit Yj is given by

$$y\_in_j = x_j + \sum_{\substack{i=1 \\ i \neq j}}^{m} y_i \cdot w_{ij} \tag{8.7}$$

Here x_j is the jth component of the input pattern $\mathbf{x} = [x_1, x_2, \ldots, x_m]$ and y_i is the current activation of unit Y_i. The structure of a four-unit Hopfield net is shown in Fig. 8.3. The notable points regarding the Hopfield net discussed here are given below.

(i) The net is fully connected with symmetric weights but without any self-loop.
(ii) The net is trained with bipolar patterns so that the weight matrix is also bipolar. However, during application binary inputs are used.
(iii) Hebb rule is used to obtain the weight matrix.
(iv) During application, activation of a single unit Y_i is updated on the basis of the signal it receives from other units, and the input x_j to that unit.
(v) The units update their activations in random order.
(vi) The update of the activations of the units stops when the units reach a stable state. The stabilized set of activations of the units is taken as the output of the net.

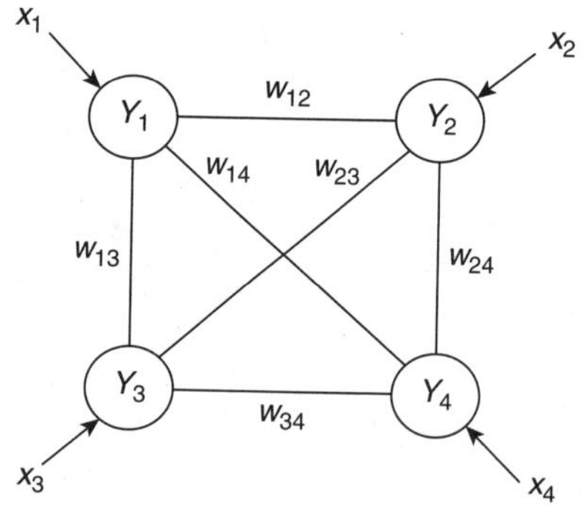

Fig. 8.3. *Structure of a four-unit Hopfield net*

8.3.2 Training

There are several versions of Hopfield network, of which we consider the one with bipolar inputs at the time of training. Let $\mathbf{s} = [s_1, s_2, \ldots, s_m]$ be an input pattern presented in bipolar form. Then the weight matrix of the Hopfield net storing the pattern $\mathbf{s}$ is obtained as:

$$w_{ij} = \begin{cases} s_i \times s_j, & \text{if } i \neq j \\ 0, & \text{if } i = j \end{cases} \tag{8.8}$$

In matrix notation, $$W = \mathbf{s}^{T} \times \mathbf{s}, \quad w_{ij} = 0 \ \forall\ i = 1, \ldots, m \tag{8.9}$$

In order to store several patterns **s**(1), **s**(2), …, **s**(k), the corresponding weight matrices are to be added as in Equation (8.6) to compute the weight matrix of the required net

$$W = W_1 + W_2 + \cdots + W_k = \sum_{i=1}^{k} W_i \tag{8.10}$$

Let $\boldsymbol{x} = [x_1, x_2, \ldots, x_m]$ be an input pattern for a given Hopfield net. To obtain the output of the net, the steps described in the **Procedure** *Hopfield-Pattern-Association* are executed. As mentioned earlier, there are many variations of Hopfield networks. A simplified version is presented here that conveys the essential features of the net without going into incidental details.

```
Procedure Hopfield-Pattern-Association

// Given an m-unit Hopfield net with weight matrix W, to find the output of
the net for the input pattern x = [ x1, x2, …, xm ]. //

Step 1.  Initialize the activations of the units with the input signals.

              Y_outi = xi        (i =1, …, m )

Step 2.  Update the activations of the units in random order by executing
         Steps 3 to 4 for each unit Yj , j =1, …, m.

Step 3.  Find the net input y_inj to Yj.
```

$$y\_in_j = x_j + \sum_{i \neq j} y\_out_i \times w_{ij}$$

```
Step 4.  Find the activation of the unit Yj.
```

$$y\_out_j = \begin{cases} 1, & \text{if } y\_in_j > 0 \\ y\_out_j, & \text{if } y\_in_j = 0 \\ 0, & \text{if } y\_in_j < 0 \end{cases}$$

```
         Once the activation of Yj, i.e., y_outj, is updated, it is broad-
         cast to all other units for further updation of the activations
         of those units.

Step 5.  Test for convergence. If there is no change in the activation of
         the units Y1, …, Ym, then the net has reached a stable state and
         therefore stop. Otherwise, go to Step 2.
```

Fig. 8.4. *Procedure Hopfield-pattern-association*

Example 8.10 *(Computing the weight matrix of a Hopfield net and testing its performance)*

Let us construct a Hopfield net to store the pattern [1, 0, 0, 1]. When put in bipolar form, it is presented as $\boldsymbol{s} = [1, -1, -1, 1]$. Applying Equation 8.9, the weight matrix of the net is obtained as

$$W = \mathbf{s}^{\mathrm{T}} \times \mathbf{s} = \begin{pmatrix} 1 \\ -1 \\ -1 \\ 1 \end{pmatrix} \times [1 \ -1 \ -1 \ 1] = \begin{pmatrix} 1 & -1 & -1 & 1 \\ -1 & 1 & 1 & -1 \\ -1 & 1 & 1 & -1 \\ 1 & -1 & -1 & 1 \end{pmatrix}$$

However, the diagonal elements of W are to be set to zeros. Therefore, the weight matrix is finally computed as

$$W = \begin{pmatrix} 0 & -1 & -1 & 1 \\ -1 & 0 & 1 & -1 \\ -1 & 1 & 0 & -1 \\ 1 & -1 & -1 & 0 \end{pmatrix}$$

To verify the performance of the net, we apply the input vector $\boldsymbol{x} = [1, 0, 0, 1]$ and let the units of the net update their activations iteratively. The computational steps are described below.

1. Let the input vector be $\boldsymbol{x} = [x_1, x_2, x_3, x_4] = [1, 0, 0, 1]$.
2. Initialize the activations of the units as

$$\boldsymbol{Y} = [y\_out_1, y\_out_2, y\_out_3, y\_out_4] = [1, 0, 0, 1].$$

3. In the first epoch, let us update the activations of the units in the random order Y_3, Y_1, Y_4, Y_2.

   3.1 Update the activation y_out_3 of Y_3.

$$y\_in_3 = x_3 + \sum_{i=1}^{4} y\_out_i \times w_{i3}$$

$$= 0 + (1 \times (-1) + 0 \times 1 + 0 \times 0 + 1 \times (-1))$$

$$= -2$$

$$\therefore y\_out_3 = 0$$

   3.2. Update the activation y_out_1 of Y_1.

$$y\_in_1 = x_1 + \sum_{i=1}^{4} y\_out_i \times w_{i1}$$

$$= 1 + (1 \times 0 + 0 \times (-1) + 0 \times (-1) + 1 \times 1)$$

$$= 2$$

$$\therefore y\_out_1 = 1$$

   3.3. Update the activation y_out_4 of Y_4.

$$y\_in_4 = x_4 + \sum_{i=1}^{4} y\_out_i \times w_{i4}$$

$$= 1 + (1 \times 1 + 0 \times (-1) + 0 \times (-1) + 1 \times 0)$$

$$= 2$$

$$\therefore y\_out_4 = 1$$

3.4. Update the activation y_out_2 of Y_2.

$$y\_in_2 = x_2 + \sum_{i=1}^{4} y\_out_i \times w_{i2}$$

$$= 0 + (1 \times (-1) + 0 \times 0 + 0 \times 1 + 1 \times (-1))$$

$$= -2$$

$$\therefore y\_out_2 = 0$$

Hence, $\boldsymbol{Y} = [y\_out_1, y\_out_2, y\_out_3, y\_out_4] = [1, 0, 0, 1]$.

4. Calculations of Steps 3.1 to 3.4 reveal that none of the units had to modify its activation during the application of the input pattern. This implies that the net has converged to a stable state and the process stops here. The activation vector $\boldsymbol{Y} = [1, 0, 0, 1]$ is accepted as the output of the net.

Hence, this Hopfield net can recognize the 'known' pattern [1, 0, 0, 1].

Performance of this Hopfield net under noisy input is illustrated in Problem 8.5, in the section 'Solved Problems'.

8.4 BIDIRECTIONAL ASSOCIATIVE MEMORY

A hetero-associative iterative neural net containing two layers of processing elements interconnected by bidirectional paths and storing a collection of pairs of patterns is known as a *bidirectional associative memory* (*BAM*). It was developed by Kosko in 1988. Other associative networks are one-way, i.e., if $\boldsymbol{s} : \boldsymbol{t}$ is the stored association, then the net can remember the pattern $\boldsymbol{t}$ when presented with $\boldsymbol{s}$ as the input pattern. However, these nets are unable to function in the reverse direction. The distinctive feature of *BAM* is, it is bidirectional. Hence, it can remember the association $\boldsymbol{s} : \boldsymbol{t}$ when presented with any of the two associated patterns $\boldsymbol{s}$, or $\boldsymbol{t}$, as the input. The following subsections provide the basic features of *BAM*.

8.4.1 Architecture

Figure 8.5 shows the structure of a *BAM*. It consists of two layers of processing units, the *X*-layer and the *Y*-layer. Signals propagate back and forth between the two layers and none of these layers is distinguished as the input, or the output, layer. Patterns may be fed to the net through any of the two layers. When the net reaches the equilibrium state, the activation vector obtained from the other layer is taken as the output. Each processing unit of a layer is connected to each unit of the other layer through weighted bidirectional paths. During operation, each layer acts as the input to the other layer. The two layers iteratively and alternately update the activations of their units using the signals obtained from the units of the other layer until they reach a stable state. There are a number of variations of *BAM*. In this text we consider the simplest among them.

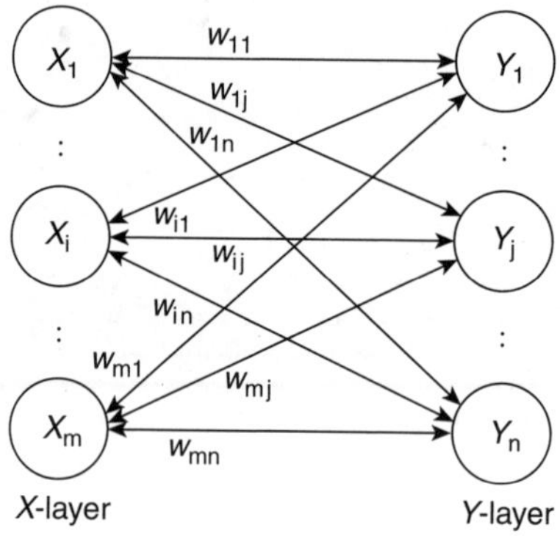

Fig. 8.5. *Structure of a bidirectional associative memory (BAM)*

8.4.2 Training

Let $\boldsymbol{s} : \boldsymbol{t}$ be an association of a pair of bipolar patterns where $\boldsymbol{s} = [s_1, s_2, \ldots, s_m]$ and $\boldsymbol{t} = [t_1, t_2, \ldots, t_n]$. Obviously, the BAM that stores this association must have m units in the X-layer, and n units in the Y-layer, assuming that during application, the vectors $\boldsymbol{s}$ and $\boldsymbol{t}$ would be fed to the X-layer and the Y-layer, respectively. Then the weight matrix W for signals sent from the X-layer to the Y-layer is obtained by using the Hebb rule as

$$W = \boldsymbol{s}^{\mathrm{T}} \times \boldsymbol{t}$$

The weight matrix for the signals in the reverse direction, i.e., from Y-layer to the X-layer, is the transpose of W, i.e., W^{T}. And, in case there are a number of associations $\boldsymbol{s}(1) : \boldsymbol{t}(1)$, $\boldsymbol{s}(2) : \boldsymbol{t}(2)$, …, $\boldsymbol{s}(k) : \boldsymbol{t}(k)$ and $W_1, W_2, \ldots, W_k$ are the corresponding weight matrices then the weight matrix W of the *BAM* storing all these associations is obtained as the algebraic sum of the individual matrices.

$$W = W_1 + W_2 + \cdots + W_k = \sum_{i=1}^{k} W_i \tag{8.11}$$

8.4.3 Application

Given the weight matrix W of a *BAM*, the algorithm for application of the *BAM* is described in **Procedure** *BAM-Pattern-Association* (Fig. 8.6). A notable point regarding **Procedure** *BAM-Pattern-Association* is that if the net input to a unit is 0 then the activation of the unit is kept unaltered. Moreover, according to **Procedure** *BAM-Pattern-Association*, initially the signals are propagated from the X-layer to the Y-layer and then in the reverse direction, and so on. What happens when the input is applied to the Y-layer, instead of the X-layer? Since the X-layer is already initialized to all 0s, the net input to the units of the Y-layer would also be 0s. As a result, the activations of the Y-layer will remain unaltered. In the next step the units of the X-layer are updated with the help of the signals from the Y-layer. Hence, effectively, the computation starts with the Y-layer as the input layer.

Procedure *BAM-Pattern-Association*

Step 1. Initialize activations of all units with 0s.

$$x\_out_i = 0, \qquad (i = 1, \ldots, m)$$

$$y\_out_j = 0, \qquad (j = 1, \ldots, n)$$

Step 2. Let $\mathbf{x} : \mathbf{y}$ be the pair of patterns to be applied where $\mathbf{x} = [x_1, x_2, \ldots, x_m]$ and $\mathbf{y} = [y_1, y_2, \ldots, y_n]$. Set the activations of the *X*-layer to $\mathbf{x}$ and the activations of the *Y*-layer to $\mathbf{y}$. If the input is provided for one layer only then the activations of the other layer remain all zeros, as set in Step 1.

Step 3. Update the activations of the *Y*-layer units using the activation signals of the *X*-layer.

The net input to unit Y_j is obtained as

$$y\_in_j = \sum_{i=1}^{m} x_i \times w_{ij} \qquad (j = 1, \ldots, n)$$

Compute the activations of the *Y*-layer units using the following function.

$$y\_out_j = \begin{cases} 1, & \text{if } y\_in_j > 0 \\ y\_out_j, & \text{if } y\_in_j = 0 \\ -1, & \text{if } y\_in_j < 0 \end{cases}$$

Step 4. Update the activations of the *X*-layer units using the activation signals of the *Y*-layer.

The net input to unit X_i is obtained as

$$x\_in_i = \sum_{j=1}^{n} y_j \times w_{ij} \qquad (i = 1, \ldots, m)$$

Compute the activations of the *X*-layer units using the following function.

$$x\_out_i = \begin{cases} 1, & \text{if } x\_in_i > 0 \\ x\_out_i, & \text{if } x\_in_i = 0 \\ -1, & \text{if } x\_in_i < 0 \end{cases}$$

Step 5. Test for convergence. Has the net arrived at an equilibrium, i.e., was there any change in the activations of the *X*-layer units or *Y*-layer units while executing the Steps 3 and 4? If yes, then the net is yet to stabilize. Go to Step 3. Otherwise stop.

Fig. 8.6. *Procedure BAM-Pattern-Association*

Example 8.11 *(Storage of pattern association in bidirectional associative memory)*

Suppose we want to create a *BAM* to store the association $\boldsymbol{s} : \boldsymbol{t} \equiv [s_1, s_2, s_3, s_4] : [t_1, t_2] \equiv [1, 1, -1, -1]: [1, -1]$. We first calculate the weight matrix of the *BAM* for signals propagating from the *X*-layer to the *Y*-layer.

$$W = s^{\mathrm{T}} \times t = \begin{pmatrix} 1 \\ 1 \\ -1 \\ -1 \end{pmatrix} \times (1 \ -1) = \begin{pmatrix} 1 & -1 \\ 1 & -1 \\ -1 & 1 \\ -1 & 1 \end{pmatrix}$$

The weight matrix for signals propagating in the reverse direction is W^{T} so that

$$W^{\mathrm{T}} = \begin{pmatrix} 1 & 1 & -1 & -1 \\ -1 & -1 & 1 & 1 \end{pmatrix}$$

In order to test the performance of the *BAM*, we apply the pattern [1, 1, −1, −1] to the *X*-layer and see the output from the *Y*-layer in the first phase and then in the second phase apply the pattern [1, −1] to the *Y*-layer and get the output from the *X*-layer. The stepwise calculations are described below.

(a) Case A, Input at the *X*-layer, $\boldsymbol{x} = [1, 1, -1, -1]$, $\boldsymbol{y} = ?$

(i) Initially all activations are set to 0s. Therefore,

$$x\_out_i = 0 \qquad (i = 1, \ldots, 4)$$

$$y\_out_j = 0 \qquad (j = 1, 2)$$

(ii) Apply the pattern $\boldsymbol{x} = [1, 1, -1, -1]$ to the *X*-layer, so that

$$x\_out_1 = 1,\ x\_out_2 = 1, y\_out_3 = -1,\ x\_out_4 = -1.$$

(iii) Compute the net inputs to the *Y*-layer and hence its activations.

$$\boldsymbol{Y\_in} = X\_out \times W = [1\ 1\ -1\ -1] \times \begin{pmatrix} 1 & -1 \\ 1 & -1 \\ -1 & 1 \\ -1 & 1 \end{pmatrix}$$

$$= [4, -4].$$

$$\therefore \boldsymbol{Y\_out} = [y\_out_1,\ y\_out_2] = [1, -1]$$

Now, the signals from the *Y*-layer is to be applied to the *X*-layer to modify (if necessary) its activations.

(iv) Compute the net inputs to the *X*-layer using the signals from *Y*-layer.

$$\boldsymbol{X\_in} = \boldsymbol{Y\_out} \times W^{\mathrm{T}} = [1\ -1] \times \begin{pmatrix} 1 & 1 & -1 & -1 \\ -1 & -1 & 1 & 1 \end{pmatrix}$$

$$= [2, 2, -2, -2]$$

$$\therefore \boldsymbol{X\_out} = [x\_out_1,\ x\_out_2,\ x\_out_3,\ x\_out_{4]} = [1, 1, -1, -1]$$

This shows that the net has reached an equilibrium state. As $\boldsymbol{Y\_out} = [y\_out_1,\ y\_out_2] = [1, -1] = \boldsymbol{t}$, we conclude that the *BAM* can associate the input pattern $\boldsymbol{s} = [1, 1, -1, -1]$ to $\boldsymbol{t} = [1, -1]$.

(b) Case B, Input at the *Y*-layer, $\boldsymbol{y} = [1, -1]$, $\boldsymbol{x} = ?$

(i) Initially all activations are set to 0s. Therefore,

$$x\_out_i = 0, \qquad (i = 1, \ldots, 4)$$

$$y\_out_j = 0, \qquad (j = 1, 2)$$

(ii) Apply the pattern $\boldsymbol{y} = [1, -1]$ to the *Y*-layer, so that

$$y\_out_1 = 1,\ y\_out_2 = -1.$$

(iii) Compute the net inputs to the *Y*-layer and hence its activations.

$$\boldsymbol{Y\_in} = \boldsymbol{X\_out} \times W = [0\ 0\ 0\ 0] \times \begin{pmatrix} 1 & -1 \\ 1 & -1 \\ -1 & 1 \\ -1 & 1 \end{pmatrix}$$

$$= [0, 0].$$

As the net input to the units of the *Y*-layer is 0, their activations remain unaltered.

$$\therefore \boldsymbol{Y\_out} = [y\_out_1,\ y\_out_2] = [1, -1]$$

Now, the signals from the *Y*-layer are to be applied to the *X*-layer to modify (if necessary) its activations.

(iv) Compute the net inputs to the *X*-layer using the signals from *Y*-layer.

$$\boldsymbol{X\_in} = \boldsymbol{Y\_out} \times W^{T} = [1\ -1] \times \begin{pmatrix} 1 & 1 & -1 & -1 \\ -1 & -1 & 1 & 1 \end{pmatrix}$$

$$= [2, 2, -2, -2]$$

$$\therefore \boldsymbol{X\_out} = [x\_out_1,\ x\_out_2,\ x\_out_3,\ x\_out_4] = [1, 1, -1, -1]$$

(v) Update the activations of the *Y*-layer with this new set of *X*-layer activations.

$$\boldsymbol{Y\_in} = \boldsymbol{X\_out} \times W = [1, 1, -1, -1] \times W = [4, -4]$$

$$\therefore \boldsymbol{Y\_out} = [y\_out_1,\ y\_out_2] = [1, -1]$$

(vi) Update the activations of the *X*-layer with *Y*-layer activations. The computations are the same as carried out in step (iv) above. As both the *X*-layer and the *Y*-layer retain their activations, the *BAM* has reached the stable state and the iterations stop here. At equilibrium state, the *X*-layer and the *Y*-layer attain the stored patterns.

Hence, the BAM can remember the stored association $\boldsymbol{s} : \boldsymbol{t} \equiv [s_1, s_2, s_3, s_4] : [t_1, t_2] \equiv [1, 1, -1, -1] : [1, -1]$ irrespective of whether it is presented with the pattern $\boldsymbol{s}$ (at the *X*-layer) or $\boldsymbol{t}$ (at the *Y*-layer).

Example 8.12 (*Performance of the BAM under noisy patterns*)

Let us now see if the *BAM* cited in the previous example is able to work under noisy inputs. Two kinds of noises are considered, *viz.*, (a) inputs with missing elements and (b) inputs with corrupt, or erroneous, elements.

(*a*) *Inputs with missing elements*

We apply the noisy input $\boldsymbol{x} = [1, 1, 0, -1]$ and see how the net behaves.

The response of the *Y*-layer to the *X*-input is obtained as

$$\boldsymbol{Y\_in} = \boldsymbol{X\_out} \times W = [1\ 1\ 0\ {-1}] \times W = [3, -3]$$

$$\therefore Y\_out = [y\_out_1,\ y\_out_2] = [1, -1]$$

The activations of the *Y*-layer are propagated to the *X*-layer.

$$\boldsymbol{X\_in} = \boldsymbol{Y\_out} \times W^{T} = [1, -1] \times \begin{pmatrix} 1 & 1 & -1 & -1 \\ -1 & -1 & 1 & 1 \end{pmatrix}$$

$$= [2, 2, -2, -2]$$

$$\therefore \boldsymbol{X\_out} = [x\_out_1,\ x\_out_2,\ x\_out_3,\ x\_out_4] = [1, 1, -1, -1]$$

So the *BAM* has already corrected the noisy input and the two layers of the net now contains the association $\boldsymbol{s} : \boldsymbol{t} \equiv [1, 1, -1, -1] : [1, -1]$. We saw in the previous examples that this state is stable and no further iterations are needed.

The *BAM* is able to tolerate a missing element in the *t* vector too. To verify this we take $\boldsymbol{y} = [1, 0]$ as the input to the net fed through the *Y*-layer. The activation induced by this *Y*-layer input to the *X*-layer is computed as

$$\boldsymbol{X\_in} = \boldsymbol{Y\_out} \times W^{T} = [1\ 0] \times \begin{pmatrix} 1 & 1 & -1 & -1 \\ -1 & -1 & 1 & 1 \end{pmatrix}$$

$$= [1, 1, -1, -1]$$

$$\therefore \boldsymbol{X\_out} = [x\_out_1,\ x\_out_2,\ x\_out_3,\ x\_out_4] = [1, 1, -1, -1]$$

In the next step, when this $\boldsymbol{X\_out} = [1, 1, -1, -1]$ is propagated to the *Y*-layer units, the signals at the *Y*-layer are corrected to $[1, -1]$. Verification of the behaviour of the *BAM* under other possible missing elements is being left as an exercise.

(*b*) *Inputs with corrupt, or erroneous, elements.*

Let $\boldsymbol{x} = [1, 1, 1, -1]$ be the input vector where the third element is erroneously set to 1, instead of -1, as stored in $\boldsymbol{s} = [1, 1, -1, -1]$. When the *BAM* is set to work, it first produces the activations of the *Y*-layer units.

$$\boldsymbol{Y\_in} = \boldsymbol{X\_out} \times W = [1\ 1\ 1\ {-1}] \times \begin{pmatrix} 1 & -1 \\ 1 & -1 \\ -1 & 1 \\ -1 & 1 \end{pmatrix}$$

$$= [2, -2]$$

$$\therefore \boldsymbol{Y\_out} = [y\_out_1, y\_out_2] = [1, -1]$$

When these Y-layer activations are sent to the X-layer, it attains the pattern $\boldsymbol{X\_out} = [1, 1, -1, -1]$, which implies that the net has corrected the noisy pattern $\boldsymbol{x} = [1, 1, 1, -1]$ to the stored pattern $\boldsymbol{s} = [1, 1, -1, -1]$. Hence, the *BAM* under consideration can tolerate single element error in its input.

Example 8.13 *(Storage of multiple associations on a BAM)*

Multiple associations can be stored on a *BAM*. As usual, the weight matrix of the resultant *BAM* is obtained by adding up the individual weight matrices corresponding to each association. For example, suppose, along with the association $\boldsymbol{s}(1) : \boldsymbol{t}(1) \equiv [1, 1, -1, -1] : [1, -1]$, we want to store the additional association $\boldsymbol{s}(2) : \boldsymbol{t}(2) = [1, -1, 1, -1] : [1, 1]$. Obviously, the two individual weight matrices W_1, W_2 are

$$W_1 = \begin{pmatrix} 1 & -1 \\ 1 & -1 \\ -1 & 1 \\ -1 & 1 \end{pmatrix}, \text{ and } W_2 = \begin{pmatrix} 1 & 1 \\ -1 & -1 \\ 1 & 1 \\ -1 & -1 \end{pmatrix}$$

Hence, the overall weight matrix is

$$W = W_1 + W_2 = \begin{pmatrix} 2 & 0 \\ 0 & -2 \\ 0 & 2 \\ -2 & 0 \end{pmatrix}$$

The following calculations show that the net is able to recall the appropriate association when presented with any of the stored vectors.

(*a*) $\boldsymbol{x} = [1, 1, -1, -1]$, $\boldsymbol{y} = ?$

$$\boldsymbol{Y\_in} = \boldsymbol{X\_out} \times W = [1\ 1\ -1\ -1] \times \begin{pmatrix} 2 & 0 \\ 0 & -2 \\ 0 & 2 \\ -2 & 0 \end{pmatrix}$$

$$= [4, -4]$$

$$\therefore \boldsymbol{Y\_out} = [y\_out_1, y\_out_2] = [1, -1]$$

So the *BAM* remembers the pattern $\boldsymbol{t}(1) = [1, -1]$ associated with the pattern $\boldsymbol{s}(1) = [1, 1, -1, -1]$. Verification of the reverse association, i.e., $\boldsymbol{s}(1)$ given $\boldsymbol{t}(1)$, is left as an exercise.

(*b*) $\boldsymbol{y} = [1, 1]$, $\boldsymbol{x} = ?$

Here, $$\boldsymbol{X\_in} = \boldsymbol{Y\_out} \times W^T = [1\ 1] \times \begin{pmatrix} 2 & 0 & 0 & -2 \\ 0 & -2 & 2 & 0 \end{pmatrix}$$

$$= [2, -2, 2, -2]$$

$$\therefore \boldsymbol{X\_out} = [x\_out_1, x\_out_2, x\_out_3, x\_out_4] = [1, -1, 1, -1]$$

Obviously, the *BAM* remembers the pattern **s** (2) = [1, −1, 1, −1] associated with the pattern **t** (1) = [1, 1]. Verification of the reverse association, i.e., **t** (2) given **s** (2), is left as an exercise.

Performance of BAM storing multiple associations under noisy inputs is illustrated in Problem 8.7 in the section 'Solved Problems'.

CHAPTER SUMMARY

Relating a given pattern to one already stored in memory is known as pattern association. We, the human beings, associate patterns in our daily life almost effortlessly. Artificial neural nets are suitable for pattern association. Some important associative neural nets are auto-associtive nets, hetero-associative nets, Hopfield nets, and Bidirectional Associative Memory (BAM). The main points of this chapter are as follows.

- The input and output patterns of an auto-associative net are the same. Presented with an input pattern, perhaps noisy, an auto-associative net returns the same pattern (this time without any noise) if the input matches one of the stored patterns.
- The diagonal elements of an auto-associative net are set to 0s to ensure that these elements do not dominate during application of the net. Otherwise, the net has a tendency to reproduce the input pattern rather than the stored pattern.
- Strength of a neural net lies in its tolerance of noisy input pattern, provided, that the input is sufficiently close to the stored pattern in spite of it being noisy. Two kinds of noises, missing elements, or erroneous element, may appear in the input pattern. While a missing element is represented by 0, instead of a 1 or −1, an erroneous element presents the complement of the correct value, i.e., 1 (−1) in place of −1 (1).
- An auto-associative neural net may store several patterns. The *capacity* of such a net is defined as the number of patterns it can store and recall. If we try to store more patterns than its capacity, then the net tends to *forget* the stored patterns.
- The weight matrix of the net storing several patterns is the sum of the individual weight matrices. Let $s_1, s_2, \ldots, s_k$ be k mutually orthogonal vectors and $W_1, W_2, \ldots, W_k$ be the weight matrices for the auto-associative nets recognizing the vectors $s_1, s_2, \ldots, s_k$, respectively. The diagonal elements of all the weight matrices are all set to zeros. Then the weight matrix W of the auto-associative net recognizing the given patterns is obtained by adding the individual weight matrices $W_1, W_2, \ldots, W_k$.
- An n-input auto-associative net can store at most $n-1$ number of mutually orthogonal vectors, each of which consists of n components.
- A hetero-associative net is used to store the associations between pairs of patterns that are not identical. This means, if **s** : **t** is a pair of associated patterns and this association is stored in a hetero-associative net, then **s** ≠ **t**.
- A Hopfield net is a fully interconnected net with symmetric weights and without any self-loop. Hebb rule is used to obtain the weight matrix of a Hopfield net.
- A hetero-associative neural net with two layers interconnected by bidirectional paths and storing a number of pairs of patterns is called as a *Bidirectional Associative Memory* (*BAM*). It can recall the association **s** : **t** when presented with any of the two associated patterns **s** or **t** as the input.

SOLVED PROBLEMS

Problem 8.1 (*Auto-associative nets: Recognition of noisy input with two missing elements*) Consider the auto-associative net of Example 8.3 and 8.4 whose weight matrix is given by

$$W = \begin{bmatrix} 0 & -1 & -1 & 1 \\ -1 & 0 & 1 & -1 \\ -1 & 1 & 0 & -1 \\ 1 & -1 & -1 & 0 \end{bmatrix}$$

The net is able to recognize the pattern $[1, -1, -1, 1]$. Moreover, we have seen that the net has the capacity to recognize correctly noisy patterns with a single missing element. Can the net withstand two missing entries?

Solution 8.1 Let us consider the case of first two elements of the pattern $[1, -1, -1, 1]$ missing, so that the input pattern is $[0, 0, -1, 1]$. The net input to the output units are computed as

$$\boldsymbol{Y\_in} = [y\_in_1, y\_in_2, y\_in_3, y\_in_4]$$

$$= [0\ 0\ -1\ 1] \times \begin{pmatrix} 0 & -1 & -1 & 1 \\ -1 & 0 & 1 & -1 \\ -1 & 1 & 0 & -1 \\ 1 & -1 & -1 & 0 \end{pmatrix}$$

$$= [2, -2, -1, 1]$$

And the output vector is obtained as

$$\boldsymbol{Y\_out} = [y\_out_1, y\_out_2, y\_out_3, y\_out_4]$$

$$= [1, -1, -1, 1]$$

Hence, the net is able to recognize the stored pattern even if the first two elements are missing. Calculations shown in Table 8.3 present the performance of the net with various combinations of a pair of missing elements.

Table 8.3. *Recognition of noisy input with two missing elements*

#	Input pattern (noisy)	Net input to the output layer ($\boldsymbol{Y\_in} = \mathbf{s} \times W$)	Output pattern
i	[0, 0, −1, 1]	[2, −2, −1, 1]	[1, −1, −1, 1]
ii	[0, −1, 0, 1]	[2, −1, −2, 1]	[1, −1, −1, 1]
iii	[0, −1, −1, 0]	[2, −1, −1, 2]	[1, −1, −1, 1]
iv	[1, 0, 0, 1]	[1, −2, −2, 1]	[1, −1, −1, 1]
v	[1, 0, −1, 0]	[1, −2, −1, 2]	[1, −1, −1, 1]
vi	[1, −1, 0, 0]	[1, −1, −2, 2]	[1, −1, −1, 1]

It shows that the net can correctly recognize all noisy input patterns with two missing elements.

Table 8.4. *Recognition of noisy input with one erroneous element*

#	Input pattern (noisy)	Net input to the output layer (Y_in = s × W)	Output pattern
i	[−1, −1, −1, 1]	[3, −1, −1, 1]	[1, −1, −1, 1]
ii	[1, 1, −1, 1]	[1, −3, −1, 1]	[1, −1, −1, 1]
iii	[1, −1, 1, 1]	[1, −1, −3, 1]	[1, −1, −1, 1]
iv	[1, −1, −1, −1]	[1, −1, −1, 3]	[1, −1, −1, 1]

Problem 8.2 (*Recognition of noisy inputs with one erroneous entry*) Problem 8.1 illustrates that the net can withstand up to two missing elements in the input pattern. See the behaviour of the net with one and two errors.

Solution 8.2 There are four possible one-element errors in the pattern [1, −1, −1, 1]. These are [−1, −1, −1, 1], [1, 1, −1, 1], [1, −1, 1, 1], and [1, −1, −1, −1] corresponding to errors in the first, second, third, and the fourth element of the input vector. The behaviour of the net with respect to these inputs is shown in Table 8.4. We see that the net can tolerate one error in the input pattern. Can it withstand two erroneous elements? To verify we consider the noisy pattern where the first two elements are erroneous, i.e., the input pattern is [−1, 1, −1, 1] instead of [1, −1, −1, 1]. Application of this pattern to the given net results in

$$[-1, 1, -1, 1] \times W = [1, -1, 1, -1] \neq [1, -1, -1, 1]$$

Hence, the net cannot recognize input patterns with two erroneous entries.

Problem 8.3 (*Storage of non-orthogonal patterns in auto-associative net*) Consider two non-orthogonal patterns $\mathbf{s}_1 = [1, -1, 1, -1]$ and $\mathbf{s}_2 = [-1, 1, 1, 1]$. These are not orthogonal because their inner product $\mathbf{s}_1 \cdot \mathbf{s}_2 = -2 \neq 0$. Can you design an auto-associative net to store these patterns?

Solution 8.3 Assuming that there exists such an auto-associative net, we calculate the weight matrix of as follows.

$$W = W_1 + W_2 = \begin{bmatrix} 0 & -1 & 1 & -1 \\ -1 & 0 & -1 & 1 \\ 1 & -1 & 0 & -1 \\ -1 & 1 & -1 & 0 \end{bmatrix} + \begin{bmatrix} 0 & -1 & -1 & -1 \\ -1 & 0 & 1 & 1 \\ -1 & 1 & 0 & 1 \\ -1 & 1 & 1 & 0 \end{bmatrix} = \begin{bmatrix} 0 & -2 & 0 & -2 \\ -2 & 0 & 0 & 2 \\ 0 & 0 & 0 & 0 \\ -2 & 2 & 0 & 0 \end{bmatrix}$$

Now, let us see if the resultant net can recognize the stored patterns.

$$\mathbf{s}_1 \times W = [1, -1, 1, -1] \times W = [4, -4, 0, -4] \rightarrow [1, -1, -1, -1] \neq s_1$$

and,

$$\mathbf{s}_2 \times W = [-1, 1, 1, 1] \times W = [-4, 4, 0, 4] \rightarrow [-1, 1, -1, 1] \neq s_2$$

Hence, the net fails to recognize the stored patterns.

Problem 8.4 (*Storage of n orthogonal patterns in n-node auto-associative net*) Obtain a net to store four mutually orthogonal patterns $\mathbf{s}_1 = [1, 1, 1, 1]$, $\mathbf{s}_2 = [-1, 1, -1, 1]$, and $\mathbf{s}_3 = [-1, -1, 1, 1]$, $\mathbf{s}_4 = [1, -1, -1, 1]$.

Solution 8.4 The first three patterns are already tested to be orthogonal in Example 8.5 and the weight matrix for them has been computed as

$$\begin{bmatrix} 0 & 1 & 1 & -1 \\ 1 & 0 & -1 & 1 \\ 1 & -1 & 0 & 1 \\ -1 & 1 & 1 & 0 \end{bmatrix}$$

It can be readily verified that s_4 is orthogonal to the rest three patterns. To store the four patterns s_1, s_2, s_3 and s_4 on a four-input auto-associative net, the corresponding weight matrix would be

$$W = (W_1 + W_1 + W_1) + W_4 = \begin{bmatrix} 0 & 1 & 1 & -1 \\ 1 & 0 & -1 & 1 \\ 1 & -1 & 0 & 1 \\ -1 & 1 & 1 & 0 \end{bmatrix} + \begin{bmatrix} 0 & -1 & -1 & 1 \\ -1 & 0 & 1 & -1 \\ -1 & 1 & 0 & -1 \\ 1 & -1 & -1 & 0 \end{bmatrix} = \begin{bmatrix} 0 & 0 & 0 & 0 \\ 0 & 0 & 0 & 0 \\ 0 & 0 & 0 & 0 \\ 0 & 0 & 0 & 0 \end{bmatrix}$$

Obviously, the net is unable to recognize any of the four patterns.

Problem 8.5 (*Storage of multiple associations on a hetero-associative net*) Find a hetero-associative net to store three associations between pairs of patterns given below.

(vii) $[1, -1, 1, -1] : [-1, 1, -1]$
(viii) $[1, 1, 1, -1] : [1, 1, -1]$
(ix) $[1, -1, 1, 1] : [-1, 1, 1]$

Solution 8.5 The corresponding weight matrices W_1, W_2, W_3 are

$$W_1 = \begin{bmatrix} -1 & 1 & -1 \\ 1 & -1 & 1 \\ -1 & 1 & -1 \\ 1 & -1 & 1 \end{bmatrix},\ W_2 = \begin{bmatrix} 1 & 1 & -1 \\ 1 & 1 & -1 \\ 1 & 1 & -1 \\ -1 & -1 & 1 \end{bmatrix},\ \text{and } W_3 = \begin{bmatrix} -1 & 1 & 1 \\ 1 & -1 & -1 \\ -1 & 1 & 1 \\ -1 & 1 & 1 \end{bmatrix}.$$

Therefore, the weight matrix of the desired net for storing the three associations is computed as

$$W = W_1 + W_2 + W_3 = \begin{bmatrix} -1 & 3 & -1 \\ 3 & -1 & -1 \\ -1 & 3 & -1 \\ -1 & -1 & 3 \end{bmatrix}$$

The following calculations show that the resultant net correctly associates the input vector $[1, -1, 1, -1]$ to the corresponding output vector $[-1, 1, -1]$.

Input pattern : $\boldsymbol{x} = [1, -1, 1, -1]$
Net input to the output layer : $\boldsymbol{Y\_in} = \boldsymbol{x} \times W = [1, -1, 1, -1] \times W = [-4, 8, -4]$
Activation at the output layer : $\boldsymbol{Y\_out} = [-1, 1, -1]$

Verification of the performance of the net for the rest of the patterns is left as an exercise.

Problem 8.6 (*Performance of a Hopfield net under noisy input*) Consider the Hopfield net developed in Example 8.10. We would like to verify if it is able to recognize a known but noisy input pattern. See if the net can recognize the input vector $\boldsymbol{x} = [1, 1, 0, 1]$ which differs from the stored vector $\boldsymbol{s} = [1, 0, 0, 1]$ in the second component x_2.

Solution 8.6 The verification process consists of application of the given input pattern to the net and computation of the output when it reaches the stable state. The computations are shown below.

1. The input vector is $\boldsymbol{x} = [x_1, x_2, x_3, x_4] = [1, 1, 0, 1]$.
2. Initialize the activations of the units as

$$\boldsymbol{Y} = [y\_out_1, y\_out_2, y\_out_3, y\_out_4] = [1, 1, 0, 1].$$

3. In the first epoch, the units are updated in the random order Y_4, Y_1, Y_3, Y_2.

3.1 Update the activation y_out_4 of Y_4.

$$y\_in_4 = x_4 + \sum_{i=1}^{4} y\_out_i \times w_{i4}$$
$$= 1 + (1 \times 1 + 1 \times (-1) + 0 \times (-1) + 1 \times 0)$$
$$= 1.$$
$$\therefore y\_out_4 = 1.$$

3.2 Update the activation y_out_1 of Y_1.

$$y\_in_1 = x_1 + \sum_{i=1}^{4} y\_out_i \times w_{i1}$$
$$= 1 + (1 \times 0 + 1 \times (-1) + 0 \times (-1) + 1 \times 1)$$
$$= 1.$$
$$\therefore y\_out_1 = 1.$$

3.3 Update the activation y_out_3 of Y_3.

$$y\_in_3 = x_3 + \sum_{i=1}^{4} y\_out_i \times w_{i3}$$
$$= 0 + (1 \times (-1) + 1 \times 1 + 0 \times 0 + 1 \times (-1))$$
$$= -1.$$
$$\therefore y\_out_3 = 0.$$

3.4 Update the activation y_out_2 of Y_2.

$$y\_in_2 = x_2 + \sum_{i=1}^{4} y\_out_i \times w_{i2}$$
$$= 1 + (1 \times (-1) + 1 \times 0 + 0 \times 1 + 1 \times (-1))$$
$$= -1.$$
$$\therefore y\_out_2 = 0.$$

Therefore, at the end of the first epoch the activation vector of the net changes from [1, 1, 0, 1] to [1, 0, 0, 1]. As some change in the activation of one of the units, Y_2, has taken place in the first epoch, the process continues to the second epoch. The computations of the second epoch are left as an exercise.

Problem 8.7 (*Performance of the BAM storing multiple associations under noisy input*) In Example 8.13, a BAM is designed to store the associations $\mathbf{s}(1) : \mathbf{t}(1) \equiv [1, 1, -1, -1] : [1, -1]$, and $\mathbf{s}(2) : \mathbf{t}(2) = [1, -1, 1, -1] : [1, 1]$. The weight matrix of the BAM is calculated as

$$\begin{pmatrix} 2 & 0 \\ 0 & -2 \\ 0 & 2 \\ -2 & 0 \end{pmatrix}$$

Suppose the *BAM* is now presented with an input pattern $x = [1, 0, 0, -1]$ (a noisy version of the pattern $s(1) = [1, 1, -1, -1]$ or, $s(2) = [1, -1, 1, -1]$ where the second and the third elements are missing) at the X-layer. Can it tolerate the lack of information and recall the associated pattern correctly?

Solution 8.7 The effects of the input pattern through successive iterations till the net reach the stable state are shown below.

1. Propagate the signals of the X-layer to the Y-layer.

$$\boldsymbol{Y\_in} = \boldsymbol{X\_out} \times W = [1\ 0\ 0\ {-1}] \times \begin{pmatrix} 2 & 0 \\ 0 & -2 \\ 0 & 2 \\ -2 & 0 \end{pmatrix}$$

$$= [4, 0]$$

$$\therefore \boldsymbol{Y\_out} = [y\_out_1, y\_out_2] = [1, 0]$$

2. Apply the signals of the Y-layer to the X-layer.

$$\boldsymbol{X\_in} = \boldsymbol{Y\_out} \times W^T = [1\ 0] \times \begin{pmatrix} 2 & 0 & 0 & -2 \\ 0 & -2 & 2 & 0 \end{pmatrix}$$

$$= [2, 0, 0, -2]$$

$$\therefore \boldsymbol{X\_out} = [x\_out_1, x\_out_2, x\_out_3, x\_out_4] = [1, 0, 0, -1]$$

Since the $\boldsymbol{X\_out}$ is back to the same pattern as it had in the previous iteration, the *BAM* has already reached a stable state and the activations of neither the X-layer nor the Y-layer match the stored patterns. Hence, the *BAM* cannot overcome this noise input.

However, the situation may improve if, along with the noisy pattern, the *BAM* is fed with some clue regarding the corresponding association. In particular, let us simultaneously present the patterns $x = [1, 0, 0, -1]$ and $y = [0, -1]$ at the X-layer and the Y-layer, respectively, and see how the net responds.

$$\boldsymbol{Y\_in} = \boldsymbol{X\_out} \times W = [1\ 0\ 0\ {-1}] \times \begin{pmatrix} 2 & 0 \\ 0 & -2 \\ 0 & 2 \\ -2 & 0 \end{pmatrix}$$

$$= [4, 0]$$

$$\therefore \boldsymbol{Y\_out} = [y\_out_1, \ y\_out_2] = [1, -1]$$

As the net input $y\_in_2 = 0$, the corresponding activation y_out_2 retains its previous value, i.e., −1. When these Y-layer activations are fed to the X-layer we get

$$\boldsymbol{X\_in} = \boldsymbol{Y\_out} \times W^{T} = (1 \ -1) \times \begin{pmatrix} 2 & 0 & 0 & -2 \\ 0 & -2 & 2 & 0 \end{pmatrix}$$

$$= [2, 2, -2, -2]$$

$$\therefore \boldsymbol{X\_out} = [x\_out_1, \ x\_out_2, \ x\_out_3, \ x\_out_4] = [1, 1, -1, -1]$$

Hence, this time, aided with appropriate clues, the *BAM* is able to remember the stored association.

Problem 8.8 (*Auto-associative net with MatLab*) Write a MatLab program to implement an auto-associative net to store the patterns [−1 −1 −1 −1] and [−1 −1 1 1]. Test the performance of the net with the test patterns [−1 −1 −1 −1] (stored pattern), [1 1 1 1] (unknown pattern), and [−1 −1 −1 1] (unknown but similar).

Solution 8.8 The MatLab code is given below. The code is followed by the outputs of the test.

```
clc;
clear;
StrVctr = [-1 -1 -1 -1;-1 -1 1 1];       % Patterns to be stored
TstVctr_Trnd = [-1 -1 -1 -1];             % CASE 1: Known Pattern
TstVctr_New = [1 1 1 1];                  % CASE 2: Unknown Pattern
TstVctr_Similar = [-1 -1 -1 1];           % CASE 3: Unknown yet similar
wt=zeros(4,4);                            % Initialize Weights

for i = 1:2                               % Calculate weight matrix
  wt = wt + StrVctr(i,1:4)'*StrVctr(i,1:4);
end
disp('The calculated weight matrix');
disp(wt);

TstOutpt = TstVctr_Trnd*wt;               % CASE 1: Testing with pattern
for i=1:4                                 % on which the net has been trained
  if TstOutpt(i)>0
     fx(i)=1;
  else
     fx(i)=-1;
  end
end
disp('***************CASE 1************');
if StrVctr(1,1:4) == fx(1:4) | StrVctr(2,1:4) == fx(1:4)
  disp('The Pattern is a Known Pattern');
else
  disp('The Pattern is an Unknown Pattern');
end
```

```
TstOutpt = TstVctr_New*wt;             % CASE 2: Testing with pattern
for i=1:4                              % on which the net has not been trained
  if TstOutpt(i)>0                     % and the pattern is not similar to
                                         those
     fx(i)=1;                          % for which the net has been trained
  else
     fx(i)=-1;
  end
end
disp('***************CASE 2***********');
if StrVctr(1,1:4) == fx(1:4) | StrVctr(2,1:4) == fx(1:4)
  disp('The Pattern is a Known Pattern');
else
  disp('The Pattern is an Unknown Pattern');
end

TstOutpt = TstVctr_Similar*wt;     % CASE 3: Testing with pattern
for i=1:4                          % on which the net has not been trained
  if TstOutpt(i)>0                 % but the pattern is similar to those
     fx(i)=1;                      % for which the net has been trained
  else
     fx(i)=-1;
  end
end
disp('***************CASE 3***********');
if StrVctr(1,1:4) == fx(1:4) | StrVctr(2,1:4) == fx(1:4)
  disp('The Pattern is a Known Pattern');
else
  disp('The Pattern is a Unknown Pattern');
end

***********OUTPUT********************
The calculated weight matrix
   2  2  0  0
   2  2  0  0
   0  0  2  2
   0  0  2  2

***************CASE 1***********
The Pattern is a Known Pattern
***************CASE 2***********
The Pattern is an Unknown Pattern
***************CASE 3***********
The Pattern is a Known Pattern
```

Problem 8.9 (*Hetero-associative net with MatLab*) Write a MatLab program to implement a hetero-associative net to map four patterns [1 1 0 0], [0 1 0 0], [0 0 1 1], and [0 0 1 0] to two output patterns [1 0], [0 1] so that the patterns [1 1 0 0] and [0 1 0 0] are associated with [1 0] and the patterns [0 0 1 1], and [0 0 1 0] are associated with [0 1].

Solution 8.9 The MatLab code is given below. The designed net is tested with the pattern [1 1 0 0] which results in an output [1 0].

```
%Hetero associative neural net for mapping input vectors to output
vectors
clc;
clear;
Inp = [1 1 0 0;0 1 0 0;0 0 1 1;0 0 1 0];      % Input patterns
Trgt = [1 0;1 0;0 1;0 1];                      % Target outputs
wt = zeros(4,2);                               % Initialize all weights to 0
for i = 1:4                                    % Training the weights
  wt = wt + Inp(i,1:4)' * Trgt(i,1:2);       %
end                                          %
disp('Displaying Weight Matrix');
disp(wt);
Test_Inp = [1 1 0 0];
Test_Outpt = Test_Inp*wt;                    % Testing response for Input
for i = 1:2                                  % Mapping through Activation Fn.
  if Test_Outpt(1,i) > 0
     fx(1,i) = 1;
  else fx(1,i) = 0;
  end
end
disp('Displaying Output mapped through Activation Function');
disp(fx);
**************OUTPUT*************************
Displaying Weight Matrix
   1  0
   2  0
   0  2
   0  1
Displaying Output mapped through Activation Function
   1  0
```

Problem 8.10 (*Hetero-associative net with MatLab*) Write a MatLab program to store the pattern shown as Stored Pattern in the following 11 × 7 matrix with the help of an auto-associative net. The resultant net is to be tested with the Test Pattern #1 and Test Pattern #2. It may be noted that while neither Test Pattern #1 nor Test Pattern #2 exactly matches with the Stored Pattern, the former closely resembles the Stored Pattern though the latter one, Test Pattern #2, is clearly a mismatch.

Stored Pattern

0	**1**	0	0	0	0	0
0	**1**	0	0	0	0	0
0	**1**	0	0	0	0	0
0	**1**	0	0	0	0	0
0	**1**	0	0	0	0	0
0	**1**	0	0	0	0	0
0	**1**	0	**1**	**1**	**1**	0
0	**1**	**1**	0	0	0	**1**
0	**1**	0	0	0	0	**1**
0	**1**	0	0	0	**1**	0
0	**1**	**1**	**1**	**1**	0	0

Test Pattern #1

0	**1**	0	0	0	0	0
0	**1**	0	0	0	0	0
0	**1**	0	0	0	0	0
0	**1**	0	0	0	0	0
0	**1**	0	0	0	0	0
0	**1**	0	0	0	0	0
0	**1**	0	**1**	**1**	**1**	0
0	**1**	0	0	0	0	**1**
0	**1**	0	0	0	0	**1**
1	**1**	0	0	0	**1**	0
0	**1**	**1**	**1**	**1**	0	0

Test Pattern #2

0	0	0	0	0	0	0
0	0	0	0	0	0	0
0	0	0	0	0	0	0
0	0	0	0	0	0	0
1	0	0	0	0	0	**1**
0	**1**	0	0	0	**1**	0
0	0	**1**	0	**1**	0	0
0	0	0	**1**	0	0	0
0	0	**1**	0	**1**	0	0
0	**1**	0	0	0	**1**	0
1	0	0	0	0	0	**1**

Solution 8.10 The entire MatLab code is given below. It is seen that while the designed net accepts Test Pattern #1 and returns the original stored pattern correctly, it rejects Test Pattern #2 as an unknown pattern.

```
clc;
clear;
% Original pattern 11x7 matrix
Stored_Ptrn = [  -1     1    -1    -1    -1    -1    -1
                 -1     1    -1    -1    -1    -1    -1
                 -1     1    -1    -1    -1    -1    -1
                 -1     1    -1    -1    -1    -1    -1
                 -1     1    -1    -1    -1    -1    -1
                  1    -1    -1    -1    -1    -1    -1
                 -1     1    -1     1     1     1    -1
                 -1     1     1    -1    -1    -1     1
                 -1     1    -1    -1    -1    -1     1
                 -1     1    -1    -1    -1     1    -1
                 -1     1     1     1     1    -1    -1   ];

% Test pattern 11x7 matrix
Test_Ptrn_1 = [  -1     1    -1    -1    -1    -1    -1
                 -1     1    -1    -1    -1    -1    -1
                 -1     1    -1    -1    -1    -1    -1
                 -1     1    -1    -1    -1    -1    -1
                 -1     1    -1    -1    -1    -1    -1
                 -1     1    -1    -1    -1    -1    -1
                 -1     1    -1     1     1     1    -1
                 -1     1    -1    -1    -1    -1     1
                 -1     1    -1    -1    -1    -1     1
                  1     1    -1    -1    -1     1    -1
                 -1     1     1     1     1    -1    -1   ];
```

```
Test_Ptrn_2 = [  -1    -1    -1    -1    -1    -1    -1
                 -1    -1    -1    -1    -1    -1    -1
                 -1    -1    -1    -1    -1    -1    -1
                 -1    -1    -1    -1    -1    -1    -1
                  1    -1    -1    -1    -1    -1     1
                 -1     1    -1    -1    -1     1    -1
                 -1    -1     1    -1     1    -1    -1
                 -1    -1    -1     1    -1    -1    -1
                 -1    -1     1    -1     1    -1    -1
                 -1     1    -1    -1    -1     1    -1
                  1    -1    -1    -1    -1    -1     1   ];
wt=zeros(77,77);                          % Initializing weights
wt = wt + Stored_Ptrn'*Stored_Ptrn;
disp('TESTING WITH STORED PATTERN');
TstOutpt = Stored_Ptrn*wt;                % Test association of stored
                                            pattern
for i-1:77
  if TstOutpt(i)>5
     fx(i)=1;
  else
     fx(i)=-1;
  end
end
if Stored_Ptrn(1:77) == fx(1:77)
  disp('The Pattern is associated with the following pattern');
  disp('0   1   0   0   0   0   0');
  disp('0   1   0   0   0   0   0');
  disp('0   1   0   0   0   0   0');
  disp('0   1   0   0   0   0   0');
  disp('0   1   0   0   0   0   0');
  disp('0   1   0   0   0   0   0');
  disp('0   1   0   1   1   1   0');
  disp('0   1   1   0   0   0   1');
  disp('0   1   0   0   0   0   1');
  disp('0   1   0   0   0   1   0');
  disp('0   1   1   1   1   0   0');
else
  disp('The Pattern is an Unknown Pattern');
end
disp('TESTING WITH TEST PATTERNS 1 AND 2');
disp('TEST PATTERN 1');
TstOutpt = Test_Ptrn_1*wt;      % Test association of Test Pattern
for i=1:77
  if TstOutpt(i)>5
     fx(i)=1;
  else
     fx(i)=-1;
  end
end
```

```
if Stored_Ptrn(1:77) == fx(1:77)
  disp('The Test Pattern is associated with the following pattern');
  disp('0   1     0     0     0     0     0');
  disp('0   1     0     0     0     0     0');
  disp('0   1     0     0     0     0     0');
  disp('0   1     0     0     0     0     0');
  disp('0   1     0     0     0     0     0');
  disp('0   1     0     0     0     0     0');
  disp('0   1     0     1     1     1     0');
  disp('0   1     1     0     0     0     1');
  disp('0   1     0     0     0     0     1');
  disp('0   1     0     0     0     1     0');
  disp('0   1     1     1     1     0     0');
else
  disp('The Pattern is an Unknown Pattern');
end
disp('TEST PATTERN 2');
TstOutpt = Test_Ptrn_2*wt;      % Test association of Test Pattern
for i=1:77
  if TstOutpt(i)>5
     fx(i)=1;
  else
     fx(i)=-1;
  end
end
if Stored_Ptrn(1:77) == fx(1:77)
  disp('The Test Pattern is associated with the following pattern');
  disp('0   1     0     0     0     0     0');
  disp('0   1     0     0     0     0     0');
  disp('0   1     0     0     0     0     0');
  disp('0   1     0     0     0     0     0');
  disp('0   1     0     0     0     0     0');
  disp('0   1     0     0     0     0     0');
  disp('0   1     0     1     1     1     0');
  disp('0   1     1     0     0     0     1');
  disp('0   1     0     0     0     0     1');
  disp('0   1     0     0     0     1     0');
  disp('0   1     1     1     1     0     0');
else
  disp('The Pattern is an Unknown Pattern');
end

******************OUTPUT****************************

TESTING WITH STORED PATTERN
The Pattern is associated with the following pattern
0     1    0     0    0     0    0
0     1    0     0    0     0    0
0     1    0     0    0     0    0
```

```
0    1    0    0    0    0    0
0    1    0    0    0    0    0
0    1    0    0    0    0    0
0    1    0    1    1    1    0
0    1    1    0    0    0    1
0    1    0    0    0    0    1
0    1    0    0    0    1    0
0    1    1    1    1    0    0

TESTING WITH TEST PATTERNS 1 AND 2
TEST PATTERN 1
The Test Pattern is associated with the following pattern
0    1    0    0    0    0    0
0    1    0    0    0    0    0
0    1    0    0    0    0    0
0    1    0    0    0    0    0
0    1    0    0    0    0    0
0    1    0    0    0    0    0
0    1    0    1    1    1    0
0    1    1    0    0    0    1
0    1    0    0    0    0    1
0    1    0    0    0    1    0
0    1    1    1    1    0    0
TEST PATTERN 2
The Pattern is an Unknown Pattern
```

Problem 8.11 (*Pattern recognition with bidirectional associative memory*) Figs. 8.7 and 8.8 show two faces, one smiling and the other frowning, and the corresponding encoding in 12×7 matrices filled with 0s and 1s. Fig. 8.9 shows a test pattern which neither matches with the smiling face nor the frowning face. Design a BAM, with MatLab program, to store the smiling face and the frowning face. Test the performance of the BAM with the smiling face as input and also with the pattern given in Fig. 8.9.

Smiling Face

```
  * * * * *
*           *
*           *
* * *   * * *
*           *
*     *     *
*     *     *
*     *     *
* *       * *
*   * * *   *
*           *
  * * * * *
```

Smiling Face

```
0 1 1 1 1 1 0
1 0 0 0 0 0 1
1 0 0 0 0 0 1
1 1 1 0 1 1 1
1 0 0 0 0 0 1
1 0 0 1 0 0 1
1 0 0 1 0 0 1
1 0 0 1 0 0 1
1 1 0 0 0 1 1
1 0 1 1 1 0 1
1 0 0 0 0 0 1
0 1 1 1 1 1 0
```

Fig. 8.7. *Smiling face and its binary encoding*

Frowning Face

```
  * * * * *
*           *
*           *
* * *   * * *
*           *
*     *     *
*     *     *
*     *     *
*   * * *   *
* *       * *
*           *
  * * * * *
```

Frowning Face

```
0 1 1 1 1 1 0
1 0 0 0 0 0 1
1 0 0 0 0 0 1
1 1 1 0 1 1 1
1 0 0 0 0 0 1
1 0 0 1 0 0 1
1 0 0 1 0 0 1
1 0 0 1 0 0 1
1 0 1 1 1 0 1
1 1 0 0 0 1 1
1 0 0 0 0 0 1
0 1 1 1 1 1 0
```

Fig. 8.8. *Frowning face and its binary encoding*

Circle

```
  * * * * *
*           *
*           *
*           *
*           *
*           *
*           *
*           *
*           *
*           *
*           *
  * * * * *
```

Circle

```
0 1 1 1 1 1 0
1 0 0 0 0 0 1
1 0 0 0 0 0 1
1 0 0 0 0 0 1
1 0 0 0 0 0 1
1 0 0 0 0 0 1
1 0 0 0 0 0 1
1 0 0 0 0 0 1
1 0 0 0 0 0 1
1 0 0 0 0 0 1
1 0 0 0 0 0 1
0 1 1 1 1 1 0
```

Fig. 8.9. *Test pattern*

Solution 8.11 The required MatLab program is given below. The BAM is tested with the patterns mentioned in the problem statement. While the BAM correctly recognizes the first test pattern, it diagnoses the second pattern as unknown as it does not match with any of the two stored patterns. Hence, the BAM functions correctly.

```
%Bidirectional Associative Memory neural net
clc;
clear;
% Patterns Associated with the network
Stored_Patterns =
[0111110100000110000011110111110000011001001100100110010011100011101110110
000010111110;0111110100000110000011110111110000011001001100100110010011011
1011100011100000101111 10];
Target_Output=[1 0;0 1];
Test_Pattern_1 = [01111101000001100000111101111100000110010011001001100100
1110001110111011000001011111 0];
Test_Pattern_2 = [01111101000001100000110000011000001100000110000011000000
1100000110000011000001011111 0];
```

```
Inter_x=2*Stored_Patterns-1;
Inter_y=2*Target_Output-1;
weights=zeros(84,2);
for i=1:2
  weights=weights+Inter_x(i,:)'*Inter_y(i,:);
end

Test_Output = Test_Pattern_1*weights;
for(i = 1:2)
if(Test_Output(i)>0)
  Test_Output(i) = 1;
else
  Test_Output(i) = 0;
end
end
disp('Testing with Test Pattern 1');
if (Test_Output == Target_Output(1,1:2))
  disp('Pattern Associated with Stored Pattern 1');
  disp(' SMILING FACE ');
  disp('         *      *      *      *      *      ');
  disp('*                                            *');
  disp('*                                            *');
  disp('*        *      *             *      *       *');
  disp('*                      *                     ');
  disp('*        *             *                     ');
  disp('*                      *                     *');
  disp('*               *                            *');
  disp('*        *             *                     *');
  disp('*               *      *      *              *');
  disp('*                                            *');
  disp('    *    *      *      *      *      ');
elseif (Test_Output == Target_Output(2,1:2))
  disp('Pattern Associated with Stored Pattern 2');
  disp(' FROWNING FACE   ');
    disp('   *    *    *    *    *    ');
  disp('*                 *');
  disp('*                 *');
  disp('*  *    *    *    *    *');
  disp('*                 *');
  disp('*       *         *');
  disp('*       *         *');
  disp('*       *         *');
  disp('*  *    *    *    *');
  disp('*  *         *    *');
  disp('*                 *');
  disp(' * *    *    *    * ');
else
  disp('Unknown Pattern');
end
Test_Output = Test_Pattern_2*weights;
```

```
for(i = 1:2)
if(Test_Output(i)>0)
  Test_Output(i) = 1;
else
  Test_Output(i) = 0;
end
end
disp('Testing with Test Pattern 2');
if (Test_Output == Target_Output(1,1:2))
  disp('Pattern Associated with Stored Pattern 1');
  disp(' SMILING FACE ');
  disp('   *      *      *      *      *      ');
  disp('*                *');
  disp('*                *');
  disp('*  *      *      *      *      *');
  disp('*                *');
  disp('*         *             *');
  disp('*         *             *');
  disp('*         *             *');
  disp('*  *             *      *');
  disp('*  *      *      *      *');
  disp('*                *');
  disp(' *  *      *      *      *      ');
elseif (Test_Output == Target_Output(2,1:2))
  disp('Pattern Associated with Stored Pattern 2');
  disp(' FROWNING FACE    ');
     disp('   *      *      *      *      *');
  disp('*                *');
  disp('*                *');
  disp('*  *      *      *      *      *');
  disp('*                *');
  disp('*         *             *');
  disp('*         *             *');
  disp('*         *             *');
  disp('*  *      *      *      *');
  disp('*  *             *      *');
  disp('*                *');
  disp(' * *      *      *      *');
else
  disp('Unknown Pattern');
end
*******************OUTPUT**********************************
Testing with Test Pattern 1
Pattern Associated with Stored Pattern 1
   SMILING FACE
 *  *     *     *     *
*         *
*         *
**  *     *     *     *
```

```
*           *
*    *            *
*    *            *
*    *            *
**          *     *
**   *      *     *
*           *
     *       *     *      *      *
Testing with Test Pattern 2
Unknown Pattern
```

Problem 8.12 (*Hopfield net*) Design and train a Hopfield network for the following training patterns

i) 1 1 −1 −1
ii) −1 1 −1 −1
ii) −1 −1 −1 1

Determine the pattern to which [0.9, 0.87,–0.9, –0.89] associates.

Solution 8.12 The MatLab code for the required network and its application are given below.

```
% Design and train a Hopfield Network for the following training
patterns
% (1)  1  1 -1 -1
% (2) -1  1 -1 -1
% (3) -1 -1 -1  1
% Determine the pattern to which [0.9, 0.87,-0.9,-0.89] associates
clc;
clear;
T = [1 1-1-1;-1 1-1-1;-1-1-1 1]';          % Training patterns
net = newhop(T);                          % Creating Hopfield Network
Ai = T;
[Y,Pf,Af] = sim(net,3,[],Ai);             % Simulating network
Trained = Y;
disp(Y);                                  % Displaying result
Ai = {[0.9; 0.87;-0.9;-0.89]};            % Testing pattern
[Y,Pf,Af] = sim(net,{1 5},{},Ai);         % Simulating test pattern
disp('ans = ');
disp(Y{1});                               % Displaying result of test
Tested = Y{1};
Tested = Tested';
Trained = Trained';
if (Trained(1,:) == Tested)               % Matching with stored pattern
  disp('Associated with pattern  1 1-1-1');
elseif (Trained(2,:) == Tested)
  disp('Associated with pattern-1 1-1-1');
elseif (Trained(3,:) == Tested)
  disp('Associated with pattern-1-1-1 1');
```

```
else disp('Unknown pattern');
end

**********************OUTPUT***************************************
**********************
    1 -1 -1
    1  1 -1
   -1 -1 -1
   -1 -1  1

ans =
    1
    1
   -1
   -1

Associated with pattern  1 1 -1 -1
```

✓ TEST YOUR KNOWLEDGE

8.1 Which of the following is not a recurrent network?

a) Hopfield network
b) Bidirectional associative memory
c) Both (*a*) and (*b*)
d) None of the above

8.2 In auto-associative networks, the diagonal elements of the weight matrix are set to 0s in order to prevent

a) Reproducing the input rather than the associated pattern
b) Self-loops in the auto-associative networks
c) Both (*a*) and (*b*)
d) None of the above

8.3 Which of the following neural nets can recognize noisy patterns?

a) Auto-associative nets
b) Hetero-associative nets
c) Both (*a*) and (*b*)
d) None of the above

8.4 Two patterns can be stored in the same auto-associative networks if they are

a) Mutually orthogonal
b) Complementary
c) Both (*a*) and (*b*)
d) None of the above

8.5 The highest number of patterns an n-input n-output auto-associative net can store is

a) 2^n
b) n
c) $n-1$
d) None of the above

8.6 Which of the following neural nets can have inequal number of input and output units?

a) Auto-associative nets
b) Hetero-associative nets
c) Both (*a*) and (*b*)
d) None of the above

8.7 Which of the following is a fully connected neural net?

a) Bidirectional associative memory (*BAM*)
b) Hopfield networks
c) Both (*a*) and (*b*)
d) None of the above

8.8 During application, the units of a Hopfield net are updated
a) In predetermined order
b) In parallel
c) In random order
d) None of the above

8.9 Number of layers of processing units in a bidirectional associative memory (*BAM*) is
a) 1
b) 2
c) More than 2
d) None of the above

8.10 The associative network that allows any of its layers of processing units to be used as the input layer is
a) Hopfield networks
b) Bidirectional associative memory (*BAM*)
c) Both (*a*) and (*b*)
d) None of the above

8.11 The associative network that allows any of its layers of processing units to be used as the output layer is
a) Hopfield networks
b) Bidirectional associative memory (*BAM*)
c) Both (*a*) and (*b*)
d) None of the above

8.12 Let the present activation of a unit in a bidirectional associative memory (*BAM*) be 1. If the present net input to the unit is 0, then the next activation of the unit will be
a) 0
b) 1
c) Undefined
d) None of the above

8.13 Let the weight matrix of a bidirectional associative memory (BAM) be given by

$$W = \begin{bmatrix} 1 & -1 & 1 \\ -1 & 1 & -1 \\ -1 & 1 & -1 \\ -1 & 1 & -1 \end{bmatrix}$$

If the vector [1, −1, −1] is applied to the *Y*-layer of the *BAM*, then what will be the corresponding activation of the *X*-layer?
a) [1, −1, −1, −1]
b) [−1, −1, −1, 1]
c) Undefined
d) None of the above

8.14 Which of the following pairs of patterns cannot be stored in an auto-associative neural net?
a) [1, 1, 1, 1] and [1, −1, 1, −1]
b) [1, 1, −1, −1] and [−1, 1, −1, 1]
c) Both (*a*) and (*b*)
d) None of the above

8.15 Which of the following pairs of patterns can be stored in an auto-associative neural net?
a) [1, −1, 1, −1] and [-1, 1, −1, 1]
b) [1, −1, 1, −1] and [1, −1, −1, 1]
c) Both (*a*) and (*b*)
d) None of the above

Answers

8.1 (d)	8.2 (c)	8.3 (c)	8.4 (a)	8.5 (c)
8.6 (b)	8.7 (b)	8.8 (c)	8.9 (b)	8.10 (b)
8.11 (b)	8.12 (b)	8.13 (a)	8.14 (d)	8.15 (b)

EXERCISES

8.1 Let [−1, −1, −1, −1], [1, −1, 1, 1], and [1, −1, −1, 1] be three patterns. Identify two among these, say **s** (1) and **s** (2), which can be stored in a 4-input auto-associative neural net. Find the weight matrix of the net and set its diagonal elements to 0s. Then carry out the following tasks with the net obtained.

(i) Test the net with the two stored vectors s_1 and s_2.

(ii) Set the third element of s_1 and the first element of s_2 to 0s, indicating that values for these elements are missing in the input. Test the network with these noisy inputs.

(iii) Carry out the task mentioned above with two, instead of one, arbitrarily chosen missing elements.

(iv) Insert a mistake in each of the positions mentioned above by flipping the corresponding values (replacing 1 by −1, and vice versa). Test the network with these erroneous inputs.

8.2 Let us consider four pairs of associated patterns as described below.

(i) **s** (1) = [−1, −1, −1], and **t** (1) = [−1, −1]

(ii) **s** (2) = [−1, −1, 1], and **t** (2) = [−1, 1]

(iii) **s** (3) = [−1, 1, −1], and **t** (3) = [1, −1]

(iv) **s** (4) = [1, −1, −1], and **t** (4) = [1, 1]

Construct a hetero-associative net to store these associated vectors. Carry out the following tasks with the net thus constructed.

(i) Test the net with **s** (1), **s** (2), **s** (3) and **s** (4) as inputs.

(ii) Set the middle element of each of the vectors **s** (1), **s** (2), **s** (3) and **s** (4) to 0s. Then test if the net is able to tolerate these noisy inputs and recall the correct associations.

(iii) Carry out the task mentioned above with two, instead of one, arbitrarily chosen missing elements.

(iv) Flip the middle element of each of the vectors **s** (1), **s** (2), **s** (3) and **s** (4), i.e., replace a 1 by −1 and vice versa. Then test if the net is able to tolerate these erroneous inputs and recall the correct associations.

8.3 Obtain a discrete Hopfield network to store the pattern [1, 1, 1, 0]. Do the following with the net thus created.

(i) Test the net with the given pattern.

(ii) Test the net with one erroneous element, say, with [1, 1, 1, 1].

(iii) Test the net with two erroneous elements, say, with [0, 1, 1, 1].

8.4 Design a Bidirectional associative memory (*BAM*) to store the following associations.

(a) **s** (1) = [−1, −1, 1, 1], and **t** (1) = [−1, −1]

(b) **s** (2) = [1, −1, 1, −1], and **t** (2) = [−1, 1]

Perform the following tasks with the *BAM* obtained above.

(i) Test the *BAM* with the given vectors both ways, i.e., using the *X*-layer as the input layer, and also, using the *Y*-layer as the input layer.

(ii) Test the *BAM* with one missing element in the input patterns.

(iii) Test the *BAM* with the input [0, −1, 1, 0]. What is your observation? How does the *BAM* behave if you apply the pattern [0, −1] simultaneously to the *Y*-layer, along with the pattern [0, −1, 1, 0] applied to the *X*-layer?

BIBLIOGRAPHY AND HISTORICAL NOTES

The fundamental ideas of pattern association with neural nets can be traced to the works of Hebb in late 1940s. Later, this was strengthened by the works of stalwarts like Hopfield, Kosko, Kohonen and others. Hopfield proposed his networks, popularly known as Hopfield nets, in 1982. Bidirectional Associative Memories (BAM), another important class of associative memories, was introduced by B. Kosko in 1988. A selected list of works in this area is given below.

Hebb, D. O. (1949). *The Organization of Behaviour*. New York: John Wiley and Sons.

Hopfield, J. J. (1982). Neural networks and physical systems with emergent collective computational abilities. *Proceedings of the National Academy of Sciences of the USA*, Vol. 79, No. 8, pp. 2554–2558.

Kohonen, T. (1989). *Self-organization* and *Associative Memory*. Berlin: Springer-Verlag.

Kosko, B. (1988). Bidirectional associative memories. *IEEE Transactions on Systems, Man and Cybernetics*, Vol. 18, No. 1, pp. 49–60.

Kosko, B. (1990). Unsupervised learning in noise. *IEEE Transactions on Neural Networks*, Vol. 1, No. 1, pp. 44–57.

Kosko, B. (1991). *Neural Networks for Signal Processing*. Englewood Cliffs, NJ: Prentice Hall.

Kosko, B. (1992). *Neural Networks and Fuzzy Systems: A Dynamical Systems Approach to Machine Intelligence*. Englewood Cliffs, NJ: Prentice Hall.

Xu, Z. B., Leung, Y. and He, X. W. (1994). Asymmetrical bidirectional associtive memories. *IEEE Transactions on Systems, Man and Cybernetics*, Vol. 24, pp. 1558–1564.

9

COMPETITIVE NEURAL NETS

Key Concepts

Adaptive resonance theory (ART), ART–1, ART–2, Clustering, Code vector, Competition, Exemplar, Inhibitory weight, Learning vector quantization (LVQ), MaxNet, Self-organizing map (SOM), Stability-plasticity dilemma, Topological neighbourhood, Vigilance parameter, Winner-takes-all

Chapter Outline

The last two chapters presented certain neural networks for pattern classification and pattern association. Artificial neural nets are inherently structured to suit such purposes. However, there are situations when the net is responded by more than one outputs even though it is known that only one of several neurons should respond. Therefore, such nets must be designed in a way so that it is forced to make a decision as to which unit would respond. This is achieved through a mechanism called *competition* and neural networks which employ competition are called competitive neural nets.

Winner-takes-all is a form of competition where only one among a group of competing neurons has a non-zero output at the end of computation. However, quite often the long iterative process of competition is replaced with a simple search for the neuron with the largest input, or some other criteria, to select as the winner.

There are various forms of learning by competitive nets. *Maxnet*, an elementary competitive net, does not require any training because its weights are fixed and pre-determined. *Learning Vector Quantization* (LVQ) nets avail training pairs to learn and therefore, the learning is supervised. However, an important type of competitive nets called the *self-organizing map* (SOM) which groups data into clusters employs *unsupervised* learning. A net employing unsupervised learning seeks to find patterns, or regularity, in the input data. *Adaptive Resonance Theory* (ART) nets are also clustering nets.

There are two methods to determine the closeness of a pattern vector to the weight vector. These are, Euclidean distance, and the dot product. The largest dot product corresponds to the smallest angle between the input and the weight vector if they are both of unit length.

The rest of this chapter presents brief discussions on four important competitive networks, viz., the Maxnet, Kohonen's self-organizing maps, Learning Vector Quantization (LVQ) nets, and the Adaptive Resonance Theory (ART) nets.

9.1 THE MAXNET

MAXNET is the simplest artificial neural net that works on the principle of competition. It is a fully connected network with symmetric interconnections and self-loops. The architecture of an m-unit MAXNET is shown in Fig. 9.1. It consists of m number of cluster units denoted as $Y_1,\ldots, Y_m$. Each unit is directly connected to each other through a link. All the links have the same, fixed, inhibitory weight $-\delta$. Each unit has a self-loop. The weight of a self-loop is 1. Each unit of a MAXNET represents a cluster. When the net is presented with an unknown pattern, the net iteratively modifies the activations of its units until all units except one attain zero activation. The remaining unit with positive activation is the winner.

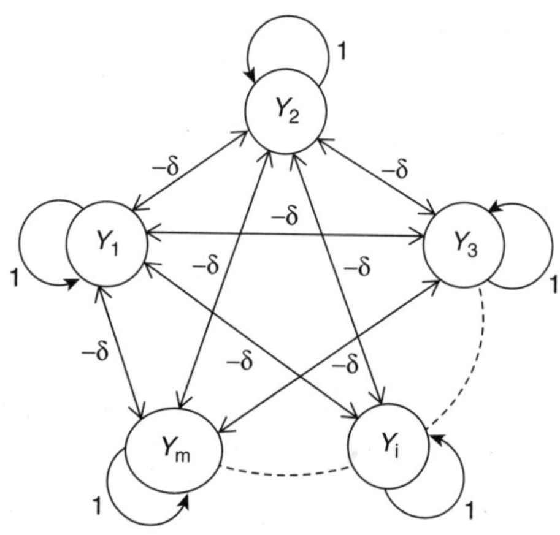

Fig. 9.1. *Architecture of an m-node MAXNET*

9.1.1 Training a MAXNET

There is no need to train a MAXNET because all weights are fixed. While the self-loops have the weight 1, other interconnection paths have the same inhibitory weight $-\delta$, where δ has to satisfy the condition $0 < \delta < \frac{1}{m}$, m being the number of units in the net.

9.1.2 Application of MAXNET

During application, the MAXNET is presented with an input vector $\boldsymbol{x} = [x_1,\ldots, x_m]$ by initializing the activation of the ith unit Y_i by x_i, for all $i = 1$ to m. It then iteratively updates the activations of the cluster units using the activation function

$$y\_out_i = f(y\_in_i) = \begin{cases} y\_in_i, & \text{if } y\_in_i \geq 0 \\ 0, & \text{otherwise} \end{cases} \tag{9.1}$$

Algorithm MAXNET-Clustering
/* A MAXNET of size m, with cluster units $Y_1, \ldots, Y_m$ is given. All interconnection links have an inhibitory weight of $-\delta$ and all self loops have weight 1. The given pattern $\mathbf{x} = [x_1, \ldots, x_m]$ is to be clustered. */

Step 0. Initialize the net inputs to the cluster units.

For i = 1 **To** m **Do** $y\_in_i = x_i$

Step 1. Compute the activation of each cluster unit.

For i = 1 **To** m **Do** $y\_out_i = f(y\_in_i) = \begin{cases} y\_in_i, & \text{if } y\_in_i \geq 0 \\ 0, & \text{otherwise} \end{cases}$

Step 2. Test for stopping condition. **If** all units except one have 0 activation **Then** return the unit with non-zero activation as the winner. **Stop.**

Step 3. Update the net input to each cluster unit.

For i = 1 **To** m **Do** $y\_in_i = y\_out_i - \delta \sum_{j \neq i} y\_out_j$

Step 4. **Go to** Step 1.

Fig. 9.2. *Algorithm MAXNET Clustering*

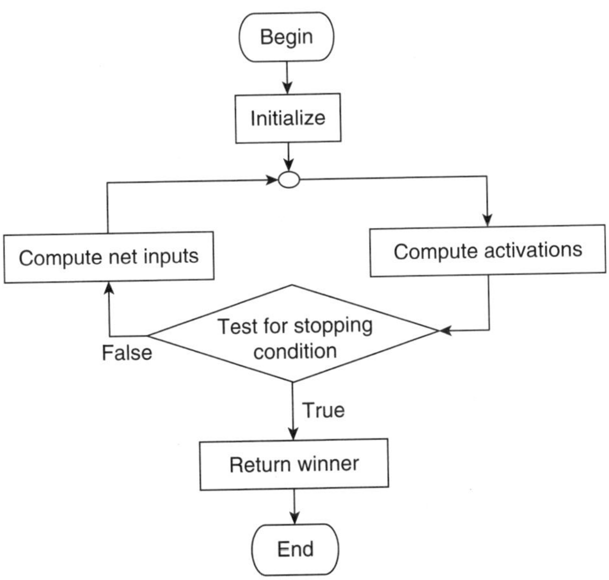

Fig. 9.3. *Flow chart for MAXNET Clustering*

The net input to a cluster unit Y_i is computed as

$$y\_in_i = y\_out_i - \delta \sum_{j \neq i} y\_out_j \tag{9.2}$$

As the clustering process advances, more and more clustering units get deactivated (by attaining an activation of value 0) until all units except one are deactivated. The only one remaining positively activated unit is the winner. The procedure followed by MAXNET to identify the cluster to which a given pattern $\boldsymbol{x} = [x_1, \ldots, x_m]$ belongs is described in **Algorithm** `MAXNET-Clustering` (Fig. 9.2). Fig. 9.3 presents a flowchart of the procedure. Example 9.1 illustrates the procedure followed by a MAXNET.

Example 9.1 *(Clustering by MAXNET)*

Let us consider the 4-unit MAXNET shown in Fig. 9.4. The inhibitory weight is taken as $\delta = 0.2$ which satisfies the condition $0 < \delta < \frac{1}{4}$. The input pattern $\boldsymbol{x} = [x_1, x_2, x_3, x_4] = [0.5, 0.8, 0.3, 0.6]$ is to be clustered. The step-by-step execution of **Algorithm** `MAXNET-Clustering` is given below.

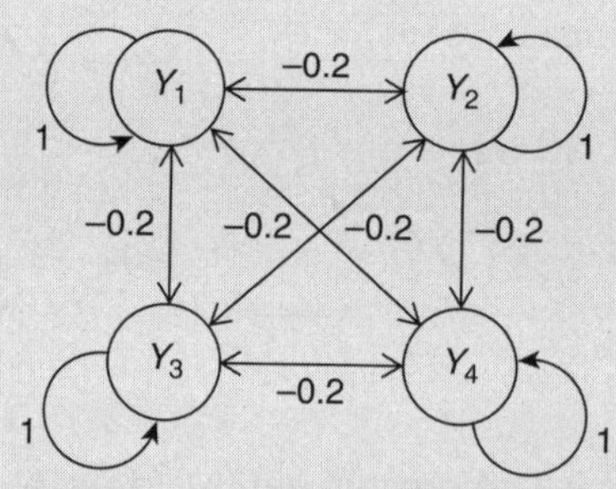

Fig. 9.4. *A 4-unit MAXNET*

Step 0. `Initialize the net inputs to the cluster units.`

$$y\_in_1 = 0.5,\ y\_in_2 = 0.8,\ y\_in_3 = 0.3,\ y\_in_4 = 0.6$$

Iteration #1

Step 1. `Compute the activation of each cluster unit.`

$$y\_out_1 = 0.5,\ y\_out_2 = 0.8,\ y\_out_3 = 0.3,\ y\_out_4 = 0.6.$$

Step 2. `Test for stopping condition.` **If** `all units except one have 0 activation` **Then** `return the unit with non-zero activation as the winner.` **Stop.**

There are four units with non-zero activations. Therefore the stopping criterion (that all units except one have zero activations) is not satisfied. Hence, continue to Step 3.

Step 3. `Update the net input to each cluster unit.`

$$y\_in_1 = y\_out_1 - \delta \sum_{j \neq 1} y\_out_j = 0.5 - 0.2 \times (0.8 + 0.3 + 0.6)$$

$$= 0.5 - 0.2 \times 1.7 = 0.5 - 0.34 = 0.16$$

Similarly,

$$y\_in_2 = 0.8 - 0.2 \times (0.5 + 0.3 + 0.6) = 0.8 - 0.28 = 0.52$$
$$y\_in_3 = 0.3 - 0.2 \times (0.5 + 0.8 + 0.6) = 0.3 - 0.38 = -0.08$$
$$y\_in_4 = 0.6 - 0.2 \times (0.5 + 0.8 + 0.3) = 0.6 - 0.32 = 0.28$$

Step 4. **Go to** Step 1.

Iteration #2

Step 1. Compute the activation of each cluster unit.

$$y\_out_1 = 0.16, y\_out_2 = 0.52, y\_out_3 = 0, y\_out_4 = 0.28$$

Step 2. Test for stopping condition. **If** all units except one have 0 activation **Then** return the unit with non-zero activation as the winner. **Stop.**

There are three units with non-zero activations. Therefore the stopping criterion (that all units except one have zero activations) is not satisfied. Hence, continue to Step 3.

Step 3. Update the net input to each cluster unit.

$$y\_in_1 = y\_out_1 - \delta \sum_{j \neq 1} y\_out_j = 0.16 - 0.2 \times (0.52 + 0 + 0.28)$$
$$= 0.16 - 0.2 \times 0.8 = 0.16 - 0.16 = 0$$

Similarly,

$$y\_in_2 = 0.432$$
$$y\_in_3 < 0$$
$$y\_in_4 = 0.144$$

Step 4. **Go to** Step 1.

The calculations till the net comes to a halt is shown in Table 9.1. We see that the net successfully identifies the unit Y_2 as having maximum input as all the other activations have been reduced to 0. Hence Y_2 is the winner and the given input pattern is clustered to the cluster unit Y_2.

Table 9.1. *Clustering by MAXNET*

#	y_in				y_out			
	y_in_1	y_in_2	y_in_3	y_in_4	y_out_1	y_out_2	y_out_3	y_out_4
0	0.5	0.8	0.3	0.6	0.5	0.8	0.3	0.6
1	0.16	0.52	< 0	0.28	0.16	0.52	0	0.28
2	0	0.432	< 0	0.144	0	0.432	0	0.144
3	< 0	0.403	< 0	0.058	0	0.403	0	0.058
4	< 0	0.391	< 0	< 0	0	0.391	0	0

9.2 KOHONEN'S SELF-ORGANIZING MAP (SOM)

Kohonen's self-organizing map (SOM) is a clustering neural net that works on the principle of winner-takes-all. The unique feature of Kohonen's self-organizing map is the existence of a topological structure among the cluster units. It is assumed that the output (or, cluster) units are arranged in one- or two-dimensional arrays. Given a cluster unit Y_j, its neighborhood of radius R is the set of all units within a distance of R around Y_j. The idea is, patterns close to each other should be mapped to clusters with physical proximity.

A SOM that is used to cluster patterns of length m into n clusters should have m number of input units and n number of output, or cluster, units. The number of clusters is restricted by the number of output units n. Learning takes place with the help of a given set of patterns, and the given number of clusters into which the patterns are to be clustered. Initially, the clusters are unknown, *i.e.*, the knowledge about the patterns that form a particular cluster, or the cluster to which a pattern belongs, is absent at the beginning. During the clustering process, the network organizes itself gradually so that patterns those are close to each other form a cluster. Hence, the learning here is unsupervised. The weight vector associated with a cluster unit acts as the *exemplar* for all patterns belonging to the cluster. During training, the cluster unit whose weight vector is closest to the given input pattern is the winner. The weight vectors of all cluster units in the neighborhood of the winner are updated.

Let $\mathbf{s}_1, \mathbf{s}_2, \ldots, \mathbf{s}_p$ be a set of p number of patterns of the form $\mathbf{s}_i = [x_{i1}, x_{i2}, \ldots, x_{im}]$, to be clustered into n clusters $C_1, C_2, \ldots, C_n$. The subsequent neural net architecture and algorithm enables a Kohonen's SOM to accomplish the clustering task stated above.

9.2.1 SOM Architecture

The architecture of a SOM is shown in Fig. 9.5. It consists of m input units $X_1, X_2, \ldots, X_m$ and n output units $Y_1, Y_2, \ldots, Y_n$. Each input unit X_i is connected to each output unit Y_j through an edge with weight w_{ij}. Each output unit represents a cluster and these cluster units may be arranged in one, or two, dimensional arrays. The topological neighbourhood of a cluster unit in the Kohonen's SOM is shown in Fig. 9.6. Fig. 9.6(a), (b), and (c) show 0, 1, 2 neighbourhood of a given cluster (represented as ⊗) in one and two dimensional array.

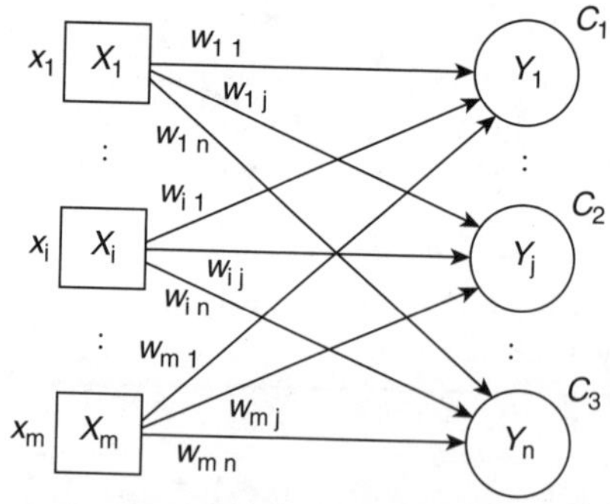

Fig. 9.5. *Architecture of an m-input n-output SOM net*

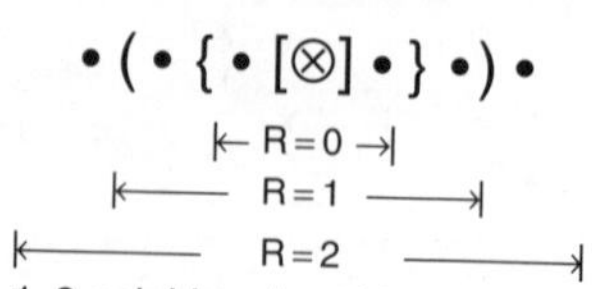

(a) 0, 1, 2 neighbourhood in one dimension

Fig. 9.6. *Neighbourhood of a cluster unit in SOM*

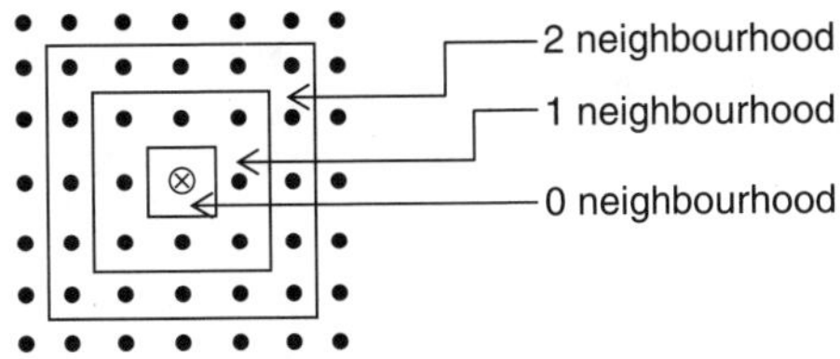

(b) 0, 1, 2 neighbourhood in two dimensional rectangular grid

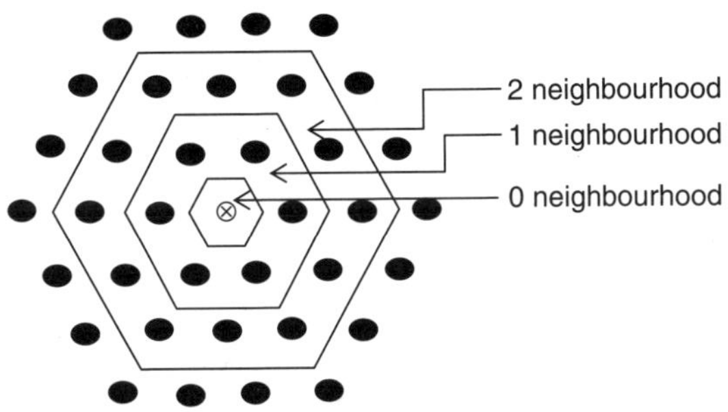

(c) 0, 1, 2 neighbourhood in two dimensional hexagonal grid

Fig. 9.6. *(Continued)*

Algorithm Learning-by-SOM

/* Given a SOM with m input units X_1, X_2, ..., X_m and n output units Y_1, Y_2, ..., Y_n. It is to be trained with a set of p number of patterns $\mathbf{s}_1$, $\mathbf{s}_2$, ..., $\mathbf{s}_p$. */

Step 0. Initialize

i) weight matrix, i.e., w_{ij} for all i and j

ii) Topological neighbourhood R

iii) Learning rate η.

Step 1. **While** stopping condition is not satisfied **Do** Steps 2-8.

Step 2. **For** each training vector $\mathbf{s}_i$ **Do** Step 3 to 5.

Step 3. **For** each exemplar /code vector $\mathbf{w}_{*j}$ **Do** find the distance $D(j)$ between $\mathbf{s}_i$ and $\mathbf{w}_{*j}$.

$$D(j)=\sum_i (x_i - w_{ij})^2$$

Step 4. Find index J so that $D(J)$ is minimum.

Step 5. Update the weights of all units within the specified neighbourhood of J.

For all J, such that $J - R \le j \le J + R$ **Do**

For all i = 1 to m **Do**

$$w_{ij}(new)=w_{ij}(old)+\eta\times[x_i - w_{ij}(old)]$$

Step 6. Update the learning rate, $\eta = k \times \eta$, $0 < k < 1$.

```
Step 7.    If required, reduce R.
Step 8.    Test whether the stopping condition is satisfied or not.
```

Fig. 9.7. *Algorithm Learning-by-SOM*

9.2.2 Learning by Kohonen's SOM

Let $\{s_1, s_2, \ldots, s_p\}$ be the set of training patterns where each $s_i = [x_{i1}, x_{i2}, \ldots, x_{im}]$ is an m-dimensional vector. Learning by the SOM net starts with initializing the weights, the topological neighbourhood parameters, and the learning rate parameters. As mentioned earlier, SOM employs winner-takes-all strategy to organize itself into the desired clusters. The weight vector associated with a cluster unit represents an exemplar, or code-vector. Training takes place through a number of epochs. During an epoch of training, each training vector is compared with the exemplars and its distance from each exemplar is calculated. The cluster unit with least distance is the winner. The weight vector of the winner, along with the weight vectors of all units in its neighbourhood, is updated. After each epoch, the learning rate, and if necessary, the topological neighbourhood parameter, are updated. The learning algorithm is presented in **Algorithm** `Learning-by-SOM` (Fig. 9.7). The corresponding flowchart is given in Fig. 9.8.

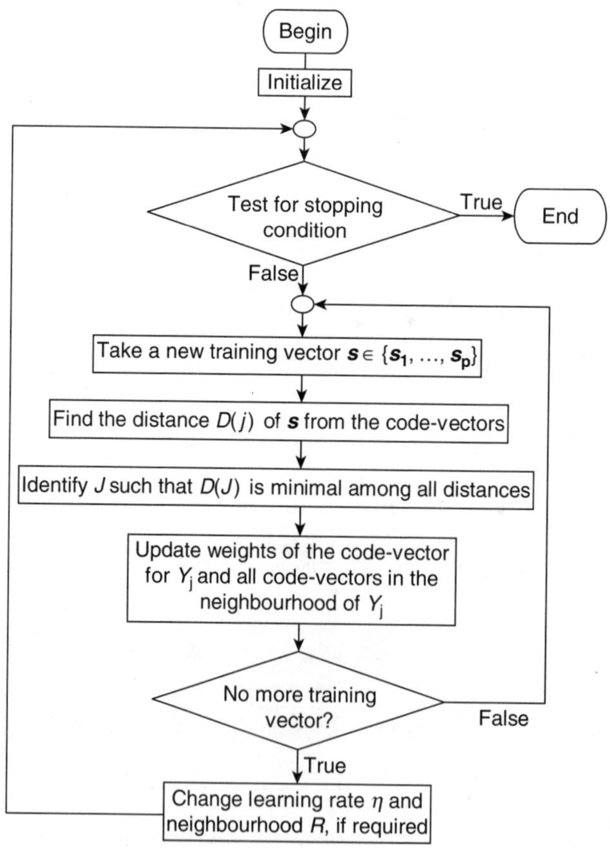

Fig. 9.8. *Flow chart for SOM learning*

9.2.3 Application

During application, the input pattern is compared with the exemplar/code vector in terms of the distance between them. The cluster unit whose code vector is at a least distance from the input pattern is the winner. The input pattern belongs to the corresponding cluster.

The learning and application process of Kohonen's self-organizing map are illustrated in Example 9.2 and Problem 9.1 in the Solved Problems section respectively.

Example 9.2 *(Learning by Kohonen's self-organizing map)*

Suppose there are four patterns $s_1 = [1, 0, 0]$, $s_2 = [0, 0, 1]$, $s_3 = [1, 1, 0]$ and $s_4 = [0, 1, 1]$ to be clustered into two clusters. The target SOM, as shown in Fig. 9.9, consists of three input units and two output units.

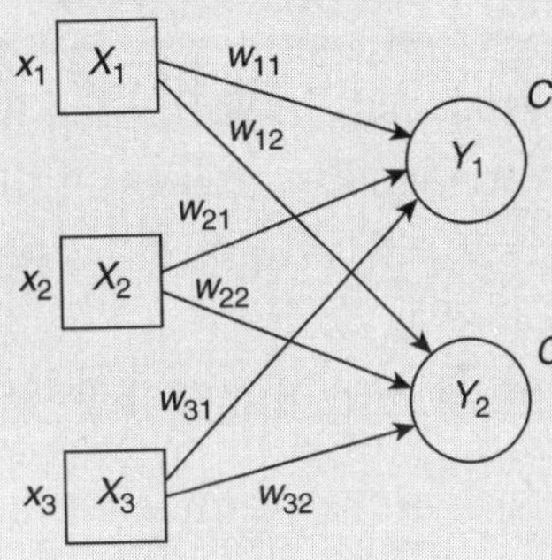

Fig. 9.9. *Target SOM network*

The exemplar, or code-vector, for the clusters C_1 and C_2, represented by the cluster units Y_1 and Y_2 respectively, are given by the 1st and the 2nd column of the weight matrix

$$W = \begin{bmatrix} w_{11} & w_{12} \\ w_{21} & w_{22} \\ w_{31} & w_{32} \end{bmatrix}$$

Hence $\mathbf{W}_{*1} = [w_{11}, w_{21}, w_{31}]^T$ and $\mathbf{W}_{*2} = [w_{12}, w_{22}, w_{32}]^T$ are the code-vectors for the clusters C_1 and C_2 respectively. Now les us denote the input vectors as $s_1 = [1, 0, 0]$, $s_2 = [0, 0, 1]$, $s_3 = [1, 1, 0]$ and $s_4 = [0, 1, 1]$. The successive steps of the learning process are described below.

Step 0. `Initialize`

(i) Weight matrix W is randomly initialized as

$$W = \begin{bmatrix} .5 & .3 \\ .8 & .5 \\ .4 & .3 \end{bmatrix}$$

(ii) Topological neighbourhood is initialized to $R = 0$, because there are only two cluster units.

(iii) Learning rate $\eta = 0.8$. It will be geometrically decreased with a factor of 0.5 after each epoch of training.

Step 1. `While stopping condition is not satisfied`

`Do Steps 2-8.`

When the weight adjustment $\Delta w_{ij} < 0.01$ the net is assumed to have converged. Initially the stopping condition is obviously false. Hence we continue to Step 2.

Step 2. `For each training vector` s_i `Do Step 3 to 5.`

We start training with the first vector $s_1 = [1, 0, 0]$.

Step 3. `For each exemplar /code vector` w_{*j}
`Do find the distance` $D(j)$ `between` s_i `and` w_{*j}.

$$D(j)=\sum_i (x_i - w_{ij})^2$$

$$\begin{aligned}D(1) &= \text{distance between } s_1 \text{ and } W_{*1}\\ &= (1-0.5)^2 + (0-0.8)^2 + (0-0.4)^2\\ &= 0.25 + 0.64 + 0.16\\ &= 1.05\end{aligned}$$

$$\begin{aligned}D(2) &= \text{distance between } s_1 \text{ and } W_{*2}\\ &= (1-0.3)^2 + (0-0.5)^2 + (0-0.3)^2\\ &= 0.49 + 0.25 + 0.09\\ &= 0.83\end{aligned}$$

Step 4. `Find index` J `so that` $D(J)$ `is minimum.`

Since, $D(2) < D(1)$, s_1 is closer to C_2, and Y_2 is the winner. Therefore, the code vector W_{*2} is to be adjusted.

Step 5. `Update the weights of all units within the specified neighbourhood of` J.

`For all` J, `such that` $J - R \le j \le J + R$ `Do`
　　`For all` i = `1 to` m `Do`

$$w_{ij}(new)=w_{ij}(old)+\eta\times[x_i - w_{ij}(old)]$$

Since $R = 0$, we need to adjust the weight vector of the winner only.

$$\begin{aligned}w_{12}\,(\text{new}) &= w_{12}\,(\text{old}) + \eta\times(x_1 - w_{12}\,(\text{old}))\\ &= 0.3 + 0.8\times(1-0.3)\\ &= 0.3 + 0.8\times 0.7\\ &= 0.86\end{aligned}$$

$$\begin{aligned}w_{22}\,(\text{new}) &= w_{22}\,(\text{old}) + \eta\times(x_2 - w_{22}\,(\text{old}))\\ &= 0.5 + 0.8\times(0-0.5)\\ &= 0.5 - 0.4\\ &= 0.1\end{aligned}$$

$$w_{32}\text{ (new)} = w_{32}\text{ (old)} + \eta \times (x_3 - w_{32}\text{ (old)})$$
$$= 0.3 + 0.8 \times (0 - 0.3)$$
$$= 0.3 - 0.24$$
$$= 0.06$$

Hence, the weight matrix after training with the 1st input vector in the 1st epoch is

$$W = \begin{bmatrix} 0.5 & 0.86 \\ 0.8 & 0.1 \\ 0.4 & 0.06 \end{bmatrix}$$

We now proceed to train the SOM with the second pattern.

Step 2. **For** each training vector $\mathbf{s}_i$ **Do** Step 3 to 5.

After training with the first vector $\mathbf{s}_1 = [1, 0, 0]$, we proceed with the second pattern $\mathbf{s}_2 = [0, 0, 1]$.

Step 3. **For** each exemplar /code vector $\mathbf{w}_{*j}$

Do find the distance $D(j)$ between $\mathbf{s}_i$ and $\mathbf{w}_{*j}$.

$$D(j) = \sum_i (x_i - w_{ij})^2$$

$$D(1) = \text{distance between } \mathbf{s}_2 \text{ and } \mathbf{W}_{*1}$$
$$= (0 - 0.5)^2 + (0 - 0.8)^2 + (1 - 0.4)^2$$
$$= 0.25 + 0.64 + 0.36$$
$$= 1.25$$
$$D(2) = \text{distance between } \mathbf{s}_2 \text{ and } \mathbf{W}_{*2}$$
$$= (0 - 0.86)^2 + (0 - 0.1)^2 + (1 - 0.06)^2$$
$$= 0.74 + 0.01 + 0.88$$
$$= 1.63$$

Step 4. Find index J so that $D(J)$ is minimum.

Since, $D(1) < D(2)$, $\mathbf{s}_2$ is closer to C_1, and Y_1 is the winner. Therefore, the code vector $\mathbf{W}_{*1}$ is to be adjusted.

Step 5. Update the weights of all units within the specified neighbourhood of J.

For all J, such that $J - R \le j \le J + R$ **Do**
  For all i = 1 to m **Do**

$$w_{ij}(new) = w_{ij}(old) + \eta \times [x_i - w_{ij}(old)]$$

Since $R = 0$, we need to adjust the weight vector of the winner only.

$$w_{11}(\text{new}) = w_{11}(\text{old}) + \eta \times (x_1 - w_{11}(\text{old}))$$
$$= 0.5 + 0.8 \times (0 - 0.5)$$
$$= 0.5 - 0.8 \times 0.5$$
$$= 0.1$$
$$w_{21}(\text{new}) = w_{21}(\text{old}) + \eta \times (x_2 - w_{21}(\text{old}))$$
$$= 0.8 + 0.8 \times (0 - 0.8)$$
$$= 0.8 - 0.64$$
$$= 0.16$$
$$w_{31}(\text{new}) = w_{31}(\text{old}) + \eta \times (x_3 - w_{31}(\text{old}))$$
$$= 0.4 + 0.8 \times (1 - 0.4)$$
$$= 0.4 + 0.48$$
$$= 0.88$$

Hence, the weight matrix W after training with the second vector in the first epoch is

$$W = \begin{bmatrix} 0.1 & 0.86 \\ 0.16 & 0.1 \\ 0.88 & 0.06 \end{bmatrix}$$

In this way learning with the rest of the patterns $s_3 = [1, 1, 0]$ and $s_4 = [0, 1, 1]$ takes place by repeating Steps 3–5. Table 9.2 shows the outline of learning during the first epoch.

Table 9.2. *Learning by the SOM during the first epoch*

#	Training Patterns $s = (x_1, x_2, x_3)$	Squared Euclidean Distance		Winner	New Code Vectors	
		$D(1)$	$D(2)$		C_1 (w_{11}, w_{21}, w_{31})	C_2 (w_{12}, w_{22}, w_{32})
0					(0.5, 0.8, 0.4)	(0.3, 0.5, 0.3)
1	$s_1 = (1, 0, 0)$	1.05	0.83	C_2	No change	(0.86, 0.1, 0.06)
2	$s_2 = (0, 0, 1)$	1.25	1.63	C_1	(0.1, 0.16, 0.88)	No change
3	$s_3 = (1, 1, 0)$	2.29	1.71	C_2	No change	(0.97, 0.82, 0.01)
4	$s_4 = (0, 1, 1)$	1.53	1.95	C_1	(0.02, 0.83, 0.98)	No change

So, code-vector W_{*2} gets modified as a result of training with the patterns s_1 and s_3 while training with the patterns s_2 and s_4 results in adjustment of the code-vector W_{*1}.
The weight matrix obtained after the first epoch is

$$W_1 = \begin{bmatrix} 0.02 & 0.97 \\ 0.83 & 0.82 \\ 0.98 & 0.01 \end{bmatrix}$$

On further computation, the weight matrix after the second epoch becomes

$$W_2 = \begin{bmatrix} 0.01 & 0.99 \\ 0.7 & 0.7 \\ 0.99 & 0 \end{bmatrix}$$

The training process converges after 19 epochs when the weight matrix becomes (approximately)

$$W_{19} = \begin{bmatrix} 0 & 1 \\ 0.6 & 0.6 \\ 1 & 0 \end{bmatrix}$$

Fig. 9.10 shows the SOM obtained for the given clustering problem.

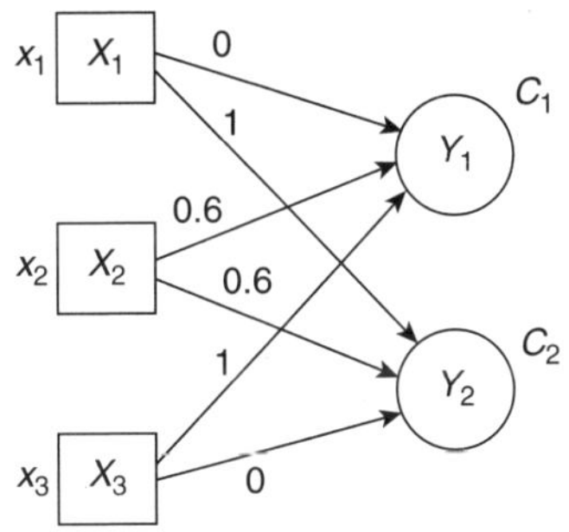

Fig. 9.10. *Resultant net after training*

9.3 LEARNING VECTOR QUANTIZATION (LVQ)

Another pattern clustering net based on the winner-takes-all strategy is Learning Vector Quantization (LVQ) nets. However, unlike Kohonen's SOM, LVQ follows supervised learning, instead of unsupervised learning. The architecture of LVQ is essentially same as that of SOM except that the concept of topological neighbourhood is absent here. There are as many input units as the number of components in the input patterns and each output unit represents a known cluster. The details of LVQ learning are described below.

9.3.1 LVQ Learning

LVQ nets undergo a supervised learning process. The training set consists of a number of training vectors, each of which is designated with a known cluster. After initializing the weight matrix of the LVQ net, it undergoes training through a number of epochs. During each epoch, the weights are adjusted to accommodate the training vectors on the basis of their known clusters. The objective is to find the output unit that is closest to the input vector. In order to ensure this the algorithm finds the code vector $\boldsymbol{w}$ closest to the input vector $\boldsymbol{s}$. If $\boldsymbol{s}$ and $\boldsymbol{w}$ map to the same cluster, then $\boldsymbol{w}$ is moved closer to $\boldsymbol{s}$. Otherwise, $\boldsymbol{w}$ is moved away from $\boldsymbol{x}$. Let $\boldsymbol{t}$ be the cluster for the training vector $\boldsymbol{s}$, and C_j

be the cluster represented by Y_j, the jth output unit of the LVQ net. The procedure followed by LVQ learning is presented in **Algorithm** LVQ-Learning (Fig. 9.11). Fig. 9.12 presents the LVQ learning process in flowchart form.

```
Algorithm LVQ-Learning

/* There are p number of m-dimensional training patterns s1, s2, ..., sp, and
n number of clusters C1, ..., Cn. The training set consists of the pairs (s1,
t1), (s2, t2), ..., (sp, tp) where the pair (si, ti) indicates that pattern si
belongs to cluster ti ∈ { C1, ..., Cn}. We have to make an m-input n-output LVQ
net learn these training set. */

Step 0.    Initialize
             i)  The weight matrix, i.e., wij for all i and j. A simple
                 technique is to select one training vector from each
                 known cluster and assign them directly to the columns of
                 the weight matrix so that each of them becomes a code
                 vector. Rest of the input patterns are used for train-
                 ing.)
            ii)  The learning rate.

Step 1.    While stopping condition is not satisfied Do
           Step 2 to Step 7.

Step 2.    For each input training vector s Do Steps 3 to Step 5.

Step 3.    Find the distance D(j) of s from each exemplar / code-vector
           W*j.
```

$$D(j) = \sum_{i=1}^{m} (x_i - w_{ij})^2$$

```
Step 4.    Find the index J for which D(J) is minimum.

Step 5.    Update code-vector W*J.
           If t = = Cj Then /* bring Cj closer to s */
```

$$w_{*J}(new) = w_{*J}(old) + \eta \times [s - w_{*j}(old)]$$

```
           Else /* take Cj away from s */
```

$$w_{*J}(new) = w_{*J}(old) - \eta \times [s - w_{*j}(old)]$$

```
Step 6.    Reduce the learning rate, η = k × η, 0 < k < 1.

Step 7.    Test for stopping condition.
```

Fig. 9.11. *Algorithm LVQ-Learning*

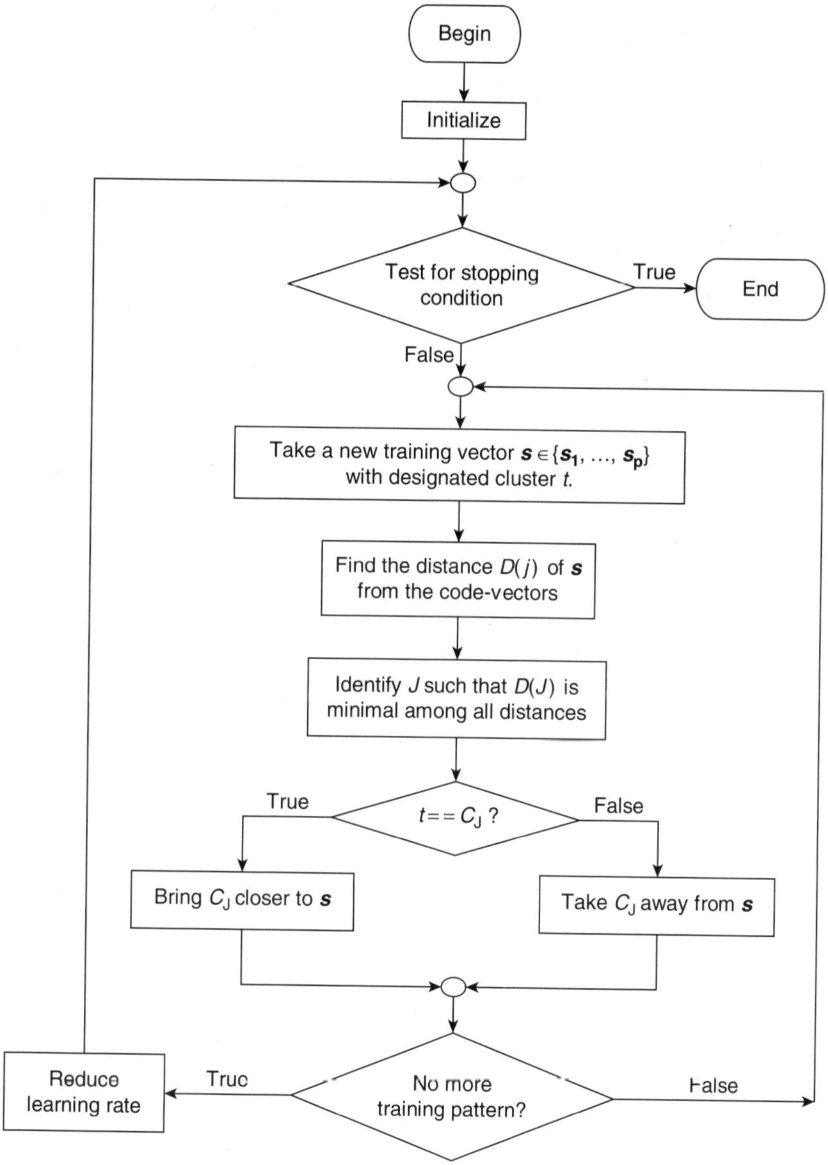

Fig. 9.12. *Flow chart for LVQ Learning*

9.3.2 Application

During application, the input pattern is compared with the exemplar/code vector in terms of the distance between them. The cluster unit whose code vector is at a least distance from the input pattern is the winner. The input pattern belongs to the corresponding cluster.

The learning and application process of LVQ nets are illustrated in Examples 9.3 and 9.4 respectively.

Example 9.3 *(Learning by LVQ net)*

Five patterns and their corresponding designated clusters are given in Table 9.3. A neural net is to be obtained through Learning Vector Quantization (LVQ) method for the given set of vectors.

As there are 4 components in the training vectors and two clusters, the target net shall have 4 inputs and 2 cluster units. The exemplars, or code vectors, are initialized with the input vectors 1 and 4. The rest of the vectors, *i.e.*, 2, 3, 5 are used for training. Fig. 9.13 shows the initial situation. Subsequent steps of the learning process are described below.

Table 9.3. *Training set*

#	Training Vector $s = [x_1, x_2, x_3, x_2]$	Cluster
1	$\mathbf{s}_1 = [1, 0, 0, 0]$	C_1
2	$\mathbf{s}_2 = [0, 1, 0, 0]$	C_1
3	$\mathbf{s}_3 = [1, 1, 0, 0]$	C_1
4	$\mathbf{s}_4 = [0, 0, 0, 1]$	C_2
5	$\mathbf{s}_5 = [0, 0, 1, 1]$	C_2

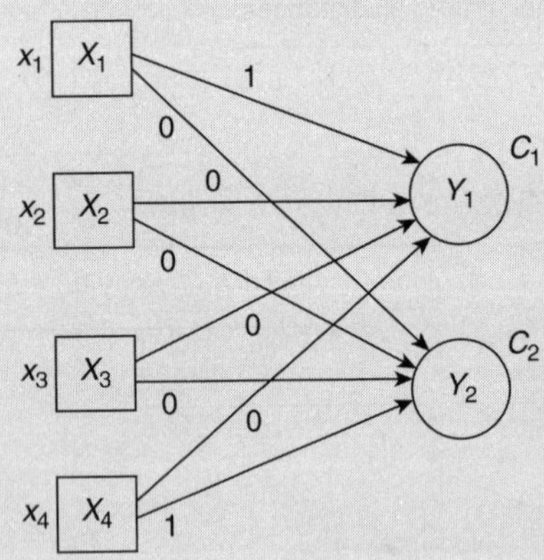

$$W = \begin{bmatrix} w_{11} & w_{12} \\ w_{21} & w_{22} \\ w_{31} & w_{32} \\ w_{41} & w_{42} \end{bmatrix} = \begin{bmatrix} 1 & 0 \\ 0 & 0 \\ 0 & 0 \\ 0 & 1 \end{bmatrix}$$

Training Vectors :

$\mathbf{s}_2 = [0, 1, 0, 0]$: Cluster C_1
$\mathbf{s}_3 = [1, 1, 0, 0]$: Cluster C_1
$\mathbf{s}_5 = [0, 0, 1, 1]$: Cluster C_2

Fig. 9.13. *Initial configuration*

Step 0. Initialize the weight matrix, and the learning rate.

The weight matrix is initialized with the patterns $\mathbf{s}_1 = [1, 0, 0, 0]$ and $\mathbf{s}_4 = [0, 0, 0, 1]$. The resultant weight vector is shown in Fig. 9.13. We fix the learning rate $\eta = 0.2$ and decrease it geometrically after each iteration by a factor of 0.5.

Step 1. **While** stopping condition is not satisfied **Do** Step 2 to Step 7.

We stop when the process converges, *i.e.*, there is no perceptible change in the code vectors. Obviously, initially the stopping condition is false.

Step 2. **For** each input training vector ***s*** **Do** Step 3 to Step 5.
The first training vector is $\mathbf{s}_2 = [0, 1, 0, 0]$ that maps to cluster C_1.

Step 3. Find the distance $D(j)$ of ***s*** from each exemplar / code-vector $\mathbf{W}_{*j}$.

$$D(j)=\sum_{i=1}^{m}(x_i - w_{ij})^2$$

The distance of $\mathbf{s}_2 = (0, 1, 0, 0)$ from the two code-vectors are calculated.

$$D(1)=\sum_{i=1}^{4}(x_i - w_{i1})^2 = (0-1)^2 + (1-0)^2 + (0-0)^2 + (0-0)^2 = 2$$

$$D(2)=\sum_{i=1}^{4}(x_i - w_{i2})^2 = (0-0)^2 + (1-0)^2 + (0-0)^2 + (0-1)^2 = 2$$

Step 4. Find the index J for which $D(J)$ is minimum.

As $D(1) = D(2)$, we resolve the tie by arbitrarily selecting $J = 2$.

Step 5. Update code-vector $\mathbf{W}_{*J}$.

If $t == Cj$ **Then** /* bring Cj closer to ***s*** */

$$w_{*J}(new)=w_{*J}(old)+\eta\times[s - w_{*j}(old)]$$

Else /* take Cj away from ***s*** */

$$w_{*J}(new)=w_{*J}(old)-\eta\times[s - w_{*j}(old)]$$

As per Table 9.4, $t = C_1$ and therefore, $t \neq Cj$ here. Hence, the code vector $\mathbf{W}_{*2}$ should be moved away from the training pattern $\mathbf{s}_2 = (0, 1, 0, 0)$. Therefore,

$$w_{12}(\text{new}) = w_{12}(\text{old}) - \eta \times [x_1 - w_{12}(\text{old})]$$

$$= 0 - 0.2 \times (0 - 0)$$

$$= 0.$$

$$w_{22}(\text{new}) = w_{22}(\text{old}) - \eta \times [x_2 - w_{22}(\text{old})]$$

$$= 0 - 0.2 \times (1 - 0)$$

$$= -0.2$$

Similarly, $w_{32}(\text{new}) = 0$, and $w_{42}(\text{new}) = 1.2$.
Hence the new weight matrix is,

$$W(new)=\begin{bmatrix} w_{11} & w_{12} \\ w_{21} & w_{22} \\ w_{31} & w_{32} \\ w_{41} & w_{42} \end{bmatrix}=\begin{bmatrix} 1 & 0 \\ 0 & -0.2 \\ 0 & 0 \\ 0 & 1.2 \end{bmatrix}$$

We now go back to Step 2 to train the net with the next training pattern.

Step 2. **For** each input training vector ***s*** **Do** Steps 3 to Step 5.
The second training pattern is $\mathbf{s}_3 = [1, 1, 0, 0]$ that maps to cluster C_1.

Step 3. Find the distance *D*(j) of ***s*** from each exemplar / code-vector $\mathbf{W}_{*j}$.

$$D(j)=\sum_{i=1}^{m}(x_i - w_{ij})^2$$

The distance of $\mathbf{s}_3 = [1, 1, 0, 0]$ from the two code-vectors are calculated.

$$D(1)=\sum_{i=1}^{4}(x_i - w_{i1})^2 = (1-1)^2 + (1-0)^2 + (0-0)^2 + (0-0)^2 = 1$$

$$D(2)=\sum_{i=1}^{4}(x_i - w_{i2})^2 = (1-0)^2 + (1+0.2)^2 + (0-0)^2 + (0-1.2)^2 = 3.88$$

Step 4. Find the index *J* for which *D*(*J*) is minimum.

As $D(1) < D(2)$, $J = 1$.

Step 5. Update code-vector $\mathbf{W}_{*J}$.

If t = = Cj **Then** /* bring Cj closer to ***s*** */

$$w_{*j}(new)=w_{*j}(old)+\eta\times[s - w_{*j}(old)]$$

Else /* take Cj away from ***s*** */

$$w_{*j}(new)=w_{*j}(old)-\eta\times[s - w_{*j}(old)]$$

As per Table 9.4, $t = C_1$ and therefore, $t = Cj$ here. Hence, the code vector $\mathbf{W}_{*1}$ should be moved closer to the training pattern $\mathbf{s}_3 = [1, 1, 0, 0]$. Therefore,

$$\begin{aligned} w_{11}(\text{new}) &= w_{11}(\text{old}) + \eta\times[x_1 - w_{11}(\text{old})] \\ &= 1 - 0.2\times(1-1) \\ &= 1 \\ w_{21}(\text{new}) &= w_{21}(\text{old}) + \eta\times[x_2 - w_{21}(\text{old})] \\ &= 0 + 0.2\times(1-0) \\ &= 0.2 \end{aligned}$$

Similarly, $w_{31}(\text{new}) = 0$, and $w_{41}(\text{new}) = 0$.

Hence the new weight matrix is,

$$W(new) = \begin{bmatrix} w_{11} & w_{12} \\ w_{21} & w_{22} \\ w_{31} & w_{32} \\ w_{41} & w_{42} \end{bmatrix} = \begin{bmatrix} 1 & 0 \\ 0.2 & -0.2 \\ 0 & 0 \\ 0 & 1.2 \end{bmatrix}$$

The calculations go on in this way. Details of the training during the first epoch are shown in Table 9.4.

Table 9.4. *First epoch of LVQ learning*

#	Training Pattern (s)	Squared Euclidean Distance		Winner	Designated cluster	New Code Vectors	
		D(1)	D(2)			C_1	C_2
0						(1, 0, 0, 0,)	(0, 0, 0, 1)
1	(0, 1, 0, 0)	2	2	C_2	C_1	-	(0, −.2, 0, 1.2)
2	(1, 1, 0, 0)	1	3.88	C_1	C_1	(1, .2, 0, 0)	-
3	(0, 0, 1, 1)	3.04	1.08	C_2	C_2	-	(0, −.16, .2, 1.16)

Hence, the weight matrix after the first epoch is

$$W_1 = \begin{bmatrix} w_{11} & w_{12} \\ w_{21} & w_{22} \\ w_{31} & w_{32} \\ w_{41} & w_{42} \end{bmatrix} = \begin{bmatrix} 1 & 0 \\ 0.2 & -0.16 \\ 0 & 0.2 \\ 0 & 1.16 \end{bmatrix}$$

Through calculations we see that the weight matrices W_2 and W_3 after the second and the third epoch, respectively, take the forms

$$W_2 = \begin{bmatrix} 0.91 & 0 \\ 0.352 & -0.144 \\ 0 & 0.28 \\ 0 & 1.14 \end{bmatrix}, \; W_3 = \begin{bmatrix} 0.871 & 0 \\ 0.415 & -0.137 \\ 0 & 0.316 \\ 0 & 1.14 \end{bmatrix}$$

The process takes 12 epochs to converge, when the weight matrix becomes

$$W = \begin{bmatrix} 0.836 & 0 \\ 0.471 & -0.13 \\ 0 & 0.35 \\ 0 & 1.13 \end{bmatrix}$$

Hence the code vectors arrived at are $W_{*1} = [0.836, 0.471, 0, 0]^T$, and $W_{*2} = [0, -0.13, 0.35, 1.13]^T$ representing the clusters C_1 and C_2, respectively. Fig. 9.14 shows the LVQ net obtained.

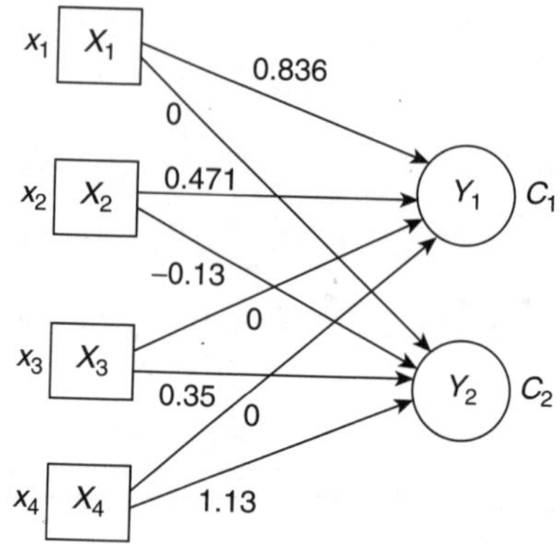

Fig. 9.14. *Final LVQ net obtained*

Example 9.4 *(Clustering application of LVQ net)*

The LVQ net constructed in Example 9.3 can now be tested with the input patterns given in Table 9.3. Moreover, we apply a new input pattern **s** = [1, 1, 1, 0] which is to be clustered by the resultant net. The clustering method is rather simple and is based on the principle of the winner-takes-all. It consists of finding the distance of the given input pattern from each of the code vectors. The nearest code vector, i.e., the code vector have least distance, is the winner. Table 9.5 presents the summary of calculations for these patterns.

Results shown in Table 9.5 reveal that the LVQ net arrived at through the aforesaid learning process is working correctly. All the input patterns are clustered by the net in expected manner. Clusters returned by the net for patterns $\mathbf{s}_1$ to $\mathbf{s}_5$ match with their designated clusters in the training data. The new pattern **s** = [1, 1, 1, 0] is placed in cluster C_1. This is expected because this pattern has greater similarity with patterns $\mathbf{s}_1$, $\mathbf{s}_2$, and $\mathbf{s}_3$, than with the rest of the patterns $\mathbf{s}_4$ and $\mathbf{s}_5$.

Table 9.5. *Clustering application of LVQ net*

#	Input Pattern	Squared Euclidean Distance		Winner
		D(1)	D(2)	
1	(1, 0, 0, 0)	0.249	2.416	C_1
2	(0, 1, 0, 0)	0.979	2.676	C_1
3	(1, 1, 0, 0)	0.805	3.676	C_1
4	(0, 0, 0, 1)	1.921	0.156	C_2
5	(0, 0, 1, 1)	2.921	0.456	C_2
6	(1, 1, 1, 0)	1.805	3.976	C_1

9.4 ADAPTIVE RESONANCE THEORY (ART)

Adaptive Resonance Theory (ART) nets were introduced by Carpenter and Grossberg (1987, 1991) to resolve the so called *stability-plasticity* dilemma. ART nets learn through unsupervised learning where the input patterns may be presented in any order. Moreover, ART nets allow the user to control the degree of similarity among the patterns placed in the same cluster. It provides a mechanism to include a new cluster unit for an input pattern which is sufficiently different from all the exemplars of the clusters corresponding to the existing cluster units. Hence, unlike other ANNs, ART nets are capable of adaptive expansion of the output layer of clustering units subject to some upper bound.

9.4.1 The Stability-Plasticity Dilemma

Usually, a neural net is trained with the help of a training set of fixed number of patterns. Learning by the net is accomplished through a number of epochs, where each epoch consists of application of the training patterns in a certain sequence and making suitable adjustments in the interconnection weights under the influence of each of these training patterns.

Depending on the number of epochs of training, a training pattern is presented to the net multiple times. As the interconnection weights of a net change with each pattern during learning, a training pattern that is placed in a cluster may be placed on a different cluster later on. Therefore, a training pattern may oscillate among the clusters during net learning. In this situation, the net is said to be unstable. Hence, a net is said to be **stable** if it attains the interconnection weights (i.e., the exemplars) which prevent the training patterns from oscillating among the clusters. Usually, stability is achieved by a net by monotonically decreasing the learning rate as it is subjected to the same set of training patterns over and over again.

However, while attaining stability in the way mentioned above, the net may lose the capacity to readily learn a pattern presented for the first time to the net after a number of epochs have already taken place. In other words, as the net attains stability, it loses plasticity. By **plasticity** of a net we mean its readiness to learn a new pattern equally well at any stage of training.

ART nets are designed to be stable as well as plastic. It employs a feedback mechanism to enable the net learn a new pattern at any stage of learning without jeopardizing the patterns already learnt. Therefore, practically, it is able to switch automatically between the stable and plastic mode.

9.4.2 Features of ART Nets

The main features of ART nets are summarized below.

(i) ART nets follow unsupervised learning where the training patterns may be presented in any order.

(ii) ART nets allow the user to control the degree of similarity of patterns placed on the same cluster. The decision is taken on the basis of the *relative similarity* of an input pattern to a code-vector (or, exemplar), rather than the *distance* between them.

(iii) There is scope for inclusion of additional cluster units during the learning phase. If an input pattern is found to be sufficiently different from the code-vector of the existing clusters, a new cluster unit is introduced and the concerned input vector is placed on this new cluster.

(iv) ART nets try to solve the *stability-plasticity* dilemma with the help of a feedback mechanism between it's two layers of processing units one of which is the processing layer while the other is the output, or the competitive clustering layer. The feedback mechanism empowers the net to learn new information without destroying old information. Hence the system is capable of automatically switching between stability and plasticity.

(v) ART nets are able to learn only in their resonant states. The ART net is in resonant state when the current input vector matches the winner code-vector (exemplar) so close that a *reset signal* is not generated. The reset signal inhibits the ART to learn.

(vi) There are two kinds of ARTs, *viz.*, ART1 and ART2. ART1 works on binary patterns and ART2 is designed for patterns with real, or continuous, values.

9.4.3 ART 1

As stated earlier, ART1 is designed to cluster binary input patterns. It provides the user the power to control the degree of similarity among the patterns belonging to the same cluster. This is achieved with the help of the so called *vigilance parameter* ρ. One important feature of ART1 is, it allows the training patterns to be presented in any order. Moreover, the number of patterns used for training is not necessarily known in advance. Hence, a pattern may be presented to the net for the first time at an intermediate stage of ART1 learning. The architecture and learning technique of ART1 nets are given below.

Architecture Fig. 9.15 shows a simplified view of the structure of an m-input n-output (expandable) ART1 net. It includes the following constituent parts :

1. A combination of two layers of neurons, known together as the *comparison layer*, and symbolically expressed as the F_1 layer
2. An output, or clustering, layer of neurons known as the *recognition layer*, referred to as the F_2 layer. This is the *competitive* layer of the net.
3. A *reset* unit R.
4. Various interconnections.

The comparison layer includes two layers of neurons, the *Input Layer* $F_1(a)$ consisting of the units $S_1, S_2, \ldots, S_m$ and the *Interface Layer* $F_1(b)$ with the units $X_1, X_2, \ldots, X_m$. The input layer $F_1(a)$ do not process the input pattern but simply pass it on to be interface layer $F_1(b)$. Each unit S_i of $F_1(a)$ layer is connected to the corresponding unit X_i of the interface layer.

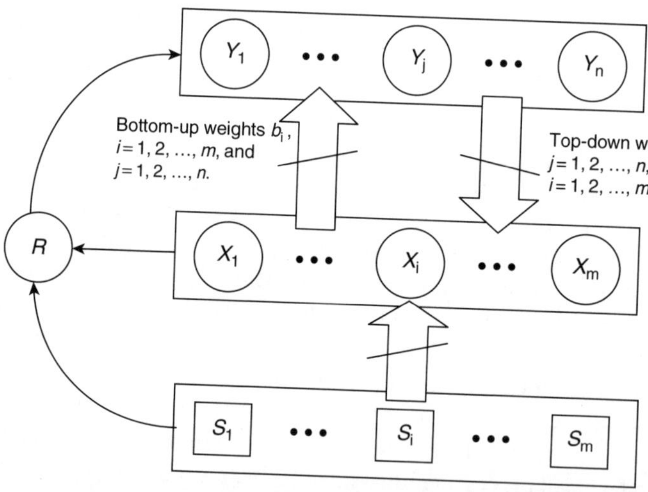

Fig. 9.15. *Simplified ART1 architecture*

The role of the *interface layer* $F_1(b)$ is to broadcast the input pattern to the recognition layer F_2. Moreover, the $F_1(b)$ layer takes part in comparing the input pattern with the winning code-vector. If the input pattern and the winning code-vector matches sufficiently closely, which is determined with the help of the vigilance parameter ρ, the winning cluster unit is allowed to learn the pattern. Otherwise, the reset signal is switched on, and the cluster unit is inhibited to learn the input pattern.
The *recognition layer* F_2 is the competitive layer of ART1. Each unit of F_2 represents a distinct cluster. As

ART1 provides scope for expansion of the number of clusters, the number of units in the F_2 layer is not fixed. While the net is learning a pattern, an F_2 unit may be in any one of the three states, *viz.*, *active*, *inactive*, and *inhibited*. These states are described below:

Active The unit is 'on' and has a positive activation. For ART1, the activation is 1, and for ART2, it is between 0 and 1.

Inactive The unit is 'off' and activation = 0. However, the unit takes part in competition.

Inhibited The unit is 'off' and activation = 0. Moreover, it is not allowed to further participate in a competition during the learning process with the current input pattern.

The *reset* unit R is used to control vigilance matching. It receives excitatory signals from $F_1(a)$ units that are on and inhibitory signals from $F_1(b)$ units that are on. Depending on whether sufficient number of $F_1(b)$ interface units are on, which is determined with the help of the vigilance parameter set by the user, the reset unit R is either not fired, or fired. In case the reset unit R fires, the active F_2 clustering unit is inhibited.

There are various kinds of interconnections in ART1. Each $F_1(a)$ input unit S_i is connected to the corresponding $F_1(b)$ interface unit X_i. There are two types of interconnections between the interface layer $F_1(b)$ and the recognition layer F_2. The *botton-up* interconnections are directed from the $F_1(b)$ units to F_2 units. Each bottom-up interconnection has an weight b_{ij}, $i = 1, \ldots, m$ and $j = 1, \ldots, n$. Similarly, each F_2 unit Y_j is connected to each $F_1(b)$ unit X_i with the help of a *top-down* interconnection with weight t_{ji}, $j = 1, \ldots, n$ and $i = 1, \ldots, m$. While the bottom-up weights are real valued, the top-down weights are binary. The notations used here relating to ART1 are given in Table 9.6.

Table 9.6. *Notational conventions*

L	Learning parameter
m	Number of input units (components in the input pattern)
n	Maximum number of cluster units (units at layer F_2)
b_{ij}	Bottom-up weight from F_1(b) unit X_i to F_2 unit Y_j, b_{ij} is real valued
t_{ji}	Top-down weight from F_2 unit Y_j to F_1(b) unit X_i, t_{ji} is binary
ρ	Vigilance parameter
s	Training pattern (binary), $s = [s_1, s_2, \ldots, s_m]$
x	$x = [x_1, x_2, \ldots, x_m]$ is the activation vector at the F_1(b) layer
$\lVert x \rVert$	Norm of vector x, $\lVert x \rVert = \sum_{i=1}^{m} x_i$

Learning As stated earlier, ART1 adopts unsupervised learning for clustering binary patterns. It permits the training set of patterns to be presented in any order. The number of clustering units in the recognition layer is flexible. If the net finds a pattern sufficiently different from existing clusters, a new cluster unit is incorporated at the output layer and the concerned pattern is placed in that cluster.

Learning a pattern starts by presenting the pattern to the $F_1(a)$ layer which passes it on to the $F_1(b)$ layer. $F_1(b)$ layer sends it to the F_2 layer through the bottom-up interconnection paths. The F_2 units compute the net inputs to them. The unit with the largest net input is the winner and has an activation of 1. All other F_2 units have 0 activations. The winning F_2 unit is the candidate to learn the input pattern. However, it is allowed to do so only if the input pattern is sufficiently close to this cluster.

Algorithm ART1-Learning

Step 0. Initialize the learning parameters and the interconnection weights

$$L > 1, 0 < \rho \leq 1,$$

$$0 < b_{ij}(0) < \frac{L}{L-1+m}, t_{ji}(0)=1, \quad \textit{for all } i=1 \textit{ to } m, j=1 \textit{ to } n$$

Step 1. **Do** Steps 2 to 14 **While** stopping criteria is not satisfied.

Step 2. **For** each training pattern ***s*** **Do** Steps 3 to 13.

Step 3. Apply the input pattern *s* to $F_1(a)$ layer, i.e., set the activations of the $F_1(a)$ units to the input training pattern ***s***.

Step 4. Set the activations of F_2 layer to all 0.

Step 5. Find the norm of ***s***.

$$\|s\| = \sum_{i=1}^{m} s_i$$

Step 6. Propagate input from $F_1(a)$ layer to interface layer $F_1(b)$ so that $x_i = s_i$, for all $i = 1$ to m.

Step 7. Compute the net inputs to each uninhibited unit of the F_2 layer.

For $j = 1$ **To** n **Do**

If $y_j \neq -1$ **Then** $y_j = \sum_{i=1}^{m} b_{ij} \times x_i$

Step 8. **While** reset is True **Do** Steps 9 To 12.

Step 9. **If** $y_j = -1$ for all cluster units, then all of them are inhibited and the pattern cannot be learnt by the net. Otherwise, find the J such that $y_J \geq y_j$ for all $j = 1$ to n. Then the Jth cluster unit is the winner. In case of a tie, take the smallest J.

Step 10. Update ***x*** : $x_i = s_i \times t_{Ji}$ for all $i = 1$ to m.

Step 11. Find the norm of ***x*** : $\|x\| = \sum_{i=1}^{m} x_i$

Step 12. Test for Reset : If $\frac{\|x\|}{\|s\|} < \rho$ Then inhibit the Jth cluster unit by setting $y_J = -1$. Go To Step 8. Otherwise $\frac{\|x\|}{\|s\|} \geq \rho$ and proceed to Step 13.

Step 13. Update the weights (top-down and bottom-up) attached to unit J of the F_2 layer.

$$b_{iJ} = \frac{L \cdot x_i}{L - 1 + \|x\|}, \text{ for all } i = 1 \text{ to } m$$

$$t_{Ji} = x_i, \text{ for all } i = 1 \text{ to } m$$

Step 14. Test for stopping condition.

Fig. 9.16. *Algorithm ART1-Learning*

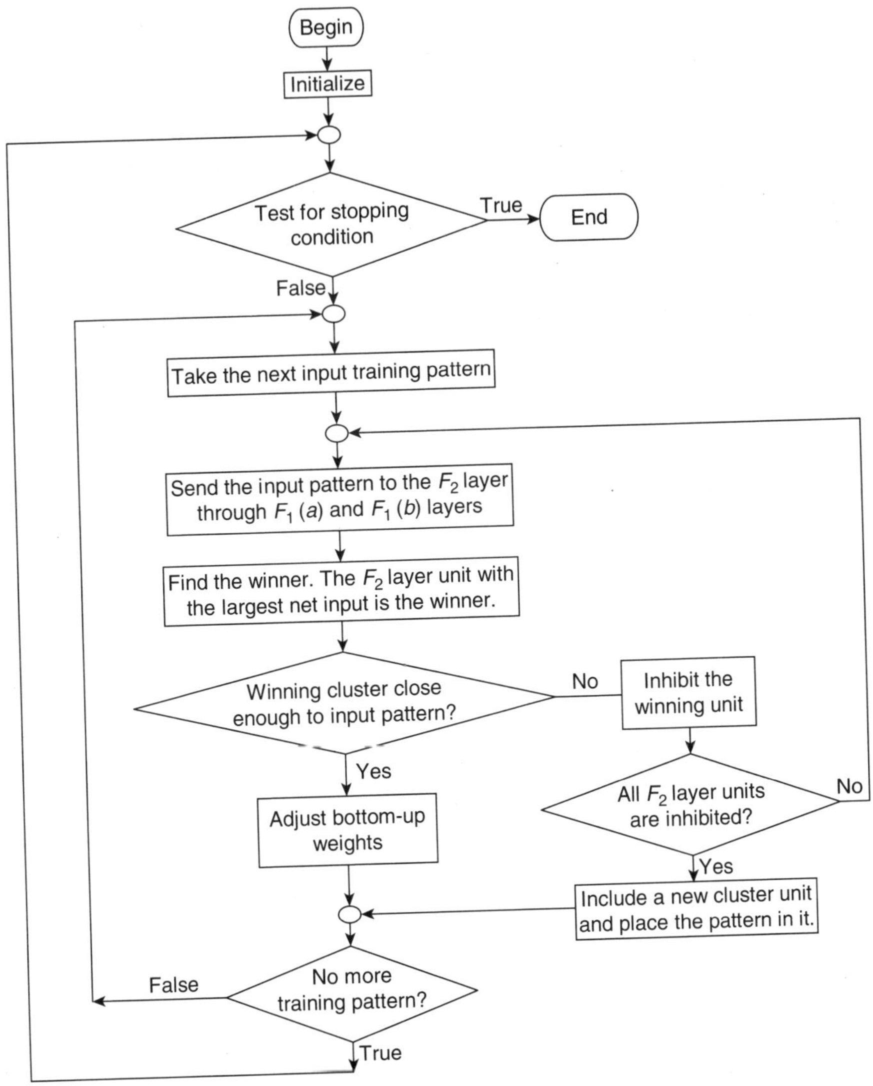

Fig. 9.17. *Flow chart of ART1 learning process*

To ensure this, the activation of the winning unit is sent back to $F_1(b)$ layer through the top-down interconnections (having binary weights). An $F_1(b)$ layer unit remains 'on' only if it receives a 1 from both the $F_1(a)$ layer and the F_2 layer. The norm $||x||$ of the vector x at the $F_1(b)$ layer gives the number of components where both the $F_1(a)$ signal and F_2 signal are 1s. The ratio of $||x||$ and norm of the input pattern $||s||$ gives the degree of similarity between the input pattern and the winning cluster. The ratio $||x||/||s||$ is known as the *match ratio*. If the ratio is sufficiently high, which is determined with the help of the vigilance parameter ρ, the winning cluster is allowed to learn the input pattern. Otherwise, it is inhibited and the net takes appropriate action.

Algorithm `ART1-Learning` (Fig. 9.16) presents the detailed procedure. The outline of the ART1 learning process is shown in Fig. 9.17 in the form of a flow chart. A few notable points regarding ART1 learning are stated below.

(i) Learning starts with removing all inhibitions from the units of the clustering layer. This is ensured in Step 4 of **Algorithm** `ART1-Learning` by setting the activations of all F_2 layer units to 0. An inhibited node has an activation of -1.
(ii) In order to prevent a node from being a winner its activation is set to -1 (Step 12).
(iii) Step 10 ensures that an interface unit X_i is 'on' only if s_i (the training signal) and t_{Ji} (the top-down signal sent by the winning unit) are both 1.
(iv) Any one of the following may be used as the stopping condition mentioned in Step 14.
   (a) A predefined maximum number of training epochs have been executed.
   (b) No interconnection weights have changed.
   (c) None of the cluster units resets.
(v) For the sake of simplicity, the activation of the winning cluster unit is not explicitly made 1. However, the computational procedure implicitly embodies this step and the results are not affected by this omission.
(vi) Step 10 concerns the event of all cluster units being inhibited. The user must specify the action to be taken under such situation. The possible options are
   (d) Add more cluster units.
   (e) Reduce vigilance.
   (f) Classify the pattern as outside of all clusters.
(vii) Table 9.7 shows the permissible range and sample values of various user-defined parameters in ART1 learning.

Table 9.7. *ART-1 parameter values*

#	Parameter	Constraints	Typical values
1.	L	$L > 1$	2
2.	ρ (vigilance parameter)	$0 < \rho \leq 1$	0.8
3.	b_{ij} (bottom-up weights)	$0 < b_{ij}(0) < \dfrac{L}{L-1+m}$	$\dfrac{1}{1+m}$
4.	t_{ji} (top-down weights)	Binary, i.e., 0, or 1	1, or 1

Example 9.5 *(Learning by ART1 net)*

Suppose we want to cluster the patterns [1, 1, 1, 0], [1, 1, 0, 0], [0, 1, 1, 0], [0, 0, 0, 1] and [0, 0, 1, 1] into a maximum of three clusters using the ART-1 learning algorithm. The following set of parameter values are used in this example.

$m = 4$	Number of units in the input layers F_1(a) and F_1(b)
$n = 3$	Number of units in the clustering layers F_2
$\rho = 0.5$	Vigilance parameter
$L = 2$	Learning parameter, used in updating the bottom-up weights
$b_{ij}(0) = \frac{1}{1+m} = 0.2$	Initial bottom-up weights (half of the maximum value allowed)
$t_{ji}(0) = 1$	Initial top-down weights (initially all set to 1)

Execution of the first epoch of ART—1 training is traced below.

Step 0. Initialize the learning parameters and the interconnection weights

$$L = 2,\ \rho = .5,\ b_{ij}(0) = \frac{1}{1+4} = 0.2,\ t_{ji}(0) = 1,\quad for\ all\ i = 1\ to\ 4,\ j = 1\ to\ 3$$

$$\therefore\ B_{4\times3} = \begin{bmatrix} .2 & .2 & .2 \\ .2 & .2 & .2 \\ .2 & .2 & .2 \\ .2 & .2 & .2 \end{bmatrix},\ T_{3\times4} = \begin{bmatrix} 1 & 1 & 1 & 1 \\ 1 & 1 & 1 & 1 \\ 1 & 1 & 1 & 1 \end{bmatrix}$$

Step 1. **Do** Steps 2 to 14 **While** stopping criteria is not satisfied.

/* Epoch No. 1, Pattern No. 1 */

Step 2. **For** each training pattern ***s*** **Do** Steps 3 to 13.

Training pattern no. 1 is ***s*** = [1, 1, 1, 0]

Step 3. Apply the input pattern *s* to F_1(*a*) layer, *i.e.*, set the activations of the F_1(*a*) units to the input training pattern ***s***.

Set the activations of the $F_1(a)$ units to ***s*** = [1, 1, 1, 0].

Step 4. Set the activations of F_2 layer to all 0.

$$y_1 = y_2 = y_3 = 0.$$

Step 5. Find the norm of ***s***.

$$\|s\| = \sum_{i=1}^{m} s_i = 3$$

Step 6. Propagate input from $F_1(a)$ layer to interface layer $F_1(b)$ so that $x_i = s_i$, for all i = 1 to m.

$$\boldsymbol{x} = \boldsymbol{s} = [1, 1, 1, 0]$$

Step 7. Compute the net inputs to each uninhibited unit of the F_2 layer.
For j = 1 **To** n **Do**

If $y_j \neq -1$ **Then** $y_j = \sum_{i=1}^{m} b_{ij} \times x_i$

$$Y = [y_1, y_2, y_3] = \boldsymbol{x} \times B = [1, 1, 1, 0] \times \begin{bmatrix} .2 & .2 & .2 \\ .2 & .2 & .2 \\ .2 & .2 & .2 \\ .2 & .2 & .2 \end{bmatrix} = [.6, .6, .6]$$

Step 8. While reset is True Do Steps 9 To 12.

Step 9. If $y_j = -1$ for all cluster units, then all of them are inhibited and the pattern cannot be learnt by the net. Otherwise, find the J such that $y_J \geq y_j$ for all j = 1 to n. Then the Jth cluster unit is the winner. In case of a tie, take the smallest J.

None of the cluster units is inhibited and all of them have the same activation value of 0.6. So winner is the lowest indexed unit, so that $J = 1$.

Step 10. Update $\boldsymbol{x}$: $x_i = s_i \times t_{Ji}$ for all i =1 to m.

$$\boldsymbol{x} = \boldsymbol{s} \cdot T_{1*} = [1, 1, 1, 0] \cdot [1, 1, 1, 1] = [1, 1, 1, 0]$$

Step 11. Find the norm of $\boldsymbol{x}$: $\|x\| = \sum_{i=1}^{m} x_i$

$$\|x\| = \sum_{i=1}^{m} x_i = 3$$

Step 12. Test for Reset : If $\frac{\|x\|}{\|s\|} < \rho$ Then inhibit the Jth cluster unit by setting $y_J = -1$. Go To Step 8. Otherwise $\frac{\|x\|}{\|s\|} \geq \rho$ and proceed to Step 13.

$\frac{\|x\|}{\|s\|} = \frac{3}{3} = 1.0 \geq 0.5 = \rho$, hence proceed to Step 13.

Step 13. Update the weights (top-down and bottom-up) attached to unit J of the F_2 layer.

$$b_{iJ} = \frac{L \cdot x_i}{L - 1 + \|x\|}, \text{ for all } i = 1 \text{ to } m$$

$$t_{Ji} = x_i, \text{ for all } i = 1 \text{ to } m$$

$b_{i1}(new) = \frac{L \cdot x_i}{L - 1 + \|x\|} = \frac{2x_i}{1 + \|x\|}$, $\therefore$ b_{11}(new) = b_{21}(new) = b_{31}(new) = 0.5, and b_{41}(new) = 0. Therefore the new bottom-up weight matrix is

$$B_{4\times3} = \begin{bmatrix} .5 & .2 & .2 \\ .5 & .2 & .2 \\ .5 & .2 & .2 \\ 0 & .2 & .2 \end{bmatrix}$$

We now update $T_{3\times4}$, the top-down weight matrix. We have, $t_{Ji} = t_{1i} = x_i$, so that T_{1*} (new) = $\boldsymbol{x}$ = [1, 1, 1, 0].

$$\therefore T_{3\times4}(new) = \begin{bmatrix} 1 & 1 & 1 & 0 \\ 1 & 1 & 1 & 1 \\ 1 & 1 & 1 & 1 \end{bmatrix}$$

This completes training with the first pattern in the first epoch.

/* Epoch No. 1, Pattern No. 2 */

Step 2. For each training pattern $\boldsymbol{s}$ Do Steps 3 to 13.
The second training pattern $\boldsymbol{s}$ = [1, 1, 0, 0]

Step 3. Apply the input pattern s to $F_1(a)$ layer, *i.e.*, set the activations of the $F_1(a)$ units to the input training pattern $\boldsymbol{s}$.

Set the activations of the $F_1(a)$ units to $\boldsymbol{s}$ = [1, 1, 0, 0].

Step 4. Set the activations of F_2 layer to all 0.

$$y_1 = y_2 = y_3 = 0.$$

Step 5. Find the norm of $\boldsymbol{s}$. $\|s\| = \sum_{i=1}^{m} s_i = 2$

Step 6. Propagate input from $F_1(a)$ layer to interface layer $F_1(b)$ so that $x_i = s_i$, for all i = 1 to m.

$$\boldsymbol{x} = \boldsymbol{s} = [1, 1, 0, 0]$$

Step 7. Compute the net inputs to each uninhibited unit of the F_2 layer.

For $j = 1$ **To** n **Do**

If $y_j \neq -1$ **Then** $y_j = \sum_{i=1}^{m} b_{ij} \times x_i$

$$Y = [y_1, y_2, y_3] = \boldsymbol{x} \times B = [1, 1, 0, 0] \times \begin{bmatrix} .5 & .2 & .2 \\ .5 & .2 & .2 \\ .5 & .2 & .2 \\ 0 & .2 & .2 \end{bmatrix} = [1, .4, .4]$$

Step 8. **While** reset is True **Do** Steps 9 To 12.

Step 9. **If** $y_j = -1$ for all cluster units, then all of them are inhibited and the pattern cannot be learnt by the net. Otherwise, find the J such that $y_J \geq y_j$ for all $j = 1$ to n. Then the Jth cluster unit is the winner. In case of a tie, take the smallest J.

None of the cluster units is inhibited and the cluster unit Y_1 has the largest activation 1. So winner is Y_1, and $J = 1$.

Step 10. Update $\boldsymbol{x}$: $x_i = s_i \times t_{Ji}$ for all $i = 1$ to m.

$$\boldsymbol{x} = \boldsymbol{s} \cdot T_{1*} = [1, 1, 0, 0] \cdot [1, 1, 1, 0] = [1, 1, 0, 0]$$

Step 11. Find the norm of $\boldsymbol{x}$: $\|x\| = \sum_{i=1}^{m} x_i$

$$\|x\| = \sum_{i=1}^{m} x_i = 2$$

Step 12. Test for Reset : If $\frac{\|x\|}{\|s\|} < \rho$ Then inhibit the Jth cluster unit by setting $y_J = -1$. Go To Step 8. Otherwise $\frac{\|x\|}{\|s\|} \geq \rho$ and proceed to Step 13.

$\frac{\|x\|}{\|s\|} = \frac{2}{2} = 1.0 \geq 0.5 = \rho$, hence proceed to Step 13.

Step 13. Update the weights (top-down and bottom-up) attached to unit J of the F_2 layer.

$$b_{iJ} = \frac{L \cdot x_i}{L - 1 + \|x\|}, \text{ for all } i = 1 \text{ to } m$$

$$t_{Ji} = x_i, \text{ for all } i = 1 \text{ to } m$$

$$b_{i1}(new) = \frac{L \cdot x_i}{L - 1 + \|x\|} = \frac{2x_i}{1 + \|x\|}, \therefore b_{11}(\text{new}) = b_{21}(\text{new}) = .67,\ b_{31}(\text{new}) = b_{41}(\text{new}) = 0.$$

Therefore the new bottom-up weight matrix is

$$B_{4\times3} = \begin{bmatrix} .67 & .2 & .2 \\ .67 & .2 & .2 \\ 0 & .2 & .2 \\ 0 & .2 & .2 \end{bmatrix}$$

We now update $T_{3\times4}$, the top-down weight matrix. We have, $t_{Ji} = t_{1i} = x_i$, so that T_{1*} (new) $= \boldsymbol{x} = [1, 1, 0, 0]$.

$$\therefore T_{3\times4}(new) = \begin{bmatrix} 1 & 1 & 0 & 0 \\ 1 & 1 & 1 & 1 \\ 1 & 1 & 1 & 1 \end{bmatrix}$$

This completes training with the second pattern in the first epoch.

/* Epoch No. 1, Pattern No. 3 */

Step 2. `For each training pattern` ***s*** `Do Steps 3 to 13.`

The third training pattern $\boldsymbol{s} = [0, 1, 1, 0]$

Step 3. `Apply the input pattern` *s* `to` $F_1(a)$ `layer,` *i.e.*, `set the activations of the` $F_1(a)$ `units to the input training pattern` ***s***.

Set the activations of the $F_1(a)$ units to [0, 1, 1, 0].

Step 4. `Set the activations of` F_2 `layer to all 0.`

$$y_1 = y_2 = y_3 = 0.$$

Step 5. `Find the norm of` ***s***. $\|s\| = \sum_{i=1}^{m} s_i = 2$

Step 6. `Propagate input from` $F_1(a)$ `layer to interface layer` $F_1(b)$ `so that` $x_i = s_i$, `for all` $i = 1$ `to` m.

$$\boldsymbol{x} = \boldsymbol{s} = [0, 1, 1, 0]$$

Step 7. `Compute the net inputs to each uninhibited unit of the` F_2 `layer.`

For $j = 1$ **To** n **Do**

If $y_j \neq -1$ **Then** $y_j = \sum_{i=1}^{m} b_{ij} \times x_i$

$$Y = [y_1, y_2, y_3] = \mathbf{x} \times B = [0, 1, 1, 0] \times \begin{bmatrix} .67 & .2 & .2 \\ .67 & .2 & .2 \\ 0 & .2 & .2 \\ 0 & .2 & .2 \end{bmatrix} = [0, .67, 0]$$

Step 8. **While** reset is True **Do** Steps 9 To 12.

Step 9. **If** $y_j = -1$ for all cluster units, then all of them are inhibited and the pattern cannot be learnt by the net. Otherwise, find the J such that $y_J \geq y_j$ for all j = 1 to n. Then the Jth cluster unit is the winner. In case of a tie, take the smallest J.

None of the cluster units is inhibited and the cluster unit Y_2 has the largest activation 0.67. So winner is Y_2, and $J = 2$.

Step 10. Update **x** : $x_i = s_i \times t_{Ji}$ for all i =1 to m.

$$\mathbf{x} = \mathbf{s} \cdot T_{2*} = [0, 1, 1, 0] \cdot [1, 1, 1, 1] = [0, 1, 1, 0]$$

Step 11. Find the norm of **x** : $\|x\| = \sum_{i=1}^{m} x_i$

$$\|x\| = \sum_{i=1}^{m} x_i = 2$$

Step 12. Test for Reset : If $\frac{\|x\|}{\|s\|} < \rho$ Then inhibit the Jth cluster unit by setting $y_J = -1$. Go To Step 8. Otherwise $\frac{\|x\|}{\|s\|} \geq \rho$ and proceed to Step 13.

$$\frac{\|x\|}{\|s\|} = \frac{2}{2} = 1.0 \geq 0.5 = \rho, \text{ hence proceed to Step 13.}$$

Step 13. Update the weights (top-down and bottom-up) attached to unit J of the F_2 layer.

$$b_{iJ} = \frac{L \cdot x_i}{L - 1 + \|x\|}, \textit{for all } i = 1 \textit{ to } m$$

$$t_{Ji} = x_i, \textit{ for all } i = 1 \textit{ to } m$$

$$b_{i2}(new) = \frac{L \cdot x_i}{L-1+\|x\|} = \frac{2x_i}{1+\|x\|}, \therefore b_{22}(\text{new}) = b_{32}(\text{new}) = .67, b_{12}(\text{new}) = b_{42}(\text{new}) = 0.$$

Therefore the new bottom-up weight matrix is

$$B_{4\times3} = \begin{bmatrix} .67 & 0 & .2 \\ .67 & .67 & .2 \\ 0 & .67 & .2 \\ 0 & 0 & .2 \end{bmatrix}$$

We now update $T_{3\times4}$, the top-down weight matrix. We have, $t_{Ji} = t_{2i} = x_i$, so that $T_{2*}(\text{new}) = \boldsymbol{x} = [0, 1, 1, 0]$.

$$\therefore T_{3\times4}(new) = \begin{bmatrix} 1 & 1 & 0 & 0 \\ 0 & 1 & 1 & 0 \\ 1 & 1 & 1 & 1 \end{bmatrix}$$

This completes training with the third pattern in the first epoch.

/* Epoch No. 1, Pattern No. 4 */

Step 2. **For** each training pattern ***s*** **Do** Steps 3 to 13.

The fourth training pattern $\boldsymbol{s} = [0, 0, 0, 1]$

Step 3. Apply the input pattern *s* to $F_1(a)$ layer, *i.e.*, set the activations of the $F_1(a)$ units to the input training pattern ***s***.

Set the activations of the $F_1(a)$ units to (0, 0, 0, 1).

Step 4. Set the activations of F_2 layer to all 0.

$$y_1 = y_2 = y_3 = 0.$$

Step 5. Find the norm of ***s***. $\|s\| = \sum_{i=1}^{m} s_i = 1$

Step 6. Propagate input from $F_1(a)$ layer to interface layer $F_1(b)$ so that $x_i = s_i$, for all i = 1 to m.

$$\boldsymbol{x} = \boldsymbol{s} = [0, 0, 0, 1]$$

Step 7. Compute the net inputs to each uninhibited unit of the F_2 layer.

For j = 1 **To** n **Do**

If $y_j \neq -1$ **Then** $y_j = \sum_{i=1}^{m} b_{ij} \times x_i$

$$Y = [y_1, y_2, y_3] = \boldsymbol{x} \times B = [0, 0, 0, 1] \times \begin{bmatrix} .67 & 0 & .2 \\ .67 & .67 & .2 \\ 0 & .67 & .2 \\ 0 & 0 & .2 \end{bmatrix} = [0, 0, .2]$$

Step 8. **While** reset is True **Do** Steps 9 To 12.

Step 9. **If** $y_j = -1$ for all cluster units, then all of them are inhibited and the pattern cannot be learnt by the net. Otherwise, find the J such that $y_J \geq y_j$ for all $j = 1$ to n. Then the Jth cluster unit is the winner. In case of a tie, take the smallest J.

None of the cluster units is inhibited and the cluster unit Y_3 has the largest activation 0.2. So winner is Y_3, and $J = 3$.

Step 10. Update $\boldsymbol{x}$: $x_i = s_i \times t_{Ji}$ for all $i = 1$ to m.

$$\boldsymbol{x} = \boldsymbol{s} \cdot T_{3*} = [0, 0, 0, 1] \cdot [1, 1, 1, 1] = [0, 0, 0, 1]$$

Step 11. Find the norm of $\boldsymbol{x}$: $\|x\| = \sum_{i=1}^{m} x_i$

$$\|x\| = \sum_{i=1}^{m} x_i = 1$$

Step 12. Test for Reset : If $\frac{\|x\|}{\|s\|} < \rho$ Then inhibit the Jth cluster unit by setting $y_J = -1$. Go To Step 8. Otherwise $\frac{\|x\|}{\|s\|} \geq \rho$ and proceed to Step 13.

$\frac{\|x\|}{\|s\|} = \frac{1}{1} = 1.0 \geq 0.5 = \rho$, hence proceed to Step 13.

Step 13. Update the weights (top-down and bottom-up) attached to unit J of the F_2 layer.

$$b_{iJ} = \frac{L \cdot x_i}{L - 1 + \|x\|}, \textit{ for all } i = 1 \textit{ to } m$$

$$t_{Ji} = x_i, \textit{ for all } i = 1 \textit{ to } m$$

$b_{i3}(new) = \frac{L \cdot x_i}{L - 1 + \|x\|} = \frac{2x_i}{1 + \|x\|}$, $\therefore$ b_{13}(new) = b_{23}(new) = b_{33}(new) = 0, b_{43}(new) = 1.

Therefore the new bottom-up weight matrix is

$$B_{4\times3}=\begin{bmatrix} .67 & 0 & 0 \\ .67 & .67 & 0 \\ 0 & .67 & 0 \\ 0 & 0 & 1 \end{bmatrix}$$

We now update $T_{3\times4}$, the top-down weight matrix. We have, $t_{Ji} = t_{3i} = x_i$, so that T_{3*} (new) = $\boldsymbol{x}$ = [0, 0, 0, 1].

$$\therefore\ T_{3\times4}(new)=\begin{bmatrix} 1 & 1 & 0 & 0 \\ 0 & 1 & 1 & 0 \\ 0 & 0 & 0 & 1 \end{bmatrix}$$

This completes training with the fourth pattern in the first epoch.

/* Epoch No. 1, Pattern No. 5 */

Step 2. **For** each training pattern ***s*** **Do** Steps 3 to 13.

The fifth training pattern $\boldsymbol{s}$ = [0, 0, 1, 1]

Step 3. Apply the input pattern *s* to $F_1(a)$ layer, *i.e.*, set the activations of the $F_1(a)$ units to the input training pattern ***s***.

Set the activations of the $F_1(a)$ units to [0, 0, 1, 1].

Step 4. Set the activations of F_2 layer to all 0.

$$y_1 = y_2 = y_3 = 0.$$

Step 5. Find the norm of ***s***. $\|s\| = \sum_{i=1}^{m} s_i = 2$

Step 6. Propagate input from $F_1(a)$ layer to interface layer $F_1(b)$ so that $x_i = s_i$, for all i = 1 to m.

$$\boldsymbol{x} = \boldsymbol{s} = [0, 0, 1, 1]$$

Step 7. Compute the net inputs to each uninhibited unit of the F_2 layer.

For j = 1 **To** n **Do**

If $y_j \neq -1$ **Then** $y_j = \sum_{i=1}^{m} b_{ij} \times x_i$

$$Y = [y_1,\ y_2,\ y_3] = \boldsymbol{x} \times B = [0, 0, 1, 1] \times \begin{bmatrix} .67 & 0 & 0 \\ .67 & .67 & 0 \\ 0 & .67 & 0 \\ 0 & 0 & 1 \end{bmatrix} = [0, .67, 1]$$

Step 8. **While** reset is True **Do** Steps 9 To 12.

Step 9. **If** $y_j = -1$ for all cluster units, then all of them are inhibited and the pattern cannot be learnt by the net. Otherwise, find the J such that $y_J \geq y_j$ for all $j = 1$ to n. Then the Jth cluster unit is the winner. In case of a tie, take the smallest J.

None of the cluster units is inhibited and the cluster unit Y_3 has the largest activation 1. So winner is Y_3, and $J = 3$.

Step 10. Update $\boldsymbol{x}$: $x_i = s_i \times t_{Ji}$ for all i =1 to m.

$$\boldsymbol{x} = \boldsymbol{s} \cdot T_{3*} = [0, 0, 1, 1] \cdot [0, 0, 0, 1] = [0, 0, 0, 1]$$

Step 11. Find the norm of $\boldsymbol{x}$: $\|x\| = \sum_{i=1}^{m} x_i$

$$\|x\| = \sum_{i=1}^{m} x_i = 1$$

Step 12. Test for Reset : If $\frac{\|x\|}{\|s\|} < \rho$ Then inhibit the Jth cluster unit by setting $y_J = -1$. Go To Step 8. Otherwise $\frac{\|x\|}{\|s\|} \geq \rho$ and proceed to Step 13.

$\frac{\|x\|}{\|s\|} = \frac{1}{2} = 0.5 \geq 0.5 = \rho$, hence proceed to Step 13.

Step 13. Update the weights (top-down and bottom-up) attached to unit J of the F_2 layer.

$$b_{iJ} = \frac{L \cdot x_i}{L - 1 + \|x\|}, \textit{ for all } i = 1 \textit{ to } m$$

$$t_{Ji} = x_i, \textit{ for all } i = 1 \textit{ to } m$$

$b_{i3}(new) = \frac{L \cdot x_i}{L - 1 + \|x\|} = \frac{2x_i}{1 + \|x\|}$, $\therefore$ $b_{13}(\text{new}) = b_{23}(\text{new}) = b_{33}(\text{new}) = 0$, $b_{43}(\text{new}) = 1$.

Therefore the new bottom-up weight matrix is

$$B_{4\times3}(new) = \begin{bmatrix} .67 & 0 & 0 \\ .67 & .67 & 0 \\ 0 & .67 & 0 \\ 0 & 0 & 1 \end{bmatrix}$$

We now update $T_{3\times4}$, the top-down weight matrix. We have, $t_{Ji} = t_{3i} = x_i$, so that T_{3*} (new) = $\boldsymbol{x}$ = [0, 0, 0, 1].

$$\therefore T_{3\times4}(new) = \begin{bmatrix} 1 & 1 & 0 & 0 \\ 0 & 1 & 1 & 0 \\ 0 & 0 & 0 & 1 \end{bmatrix}$$

This completes training with the fifth pattern in the first epoch.

Step 14. `Test for stopping condition.`

The reader may verify that this set of weights is stable and no learning takes place even on further training with the given set of patterns.

Example 9.6 *(ART1 net operation)*

Let us consider an ART-1 net with 5 input units and 3 cluster units. After some training the net attains the bottom-up and top-down weight matrices as shown below.

$$B_{5\times3} = \begin{bmatrix} .2 & 0 & .2 \\ .5 & .8 & .2 \\ .5 & .5 & .2 \\ .5 & .8 & .2 \\ .1 & 0 & .2 \end{bmatrix}, \text{ and } T_{3\times5} = \begin{bmatrix} 1 & 1 & 1 & 1 & 1 \\ 0 & 1 & 1 & 1 & 0 \\ 1 & 1 & 1 & 1 & 1 \end{bmatrix}$$

Show the behaviour of the net if it is presented with the training pattern **s** = [0, 1, 1, 1, 1]. Assume $L = 2$, and $\rho = .8$.

We start the training process from Step 2 of the ATR-1 learning procedure.

Step 2. **For** each training pattern ***s*** **Do** Steps 3 to 13.

Here ***s*** = [0, 1, 1, 1, 1]

Step 3. Apply the input pattern *s* to $F_1(a)$ layer, *i.e.*, set the activations of the $F_1(a)$ units to the input training pattern ***s***.

Set the activations of the $F_1(a)$ units to [0, 1, 1, 1, 1].

Step 4. Set the activations of F_2 layer to all 0.

$$y_1 = y_2 = y_3 = 0.$$

Step 5. Find the norm of ***s***. $\|s\| = \sum_{i=1}^{m} s_i = 4$

Step 6. Propagate input from $F_1(a)$ layer to interface layer $F_1(b)$ so that $x_i = s_i$, for all i = 1 to m.

$$\boldsymbol{x} = \boldsymbol{s} = [0, 1, 1, 1, 1]$$

Step 7. Compute the net inputs to each uninhibited unit of the F_2 layer.

For j = 1 **To** n **Do**

If $y_j \neq -1$ **Then** $y_j = \sum_{i=1}^{m} b_{ij} \times x_i$

$$Y = [y_1, y_2, y_3] = \boldsymbol{x} \times B = [0, 1, 1, 1, 0] \times \begin{bmatrix} .2 & 0 & .2 \\ .5 & .8 & .2 \\ .5 & .5 & .2 \\ .5 & .8 & .2 \\ .1 & 0 & .2 \end{bmatrix} = [1.6, 2.1, .8]$$

Step 8. **While** reset is True **Do** Steps 9 To 12.

Step 9. **If** $y_j = -1$ for all cluster units, then all of them are inhibited and the pattern cannot be learnt by the net. Otherwise, find the J such that $y_J \geq y_j$ for all j = 1 to n. Then the Jth cluster unit is the winner. In case of a tie, take the smallest J.

None of the cluster units is inhibited and the cluster unit Y_2 has the largest activation 1.6. So winner is Y_2, and $J = 2$.

Step 10. Update $\boldsymbol{x}$: $x_i = s_i \times t_{Ji}$ for all i =1 to m.

$$\boldsymbol{x} = \boldsymbol{s} \cdot T_{2*} = [0, 1, 1, 1, 1] \cdot [0, 1, 1, 1, 0] = [0, 1, 1, 1, 0]$$

Step 11. Find the norm of $\boldsymbol{x}$: $\|x\| = \sum_{i=1}^{m} x_i$

$$\|x\| = \sum_{i=1}^{m} x_i = 3$$

Step 12. Test for Reset : If $\frac{\|x\|}{\|s\|} < \rho$ Then inhibit the Jth cluster unit by setting $y_J = -1$. Go To Step 8. Otherwise $\frac{\|x\|}{\|s\|} \geq \rho$ and proceed to Step 13.

$\frac{\|x\|}{\|s\|} = \frac{3}{4} = 0.75 < 0.8 = \rho$. Hence Y_2 must be inhibited. $\therefore$ $y_2 = -1$. Reset = True, Go to Step 8.

Step 8. **While** reset is True **Do** Steps 9 To 12.

Step 9. **If** $y_j = -1$ for all cluster units, then all of them are inhibited and the pattern cannot be learnt by the net. Otherwise, find the J such that $y_J \ge y_j$ for all $j = 1$ to n. Then the Jth cluster unit is the winner. In case of a tie, take the smallest J.

Since Y_2 is inhibited, we have $[y_1, y_2, y_3] = [1.6, -1, .8]$. Therefore unit Y_1 has the largest activation 1.6 and winner is Y_1, so that $J = 1$.

Step 10. Update **x** : $x_i = s_i \times t_{Ji}$ for all $i = 1$ to m.

$$\boldsymbol{x} = \boldsymbol{s} \cdot T_{1*} = [0, 1, 1, 1, 1] \cdot [1, 1, 1, 1, 1] = [0, 1, 1, 1, 1]$$

Step 11. Find the norm of **x** : $\|x\| = \sum_{i=1}^{m} x_i$

$$\|x\| = \sum_{i=1}^{m} x_i = 4$$

Step 12. Test for Reset : If $\frac{\|x\|}{\|s\|} < \rho$ Then inhibit the Jth cluster unit by setting $y_J = -1$. Go To Step 8. Otherwise $\frac{\|x\|}{\|s\|} \ge \rho$ and proceed to Step 13.

$\frac{\|x\|}{\|s\|} = \frac{4}{4} = 1 > 0.8 = \rho$, hence Reset = False. Go to Step 13.

Step 13. Update the weights (top-down and bottom-up) attached to unit J of the F_2 layer.

$$b_{iJ} = \frac{L \cdot x_i}{L - 1 + \|x\|}, \textit{for all } i = 1 \textit{ to } m$$

$$t_{Ji} = x_i, \textit{ for all } i = 1 \textit{ to } m$$

$b_{i1}(new) = \frac{L \cdot x_i}{L - 1 + \|x\|} = \frac{2x_i}{1 + \|x\|}$, $\therefore$ $b_{11}(\text{new}) = 0$, and $b_{21}(\text{new}) = b_{31}(\text{new}) = b_{41}(\text{new}) = b_{51}(\text{new}) = .4$.

Therefore the new bottom-up weight matrix is

$$B_{5\times3} = \begin{bmatrix} .2 & 0 & .2 \\ .4 & .8 & .2 \\ .4 & .5 & .2 \\ .4 & .8 & .2 \\ .4 & 0 & .2 \end{bmatrix}$$

We now update $T_{3\times5}$, the top-down weight matrix. We have, $t_{Ji} = t_{1i} = x_i$, so that T_{1*} (new) $= x = [0, 1, 1, 1, 1]$.

$$\therefore T_{3\times5} = \begin{bmatrix} 0 & 1 & 1 & 1 & 1 \\ 0 & 1 & 1 & 1 & 0 \\ 1 & 1 & 1 & 1 & 1 \end{bmatrix}$$

This completes training with the given pattern **s** = (0, 1, 1, 1, 1).

CHAPTER SUMMARY

Basic concepts of competitive networks and brief descriptions of certain elementary competitive networks are discussed in this chapter. The main points are summarized below.

- A competitive neural net is a clustering net that selects the output clustering unit through competition. Usually the competition is in terms of the distance between the input pattern and the weight vector associated with the output unit. Quite frequently, the distance is measured either as the Euclidean distance between two points in a hyperplane or the dot product of the input vector and the weight vector.
- MAXNET is the simplest competitive ANN. It is a fully connected network with symmetric interconnections and self-loops. All the links have the same, fixed, inhibitory weight $-\delta$. Each unit has a self-loop. The weight of a self-loop is 1. A MAXNET do not required to be trained because all weights are fixed. During application, as the MAXNET is presented with an input vector, it iteratively updates the activations of the cluster units until all units except one are deactivated. The only remaining positively activated unit is the winner.
- Kohonen's self-organizing map (SOM) works on the principle of winner-takes-all and follows unsupervised learning. Here the weight vector associated with a cluster unit acts as the exemplar. During learning, the cluster unit whose weight vector is closest to the given input pattern is declared the winner. The weight vectors of all cluster units in the neighbourhood of the winner are updated. During application, the input pattern is compared with the exemplar / code vector. The unit whose code vector is at a least distance from the input pattern is the winner.
- Learning Vector Quantization (LVQ) nets are also based on the winner-takes-all strategy, though, unlike Kohonen's SOM, LVQ follows supervised learning. There are as many input units as the number of components in the input patterns and each output unit represents a known cluster. During each epoch of training, the LVQ net adjusts its weights to accommodate the training vectors on the basis of the known clusters. During training, the net identifies the code vector ***w*** closest to the input vector ***s***. If ***s*** and ***w*** are from the same cluster, then ***w*** is moved closer to ***s***. Otherwise, ***w*** is moved away from ***x***. During application, the cluster unit whose code vector is at a least distance from the input pattern is the winner.
- Adaptive Resonance Theory (ART) nets were introduced to resolve the *stability-plasticity* dilemma. These nets learn through unsupervised learning where the input patterns may be presented in any order. Moreover, ART nets allow the user to control the degree of similarity among the patterns placed in the same cluster. It provides a mechanism to include a new cluster unit for an input pattern which is sufficiently different from all the exemplars of the clusters corresponding to the existing cluster units. Hence, unlike other ANNs, ART nets are capable of adaptive expansion of the output layer of clustering units subject to some upper bound. ART

nets are able to learn only in their resonant states. The ART net is in resonant state when the current input vector matches the winner code-vector (exemplar) so close that a *reset signal* is not generated. The reset signal inhibits the ART to learn. There are two kinds of ARTs, *viz.*, ART1 and ART2. ART1 works on binary patterns and ART2 is designed for patterns with real, or continuous, values.

SOLVED PROBLEMS

Problem 9.1 *(Clustering application of SOM)* Consider the SOM constructed in Example 9.2. The weight matrix of the resultant SOM is given by

$$W = \begin{bmatrix} 0 & 1 \\ 0.6 & 0.6 \\ 1 & 0 \end{bmatrix}$$

Fig. 9.18 shows the SOM obtained for the given clustering problem.

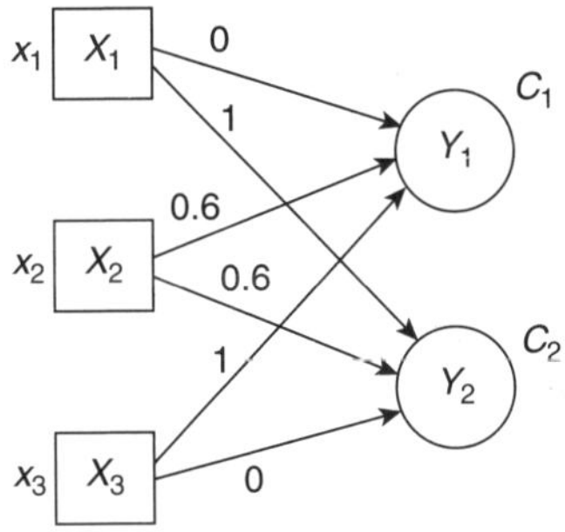

Fig. 9.18. *The SOM obtained in Example 9.2*

Test the performance of this net with the input vectors [1, 0, 0], [0, 0, 1], [1, 1, 0] and [0, 1, 1].

Solution 9.1 Table 9.8 shows the calculations to identify the cluster to which each vector belongs, the decision being made on the basis of Winner-takes-all policy. It is seen that the SOM clusters the patterns (1, 0, 0) and (1, 1, 0) at unit C_2 and the patterns (0, 0, 1) and (0, 1, 1) at unit C_1 (Fig. 9.19). Considering the relative positions of the vectors in a 3-dimensional space, this is the correct clustering for these patterns.

Table 9.8. *Calculations to identify the cluster*

#	Input Patterns $s = [x_1, x_2, x_3]$	Squared Euclidean Distance		Winner
		$D(1)$	$D(2)$	
1	[1, 0, 0]	2.36	.36	C_2
2	[0, 0, 1]	.36	2.36	C_1
3	[1, 1, 0]	2.16	.16	C_2
4	[0, 1, 1]	.16	2.16	C_1

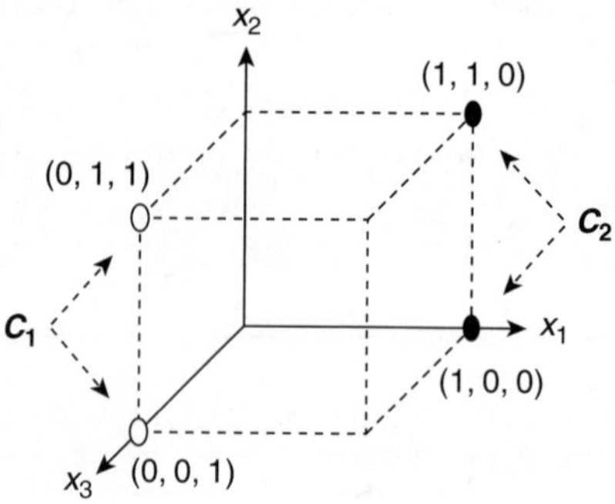

Fig. 9.19. *Clusters formed*

Problem 9.2 *(Creating and training an ART1 net)* Create an ART-1 net initially with 7 inputs and 3 clusters. Then apply the ART-1 procedure to train the net with the following patterns: [1, 1, 1, 1, 0, 0, 0], [1, 1, 1, 0, 0, 0, 0], [0, 0, 0, 0, 0, 1, 1], [0, 0, 0, 0, 1, 1, 1], [0, 0, 1, 1, 1, 0, 0] and [0, 0, 0, 1, 0, 0, 0].

Solution 9.2 Execution of the first epoch of ART-1 training is traced below.

Step 0. Initialize the learning parameters and the interconnection weights

$$L = 2, \rho = .9, b_{ij}(0) = \frac{1}{1+7} = 0.125, t_{ji}(0) = 1, \quad for\,all\, i = 1\, to\, 7, j = 1\, to\, 3$$

$$\therefore B_{7\times 3} = \begin{bmatrix} .125 & .125 & .125 \\ .125 & .125 & .125 \\ .125 & .125 & .125 \\ .125 & .125 & .125 \\ .125 & .125 & .125 \\ .125 & .125 & .125 \\ .125 & .125 & .125 \end{bmatrix}, T_{3\times 7} = \begin{bmatrix} 1 & 1 & 1 & 1 & 1 & 1 & 1 \\ 1 & 1 & 1 & 1 & 1 & 1 & 1 \\ 1 & 1 & 1 & 1 & 1 & 1 & 1 \end{bmatrix}$$

Step 1. **Do** Steps 2 to 14 **While** stopping criteria is not satisfied.

/* Epoch No. 1, Pattern No. 1 */

Step 2. **For** each training pattern **s** **Do** Steps 3 to 13.

The first training pattern **s** = [1, 1, 1, 1, 0, 0, 0]

Step 3. Apply the input pattern **s** to $F_1(a)$ layer, *i.e.*, set the activations of the $F_1(a)$ units to the input training pattern **s**.

Set the activations of the $F_1(a)$ units to [1, 1, 1, 1, 0, 0, 0].

Step 4. Set the activations of F_2 layer to all 0.

$$y_1 = y_2 = y_3 = 0.$$

Step 5. Find the norm of **s**. $\|s\| = \sum_{i=1}^{m} s_i = 4$

Step 6. Propagate input from $F_1(a)$ layer to interface layer $F_1(b)$ so that $x_i = s_i$, for all i = 1 to m.

$$x = s = [1, 1, 1, 1, 0, 0, 0]$$

Step 7. Compute the net inputs to each uninhibited unit of the F_2 layer.

For j = 1 **To** n **Do**

If $y_j \neq -1$ **Then** $y_j = \sum_{i=1}^{m} b_{ij} \times x_i$

$$Y = [y_1, y_2, y_3] = x \times B = [1, 1, 1, 1, 0, 0, 0] \times \begin{bmatrix} .125 & .125 & .125 \\ .125 & .125 & .125 \\ .125 & .125 & .125 \\ .125 & .125 & .125 \\ .125 & .125 & .125 \\ .125 & .125 & .125 \\ .125 & .125 & .125 \end{bmatrix} = [.5, .5, .5]$$

Step 8. **While** reset is True **Do** Steps 9 To 12.

Step 9. **If** $y_j = -1$ for all cluster units, then all of them are inhibited and the pattern cannot be learnt by the net. Otherwise, find the J such that $y_J \geq y_j$ for all j = 1 to n. Then the Jth cluster unit is the winner. In case of a tie, take the smallest J.

None of the cluster units is inhibited and all of them have the same activation value of 0.5. So the winner is the lowest indexed unit, so that $J = 1$.

Step 10. Update $\boldsymbol{x}$: $x_i = s_i \times t_{Ji}$ for all i =1 to m.

$$x = s \cdot T_{1*} = [1, 1, 1, 1, 0, 0, 0] \cdot [1, 1, 1, 1, 1, 1, 1] = [1, 1, 1, 1, 0, 0, 0].$$

Step 11. Find the norm of $\boldsymbol{x}$: $\|x\| = \sum_{i=1}^{m} x_i$

$$\|x\| = \sum_{i=1}^{m} x_i = 4$$

Step 12. Test for Reset : If $\frac{\|x\|}{\|s\|} < \rho$ Then inhibit the Jth cluster unit by setting $y_J = -1$. Go To Step 8. Otherwise $\frac{\|x\|}{\|s\|} \geq \rho$ and proceed to Step 13.

$\frac{\|x\|}{\|s\|}=\frac{4}{4}=1.0 \geq 0.9=\rho$, hence Reset = False. Proceed to Step 13.

Step 13. Update the weights (top-down and bottom-up) attached to unit J of the F_2 layer.

$$b_{iJ} = \frac{L \cdot x_i}{L-1+\|x\|}, \text{ for all } i = 1 \text{ to } m$$

$$t_{Ji} = x_i, \text{ for all } i = 1 \text{ to } m$$

$b_{i1}(new) = \frac{L \cdot x_i}{L-1+\|x\|} = \frac{2x_i}{1+\|x\|}$, $\therefore$ b_{11}(new) = b_{21}(new) = b_{31}(new) = b_{41}(new) = 0.4, and b_{51}(new) = b_{61}(new) = b_{71}(new) = 0.

Therefore, the new bottom-up weight matrix is

$$B_{7\times3} = \begin{bmatrix} .4 & .125 & .125 \\ .4 & .125 & .125 \\ .4 & .125 & .125 \\ .4 & .125 & .125 \\ 0 & .125 & .125 \\ 0 & .125 & .125 \\ 0 & .125 & .125 \end{bmatrix}$$

We now update $T_{3\times7}$, the top-down weight matrix. We have, $t_{Ji} = t_{1i} = x_i$, so that T_{1*} (new) = $\boldsymbol{x}$ = [1, 1, 1, 1, 0, 0, 0].

$$\therefore T_{3\times7} = \begin{bmatrix} 1 & 1 & 1 & 1 & 0 & 0 & 0 \\ 1 & 1 & 1 & 1 & 1 & 1 & 1 \\ 1 & 1 & 1 & 1 & 1 & 1 & 1 \end{bmatrix}$$

This completes training with the first pattern in the first epoch.

/* Epoch No. 1, Pattern No. 2 */

Step 2. **For** each training pattern **s** **Do** Steps 3 to 13.

The second training pattern **s** = [1, 1, 1, 0, 0, 0, 0]

Step 3. Apply the input pattern **s** to $F_1(a)$ layer, *i.e.*, set the activations of the $F_1(a)$ units to the input training pattern **s**.

Set the activations of the $F_1(a)$ units to [1, 1, 1, 0, 0, 0, 0].

Step 4. Set the activations of F_2 layer to all 0.

$$y_1 = y_2 = y_3 = 0.$$

Step 5. Find the norm of **s**. $\|s\| = \sum_{i=1}^{m} s_i = 3$

Step 6. Propagate input from $F_1(a)$ layer to interface layer $F_1(b)$ so that $x_i = s_i$, for all $i = 1$ to m.

$$\boldsymbol{x} = \boldsymbol{s} = [1, 1, 1, 0, 0, 0, 0]$$

Step 7. Compute the net inputs to each uninhibited unit of the F_2 layer.
For $j = 1$ **To** n **Do**

If $y_j \neq -1$ **Then** $y_j = \sum_{i=1}^{m} b_{ij} \times x_i$

$$Y = [y_1, y_2, y_3] = \boldsymbol{x} \times B = [1, 1, 1, 0, 0, 0, 0] \times \begin{bmatrix} .4 & .125 & .125 \\ .4 & .125 & .125 \\ .4 & .125 & .125 \\ .4 & .125 & .125 \\ 0 & .125 & .125 \\ 0 & .125 & .125 \\ 0 & .125 & .125 \end{bmatrix}$$

$$= [1.2, .375, .375]$$

Step 8. **While** reset is True **Do** Steps 9 To 12.

Step 9. **If** $y_j = -1$ for all cluster units, then all of them are inhibited and the pattern cannot be learnt by the net. Otherwise, find the J such that $y_J \geq y_j$ for all $j = 1$ to n. Then the Jth cluster unit is the winner. In case of a tie, take the smallest J.

None of the cluster units is inhibited and y_1 has the highest activation value of 1.2. So winner is the lowest indexed unit Y_1, so that $J = 1$.

Step 10. Update $\boldsymbol{x}$: $x_i = s_i \times t_{Ji}$ for all $i = 1$ to m.

$$\boldsymbol{x} = \boldsymbol{s} \cdot T_{1*} = [1, 1, 1, 0, 0, 0, 0] \cdot [1, 1, 1, 1, 0, 0, 0] = [1, 1, 1, 0, 0, 0, 0].$$

Step 11. Find the norm of $\boldsymbol{x}$: $\|x\| = \sum_{i=1}^{m} x_i$

$$\|x\| = \sum_{i=1}^{m} x_i = 3$$

Step 12. Test for Reset : If $\frac{\|x\|}{\|s\|} < \rho$ Then inhibit the Jth cluster unit by setting $y_J = -1$. Go To Step 8. Otherwise $\frac{\|x\|}{\|s\|} \geq \rho$ and proceed to Step 13.

$\frac{\|x\|}{\|s\|}=\frac{3}{3}=1.0 \geq 0.9=\rho$, hence Reset = False. Proceed to Step 13.

Step 13. `Update the weights (top-down and bottom-up) attached to unit` J `of the` F_2 `layer.`

$$b_{iJ} = \frac{L \cdot x_i}{L-1+\|x\|}, \text{ for all } i = 1 \text{ to } m$$

$$t_{Ji} = x_i, \text{ for all } i = 1 \text{ to } m$$

$b_{i1}(new)=\frac{L \cdot x_i}{L-1+\|x\|}=\frac{2x_i}{1+\|x\|}$, $\therefore$ b_{11}(new) = b_{21}(new) = b_{31}(new) = 0.5, and b_{41}(new) = $b_{51}(\text{new}) = b_{61}(\text{new}) = b_{71}(\text{new}) = 0$.

Therefore the new bottom-up weight matrix is

$$B_{7\times3} = \begin{bmatrix} .5 & .125 & .125 \\ .5 & .125 & .125 \\ .5 & .125 & .125 \\ 0 & .125 & .125 \\ 0 & .125 & .125 \\ 0 & .125 & .125 \\ 0 & .125 & .125 \end{bmatrix}$$

We now update $T_{3\times7}$, the top-down weight matrix. We have, $t_{Ji} = t_{1i} = x_i$, so that T_{1*} (new) = $\boldsymbol{x}$ = [1, 1, 1, 0, 0, 0, 0].

$$\therefore T_{3\times7} = \begin{bmatrix} 1 & 1 & 1 & 0 & 0 & 0 & 0 \\ 1 & 1 & 1 & 1 & 1 & 1 & 1 \\ 1 & 1 & 1 & 1 & 1 & 1 & 1 \end{bmatrix}$$

This completes training with the second pattern in the first epoch.

/* Epoch No. 1, Pattern No. 3 */

Similarly, training with the third training pattern **s** = [0, 0, 0, 0, 0, 1, 1] yields the bottom-up and top-down weight matrices as follows:

$$B_{7\times3} = \begin{bmatrix} .5 & 0 & .125 \\ .5 & 0 & .125 \\ .5 & 0 & .125 \\ 0 & 0 & .125 \\ 0 & 0 & .125 \\ 0 & .67 & .125 \\ 0 & .67 & .125 \end{bmatrix}$$

$$\therefore T_{3\times7} = \begin{bmatrix} 1 & 1 & 1 & 0 & 0 & 0 & 0 \\ 0 & 0 & 0 & 0 & 0 & 1 & 1 \\ 1 & 1 & 1 & 1 & 1 & 1 & 1 \end{bmatrix}$$

Now we proceed to train with the fourth pattern [0, 0, 0, 0, 1, 1, 1].

/* Epoch No. 1, Pattern No. 4 */

Step 2. **For** each training pattern ***s*** **Do** Steps 3 to 13.

The fourth training pattern ***s*** = [0, 0, 0, 0, 1, 1, 1]

Step 3. Apply the input pattern ***s*** to $F_1(a)$ layer, *i.e.*, set the activations of the $F_1(a)$ units to the input training pattern ***s***.

Set the activations of the $F_1(a)$ units to [0, 0, 0, 0, 1, 1, 1].

Step 4. Set the activations of F_2 layer to all 0.

$$y_1 = y_2 = y_3 = 0.$$

Step 5. Find the norm of ***s***. $\|s\| = \sum_{i=1}^{m} s_i = 3$

Step 6. Propagate input from $F_1(a)$ layer to interface layer $F_1(b)$ so that $x_i = s_i$, for all $i = 1$ to m.

$$\boldsymbol{x} = \boldsymbol{s} = [0, 0, 0, 0, 1, 1, 1]$$

Step 7. Compute the net inputs to each uninhibited unit of the F_2 layer.

For $j = 1$ **To** n **Do**

If $y_j \neq -1$ **Then** $y_j = \sum_{i=1}^{m} b_{ij} \times x_i$

$$Y = [y_1, y_2, y_3] = \boldsymbol{x} \times B = [0, 0, 0, 0, 1, 1, 1] \times \begin{bmatrix} .5 & 0 & .125 \\ .5 & 0 & .125 \\ .5 & 0 & .125 \\ 0 & 0 & .125 \\ 0 & 0 & .125 \\ 0 & .67 & .125 \\ 0 & .67 & .125 \end{bmatrix}$$

$$= [0, .1.34, .375]$$

Step 8. **While** reset is True **Do** Steps 9 To 12.

Step 9. **If** $y_j = -1$ for all cluster units, then all of them are inhibited and the pattern cannot be learnt by the net. Otherwise, find the J such that $y_J \geq y_j$ for all $j = 1$ to n. Then the Jth cluster unit is the winner. In case of a tie, take the smallest J.

None of the cluster units is inhibited and y_2 has the highest activation value of 1.34. So winner is the lowest indexed unit Y_2, so that $J = 2$.

Step 10. Update $\mathbf{x}$: $x_i = s_i \times t_{Ji}$ for all $i = 1$ to m.

$$\mathbf{x} = \mathbf{s} \cdot T_{2*} = [0, 0, 0, 0, 1, 1, 1] \cdot [0, 0, 0, 0, 0, 1, 1] = [0, 0, 0, 0, 0, 1, 1].$$

Step 11. Find the norm of $\mathbf{x}$: $\|x\| = \sum_{i=1}^{m} x_i$

$$\|x\| = \sum_{i=1}^{m} x_i = 2$$

Step 12. Test for Reset : If $\frac{\|x\|}{\|s\|} < \rho$ Then inhibit the Jth cluster unit by setting $y_J = -1$. Go To Step 8. Otherwise $\frac{\|x\|}{\|s\|} \geq \rho$ and proceed to Step 13.

$\frac{\|x\|}{\|s\|} = \frac{2}{3} = 0.67 < 0.9 = \rho$, hence inhibit cluster unit 2 by making $y_2 = -1$. Reset = True. Go to Step 9.

Step 9. **If** $y_j = -1$ for all cluster units, then all of them are inhibited and the pattern cannot be learnt by the net. Otherwise, find the J such that $y_J \geq y_j$ for all $j = 1$ to n. Then the Jth cluster unit is the winner. In case of a tie, take the smallest J.

Cluster units Y_2 is inhibited and between Y_1 and Y_3, Y_3 has the highest activation value of 0.375. So winner is the lowest indexed unit Y_3, so that $J = 3$.

Step 10. Update $\mathbf{x}$: $x_i = s_i \times t_{Ji}$ for all $i = 1$ to m.

$$\mathbf{x} = \mathbf{s} \cdot T_{3*} = [0, 0, 0, 0, 1, 1, 1] \cdot [1, 1, 1, 1, 1, 1, 1] = [0, 0, 0, 0, 1, 1, 1].$$

Step 11. Find the norm of $\mathbf{x}$: $\|x\| = \sum_{i=1}^{m} x_i$

$$\|x\| = \sum_{i=1}^{m} x_i = 3$$

Step 12. Test for Reset : If $\frac{\|x\|}{\|s\|} < \rho$ Then inhibit the Jth cluster unit by setting $y_J = -1$. Go To Step 8. Otherwise $\frac{\|x\|}{\|s\|} \geq \rho$ and proceed to Step 13.

$\frac{\|x\|}{\|s\|} = \frac{3}{3} = 1.0 \geq 0.9 = \rho$, hence Reset = False. Go to Step 13.

Step 13. Update the weights (top-down and bottom-up) attached to unit J of the F_2 layer.

$$b_{iJ} = \frac{L \cdot x_i}{L - 1 + \|x\|}, \, for\, all\ i = 1\ to\ m$$

$$t_{Ji} = x_i, \, for\, all\ i = 1\ to\ m$$

$b_{i1}(new) = \frac{L \cdot x_i}{L - 1 + \|x\|} = \frac{2x_i}{1 + \|x\|}$, $\therefore b_{13}(\text{new}) = b_{23}(\text{new}) = b_{33}(\text{new}) = b_{43}(\text{new}) = 0$. $b_{53}(\text{new}) = b_{63}(\text{new}) = b_{73}(\text{new}) = 0.5$.

Therefore the new bottom-up weight matrix is

$$B_{7\times3} = \begin{bmatrix} .5 & 0 & 0 \\ .5 & 0 & 0 \\ .5 & 0 & 0 \\ 0 & 0 & 0 \\ 0 & 0 & .5 \\ 0 & .67 & .5 \\ 0 & .67 & .5 \end{bmatrix}$$

We now update $T_{3\times7}$, the top-down weight matrix. We have, $t_{Ji} = t_{1i} = x_i$, so that T_{3*} (new) $= \boldsymbol{x} = [0, 0, 0, 0, 1, 1, 1]$.

$$\therefore T_{3\times7} = \begin{bmatrix} 1 & 1 & 1 & 0 & 0 & 0 & 0 \\ 0 & 0 & 0 & 0 & 0 & 1 & 1 \\ 0 & 0 & 0 & 0 & 1 & 1 & 1 \end{bmatrix}$$

This completes training with the fourth pattern in the first epoch.

/* Epoch No. 1, Pattern No. 5 */

Step 2. **For** each training pattern ***s*** **Do** Steps 3 to 13.

The fifth training pattern is $\boldsymbol{s} = [0, 0, 1, 1, 1, 0, 0]$

Step 3. Apply the input pattern ***s*** to $F_1(a)$ layer, *i.e.*, set the activations of the $F_1(a)$ units to the input training pattern ***s***.

Set the activations of the $F_1(a)$ units to (0, 0, 1, 1, 1, 0, 0).

Step 4. Set the activations of F_2 layer to all 0.

$$y_1 = y_2 = y_3 = 0.$$

Step 5. Find the norm of **s**. $\|s\| = \sum_{i=1}^{m} s_i = 3$

Step 6. Propagate input from $F_1(a)$ layer to interface layer $F_1(b)$ so that $x_i = s_i$, for all $i = 1$ to m.

$$\mathbf{x} = \mathbf{s} = [0, 0, 1, 1, 1, 0, 0]$$

Step 7. Compute the net inputs to each uninhibited unit of the F_2 layer.

For $j = 1$ **To** n **Do**

If $y_j \neq -1$ **Then** $y_j = \sum_{i=1}^{m} b_{ij} \times x_i$

$$Y = [y_1, y_2, y_3] = \mathbf{x} \times B = [0, 0, 1, 1, 1, 0, 0] \times \begin{bmatrix} .5 & 0 & 0 \\ .5 & 0 & 0 \\ .5 & 0 & 0 \\ 0 & 0 & 0 \\ 0 & 0 & .5 \\ 0 & .67 & .5 \\ 0 & .67 & .5 \end{bmatrix}$$

$$= [.5, 0, .5]$$

Step 8. **While** reset is True **Do** Steps 9 To 12.

Step 9. **If** $y_j = -1$ for all cluster units, then all of them are inhibited and the pattern cannot be learnt by the net. Otherwise, find the J such that $y_J \geq y_j$ for all $j = 1$ to n. Then the Jth cluster unit is the winner. In case of a tie, take the smallest J.

None of the cluster units is inhibited and both Y_1 and Y_3 has the highest activation value of .5. So winner is the lowest indexed unit Y_1, so that $J = 1$.

Step 10. Update **x** : $x_i = s_i \times t_{Ji}$ for all $i = 1$ to m.

$$\mathbf{x} = \mathbf{s} \cdot T_{1*} = [0, 0, 1, 1, 1, 0, 0] \cdot [1, 1, 1, 0, 0, 0, 0] = [0, 0, 1, 0, 0, 0, 0].$$

Step 11. Find the norm of **x** : $\|x\| = \sum_{i=1}^{m} x_i$

$$\|x\| = \sum_{i=1}^{m} x_i = 1$$

Step 12. Test for Reset : If $\frac{\|x\|}{\|s\|} < \rho$ Then inhibit the *J*th cluster unit by setting $y_J = -1$. Go To Step 8. Otherwise $\frac{\|x\|}{\|s\|} \geq \rho$ and proceed to Step 13.

$\frac{\|x\|}{\|s\|} = \frac{1}{3} = 0.33 < 0.9 = \rho$, hence inhibit cluster unit 1 by making $y_1 = -1$. Reset = True.

Go to Step 9.

Step 9. **If** $y_j = -1$ for all cluster units, then all of them are inhibited and the pattern cannot be learnt by the net. Otherwise, find the *J* such that $y_J \geq y_j$ for all $j = 1$ to n. Then the *J*th cluster unit is the winner. In case of a tie, take the smallest *J*.

Cluster unit Y_1 is inhibited and between Y_2 and Y_3, Y_3 has the highest activation value of 0.5. So winner is the lowest indexed unit Y_3, and $J = 3$.

Step 10. Update **x** : $x_i = s_i \times t_{Ji}$ for all $i = 1$ to m.

$$\boldsymbol{x} = \boldsymbol{s} \cdot T_{3*} = [0, 0, 1, 1, 1, 0, 0] \cdot [0, 0, 0, 0, 1, 1, 1] = [0, 0, 0, 0, 1, 0, 0].$$

Step 11. Find the norm of **x** : $\|x\| = \sum_{i=1}^{m} x_i = 1$

Step 12. Test for Reset : If $\frac{\|x\|}{\|s\|} < \rho$ Then inhibit the *J*th cluster unit by setting $y_J = -1$. Go To Step 8. Otherwise $\frac{\|x\|}{\|s\|} \geq \rho$ and proceed to Step 13.

$\frac{\|x\|}{\|s\|} = \frac{1}{3} = .33 \leq 0.9 = \rho$, hence Reset = True. Go to Step 9.

Step 9. **If** $y_j = -1$ for all cluster units, then all of them are inhibited and the pattern cannot be learnt by the net. Otherwise, find the *J* such that $y_J \geq y_j$ for all $j = 1$ to n. Then the *J*th cluster unit is the winner. In case of a tie, take the smallest *J*.

Cluster units Y_1 and Y_3 are inhibited so that Y_2 has the highest activation value of 0. So winner is the unit Y_2, so that $J = 2$.

Step 10. Update $\boldsymbol{x}$: $x_i = s_i \times t_{Ji}$ for all i =1 to m.

$$\boldsymbol{x} = \boldsymbol{s} \cdot T_{2*} = [0, 0, 1, 1, 1, 0, 0] \cdot [0, 0, 0, 0, 0, 1, 1] = [0, 0, 0, 0, 0, 0, 0].$$

Step 11. Find the norm of $\boldsymbol{x}$: $\|x\| = \sum_{i=1}^{m} x_i = 0$

Step 12. Test for Reset : If $\frac{\|x\|}{\|s\|} < \rho$ Then inhibit the Jth cluster unit by setting $y_J = -1$. Go To Step 8. Otherwise $\frac{\|x\|}{\|s\|} \geq \rho$ and proceed to Step 13.

$\frac{\|x\|}{\|s\|} = \frac{0}{3} = 0 \leq 0.9 = \rho$, hence Reset = True. Go to Step 9.

Step 9. **If** $y_j = -1$ for all cluster units, then all of them are inhibited and the pattern cannot be learnt by the net. Otherwise, find the J such that $y_J \geq y_j$ for all $j = 1$ to n. Then the Jth cluster unit is the winner. In case of a tie, take the smallest J.

All cluster units are now inhibited. So we introduce a new cluster unit Y_4. The modified bottom-up and top-down weight matrices are now:

$$B_{7\times4} = \begin{bmatrix} .5 & 0 & 0 & .125 \\ .5 & 0 & 0 & .125 \\ .5 & 0 & 0 & .125 \\ 0 & 0 & 0 & .125 \\ 0 & 0 & .5 & .125 \\ 0 & .67 & .5 & .125 \\ 0 & .67 & .5 & .125 \end{bmatrix}$$

$$\therefore T_{4\times7} = \begin{bmatrix} 1 & 1 & 1 & 0 & 0 & 0 & 0 \\ 0 & 0 & 0 & 0 & 0 & 1 & 1 \\ 0 & 0 & 0 & 0 & 1 & 1 & 1 \\ 1 & 1 & 1 & 1 & 1 & 1 & 1 \end{bmatrix}$$

As the cluster units Y_1, Y_2, and Y_3 are all inhibited the remaining new unit Y_4 has the highest activation value of 0.375. So winner is the unit Y_4, so that $J = 4$.

Step 10. Update $\boldsymbol{x}$: $x_i = s_i \times t_{Ji}$ for all i =1 to m.

$$\boldsymbol{x} = \boldsymbol{s} \cdot T_{4*} = [0, 0, 1, 1, 1, 0, 0] \cdot [1, 1, 1, 1, 1, 1, 1] = [0, 0, 1, 1, 1, 0, 0].$$

Step 11. Find the norm of $\boldsymbol{x}$: $\|x\| = \sum_{i=1}^{m} x_i = 3$

Step 12. Test for Reset : If $\frac{\|x\|}{\|s\|} < \rho$ Then inhibit the Jth cluster unit by setting $y_J = -1$. Go To Step 8. Otherwise $\frac{\|x\|}{\|s\|} \geq \rho$ and proceed to Step 13.

$\frac{\|x\|}{\|s\|} = \frac{3}{3} = 1 \geq 0.9 = \rho$, hence Reset = False. Go to Step 13.

Step 13. Update the weights (top-down and bottom-up) attached to unit J of the F_2 layer.

$$b_{iJ} = \frac{L \cdot x_i}{L - 1 + \|x\|}, \textit{ for all } i = 1 \textit{ to } m$$

$$t_{Ji} = x_i, \textit{ for all } i = 1 \textit{ to } m$$

$b_{i4}(new) = \frac{L \cdot x_i}{L - 1 + \|x\|} = \frac{2x_i}{1 + \|x\|}$, $\therefore$ $b_{14}(\text{new}) = b_{24}(\text{new}) = b_{64}(\text{new}) = b_{74}(\text{new}) = 0$. $b_{34}(\text{new}) = b_{44}(\text{new}) = b_{54}(\text{new}) = 0.5$.

Therefore the new bottom-up weight matrix is

$$B_{7\times4} = \begin{bmatrix} .5 & 0 & 0 & 0 \\ .5 & 0 & 0 & 0 \\ .5 & 0 & 0 & .5 \\ 0 & 0 & 0 & .5 \\ 0 & 0 & .5 & .5 \\ 0 & .67 & .5 & 0 \\ 0 & .67 & .5 & 0 \end{bmatrix}$$

We now update $T_{4\times7}$, the top-down weight matrix. We have, $t_{Ji} = t_{1i} = x_i$, so that T_{4*} (new) $= \boldsymbol{x} = [0, 0, 1, 1, 1, 0, 0]$.

$$\therefore T_{4\times7} = \begin{bmatrix} 1 & 1 & 1 & 0 & 0 & 0 & 0 \\ 0 & 0 & 0 & 0 & 0 & 1 & 1 \\ 0 & 0 & 0 & 0 & 1 & 1 & 1 \\ 0 & 0 & 1 & 1 & 1 & 0 & 0 \end{bmatrix}$$

This completes training with the fifth pattern in the first epoch.

Training with the last pattern (0, 0, 0, 1, 0, 0, 0) is left as an exercise. We will see that none of the existing four cluster units is able to learn this pattern. Providing one more cluster unit Y_5 to accommodate this pattern, we finally have

$$B_{7\times5} = \begin{bmatrix} .5 & 0 & 0 & 0 & 0 \\ .5 & 0 & 0 & 0 & 0 \\ .5 & 0 & 0 & .5 & 0 \\ 0 & 0 & 0 & .5 & 1 \\ 0 & 0 & .5 & .5 & 0 \\ 0 & .67 & .5 & 0 & 0 \\ 0 & .67 & .5 & 0 & 0 \end{bmatrix}$$

$$T_{5\times7} = \begin{bmatrix} 1 & 1 & 1 & 0 & 0 & 0 & 0 \\ 0 & 0 & 0 & 0 & 0 & 1 & 1 \\ 0 & 0 & 0 & 0 & 1 & 1 & 1 \\ 0 & 0 & 1 & 1 & 1 & 0 & 0 \\ 0 & 0 & 0 & 1 & 0 & 0 & 0 \end{bmatrix}$$

Problem 9.3 *(Creating and training an ART1 net)* Repeat the previous problem with $\rho = .3$.

Solution 9.3 The ART-1 net initially consists of 7 inputs and 3 clusters. The training set comprises the patterns: [1, 1, 1, 1, 0, 0, 0], [1, 1, 1, 0, 0, 0, 0], [0, 0, 0, 0, 0, 1, 1], [0, 0, 0, 0, 1, 1, 1], [0, 0, 1, 1, 1, 0, 0] and [0, 0, 0, 1, 0, 0, 0]. The vigilance parameter $\rho = .3$. Execution of the first epoch of ART-1 training is traced below.

Step 0. `Initialize the learning parameters and the interconnection weights`

$$L = 2,\ \rho = .3,\ b_{ij}(0) = \frac{1}{1+7} = 0.125,\ t_{ji}(0) = 1,\quad for\ all\ i = 1\ to\ 7, j = 1\ to\ 3$$

$$\therefore\ B_{7\times3} = \begin{bmatrix} .125 & .125 & .125 \\ .125 & .125 & .125 \\ .125 & .125 & .125 \\ .125 & .125 & .125 \\ .125 & .125 & .125 \\ .125 & .125 & .125 \\ .125 & .125 & .125 \end{bmatrix},\ T_{3\times7} = \begin{bmatrix} 1 & 1 & 1 & 1 & 1 & 1 & 1 \\ 1 & 1 & 1 & 1 & 1 & 1 & 1 \\ 1 & 1 & 1 & 1 & 1 & 1 & 1 \end{bmatrix}$$

Step 1. **Do** `Steps 2 to 14` **While** `stopping criteria is not satisfied.`

/* Epoch No. 1, Pattern No. 1 */

This is same in the previous example. The new bottom-up weight matrix and the top-down weight matrix at the end of training with the first pattern are

$$B_{7\times3} = \begin{bmatrix} .4 & .125 & .125 \\ .4 & .125 & .125 \\ .4 & .125 & .125 \\ .4 & .125 & .125 \\ 0 & .125 & .125 \\ 0 & .125 & .125 \\ 0 & .125 & .125 \end{bmatrix}$$

$$\therefore T_{3\times7} = \begin{bmatrix} 1 & 1 & 1 & 1 & 0 & 0 & 0 \\ 1 & 1 & 1 & 1 & 1 & 1 & 1 \\ 1 & 1 & 1 & 1 & 1 & 1 & 1 \end{bmatrix}$$

/* Epoch No. 1, Pattern No. 2 */

The training is again same as in the previous example. The resultant bottom-up and top-down weight matrices are given by

$$B_{7\times3} = \begin{bmatrix} .5 & .125 & .125 \\ .5 & .125 & .125 \\ .5 & .125 & .125 \\ 0 & .125 & .125 \\ 0 & .125 & .125 \\ 0 & .125 & .125 \\ 0 & .125 & .125 \end{bmatrix}$$

$$\therefore T_{3\times7} = \begin{bmatrix} 1 & 1 & 1 & 0 & 0 & 0 & 0 \\ 1 & 1 & 1 & 1 & 1 & 1 & 1 \\ 1 & 1 & 1 & 1 & 1 & 1 & 1 \end{bmatrix}$$

Similarly, the bottom-up and top-down weight matrices after training with the third pattern in the first epoch are given by

$$B_{7\times3} = \begin{bmatrix} .5 & 0 & .125 \\ .5 & 0 & .125 \\ .5 & 0 & .125 \\ 0 & 0 & .125 \\ 0 & 0 & .125 \\ 0 & .67 & .125 \\ 0 & .67 & .125 \end{bmatrix}$$

$$\therefore T_{3\times7} = \begin{bmatrix} 1 & 1 & 1 & 0 & 0 & 0 & 0 \\ 0 & 0 & 0 & 0 & 0 & 1 & 1 \\ 1 & 1 & 1 & 1 & 1 & 1 & 1 \end{bmatrix}$$

Now we proceed to train with the fourth pattern [0, 0, 0, 0, 1, 1, 1].

/* Epoch No. 1, Pattern No. 4 */

Step 2. **For** each training pattern ***s*** **Do** Steps 3 to 13.

The fourth training pattern $\mathbf{s} = [0, 0, 0, 0, 1, 1, 1]$

Step 3. Apply the input pattern ***s*** to $F_1(a)$ layer, *i.e.*, set the activations of the $F_1(a)$ units to the input training pattern ***s***.

Set the activations of the $F_1(a)$ units to [0, 0, 0, 0, 1, 1, 1].

Step 4. Set the activations of F_2 layer to all 0.

$$y_1 = y_2 = y_3 = 0.$$

Step 5. Find the norm of ***s***. $\|s\| = \sum_{i=1}^{m} s_i = 3$

Step 6. Propagate input from $F_1(a)$ layer to interface layer $F_1(b)$ so that $x_i = s_i$, for all $i = 1$ to m.

$$\mathbf{x} = \mathbf{s} = [0, 0, 0, 0, 1, 1, 1]$$

Step 7. Compute the net inputs to each uninhibited unit of the F_2 layer.

For $j = 1$ **To** n **Do**

If $y_j \neq -1$ **Then** $y_j = \sum_{i=1}^{m} b_{ij} \times x_i$

$$Y = [y_1, y_2, y_3] = \mathbf{x} \times B = [0, 0, 0, 0, 1, 1, 1] \times \begin{bmatrix} .5 & 0 & .125 \\ .5 & 0 & .125 \\ .5 & 0 & .125 \\ 0 & 0 & .125 \\ 0 & 0 & .125 \\ 0 & .67 & .125 \\ 0 & .67 & .125 \end{bmatrix}$$

$$= [0, .1.34, .375]$$

Step 8. **While** reset is True **Do** Steps 9 To 12.

Step 9. **If** $y_j = -1$ for all cluster units, then all of them are inhibited and the pattern cannot be learnt by the net. Otherwise, find the J such that $y_J \geq y_j$ for all $j = 1$ to n. Then the Jth cluster unit is the winner. In case of a tie, take the smallest J.

None of the cluster units is inhibited and y_2 has the highest activation value of 1.34. So winner is the lowest indexed unit Y_2, so that $J = 2$.

Step 10. Update $\boldsymbol{x}$: $x_i = s_i \times t_{Ji}$ for all i =1 to m.

$$\boldsymbol{x} = \boldsymbol{s} \cdot T_{2*} = [0, 0, 0, 0, 1, 1, 1] \cdot [0, 0, 0, 0, 0, 1, 1] = [0, 0, 0, 0, 0, 1, 1].$$

Step 11. Find the norm of $\boldsymbol{x}$: $\|x\| = \sum_{i=1}^{m} x_i = 2$

Step 12. Test for Reset : If $\frac{\|x\|}{\|s\|} < \rho$ Then inhibit the Jth cluster unit by setting $y_J = -1$. Go To Step 8. Otherwise $\frac{\|x\|}{\|s\|} \geq \rho$ and proceed to Step 13.

$$\frac{\|x\|}{\|s\|} = \frac{2}{3} = 0.67 \geq 0.3 = \rho, \text{ hence Reset} = \text{False. Go to Step 13.}$$

Step 13. Update the weights (top-down and bottom-up) attached to unit J of the F_2 layer.

$$b_{iJ} = \frac{L \cdot x_i}{L - 1 + \|x\|}, \textit{for all } i = 1 \textit{ to } m$$

$$t_{Ji} = x_i, \textit{ for all } i = 1 \textit{ to } m$$

$b_{i1}(new) = \frac{L \cdot x_i}{L - 1 + \|x\|} = \frac{2x_i}{1 + \|x\|}$, $\therefore$ b_{12}(new) = b_{22}(new) = b_{32}(new) = b_{42}(new) = b_{52}(new) = 0. b_{62}(new) = b_{72}(new) = 0.67.

Therefore there is no change in the new bottom-up weight matrix and top-down weight matrix.

$$B_{7\times3} = \begin{bmatrix} .5 & 0 & .125 \\ .5 & 0 & .125 \\ .5 & 0 & .125 \\ 0 & 0 & .125 \\ 0 & 0 & .125 \\ 0 & .67 & .125 \\ 0 & .67 & .125 \end{bmatrix}$$

$$\therefore T_{3\times7} = \begin{bmatrix} 1 & 1 & 1 & 0 & 0 & 0 & 0 \\ 0 & 0 & 0 & 0 & 0 & 1 & 1 \\ 1 & 1 & 1 & 1 & 1 & 1 & 1 \end{bmatrix}$$

This completes training with the fourth pattern in the first epoch.

/* Epoch No. 1, Pattern No. 5 */

Step 2. **For** each training pattern ***s*** **Do** Steps 3 to 13.

The fifth training pattern $\mathbf{s} = [0, 0, 1, 1, 1, 0, 0]$

Step 3. Apply the input pattern ***s*** to $F_1(a)$ layer, *i.e.*, set the activations of the $F_1(a)$ units to the input training pattern ***s***.

Set the activations of the $F_1(a)$ units to $[0, 0, 1, 1, 1, 0, 0]$.

Step 4. Set the activations of F_2 layer to all 0.

$$y_1 = y_2 = y_3 = 0.$$

Step 5. Find the norm of ***s***. $\|s\| = \sum_{i=1}^{m} s_i = 3$

Step 6. Propagate input from $F_1(a)$ layer to interface layer $F_1(b)$ so that $x_i = s_i$, for all i = 1 to m.

$$\mathbf{x} = \mathbf{s} = [0, 0, 1, 1, 1, 0, 0]$$

Step 7. Compute the net inputs to each uninhibited unit of the F_2 layer.

For j = 1 **To** n **Do**

If $y_j \neq -1$ **Then** $y_j = \sum_{i=1}^{m} b_{ij} \times x_i$

$$Y = [y_1,\ y_2, y_3] = \mathbf{x} \times B = [0, 0, 1, 1, 1, 0, 0] \times \begin{bmatrix} .5 & 0 & .125 \\ .5 & 0 & .125 \\ .5 & 0 & .125 \\ 0 & 0 & .125 \\ 0 & 0 & .125 \\ 0 & .67 & .125 \\ 0 & .67 & .125 \end{bmatrix}$$

$$= [.5, 0, .375]$$

Step 8. **While** reset is True **Do** Steps 9 To 12.

Step 9. **If** $y_j = -1$ for all cluster units, then all of them are inhibited and the pattern cannot be learnt by the net. Otherwise, find the J such that $y_J \geq y_j$ for all j = 1 to n. Then the Jth cluster unit is the winner. In case of a tie, take the smallest J.

None of the cluster units is inhibited and Y_1 has the highest activation value of .5. So winner is the lowest indexed unit Y_1, so that $J = 1$.

Step 10. Update **x** : $x_i = s_i \times t_{Ji}$ for all i =1 to m.

$$\boldsymbol{x} = \boldsymbol{s} \cdot T_{1*} = [0, 0, 1, 1, 1, 0, 0] \cdot [1, 1, 1, 0, 0, 0, 0] = [0, 0, 1, 0, 0, 0, 0].$$

Step 11. Find the norm of **x** : $\|x\| = \sum_{i=1}^{m} x_i = 1$

Step 12. Test for Reset : If $\frac{\|x\|}{\|s\|} < \rho$ Then inhibit the Jth cluster unit by setting $y_J = -1$. Go To Step 8. Otherwise $\frac{\|x\|}{\|s\|} \geq \rho$ and proceed to Step 13.

$\frac{\|x\|}{\|s\|} = \frac{1}{3} = 0.33 \geq 0.3 = \rho$, hence Reset = False. Go to Step 13.

Step 13. Update the weights (top-down and bottom-up) attached to unit J of the F_2 layer.

$$b_{iJ} = \frac{L \cdot x_i}{L - 1 + \|x\|}, \textit{ for all } i = 1 \textit{ to } m$$

$$t_{Ji} = x_i, \textit{ for all } i = 1 \textit{ to } m$$

$b_{i1}(new) = \frac{L \cdot x_i}{L - 1 + \|x\|} = \frac{2x_i}{1 + \|x\|}$, $\therefore$ b_{11}(new) = b_{21}(new) = b_{41}(new) = b_{51}(new) = b_{61}(new) = b_{71}(new) = 0, b_{34}(new) = 1.

Therefore the new bottom-up weight matrix is

$$B_{7\times3} = \begin{bmatrix} 0 & 0 & .125 \\ 0 & 0 & .125 \\ 1 & 0 & .125 \\ 0 & 0 & .125 \\ 0 & 0 & .125 \\ 0 & .67 & .125 \\ 0 & .67 & .125 \end{bmatrix}$$

$$\therefore T_{3\times7} = \begin{bmatrix} 0 & 0 & 1 & 0 & 0 & 0 & 0 \\ 0 & 0 & 0 & 0 & 0 & 1 & 1 \\ 1 & 1 & 1 & 1 & 1 & 1 & 1 \end{bmatrix}$$

This completes training with the fifth pattern in the first epoch.

/* Epoch No. 1, Pattern No. 6 */

Step 2. **For** each training pattern ***s*** **Do** Steps 3 to 13.

The sixth training pattern $\boldsymbol{s}$ = [0, 0, 0, 1, 0, 0, 0]

Step 3. Apply the input pattern ***s*** to $F_1(a)$ layer, *i.e.*, set the activations of the $F_1(a)$ units to the input training pattern ***s***.

Set the activations of the $F_1(a)$ units to [0, 0, 0, 1, 0, 0, 0].

Step 4. Set the activations of F_2 layer to all 0.

$$y_1 = y_2 = y_3 = 0.$$

Step 5. Find the norm of **s**. $\|s\| = \sum_{i=1}^{m} s_i = 1$

Step 6. Propagate input from $F_1(a)$ layer to interface layer $F_1(b)$ so that $x_i = s_i$, for all $i = 1$ to m.

$$\boldsymbol{x} = \boldsymbol{s} = [0, 0, 0, 1, 0, 0, 0]$$

Step 7. Compute the net inputs to each uninhibited unit of the F_2 layer.

For $j = 1$ **To** n **Do**

If $y_j \neq -1$ **Then** $y_j = \sum_{i=1}^{m} b_{ij} \times x_i$

$$Y = [y_1, y_2, y_3] = \boldsymbol{x} \times B = [0, 0, 0, 1, 0, 0, 0] \times \begin{bmatrix} .5 & 0 & .125 \\ .5 & 0 & .125 \\ .5 & 0 & .125 \\ 0 & 0 & .125 \\ 0 & 0 & .125 \\ 0 & .67 & .125 \\ 0 & .67 & .125 \end{bmatrix}$$

$$= [0, 0, .125]$$

Step 8. **While** reset is True **Do** Steps 9 To 12.

Step 9. **If** $y_j = -1$ for all cluster units, then all of them are inhibited and the pattern cannot be learnt by the net. Otherwise, find the J such that $y_J \geq y_j$ for all $j = 1$ to n. Then the Jth cluster unit is the winner. In case of a tie, take the smallest J.

None of the cluster units is inhibited and Y_3 has the highest activation value of .125. So winner is the lowest indexed unit Y_3, so that $J = 3$.

Step 10. Update **x** : $x_i = s_i \times t_{Ji}$ for all $i = 1$ to m.

$$\boldsymbol{x} = \boldsymbol{s} \cdot T_{3*} = [0, 0, 0, 1, 0, 0, 0] \cdot [1, 1, 1, 1, 1, 1, 1] = [0, 0, 0, 1, 0, 0, 0].$$

Step 11. Find the norm of **x** : $\|x\| = \sum_{i=1}^{m} x_i = 1$

Step 12. `Test for Reset : If` $\frac{\|x\|}{\|s\|} < \rho$ `Then inhibit the Jth cluster unit by setting` y_J `= −1. Go To Step 8. Otherwise` $\frac{\|x\|}{\|s\|} \geq \rho$ `and proceed to Step 13.`

$\frac{\|x\|}{\|s\|} = \frac{1}{1} = 1 \geq 0.3 = \rho$, hence Reset = False. Go to Step 14.

Step 13. `Update the weights (top-down and bottom-up) attached to unit J of the` F_2 `layer.`

$$b_{iJ} = \frac{L \cdot x_i}{L - 1 + \|x\|}, \, for\, all\; i = 1 \; to \; m$$

$$t_{Ji} = x_i, \; for\, all\; i = 1 \; to \; m$$

$b_{i1}(new) = \frac{L \cdot x_i}{L - 1 + \|x\|} = \frac{2x_i}{1 + \|x\|}$, $\therefore$ $b_{13}(\text{new}) = b_{23}(\text{new}) = b_{33}(\text{new}) = b_{53}(\text{new}) = b_{63}(\text{new}) =$
$b_{73}(\text{new}) = 0, = b_{43}(\text{new}) = 1.$

Therefore the new bottom-up weight matrix is

$$B_{7\times 3} = \begin{bmatrix} 0 & 0 & 0 \\ 0 & 0 & 0 \\ 1 & 0 & 0 \\ 0 & 0 & 1 \\ 0 & 0 & 0 \\ 0 & .67 & 0 \\ 0 & .67 & 0 \end{bmatrix}$$

$$\therefore \; T_{3\times 7} = \begin{bmatrix} 0 & 0 & 1 & 0 & 0 & 0 & 0 \\ 0 & 0 & 0 & 0 & 0 & 1 & 1 \\ 0 & 0 & 0 & 1 & 0 & 0 & 0 \end{bmatrix}$$

This completes training with the sixth pattern in the first epoch.

Problem 9.4 *(Implementation of LVQ net through MatLab)* Write a MatLab program to design and implement an LVQ net with two inputs and two outputs. The two outputs should correspond to two clusters, cluster 1 and cluster 2. The training set consists of the training pairs { [0 −2] : 1, [+2 −1] : 1, [−2 +1] : 1, [0 +2] : 2, [+1 +1] : 2, [0 +1] : 2, [+1 +3] : 2, [−3 +1] : 1, [3 −1] : 1, [−3, 0] : 1}. Test the net with the input pattern [0.2, −1].

Solution 9.4 The MatLab code for the net, its training and testing, is given below.

*****************CODE FOR LEARNING VECTOR QUANTIZATION NETWORKS***********

```
clc;
clear;

Input_Vector = [0 +2 −2  0 +1  0 +1 −3  3 −3;
               −2 −1 +1 +2 +1 +1 +3 +1 −1  0];
% Input Vector comsists of 10 samples having 2 inputs each.
Target_Class = [1  1  1  2  2  2  2  1  1  1];
% The Input Vector has to be classified into two classes, namely Class 1
% and Class 2. 6 inputs belong to Class 1 and 4 belong to Class 2.
Target_Vector = ind2vec(Target_Class);
% Converting indices to vector
net = newlvq(minmax(Input_Vector),4,[.6 .4],0.1);
% Creating new LVQ network. The network takes input from P, has 4 hidden
% neurons and two classes having percentages of 0.6 and 0.4 respectively.
% The learning rate is 0.1.
net.trainParam.epochs = 150; % Setting maximum number of epochs to 150
net=train(net,Input_Vector,Target_Vector); % Train the network
Test_Vector_1 = [0.2; 1];
a = vec2ind(sim(net,Test_Vector_1));    % Simulate network with test vector
disp('Test_Vector_1 [0.2; 1] has been classified as belonging to Class -');
disp(a);
Test_Vector_2 = [0.2; −1];
a = vec2ind(sim(net,Test_Vector_2));
disp('Test_Vector_2 [0.2; −1] has been classified as belonging to Class
−');
disp(a);
```

*********************************OUTPUT*************************************

```
Test_Vector_1 [0.2; 1] has been classified as belonging to Class - 2
Test_Vector_2 [0.2; −1] has been classified as belonging to Class - 1
```

Problem 9.5 *(Self-organizing maps)* The Iris dataset on flowers consists of 150 sample data. It is based on four attributes, sepal length in cm, sepal width in cm, petal length in cm, and petal width in cm, along with the type of flower. This dataset can be copied from the webpage http://mlg.eng.cam.ac.uk/

teaching/3f3/1011/iris.data or downloaded from: http://www2.acae.cuhk.edu.hk/~cvl/main_database.htm. Design a SOM in MatLab for this dataset.

Solution 9.5 The MatLab code along with various outputs are given below.

MatLab code

```
%    SOM on Iris Data Set mds3.txt
%    Classify iris flowers based on four attributes.
%    The data set consists of 150 samples.
%    "irisInputs" is an 4x150 matrix, whose rows are:
%    1. Sepal length in cm
%    2. Sepal width in cm
%    3. Petal length in cm
%    4. Petal width in cm

clc;
clear();
load mdstrain.txt;              % Load the training file containing 150 samples
                                % having 4 fields

r = mdstrain(:,1:4);            % Bring the contents of the text file to matrix
r
r = r';                         % Transpose r to bring in order of rows
net = newsom(r,[10 10]);        % Create new SOM for r with 10 x 10 hidden
                                % neurons. The other parameters are kept at
                                % default values.
%    The syntax for newsom is net = newsom(P,[D1,D2,...],TFCN,DFCN,
     STEPS,IN)
%    where P = R x Q matrix of Q representative input vectors.
%    Di = Size of ith layer dimension. Defaults = [5 8]. Here it is [10 10]
%    TFCN = Topology function. Default = 'hextop'. May be made 'gridtop' or
%    'randtop'
%    DFCN = Distance function. Default = 'linkdist'. Can be made 'dist' or
%    'mandist'. 'linkdist' is a layer distance function used to find the
%    distances between the layer's neurons given their positions.'dist' is
     the Eucledian distance function while 'mandist'is the Manhattan dis-
     tance function.
%    STEPS = Steps for neighborhood to shrink to 1. Default = 100.
%    IN = Initial neighborhood size. default = 3.
net = train(net,r);             % Train the network. train(net,r) opens up the
                                % nntraintool from which the plots can be
                                % generated.
```

Snapshots of MatLab outputs

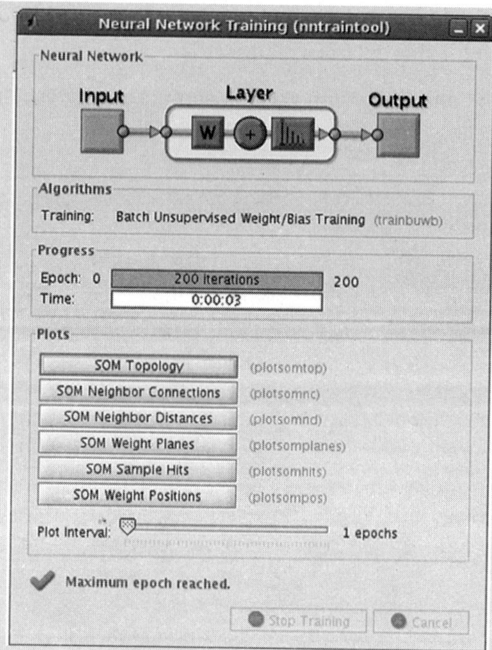

Fig. 9.20. *The 'nntraintool' window of MatLab*

Various SOM profiles are generated by clicking the respective buttons on the nntraintool. These are shown below as Fig. 9.21–9.26

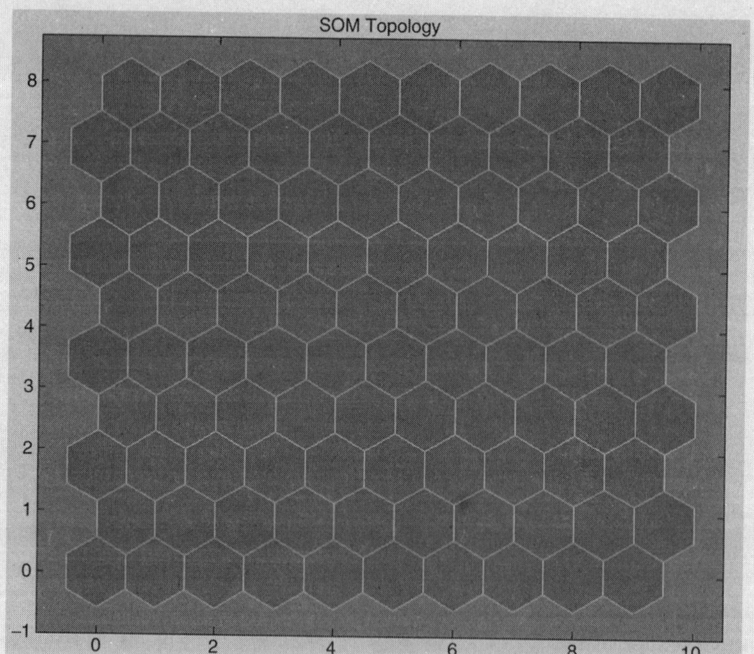

Fig. 9.21. *SOM Topology, plotted by function 'plotsomtop'.*

This shows the topology of the SOM

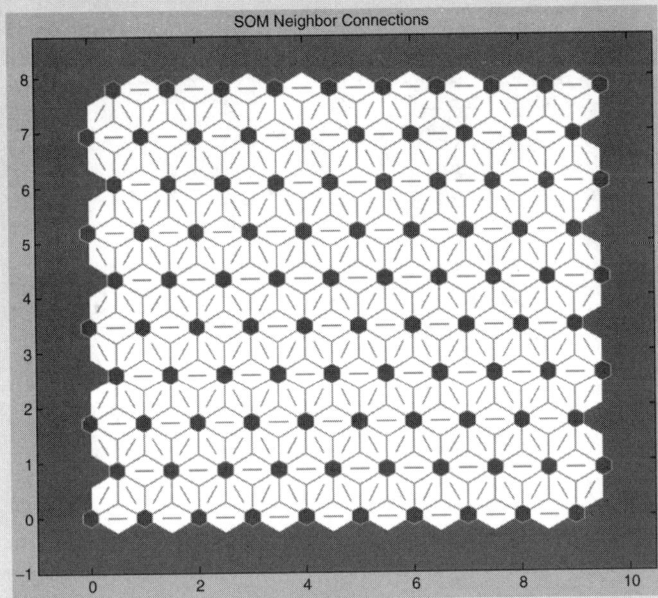

Fig. 9.22. *SOM neighbor connections, plotted by the function 'plotsomnc'. This plot shows the SOM layer, with the neurons denoted as dark patches and their connections with their direct neighbours denoted as line segments.*

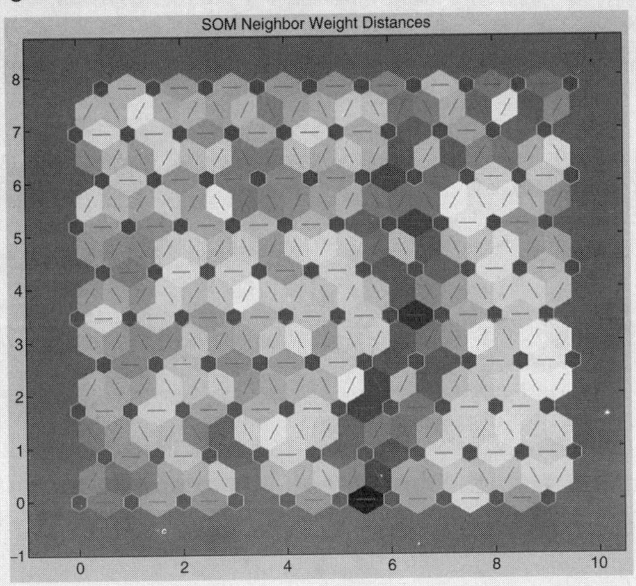

Fig. 9.23. *SOM neighbor weight distances, plotted by the function 'plotsomnd'. This plot depicts the SOM layer with the neurons as standard dark central patches and their direct neighbour relations with line segments. The neighbouring patches are presented here with various shades of grey to show how close each neuron's weight vector is to its neighbours.*

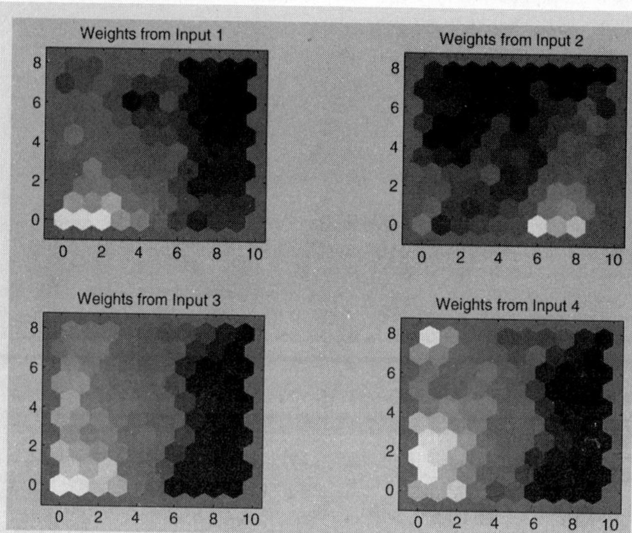

Fig. 9.24. *SOM weight planes, plotted by the function 'plotsomplanes'. The 'plotsomplanes' generates a set of subplots where each subplot shows the weights from the i-th input to the layer's neurons. The various connections are shown with different shades of grey (black for zero connection)*

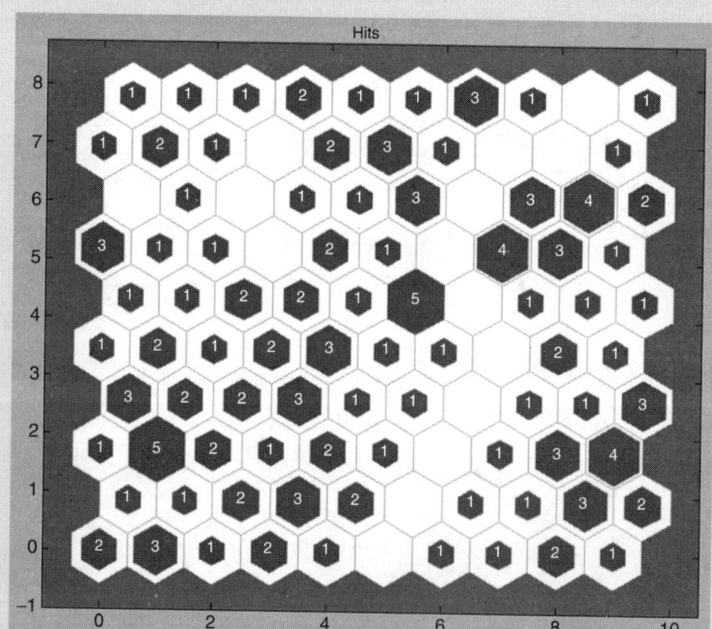

Fig. 9.25. *SOM sample hits, plotted by function 'plotsomhits'. This plot shows a SOM layer, with each neuron and the number of input vectors that are classified by it. This is shown as a number inside the cells.*

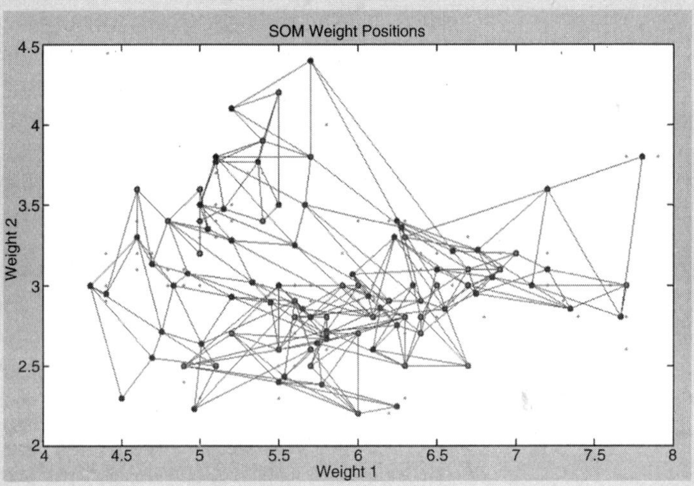

Fig. 9.26. *SOM weight positions, plotted by function 'plotsompos'. This plot shows how the classification of the input space is done by the SOM. It shows dots for each neuron's weight vector and the connecting neighbouring neurons with the lines.*

✓ TEST YOUR KNOWLEDGE

9.1 Which of the following ANNs do not work on the principle of competition?
   a) MAXNET b) Learning Vector Quantization (LVQ)
   c) ART nets d) None of the above

9.2 Which of the following ANNs is fully connected?
   a) MAXNET b) Learning Vector Quantization (LVQ)
   c) ART nets d) None of the above

9.3 Which of the following ANNs do not require any training?
   a) MAXNET b) Learning Vector Quantization (LVQ)
   c) ART nets d) None of the above

9.4 Let us suppose a MAXNET have a weight $-\delta$ at each non-self loop interconnection path and m number of units. Which of the following conditions is satisfied by δ and m?
   a) $\delta > \frac{1}{m}$ b) $\delta = \frac{1}{m}$
   c) $0 < \delta < \frac{1}{m}$ d) None of the above

9.5 Which of the following competitive nets is based on the idea that patterns close to each other should be mapped to clusters with physical proximity.
   a) MAXNET b) Kohonen's self-Organizing Map (SOM)
   c) Learning Vector Quantization (LVQ) d) None of the above

9.6 Which of the following nets employ unsupervised learning?
   a) Kohomen's Self-Organizing Map (SOM) b) Learning Vector Quantization (LVQ)
   c) Both (*a*) and (*b*) d) None of the above

9.7 Which of the following nets employ supervised learning?
  a) Kohomen's Self-Organizing Map (SOM)
  b) Learning Vector Quantization (LVQ)
  c) Both (*a*) and (*b*)
  d) None of the above

9.8 Given a pattern applied to a Kohomen's Self-Organizing Map (SOM), winner is the output unit whose weight vector is
  a) Furthest from the given pattern
  b) Closest to the given pattern
  c) Unrelated to the distance from the given pattern
  d) None of the above

9.9 Which of the following nets is intended to solve the stability-plasticity dilemma?
  a) Kohomen's Self-Organizing Map (SOM)
  b) Learning Vector Quantization (LVQ)
  c) Adaptive Resonance Theory (ART) net
  d) None of the above

9.10 Which of the following ANNs allow inclusion of a new clustering unit during the learning process?
  a) Adaptive Resonance Theory (ART)
  b) Kohomen's Self-Organizing Map (SOM)
  c) Learning Vector Quantization (LVQ)
  d) Name of the above

9.11 ART1 nets are applicable for clustering
  a) Binary patterns
  b) Real valued patterns
  c) Both (*a*) and (*b*)
  d) None of the above

9.12 ART2 nets are applicable for clustering
  a) Binary patterns
  b) Real valued patterns
  c) Both (*a*) and (*b*)
  d) None of the above

9.13 In ART nets, the degree of similarity among the patterns belonging to the same cluster is controlled with
  a) The Reset signal
  b) The learning rate
  c) The vigilance parameter
  d) None of the above

9.14 In ART1 nets, the bottom-up interconnections are directed
  a) From the comparison layer to the recognition layer
  b) From the recognition layer to the comparison layer
  c) Both ways between the recognition and the comparison layers
  d) None of the above.

9.15 In ART1 nets, the top-down interconnections are directed
  a) From the comparison layer to the recognition layer
  b) from the recognition layer to the comparison layer
  c) both ways between the recognition and the comparison layers
  d) None of the above.

9.16 A recognition layer unit of an ART1 net is not allowed to participate in a competition when it is in
  a) Active state
  b) Inactive state
  c) Inhibited stated
  d) None of the above.

9.17 Which of the following weights in an ART1 net is binary?
a) Bottom-up weights b) Top-down weights
c) Both (*a*) and (*b*) d) None of the above

9.18 Which of the following weights in an ART1 net is real valued?
a) Bottom-up weights b) Top-down weights
c) Both (*a*) and (*b*) d) None of the above

9.19 Which of the following is a competitive learning strategy for ANNs?
a) Hebb learning b) LMS Learning
c) Winner-takes-all d) None of the above

9.20 Which of the following is a possible action during ART1 learning in case all the cluster units are inhibited?
a) Add more cluster unit
b) Reduce vigilance
c) Classify the pattern as outside all clusters
d) All of the above

Answers

9.1 (d)	9.2 (a)	9.3 (a)	9.4 (c)	9.5 (b)
9.6 (a)	9.7 (b)	9.8 (b)	9.9 (c)	9.10 (a)
9.11 (a)	9.12 (b)	9.13 (c)	9.14 (a)	9.15 (b)
9.16 (c)	9.17 (b)	9.18 (a)	9.19 (c)	9.20 (d)

EXERCISES

9.1 Design a MaxNet with $\delta = 0.15$ to cluster the input pattern $\boldsymbol{x} = [x_1, x_2, x_3, x_4] = [0.7, 0.6, 0.1, 0.8]$. Show the step-by-step execution of the clustering algorithm you follow.

9.2 Design a Self-Organizing Map (SOM) to cluster the patterns $s_1 = [1, 0, 0, 0]$, $s_2 = [0, 0, 0, 1]$, $s_3 = [1, 1, 0, 0]$ and $s_4 = [0, 0, 1, 1]$ into two clusters. Apply the resultant SOM to the patterns [0, 1, 1, 1] to determine the cluster to which it belongs.

9.3 Six patterns and their corresponding designated clusters are given in Table 9.8. Obtain a Learning Vector Quantization (LVQ) neural net for the given set of vectors. Test the resultant LVQ net with the patterns [1, 0, 1, 0] and [1, 0, 1, 1].

Table 9.8. *Training set*

#	Training Vector $s = [x_1, x_2, x_3, x_2]$	Cluster
1	$\mathbf{s}_1 = [1, 0, 0, 0]$	C_1
2	$\mathbf{s}_2 = [1, 1, 0, 0]$	C_1
3	$\mathbf{s}_3 = [1, 1, 1, 0]$	C_1
4	$\mathbf{s}_4 = [0, 0, 0, 1]$	C_2
5	$\mathbf{s}_5 = [0, 0, 1, 1]$	C_2
6	$\mathbf{s}_6 = [0, 1, 1, 1]$	C_2

9.4 Apply the ART-1 learning algorithm to cluster six patterns [1, 0, 0, 0, 0], [1, 1, 0, 0, 0], [0, 0, 1, 0, 0], [0, 1, 1, 1, 0], [0, 0, 0, 1, 1] and [0, 0, 0, 0, 1] into at most three clusters. The following set of parameter values are to be used.

$m = 4$	Number of units in the input layers F_1(a) and F_1(b)
$n = 3$	Number of units in the clustering layers F_2
$\rho = 0.5$	Vigilance parameter
$L = 2$	Learning parameter, used in updating the bottom-up weights
$b_{ij}(0) = \frac{1}{1+m} = 0.2$	Initial bottom-up weights (half of the maximum value allowed)
$t_{ji}(0) = 1$	Initial top-down weights (initially all set to 1)

9.5 Consider an ART-1 net referred in Example 9.6 with 5 input units and 3 cluster units. After some training the net attains the bottom-up and top-down weight matrices as shown below.

$$B_{5\times3} = \begin{bmatrix} .2 & 0 & .2 \\ .5 & .8 & .2 \\ .5 & .5 & .2 \\ .5 & .8 & .2 \\ .1 & 0 & .2 \end{bmatrix}, \text{ and } T_{3\times5} = \begin{bmatrix} 1 & 1 & 1 & 1 & 1 \\ 0 & 1 & 1 & 1 & 0 \\ 1 & 1 & 1 & 1 & 1 \end{bmatrix}$$

Show the behaviour of the net when it is presented with the training pattern $\mathbf{s}$ = [1, 1, 1, 1, 0]. Assume $L = 2$, and $\rho = .8$.

BIBLIOGRAPHY AND HISTORICAL NOTES

Stalwarts like R. Lippman, G. A. Carpenter, S. Grossberg, T. Kohonen etc. worked on various competitive neural nets over the years. MaxNet was introduced by Lippman in 1987. Adaptive Resonance Theory was developed by Stephen Grossberg and Gail Carpenter towards late eighties. SOM was developed by Kohonen. A selected list of publications in the field of competitive networks is presented below.

Carpenter, G.A. and Grossberg, S. (1987). *A massively parallel architecture for a self-organizing neural pattern recognition machine*. Computer Vision, Graphics, and Image Processing.

Carpenter, G.A. and Grossberg, S. (2003). *Adaptive Resonance Theory*. In M. A. Arbib (ed.), *The Handbook of Brain Theory and Neural Networks*, Second Edition, pp. 87–90. MIT Press.

Carpenter, G.A., Grossberg, S., and Reynolds, J.H. (1991). ARTMAP: Supervised real-time learning and classification of nonstationary data by a self-organizing neural network. *Neural Networks*, Vol. 4, pp. 565–588.

Grossberg, S. (1987). Competitive learning: From interactive activation to adaptive resonance. *Cognitive Science*, Vol. 11, pp. 23–63.

Kohonen, T. (1984). *Self-Organization and Associative Memory*. Springer, Berlin.

Kohonen, T. (1982). Self-organized formation of topologically correct feature maps. *Biological Cybernetics*, Vol. 43, pp. 59–69.

Kohonen, T. (1995). *Learning vector quantization.* In M.A. Arbib, (ed), *The Handbook of Brain Theory and Neural Networks*, pp. 537–540. MIT Press.

Kohonen, T. (1997). *Self-Organizing Maps*. Springer, Berlin.

Kohonen, T., Kaski, S. and Lappalainen, H. (1997). Self-organized formation of various invariant-feature filters in the adaptive-subspace SOM. *Neural Computation*, Vol. 9, pp. 1321–1344.

Lippman, R, (1987). An introduction to computing with neural nets. *IEEE Transactions on Acoustics, Speech, Signal Processing*, Vol. 35, pp. 2–44.

10

BACKPROPAGATION

Key Concepts

Backpropagation of error, Feedforward neural net, Generalized delta rule, Hidden layer, Hyperbolic tangent function, Multilayer perceptron, Nguyen-Widrow initialization, Random initialization, Sigmoid function, Steepness parameter

Chapter Outline

Backpropagation net is an important class of artificial neural nets which is used in a wide range of applications. The early enthusiasm over neural networks received a severe blow when Minsky and Papert (1969) demonstrated that perceptrons are unable to implement an elementary function like a 2-input XOR. Research community lost interest in the subject and no further development took place for several years. Discovery of multilayered perceptron (also referred to as multilayered networks) independently by several researchers (Rumelhart, Ivilliams, McClelland etc.) eventually restored interest in this field. The limitation of a single layer perceptron is overcome by multilayer neural nets. It is proved that a multilayer feedforward net can be made to learn any continuous function to any extent of desired accuracy. The learning method called the generalized delta rule, or back-propagation (of errors), is employed to train the multilayer feedforward networks. It is essentially a gradient descent method to minimize the total squared error of the output computed by the net. The learning is supervised. This chapter presents the basic features of backpropagation networks.

10.1 MULTI-LAYER FEEDFORWARD NET

As stated earlier, a single layer net has very limited capability. It is unable to learn such a simple function as the 2-input XOR. Multilayer perceptron has the capacity to overcome this limitation. A multilayer network with one or more *hidden layers* can learn any continuous mapping to an arbitrary accuracy. Moreover, it is proved that one hidden layer is sufficient for a multilayer perceptron to implement any continuous function. However, in some cases, more than one hidden layer may be advantageous. The features of multilayer feed forward net are discussed below in brief.

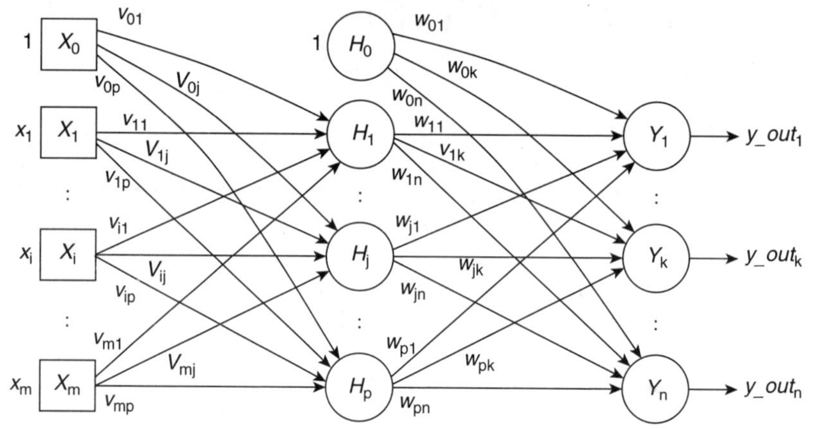

Fig. 10.1. *Structure of a multi-layered feed forward network with one hidden layer*

10.1.1 Architecture

The processing elements of a multi-layer feedforward neural net are arranged in a number of layers. The layers between the input and the output layers are called the **hidden layers**. The connecting paths are unidirectional. They are directed from the input layer to the output layer. Signals flow from the input to the output through the hidden layers and not in the reverse direction. The name *feedforward* is due to the unidirectional flow of signal from the input to the output layer. During learning, the net adjusts its inter-connection weights on the basis of the errors in computation. Calculation of errors starts at the output layer and the errors are propagated backward, i.e., from the output layer towards the input layer. Because of this backward propagation of errors during the learning phase these nets are called backpropagation nets. The structure of an *m-p-n* multilayer net with one hidden layer is shown in Fig.10.1. It can be easily generalized to nets having more than hidden layers. The biases to the hidden units and the output units are provided by the units X_0 and H_0 respectively, each of which is permanently fed with the signal 1. The biases to the hidden units $H_1, \ldots, H_p$ are shown in Fig.10.1 as $v_{01}, v_{02}, \ldots, v_{0p}$. Similarly, those to the output units $Y_1, \ldots, Y_n$ are given by $w_{01}, \ldots, w_{0n}$.

10.1.2 Notational Convention

The symbols used to describe the multilayer feed forward net, and its learning algorithm, are listed below.

$\boldsymbol{x}$	The input training pattern of length m. $\boldsymbol{x} = [\, x_{1,\ldots}, x_i, \ldots, x_m \,]$
y_out	Output pattern produced by the activations of the output units $Y_1, \ldots., Y_n$. ***y_out*** = [*y_out*$_1$, …, *y_out*$_k$, …, *y_out*$_n$]
$\boldsymbol{t}$	Target output pattern for input pattern $\boldsymbol{x}$. $\boldsymbol{t} = [\, t_1, \ldots, t_k, \ldots, t_n \,]$

h_out Pattern produced by the activations of the hidden units $H_1, \ldots, H_p$.
$\boldsymbol{h\_out} = [\, h\_out_1, \ldots, h\_out_j, \ldots, h\_out_p \,]$

X_i The ith input unit. The signal to input unit X_i is symbolized as x_i. The activation of X_i is also x_i, as it simply broadcasts the input signal x_i, without any processing, to the units of the hidden layer.

H_j The jth hidden unit, $j = 1, .., p$. The total input signal to H_j is given by

$$h\_in_j = \sum_{i=0}^{m} v_{ij} x_i = v_{0j} + \sum_{j=1}^{m} v_{ij} x_i$$

Where v_{ij} is the interconnection weight between the input unit X_i and the hidden unit H_j, and v_{oj} is the bias on the hidden unit H_j.

h_out_j The activation of the jth hidden unit H_j.
$h\_out_j = f_h(\, h\_in_j\,)$, where f_h is the activation function for the hidden units.

Y_k The kth output unit, $k = 1, \ldots, n$. The total input signal to Y_k is given by

$$y\_in_k = \sum_{j=0}^{p} w_{jk} h\_out_j = w_{0k} + \sum_{i=1}^{p} w_{jk} h\_out_j$$

Where w_{jk} is the interconnection weight between the hidden unit H_j and the output unit Y_k, and w_{ok} is the bias on the output unit Y_k.

y_out_k The activation of the output unit Y_k.
$y\_out_k = f_o(\, y\_in_k\,)$, where f_o is the activation function for the output units.

$\delta(w_k)$ A component of error correction weight adjustment for w_{jk}, $j = 0, \ldots, p$, that is due to an error at output Y_k. Moreover, δ_k is propagated to the hidden units to further calculate the error terms at the hidden units.

$\delta(v_j)$ A component of error correction weight adjustment for v_{ij}, $i = 0, \ldots, m$. $\delta(v_j)$ results from the backpropagation of error information from the output units to the hidden unit H_j.

α Learning rate

10.1.3 Activation Functions

The activation function employed in a backpropagation net must satisfy certain properties. It must be continuous, differentiable, and monotonically non-decreasing. Moreover, it is desirable that the first derivative of the activation function be easily computable. Some of the widely used activation functions are mentioned below.

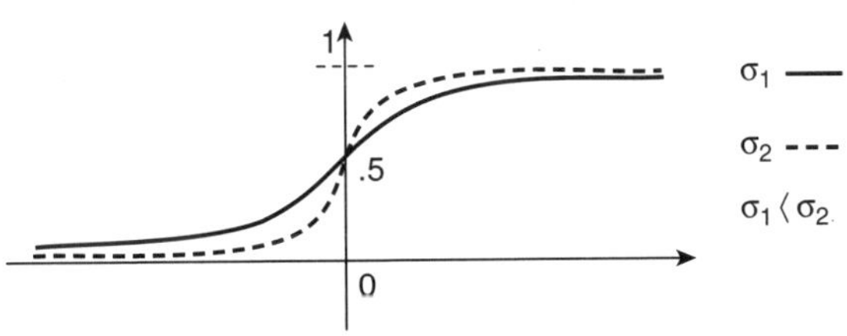

Fig. 10.2. *Binary sigmoid function*

(a) Binary sigmoid function

This is one of the most popular activation function with a range of (0, 1). The binary sigmoid function and its first derivative are given below.

$$f(x)=\frac{1}{1+e^{-\sigma x}} \tag{10.1}$$

$$f'(x)=\sigma f(x)(1-f(x)) \tag{10.2}$$

The parameter σ in Equation 10.1 is known as the *steepness parameter*. The shape of the sigmoid function is shown in Fig. 10.2. The transition from 0 to 1 could be made as steep as desired by increasing the value of σ to appropriate extent.

(b) Bipolar sigmoid function

Depending on the requirement, the binary sigmoid function can be scaled to any range of values appropriate for a given application. The most widely used range is from −1 to +1, and the corresponding sigmoid function is referred to as the *bipolar* sigmoid function. The formulae for the bipolar sigmoid function and its first derivative are given below as Equations 10.3 and 10.4 respectively. Fig. 10.3 presents the form of a bipolar sigmoid function graphically.

$$g(x)=\frac{1-e^{-\sigma x}}{1+e^{-\sigma x}} \tag{10.3}$$

$$g'(x)=\frac{\sigma}{2}(1+g(x))(1-g(x)) \tag{10.4}$$

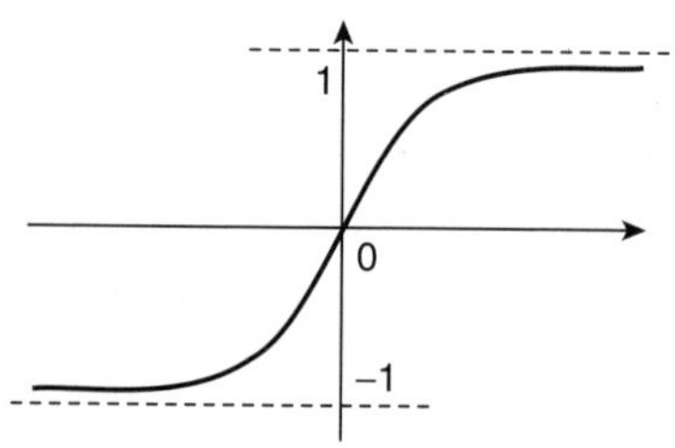

Fig. 10.3. *Bipolar sigmoid function*

(c) Hyperbolic tangent function

Another bipolar activation function that is widely employed in backpropagation nets is the hyperbolic tangent function. The function and its first derivative are expressed by Equations 10.5 and 10.6 respectively.

$$h(x)=\frac{e^{x}-e^{-x}}{e^{x}+e^{-x}} \tag{10.5}$$

$$h'(x)=(1+h(x))(1-h(x)) \tag{10.6}$$

The hyperbolic tangent function is closely related to the bipolar sigmoid function. When the input data is binary and not continuously valued in the range from 0 to 1, they are generally converted to bipolar form and then a bipolar sigmoid or hyperbolic tangent activation is applied on them by the processing units.

10.2 THE GENERALIZED DELTA RULE

As stated earlier, the backpropagation nets follow the generalized delta rule for learning. It is a supervised learning method which is essentially a gradient descent method that tries to minimize the total squared error of the output computed by the net. The learning algorithm is presented in Section 10.3. This section provides a derivation of the generalized delta rule.

Let v_{ij} be the interconnection weight between the input unit X_i and the hidden unit H_j and w_{jk} be the interconnection weight between the hidden unit H_j and the output unit Y_k. Then the total input signal h_in_j to the hidden unit H_j is given by

$$h\_in_j = \sum_{i=0}^{m} v_{ij}x_i = v_{0j} + \sum_{i=1}^{m} v_{ij}x_i \tag{10.7}$$

The activation of the hidden unit H_j is obtained with the help of an activation function f_h.

$$h\_out_j = f_h\,(h\_in_j) \tag{10.8}$$

The total input y_in_k to the output unit Y_k is given by

$$y\_in_k = \sum_{j=0}^{p} w_{jk}h\_out_j = w_{0k} + \sum_{i=1}^{p} w_{jk}h\_out_j \tag{10.9}$$

Where w_{0k} is the bias on the output unit Y_k. The activation of the output unit Y_k is obtained with the help of an activation function f_o.

$$y\_out_k = f_o\,(h\_in_k) \tag{10.10}$$

The squared error at the output layer is given by

$$E = \frac{1}{2}.\sum_{k=1}^{n}(t_k - y\_out_k)^2 = \frac{1}{2}\sum_{k=1}^{n}(t_k - f_0(y\_in_k))^2 \tag{10.11}$$

Equation 10.9 provides the expression for y_in_k. Equation 10.11, together with Equation 10.9, indicates that E is a function of the interconnection weights. Now, taking the partial derivative of E with respect to w_{jk}, i.e., the interconnection weight between the hidden unit H_j and the output unit Y_k, we get

$$\frac{\partial E}{\partial w_{jk}} = \frac{\partial}{\partial w_{jk}}\left\{\frac{1}{2}\sum_{k=1}^{n}(t_k - y\_out_k)^2\right\} = \frac{\partial}{\partial w_{jk}}\left\{\frac{1}{2}\sum_{k=1}^{n}(t_k - f_0(y\_in_k)^2\right\}$$

$$= -(t_k - f_o(y\_in_k))\frac{\partial}{\partial w_{jk}} f_0(y\_in_k). = -(t_k - y\_out_k)f_o'(y\_in_k)\frac{\partial}{\partial w_{jk}}(y\_in_k)$$

$$= -(t_k - y\_out_k)f_o'(y\_in_k)\frac{\partial}{\partial w_{jk}}\left(\sum_{J=0}^{p} w_{Jk}h\_out_J\right)$$

$$= -(t_k - y\_out_k)f_o'(y\_in_k)h\_out_j$$

We denote, $\delta w_k = -(t_k - y\_out_k)f_o'(y\_in_k)$, so that $\dfrac{\partial E}{\partial w_{jk}} = \delta w_k \cdot h\_out_j$ (10.12)

Regarding weights of the paths between the input layer and the hidden layer we have

$$\frac{\partial E}{\partial v_{ij}} = \frac{\partial}{\partial v_{ij}}\left\{\frac{1}{2}\sum_{k=0}^{n}(t_k - y\_out_k)^2\right\} = -\sum_{k=1}^{n}(t_k - y\_out_k).\frac{\partial}{\partial v_{ij}}(y\_out_k)$$

$$= -\sum_{k=1}^{n}(t_k - y\_out_k).\frac{\partial}{\partial v_{ij}}(f_o(y\_in_k))$$

$$= -\sum_{k=1}^{n}(t_k - y\_out_k)f_o'(y\_in_k)\frac{\partial}{\partial v_{ij}}(y\_in_k)$$

$$= -\sum_{k=1}^{n}\delta w_k \frac{\partial}{\partial v_{ij}}(y\_in_k) = -\sum_{k=1}^{n}\delta w_k \frac{\partial}{\partial v_{ij}}\sum_{J=0}^{p} w_{Jk}\cdot h\_out_J$$

$$= -\sum_{k=1}^{n}\delta w_k \cdot w_{jk}\cdot \frac{\partial}{\partial v_{ij}}(h\_out_j) = -\sum_{k=1}^{n}\delta w_k \cdot w_{jk}\frac{\partial}{\partial v_{ij}}(f_h(h\_in_j))$$

$$= -\sum_{k=1}^{n}\delta w_k . w_{jk}\frac{\partial}{\partial v_{ij}}(f_h(\sum_{I=0}^{m} v_{Ij}x_I)) = -\sum_{k=1}^{n}\delta w_k \cdot w_{jk}\cdot f_h'(h\_in_j)\cdot x_i$$

$$= -\delta v_j \cdot x_i ,$$

where $$\delta v_j = \sum_{k=1}^{n}\delta w_k \cdot w_{jk}\cdot f_h'(h\_in_j)$$

Therefore, the formulae for weight update are

$$\Delta w_{jk} = -\alpha\frac{\partial E}{\partial w_{jk}} = -\alpha\cdot\delta w_k \cdot h\_out_j = \alpha\cdot(t_k - y\_out_k)\cdot f_o'(y\_in_k)\cdot h\_out_j$$

Hence $$\Delta w_{jk} = \alpha\cdot(t_k - y\_out_k)\cdot f_o'(y\_in_k)\cdot h\_out_j \tag{10.13}$$

Similarly, $$\Delta v_{ij} = -\alpha\frac{\partial E}{\partial v_{ij}} = \alpha\cdot\delta v_j \cdot x_i = \alpha\cdot\left[\sum_{k=1}^{n}\delta w_k . w_{jk} f_h'(h\_in_j)\right]\cdot x_i$$

$$= \alpha\cdot f_h'(h\_in_j)\cdot x_i \cdot\left[\sum_{k=1}^{n}\delta w_k . w_{jk}\right]$$

Therefore, $$\Delta v_{ij} = \alpha\cdot f_h'(h\_in_j)\cdot x_i \cdot\left[\sum_{k=1}^{n}\delta w_k . w_{jk}\right] \tag{10.14}$$

The backpropagation algorithm applies formulae 10.13 and 10.14 for adjustment of the interconnection weights during the learning process. The details of the bachpropagation algorithm are discussed below.

10.3 THE BACKPROPAGATION ALGORITHM

Backpropagation is a supervised learning method where the net repeatedly adjusts its interconnection weights on the basis of the error, or deviation from the target output, in response to the training patterns. As usual, learning takes place through a number of epochs. During each epoch the training patterns are applied at the input layer and the signals flow from the input to the output through the hidden layers. Calculation of errors starts at the output layer and the errors are propagated backward, *i.e.*, from the output layer towards the input layer. The error terms for the interconnection weights between various layers of neurons are derived in Section 10.2 and are given by Equations 10.13, and 10.14. The step-by-step procedure is given in **`Algorithm Backpropagation`** (Fig. 10.4). The corresponding flowchart is shown in Fig. 10.5.

Algorithm Backpropagation

/* To train a multilayer feedforward net having a single hidden layer with a set of training pairs {($\mathbf{x}$, $\mathbf{t}$) | $\mathbf{x}$ = [x_1, …, x_m], $\mathbf{t}$ = [t_1, …, t_n]} */

Step 0. **Initialize** weights v_{ij} and w_{jk} with small random values.

Step 1. **While** stopping condition is false, **Do** Steps 2 to 9.

Step 2. **For** each training pair, **Do** Steps 3 to 8.

/* Feed forward the input pattern */

Step 3. **Apply** pattern $\mathbf{x}$ = [x_1, …, x_m] to the input layer [X_1, …, X_m] and broadcast the signals x_1, …, x_m to the hidden layer units.

Step 4. **Compute** the total input h_in_j to each hidden layer unit H_j:

$$h\_in_j = \sum_{i=0}^{m} x_i \cdot v_{ij} = v_{0j} + \sum_{i=1}^{m} x_i \cdot v_{ij}, \quad j = 1, \ldots, p.$$

Compute the activation of each hidden unit as $h\_out_j = f_h(h\_in_j)$. Broadcast h_out_j to each unit Y_k of the output layer.

Step 5. **Compute** the total input y_in_k to each output layer unit Y_k :

$$y\_in_k = \sum_{j=0}^{p} h\_out_j \cdot w_{jk} = w_{0k} + \sum_{j=1}^{p} h\_out_j \cdot w_{jk}, \quad k = 1, \ldots, n.$$

Compute the activation of each output unit $y\_out_j = f_o(y\_in_k)$.

/* Backpropagate the errors and adjust weights. */

Step 6. **Compute** the error term at the output layer as

$\delta w_k = (t_k - y\_out_k) \cdot f_o'(y\_in_k)$, $k = 1, \ldots, n$.

Compute the weight adjustment terms for weights w_{jk}

$\Delta w_{jk} = \alpha \cdot \delta w_k \cdot h\_out_j$, and $\Delta w_{0k} = \alpha \cdot \delta w_k$, $j = 1, \ldots, p$, and $k = 1, \ldots, n$.

Broadcast the error terms δw_k backward to the hidden layer.

Step 7. **For** each hidden unit H_j, $j = 1, .., p$, **compute** the total error obtained from the output layer.

$$\delta v\_in_j = \sum_{k=1}^{n} \delta_k \cdot w_{jk}$$

Compute the error term at the hidden layer as

$$\delta v_j = \delta v\_in_j \cdot f_h'(h\_in_j), \quad j = 1, \ldots, p.$$

Compute the weight correction terms for updating weights V_{ij}.

$$\Delta v_{ij} = \alpha \cdot \delta v_j \cdot x_i, \text{ and } \Delta v_{0j} = \alpha \cdot \delta v_j$$

```
        /* adjust the weights of interconnections */
Step 8. Compute the new weights as:
         i) Wjk(new) = Wjk(old) + Δwjk , for j = 0,... , P, and k = 1,..., n
        ii) vij(new) = vij(old) + Δvij , for i =0,.., m, and j = 1,..., p
Step 9. Test for the stopping condition
```

Fig. 10.4. *Algorithm backpropagation*

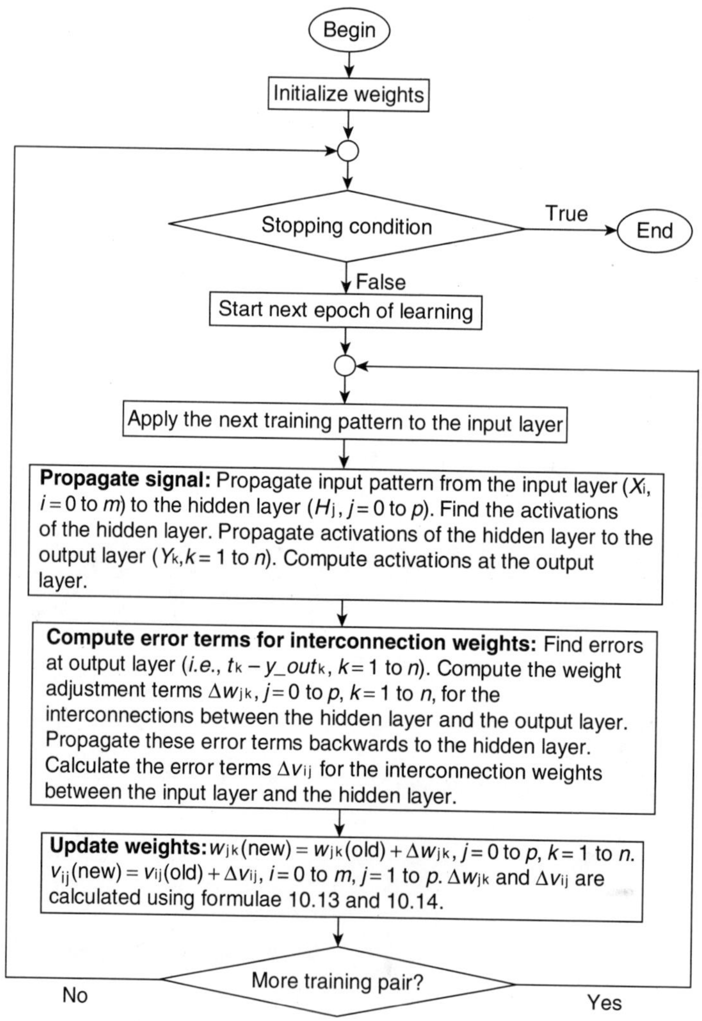

Fig. 10.5. *Flowchart of backpropagation training algorithm*

10.3.1 Choice of Parameters

Performance of the Backpropagation learning procedure with respect to a problem instance requires fine tuning of certain parameters. Important parameters include the initial interconnection weights and biases, size of the training set, data representation, number of hidden layers etc. These issues are briefly discussed in the rest of this subsection.

(a) Initial weights and biases

Choosing the appropriate initial interconnection weights highly influence the quality of the solution. Quality of a solution can be judged on the basis of whether a global minima is reached or the learning process gets stuck at a local minima, or the efficiency of search process. The popular ways to choose the initial weights are described below.

Random Initialization In this method, random real values within the range – 0.5 to + 0.5, or – 1.0 to + 1.0, or some other suitable range, are assigned to the interconnection weights initially. The initial weights should neither be too large nor be too small. This is because in both these cases learning becomes slow.

```
Procedure Nguyen-Widrow Initialization.

Step 1.   Compute a scale function β = 0.7(p) β=0.7×p^(1/m), where p is the
          number of units in the hidden layer and m is the number of units
          in the input layer.

Step 2.   Initialize the biases v_0j, j =1, .., p, by random number within
          the range -β to β.

Step 3.   Initialize each interconnection weight v_ij, i = 1, …, m, and j =
          1, …, p with a random number within the range - 0.5 to +0.5.

Step 4.   For each j = 1, …, p compute ||v_j|| = sqrt(v_1j^2 + v_2j^2 + ... + v_mj^2)

Step 5.   Final initialization of v_ij, i = 1, …, m, and j = 1, …, p is ac-
          complished with the help of the formula

                    v_ij = β.v_ij / ||v_j||
```

Fig. 10.6. *Procedure Nguyen-Widrow initialization*

Nguyen-Widrow Initialization. Nguyen-Widrow proposed an initialization technique that accelerates the learning rate to a great extent. It is based on the hyperbolic tangent activation function

$$h(x) = \frac{e^x - e^{-x}}{e^x + e^{-x}} \tag{10.15}$$

We know that this function is closely related to the bipolar sigmoid activation function. In Nguyen-Widrow initialization, the weights between the hidden layer and the output layer, i.e., the w_{jk} weights, are randomly initialized to values in the range – 0.5 to + 0.5. However, the interconnection weights between the input layer and hidden layer, i.e., v_{ij} weights, are assigned differently. The method is presented as **Procedure Nguyen-Widrow Initialization** (Fig. 10.6).

(b) Stopping criteria

Hecht and Nielsen have proposed a very effective criterion for the termination of the backpropagation learning process. The technique requires use of two sets of patterns during training, viz., a set of training patterns, together with a set of training *testing* patterns. These sets are disjoint. The training patterns are used to train the net as usual. However, the training-testing patterns play a somewhat different role. These are employed to compute the errors at regular intervals. Training is continued as long as the error for the training-testing patterns goes on decreasing. When this trend reverses, i.e., instead of decreasing the error begins to increase, training is terminated.

(c) Size of training set

Let p be the size of the training set, i.e., number of training pairs, w be the number of weights to be adjusted, and e the accuracy of classification. Then the expression for 'enough' training pairs is given by

$$P = \frac{w}{e} \tag{10.16}$$

This implies that if the net is trained to classify $1 - \frac{e}{2}$ of the training patterns correctly, where $0 < e \le 0.125$, then it will classify i - e of the testing patterns correctly.

Example 10.1 (*Size of the training set*)

Let us suppose $e = 0.1$. Then a backpropagation net with 100 weights will require $w/e = 100/0.1 = 1000$ training patterns to classify 90% of *testing* patterns correctly, assuming that the net was trained to classify 95% of the *training* patterns correctly.

(d) Data representation

Data can be discrete, or continuous. It is found that distinct responses are learnt by neural nets more easily than continuous-valued responses. However, breaking continuous data into a number of distinct categories is not always advisable because, neural nets find it difficult to learn patterns that lie on, or near, the boundaries. On the other hand, representing discrete quantities, such as letters of the alphabet, or a set of facial images, should be avoided as far as possible. As usual, discrete data should be represented in bipolar form and the bipolar sigmoid function is to be used for the activation function so that the net may learn faster.

(e) Number of hidden layers

It is shown that for back-propagation nets one hidden layer is sufficient to approximate any continuous input-output pattern mapping to any desired degree of accuracy. In some situations, however, more than one hidden layers, say two, may make learning easier.

Algorithm Apply-Backpropagation-Net

/* An m-input n-output backpropagation neural net with one hidden layer consisting of p number of hidden units is given. The input, hidden, and the output layer units are denoted as X_0, X_1,…, X_m, H_0, H_1,…,H_p, and Y_1,…,Y_n respectively. The biases at the input and hidden layers are attached to the bias units X_0 and H_0. The input pattern is $\mathbf{x}$ = (x_1, …, x_m). The corresponding output pattern Y_out = (y_out_1,…,y_out_n) is to be computed. */

Step 1. Apply the input pattern to the input layer by setting activation of each input unit X_i to the corresponding component x_i of the input pattern $\mathbf{x}$.

Step 2. Compute the total input to each hidden layer unit

$$h\_in_j = \sum_{i=0}^{m} x_i \cdot v_{ij} = v_{oj} + \sum_{i=1}^{m} .x_i \cdot v_{ij}, j=1,\ldots,p$$

Step 3. Compute the activation of each hidden unit

$$h\_out_j = f_h(h\_in_j),\ j = 1,\ \ldots,\ p$$

Step 4. Propagate the hidden layer activations to the output layer units and compute the total input to each output layer unit

$$y\_in_k = \sum_{j=0}^{p} h\_out_j \cdot w_{jk} = w_{0k} + \sum_{j=1}^{p} h\_out_j \cdot w_{jk}.$$

Step 5. Compute the activation of each output unit

$$y\_out_k = f_o(y\_in_k),\ k = 1,\ \ldots,\ n$$

Step 6. Return the pattern y_out = (y_out_1, …, y_out_n)

End Algorithm Apply-Backpropagation-Net

Fig. 10.7. *Algorithm apply-backpropagation-net*

10.3.2 Application

Once the net is trained, it is ready for application. During application phase of a backpropagation neural net, only the feed forward phase of the training algorithm is needed. The application procedure is presented as **Algorithm Apply-Backprapagation-Net** (Fig. 10.7). Fig. 10.8 shows the flowchart of the procedure.

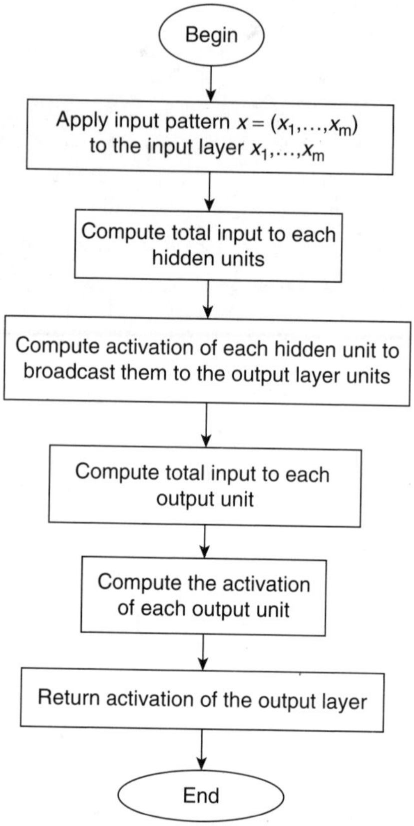

Fig. 10.8. *Flow chart for application of backpropagation net*

CHAPTER SUMMARY

The main points of the discussion on backpropagation nets are noted below.

- A multilayer feedforward neural net with one or more *hidden layers* can learn any continuous mapping to an arbitrary accuracy.
- It is proved that one hidden layer is sufficient for a multilayer perceptron to implement any continuous function.
- The processing elements of a multi-layer feedforward neural net are arranged in a number of layer. The layers intermediate between the input and the output layers are called the **hidden layers**. The connecting paths are directed from the input layer to the output layer. Signals flow from the input to the output through the hidden layers and not in the reverse direction. The name *feedforward* is due to the unidirectional flow of signal from the input to the output layer.
- During learning, the net adjusts its interconnection weights on the basis of the errors in computation. Calculation of errors starts at the output layer and the errors are propagated backward, i.e., from the output layer towards the input layer. Because of this backward propagation of errors during the learning phase these nets are called backpropagation nets.
- The activation function employed in a backpropagation net must be continuous, differentiable, and monotonically non-decreasing. The first derivative of the activation function should preferably be easily computable.

- The backpropagation nets follow the generalized delta rule for learning. It is a supervised learning method which is essentially a gradient descent method that tries to minimize the total squared error of the output computed by the net.
- The backpropagation algorithm applies the formulae 10.13 and 10.14 for adjustment of the interconnection weights during the learning process.

$$\Delta w_{jk} = \alpha \cdot (t_k - y\_out_k) \cdot f_o'(y\_in_k) \cdot h\_out_j \tag{10.13}$$

$$\Delta v_{ij} = \alpha \cdot f_h'(h\_in_j) \cdot x_i \cdot \left[\sum_{k=1}^{n} \delta w_k . w_{jk} \right] \tag{10.14}$$

- Important parameters of backpropagation algorithm include the *initial interconnection weights and biases, size of the training set, data representation, number of hidden layers* etc.

SOLVED PROBLEMS

Problem 10.1 *(Backpropagation network for diagnosis of diabetes)* Let us assume that it is possible to predict fairly correctly from the data provided in Table 10.1 below the chances of a person being a diabetic. The diagnosis field gives the inference drawn from the data given in the preceding six columns. The legend below gives the interpretation of the values in the column marked 'Diagnosis'. Use the information given in Table 10.1 to train a backpropagation network. Test the trained network with the data given in Table 10.2.

Table 10.1. *Data for diabetics*

Family History	Obese	Thirst	Increased Urination	Increased Urination (Night)	Adult	Diagnosis
1	1	1	1	1	1	1
1	1	0	0	0	1	2
1	1	1	0	0	1	2
1	1	1	1	1	0	1
0	1	1	1	1	1	1
0	0	1	1	1	1	1
0	0	0	1	1	0	0
1	0	0	0	0	1	0
0	1	1	0	0	1	0
0	0	1	0	1	1	1
0	1	0	0	1	1	0

0: Not diabetic, 1: Diabetic, 2: Probably diabetic

Table 10.2. *Test data*

Family History	Obese	Thirst	Increased Urination	Increased Urination (Night)	Adult	Diagnosis
1	1	1	1	1	1	?
0	0	0	0	0	1	?

Solution 10.1 The MatLab program for training and testing the backpropagation network is given below.

```
clc;
clear;
load ( 'Input.txt' )                    % Loading of input data ( as in Table 10.1 )
load ( 'test.txt' )                     % Loading of test data ( as in Table 10.2 )
r = Input ( :,1:6 );                    % Placing input data to matrix
r = r';
t = Input ( :,7 );                      % Placing target output from input data
t = t';
s = test ( :,1:6 );                     % Placing test data to matrix
s = s';

% ******** THESE PARAMETERS CAN BE ADJUSTED AS REQUIRED *********

numHiddenNeurons = 25;                  % Number of hidden neurons = 25
net = newpr(r,t,numHiddenNeurons); % Create new network
net.trainParam.show = 50;               % Epochs between showing progress = 50
net.trainParam.lr = 0.1;                % Learning rate = 0.1
net.trainParam.mc = 0.9;                % Momentum constant = 0.9
net.trainParam.epochs = 15000;          % Number of maximum epochs = 15000
net.trainParam.goal = 1e-15;            % Performance goal = 1e-15

%*****************************************************************

net = train ( net, r, t );              % Train the network on input data
b = sim ( net, s );                     % Test response for test data
disp ( b );                             % Display the results at command line
for i = 1:2
if ( b ( i ) < 0.7 )
  disp ( 'NOT DIABETIC' );
elseif ( 0.7 <= b ( i ) <= 1.5 )
  disp ( 'DIABETIC' );
elseif ( b ( i ) > 1.5)
  disp ( 'PROBABLY DIABETIC' );
end
end

% ************** IT IS IMPORTANT TO CLOSE ALL FILES ****************

close all;
clear all;

% ******************** THIS IS NOT PART OF CODE *******************
*******************************OUTPUT*******************************

1.5589  0.1846

DIABETIC
NOT DIABETIC
```

Problem 10.2 *(Neural Network Fitting Tool in Matlab)* Use the Neural Network Fitting Tool in Matlab to solve an input-output fitting problem with a two layer feed forward neural network.

Solution 10.2 The step-by-step process with reference to a sample dataset available in MatLab is shown below.

Step 1. Open the Neural Network Fitting Tool (nftool). (Fig. 10.9)
Then click on the→ Next button. This brings us to the Select Data interface in nftool. (Fig. 10.10)

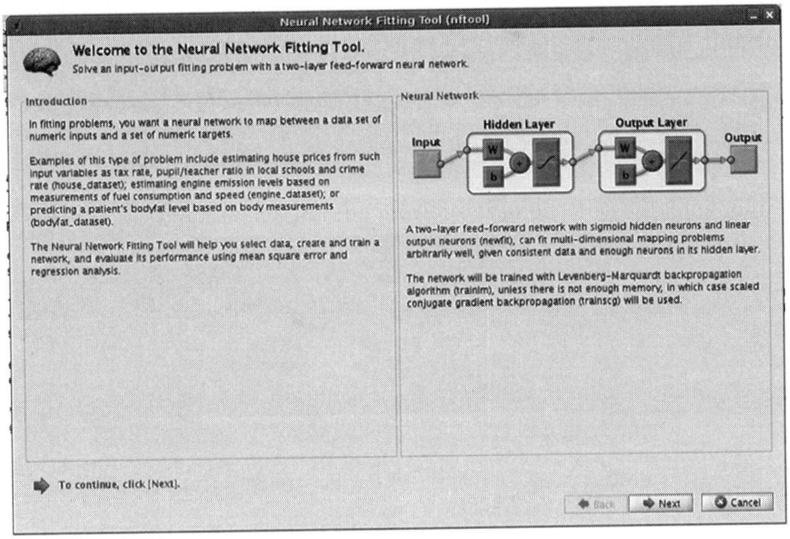

Fig. 10.9. *The neural network fitting tool (nftool)*

The page provides an introduction to the so called fitting problems where we want a neural network to map between a data set of numeric inputs and a set of numeric targets. The introduction cites a few examples of this type of problem e.g. estimating house prices from such input variables as tax rate, pupil/teacher ratio in local schools and crime rate which is provided as the house_dataset in the system, estimating engine emission levels based on measurements of fuel consumption and speed (engine_dataset); or predicting a patient's bodyfat level based on body measurements (bodyfat_dataset).

As mentioned in this page, the nftool helps to select data, create and train a network, and evaluate its performance using mean square error and regression analysis. A two-layer feed-forward network with sigmoid hidden neurons and linear output neurons (newfit) can fit multi-dimensional mapping problems arbitrarily well, given consistent data and enough neurons in its hidden layer. The network is trained with Levenberg-Marquardt backpropagation algorithm (trainlm), unless there is not enough memory, in which case scaled conjugate gradient backpropagation (trainscg) is used.

Step 2. As we are going to work with Example Data Set, load the same by selecting 'Load Example Data Set'. (Fig. 10.10)

Step 3. Select house_dataset. The description of the dataset appears on the right (Fig. 10.11). The house_dataset has 506 samples. The 'housingInputs' is a 13 × 506 matrix with rows corresponding to (i) per capita crime rate by town, (ii) proportion of residential land zoned for lots over 25,000 sq.ft., (iii) proportion of non-retail business acres per town, (iv) whether tract bounds Charles river or not, (v) nitric oxides concentration (parts per 10 million), (vi) average number of rooms per dwelling, (vii) proportion of owner-occupied units built prior to 1940, (viii) weighted distances to five Boston employment centres, (ix) index of accessibility to radial highways, (x) full-value property-tax rate per \$10,000, (xi) pupil-teacher ratio by town, (xii) $1000(Bk - 0.63)^2$, where Bk is the proportion of blacks by town, and (xiii) % lower status of the population.

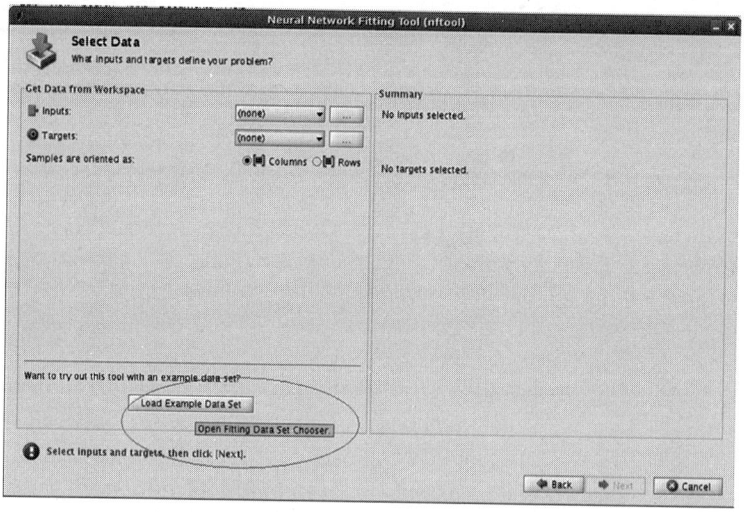

Fig. 10.10. *Select data interface in nftool*

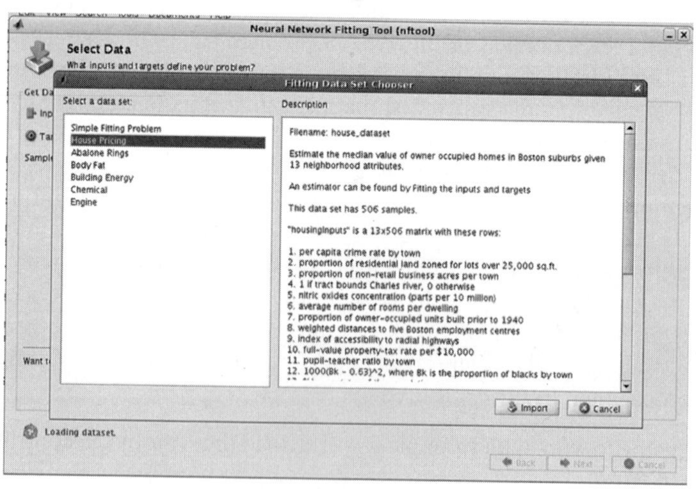

Fig. 10.11. *Selecting house_dataset*

The 'houseTargets' is a 1×506 matrix of medium values of owner-occupied homes in \$1000's. As indicated in MatLab, this data is available from the UCI Machine Learning Repository http://mlearn.ics.uci.edu/MLRepository.html Murphy, P.M., Aha, D.W. (1994). UCI Repository of machine learning databases [http://www.ics.uci.edu/~mlearn/MLRepository.html]. Irvine, CA: University of California, Department of Information and Computer Science. This dataset originated from the StatLib library which is maintained at Carnegie Mellon University.

Step 4. Load sample data, i.e., houseinputs and houseTargets (Fig. 10.12) and then click on the → Next button at the bottom.

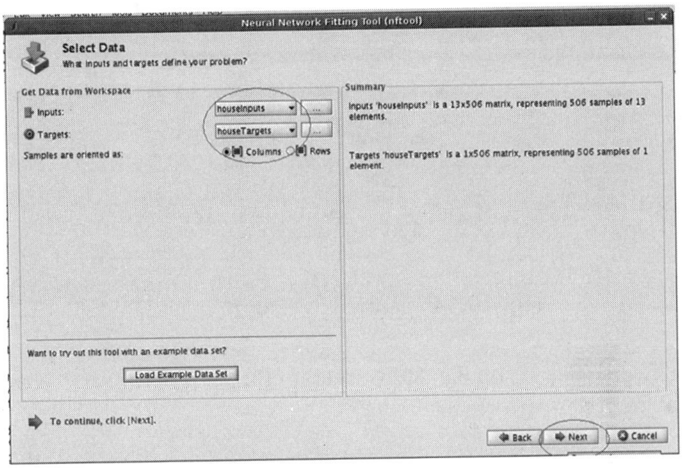

Fig. 10.12. *Sample data loaded*

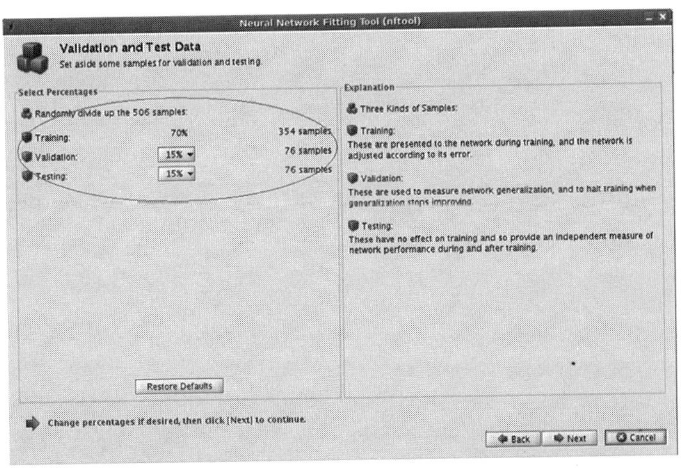

Fig. 10.13. *Training, validation and test data chosen*

Step 5. Choose the training, validation and test data (Fig. 10.13). The explanations for training, validation and test are provided in the 'explanation' window. Go to the next page.

Step 6. Determine the network size, please note the structure (Fig. 10.14). In this case the input and output sizes are 13 and 1 respectively. The size of the hidden layer is chosen to be 20.

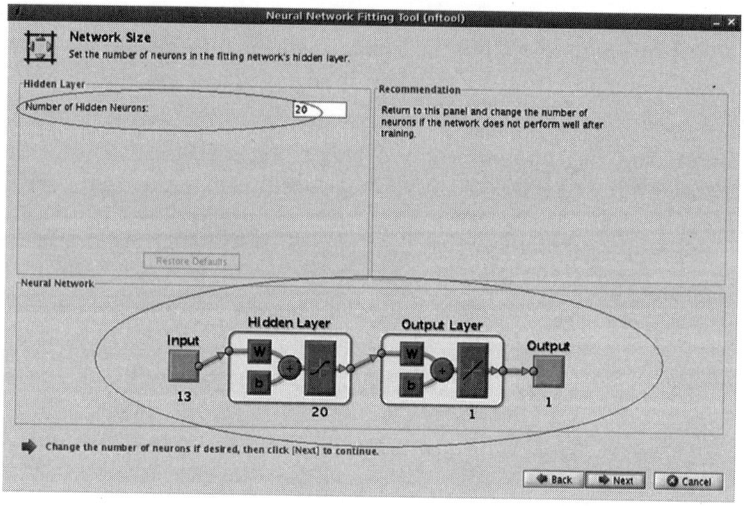

Fig. 10.14. *Network size determined*

Step 6. Train the network (Fig. 10.15, Fig. 10.16 and Fig. 10.17). It may be noted that the network may be retrained for better performance.

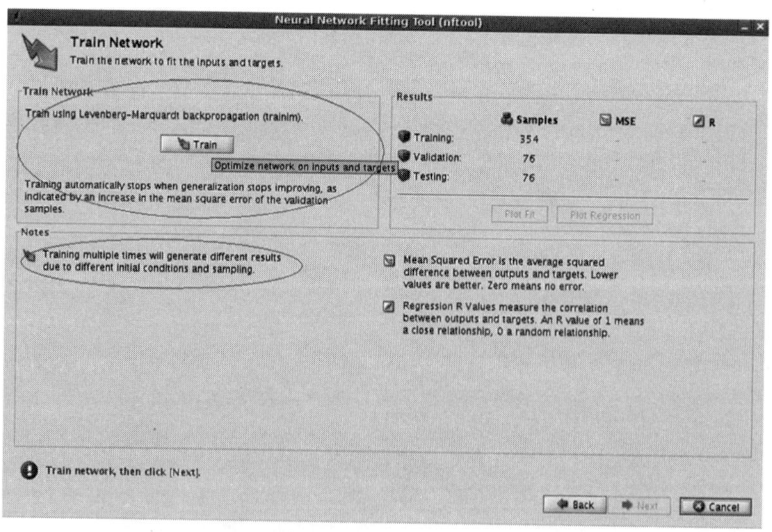

Fig. 10.15. *Training the network*

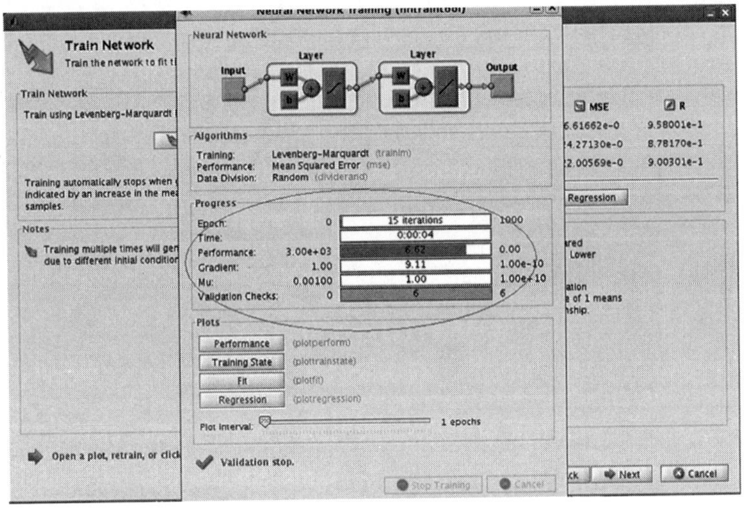

Fig. 10.16. *Training in progress*

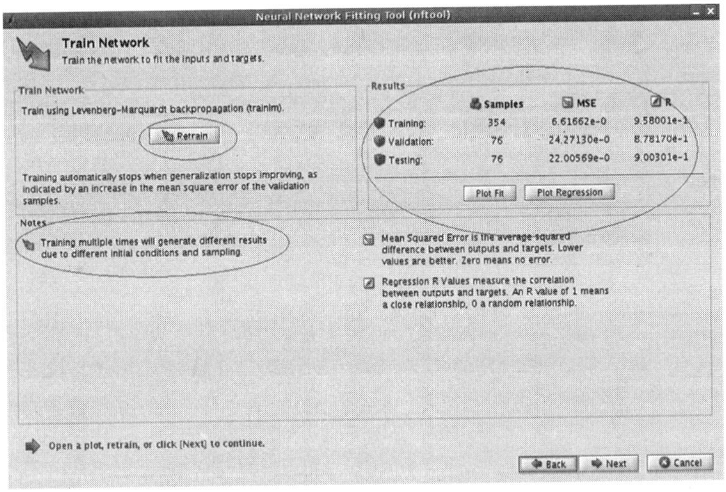

Fig. 10.17. *Training results*

If performance of the resultant network is not satisfactory then MatLab provides options for adjustment of network size and data set. This is shown in Fig. 10.18. Fig. 10.19 shows how to save the results of the process.

Fig. 10.20, Fig. 10.21 and Fig. 10.22 show various snapshots relating to the performance of the network and the training process.

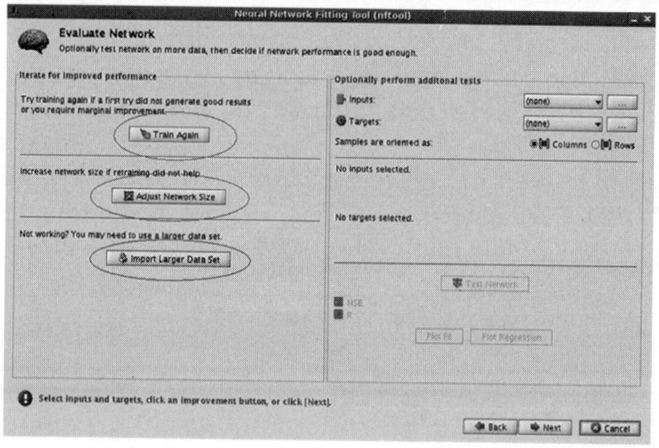

Fig. 10.18. *Network size and data set adjustment options*

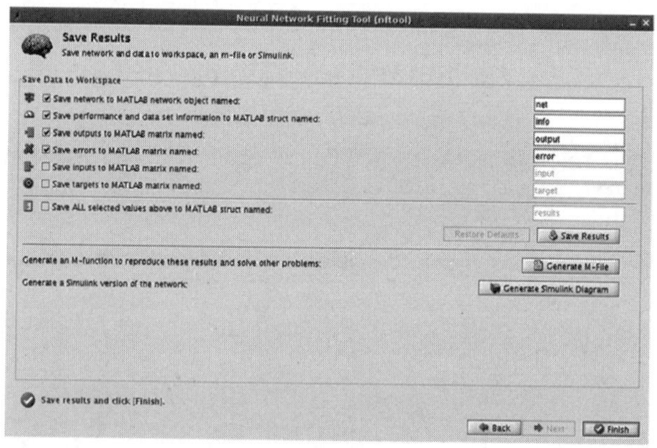

Fig. 10.19. *Saving results*

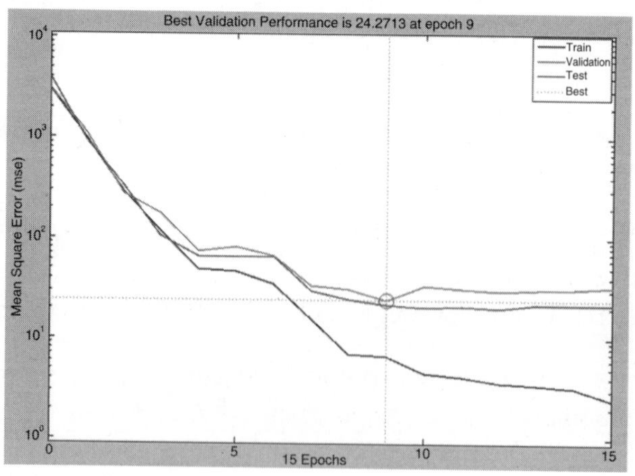

Fig. 10.20. *Performance plot*

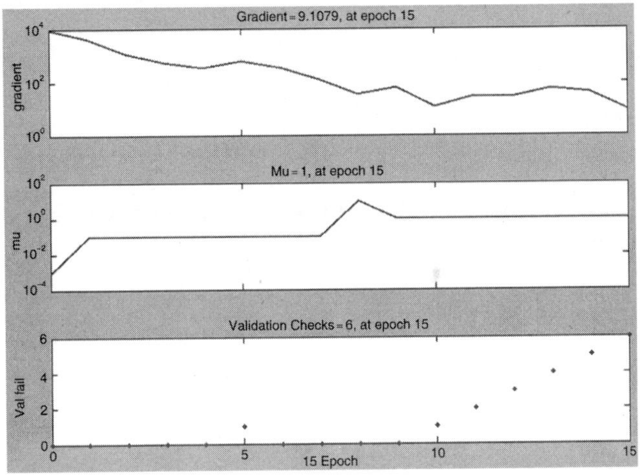

Fig. 10.21. *Training states*

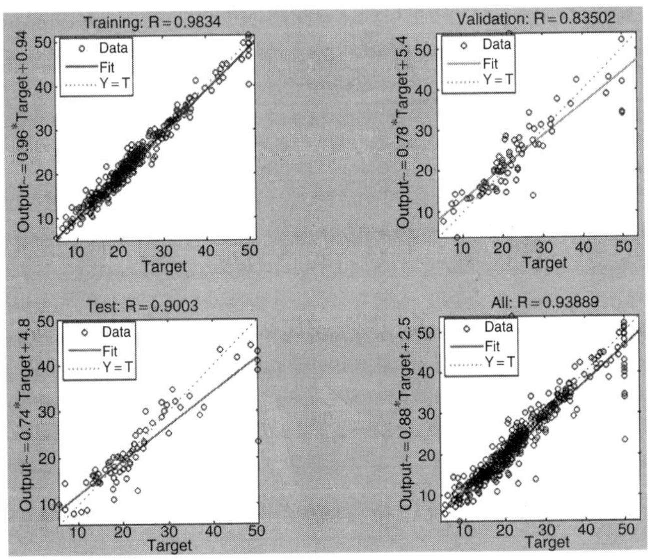

Fig. 10.22. *Regression slot*

✓ TEST YOUR KNOWLEDGE

10.1 How many hidden layers are required by a multilayer perceptron to learn an arbitrary continuous function?

a) One
b) Two
c) More than two
d) None of the above

10.2 During the learning phase of a backpropagation net, direction of flow of signals is
   a) From input to output b) From output to input
   c) Uncertain d) None of the above

10.3 During the learning phase of a backpropagation net, direction of flow of errors is
   a) From input to output b) From output to input
   c) Uncertain d) None of the above

10.4 Which of the following properties of an activation function need not be satisfied while used in a backpropagation net?
   a) Continuity b) Differentiability
   c) Monotonically non-decreasing d) None of the above

10.5 Which of the following activation functions is not suitable for backpropagation nets?
   a) Sigmoid b) Hyperbolic tangent
   c) Step function d) None of the above

10.6 Which of the following learning rules is used to train backpropagation nets?
   a) Hebb rule b) Generalized delta rule
   c) Winner-takes-all d) None of the above

10.7 While applying Hecht and Nielsen criteria for termination of the backpropagation learning process, which of the following sets of patterns is used to determine the termination condition?
   a) Training patterns b) Training-testing patterns
   c) Both (*a*) and (*b*) d) None of the above

10.8 What kind of learning is backpropagation?
   a) Supervised b) Non-supervised
   c) Semi-supervised d) None of the above

10.9 Which of the following activation functions is appropriate for Nguyen-Widrow initialization in backpropagation learning?
   a) Step function b) Hyperbolic tangent
   c) Hyperbolic d) Sigmoid function

10.10 In Nguyen-Widrow initialization, the weights between the hidden layer and the output layer, i.e., the w_{jk} weights, are randomly initialized to values in the range -
   a) -1.0 to $+1.0$ b) -1.0 to 0
   c) 0 to $+1.0$ d) -0.5 to $+0.5$

Answers

10.1 (a)	10.2 (a)	10.3 (b)	10.4 (d)	10.5 (c)
10.6 (b)	10.7 (b)	10.8 (a)	10.9 (b)	10.10 (d)

EXERCISES

10.1 Consider Problem 10.2 in the 'Solved Problems' section where Neural Network Fitting Tool in Matlab is used to solve an input-output fitting problem with a two layer feed forward neural network. Repeat the exercise with the other data sets available in the system.

10.2 A word can be misspelled in various ways. Some of these misspelled words are acceptable in the sense that we can recognize the word in spite of the spelling mistake while others are not acceptable. Table 10.3 presents a list containing various misspellings of the word 'computer' along with their acceptibilities. Use this data set to train a backpropagation net in MatLab. Test the performance of the resultant net with the words 'computrr' and 'commuter'.

Table 10.3. *Misspellings of the word 'computer'.*

#	Word	Decision
1	komputer	Yes
2	komptuer	No
3	comptuer	Yes
4	conjurer	No
5	commteer	No
6	comfuter	Yes
7	comfortr	No
8	komfuter	No
9	coomputr	Yes
10	moonliter	No
11	combuter	Yes
12	conputer	Yes

BIBLIOGRAPHY AND HISTORICAL NOTES

Backpropagation nets are deeply explored by the researchers in the past few decades. Numerous works have been published that are highly interesting both from theoretical and practical points of views. A short list of selected papers in this area is given below.

Cherkassky, V. and Vassilas, N. (1989). Performance of back-propagation networks for associative database retrieval. *In Proceedings of International Joint Conference on Neural Networks, Washington*, DC, pp. I-77–84.

Gori, M. and Tessi, A. (1992). On the problem of local minima in backpropagation. *IEEE Transactions on Pattern Analysis and Machine Intelligence*, Vol. 14, pp. 76–86.

Hecht-Niclsen, R. (1989). Theory of backpropagation neural network. *International Joint Conference on Neural Networks, Washington*, DC, pp. I-593–605.

LeCun, Y., Boser, B., Denker, J. S., Handerson, D., Howard, R. E., Hubbard, W., and Jackel, L. D. (1990). *Handwritten digit recognition with a back-propagation network*. In *Advances in Neural Information Processing Systems*, ed. Touretzky, D. S., Vol. 2, Morgan Kaufmann, San Mateo, CA, pp. 396–404.

Nguyen, D., and Widrow, B. (1990). Improving the learning speed of 2-layer neural networks by choosing initial values of the adaptive weights. *International Joint Conference on Neural Networks, San Diego*, CA., pp. III-21–26.

Pal, S. K. and Mitra, S. (1992). Multilayer perceptron, fuzzy sets, and classification. *IEEE Transactions on Neural Nets*, Vol. 3, No. 5, pp. 683–697.

Plaut, D. S., Nowlan, S. J. and Hinton, G. E. (1986). Experiments on learning by back-propagation. *Technical report CMU-CS-86-126*, Department of Computer Science, Carnegie-Mellon University, Pittsburgh, PA.

Rumelhart, D. E., Hinton, G. E. and Williams, R. J. (1986). Learning representations by back-propagating error. *Nature*, Vol. 323, 533–536.

Sarkar, M. and Yegnanarayana, B. (1997). Incorporation of fuzzy classification properties into back-propagation learning algorithms. *In Proceedings of IEEE International Conference on Fuzzy Systems*, Barcelona, Spain.

11

ELEMENTARY SEARCH TECHNIQUES

Key Concepts

8-queen problem, A algorithm, 'A' algorithm, AND-OR graph, AO* algorithm, CNF-satisfiability, Admissibility, Adversarial search, Alpha-beta cut-off, Alpha-beta pruning, Backtracking, Backtracking depth-first search, Best-first search, Bidirectional search, Binary constraint, Blind search, Block world, Book moves, Breadth-first search (BFS), Constraint, Constraint graph, Constraint hypergraph, Constraint propagation, Constraint satisfaction, Control system, Crossword puzzle, Cryptarithmetic puzzle, Degree heuristic, Depth-first iterative deepening, Depth-first search (DFS), Difference-operator-precondition table, Exhaustive search, Final state, Forward checking, Game playing, Game tree, General constraint, General problem solver (GPS), Global database, Goal state, Graph colouring problem, Greedy local search, Heuristic search, Hill climbing, Horizon effect, Informed search, Initial state, Irrevocable control strategy, Least constraining value heuristic, Local optima, Min-conflict heuristic, Minimum remaining value (MRV) heuristic, n-queen problem, Objective function, Operator subgoaling, Plan generation, Plateau, Post-condition, Pre-condition, Problem reduction, Production rules, Production system, Quiescence, Ridge, Secondary search, Start state, State space, State space search, Static evaluation function, Steepest-ascent hill climbing, Traveling salesperson problem, Unary constraint, Uninformed search, Utility function, Valley descending*

Chapter Outline

Many intelligent computational processes take the form of state space search, which is at the core of such intelligent systems. This chapter provides a review of these elementary state space search techniques. Evolutionary search techniques e.g. Genetic Algorithms (GAs), Simulated Annealing (SA) etc. are traditionally regarded as soft computational processes. These techniques are applied to tackle highly complex problems. A review of the basic search techniques is necessary for an understanding of the evolutionary search strategies stated above. In this chapter we start with the concept of a state space. Then the basic state space search algorithm is presented and explained. Exhaustive search algorithms, e.g., breadth-first search, depth-first search, depth-first iterative deepening etc., are discussed which is followed by discussions on various heuristic search strategies. The principles underlying such techniques as best-first search, hill climbing, A / A* algorithm, AO* algorithm etc. are explained with appropriate illustrative examples. Features of production systems, an important class of intelligent systems employing state space search at the core, are explained along with examples.

11.1 STATE SPACES

Many intelligent computational processes are modeled as a state space search. The concept of a state space is introduced in this section. Searching through a state space, i.e., state space search, is discussed in the next section.

Let us consider a **block world** of size three. A block world consists of a number of cubical blocks on a plane surface. The blocks are distinguishable and they may either rest on the table or stacked on it. The arrangement of the blocks constitutes a **state** of the block world. An arrangement of the blocks can be altered through a set of legal moves. An altered arrangement results in a different state. The size of the block world is given by the number of blocks in it. So, a block world of size three consists of three distinguishable blocks. Let the blocks be marked as X, Y, and Z.

Let the initial stack of the blocks be as shown in Fig. 11.1(a). They are to be rearranged into the goal stack shown in Fig. 11.1(b). The rules to manipulate the block world are:

- Only one block can be moved at a time.
- A block can be moved only if its top is clear, i.e., there is no block over it.
- A block can be placed on the table.
- A block can be placed over another block provided the latter's top is clear.

We have to find a sequence of legal moves to transform the initial stack of blocks to the goal stack.

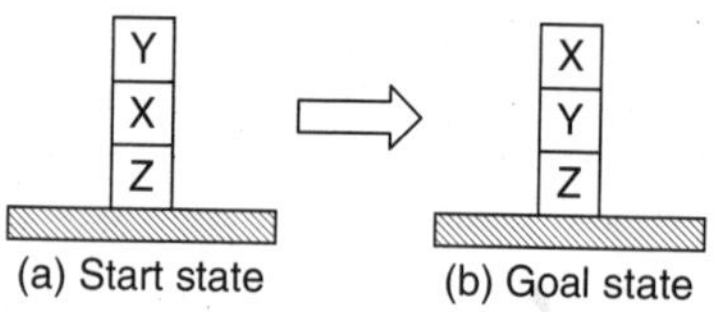

Fig. 11.1. *A block manipulation problem.*

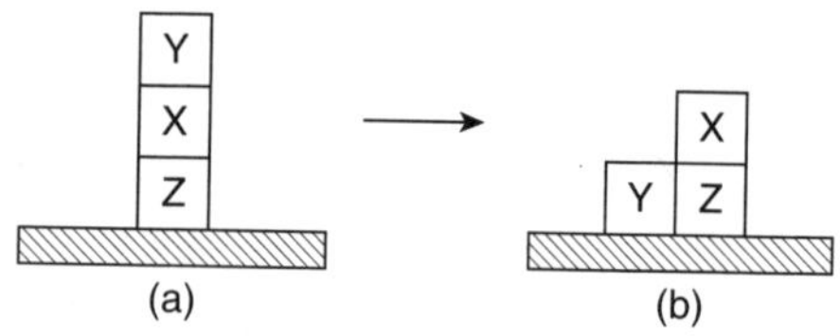

Fig. 11.2. *The first move.*

The only valid move from the initial arrangement is to lift the topmost block Y and place it on the table to obtain the state in Fig. 11.2(b).

From the state depicted in Fig. 11.2(b) the possible moves are:

- Replace block Y on top of X to return to the previous arrangement, or
- Lift block X and place it on the table, or
- Lift block X and place it on block Y.

Taking this into account, the possibilities regarding the first two moves are shown in Fig. 11.3. Bidirectional arrows indicate that the corresponding changes in the block world are reversible.

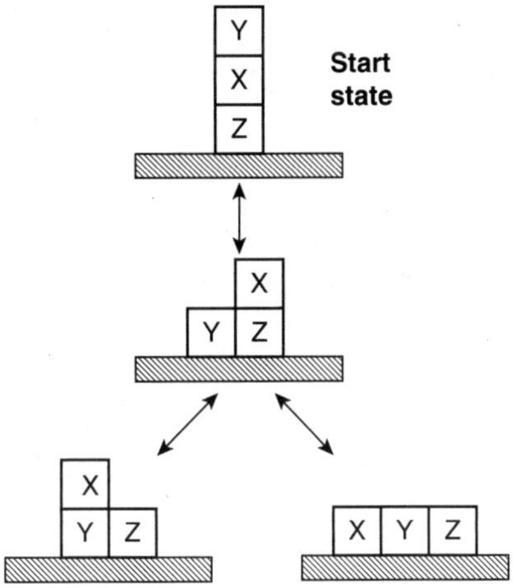

Fig. 11.3. *The first two possible moves.*

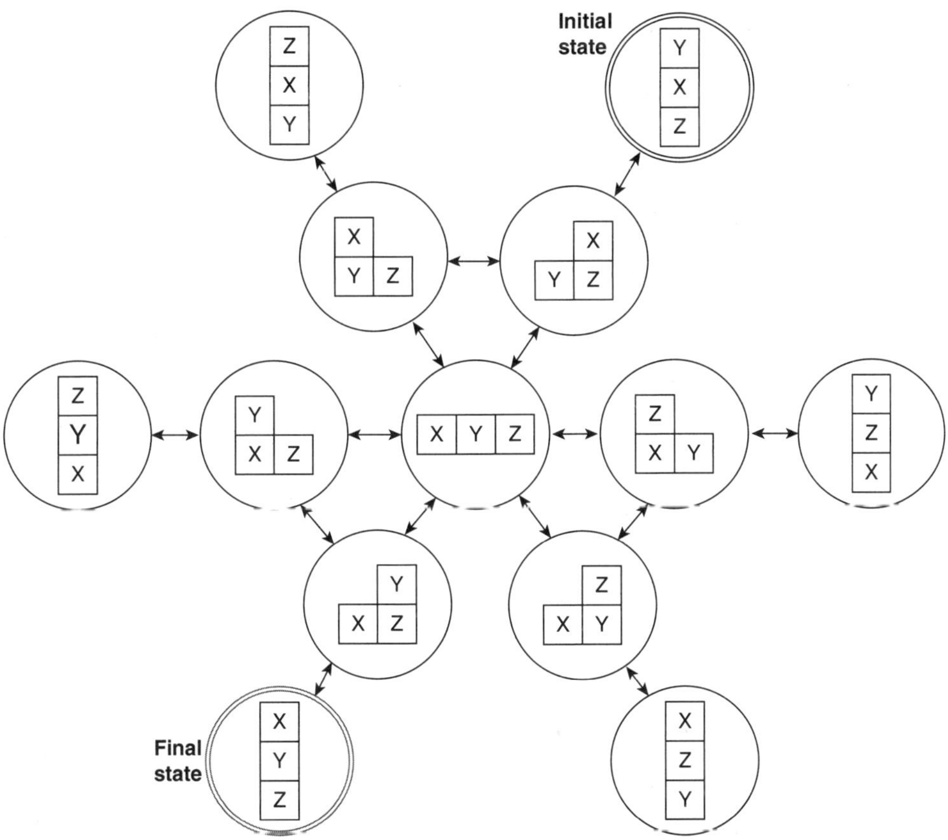

Fig. 11.4. *Movements in the block world of size 3.*

Similarly, newer block world states are generated by applying appropriate moves. The set of all possible block arrangements and their interrelations are shown in Fig. 11.4. This is a tiny **state space** of block manipulation problem of size 3.

We may represent each possible state of the block world as a node and express the transition between two states with directed arcs so that the entire set of possible states along with possible transitions among them takes the form of a graph (Fig. 11.5). Finding a solution to the given problem is tantamount to searching for a **goal** node, (or, a goal state, or final state). The search starts at the **start state** of the problem, i.e., at the start node. During the search process, newer nodes are generated from the earlier nodes by applying the rules of transformation. The generated nodes are tested for goal, or final, node. The search stops when a goal is reached, or is found to be unreachable.

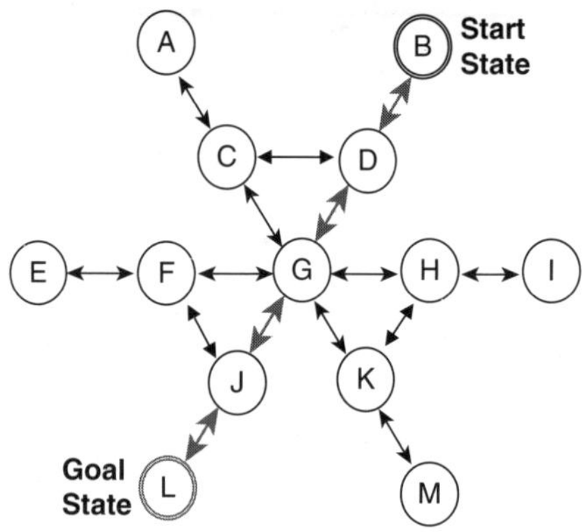

Fig. 11.5. *State space of block manipulation problem.*

Thus, a **state space** for a given problem consists of

- A directed graph $G(V, E)$ where each node $v \in V$ represents a state, and each edge e_{ij} from state v_i to v_j represents a possible transition from v_i to v_j. This graph is called the **state space** of the given problem.
- A designated state $s \in V$ referred to as the **start state**, or **start node**, of the state space. The search starts from this node.
- A **goal condition** which must be satisfied to end the search process successfully. It is expected that one or more nodes of the state space will satisfy this condition. Such nodes are called the **goal** nodes.

The following example illustrates the concept of a state space.

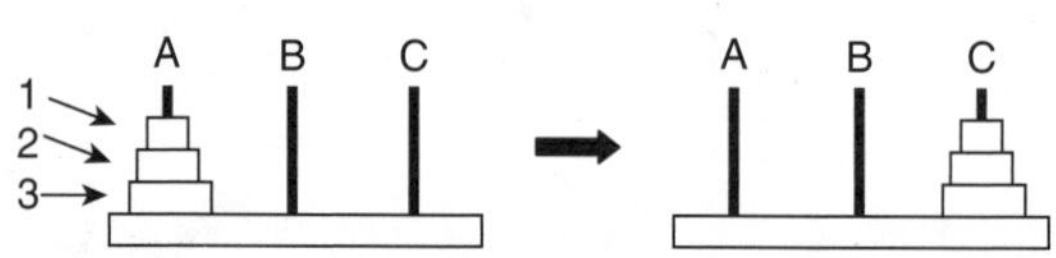

Fig. 11.6. *The Tower of Hanoi problem for three discs.*

Example 11.1 (*State space representation of the Tower of Hanoi problem*)

Let us consider the Tower of Hanoi problem for three discs 1, 2, and 3 (Fig. 11.6). Discs 1, 2, and 3 are in ascending order of diameter. Initially all the discs are in peg A and the other two pegs B and C are empty. The discs are to be transferred from peg A to peg C so that the final arrangement shown on the right side of Fig. 11.6 is achieved. Disks are transferred from peg to peg subject to the following rules:

- Only one disc may be transferred at a time.
- Under no circumstances a larger disc may be placed over a smaller disc.
- A disc can be picked for movement only if there is no other disc on it.

Let us formulate the problem as a state space search in the following way. The first thing to do is to find a suitable representation of the problem state. We employ here a 3×3 matrix to represent a state. Columns 1, 2 and 3 of the matrix correspond to the pegs A, B, and C, respectively. Similarly, the rows are used to indicate the relative positions of the discs within a peg. Thus, the start state and the goal state are expressed as in Fig. 11.7(a) and Fig. 11.7(b).

What about the transitions among the possible states? Initially all discs are in peg A with disc 3 at the bottom and disc 1 at the top. In this situation we can pick disc 1 from the top and put it either in peg B or in peg C (Fig. 11.8). Each of these two states will generate others states (including those already generated) and so on. The partial state space for this problem with one path from the start state to the goal state is shown in Fig. 11.9. The corresponding graph is given in Fig. 11.10. The graph does not show the details of a state and express them simply as nodes. The start node and the goal node are indicated with appropriate tags and the solution path, i.e., the sequence of moves from the start node to the goal node is highlighted.

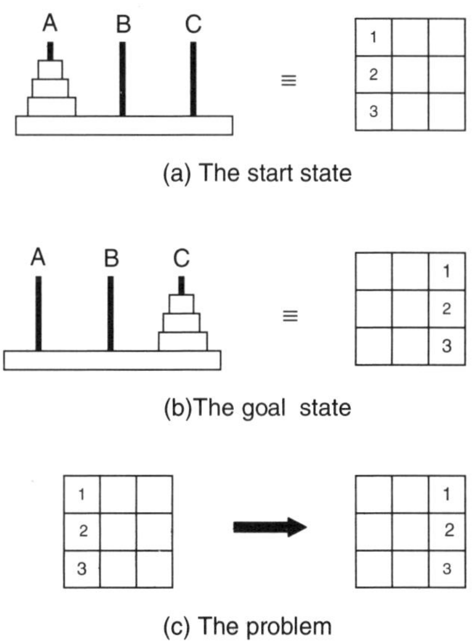

Fig. 11.7. *Formulation of Tower of Hanoi problem as a state space search.*

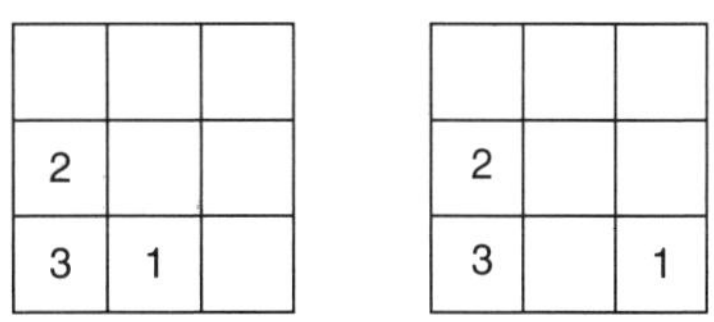

Fig. 11.8. *Probable states after the first move.*

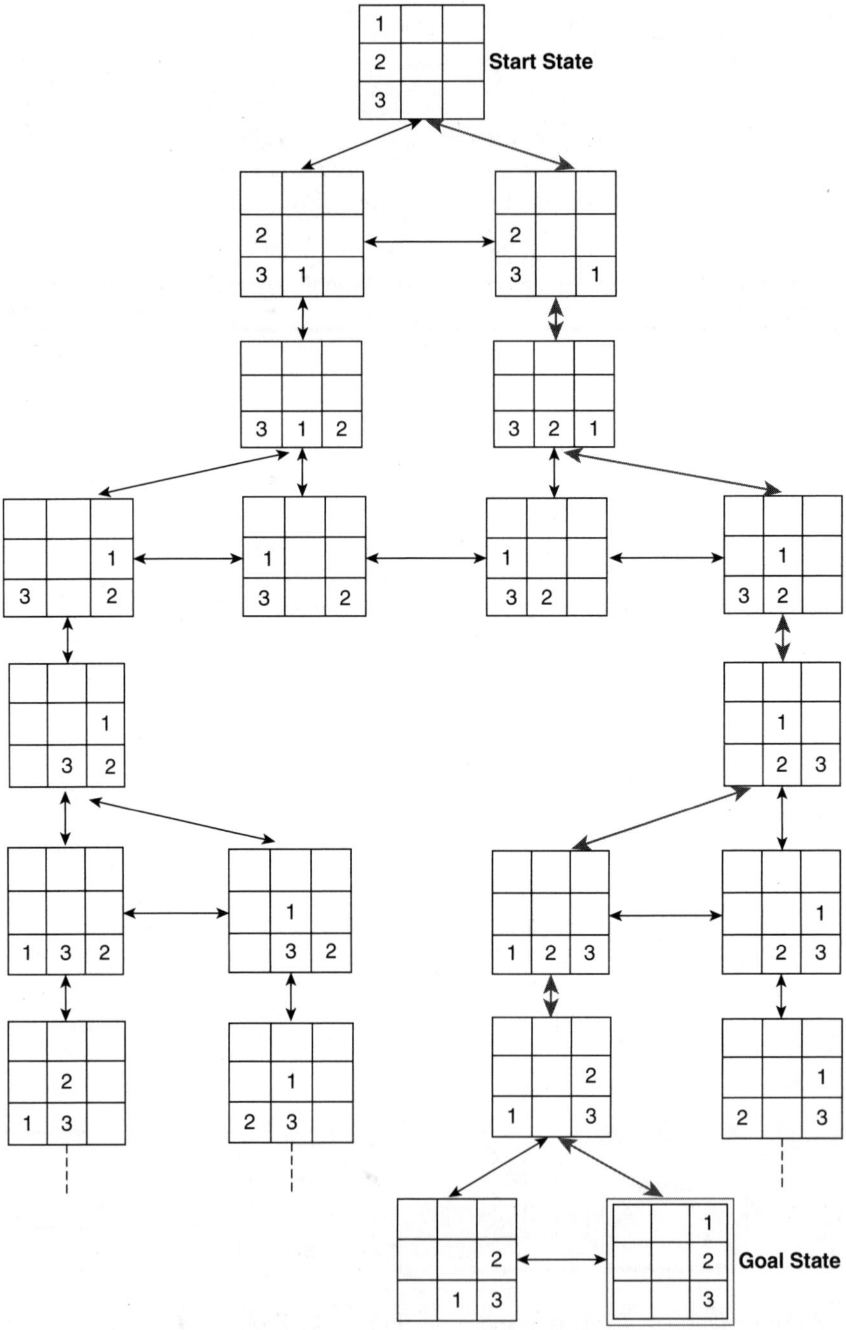

Fig. 11.9. *State space of Tower of Hanoi problem with three discs*

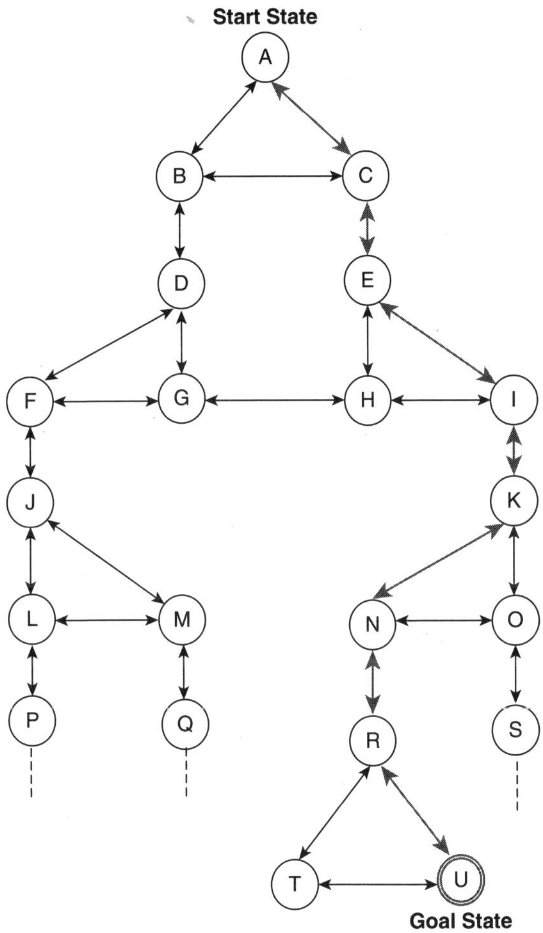

Fig. 11.10. *State space of Tower of Hanoi as a graph*

Example 11.2 (*State space representation of the 8-puzzle*)

The 8-puzzle is a combination of eight movable tiles, numbered 1 to 8, set within a 3×3 frame. Out of the $3 \times 3 = 9$ cells eight cells are occupied by the tiles and one remaining cell is empty. At any instant, a tile which is adjacent to the empty cell in the vertical or in horizontal direction, may slide into it. Equivalently, the empty cell can be moved to left, right, up, or down by one cell at a time, depending on its position. The state of the 8-puzzle can be represented with the help of a 3×3 matrix where the empty cell is indicated by blank. Given the initial and the goal states of an 8-puzzle as shown in Fig. 11.11, we are to generate the state space and a path from the start state to the goal state in it.

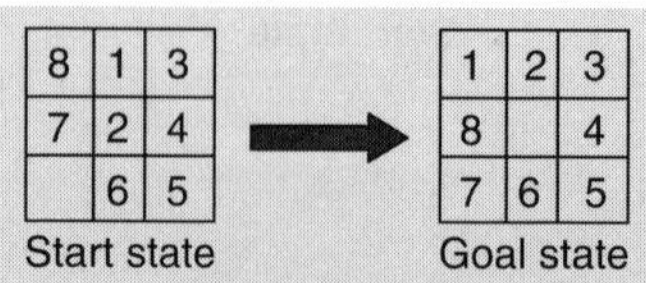

Fig. 11.11. *An instance of the 8-puzzle.*

Initially the empty cell is at the bottom-left corner. We can move it either upwards or to the right. No other movement is possible from this position. Accordingly, we get two children from the start node. From each of these children, two new states can be generated. If we go on generating newer states and the interconnections among them we get the required state space as shown in Fig. 11.12. Fig. 11.13 hides the details of the individual states and presents the said state space as a directed graph.

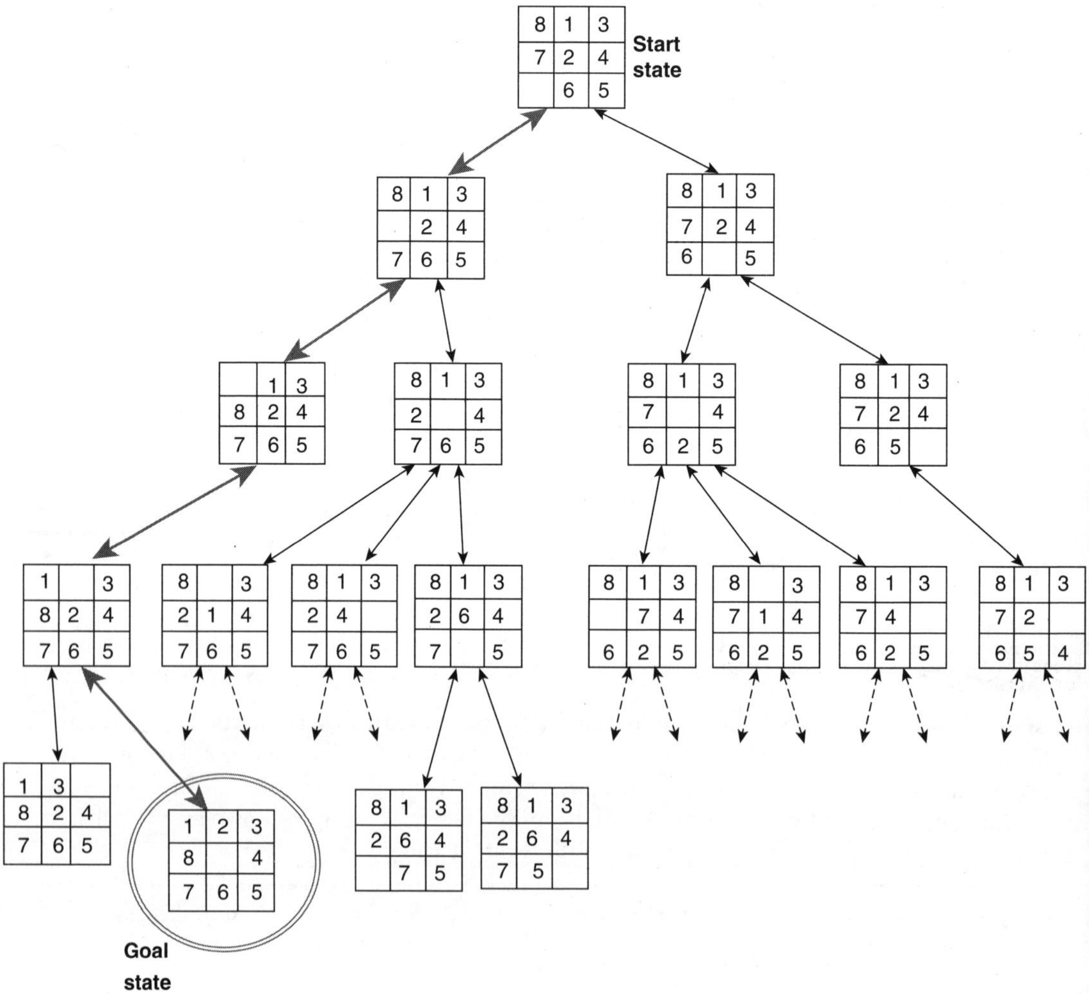

Fig. 11.12. *State space of the 8-puzzle.*

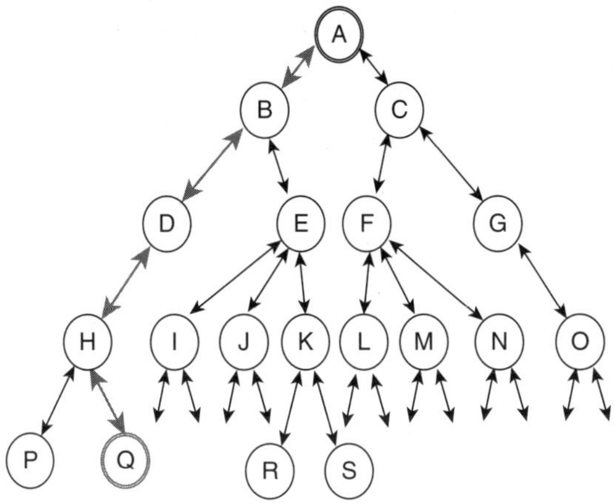

Fig. 11.13. *State space of the 8-puzzle as a graph.*

11.2 STATE SPACE SEARCH

Once the state space of a given problem is formulated, solving the problem amounts to a search for the goal in it. The basic search process is independent of the problem and has a number of common features as described below.

11.2.1 Basic Graph Search Algorithm

The search starts from the start node which represents the initial state of the problem. As the search proceeds, newer and newer nodes are produced and the search tree grows. The search tree is a subgraph of state space. It consists of the nodes generated during the search. There is a set of transformation rules that map a given node to other nodes. A node is said to be **generated** when it is obtained as a result of applying some rule on the parent node. A node is said to be **expanded** when its children are generated. Moreover, there are some conditions to ascertain whether a given node is a goal not. When a node undergoes such a test it is said to be **explored**.

During the search, two lists are maintained. One for the nodes that have been generated but neither explored, nor expanded. This list is referred to as *OPEN*. The other list, called *CLOSED*, contains all nodes that have been generated as well as explored and expanded. While the search process is on, a node from the *OPEN* list is selected for processing. It is first explored and if found to be a goal node, the search ends successfully. Otherwise, the node is expanded and the newly generated nodes are included into the search tree constructed so far. The process stops successfully when a goal node is reached. It ends unsuccessfully if the list *OPEN* is found to be empty, indicating that the goal node, if exists, is unreachable from the start node.

A simplified version of the algorithm which focuses on the essential features of state space search is given in **`Algorithm Basic-State-Space-Search`** (Fig. 11.14).

```
Algorithm Basic-State-Space-Search

/* Let OPEN be a list of states that have been generated but not yet
explored or expanded. Another list CLOSED contains the states that are
```

```
explored as well as expanded. T is the search tree, i.e., the portion of
the state space created so far. */

1. Begin
2. Initialize the search tree T with a single node S, the start state.
   Initialize OPEN with only S in it and CLOSED as an empty list.
3. If (OPEN is empty) Then the goal is unreachable and the search is un-
   successful. Exit. End-If
4. Let n be the first node on OPEN. Remove n from the list OPEN and put n
   on the list CLOSED.
5. If (n is a goal node) Then the search is successful. Exit. End-If
6. Generate all children of node n. Let us denote this set by CHLDRN(n).
7. Merge CHLDRN(n) with OPEN according to some predefined criteria.
8. Go to Step 3.
9. End Basic-State-Space-Search
```

Fig. 11.14. *Algorithm Basic-State-Space-Search.*

11.2.2 Informed and Uninformed Search

Step 7 of **Algorithm Basic-State-Space-Search** states that the newly generated nodes are to be merged with the states of the existing *OPEN* queue. But how this merging should be done is not explained. Actually, the character of a search process depends on the sequence in which the nodes are explored which, in turn, is determined by the way new nodes are merged with the current nodes of *OPEN*.

All state space searches can be classified into two broad categories, **uninformed** and **informed**. They are also referred to as **blind** search, and **heuristic** search, respectively. In an uninformed, or blind, search, no knowledge of the problem domain is employed to guide the search for a goal node. On the contrary, an informed, or heuristic, search is guided by some knowledge of the problem domain so that the process may estimate the relative merit of the unexplored nodes with respect to the attainment of a goal node through it. The crucial point is Step 7 of **Algorithm Basic-State-Space-Search** where the newly generated nodes are merged with the existing *OPEN* list. The way of merging differentiates between the various kinds of search strategies to be discussed subsequently.

11.3 EXHAUSTIVE SEARCH

An exhaustive search is a kind of blind search that tries to examine each and every node of the state space till a goal is reached or there is no way to proceed. The elementary systematic exhaustive searches are **breadth-first search** (BFS), **depth-first search**, **depth-first iterative deepening** search, and **bidirectional** search. These are discussed in this section.

11.3.1 Breadth-first Search (BFS)

Breadth-first search explores the search space laterally. It employs a queue to implement *OPEN* so that while executing Step 7 of **`Algorithm Basic-State-Space-Search`**, the newly generated nodes are added at the *end* of the *OPEN*. Consequently, the nodes generated earlier are explored earlier in a FIFO fashion. For example, consider the extremely simple and tiny state space depicted in Fig. 11.15. It consists of 13 states A, B, …, M and certain transitions among them. The states G, L and M are the goal states.

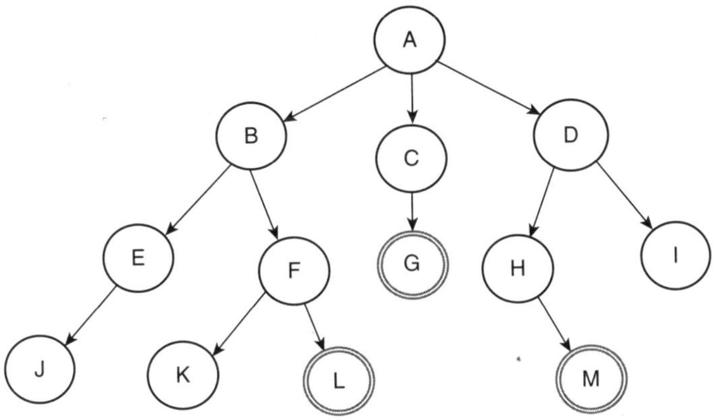

Fig. 11.15. *A tiny state space.*

Table 11.1 shows the trace of execution of breadth-first search of the state space given in Fig. 11.15. The search is initialized by putting the start state A on the *OPEN* queue. At this instant *n*, *CHLDRN* (*n*), and *CLOSED* are all empty because node A is not yet removed from *OPEN* and explored. At the 8th row we remove node G, the first node in the *OPEN* queue at that moment, and examine it. Since G is tested to be a goal node, the search stops here successfully.

Table 11.1. *Breadth-first search on Fig. 11.15*

#	n	CHLDRN (*n*)	CLOSED	OPEN
1	–	–	–	A
2	A	B, C, D	A	B, C, D
3	B	E, F	A, B	C, D, E, F
4	C	G	A, B, C	D, E, F, G
5	D	H, I	A, B, C, D	E, F, G, H, I
6	E	J	A, B, C, D, E	F, G, H, I, J
7	F	K, L	A, B, C, D, E, F	G, H, I, J, K, L
8	**G**	***(SUCCESS)***		

Step by step construction of the search tree is shown in Fig. 11.16(a)–(h). Nodes that are generated but not yet explored, or expanded, are highlighted with dotted lines. The unexplored node which is to be explored next is indicated by an arrow. Fig. 11.16(h) shows the final search tree. The dotted arrowed line shows the sequence of nodes visited during the breadth-first search. The search stops as soon as we explore the node G, a goal. It may be noted that except Fig. 11.16(h), node G is shown as an usual node and not a goal node. This is because unless a state is tested it can not be recognized as a goal node even after it has been generated.

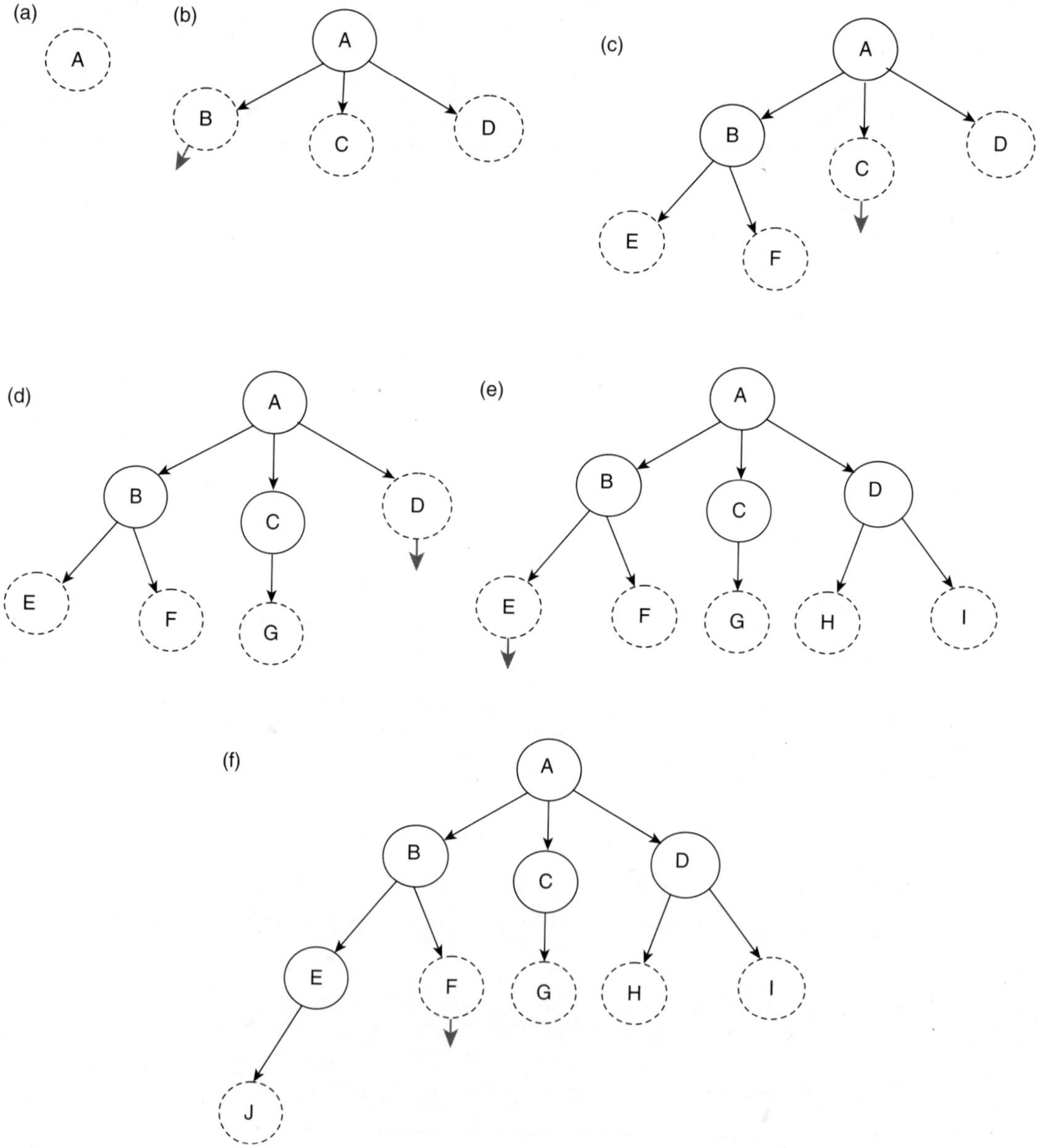

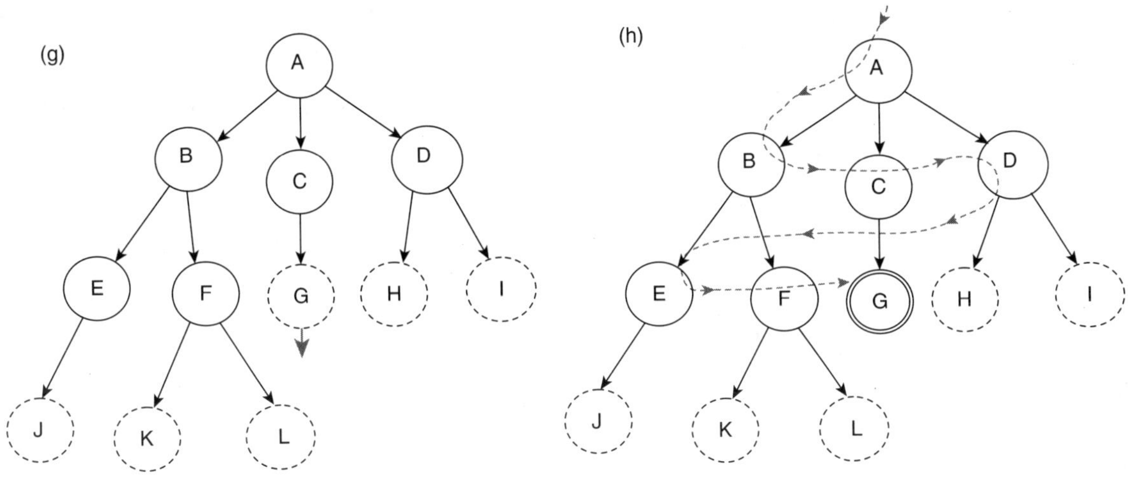

Fig. 11.16. *(a)–(h) Breadth-first search (BFS) steps*

11.3.2 Depth-first Search (DFS)

While BFS explores the search tree laterally, DFS does so vertically. In DFS, *OPEN* is implemented as a stack so that the problem states are explored in a LIFO manner. The execution of the depth-first search process can be traced as in case of BFS. As the data structure *OPEN* should now be a stack rather than a queue the nodes in *CHLDRN* (*n*) should be placed in front of *OPEN* and not at the rear. Table 11.2 depicts the trace of DFS on Fig. 11.15. The construction of the corresponding search tree is shown in Fig. 11.17(a)–(h).

Table 11.2. *Depth-first search on Fig. 11.15.*

#	*n*	CHLDRN (*n*)	CLOSED	OPEN (stack)
1	–	–	–	A
2	A	B, C, D	A	B, C, D
3	B	E, F	A, B	E, F, C, D
4	E	J	A, B, E	J, F, C, D
5	J	–	A, B, E, J	F, C, D
6	F	K, L	A, B, E, J, F	K, L, C, D
7	K	–	A, B, E, J, F, K	L, C, D
8	**L**	***(SUCCESS)***		

Please note that the DFS tree is different from its BFS counterpart. This is because the nodes explored are different. Moreover, the goals reached are also different. However, in case the state space contains only one goal state then both of these strategies will end with this unique goal. Still, the path from the start node to the goal node would be different for different search strategies.

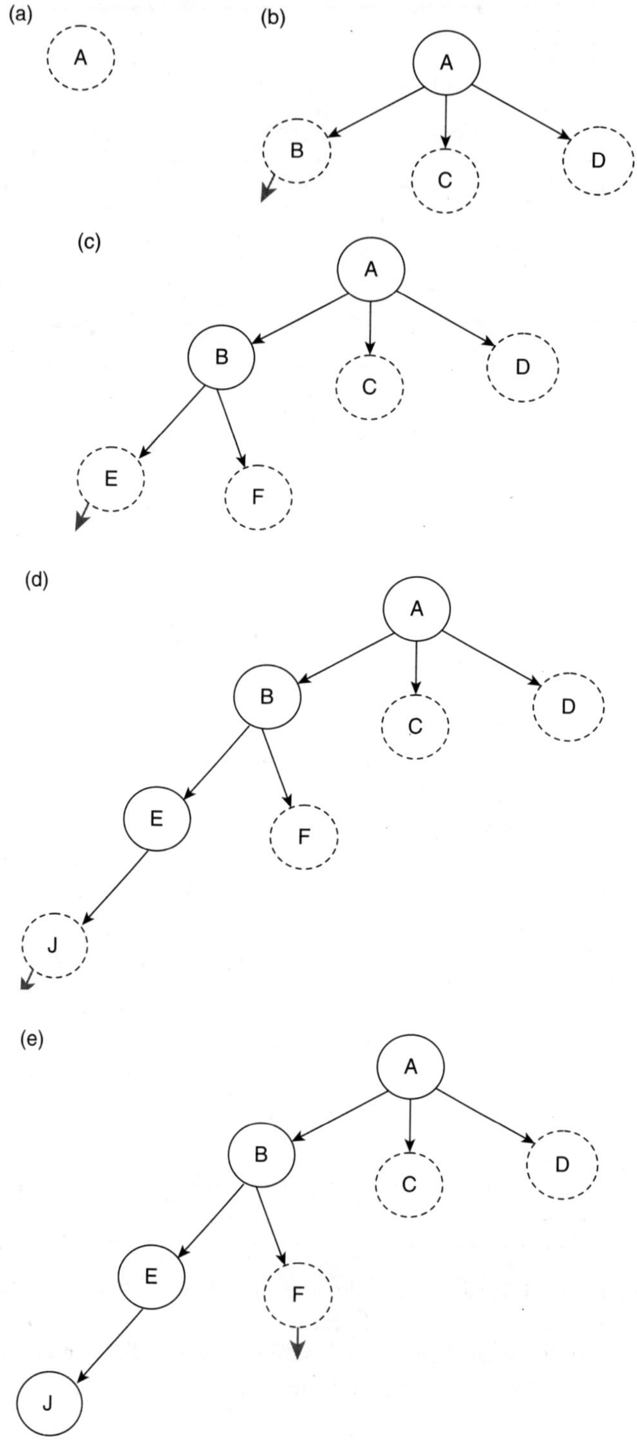

(Continued)

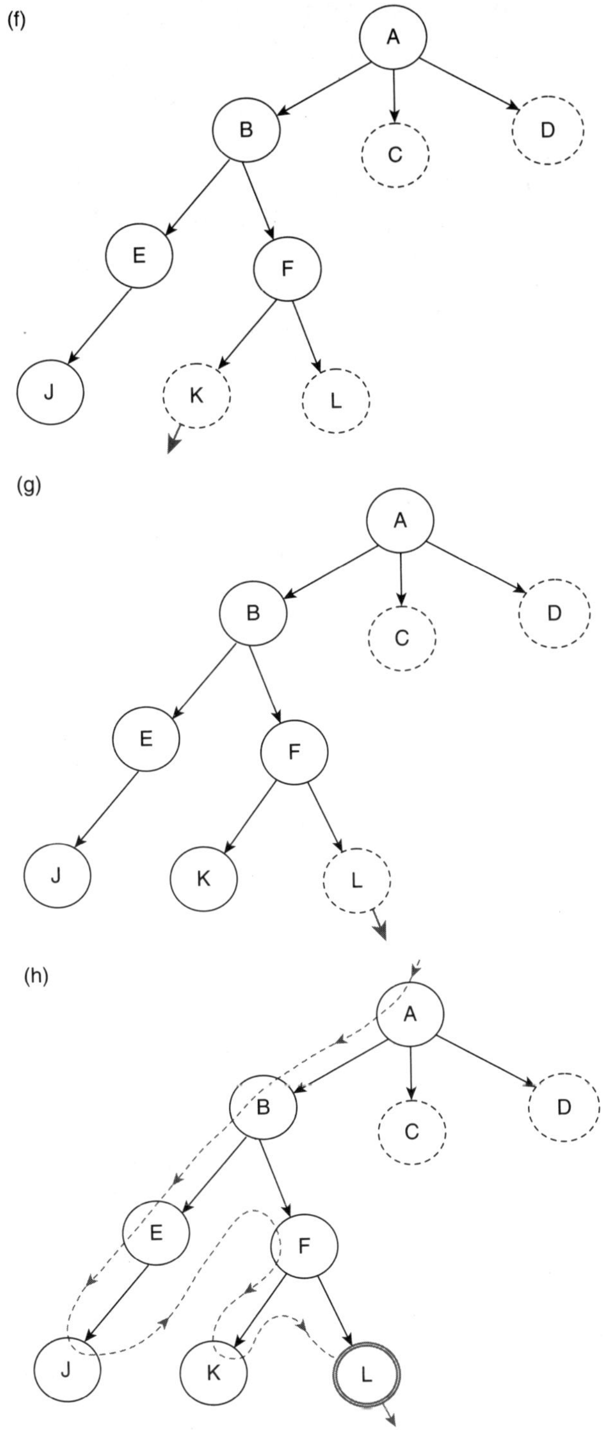

Fig. 11.17. *(a)–(h) Depth-first search steps.*

11.3.3 Comparison Between BFS and DFS

For a given search problem is it possible to anticipate à-priori which between BFS and DFS would reach a goal earlier? For example, consider the state space of Fig. 11.18(a), which is identical to Fig. 11.15 except that instead of three here we have a single goal node D. If we follow BFS on this graph, we need to explore four nodes to arrive at the goal (Fig. 11.18(b)). The same goal is attained after exploring 10 nodes if we employ DFS (Fig. 11.18(c)). Obviously, the BFS approach is better than DFS in this case. However, the situation is quite the opposite if the goal is located at J instead of D (Fig. 11.19(a)). Here the number of nodes required to explore till we reach the goal using BFS and DFS are 10 and 4, respectively (Fig. 11.19(b) and (c)).

There are some thumb rules to anticipate which, between BFS and DFS, is more efficient for a given problem. Such anticipations are based on some knowledge of the problem domain. For example, if it is known that there are a large number of goal nodes distributed over the entire state space then DFS is probably the right choice. On the other hand, if it contains only one or just a few goal nodes then BFS is perhaps better than DFS.

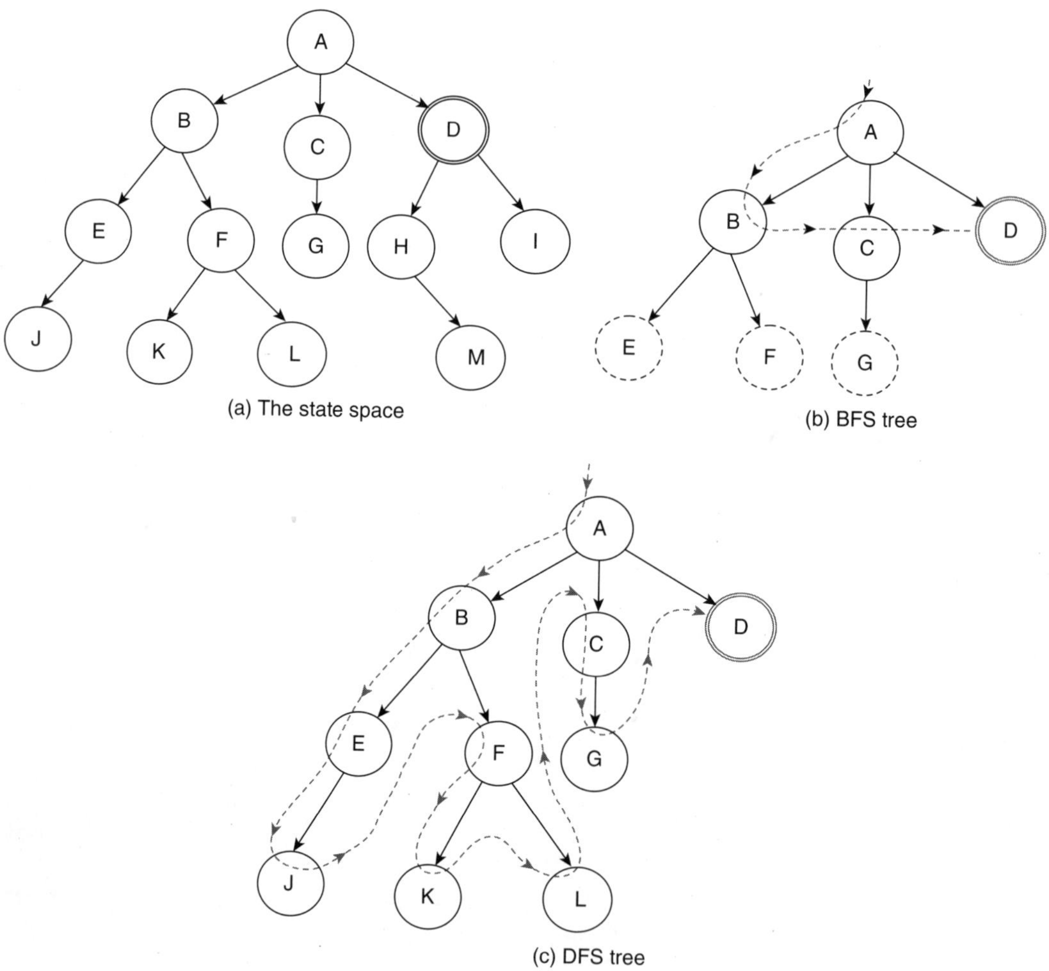

(a) The state space

(b) BFS tree

(c) DFS tree

Fig.11.18. *(a)–(c) A state space where BFS is more efficient than DFS.*

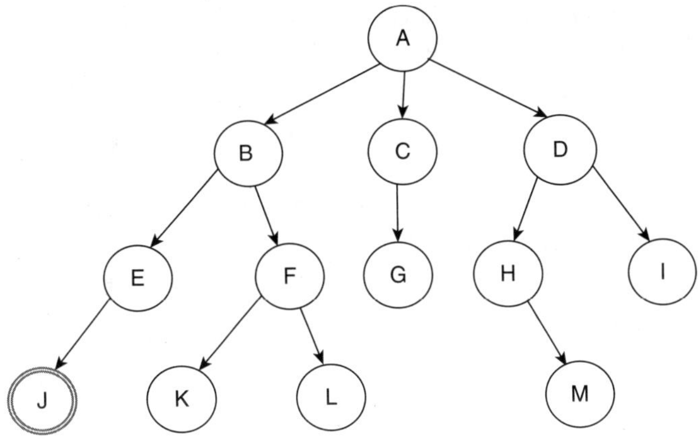

(a) The state space

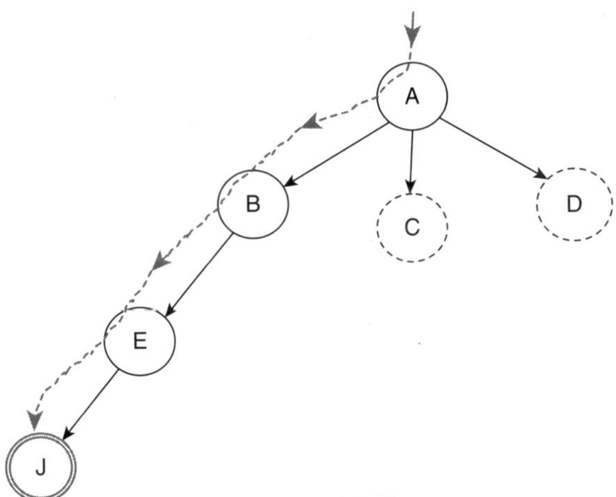

(b) DFS tree

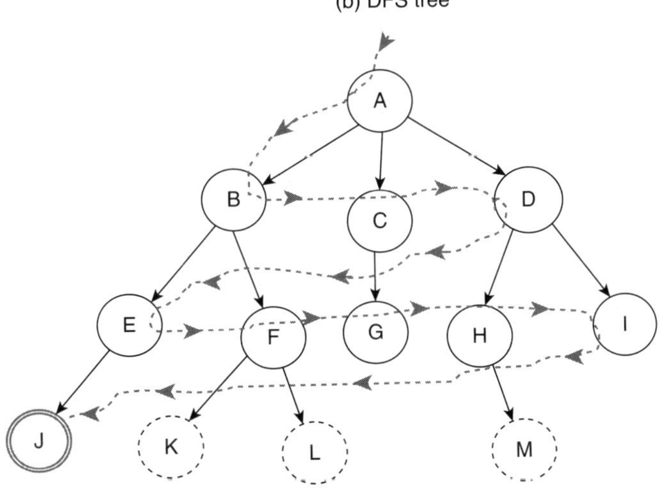

(c) BFS tree

Fig.11.19. *(a)–(c) A state space where DFS is more efficient than BFS.*

Both depth-first search and breadth-first search have their own merits and demerits. A comparative study of these two exhaustive search strategies is given in Table 11.3.

Table 11.3. *Comparison of DFS and BFS*

#	DFS	BFS
1	Requires less memory.	Requires more memory.
2	May reach a goal at level *n*+1 without exploring the entire search space till level *n*.	All parts of the search space till level *n* must be explored to reach a goal at level *n*+1.
3	Likely to reach a solution early if numerous goals exist.	Likely to reach a solution early even if few goals exist.
4	Susceptible to get stuck in an unfruitful path for a very long time while exploring a path deep into the state space.	Not susceptible to get stuck in a blind ally.
5	Does not guarantee to offer a minimal-length path from the start state to a goal node. Hence, DFS is not *admissible*.	Guarantees to find the minimal-length path from the start node to a goal node. Therefore, BFS is *admissible*.

If b is the highest number of successors obtained by expanding a node in the state space, then the time complexity of BFS is $O(b^d)$, where d is the depth of the search tree, i.e., the length of the solution path. This can be easily obtained by considering the fact that the most significant computation during the search process is the expansion of a leaf node. The number of nodes generated till depth d is $b + b^2 + \ldots + b^d$, which is $O(b^d)$. The space complexity is also $O(b^d)$ because all nodes at level d must be kept in memory in order to generate the nodes at level d+1. Hence, BFS is quite expensive in terms of space and time requirements. The time complexity of DFS is also $O(b^d)$, same as that of BFS. However, DFS is more efficient in terms of space utilization having space complexity $O(b)$. This is because only the nodes belonging to the path from the start node to the current node are to be stored in case of DFS.

The main problem with DFS is that unless we set a cutoff depth and compel the search to backtrack when the current path exceeds the cutoff, it may take too long find a goal. Setting the cutoff depth is also a tricky issue. If it is too shallow, we may miss a goal. If it is too deep, wasteful computation will be done.

11.3.4 Depth-first Iterative Deepening

We have seen that depth-first search is efficient in terms of space requirement, but runs the risk of getting trapped in an unfruitful path. Moreover, it does not guarantee a shortest path from the start state to a goal state. Breadth-first search, on the other hand, always returns a shortest solution path but requires huge memory space because all leaf nodes till the depth of the current search tree are to be preserved. **Depth-first iterative deepening** (DFID) is the algorithm that tries to combine the advantages of depth-first and breadth-first search. DFID is a version of depth-first search where the search is continued till a predefined depth d is reached. The value of d is initially 1 and is incremented by 1 after each iteration. Therefore, DFID starts with a DFS with cutoff depth 1. If a goal is attained, the search stops successfully. Otherwise, all nodes generated so far are discarded and the search starts afresh for a new cutoff depth 2. Again, if a goal is reached then the search ends successfully, otherwise the process is repeated for depth 3 and so on. The entire process is continued until a goal node is found or some predefined maximum depth is reached. Fig. 11.20(a)–(c) depict the successive iterations of a simple DFID.

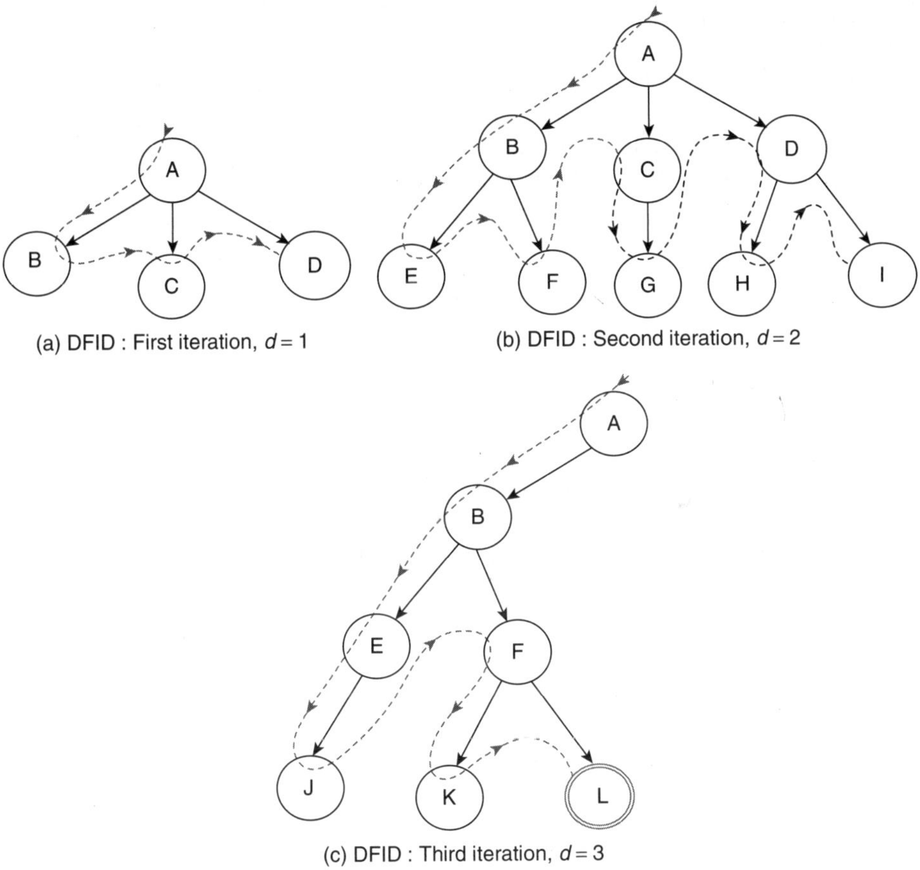

Fig. 11.20. *(a)–(c) Depth-first iterative deepening (DFID) search steps.*

The depth-first iterative deepening algorithm expands all nodes at a given depth before it goes for expanding nodes at some deeper level. Hence, DFID search is admissible, i.e., it guarantees to find a shortest solution path to the goal. However, it does perform some redundant computations before reaching the depth where a goal exists. It has been shown that both DFS and BFS require at least as much time and space as DFID, especially for increasingly large searches. The time and space complexities of depth-first iterative deepening search are $O(b^d)$ and $O(b)$, respectively.

11.3.5 Bidirectional Search

The search techniques discussed so far proceed from the start state to the goal state and never in the reverse direction. It is also possible to perform the search in the reverse direction, i.e., from the goal state towards the start state provided that the state space satisfies the following conditions:

- The goal is already known, and our aim is to find a *path* from the start state to the goal state.
- There is a single goal state and that is provided in explicit terms so that we know at the very outset exactly what the goal state is.
- The links between the states of the search space are bidirectional. This means that the operators, or rules, provided for generation of the nodes have inverses.

A search procedure which proceeds in two opposite directions, *viz.*, one from the start state towards the goal state (forward direction) and the other from the goal state towards the start state (backward direction), simultaneously, is called a **bidirectional search**. The search ends successfully when a common node is generated by both. The path from the start state to the goal state is obtained by combining the forward path from the start state to the common node α and that from the goal node to node α. The basic idea of a bidirectional search is shown in Fig. 11.21.

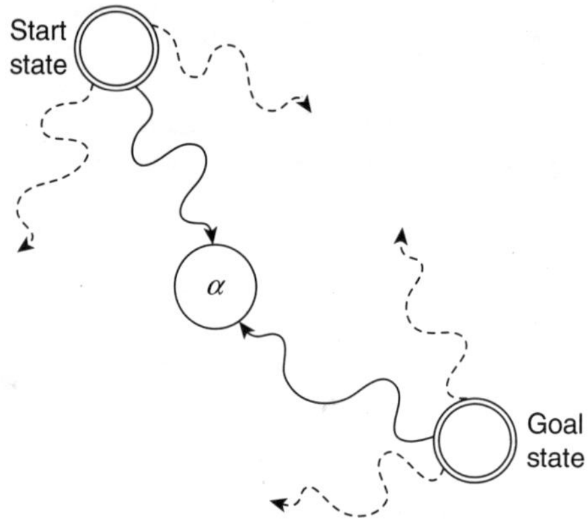

Fig. 11.21. *Bidirectional search.*

Example 11.3 (*Bidirectional search for block manipulation problem*)

Let us consider Fig. 11.5 depicting the state space of a block manipulation problem with three blocks. Assuming that node *B* is start state and node *L* the goal, we want to find a path from *A* to *L* using the bidirectional search strategy.

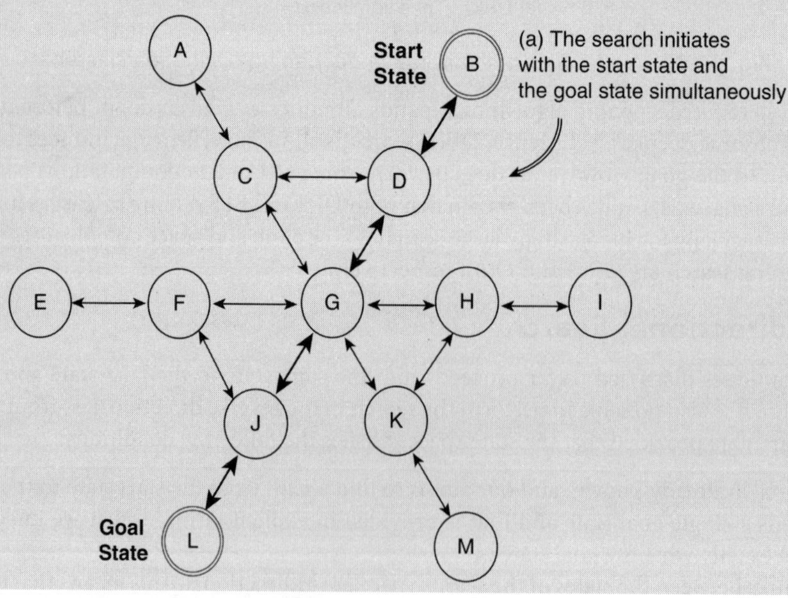

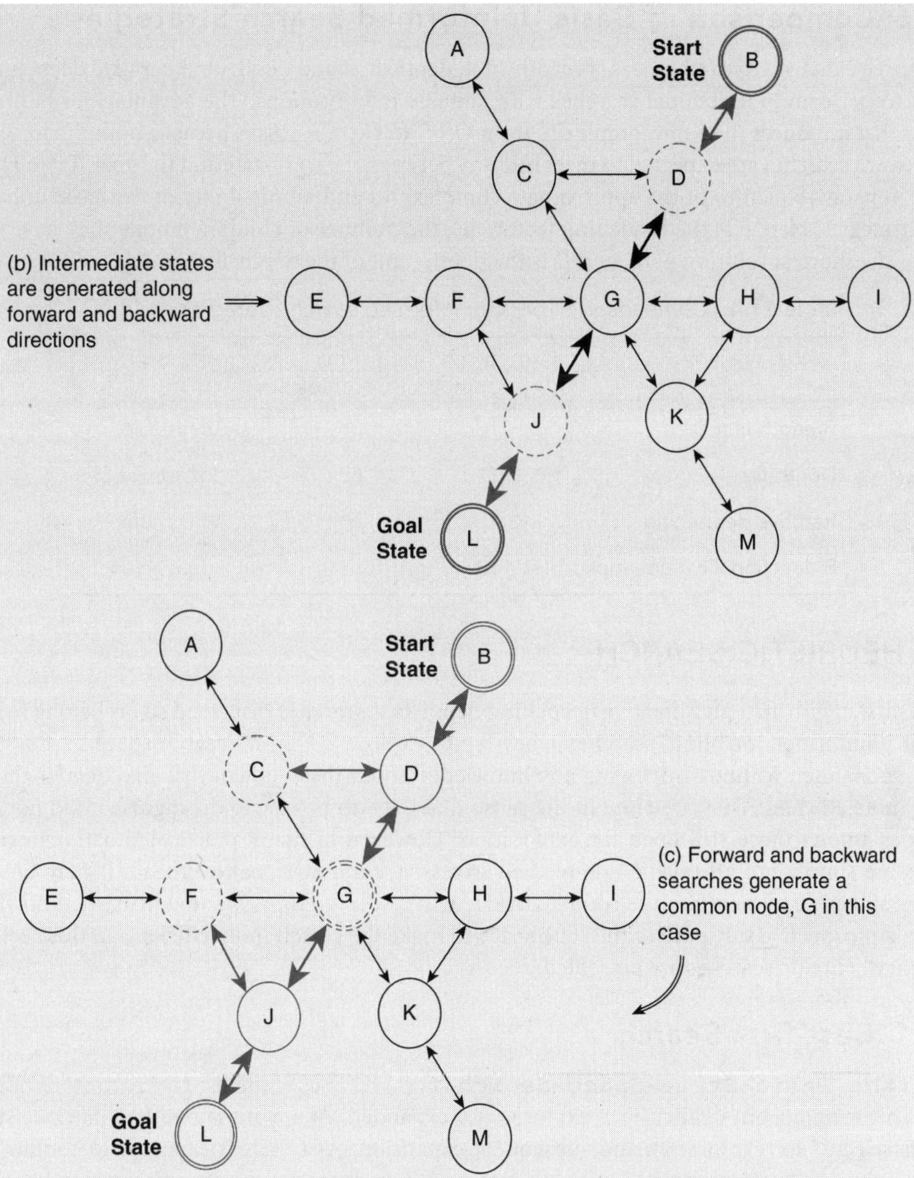

Fig. 11.22. *(a)–(c) Bidirectional search for block manipulation problem.*

The consecutive steps are shown in Fig. 11.22(a)–(c). The portion of the search space which remains unexplored at any instant appears in a lighter tone. Nodes that have been generated but not yet explored are depicted in dashed lines. The common node *G* generated by both the forward and the backward search process is drawn with double dashed lines. The path from the start node *B* to the goal node *L* consists of the sequence of nodes *B-D-G-J-L* which is constructed by combining the path *B-D-G* and *L-J-G* returned by the forward and backward searches, respectively.

11.3.6 Comparison of Basic Uninformed Search Strategies

All the three exhaustive searches, *viz.*, breadth-first, depth-first and depth-first iterative deepening, may be used to perform bidirectional searches with suitable modifications. The advantage of bidirectional search is that it reduces the time complexity from $O(b^d)$ to $O(b^{d/2})$. This is because both the forward and the backward searches are expected to meet midway between the start state and the goal. Table 11.4 presents a comparative picture of the approximate complexities and admissibility of the basic uninformed search strategies. Here b is the branching factor, i.e., the number of children a node may have, d is the length of the shortest solution path, and D is the depth limit of the depth-first search.

Table 11.4. *Comparison of basic uninformed search strategies*

Search strategy	Space complexity	Time complexity	Admissibilty
Breadth-first	b^d	b^d	Admissible
Depth-first	D	b^D	Not admissible
Iterative deepening	d	b^d	Admissible
Bidirectional (where applicable)	$b^{d/2}$	$b^{d/2}$	Admissible

11.4 HEURISTIC SEARCH

Breadth-first, depth-first and iterative deepening depth-first searches discussed so far belong to the category of uninformed, or blind, searches. They try to explore the entire search space in a systematic, exhaustive manner, without employing any knowledge about the problem that may render the search process more efficient. They are *blind* in the sense that they do not try to distinguish good nodes from bad nodes among those still open for exploration. However, in many practical situations exhaustive searches are simply not affordable due to their excessive computational overhead. It may be recalled that they all have exponential time complexity. Heuristic search employs some heuristic knowledge to focus on a prospective subspace of the state space to make the search more efficient. In this section, the elementary heuristic searches are presented.

11.4.1 Best-first Search

`Algorithm Basic-State-Space-Search` (Fig. 11.14) uses the list *OPEN* to store nodes that have been generated, but neither been explored nor expanded. At any iteration, the first node stored in *OPEN* is selected for exploration and subsequent expansion. As *OPEN* is expected to contain several nodes at a time, a strategy must be devised to determine which among the open nodes should emerge as the first. In case of BFS, *OPEN* is implemented as a queue so that the most recently generated nodes are placed at the rear of *OPEN*, and the states of the search space are processed in first-in first-out basis. In DFS and DFID, *OPEN* acts as a stack so that the states are processed in last-in first-out manner. None of these strategies make any judgment regarding the relative merits of the nodes in *OPEN*.

Best-first search is a kind of informed search that tries, at the beginning of each iteration, to estimate the prospect of an open node with respect to reaching the goal through it. It makes use of an **evaluation function** that embodies some domain-specific information to achieve this. Such information is sometimes referred to as **heuristic** knowledge and a search procedure that is guided by some heuristic is termed as a *heuristic search*. The nature and significance of heuristic knowledge will be discussed in greater details in the later parts of this section. The heuristic knowledge enables us to assign a number to each node in *OPEN* to indicate the **cost** of a path to the goal through the node. In best-first search, this cost is *estimated* for each member of *OPEN* and the members are reshuffled in ascending order of this value so that the node with the lowest estimated cost is placed at the front of the queue. Therefore, Step 7 of **Algorithm Basic-State-Space-Search** can be written for best-first search as follows (Fig. 11.23):

```
7(a).   For (each x∈SUCC(n)) Do
            Compute the estimate of the cost c(x) from x to a goal node
        End-For
7(b).   Merge CHLDRN(n) to OPEN list.
7(c).   Rearrange the elements of OPEN in ascending order of their esti-
        mated costs so that the lowest cost nodes is placed at the front
        of the queue.
```

Fig. 11.23.

The behaviour of a best-first search algorithm is illustrated in Fig. 11.24(a)–(e) with the state space of Fig. 11.15 assuming node *M* as the only goal node. The process initiates with the start node *A* with an estimated cost of, say, 10. Since this is the only node available at this moment we have no option other than expanding this node. On expanding node *A*, the successors *B*, *C* and *D* are obtained with estimated costs 6, 10 and 7, respectively. Since node *B* has the lowest estimated cost 6, it is selected for expansion (Fig. 11.24(b)). The candidature of B for processing in the next step is indicated by the small arrow coming out of it. This convention is followed in the rest of these diagrams. Nodes *E* and *F* are generated as children of *B*. As shown in Fig. 11.24(c) *E* and *F* have estimated costs 8 and 9, and consequently, node *D* with cost 7 becomes the lowest-cost unexplored node in *OPEN*. Node *D* generates the successors *H* (estimated cost 3) and *I* (estimated cost 5). There are now five nodes, *viz*., *H*, *I*, *E*, *F*, and *C* with costs 3, 5, 8, 9 and 10, respectively of which is *H* is the candidate for further expansion at this moment. On expansion, node *H* generates *M* which is a goal. In this example, for the sake of simplicity, the costs are assumed. In practice, these are to be evaluated with the help of a function embodying the heuristic knowledge.

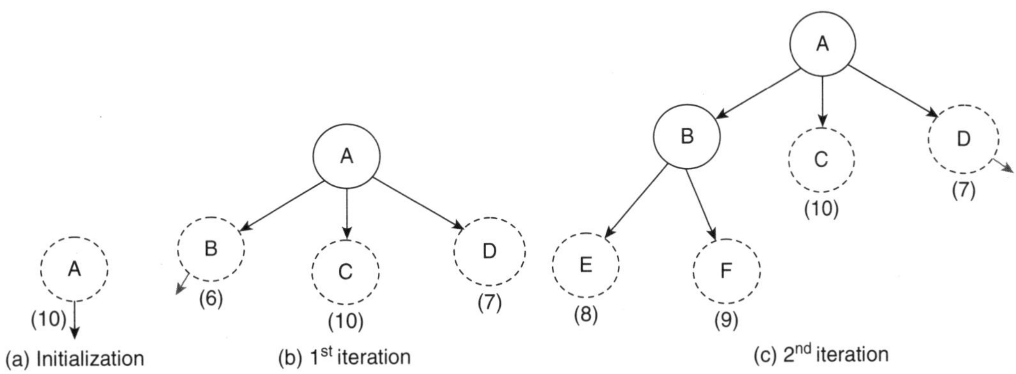

Fig. 11.24. *(a)-(e) The best-first search (BFS) process.*

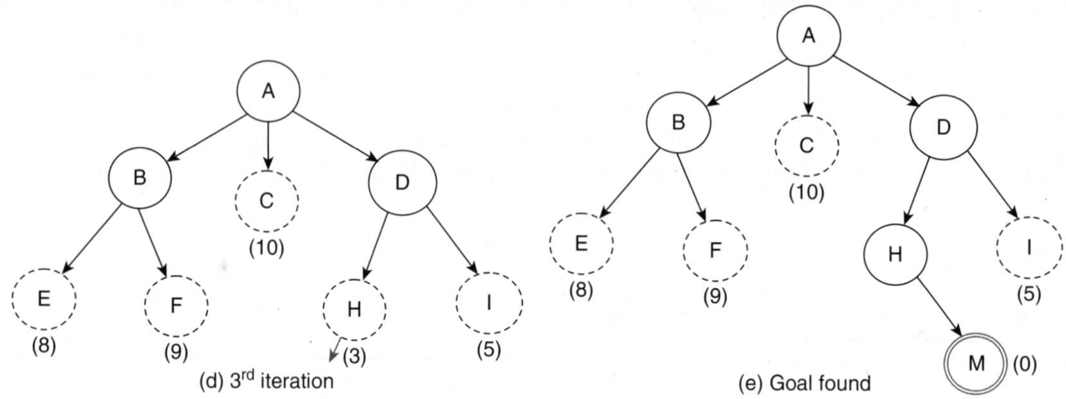

Fig. 11.24. *Continued*

11.4.2 Generalized State Space Search

`Algorithm Basic-State-Space-Search` (Fig. 11.14) hides some finer aspects of state space search for the sake of simplicity. **`Algorithm Generalized-State-Space-Search`** (Fig. 11.25) takes some of these aspects into consideration and presents a more complete picture of state space search. For example, quite often attaining a goal state alone is not sufficient. The process has to return the *path* from the start state to the goal state as well. In order to achieve this, we should keep track of the chain of ancestors of a node way up to the root. In Step 5 of **`Algorithm Generalized-State-Space-Search`** we first test the current node to determine if it is a goal and then, in case it is, we retrieve the path from the root to this goal by tracing the pointers from the goal to the root through the intermediate ancestors. Establishment of these pointers is done in Step 10 of the algorithm. Again, **`Algorithm Basic-State-Space-Search`** tacitly assumes the state space to be a tree rather than a graph so that the possibility of generating a node which is already present in the *OPEN* queue has been overlooked. As a result all nodes generated from node *n*, *CHLDRN* (*n*), are summarily put into *OPEN*. However, consider the case depicted in Fig. 11.26, where node *C* is a successor of node *A* as well as *B*. Let us assume that node *A* has been explored earlier and *B* later. When node *B* is expanded, it will produce a number of successors of which *C* is one. Since *C* is a child of *A* and *A* has been expanded earlier, *C* is already in *OPEN*. Therefore, there is no need to include *C* into the search tree. Moreover, while merging the children of *B* with the existing nodes of *OPEN* node, *C* should be left out to avoid repetitions. This is achieved in Step 8, which ensures that installation of a node and establishment of a pointer to its parent is done only if the node is not already in *G*. There is another possible adjustment to be incorporated. The existing pointer from *C* to *A* might be required to be redirected to *B*, if necessary. This depends on which among the path through *A* or *B* seems to be more promising (Step 14 of **`Algorithm Generalized-State-Space-Search`**).

11.4.3 Hill Climbing

Hill climbing is a heuristic search technique that makes use of local knowledge in its attempt to achieve global solution of a given problem. Imagine you are trying to reach the top of a hill in foggy weather. You are too small to see the peak while you are crawling on the surface of the hill and there is no clue regarding any path towards the peak. How should you proceed? One possible way would be to look around your current position and take that step which elevates you to a higher level. You continue in this way until a point is arrived from where all steps result in positions at lower heights. This point is considered to be the maximal point and corresponds to the solution to be returned. The hill climbing strategy is also applied to problems where the purpose is to reach the lowest point, and not the highest point. In such cases, steps which take us to lower heights are followed. This is sometimes referred to as **valley descending**. In this text we shall use the term hill climbing to mean both hill climbing and valley descending and interpret it in the context of the nature of the problem.

```
Algorithm Generalized-State-Space-Search

/* Let OPEN be a list of states that have been generated but not yet ex-
plored or expanded. Another list CLOSED contains the states that have al-
ready been explored and expanded. T is the search graph, i.e., the portion
of the state space that has been created so far. */

1.   Begin
2.     Initialize the search tree T with node S as the root. Initialize
       OPEN with S in it and CLOSED as an empty list.
3.     If (OPEN is empty) Then the search is unsuccessful. Exit.
4.     Let n be the 1st node on OPEN. Remove n from OPEN and put n on
       CLOSED.
5.     If (n is a goal node) Then the search is successful. Recover the
       path from the start node S to n by tracing the pointers from n to
       S along the ancestors of n. These pointers are established during
       the expansion of the search tree (Steps 8-11). Exit.
6.     Generate children of n. Let us denote this by CHLDRN(n).
7.     For (each x∈CHLDRN(n)) Do
8.       If (x is not already in T) Then
9.           Install x in T as a child of n.
10.          Establish a pointer from x to n.
11.          Add x to OPEN.
12.      Else (i.e., if x is already in T)
13.              Make x a child of n.
14.              If required redirect the pointer of x to n. (see discus-
                 sion in text)
15.      End-If
16.    End-For
17.    Rearrange the elements in OPEN according to some criteria.
18.    Go to Step 3.
19.    End-Generalized-State-Space-Search
```

Fig. 11.25. *Algorithm generalized-state-space-search.*

The hill climbing strategy is widely employed to solve complex optimization problems. A hill climbing search must have the following elements.

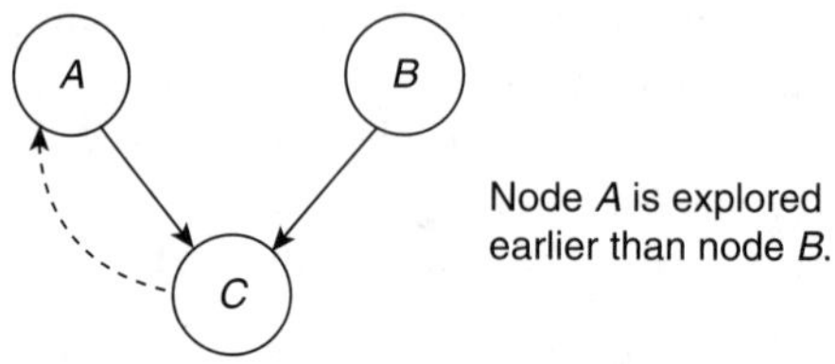

Fig. 11.26. *Two nodes having a common successor.*

- An **objective function** whose value is to be optimized. The objective function should somehow reflect the quality of a solution to the given problem so that the optimized solution corresponds to the optimal value of the objective function.
- A procedure to map a solution (perhaps sub-optimal) of the given problem to the corresponding value of the objective function.
- A procedure to generate a new solution from a given solution of the problem.

```
Algorithm Hill-Climbing (P, f(S_P), S_P)

Input: A problem P and objective function f(S_P) on a solution S_P of P.
Output: An optimal solution S_opt to P such that the objective function
f(S_opt) attains an optimal value.

1.    Begin
2.      S_new ← initial solution to P (perhaps random)
3.      S_current ← S_new
4.      Compute f(S_current), the value of the objective function for S_current
        /* Try to find a better solution */
5.      While (there is a solution obtainable from S_current) DO
6.      Begin
7.        S_new ← A new solution to P generated from S_current
8.        Compute f(S_new) and compare with f(S_current)
9.        If (S_new is a better solution than S_current) Then
10.       Go To Step 3    /* proceed along the new solution */
11.       End-if
12.     End-while  /* Discard S_new and try with another solution
        /* The peak is reached. Return the solution */
```

```
13.       S_opt ← S_current
14.       Return (S_opt)
15.    End-Hill-Climbing
```

Fig. 11.27. *Hill-climbing* (P, f(S_p), S_p)

The hill climbing strategy is presented as **Algorithm Hill-Climbing (*P*, *f*(S_P), S_P)** (Fig. 11.27). It starts with a solution, perhaps randomly generated. At each intermediate step during the search process, a new solution S_{new} is obtained from the current one $S_{current}$ (if possible). The quality of the new solution S_{new}, in terms of the evaluation function, is compared to that of the current solution. If the new solution is better than the current then the current solution is updated to the new solution (Steps 9 and 10) and the search continues along this new current solution. Otherwise, i.e., if the new solution is not better than the current solution, then it is discarded and we generate yet another new solution (if possible) and repeat the steps stated above. The process stops when none of the new solutions obtained from the current one is better than the current solution. This implies that the search process has arrived at an optimal solution. This is the output of the hill climbing process.

It may be noted that the hill climbing method does not create a solution tree. The only things it maintains are the current and the newly generated solutions. If the new solution is better than the current then it discards the current solution and update it with the new solution. In other words, hill climbing grabs a good neighbour without bothering the aftereffects. For this reason hill climbing is also referred to as **greedy local search**.

(a) *A network of cities*

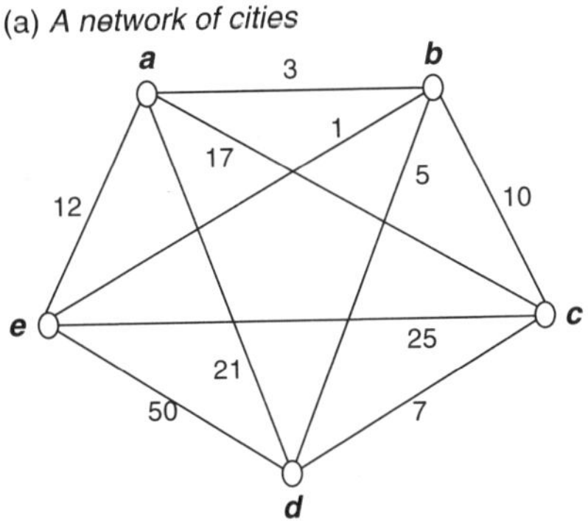

(*b*) *Travel cost between cities*

	e	d	c	b
a	12	21	17	3
b	1	5	10	
c	25	7		
d	50			

Fig. 11.28. *A tiny traveling salesperson problem (TSP) with five cities.*

Example 11.4 (*A hill climbing technique to solve the TSP*)

As an example, let us consider the traveling salesperson problem (TSP), which involves a network of cities connected to each other through paths with costs attached to them. A **tour** is defined as a path that starts from a given city, travels through the paths to visit every other city exactly once, and returns to the starting city. We are required to find a minimal cost tour.

Fig. 11.28 (a) shows a tiny TSP with five cities *a, b, c, d,* and *e*. For the sake of simplicity the cities are taken to be fully connected, i.e., an edge exists between any pair of cities. If we start at the city *a* then a tour may be represented with a permutation of the letters *a, b, c, d,* and *e* that starts and ends with the letter *a*.

The TSP is a minimization problem. Its objective function is the sum of the costs of the links in the tour. For example, if the tour is $\tau = abcdea$ then its cost $cost(\tau) = cost(ab) + cost(bc) + cost(cd) + cost(de) + cost(ea) = 3 + 10 + 7 + 50 + 12 = 82$. Mapping a solution to evaluate the objective function is also straightforward in this case. How to generate a new solution of the TSP from a given one?

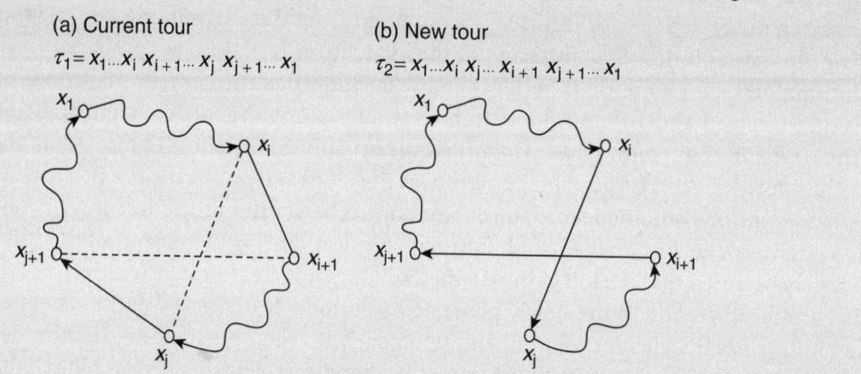

Fig. 11.29. *Generation of a new tour from a given tour.*

Let $\tau_1 = x_{1\ldots}x_i x_{i+1\ldots}x_j x_{j+1\ldots}x_1$ be an existing tour. A new tour τ_2 from τ_1 could be generated in the following manner.

1. Let $x_i x_{i+1}$ and $x_j x_{j+1}$ be two disjoint edges in τ_1 such that the cities $x_{i,}\ x_{i+1},\ x_j$ and x_{j+1} are all distinct.
2. Remove the edges $x_i x_{i+1}$ and $x_j x_{j+1}$ from the tour τ_1.
3. Join the edges $x_i x_j$ and $x_{i+1} x_{j+1}$ such that a new tour $\tau_2 = x_{1\ldots}x_i x_{j\ldots}x_{i+1}x_{j+1\ldots}x_1$ is obtained.

Fig. 11.29 shows the procedure graphically. Now, to illustrate the hill climbing procedure we may consider the of TSP presented in Fig. 11.28. The successive steps are shown in Fig. 11.30 (a)–(e). A random solution *adecba* denoting the tour $a \to d \to e \to c \to b \to a$ is considered as the initial solution (Fig. 11.30(a)). The cost of the tour is 109. To obtain a new tour the links *ad* and *ec* are are removed from the tour and are substituted by *ae* and *cd*. So we obtain the tour *abcdea* with cost 82 (Fig. 11.30(b)). Since this cost is lower (and hence, better, since we are addressing a minimization problem) we accept this solution and proceed.

In this way, we proceed to *acdbea* (Fig. 11.30(d)) having a tour cost of 42. Only three tours, *viz., acebda, abedca,* and *acbdea* shown in Fig.11.30 (e1), Fig. 11.30(e2), and Fig. 11.30(e3) can be generated from this tour. These three tours have costs 69, 78 and 94, respectively. Since all of these are higher than 42, the hill climbing procedure assumes to have reached a minimal value and the procedure stops here. It is easy to verify that the other possible tours have costs greater than 42. The solution returned by the hill climbing process is thus *acdbea* and the cost of the solution is 42. The successive steps shown in Fig. 11.30(a)–(e) are given here for the sake of understanding the process but these are not memorized by the actual hill climbing procedure.

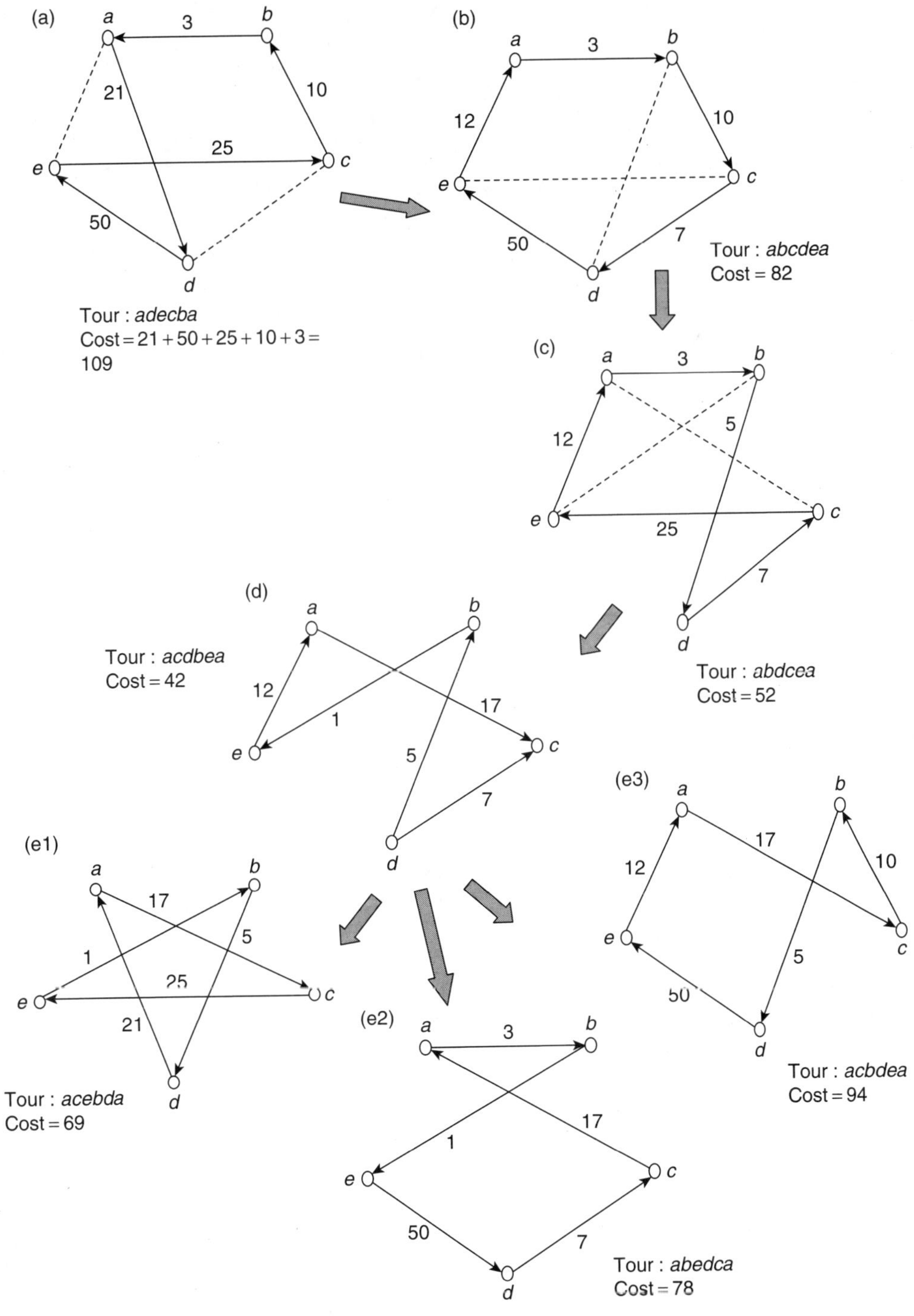

Fig. 11.30. *Solving TSP through hill climbing.*

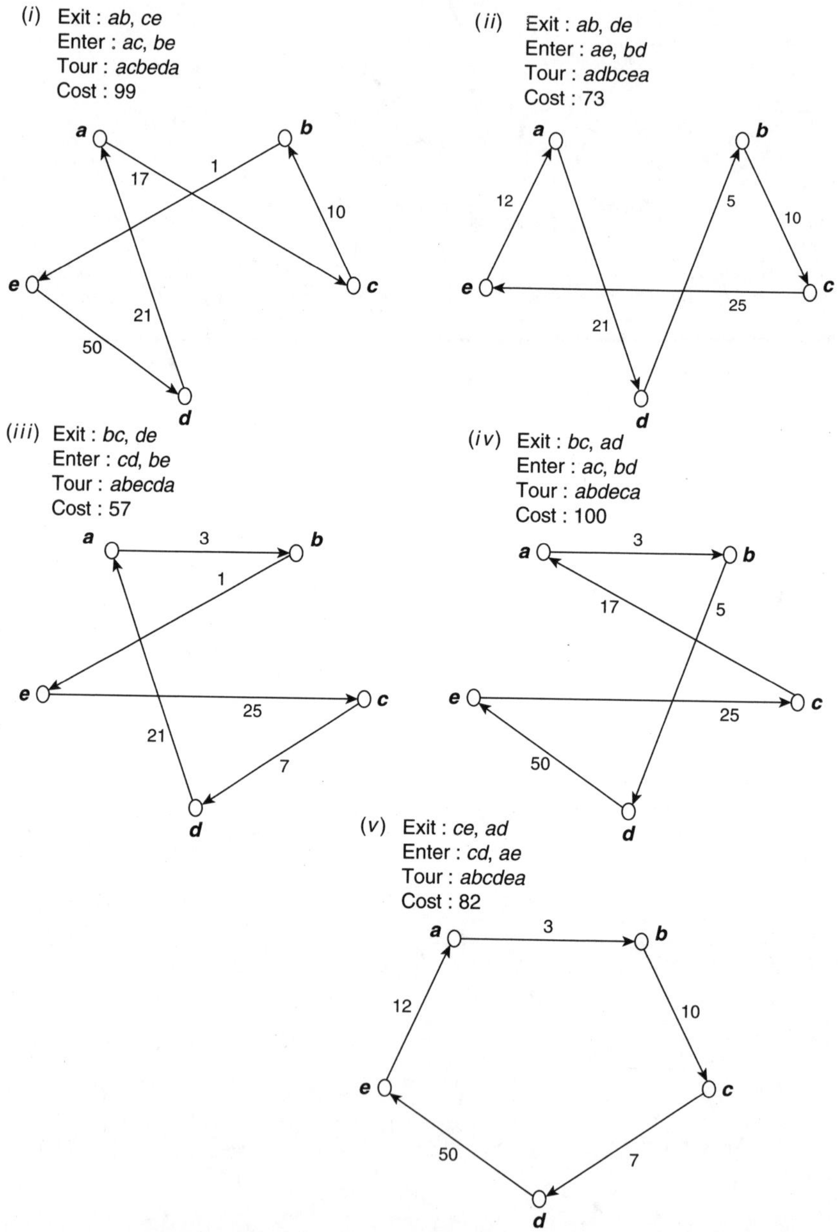

Fig. 11.31. *Various solutions obtained from the tour adecba*

Steepest ascent hill climbing In **`Algorithm Hill-Climbing`** a new solution is generated from the current solution and if it is found to be a better solution then the search proceeds along this new solution without any consideration of any other possible solution obtainable from the current one. Steepest ascent hill climbing is a variation of hill climbing, where instead of one all possible solutions from the current solution are generated and the best among these is chosen for further progress.

For example, if we follow the steepest ascent hill climbing strategy on the initial tour *adecba* shown in Fig 11.30(a), then the entire set of tours that can be obtained from *adecba* should be generated and their costs be evaluated. Five different tours, *acbeda, adbcea, abecda, abdeca,* and *abcdea*, can be generated by transforming *adecba*. These tours have costs 99, 73, 57, 100 and 82, respectively (see Fig. 11.31(i)–(v)). Obviously, tour *abecda* of cost 57 would be selected for further exploration.

Local optima / plateaux / ridges Hill climbing is usually quite efficient in the search for an optimal solution of a complex optimization problem. However, it may run into trouble under certain conditions, e.g., existence of **local optima, plateaux**, or **ridges** within the state space.

Local optima. Often the state space of a maximization problem has a peak that is higher than each of its neighbouring states but lower than the global maximum. Such a point is called a **local maximum.** Similarly a minimization problem may have *local minima.* Fig. 11.32 shows a one-dimensional objective function containing local optima and plateaux. Since the hill climbing procedure examines only the solutions in the immediate neighborhood of the current solution it will find no better solution once it reaches a locally optimal state. As a result, there is a chance that the local optima, and not the global optima, is erroneously identified as the solution of the problem.

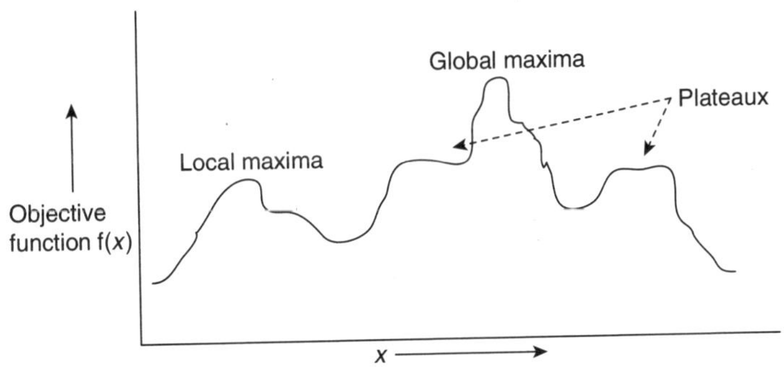

Fig. 11.32. *Problem of local optima and plateaux.*

Plateaux. A **plateau** is a flat region in the state space (Fig. 11.32) where the neighbouring states have the same value of the objective function as that of the current state. A plateau may exit at the peak, or as a shoulder, as shown in Fig. 11.32. In case it is a peak, we have reached a local maximum and there is no chance of finding a better state. However, if it is a shoulder, it is possible to survive the plateau and continue the journey along the rising side of the plateau.

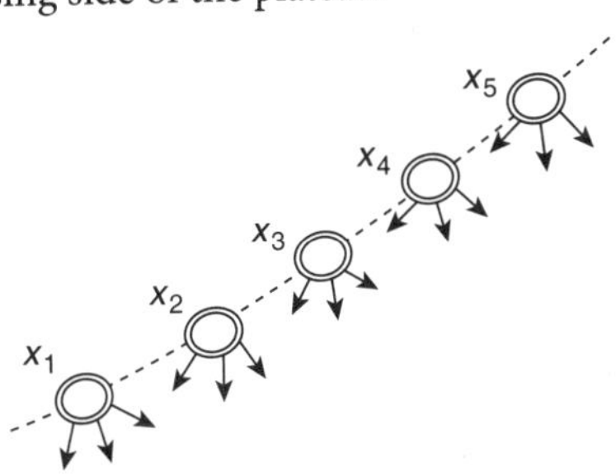

Fig. 11.33. *A ridge.*

Ridges A **ridge** is a series of local optima on a slope. Consider a situation depicted in Fig. 11.33. Each of the states x_1, x_2, x_3, x_4, and x_5 is a local maximum and they are arranged in the state space from left to right in ascending order. We would like to ascend along the path $x_1 \to x_2 \to x_3 \to x_4 \to x_5$ etc., but all the states leading from each of these states, indicated by the arrows, are at lower levels in comparison with these states. This makes it hard for the search procedure to ascend.

The problems arising out of local optima, plateaux, or ridges may be addressed by augmenting the basic hill climbing method with certain tactics. However, though these tactics help a lot, they do not guarantee to solve the problems altogether. Here is a brief description of the way outs.

- The problem of getting stuck at local optima may be tackled through backtracking to some previous state and then take a journey along a different direction but as promising, or almost as promising, as that chosen earlier.
- To escape a plateau, one may make a big jump in some direction and land on a new region of the search space. If there is no provision of making a big jump, we may repeatedly take the allowable smaller steps in the same direction until we come outside the plateau.
- A good strategy to deal with ridges is to apply several rules before doing a test so that one can move in different directions simultaneously.

11.4.4 The A/A* Algorithms

While discussing best-first search, we have seen how an evaluation function can guide the search process along a more fruitful path than exploring the entire search space blindly. However, we did not mention the form of the evaluation function. Let us define the evaluation function $f(n)$ for a given node n as

$$f(n) = g(n) + h(n) \tag{11.1}$$

where $g(n)$ is the cost of a minimal-cost path from the start node to node n and $h(n)$ is the cost of a minimal-cost path from node n to a goal node.

Therefore, $f(n)$ is the cost of a minimal-cost path from the start node to a goal node constrained to pass through node n (Fig. 11.34).

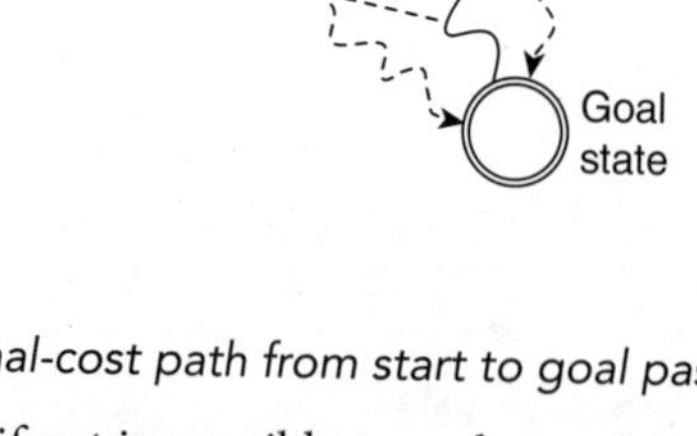

Fig. 11.34. *A minimal-cost path from start to goal passing through node n.*

However, sometimes it is difficult if not impossible to evaluate $g(n)$ and $h(n)$ accurately. Therefore some estimated values of $g(n)$ and $h(n)$ are used to guide the search process. Let $g_1(n)$ and $h_1(n)$ be the estimated values of $g(n)$ and $h(n)$. Then the estimated value of $f(n)$, written as $f_1(n)$, is defined as

$$f_1(n) = g_1(n) + h_1(n) \tag{11.2}$$

A search algorithm that uses $f_1(n)$ to order the nodes of OPEN queue and chooses the node with best value of $f_1(n)$ for further exploration is called an *A* algorithm. Moreover, if the heuristic estimation $h_1(n)$ happens to be a lower bound of $h(n)$ so that $h_1(n) \le h(n)$ for all *n*, then it is termed as *A** (pronounced as **a-star**) algorithm. An obvious example of A^* algorithm is BFS. Here $g_1(n)$ is the depth of node *n* from the root node and $h_1(n) = 0$ for all *n*. Since $h_1(n) \le h(n)$ for all *n*, BFS satisfies the basic criterion of *A** algorithm. It has been proved that an *A* algorithm satisfying the relation $h_1(n) \le h(n)$ for all *n*, is guaranteed to find an minimal-cost path from the root to a goal. Such a search algorithm is said to be **admissible** and hence *A** algorithm is admissible.

Example 11.5 *(An A-algorithm to solve 8-puzzle)*

Let us consider the 8-puzzle posed in Fig 11.11. We would like to solve it using an *A* algorithm. The first component of the evaluation function $f(n) = g(n) + h(n)$ is $g(n)$, is defined as

$$g(n) = \text{the length of the path from the start node to node } n \tag{11.3}$$

Regarding the second component, $h(n)$, we must employ some heuristic knowledge that somehow gives an idea of how far the goal node is from the given node. Presently, we take the number of tiles that are not in positions described in the goal state as the distance from the goal node. Therefore, the function $h(n)$ is defined as

$$h(n) = \text{number of misplaced tiles} \tag{11.4}$$

Now, consider the initial state of the given instance of 8-puzzle and compare it with the goal state (Fig. 11.35).

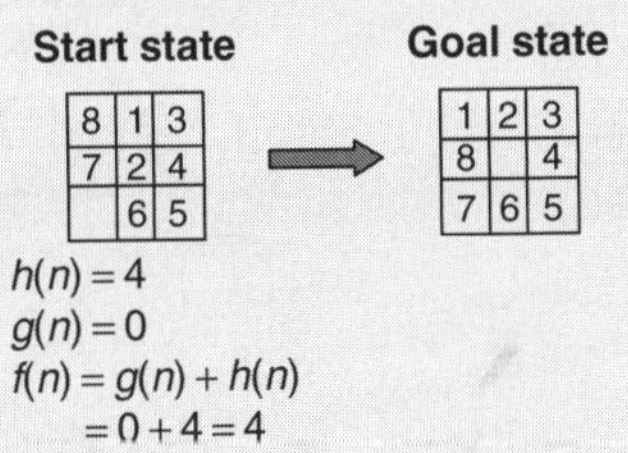

Fig. 11.35. *Evaluating the heuristic function h(n).*

Since the start state is to the root of the search tree $g(n) = 0$ for this node. To evaluate $h(n)$ we count the number of misplaced tiles. A comparison with the goal state reveals that tile no. 1, 2, 7, and 8 are not in their decimal positions. Therefore, $h(n) = 4$, so that $f(n) = 0 + 4 = 4$. Expanding the start state we get two new states with $h(n)$ values 3 and 5, respectively. Since both of these nodes are at level 1 of the search tree, $g(n) = 1$ for both of them. Hence for these two nodes $f(n) = g(n) + h(n) = 1 + 3 = 4$, and $1 + 5 = 6$, respectively. The node with the lesser $f(n)$ value 4, is chosen by the algorithm for exploration. The successive steps while constructing the search tree are shown in Fig. 11.36 (*a*)-(*e*).

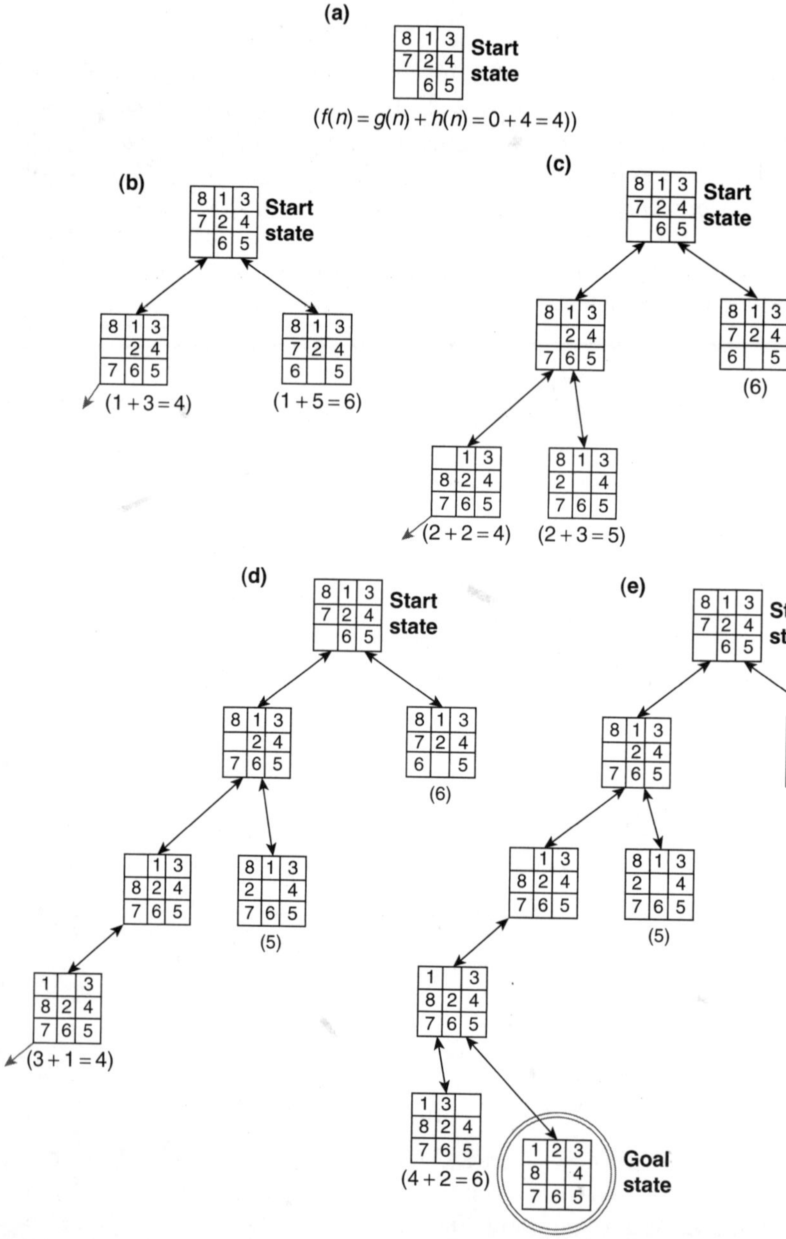

Fig. 11.36. *(a)-(e) Steps of A-algorithm to solve the 8-puzzle.*

Example 11.6 *(An A* Algorithm to solve a maze problem)*

Fig. 11.37 shows a 5×5 maze with a barrier drawn with heavy lines. We have to find a path from cell (4, 2) to cell (2, 3) avoiding the barrier. At each step of the journey we are allowed to move one cell at a time left, right, up, or down, but not along any diagonal. One or more of these movements may be blocked by the barrier. Fig. 11.38(a) and Fig. 11.38(b) explains the rules of movement. The target is to find a minimal length path from the source to the destination under the restriction imposed by the barrier. An A^* algorithm is to be found to do the job.

The length of a path from a cell (i, j) to a cell (k, l) is the number of cells traversed along the path. For example, the path shown by the dotted line of Fig. 11.39 between the cells (2, 1) and (4, 5) has a length of 10. Let us take the estimated value of $g(n)$

$$g_1(n) = \text{exact length of the path undertaken from } n_0 \text{ to } n \tag{11.5}$$

where n_0 and n are the initial and the current cell positions, respectively.

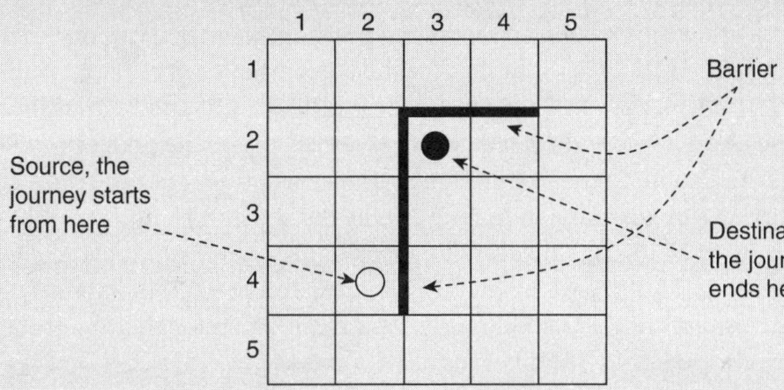

Fig. 11.37. *A maze problem to find the shortest path from the source to destination avoiding the barrier.*

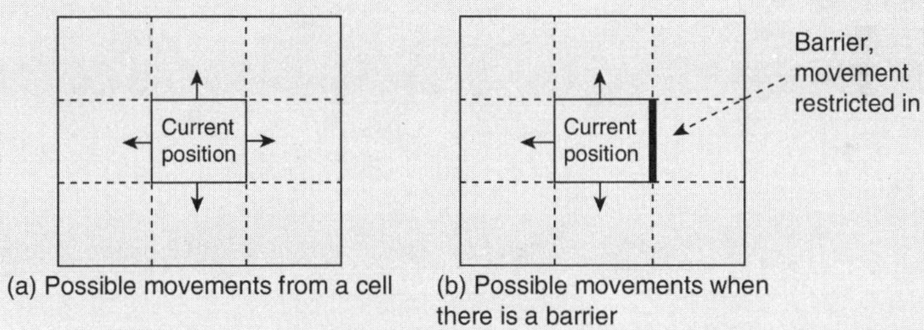

Fig. 11.38. *Possible movements from a cell.*

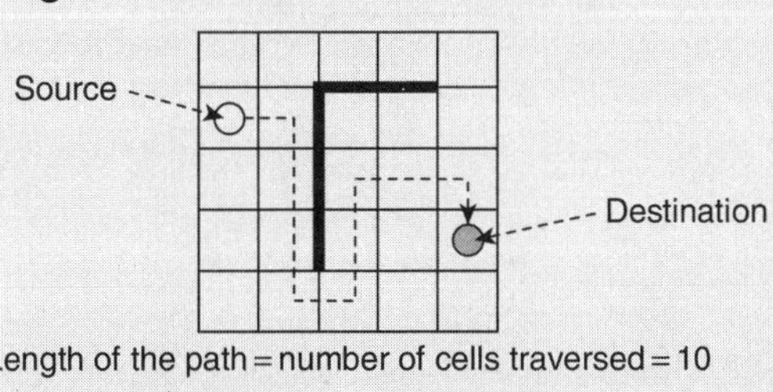

Fig. 11.39. *Length of a path.*

The heuristic estimation function $h_1(n)$ is defined as

$$h_1(n) = \text{the shortest distance between the current cell } n, \text{ and the destination } D, \text{ in absence of any barrier.} \tag{11.6}$$

Hence, if $D(i)$, $D(j)$ and $n(i)$, $n(j)$ are the row numbers and column numbers of the cells D and n, respectively, then $h_1(n)$ is calculated as

$$h_1(n) = |D(i) - n(i)| + |D(j) - n(j)| \tag{11.7}$$

It is easy to see that $h_1(n)$ is the minimum number of cells we must traverse to reach D from n in absence of any barrier. Therefore, $h_1(n) \le h(n)$ for every n. This implies that the evaluation function

$$f_1(n) = g_1(n) + h_1(n) \tag{11.8}$$

satisfies the criteria for A^* algorithm. In the present instance of the problem, the source n_0 is the cell (4, 2) and the destination D is the cell (2, 3). At the source, $g_1(n_0) = 0$, and $h_1(n) = |2 - 4| + |3 - 2| = 3$, so that $f_1(n) = 0 + 3 = 3$. From this initial position, we may try to move to cell (5, 2), (4, 1), or (3, 2). Moving to cell (4, 3) is prohibited by the barrier between cells (4, 2) and (4, 3). Now, as indicated in Fig. 11.40(*b*), the value of $f_1(n)$ for these cells are 4, 5, and 3, respectively. As 3 is the lowest among these, the corresponding cell (3, 2) is selected for further exploration.

As far as the shortest route to the destination is concerned, this is not the right choice because the intervening barrier will not allow us to take to take the shortest route. The right choice would be to proceed along the cell (5, 2). However, the merit of (5, 2) over other choices is not apparent till the step shown in Fig. 11.40(i), where all OPEN nodes except (5, 2) have cost 7 and (5, 2) have a cost of only 5. Superiority of the path along (5, 2) is maintained for the rest of the search, until we eventually reach the goal (Fig. 11.41).

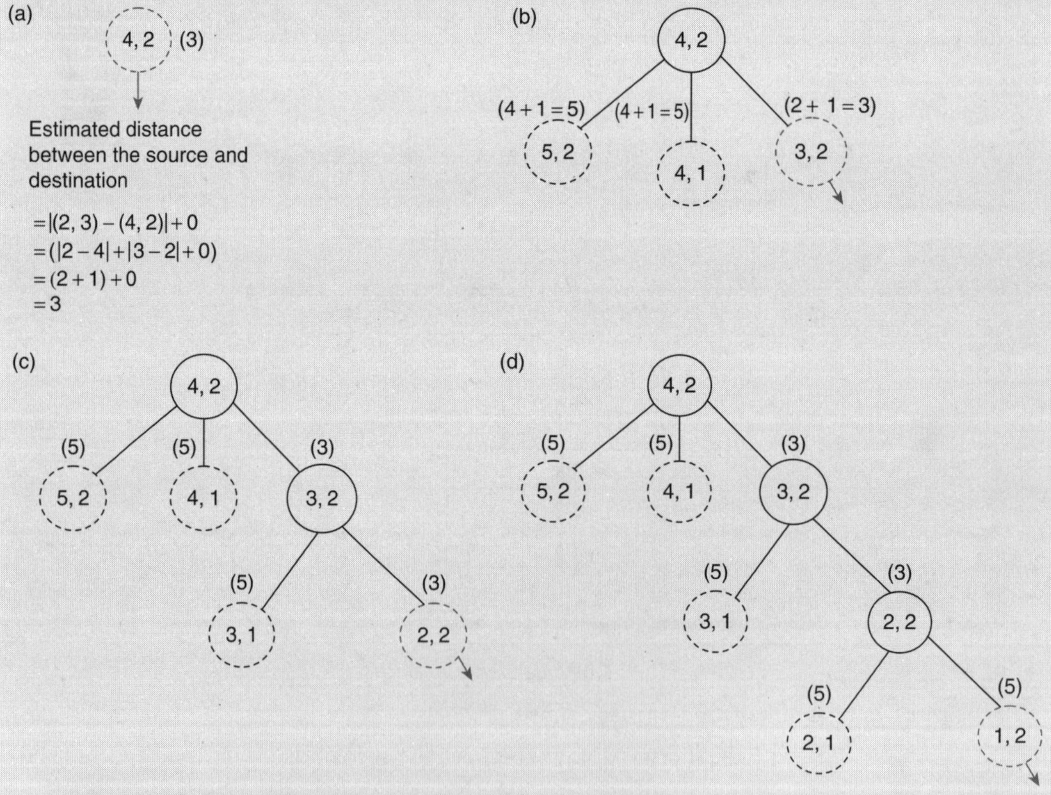

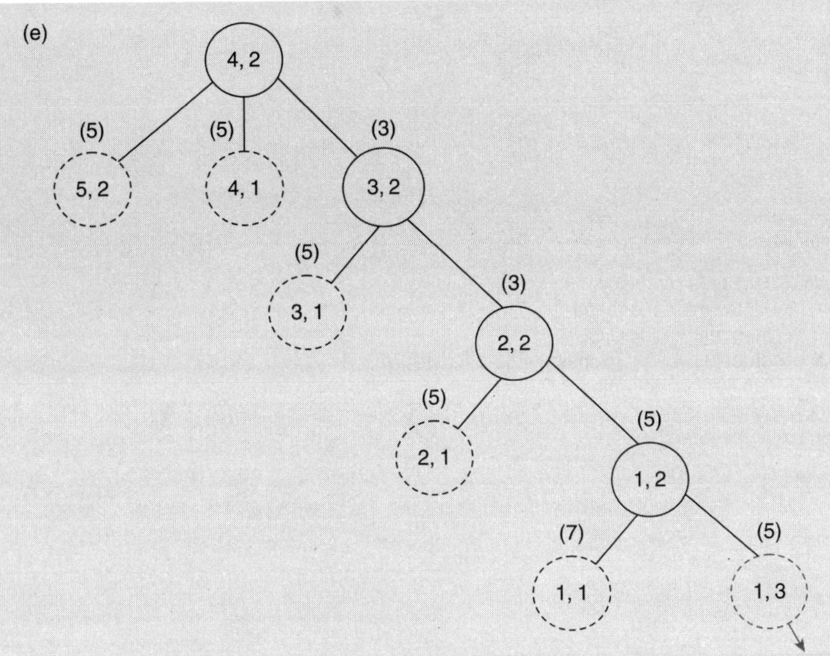
(e)
4, 2
(5)
5, 2
(5)
4, 1
(3)
3, 2
(5)
3, 1
(3)
2, 2
(5)
2, 1
(5)
1, 2
(7)
1, 1
(5)
1, 3

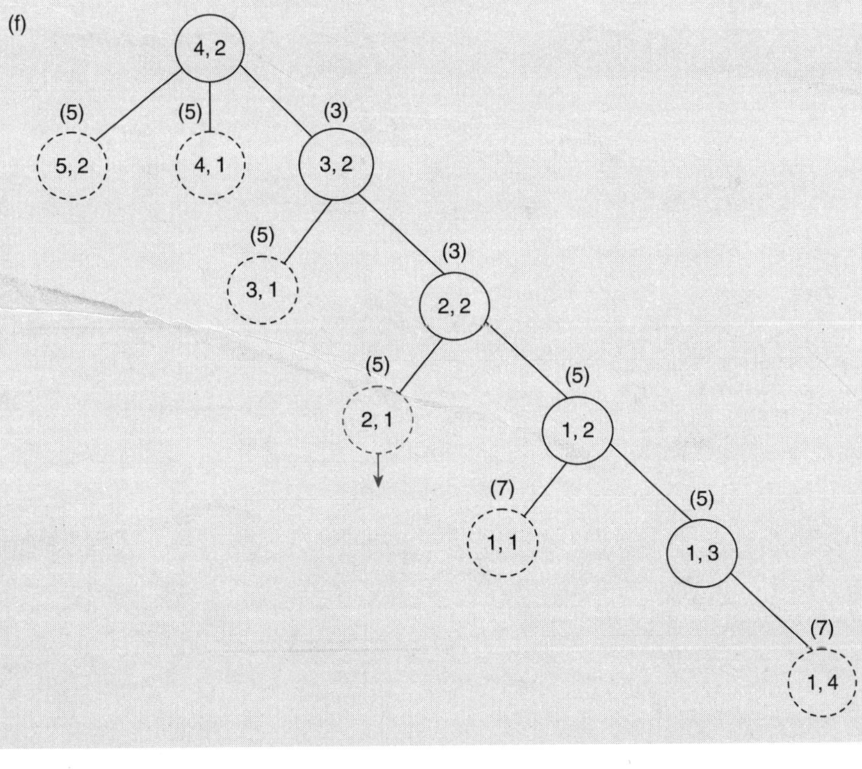
(f)
4, 2
(5)
5, 2
(5)
4, 1
(3)
3, 2
(5)
3, 1
(3)
2, 2
(5)
2, 1
(5)
1, 2
(7)
1, 1
(5)
1, 3
(7)
1, 4

(g)

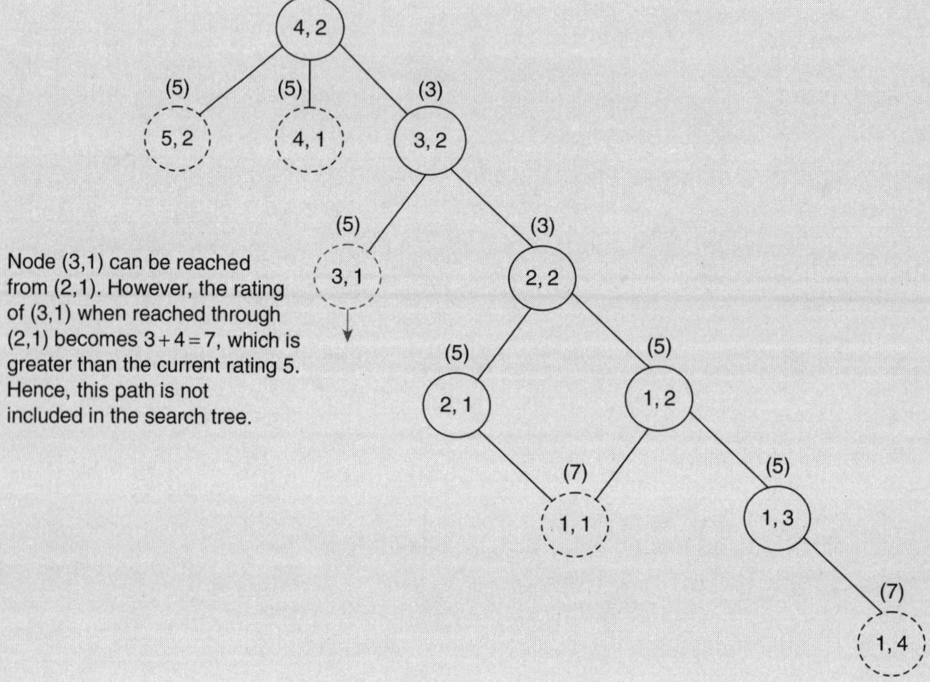
4, 2
(5)
5, 2
(5)
4, 1
(3)
3, 2
(5)
3, 1
(3)
2, 2
(5)
2, 1
(5)
1, 2
(7)
1, 1
(5)
1, 3
(7)
1, 4
Node (3,1) can be reached from (2,1). However, the rating of (3,1) when reached through (2,1) becomes 3+4=7, which is greater than the current rating 5. Hence, this path is not included in the search tree.

(h)

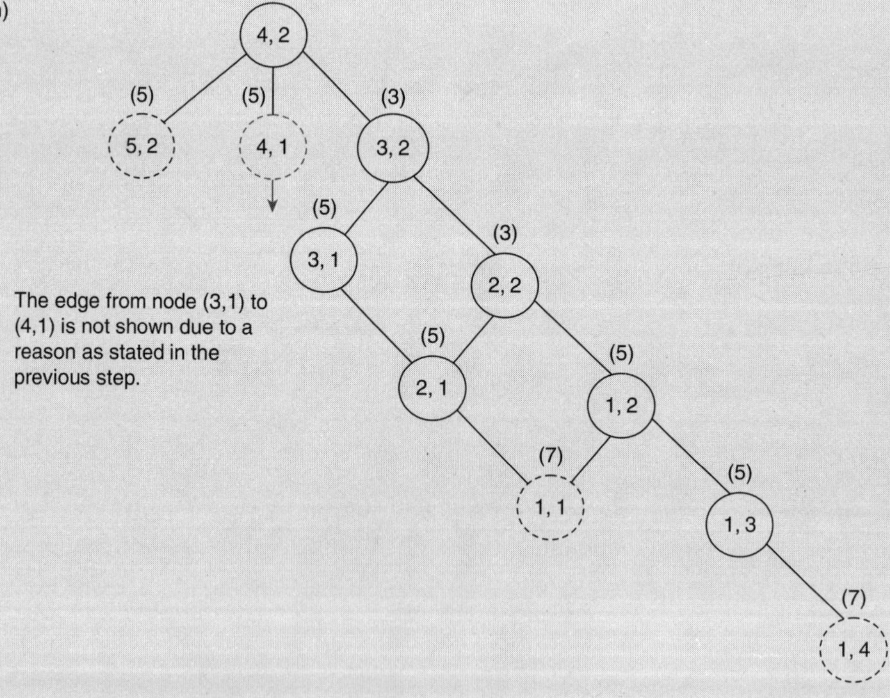
4, 2
(5)
5, 2
(5)
4, 1
(3)
3, 2
(5)
3, 1
(3)
2, 2
(5)
2, 1
(5)
1, 2
(7)
1, 1
(5)
1, 3
(7)
1, 4
The edge from node (3,1) to (4,1) is not shown due to a reason as stated in the previous step.

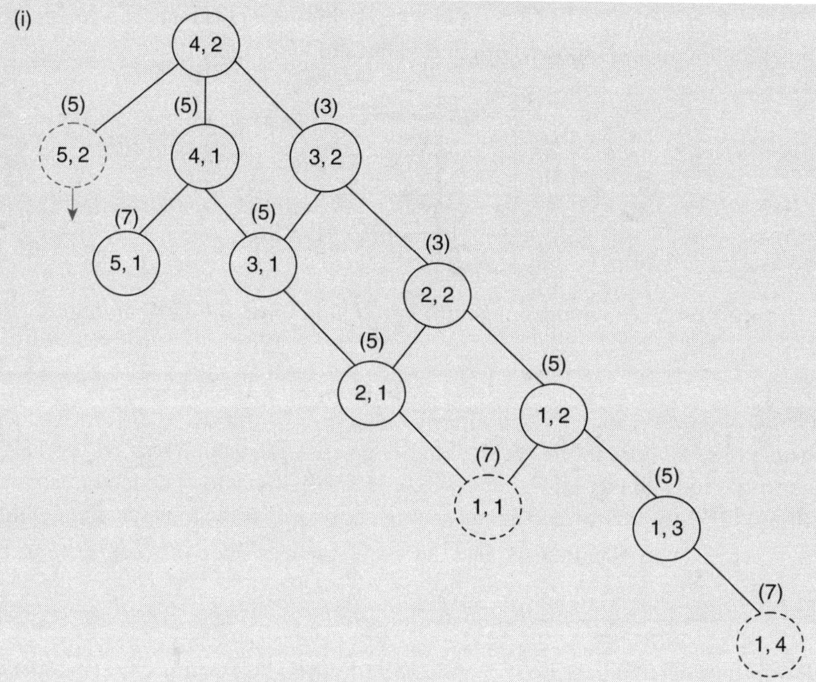

Fig. 11.40. *(a)-(i) Trace of the first nine steps of A* search for the maze problem.*

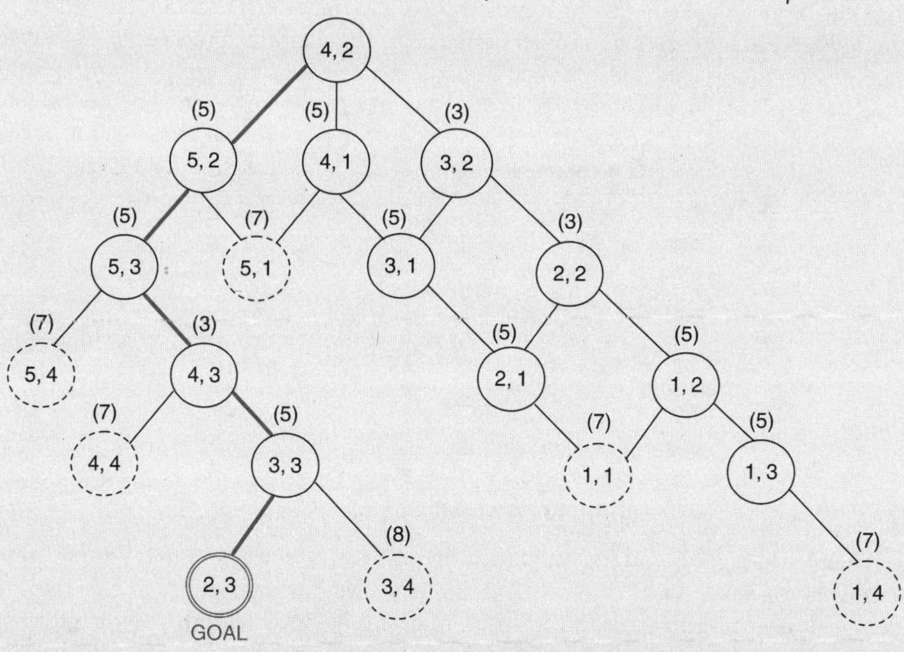

Fig. 11.41. *Search tree for the maze problem.*

The path from the root to the goal is shown with thick lines in Fig. 11.41. The corresponding minimum length path in the maze is shown with dotted lines of Fig. 11.42.

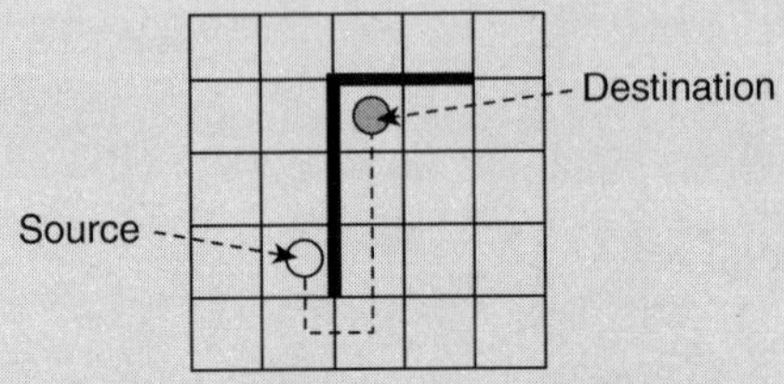

Fig. 11.42. *The minimum length path found through the A* algorithm*

Example 11.7 (*Branch-and-bound algorithm for traveling salesperson problem*)

Let us consider the TSP once more. We want to design an A* algorithm to solve the TSP and apply it on the network shown in Fig. 11.43. Let $C_1, C_2, \ldots, C_k$ be k cities and $c_{i,j}$ denotes the cost of the link between C_i and C_j. Without loss of generality, let us suppose that the tour starts at C_1 and let $\tau = C_1 \rightarrow C_2 \rightarrow \ldots \rightarrow C_i$ be a partial path generated the search process. Then the cost of the path $\tau = C_1 \rightarrow C_2 \rightarrow \ldots \rightarrow \mathbf{C}_i$ is given by

$$G(\tau) = g(C_1 \rightarrow C_2 \rightarrow \ldots \rightarrow C_i) = c_{1,2} + c_{2,3} + \ldots + c_{i-1,i} \quad (11.9)$$

In **branch-and-bound** technique, a list of possible paths from the starting city is maintained during the search process. Cost of each partial path is found and the so far minimum cost path is chosen for further expansion. While we expand a certain path, we temporarily abandon the path as soon as it is found to exceed the cost of some other partial path. The algorithm proceeds in this way until the minimum-cost tour is obtained. It should be noted that the decision to select a partial path $\tau = C_1 \rightarrow C_2 \rightarrow \ldots \rightarrow C_i$ is made solely on the basis of its cost $g(\tau)$ and no estimation of the cost for the remaining portion of the tour is done. Therefore $h_1(\tau) = 0$ for every partial path. Since $h_1(\tau) = 0 \leq h(\tau)$, this is an A* algorithm, and it guarantees to find the minimal cost tour for a given TSP.

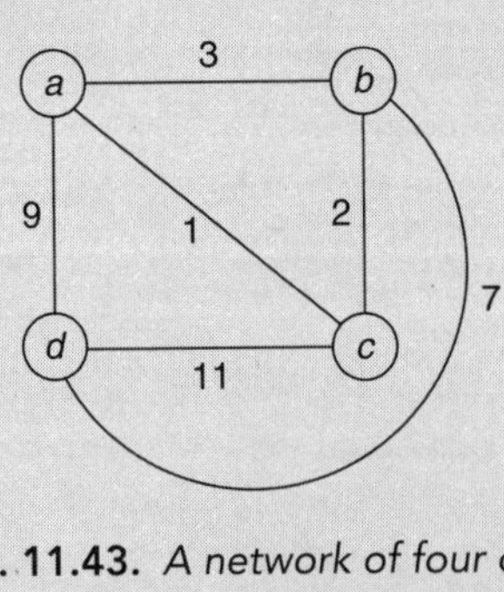

Fig. 11.43. *A network of four cities*

For this example, the algorithm starts with the starting city *a*, and since no path is yet traversed the cost attached to this node is 0 (Fig. 11.44 (*i*)) From city *a* we can go to city *b*, *c*, or *d*. The cost of the paths $a \rightarrow b$, $a \rightarrow c$, and $a \rightarrow d$ are 3, 1, and 9, respectively. Since the path $a \rightarrow c$ has the lowest cost of 1 so far, this path is chosen at this point for further extension. This is indicated by a small arrow attached to the node *c* in Fig. 11.44(ii), which shows the initial two steps of the algorithm.

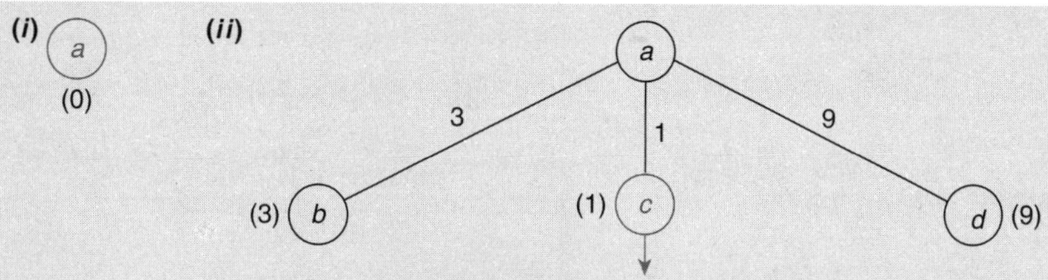

Fig. 11.44. *First two steps of branch-and-bound*

Fig. 11.45(i) shows the situation when we proceed one step further along the partial path $a \rightarrow c$. The two extended paths $a \rightarrow c \rightarrow b$ and $a \rightarrow c \rightarrow d$ have total estimated costs $1 + 2 = 3$ and $1 + 11 = 12$, respectively. As the cost of the partial path $a \rightarrow c \rightarrow b$ does not exceed that of the remaining paths (3 for $a \rightarrow b$, 12 for $a \rightarrow c \rightarrow d$, and 9 for $a \rightarrow d$) it is selected for further expansion at this point and the result of this expansion is shown in Fig. 11.45(ii). Fig. 11.45(iii) and 11.45(iv) shows two more consecutive steps.

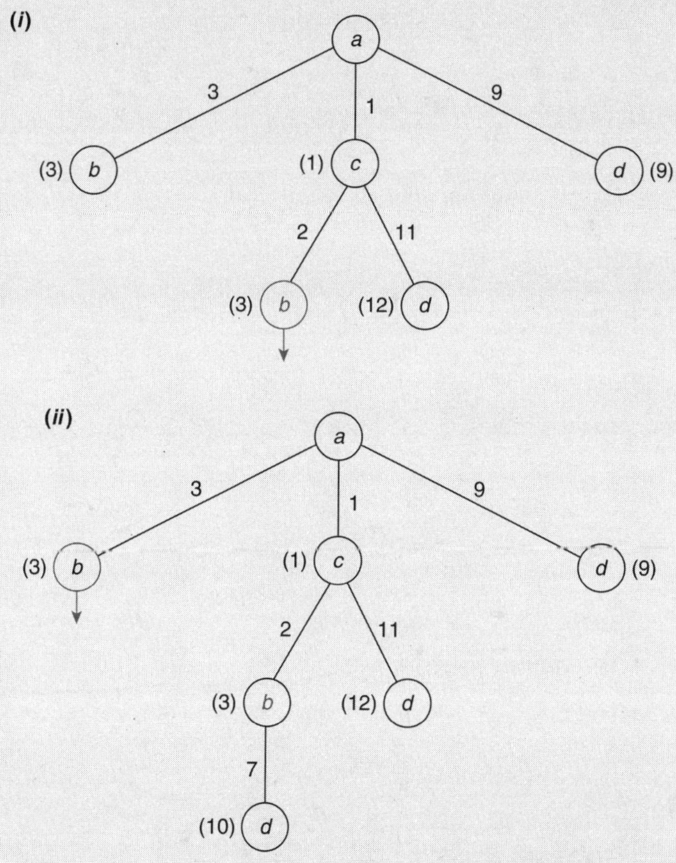

Fig. 11.45. *Further steps of TSP through branch-and-bound.*

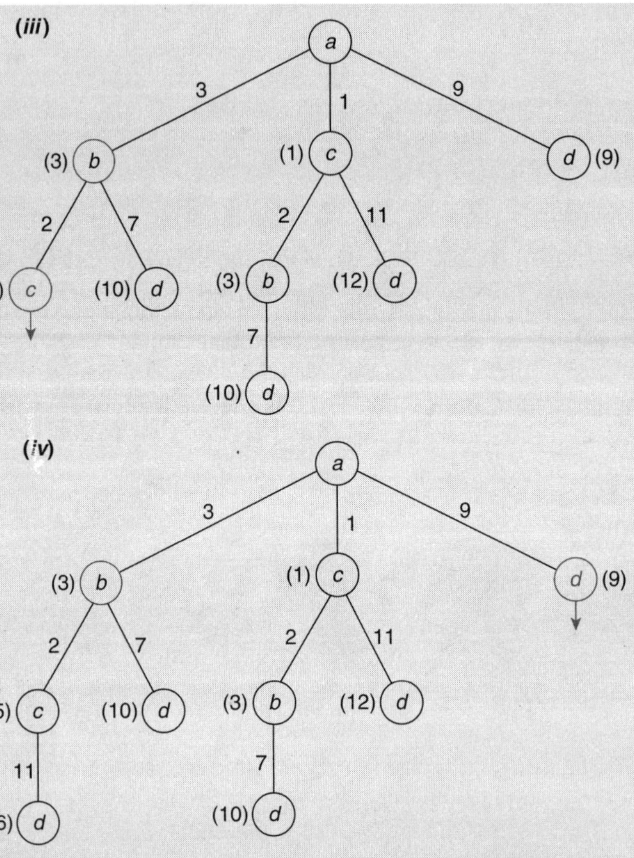

Fig. 11.45. *Further steps of TSP through branch-and-bound.*

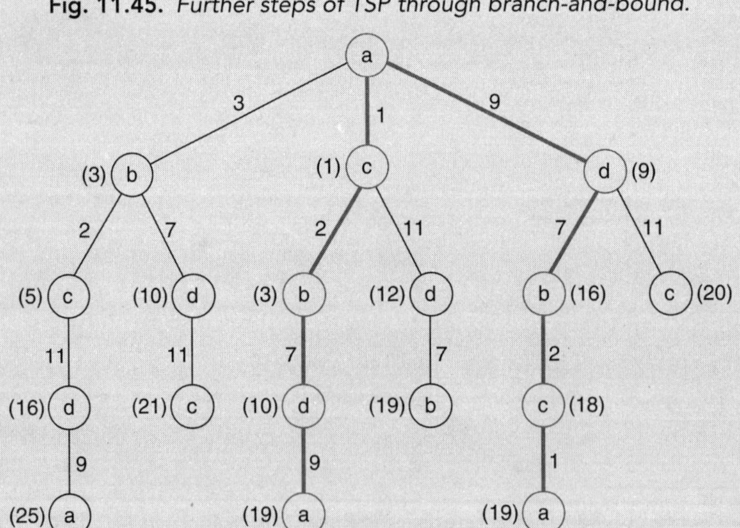

Fig. 11.46. *Final branch-and-bound search tree.*

The final branch-and-bound search tree is depicted in Fig. 11.46. The tours generated are $a \to c \to b \to d \to a$ and $a \to d \to b \to c \to a$ with the cost 19. It should be noted that these two tours are the same tour, only traversed in reverse directions. The lowest-cost tour obtained thus is shown in Fig. 11.47.

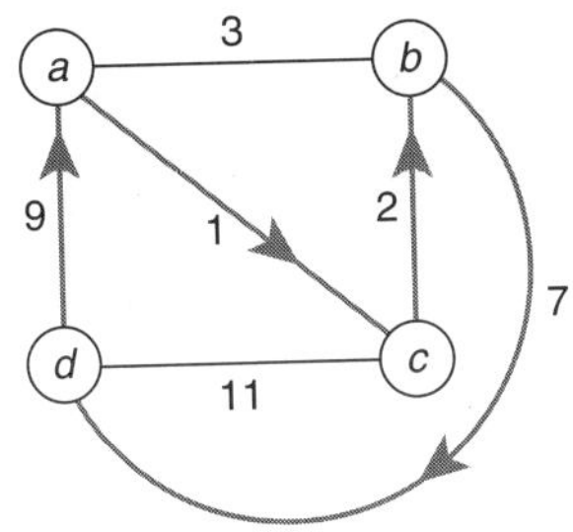

Fig. 11.47. *The lowest-cost tour.*

The efficiency of a heuristic search heavily depends upon the choice of the heuristic estimation function h_1. The function h_1 embodies some heuristic knowledge about the problem. Its objective is to guide the search for goal in the right direction. It is expected that a better heuristic will result in less amount of wasted effort in terms of the exploration of nodes that do not belong to the optimal path from the start state to a goal state. Let us consider two A* algorithms A_1 and A_2 using the heuristic functions h_1 and h_2, respectively. We say that algorithm A_1 is **more informed** than A_2 if for all nodes n except the goal node $h_1(n) > h_2(n)$. Please note that for any A* algorithm the estimate $h_1(n)$ of $h(n)$ must be a lower bound of $h(n)$, the actual cost of a minimal cost path from node n to a goal node. Combining this with the above inequality we get $0 \le h_2(n) < h_1(n) \le h(n)$. In other words, better heuristics are closer to $h(n)$ than a worse one.

11.4.5 Problem Reduction

A problem is said to be decomposable if it can be partitioned into a number of mutually independent sub-problems each of which can be solved separately. Decomposing a problem into sub-problems is advantageous because it is generally easier to solve smaller problems than larger ones. The **problem reduction** strategy is based on this characteristic. It employs a special kind of graph called AND-OR graph. The search through an AND-OR graph is known as AO* search.

AND-OR Graphs. There are two kinds of relation between the decomposed sub-problems and the problem itself. Firstly, the solution of *any* of the sub-problems may provide the solution to the original problem. This is an OR relationship. On the other hand, it might be necessary to solve *all* the sub-problems to obtain the final solution. This is called the AND relationship.

Each node of an AND-OR graph represents a problem. The root node represents the given problem while all other nodes represent sub-problems. Given a node and its children, if there is an OR relationship among them then the related arcs are called **OR-links**. In case of AND relationship these are called **AND-links**. The standard representations for these two types of links are shown in Fig. 11.48(a) and Fig. 11.48(b). It is possible that a node issues OR-links as well as AND-links simultaneously. Fig. 11.48(c) shows such a situation.

To illustrate the AND-OR graphs let us consider a network of four cities a, b, c and d and their inter connection cost as shown in Fig. 11.49. How to find a lowest-cost route from city a to city d?

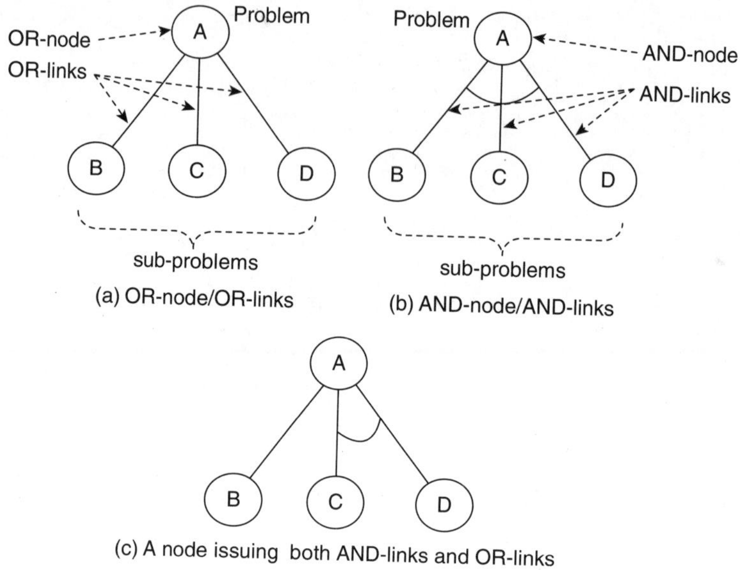

Fig. 11.48. *Representation of AND/OR nodes/links in AND-OR graphs.*

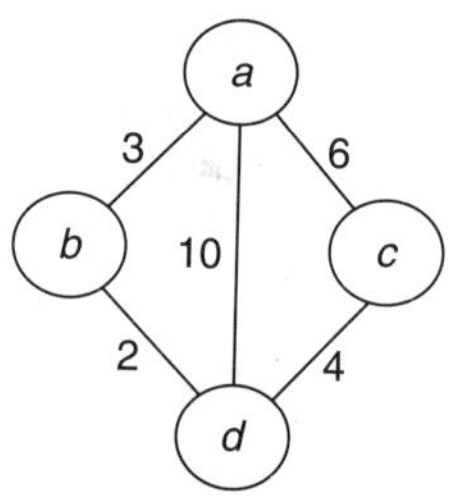

Fig. 11.49. *A network of four cities.*

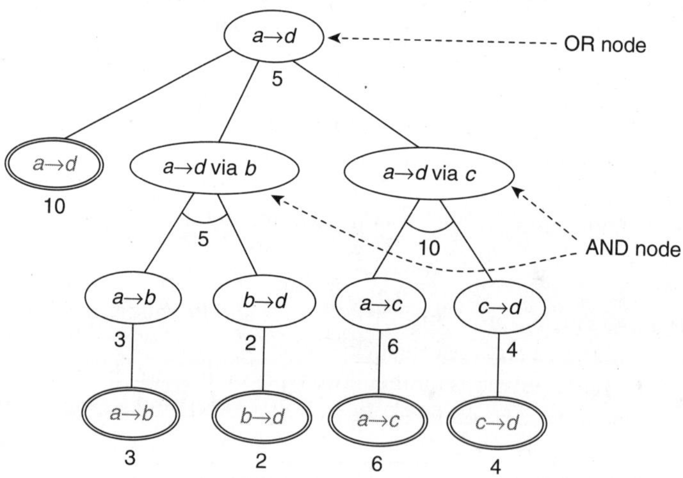

Fig. 11.50. *AND-OR tree for reaching city d from city a.*

Fig. 11.50 shows the AND-OR graph for the given problem. City d can be reached in three different ways, *viz.*, along the direct path from a to d, or, from a to d via b, or, from a to d via c. So the given problem $a \to d$ is now decomposed into three disjoint sub-problems, '$a \to d$', '$a \to d$ via b', and '$a \to d$ via c'. In Fig. 11.50 this is shown as the three children of the root node. Since the given problem can be solved through any of these three sub-problems, we have an instance of an OR node. Moreover, as there is a direct path from a to d with cost 10, a solution to the problem is readily available. This is indicated by the highlighted ovals.

Let us now focus on the sub-problem '$a \to d$ via b'. In order to reach d via b, we have to reach b from a, and then from b to d. This is indicated by the two children of the node for '$a \to d$ via b'. The fact that both of the sub-problems $a \to b$ and $b \to d$ have to be solved to obtain a solution of '$a \to d$ via b' implies that this is an AND node. Each of the two children leads to a leaf node as shown in the figure. The weights attached to an AND node is the sum of the weights of its constituent children. On the contrary, the weight attached to an OR node is the best among its children. In the present context we are looking for the minimum-cost path from a to d, and therefore, the cost 5 (among 10, 5, and 10) is attached to the root node. The entire AND-OR tree is depicted in Fig. 11.50. In the present example, the cost is attached to the nodes. However, depending on the nature of the problem addressed, one may attach such weights to the arcs also.

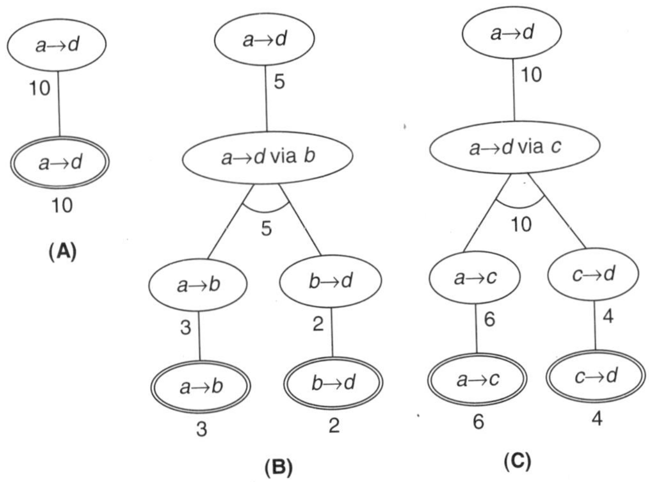

Fig. 11.51. *Solution trees for reaching city d from a.*

How to obtain the solution to a problem represented by an AND OR graph ? Since a solution must include all the sub-problems of an AND node, it has to be a subgraph, and not simply a path from the root to a leaf. The three different solutions for the present problem are shown as the solution trees A, B and C in Fig. 11.51. As we are addressing the problem of finding the minimum-cost path, Solution (B) will be preferred. We can formally define such solution graphs in the following way:

Let G be a solution graph within a given AND-OR graph. Then,

- The original problem, P, is the root node of G.
- If P is an OR node then any one of its children with its own solution graph, is in G.
- If P is an AND node then all of its children with their own solution graphs, are in G.

In this example, we have considered an AND-OR tree rather than a graph. However, AND-OR graph is the more generalized representation of a decomposable problem.

The AO* Algorithm. Typically, state space search is a search through an OR graph. The term OR graph is used to indicate the fact that if there is a node n with k number of edges $e_1, \ldots, e_k$ incident on it, then n can be reached either along the edge e_1, **or** along e_2, **or** … **or** along e_k (Fig. 11.52(a)), i.e., along *any* of the edges $e_1, \ldots, e_k$. In contrast, if there is an AND node n within an AND-OR graph with k number of edges $e_1, \ldots, e_k$ incident on it, then in order to attain n one has to reach it along the edge e_1, **and** along e_2, **and** … **and** along e_k (Fig. 11.52(b)), i.e., along *all* of the edges $e_1, \ldots, e_k$.

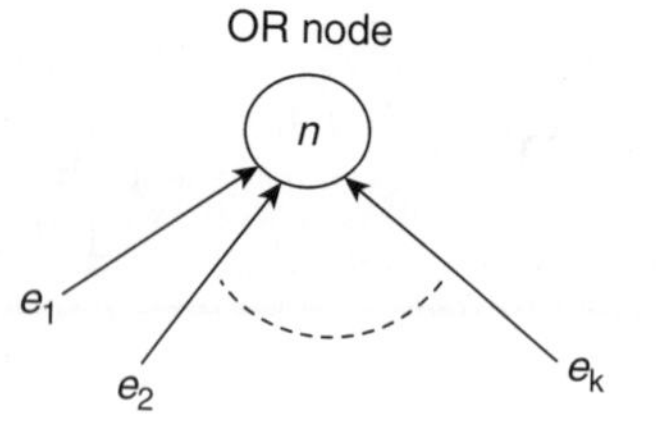

(a) Node n can be reached along *any one* of the edges $e_1, e_2, \ldots, e_k$

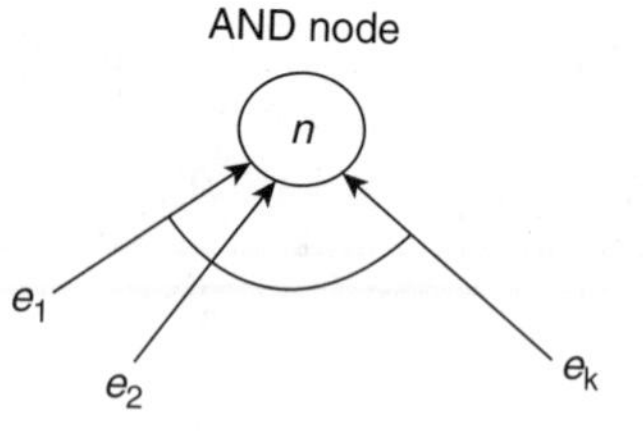

(b) Node n can be reached along *all* of the edges $e_1, e_2, \ldots, e_k$

Fig. 11.52. *Difference between OR-node and AND-node.*

Depth-first search, breadth-first search, best-first search, A* algorithm etc. are the well-known search strategies suitable for OR graphs. These can be generalized to search AND-OR graphs also. However, there are certain aspects which distinguish an AND-OR search from an OR graph search process. These are:

- An AND-OR graph represents a case of **problem reduction** through decomposition. Hence each node of such a graph represents a problem to be solved (or already solved). On the other hand a node of an OR graph represents the state of a problem within the corresponding state space.
- The goal of searching an OR graph is to find a *path* from the start node to a goal node where such a path is required, or simply to reach a goal node. On the contrary, the outcome of an AND-OR graph search is a *solution tree* rather than a path, or goal. The leaves of such trees represent the trivially solvable problems which can be combined to solve a higher-level problem and so on until we come to the root node which represents the given problem.

Before we present the algorithms for AND-OR graph search in a formal way, let us try to grasp the main idea with the help of an example.

Example 11.8 (*Searching through AND-OR graph*)

Fig. 11.53 shows a network of six cities a, b, c, d, e, and f. The weight associated with each edge denotes the cost of the link between the corresponding cities. We are to find a minimum-cost path from a to f.

The AND-OR graph representation of this problem is shown in Fig. 11.54. Here we have tried to find a path from a to f without considering the issue of finding *minimum cost* path. There must be systematic procedure to construct an AND-OR graph and moreover, once we arrive at a solution to the given problem in course of this construction process there is no need to construct the rest of the search tree. In other words, we don't have to construct the entire AND-OR graph in practice.

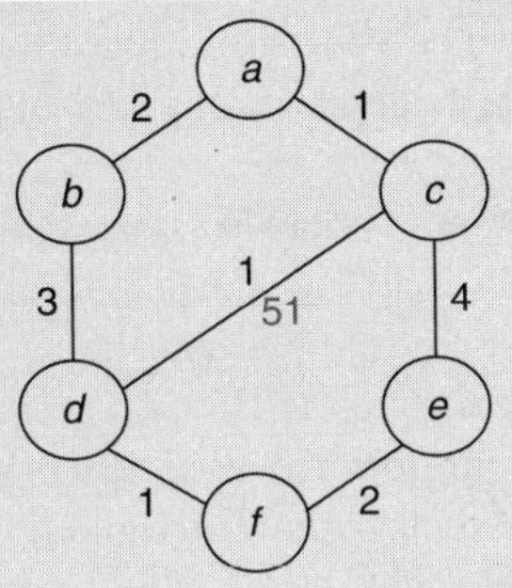

Fig. 11.53. *Interconnection of cities and related costs.*

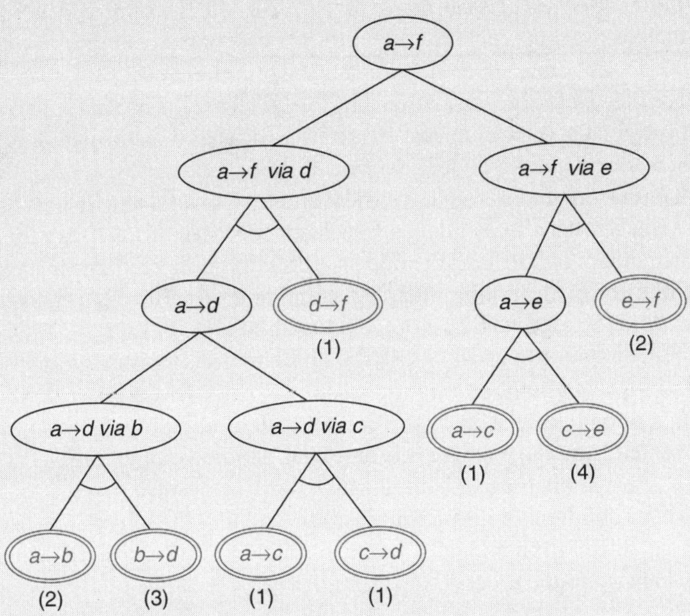

Fig. 11.54. *AND-OR graph for the problem.*

The step-by-step construction of the AND-OR graph as well as arrival at the solution of the given problem is illustrated in Fig. 11.55(a)–(f). The search for a minimum cost path from a to f starts with the root of the AND-OR graph. We employ a heuristic function h_1 associated with each node of the graph. For a node n, $h_1(n)$ estimates the cost of the path from node n to node f. Given a node n, $h_1(n)$ is estimated as

$$h_1(n) = d \times w \tag{11.10}$$

where w is the average cost of a link between two cities, and d = the estimated number of edges between node n and the goal node. The average edge-weight is calculated as

$$w = \frac{total \quad weight \quad of \quad edges}{total \quad number \quad of \quad edges} = \frac{2+1+3+1+4+1+2}{7} = \frac{14}{7} = 2$$

Moreover, we assume a uniform cost of 1 for each link of the AND-OR graph. While estimating the cost of an internal node, those of its descendant along with the costs of the links are taken into consideration.

As there are six cities, at most five edges may exist in a path between node a, and node f. Hence the estimated cost $h_1(n) = d \times w = 5 \times 2 = 10$ is attached to the root node (see Fig. 11.51(55)(a)). In the next step the initial task $a \to f$ is split into two sub-tasks ($a \to f$ *via* d) and ($a \to f$ via e) because f can be reached either through d or through e. This is represented in Fig. 11.51(55)(b) by the successors of the root node. As f can be approached along any one of the paths through d or e, the corresponding sub-tasks are attached to their parent through OR-links. The estimated cost of the node ($a \to f$ *via* d) is obtained as $h_1(a \to f \text{ via } d) = h_1(a \to d)$ + (cost of edge df) $= 4 \times 2 + 1 = 9$. Since the length of a path from a to d is 1 less than that from a to f we have taken $d = 4$. Similarly, the cost estimate of the node ($a \to f$ via e) is calculated as $4 \times 2 + 2 = 10$. If we proceed along node ($a \to f$ *via* d) then the estimated cost at the root is $(9 + 1) = 10$. The cost of traversing along the sub-problem ($a \to f$ via e) is $(10 + 1) = 11$. Since we are looking for the minimum cost path, the former is the right choice. This is indicated by the broken arrow along the link from the root node to the node ($a \to f$ *via* d). Moreover, the estimated minimum cost 10 is now associated with the parent of ($a \to f$ *via* d).

The next step is to expand the node ($a \to f$ *via* d). In order to arrive at f from a via node d one has to traverse a path from a to d (i.e., task $a \to d$) and then from d to f. Therefore node ($a \to f$ *via* d) is split into two sub-tasks $a \to d$ and $d \to f$, each attached to its parent with the help of an AND link. This is shown in Fig. 11.55(c). As the node d is directly connected to f the task $d \to f$ is readily solved. This is indicated by the doubly encircled node for $d \to f$. The cost of this task is simply the cost of the edge df, 1. The estimated cost of the other child is $(4 \times 2) = 8$.

Once we arrived at a node marked as *solved* we have to move upward along the tree to register the effect of this arrival at a solution on the ancestors of the *solved* node. The rule is, **if *each* successor of an AND node is solved, then the parent node is also solved**. And **if *any* successor of an OR node is solved then the parent node is solved.** Modification of the status of the ancestors goes on until we arrive at the root, or a node which remains unsolved even after consideration of the *solved* status of its children. In the present case the parent of the *solved* node ($d \to f$) is the AND node ($a \to f$ *via* d). Since its other child still remains unsolved the unsolved status of node ($a \to f$ *via* d) does not change and the process stops here.

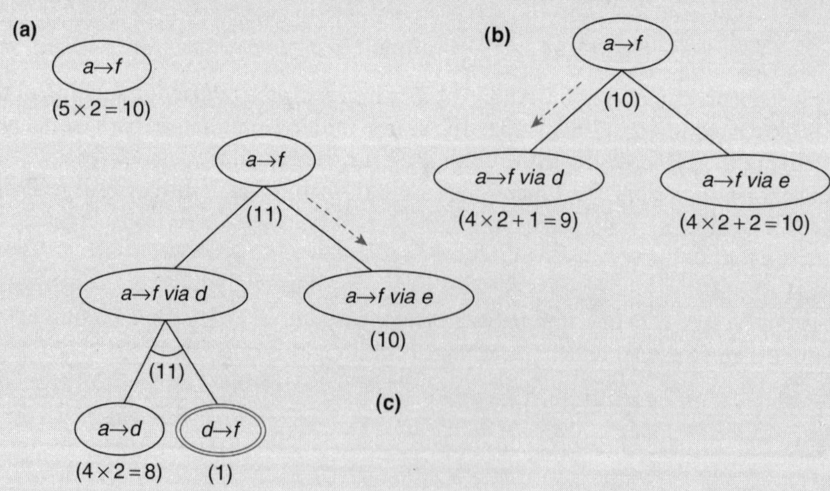

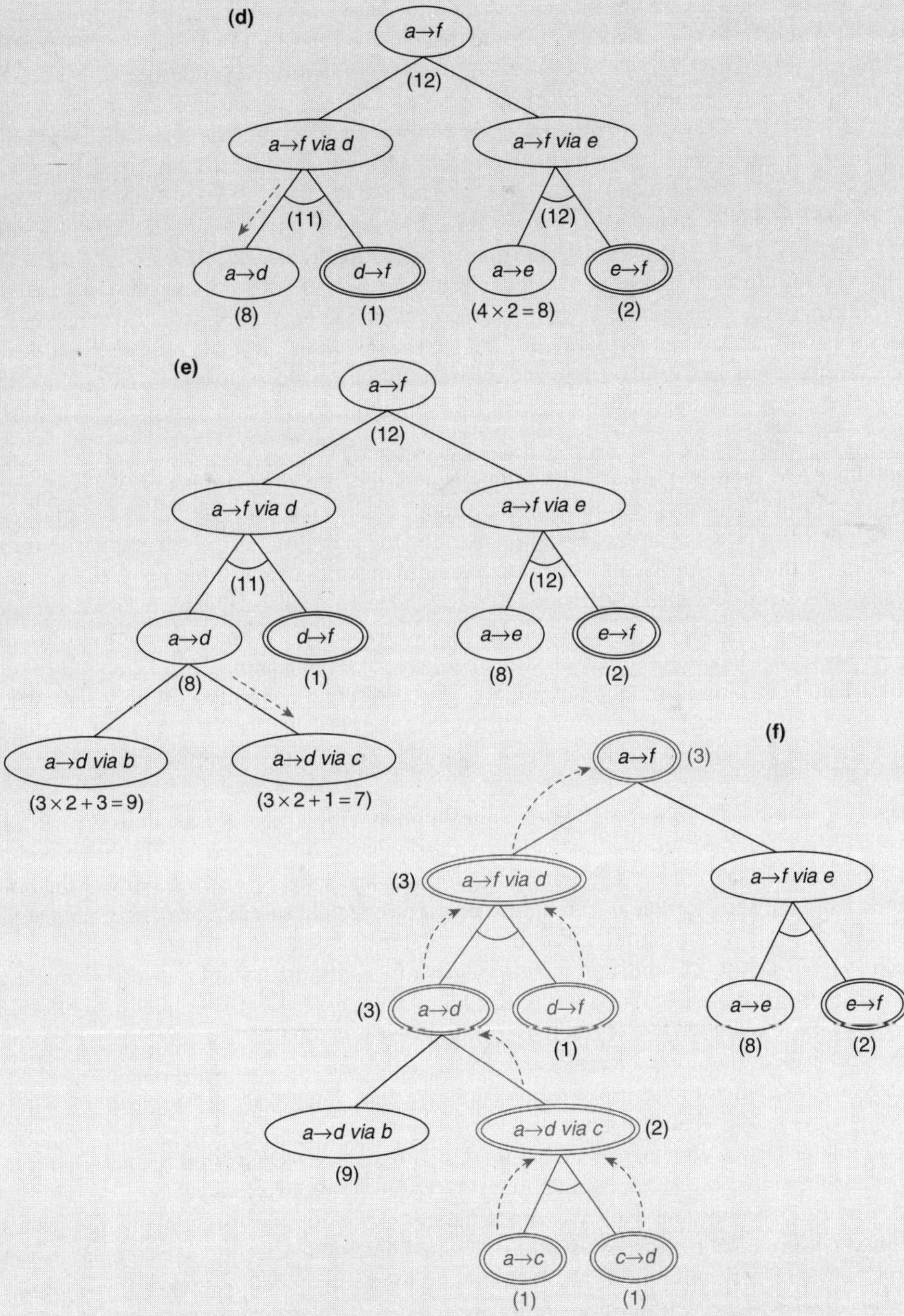

Fig. 11.55. *AND-OR search for minimum-cost path between cities*

The costs of the nodes are now to be revised on the basis of the estimates of the newly created nodes. The cost of ($a \rightarrow d$) is calculated as 8 and that of ($d \rightarrow f$) is $(0 + 1) = 1$. Here $h_1(d \rightarrow f) = 0$ because the sub-problem $d \rightarrow f$ is already solved. As ($a \rightarrow f$ *via* d) is an AND node its revised estimated cost should take into account the costs of both of its successors as well as the links. This becomes $(8 + 1) + (1 + 1) = 11$. When we try to propagate this value upwards, we find the cost of the root node to be $(11 + 1) = 12$. This is greater than the cost $(10 + 1) = 11$ when we approach the root along its other child ($a \rightarrow f$ *via* e). Thus we abandon the previous path and mark ($a \rightarrow f$ *via* e) as the most promising node to be expanded next (Fig. 11.55(c)). The subsequent steps are depicted in Fig. 11.55(d) to Fig. 11.55(f). Fig. 11.55 (*f*) conveys the outcome of the entire process. Here, when the task ($a \rightarrow d$ *via* c) is split into two sub-tasks $a \rightarrow c$ and $c \rightarrow d$ it is found that both of these sub-tasks are readily solved. This makes their parent AND node ($a \rightarrow d$ *via* c) to be marked as solved which in turn solves the parent task $a \rightarrow d$. As we go on climbing the tree in this way the root node which represents the given problem is marked as solved – a condition which indicates the end of the search process. The outcome of the entire process, i.e., the solution tree, is highlighted in Fig. 11.55(f).

A simplified AND-OR graph search technique is described in **`Algorithm AO*`** (Fig. 11.56). It starts with the given problem as the initial node and gradually constructs the AND-OR graph by decomposing a problem into sub-problems and augmenting the partially constructed graph with the nodes corresponding to those sub-problems. At any point, nodes that are generated but not yet explored or expanded are kept in a queue called OPEN and those which have already been explored and expanded are kept in a list called CLOSED. The prospect of a node with respect to the final solution is estimated with the help of a heuristic function. Moreover, two labels, *viz.*, *SOLVED*, and *FUTILE* are used to indicate the status of a node with respect to the solvability of the corresponding problem. A node that represents a readily solved problem need not be decomposed further and is labeled as *SOLVED*. On the other hand, a problem which is not solvable at all, or the solution is so costly that it is not worth trying, is labeled with *FUTILE*.

The operation of the algorithm can be best understood as a repetition of two consecutive phases. In the first phase the already constructed graph is expanded in a top-down approach. In the second phase, we revise the cost estimates of the relevant nodes, connect or change the connections of the nodes to their ancestors, see if some problems, or sub-problems, are readily solvable or not solvable at all and propagate the effect of these towards the root of the graph in a bottom-up fashion.

At each step we identify the most promising solution tree with the help of the cost estimates of the nodes. A yet-unexplored node of that tree is selected for further expansion. The children of this node are integrated into the existing AND-OR graph. Depending on the estimated costs of the newly introduced nodes, the cost estimates of their ancestors are recomputed. Moreover, if the current node is tagged as *SOLVED*, or *FUTILE*, then the status of its ancestors are also changed if necessary. The process stops when the initial node is labeled as *SOLVED* or *FUTILE*.

The example discussed above gives a simplified picture of AND-OR search because it works on a tree rather than a graph. Moreover, a node in an AND-OR graph may involve both AND-links and OR-links. Fig. 11.57 depicts few steps of an imaginary AND-OR graph search involving such a situation. In Fig. 11.57(a), node c is the lowest cost individual node. But selection of c compels us to select node d also because both of them forms an AND-arc together. Since the sum of the costs of these two nodes is greater than the other node b, it is selected at the moment for exploration and expansion. The situation changes after this step (Fig. 11.57(b)) and the AND-arc involving nodes c and d

becomes most prospective for further processing. Since *c* is cheaper than *d* the algorithm will select *c* for processing.

Algorithm AO*

1. Initialize the search tree *T* with a single node, viz. the start node *S*. Place *S* on *OPEN* queue. Initialize *CLOSED* as an empty list.
2. On the basis of the estimated costs of the nodes belonging to the search tree constructed so far, identify a sub-tree T_{best} of *T* as the most prospective solution tree at present.
3. Choose a node *n* from T_{best} that is also in *OPEN*. Remove *n* from *OPEN* and include it in *CLOSED*.
4. Is *n* a goal node? If so, label *n* with the status *SOLVED*. Propagate this status to the ancestors of node *n* in the following way:
   - Let n_1 be the parent of *n*. If the solution of *n* results in the solution of n_1 also, label n_1 with the status *SOLVED*. Repeat the procedure for n_1 and its parent, and so on.
   - The process stops when either we arrive at an ancestor of *n* which remains unsolved in spite of the solution of its descendants till *n*, or the start node of the search tree is reached.

   If the start node *S* attains the status *SOLVED* then report success and return T_{best} as the solution tree.
5. If the cost of *n* becomes prohibitively high, or *n* is simply unsolvable then label it as *FUTILE* indicating that the path through this node is blocked. Propagate this information to the ancestors of *n* in a way analogous to step 4. If the start node *S* attains the status *FUTILE* then report failure and return. From *OPEN* remove all *FUTILE* nodes along with their descendants.
6. If *n* is neither *SOLVED* nor *FUTILE*, then expand it by generating all its children, i.e., all sub-problems into which *n* could be decomposed. Maintain a back pointer from each of these children to its parent *n*. This is required to reconstruct the solution tree once the root node attains the *SOLVED* status. Compute the cost estimate for each child. Place all newly generated nodes into *OPEN*.
8. On the basis of the estimated costs of the new nodes, recompute the cost estimates of their ancestors way up to the root node. Go to Step 2.

Fig. 11.56. *Algorithm AO*.*

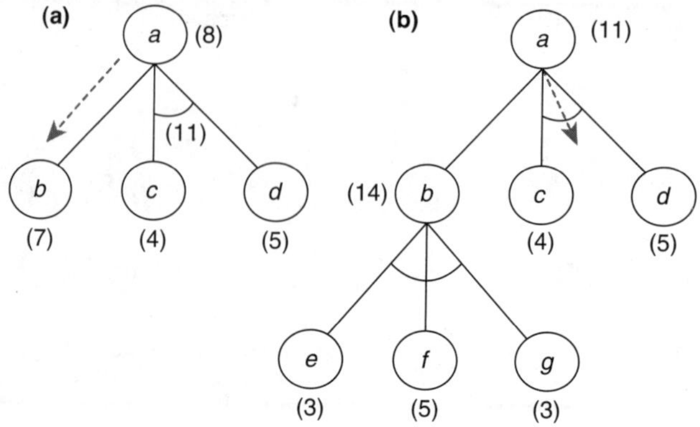

Fig. 11.57. *Characteristics of AO* search*

It has been found that AO* algorithm is admissible, i.e., it guarantees to find an optimal solution tree if one exists, provided $h_1(n) \leq h\ (n)$ for any node n, and all costs are positive. If $h(n) = 0$ then AO* algorithm becomes breadth-first search. AO* is also known as the best-first search algorithm for AND-OR graphs.

11.4.6 Means-Ends Analysis

Means-Ends Analysis (MEA) is a technique employed for generating plans for achieving goals. This technique was first exploited in sixties by a famous A.I system known as the General Problem Solver (GPS). The central idea underlying the MEA strategy is the concept of the *difference* between the start state and the goal state and in general the difference between any two states. The MEA process recursively tries to reduce the difference between two states until it reduces to zero. As a result it generates a sequence of operations or actions which transforms the start state to the goal state. The salient features of an MEA system are described below.

1. It has a problem space with an initial (start) state (object) and a final (goal) state (object).
2. It has the ability to compare two problem states and determine one or more ways in which these states differ from each other. Moreover, it has the capacity to identify the most important difference between two states which it tries to reduce in the next step.
3. It can select an operator (action) appropriate for application on the current problem state to reduce the difference between the current state and a goal. It employs a *difference-operator* table, often augmented with preconditions to the operators, for this purpose. The difference-operator table specifies the operators applicable under various kinds of differences.
4. There is a set of operators, sometimes referred to as rules. An operator can transform one problem state to another. Each operator (rule) has a set of *pre-conditions* and a set of *post-conditions*, or results. The pre-conditions of a rule describe the situation in which the rule can be applied. Similarly, the post-conditions describe the changes that will be incorporated into the problem state as a result of the operation applied.

The basic strategy of means-ends analysis is described in the pseudocode **`Algorithm Means-Ends Analysis (`$S_{current}$`, `S_{goal}`)`** (Fig. 11.58) and is illustrated in Fig. 11.59.

Suppose $S_{current}$ and S_{goal} are the initial and the goal states pertaining to the given problem. A sequence of operations is to be generated that transforms $S_{current}$ to S_{goal}. The system identifies *D* to be the most important difference between the start state and the goal state. This situation is depicted in Fig. 11.59(a). Fig. 11.59(b) shows the situation prevailing after application of an appropriate operator *OP*, which is employed to reduce the gap *D*. Let $S_{pre\text{-}op}$ be the problem state that satisfies the pre-conditions for applying the operator *OP* and $S_{post\text{-}op}$ be the problem state resultant of applying *OP* on $S_{pre\text{-}op}$. Then the portion of *D* indicated by *CD* of Fig. 11.59(b) has been filled and the original difference *D* represented by the distance *AB* in Fig. 11.59(a) and (b) is fragmented into two gaps (may be one) D_1 and D_2 represented as the distances *AC* and *DB* in Fig. 11.59(b). The differences D_1 and D_2 may further be reduced by invoking MEA($S_{current}$, $S_{pre\text{-}op}$) and MEA($S_{post\text{-}op}$ S_{goal}), respectively. It should be noted that *OP* will be actually included in the final plan only if both MEA($S_{current}$, $S_{pre\text{-}op}$) and MEA($S_{post\text{-}op}$ S_{goal}) are successful and return their own sub-plans P_1 and P_2 so that the final plan is obtained by concatenating P_1, *OP*, and P_2.

```
Algorithm Means-Ends Analysis (S_current, S_goal)
1.   IF (S_current is identical to S_goal) THEN Return SUCCESS.
2.   Let D represents the most important difference identified between
     S_current and S_goal. Reduce D through Step 3 to Step 5 until SUCCESS or
     FAILURE is returned.
3.   Select OP, an operator from the Difference-Operator-Precondition
     table which is applicable but not yet been applied to reduce D.
     IF (There is no such operator, i.e., all operators have been tried
     without success)
     THEN Return FAILURE.
4.   Generate S_pre-op and S_post-op, i.e., the states in which the pre-conditions
     and post-conditions of OP are satisfied, respectively.
5.   IF
        P1 ← Means-Ends Analysis (S_current, S_pre-op) and
        P2 ← Means-Ends Analysis (S_post-op, S_goal)
        are the plans generated through successful completion of
        MEA (S_current, S_pre-op) and MEA(S_post-op, S_goal) respectively
     THEN
        Return SUCCESS with the plan P such that
        P ← Concatenation of P1, OP, and P2.
     ELSE Go to Step 3.
```

Fig. 11.58. *Algorithm means-ends analysis ($S_{current}$, S_{goal}).*

The MEA process is a kind of backward chaining known as *operator subgoaling* that consists of selection of operators and subsequent setting up of sub-goals so that the pre-conditions of the operators are established.

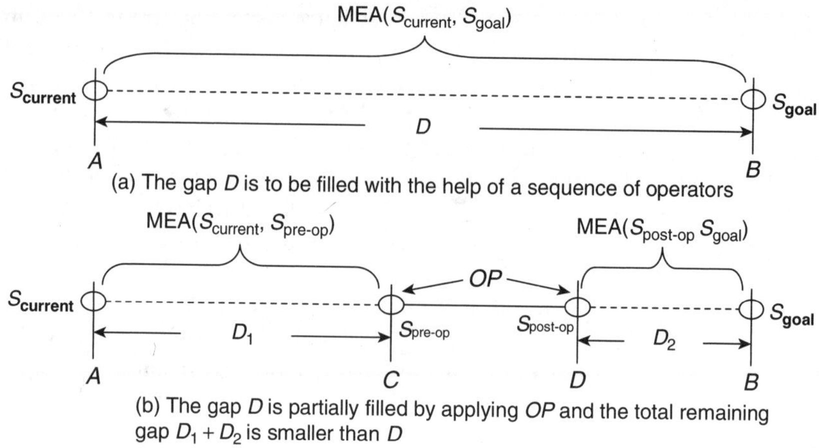

Fig. 11.59. *Basic means-ends analysis strategy.*

Example 11.9 *(Means-Ends Analysis)*

Suppose a person want to reach his friend's house at New Delhi from his home at Kolkata. The distance between Kolkata and New Delhi is about 1500 km. Depending on the distance to be traveled and subject to availability, various kinds of conveyances are used. For example, if it is a very short distance, say, less than 1 km, one should simply walk. For a destination further than 1 km but within the locality one may use a car or a bus. Similarly, to travel larger distances a train, or an aeroplane may be used. In order to board an aeroplane we have to reach the airport. Similarly, to catch a train one has to arrive at the railway station. The airport, or the railway station, may be reached through a car, or a bus, and so on. We want to generate a plan through MEA for this problem.

Here a problem state is defined as the position, or location, of the person. For the sake of simplicity, let us consider a discrete, finite set of possible locations, say, *at-home-at-K, at-the-car-at-K, at-the-car-at-ND, at-the-bus-stop-at-K, at-the-bus-stop-at-ND, at-the-station-at-K, at-the-station-at-ND, at-the-airport-at-K, at-the-airport-at-ND, at-friends-house-ND* etc. The '*K*' and '*ND*' at the tails of the name of locations given above represent Kolkata and New Delhi, respectively. The *difference* between two problem states is given by the distance between the respective locations. For example, if *d* be the distance between the airport at New Delhi and Kolkata, then the *difference* between the problem states *at-the-airport-at-ND* and *at-the-airport-at-K* is *d*. The possible actions, or operators, to reduce the differences stated above are *walk, take a bus, drive a car, use train* and *fly*. There is no pre-condition for walking, however in order to take a bus, one must be at the bus-stop. Therefore the pre-condition of *take a bus* is *be at bus-stand*. Similarly, pre-conditions for the rest of the operators are ascertained. The entire Difference-Operator-Precondition table is shown in Fig. 11.60. Table 11.5 depicts the trace of recursive application of Means-Ends Analysis process to the present problem. The plan generated through the MEA process and the recursive depths of various operators within the plan are shown in Fig. 11.61.

Initially, the applicable operation is to *fly* because the distance between the person's home at Kolkata and his friend's house at New Delhi is about 1500 km, which is greater than 500 km. In order to apply this operation, one be at the airport. So a sub-goal is created which is to reach the airport from the person's home. Similarly, when the person arrives at New Delhi airport, he has to travel from the airport to his friend's house. Both of these sub-problems are solved by invoking the same MEA process recursively.

Problem: *How to reach your friend's residence at New Delhi from your home at Kolkata.*

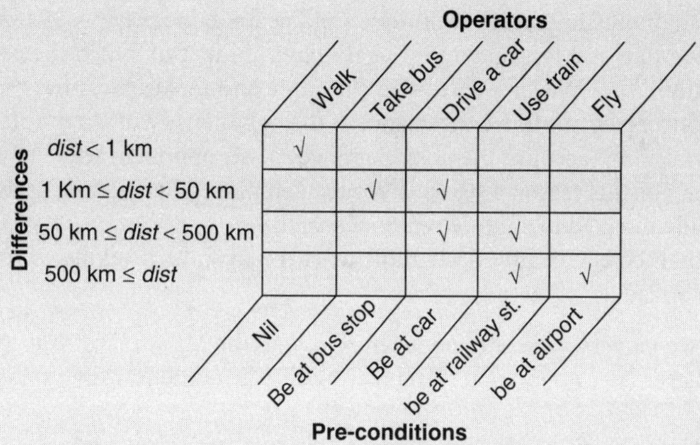

Fig. 11.60. *The difference-operator-precondition table.*

Table 11.5. *Trace of recursive application of means-ends analysis*

Difference	Applicable operator	Precondition to be satisfied
500 ≤ *dist*	*fly*	be at airport
1 ≤ *dist* <50	*drive* a car	be at car
dist <1	*walk* (to car)	nil
dist <1	*walk* (to airport)	nil
1 ≤ *dist* <50	*take* bus	be at bus stop
dist <1	*walk* (to bus)	nil
dist <1	*walk* (to friend's house)	nil

plan generated

walk (to car) → *drive* (to airport) → *walk* (to aeroplane) → *fly* (to ND airport) → *walk* (to bus stop) → *take bus* → *walk* (to friend's house)

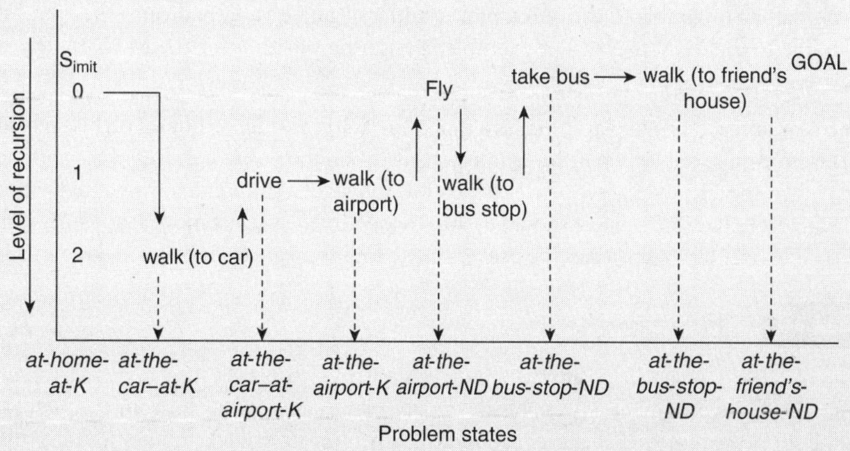

Fig. 11.61. *Plan generated through means-end analysis.*

11.4.7 Mini-Max Search

Mini-Max search is an interesting search technique suitable for game playing AI systems. A game, unless it is one-player puzzle-like, is a typically multi-agent environment in which the agents are competitive rather than cooperative. Each player tries to win the game and makes his moves so as to maximize his chance of win and conversely, minimize the chance of the opponent's win. As the players have conflicting goals, a player must take into account the possible moves of his opponent while he makes his own move against his opponent. For this reason a search algorithm employed to facilitate decision making for such a player is occasionally referred to as an *adversarial* search.

In this text, we shall consider only deterministic, two-player, turn-taking, zero-sum games. Such a game can be characterized as follows:

- There are two players. One of them is referred to as the MAX player (say, you), and the other as the MIN player (your opponent). The reason of such nomenclature of the players will be soon obvious.
- The first move is made by the MAX player.
- The moves are deterministic.
- The two players make their moves alternately.

A deterministic, two-player, turn-taking, zero-sum game as described above can be formalized as a system consisting of certain components:

1. A data structure to represent the status of the game at any moment. This is usually referred to as the *board position*. Each possible status of the game is considered as a state of the corresponding *state* space. The status of the game before the first move (by MAX) is the *initial* state.
2. A *successor function* which returns a list of legal moves from a given game state as well as the states resultant of those legal moves.
3. A *terminal condition* that defines the termination of the game. Depending on the rules of the game, it may terminate either in the win of a player (and the loss of his opponent), or a draw.
4. A function, generally termed as the *utility*, or *objective*, or *pay-off*, or *static evaluation* function. This function gives the numeric values of the terminal states. In case of *static evaluation function*, it returns a numeric value for each state of the game. Usually, a positive numeric value indicates a game status favourable to the MAX player and a negative value indicates the game status to be favourable to the MIN player. For example, a winning position for the MAX (MIN) player may have a $+\infty$ ($-\infty$), or +1 (−1) value.

As mentioned earlier, each time a player makes a move he has to consider its impact on his chance of winning the game. This is possible only when he takes into consideration the possible moves of his opponent. Starting with the first move, the entire set of sequences of possible moves of a game can be presented with the help of a *game tree*. In an ideal situation, a player should be able to identify the perfect move at any turn with the help of the game tree. Example 11.10 illustrates the use of a game tree as an aid to decision making in game playing.

Example 11.10 *(The game of NIM)*

The game of NIM is a classical example of a deterministic, two-player, turn-taking, zero-sum game. The game starts with a number of piles of sticks. Two players remove sticks from the piles alternately until all the sticks are removed. A player can remove any number of sticks from one pile of his choice when his turn of move comes. However, he should try to leave some sticks in the piles because the player who has to take the last stick loses. The status of the game at any moment may be represented with the help of a non-decreasing sequence of integers. For example, the sequence (2, 4, 4, 7) represents four piles of sticks containing 2, 4, 4, and 7 sticks in the individual piles. Now if a player removes two sticks from one pile containing 4 sticks then the resultant game status is represented by (2, 2, 4, 7). If in this situation all the sticks from the 7-stick pile are removed by a player then the game status becomes (2, 2, 4).

For the sake of simplicity, we shall consider the (1, 2, 2) NIM game. As usual the two players are denoted as the MAX (i.e., you) and the MIN (i.e., your opponent). The utility function is defined as follows:

Function Value	Interpretation	
	Won	Lost
$+\infty$	MAX	MIN
$-\infty$	MIN	MAX

It should be noted that instead of the pair ($+\infty$, $-\infty$) other numeric values, *e.g.*, (+1, −1), could also be used. However we shall see that the concept of a utility function will be generalized to that of a static evaluation function which returns an integral value for any game status and not for the winning/losing positions only. The complete game tree for (1, 2, 2) NIM is shown in Fig. 11.62.

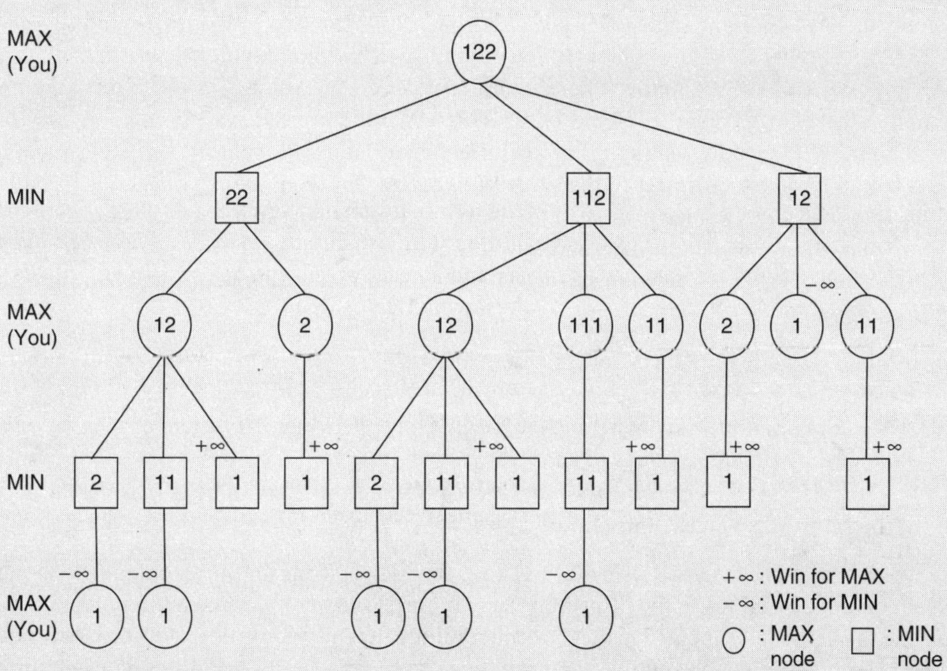

Fig. 11.62. *Complete game tree for (1, 2, 2) NIM game.*

The root node represents the initial status (1, 2, 2) of the game. Depending on whether the MAX player picks 1 or 2 sticks, the status of the game after the first move may be (2, 2), (1, 1, 2), or (1, 2). These constitute the 1st level nodes of the tree. Similarly, from (2, 2), the move by MIN player may result in the status of (1, 2), or (2), and so on. Usually the set of all game status at a certain level of the game tree which corresponds to the MAX (MIN) player's turn of move is called a MAX-ply (MIN-ply). To make the distinction clear, nodes of the MAX-ply are represented with circles and those of the MIN-ply are represented with rectangles.

Each leaf node of Fig. 11.62 represents the game status (1), i.e., the last stick. This implies defeat of the player whose turn of move it is. Hence, leaf nodes of a MAX-ply have a utility value $-\infty$ and those of MIN-plies have a value $+\infty$.

The game tree shown in Fig. 11.62 depicts the sequences of probable moves by the two players and the final outcome of those sequences with respect to the result of the game. However, the primary objective of a player is to identify and select the best possible move. The game tree, along with the utility function, may be exploited to achieve this goal.

The idea is to find the utility value, referred to as the *Mini-Max value*, of each node to decide whether the corresponding move is good or bad for the player. The underlying assumption is that each player will try to create situations best for him and worst for his opponent. Consider the MAX nodes (*j*) and (*k*) in Fig. 11.63, which show the game tree of Fig. 11.62 along with the Mini-Max values of the nodes. Nodes (*j*) and (*k*) are losing the game status for MAX. Therefore, both of them have a score of $-\infty$. Now node (*j*) is a child of node (*g*) which is a MIN node. Since MIN will definitely try to defeat MAX, it is bound to make a move that leads to game status (*j*). Hence the utility value of (*g*) is same as that of (*j*). Similarly, the utility of node (*k*) is propagated to node (*h*). However, node (*i*) of the same MIN-ply is a losing game status for a player MIN and a win for node MAX. Hence its score is $+\infty$. Now (*g*), (*h*) and (*i*) are children of node (*e*), which belongs to a MAX-ply. MAX will select a move to ensure his chance of win. Among (*g*), (*h*) and (*i*), the first two imply defeat of MAX and the last one ensures his win. Therefore, faced with situation (*e*) MAX will make a move to (*i*) only, neither (*g*) nor (*h*). Hence the Mini-Max value of node (*e*) should be same as that of (*i*), i.e., $+\infty$. However, the situation is reverse for the node (*c*). This node has three children with Mini-Max values $+\infty$, $-\infty$, and $+\infty$, respectively. Being in a MIN-ply, the opponent will try to make things worst for MAX and so will move to the game status of value $-\infty$. Hence the Mini-Max value of (*c*) is $-\infty$. Obviously, the general rule for computing the Mini-Max value of a node *N* is:

1. If *N* is a leaf node then the Mini-Max value of *N* is its score, i.e., value of the utility function at that node.
2. If *N* is a MAX-node, i.e., *N* belongs to a MAX-ply, the Mini-Max value of *N* is the *maximum* of the Mini-Max values of its children.
3. If *N* is a MIN-node, i.e., *N* belongs to a MIN-ply, the Mini-Max value of *N* is the *minimum* of the Mini-Max values of its children.

`Procedure MiniMax (N)` (Fig. 11.64) gives the pseudo-code for the technique mentioned above. In case of a MAX node, the Mini-Max value is initialized to $-\infty$ (or the minimum allowable value) and then gradually updated to the maximum value of its children. (lines 3-9). For a MIN node the value is initialized to $+\infty$ and then lowered down to the minimum value among its children. Fig 11.63 shows the Mini-Max values of each node of the game tree for (1, 2, 2) NIM game obtained by applying this procedure on the said game tree. It is easy to see that the root node attains a Mini-Max value of +∞ which implies that if properly played, the game can be won by the MAX player and in order to win he has to remove the stick from the single stick pile. Any other move may eventually lead to his losing the game, provided the opponent does not make any mistake.

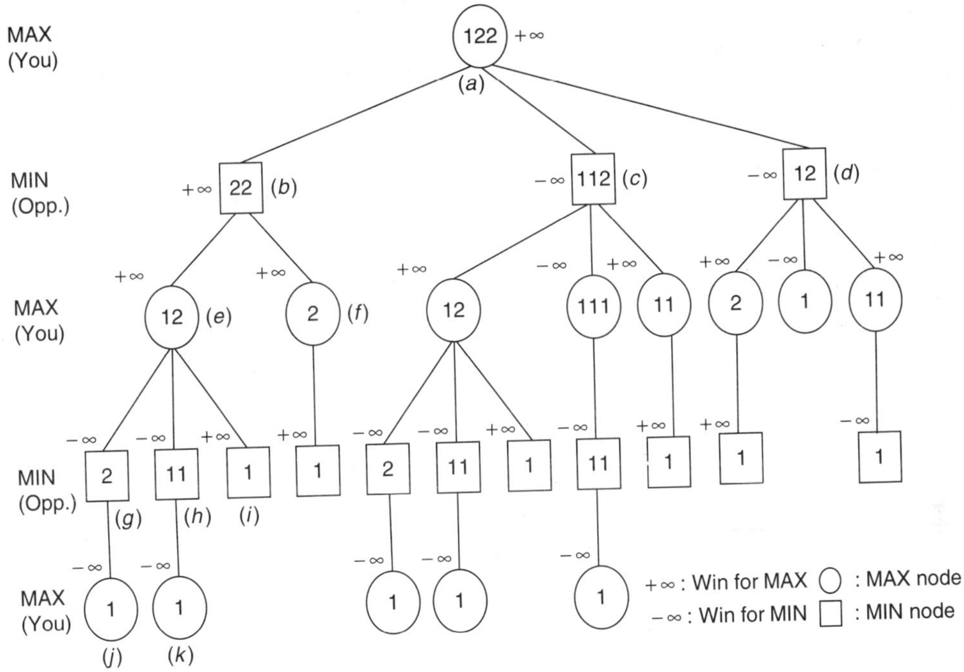

Fig. 11.63. *Utility values of different nodes of (1, 2, 2) NIM game.*

A realistic game playing system must take into consideration the facts that the real-world games are too *hard* computationally. As a classical example, consider the game of chess. The average branching factor of chess is approximately 35. If we consider a usual game with 50 moves for each player then the search tree would consist of about 35^{100} or 10^{154} nodes. Arriving at an optimal decision through exhaustive search of a tree of such dimension is not feasible. Hence `Procedure MiniMax (N)` has to be modified suitably so that effective decisions can be taken even if the entire game tree is not searched.

Static evaluator We need something more than a utility function to assist us in decision making while playing a realistic game. Recall that the utility function returned a value for terminal game status, which is percolated to their ancestors as Mini-Max values till the concerned node attains its own Mini-Max value. A **static evaluator** is a generalized utility function that returns a value for any node of the game tree and not just for the terminal modes. Equipped with a suitable static evaluator `Procedure MiniMax (N)` can now be modified to carry out the Mini-Max search to a predefined depth from the given node of the game tree and assign the Mini-Max value of the node on the basis of that limited information.

```
Procedure MiniMax (N)

INPUT: A node N of a game tree T_G. Also there is an evaluation function score(N) which returns a value indicating the relative merit of the game status corresponding to node N. Usually score(N) = -∞ if N is a winning position for MIN, and score(N) = +∞ if N is a winning position for MAX.

OUTPUT: The MiniMax value of node N.

BEGIN
    IF (N is a leaf node) THEN Return score(N) END-If
    /* code for MAX node */
    IF (N is a MAX node) THEN
        /* Initialize MiniMax value with lowest value */
        MiniMax-value ← -∞
        /* Update the MiniMax value of the current node with the highest
        MiniMax value among its children */
        FOR (each child of N) DO
            value ← MiniMax (child)
            IF value > MiniMax-value THEN MiniMax-value ← value
            END-If
        END-For
        Return MiniMax-value
    END-If

    /* code for MIN node */
    IF (N is a MIN node) THEN
        /* Initialize MiniMax value with highest possible value */
        MiniMax-value ← +∞
        /* Update the MiniMax value of the current node with the Lowest
        MiniMax value among its children */
        FOR (each child of N) DO
            value ← MiniMax (child)
            IF value < MiniMax-value THEN
                MiniMax-value ← value
            END-If
        END-For
        Return MiniMax-value
    END-If
END-MiniMax
```

Fig. 11.64. *Procedure MiniMax (N).*

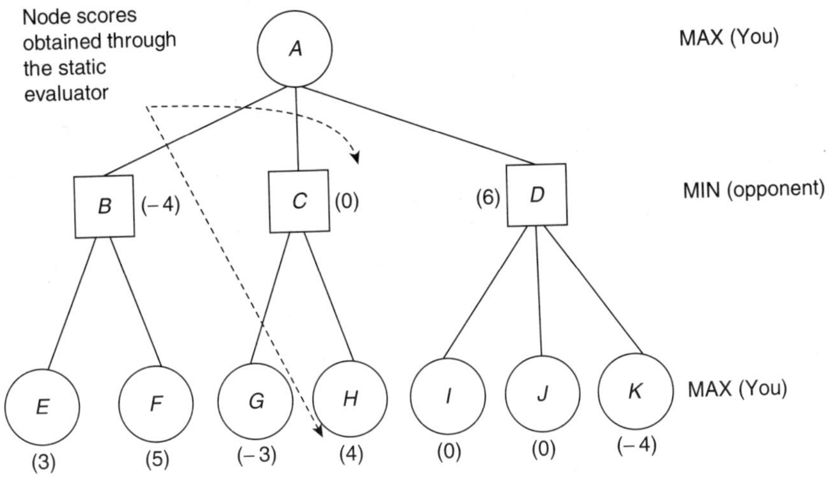

Fig. 11.65. *Scores of individual nodes based on static evaluation function.*

Depth-limited Mini-Max search As an example, let us consider a portion of an imaginary game tree as shown in Fig. 11.65. The score of each node with respect to the evaluation function is given within parentheses adjacent to the respective node. Our goal is to assign a Mini-Max value to the root node *A* on the basis of these scores. If we decide to carry out the Mini-Max search process till a depth of 1 only, then the scores of three children of *A*, i.e., nodes *B*, *C* and *D*, should be considered and no node beyond that level. As *A* is a MAX node, the maximum of these scores should be the Mini-Max value of *A* (see Fig. 11.66). Therefore node *A* attains a Mini-Max value of 6 through 1-ply MiniMax search.

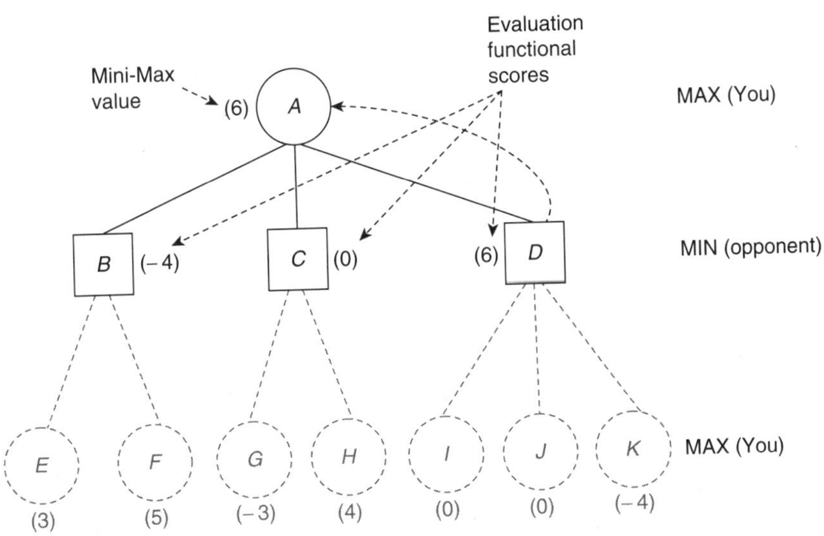

Fig. 11.66. *Finding Mini-Max value through 1-ply search.*

Now compare this with Fig. 11.67 showing the same process carried out to a depth of 2, instead of 1. Here the deepest nodes are at level 2 and these nodes are evaluated on the basis of the static evaluator. The nodes *B*, *C* and *D* being MIN nodes, each of them obtain its Mini-Max value as the lowest score among the children of the respective node. Finally, the MAX node *A* is assigned a Mini-Max value of 3, the highest score among *B*, *C* and *D*.

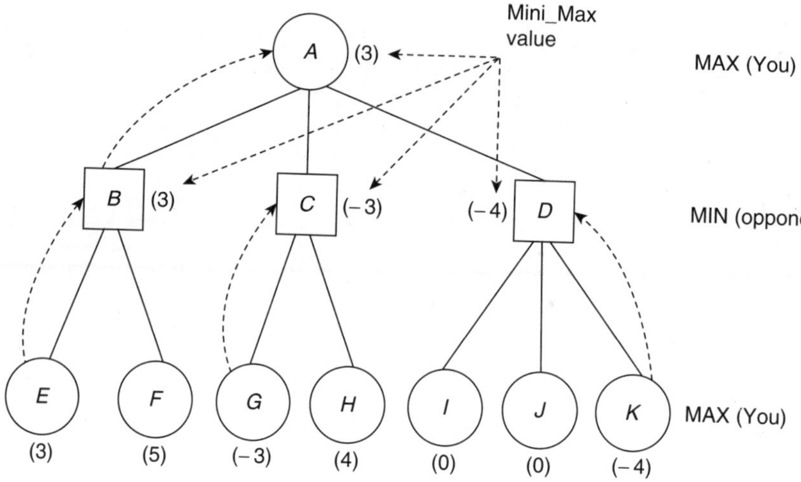

Fig. 11.67. *Finding Mini-Max value through 2-ply search.*

The pseudo-code for the technique described above is presented in **`Procedure Depth-Limited-MiniMax (N, d)`** (Fig. 11.68). The algorithm is similar to **`MiniMax (N)`** except that each time the procedure calls itself recursively the depth is reduced by 1. Therefore, *score* (*N*) is returned not only for the leaf nodes but also for the nodes at depth *d* (line #2).

```
Procedure Depth-Limited-MiniMax (N, d)

INPUT :A node N of a game tree T_G as well as the depth d to which the game
tree T_G should be explored. Also there is an evaluation function score(N)
which returns a value indicating the relative merit of the game status
corresponding to node N. Usually score(N) = -∞ if N is a winning position
for MIN, and score(N) = +∞ if N is a winning position for MAX.

OUTPUT:The MiniMax value of node N.

1.BEGIN
2.    IF (N is a leaf node) OR (d=0) THEN Return score(N) END-If
      /* code for MAX node */
3.    IF (N is a MAX node) THEN
          /* Initialize MiniMax value with lowest possible value */
4.        MiniMax-value ← -∞
          /* Update the MiniMax value of the current node with the high-
          est MiniMax value among its children */
5.        FOR (each child of N) DO
6.          value ← MiniMax (child, d-1)
```

```
            IF value > MiniMax-value THEN MiniMax-value ← value END-If
          END-For
          Return MiniMax-value
    END-If
    /* code for MIN node */
    IF (N is a MIN node) THEN
          /* Initialize MiniMax value with highest possible value */
          MiniMax-value ← +∞
          /* Update the MiniMax value of the current node with the low-
          est MiniMax value among its children */
          FOR (each child of N) DO
            value ← MiniMax (child, d-1)
            IF value < MiniMax-value THEN MiniMax-value ← value END-If
          END-For
          Return MiniMax-value
     END-If
   END-Depth-Limited-MiniMax
```

Fig. 11.68 *Procedure Depth-limited-MiniMax (N, d).*

Design issues While designing a game playing system using Mini-Max search, one has to decide two things, *viz.*, which static evaluator is to be employed, and how deeply the game tree should be searched. There is no rule regarding the first issue. It depends on the insight of the designer. However, several factors are to be taken into consideration in this regard. Most important of these are

- *Speed:* The static evaluator should compute fast. This is because time is a decisive parameter in most of the games we humans play. For example, in chess any delay in making a move is eventually severely punished.
- *Heuristic power:* The static evaluator should be powerful enough to embody sufficient knowledge regarding the game so that effective decision can be taken by the player. Again, let us consider the game of chess. A simple static evaluator would be the sum of the values of the white pieces minus the sum of the values of the black pieces, i.e.,

$$score(N) = \sum_{p_w \in N} p_W - \sum_{p_B \in N} p_B$$

where p_W and p_B are the white pieces and the black pieces remaining in board position N.

The question of how deeply should the game tree be searched is related to the speed-concern as well as the heuristic power of the static evaluator. The deeper we delve into the game tree the more informed and wise our decision, provided we have time. We may also try to compensate, so far as possible, the limitation of the evaluator by carrying out the search to deeper levels.

Alpha-beta pruning Is it possible to make MiniMax search more efficient? It has been found quite frequently that certain portions of a game tree do not play any role to decision-making in the sense that the Mini-Max value returned by the search remains the same irrespective of whether these portions are explored or not. *Alpha-Beta pruning* is a technique of making MiniMax search efficient by avoiding these parts while searching the game tree. The technique of *Alpha-Beta pruning* is explained below with reference to the game tree shown in Fig. 11.69.

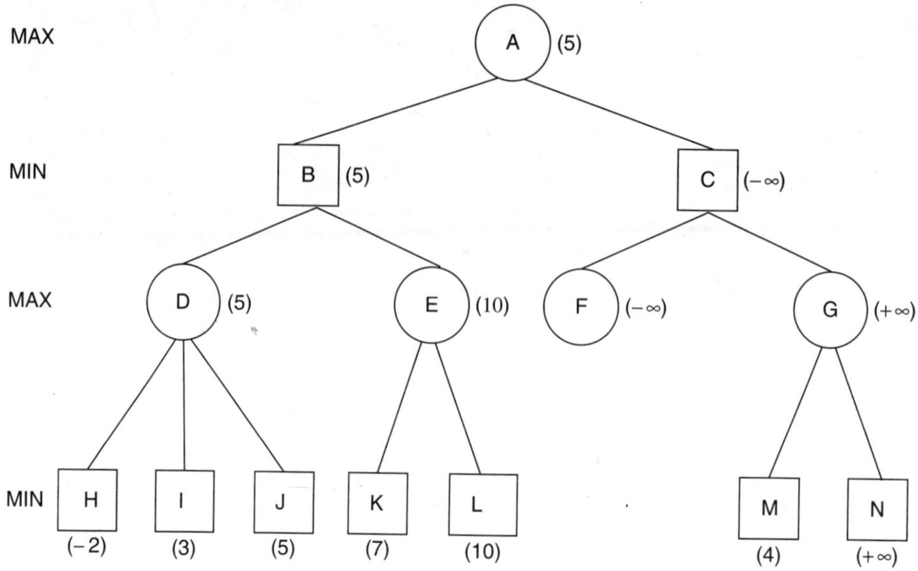

Fig. 11.69. *A 3-ply game tree with Mini-Max values.*

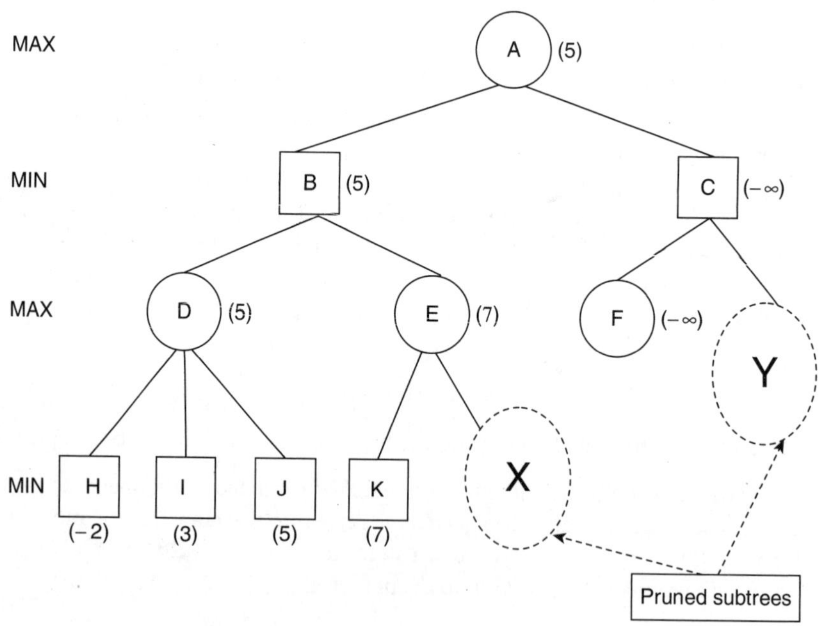

Fig. 11.70. *Alpha-Beta pruning of a game tree during Mini-Max search.*

As usual, the numbers attached to the leaf nodes are the scores of the respective game status obtained through the static evaluator and the numbers adjacent to the internal nodes give the Mini-Max values. The root node *A* obtains a Mini-Max value of 5 as a result of 3-ply Mini-Max search on the game tree mentioned above. Let us examine the Mini-Max process involved here critically. The MAX node *D* is assigned a Mini-Max value 5 as this is the highest score among its children *H*, *I* and *J*. Now, while computing the Mini-Max value of node *E*, we see that *E*'s first child *K* has a score of 7. This implies the Mini-Max value of *E* is going to be at least 7, as *E* is a MAX node. But this value is already greater that 5, the Mini-Max value of node *D*. Since the parent of *D* and *E*, i.e., node *B*, is a MIN node, the Mini-Max value of *B* will be at most 5. Hence it is useless to explore the sub-tree marked 'X' (see Fig. 11.70). Whatever be the values existing in portion 'X' of the game tree, the Mini-Max value of *B* will remain 5. Similarly, the 'Y' portion of the game tree can also be ignored because the MIN node C has already attained a Mini-Max value $-\infty$ which obviously can not be further lowered.

Procedure AlphaBeta-MiniMax (N, d, Alpha, Beta) (Fig. 11.71) presents the pseudo-code for MiniMax search made efficient by incorporating the technique of Alpha-Beta pruning explained above. Alpha and Beta are the two cutoff numbers, generally referred to as the *Alpha-Beta cut-offs*, used to prune the avoidable parts of the game tree. The Mini-Max value of node is worth computing only if it lies within the range [*Alpha*, *Beta*]. While computing the Mini-Max value of a MAX node as soon as it is found that the Mini-Max value of any of its child exceeds *Beta* then the concerned MAX node is assigned a value of *Beta* without exploring the rest of the subtree (see line #8 of **Procedure Alpha-Beta-MiniMax**). Conversely, a MIN node is assigned the Mini-Max value *Alpha* as soon as it tends to go below *Alpha*, and the search is discontinued (see line #17 of **Procedure AlphaBeta-MiniMax**). A trace of execution of **Procedure AlphaBeta-MiniMax** on the game tree of Fig. 11.69 is shown in Table 11.6. The recursive calls of **Procedure AlphaBeta-MiniMax (N, d, Alpha, Beta)** are underlined. A pictorial view of the process is presented in Fig. 11.72.

```
Procedure AlphaBeta-MiniMax (N, d, Alpha, Beta)
  /* This procedure computes the MiniMax value of node N, searched to depth
  d of the game tree T_G from node N. If the computed value is less than Alpha
  then Alpha is returned. The procedure returns Beta if the computed value
  is more than Beta. */

1. BEGIN
2.    IF (N is a leaf node) OR (d=0) THEN Return score(N) END-If

      /* code for MAX node */
3.    IF (N is a MAX node) THEN
            /* Initialize MiniMax value with Alpha */
4.          MiniMax-value ← Alpha

            /* Update MiniMax value of the current node with the highest
            MiniMax value among its children, or Beta if the computed
            value exceeds Beta. */
5.    FOR (each child of N) DO
6.             value ← MiniMax (child, d-1, MiniMax-value, Beta)
7.             IF value > MiniMax-value THEN MiniMax-value ← value END-If

               /* If Beta is exceeded then prune the rest of the sub-tree
               of T_G. */
```

```
8.      IF MiniMax-value > Beta THEN Return Beta END-If
9.     END-For
        /* Beta is not exceeded */
10.         Return MiniMax-value
11.    END-If
            /* code for MIN node */
12.    IF (N is a MIN node) THEN
            /* Initialize MiniMax value with highest possible value */
13.         MiniMax-value ← Beta
            /* Update MiniMax value of the current node with the lowest
              MiniMax value among its children or Alpha, whichever is higher.
              */
14.         FOR (each child of N) DO
15.           value ← MiniMax (child, d-1, Alpha, MiniMax-value)
16.           IF value < MiniMax-value THEN MiniMax-value ← value END-If
              /* If MiniMax-value < Alpha then prune the rest of the sub-
              tree */
17.           IF MiniMax-value < Alpha THEN Return Alpha END-If
18.         END-For
            /* MiniMax-value has not gone below Alpha */
19.         Return MiniMax-value
20.     END-If
21.    END-AlphaBeta-MiniMax
```

Fig. 11.71. *Procedure AlphaBeta-MiniMax (N, d, Alpha, Beta).*

Table 11.6. *Trace of execution of Procedure AlphaBeta-MiniMax*

Levels of recursion				
0	1	2	3	
$\alpha\beta$MiniMax (A, 3, $-\infty$, $+\infty$)		/* Initially *Alpha* = $-\infty$, *Beta* = $-\infty$		*/
MiniMax-value = $-\infty$		/* Line #4, A is a MAX node		*/
Value ←	*$\alpha\beta$MiniMax (B, 2, $-\infty$, $+\infty$)*		/* Explore the 1st child of A	*/
	MiniMax-value = $+\infty$		/* Line #13, B is a MIN node	*/
	Value ←	*$\alpha\beta$MiniMax (D, 1, $-\infty$, $+\infty$)*		
		MiniMax-value = $-\infty$		
		Value ←	*$\alpha\beta$MiniMax (H, 0, $-\infty$, $+\infty$)*	
			Return (-2)	
		Value = -2		

(Continued)

Table 11.6. *Continued*

Levels of recursion			
0	1	2	3
		MiniMax-value = –2	
		Value ←	<u>$\alpha\beta$*MiniMax* (*I*, 0, –2, +∞)</u>
			Return (3)
		Value = 3	
		MiniMax-value = 3	
		Value ←	<u>$\alpha\beta$*MiniMax* (*J*, 0, 3, +∞)</u>
			Return (5)
		Value = 5	
		MiniMax-value = 5	
		Return (5) /* All children of *D* are explored */	
	Value = 5		
	MiniMax-value = 5		
	Value ←	<u>$\alpha\beta$*MiniMax* (*E*, 1, –∞, 5)</u>	
		MiniMax-value = –∞	
		Value ←	<u>$\alpha\beta$*MiniMax* (*K*, 0, –∞, 5)</u>
			Return (7)
		Value = 7	
		MiniMax-value = 7	
		Return (5) /* see line #7, prune the rest sub-tree */	
	Value = 5		
	MiniMax-value = 5		
	Return (5) /* all children of node *B* have been explored */		
Value = 5			
MiniMax-value = 5			
Value ←	<u>$\alpha\beta$*MiniMax* (*C*, 2, 5, +∞)</u>		
	MiniMax-value = +∞		
	Value ←	<u>$\alpha\beta$*MiniMax* (*F*, 1, 5, +∞)</u> /* leaf node */	
		Return (–∞) /* score (F) = –∞ */	
	Value = –∞		
	MiniMax-value = –∞		
	Return (5) /* see line #17, prune the remaining sub-tree */		
Value = 5			
MiniMax-value = 5			
Return (5) /* The *MiniMax value* of node A */			

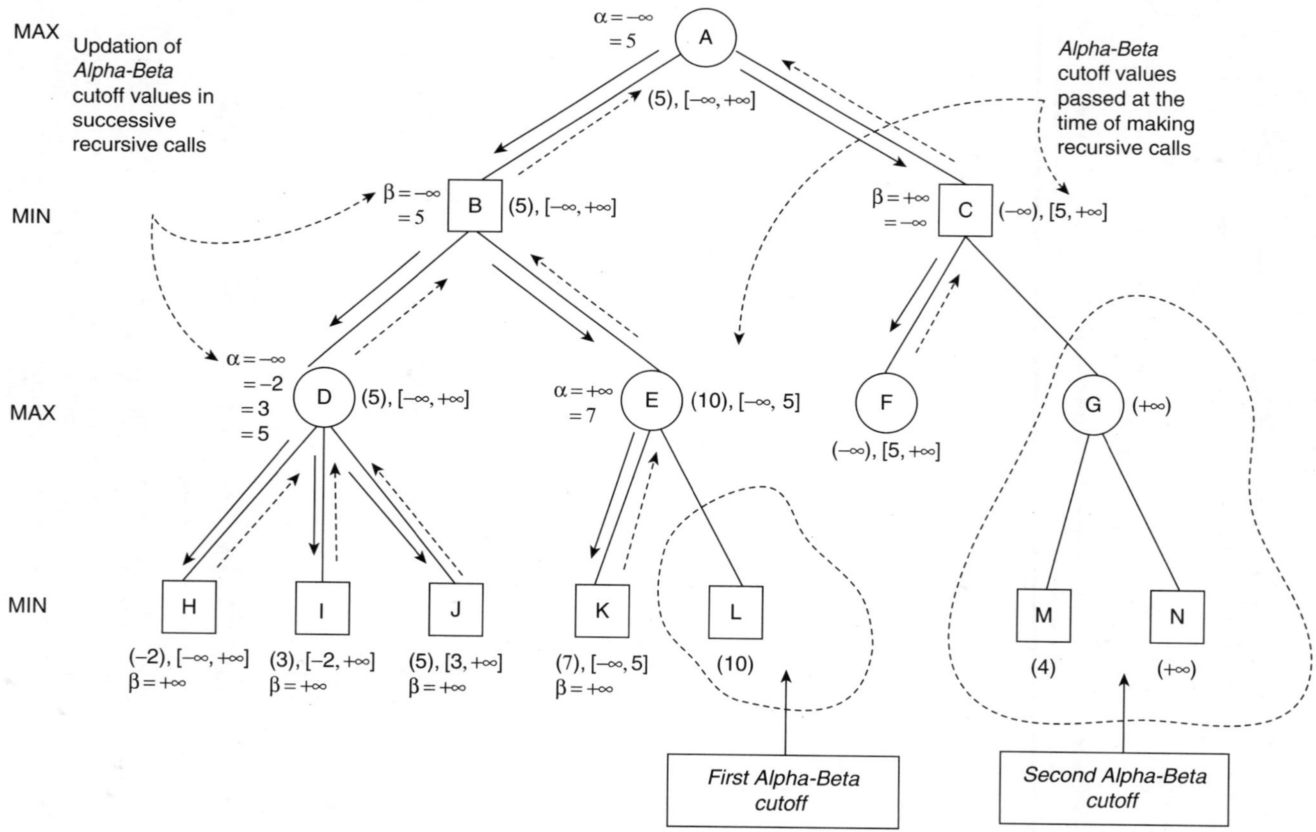

Fig. 11.72. *Alpha-Beta pruning during MiniMax search.*

The effectiveness of Alpha-Beta pruning depends on the order in which the nodes are visited. For a MAX node, the best case is exploration of the best child (best from the point of view of MAX player) first so that remaining children and sub-trees associated with them becomes irrelevant. On the other hand, visiting the worst child (worst from the point of view of MIN) is most welcome in case the concerned node is a MIN node. These correspond to pruning to the highest extent. However, there may be no pruning at all if the children are visited in the worst order.

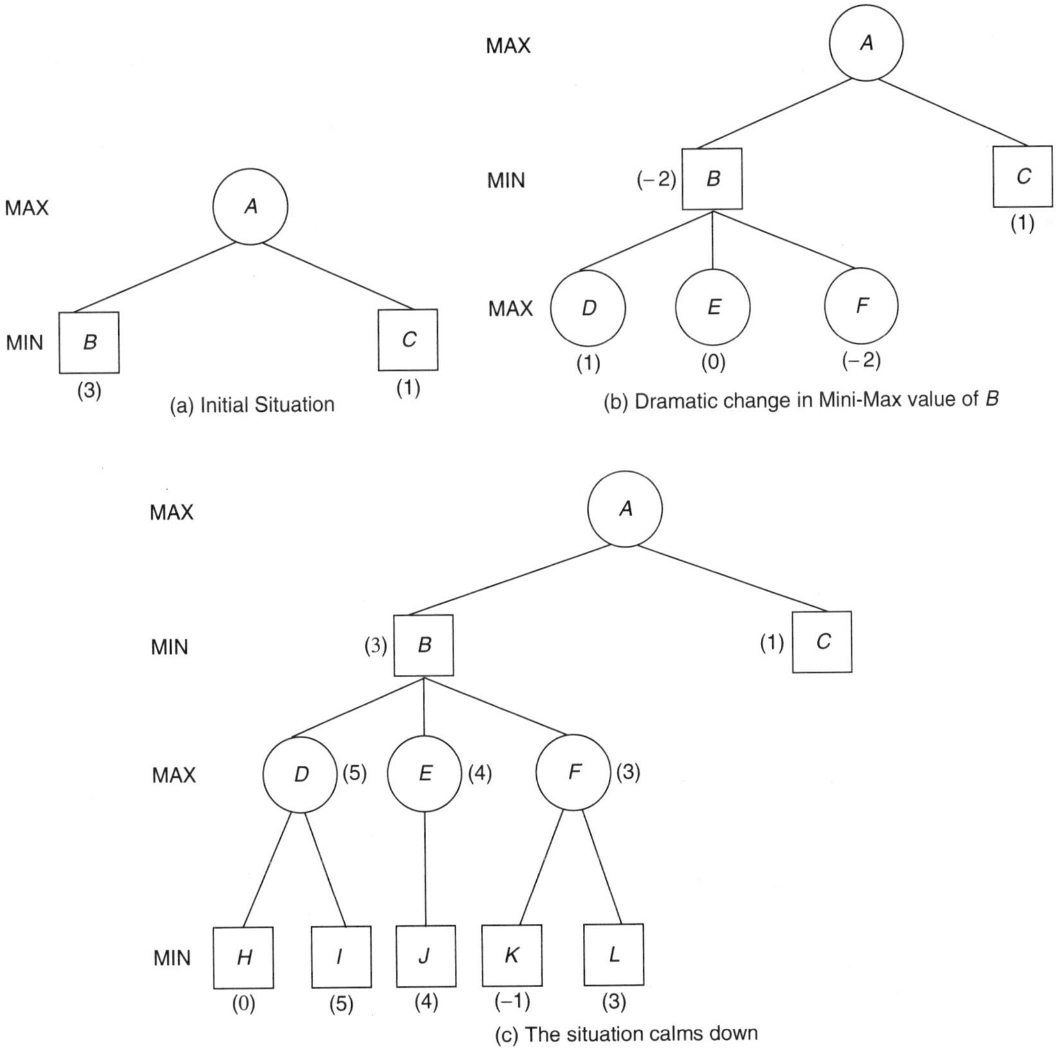

Fig. 11.73. *Waiting for quiescence.*

Quiescence How deep should we delve into the game tree while performing the depth-limited Mini-Max procedure on it? The problem is, a seemingly good move at a certain level may turn out to be a bad one, or vice versa, if the game tree is searched further. Take, for example, the situation depicted in Fig. 11.73(a), (b), and (c). Fig. 11.73(a) shows the beginning of search for the Mini-Max value of node

A. The nodes B and C are at level 1 and they have scores 3 and 1, respectively. Therefore, on the basis of the search till depth 1, the Mini-Max value of *A* should be *max* (3, 1) = 3. The situation dramatically changes when the game tree is explored one level deeper (see Fig. 11.73(b)). What was thought to be a good move represented by the node B, now appears as a very bad one because this gives the opponent an opportunity to worsen the condition of MAX player. However, if we go one level deeper into the game tree, as depicted in Fig. 11.73(c), we see that the node *B* regains its previous Mini-Max value and seems to be a good choice for MAX as earlier.

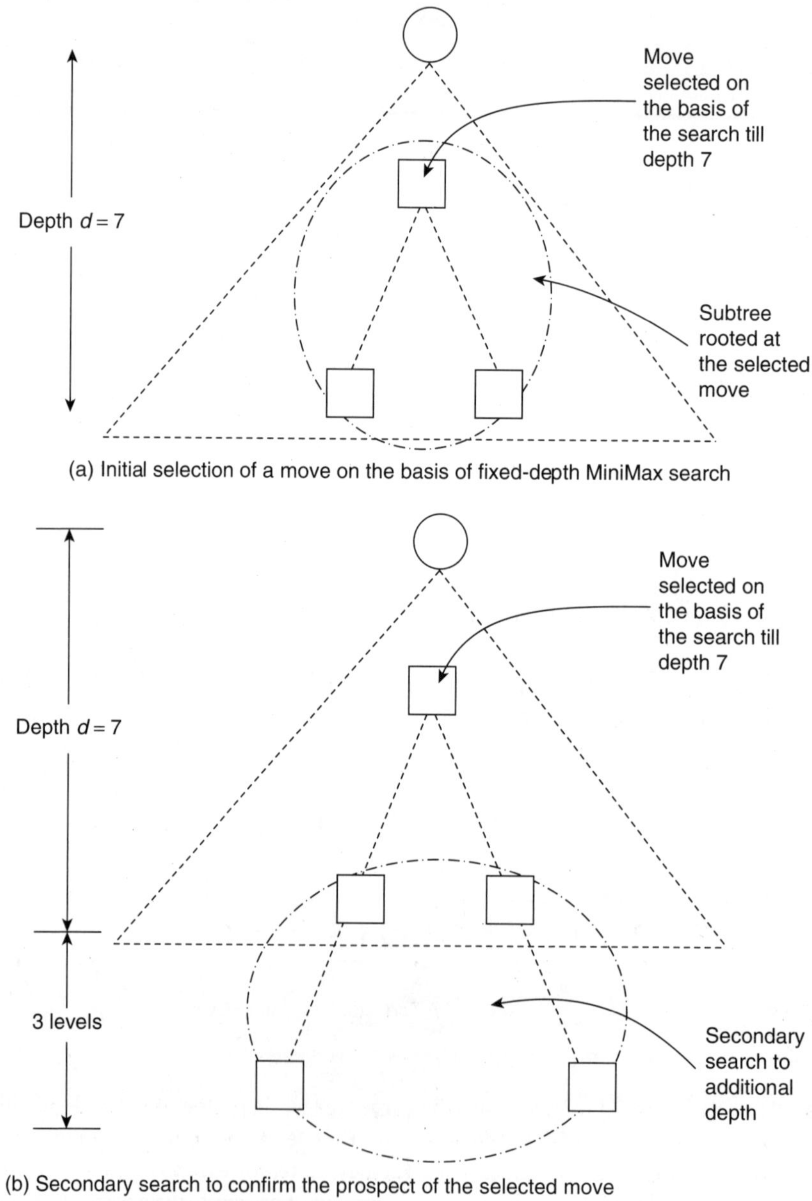

Fig. 11.74. *Secondary search to neutralize horizon effect.*

The fact is, short-term measures occasionally influence our choice of move adversely and it is not wise to take a decision without considering the long-term effects. To achieve wise selection of a move among a number of alternatives, one should go on exploring the game tree deep enough to reach a *stable* condition. The stable condition is recognized when it is found that no drastic change occurs from one level to the next. This strategy for determination of the appropriate depth to which depth-limited Mini-Max search is to be conducted is known as *waiting for quiescence*. The quiescence problems are difficult to eliminate altogether. One such example is the so-called *horizon effect*. It appears when a player is facing a move by the opponent which is bad for him but inevitable in the long run. A fixed-depth Mini-Max search may try to avoid such a fatal move by using some tactics, say a move that keeps the opponent busy for the time being. But such tactics only push the fatal move to the search horizon and merely delay the inevitable blow.

Secondary search Is there any way to tackle the *horizon effect*? A technique called *secondary search* is found to be helpful in this regard. Essentially, it consists of searching a portion of the game tree, not the entire game tree, for a few additional levels. Let us suppose that the game tree is searched to an average depth of, say seven. Let a move N be primarily selected on the basis of this search. In order to ensure that N is really a good move we may further explore the sub-tree rooted at N for additional three levels. But this additional search is not performed on any other portion of the game tree. This is called secondary search. Fig. 11.74 illustrates the technique pictorially.

Book moves In general, whenever a player has to make a move during a game, he faces a lot of alternatives among which the best, according to his own strategy of playing, is to be identified and applied. MiniMax search, empowered with appropriate heuristic knowledge, is employed to achieve this. A kind of heuristic search is practically indispensable because the other alternative is to build a catalogue of best moves corresponding to every conceivable game status and extract it during the game through a table look-up procedure. This is simply not feasible considering the immensity of the search space.

However, selective use of such moves, usually referred to as *book moves*, do enhance the performance of the program. For example, the opening and endgame sequences of chess are highly stylized. One may reasonably maintain a list of moves relevant to these parts of the game and use them directly without groping for a suitable move within the game tree through Mini-Max search. A judicious combination of book moves during the opening sequence, endgames, and Mini-Max search procedure for the midgame, would enable the program to attain a level of efficiency which neither book moves nor search alone could achieve.

11.4.8 Constraint Satisfaction

Quite often we encounter a problem in AI that can be modeled as a *constraint satisfaction problem* (CSP). Here the goal is to reach a state that satisfies certain restrictive conditions, or constraints, among the parameters of the problem. As a typical CSP, we may think of the famous **graph colouring problem**, also referred to as **map colouring problem**. An instance of this problem is shown in Fig. 11.75(a). It shows an area divided into six regions A, B, C, D, E and F. The regions are to be coloured with *red*, *blue*, or *yellow* in such a way that no two adjacent regions may have the same colour. Here the problem may be viewed as that of assigning certain values to six variables A, B, C, D, E and F, the values must be taken from the set {*red*, *blue*, *yellow*}, such that if X and Y are adjacent regions in the map, i.e., $X, Y \in \{A, B, C, D, E, F\}$, $X \neq Y$, then $v(X) \neq v(Y)$, where $v(X)$ and $v(Y)$ are the values, i.e., colours, assigned to X and Y, respectively.

The adjacency relationships among these six regions are depicted as an undirected graph in Fig. 11.75(b). Each node of the adjacency graph represents a region of the map. If two regions X and Y are adjacent in the map then there is an edge in the adjacency graph between the nodes corresponding to these regions. The adjacency graph for a given map colouring problem is also its **constraint graph** in the sense that it represents the constraints regarding the colours of the regions. An edge between two nodes *P* and *Q* of a constraint graph indicates that the regions corresponding to *P* and *Q* should have different colours.

(a) A map with 6 regions *A–F*

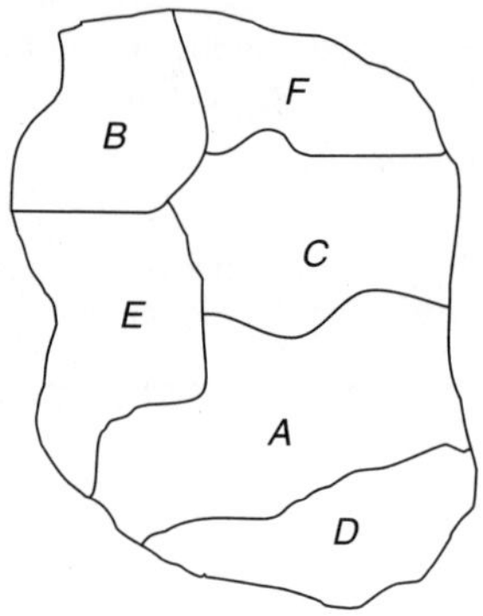

(b) The Constraint Graph

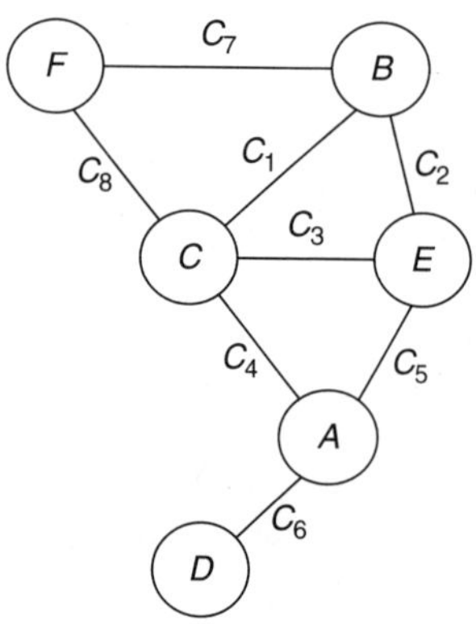

(c) Constraints

C_1	:	$v(B) \neq v(C)$
C_2	:	$v(B) \neq v(E)$
C_3	:	$v(C) \neq v(E)$
C_4	:	$v(A) \neq v(C)$
C_5	:	$v(A) \neq v(E)$
C_6	:	$v(A) \neq v(D)$
C_7	:	$v(B) \neq v(F)$
C_8	:	$v(C) \neq v(F)$

Fig. 11.75. *(a)-(c). Map coloring as a constraint satisfaction problem.*

A Constraint Satisfaction Problem (CSP) is defined by the following features:

- A set of **variables,** $X_1, X_2, \ldots, X_n$.
- For each variable X_i a non-empty domain $D(X_i)$ of possible **values** of X_i.
- A set of **constraints,** $C_1, C_2, \ldots, C_m$. Each constraint C_i involves some variables $X_p, X_q \ldots$ etc. and a specification of the allowable combination of values for these variables.

The map coloring problem presented in Fig. 11.75 can now be formulated as a CSP in the following way:

CSP Formulation of graph colouring problem

1. Variables A, B, C, D, E, F
2. Domains $D_A = D_B = D_C = D_D = D_E = D_F =$ {red, blue, yellow} = {R, B, Y}
3. Constraints C_1' :$v(B) \neq v(C) \neq v(E)$
C_2' :$v(A) \neq v(C) \neq v(E)$
C_3' :$v(B) \neq v(C) \neq v(F)$
C_4' :$v(A) \neq v(D)$

It should be noted that there are only four constraints in the CSP formulation given above even though eight constraints are depicted in Fig. 24.1(c). This is because each of the constraints C_1, C_2,..., C_8 of Fig. 11.75(c) involves only two variables whereas the constrains C_1', C_2', C_3' involve three variables each. So effectively C_1', C_2', C_3' taken together consolidates all the constraints C_1 through C_8. In fact, in CSPs we encounter three kinds of constraints, *viz.*, *unary constraints*, *binary constraints*, and *general constraints.*

A constraint that involves just one variable is termed as a **unary constraint**. A **binary constraint** involves two variables and constraints involving more that two variables are called **general constraints**. Each of the constraints C_1, C_2,..., C_8 of Fig. 11.75(c) is a binary constraint. Constraints C_1', C_2', C_3' are general constraints. There is no unary constraint in the map colouring problem stated above. However, a constraint like $v(A) \neq red$ exemplifies the category of unary constraints. A general constraint can always be broken down to an equivalent set of binary constraints.

(a) The Constraints

C_1' :$v(B) \neq v(C) \neq v(E)$
C_2' :$v(A) \neq v(C) \neq v(E)$
C_3' :$v(B) \neq v(C) \neq v(F)$
C_4' :$v(A) \neq v(D)$

(b) The constraint hypergraph

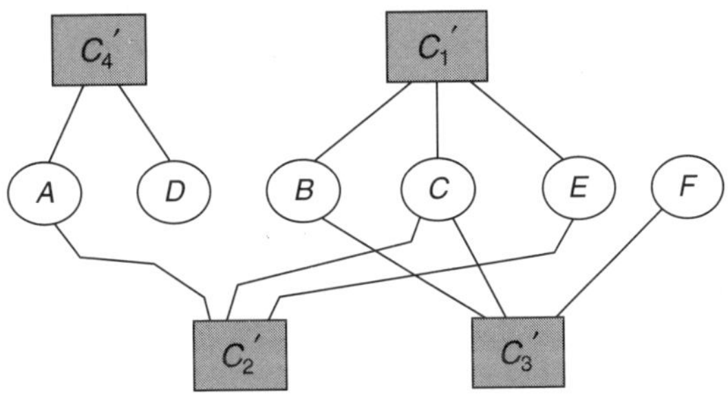

Fig. 11.76. *General constraints and constraint hypergraph.*

A **constraint hypergraph** is a graphical structure that represents the constraints involving the variables. For each variable of the given CSP there is a distinct node in the corresponding constraint hypergrah. A constraint $C(X_1, X_2, \ldots, X_k)$ involving k variables is represented by a hyperedge among the nodes X_1, X_2, ..., X_k. When all constraints are binary the corresponding constraint hypergraph becomes a constraint graph, as shown in Fig. 11.75(b). Fig. 11.76 shows the constraint hypergraph for the map colouring problem discussed above.

An **assignment** S for a given CSP, represented as $S = \{\langle X_p, v_p\rangle, \langle X_q, v_q\rangle, \ldots \langle X_r, v_r\rangle\}$, is an attachment of some legitimate values, say v_p, v_q, ... v_r to some or all variables X_p, X_q, ..., X_r such that $v_p \in D(X_p)$, $v_q \in D(X_q)$, ... , $v_r \in D(X_r)$. If none of the variables are assigned any value then it is said to be an **empty assignment**. For the map colouring problem shown in Fig. 11.75, $S = \{\langle A, blue\rangle, \langle B, yellow\rangle, \langle C, yellow\rangle, \langle D, red\rangle, \langle E, blue\rangle, \langle F, red\rangle\}$ is an assignment.

If an assignment does not violate any constraint then it is said to be **consistent** or **legal** assignment. The assignment stated above, i.e., $S_1 = \{\langle B, yellow\rangle, \langle C, yellow\rangle, \langle E, blue\rangle, \langle F, red\rangle\}$ is not consistent because it violates the first constraint $v(B) \neq v(C)$. However, it can be easily seen that $S_2 = \{\langle A, blue\rangle, \langle B, blue\rangle, \langle C, yellow\rangle, \langle D, red\rangle, \langle E, red\rangle, \langle F, red\rangle\}$ is a consistent assignment.

An assignment in which all the variables are attributed some value is said to be a **complete assignment**. For example, assignment S_2 cited above is complete, though S_1 is not a complete assignment.

Finally, a **solution** to a given CSP is a *complete assignment* that satisfies all the constraints. The assignment S_2 cited above is complete, and it satisfies all the constraints C_1, C_2, ..., C_8. Therefore S_2 is a solution to the given map colouring problem. In some CSPs, along with the basic requirement of satisfying all the constraints, there is an additional requirement of optimizing a pre-defined **objective function**.

Solving constraint satisfaction problems Once a problem is formulated as a CSP, any suitable search procedure can be employed to find a solution. Given a CSP, the suitability of a search procedure as a solution strategy is judged by the characteristics of the CSP concerned. However, two widely accepted strategies are frequently employed, *viz.*, **backtracking depth-first search** (BDFS), and **min-conflict local search**. Each of these are explained below with appropriate examples.

Backtracking depth-first search (BDFS) Consider the map coloring problem presented in Fig. 11.75 and later formulated as a CSP. A backtracking DFS would start with the empty assignment {} which corresponds to the initial state of the search space. Let us suppose that assignment of colour to the regions of the map will be made in the sequence *A*, *B*, *C*, *D*, *E*, and *F*. Since the domain D_A = {*red*, *blue*, *yellow*} = {*R*, *B*, *Y*} the region A may be assigned the color red, blue, or yellow, so that we may attain any one of the assignments, or problem states, ⟨*A*, *red*⟩, ⟨*A*, *blue*⟩, ⟨*A*, *yellow*⟩, or ⟨*A*, *R*⟩, ⟨*A*, *B*⟩, ⟨*A*, *Y*⟩. These constitute the children of the root node {} of the search tree, shown in Fig. 11.77. Each node of Fig. 11.77 represents an assignment obtained by concatenating the individual assignments along the path from the root to that node. For example node 2 corresponds to the assignment {⟨*A*, *R*⟩}, and node 5 represents the assignment {⟨*A*, *R*⟩, ⟨ *B*, *Y* ⟩, ⟨ *C*, *B* ⟩, ⟨ *D*, *B* ⟩}. Let us choose, arbitrarily, the assignment {⟨*A*, *red*⟩} among the three alternatives and proceed to assign a colour to the region *B*.

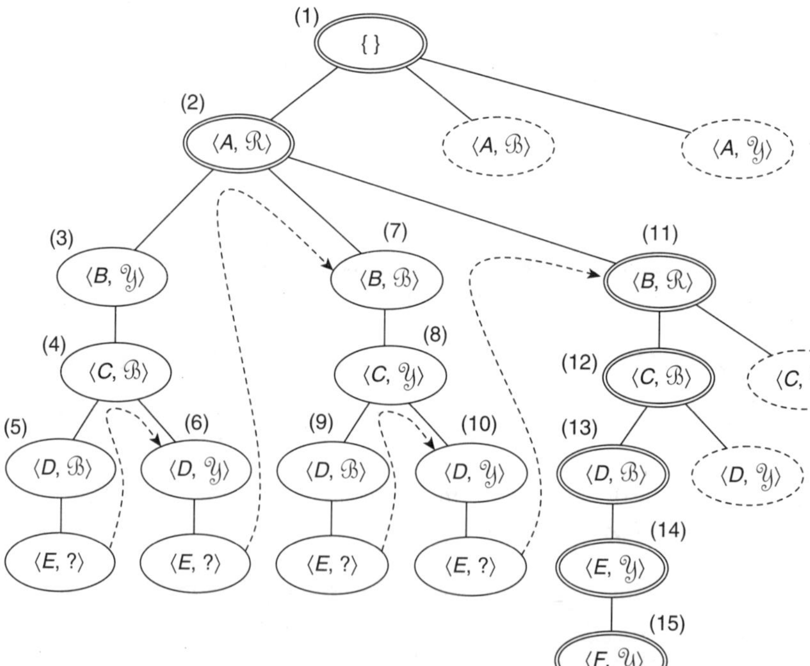

Fig. 11.77. *Backtracking depth-first search for the map colouring problem.*

As *A* and *B* are not adjacent regions the colour of *A* does not affect the choice of the colour of region *B*. Therefore, *B* can be assigned any of the values *R*, *B*, *Y* and accordingly three children of node (2) are created, viz., ⟨*B*, *Y*⟩ (node (3)), ⟨*B*, *B*⟩ (node (7)), and ⟨*B*, *R*⟩ (node (11)). The nodes of the search tree of Fig. 24.3 are numbered according to the order of exploration. Again, we arbitrarily select ⟨*B*, *Y*⟩ for further exploration. The candidate for assignment of color is now region C. Since *C* is adjacent to both A and B, its colour has to be different from that of *A* and *B*, i.e., *red* and *yellow*. Therefore the only choice left for region *C* is *blue* (node (4)). Next it is *D*'s turn. *D* is adjacent to *A* only and *A* has already been assigned red. Obviously, *D* may either be *blue* or *yellow* (see nodes (5) and (6) of Fig. 11.77). We proceed along node (5). Now when we try to assign a colour to *E* we see that as it is adjacent to *A*, *B*, and *C* and *A*, *B*, and C have the colours *red*, *yellow* and *blue*, there is no colour left for *E*. So we backtrack and explore node (6). But the situation does not change. Once again we back track and select another child of node (2), i.e., node (7).

The backtracking depth-first search proceeds in this way until it finds a complete assignment that satisfies all the constraints. In Fig. 11.77 this complete assignment is obtained by concatenating the individual assignments of nodes 1, 2, 11, 12, 13, 14, and 15 and is given by {⟨*A*, *R*⟩, ⟨*B*, *R*⟩, ⟨*C*, *B*⟩, ⟨*D*, *B*⟩, ⟨*E*, *Y*⟩, ⟨*F*, *Y*⟩}. The arrows in Fig. 11.77 show the backtracking paths.

```
Algorithm Backtracking-DFS-for-CSP (Pcs)

INPUT: A constraint satisfaction problem Pcs consisting of the following
components:

    •  Variables X1, …, Xn.
    •  Domains D(X1), …, D(Xn) of allowable values for each variable.
       If the variable Xi may assume any of the values ai1,ai2, …, aip
       then D(Xi) = {ai1,ai2, …, aip}.
    •  Constraints C1, …, Ck.

OUTPUT: SUCCESS or FAILURE, and if SUCCESS then an assignment
S = {⟨X1, v1⟩, …, ⟨ Xn, vn⟩} where v1∈ D(X1), …, vn∈ D(Xn) and all the con-
straints C1, …, Ck are satisfied.

1. BEGIN
2.     S ← { }
                 /* initialize S with the empty assignment. */
3.     result ← Recursive-Backtracking-DFS (Pcs, S)
                 /* call the recursive backtracking depth-first search
                 process for the present CSP Pcs with the partial
                 assignment S */
4.     IF (result ≠ FAILURE)
                 THEN Return SUCCESS along with updated assignment S
                 ELSE Return FAILURE
       END-if
5. END-Algorithm BDFS-for-CSP

   Procedure Recursive-Backtracking-DFS (Pcs, S)

1. BEGIN
2.     IF S is a complete assignment THEN
           Return SUCCESS along with the assignment S as the solution
       END-if
3.      Select Xi, a yet unassigned variable, for assigning a value at this
        step.
                   Let D(Xi) = {ai1,ai2, …, aip} be the domain of Xi.
4.      FOR i← 1 TO p DO
           BEGIN
5.             Xi ← ai where ai∈ D(Xi)
                 /* assign a value to Xi */
```

```
6.          IF (v(X_i) = a_i is consistent with the present partial
            assignment S and satisfies the constraints C_1, ...., C_k) THEN
            update assignment S by including ⟨X_i, a_i⟩ in it.
            END-if
7.          result ← Recursive-Backtracking-DFS (P_cs, S)
             /* recursive
               call with the updated partial assignment */
8.          IF (result ≠ FAILURE) THEN Return SUCCESS along with
               updated assignment S.
            END-if
9.          Remove ⟨X_i, a_i⟩ from S.
             /* ⟨X_i, a_i⟩ leads to failure. Try with another value for X_i,. */
10.     END-for
11.   Return FAILURE/* no valid assignment for X_i. */
12.  END-Procedure-Recursive-BDFS
```

Fig. 11.78. *Algorithm Backtracking-DFS-for-CSP (P_{cs})*

Algorithm Backtracking-DFS-for-CSP (P_{cs}) (Fig. 11.78) presents the pseudocode for the basic strategy of backtracking depth-first search for solving CSPs. The algorithm starts with empty assignment {} and progressively assign values to the variables and makes recursive calls so that if any assignment leads to inconsistency, or hinders subsequent assignments, then it may backtrack and try with some other value.

```
Procedure Heuristic-Recursive-Backtracking-DFS (P_cs, S)
1.   BEGIN
2.      IF (S is a complete assignment) THEN
           Return SUCCESS along with the assignment S as the solution
        END-if
        /* Select the next variable for assignment through minimum remaining
        value (MRV) and degree heuristics. */
3.      Let X_i be the unassigned variable with minimum number values remaining.
        If there is a tie, then resolve the tie in favour of the variable with
        largest number of constraints on other unassigned variables. If there is
        still a tie then resolve the tie arbitrarily.
4.      Select X_i for assigning a value at this step. Let D(X_i) = {a_i1,a_i2, ..., a_ip}
        be the domain of X_i.
5.      FOR i← 1 TO p DO
           BEGIN
              /* select the value of X_i through least-constraing-value
              heuristics. */
6.            Let a_i∈D(X_i)be the value that rules out the fewest choices for
              theneighbouring variables in the constraint graph. If there is
              a tie then resolve the tie arbitrarily.
```

```
7.         Xi ← ai where ai∈ D(Xi)
8.         IF (v(Xi) = ai is consistentwith the present partial assignment S
           and satisfies the constraints C1, ...., Ck) THEN update
                assignment S by including ⟨Xi, ai⟩ in it.
           END-if
           /* Constraint propagation */
9.         Propagate the effect of present assignment on the constrains of
           PCS.
10.        result ← Recursive-Backtracking-DFS (PCS, S)/* recursive
                call with the updated partial assignment */
11.        IF (result ≠ FAILURE) THEN Return SUCCESS along with
                updated assignment S.
           END-if
12.        Remove ⟨Xi, ai⟩ from S. /* ⟨Xi, ai⟩ leads to failure. Try
                         with another value for Xi,. */
13.        END-for
14.        Return FAILURE/* no valid assignment for Xi. */
15.     END-Procedure-Recursive-BDFS
```

Fig. 11.79. *Procedure heuristic-recursive-backtracking-DFS (P_{CS}, S)*

Heuristics `Algorithm Backtracking-DFS-for-CSP` described above is a simplified version of the actual procedure followed in practice. It does not consider how to make the selection when choices are there. For example

1. In step 3 of `Procedure Recursive-Backtracking-DFS` (P_{CS}, S) a variable is to be selected from the set of unassigned variables for the purpose of assigning a value. The criteria underlying this selection are not stated.
2. Step 5 of the same procedure assigns a value to the current variable. It is not clearly stated how to select an appropriate value from the corresponding domain which, in general, should contain several legal candidate values.
3. What are the implications of an assignment on the remaining unassigned variables and how to reduce the search space so that the process of legal assignment to variables is made efficient?

Regarding points 1 and 2 above, there are heuristics to facilitate selection of a variable for the purpose of value assignment as well as selection of a value to be assigned. Similarly, strategies to propagate the effect of a certain assignment to other variables are also there. **`Procedure Heuristic-Recursive-Backtracking-DFS`** (**P_{CS}, S**) (Fig. 11.79) shows the procedure after incorporation of the heuristics discussed below.

Minimum remaining value (MRV) and degree heuristic According to *minimum remaining value* (*MRV*) heuristics the variable with least number of legal values still available for assignment is to be selected for next assignment. For example, consider the assignment {⟨*A*, *blue*⟩, ⟨*E*, *red*⟩, ⟨*F*, *red*⟩}. Considering the constraints, this assignment leaves the domains of the remaining variables as D_B = {*blue*, *yellow*}, D_C = {*yellow*} D_D = {*red*, *yellow*}. As the region *C* has the least number of remaining legal values, according to the MRV heuristics, this will be selected for the next assignment.

However, MRV heuristics may not help initially because then all the variables have their domains in full capacity, or in case two or more variables have the same minimal number of remaining variables. To resolve such situation the *degree heuristics* may be employed. The degree heuristics selects the variable that is involved in the largest number of constraints on other unassigned variables. For example, consider the map colouring problem stated above. Initially all the variables have the same domain {*red, blue, yellow*} which renders the MRV heuristic ineffective. However, it is seen from the constraint graph (Fig. 11.75(b)) that region *C* is involved with four regions *A*, *B*, *E* and *F* through constraints which is the highest among all the variables. Hence, applying the degree heuristic we choose *C* as the first variable to be assigned a value.

Least constraining value Once a variable is chosen ,it is required to assign a legal value from its current domain. Since the domains normally contain several candidates the issue of selecting the most desirable value becomes relevant. Here the *least constraining value* heuristic is helpful. According to this heuristic, the value which rules out least number of candidates from the domains of the neighbouring variables is preferred. For example, suppose that at an instant the domains of *F* and *B* are D_F = {*red, yellow*} and D_B = {*yellow*} and it is *F*'s turn to be assigned a value. If we assign *yellow* then it is removed from the domain of *B*, making D_B = {}. However, if *red* then D_B remains non-empty and it is feasible for region *B* to get a legal value. Therefore, the value *red* is less constraing than *yellow* and *B* should be assigned the value *red* instead of *yellow*.

Table 11.7. *Trace of Procedure heuristic-recursive-backtracking-DFS for map colouring problem of Fig. 11.75*

	A	B	C	D	E	F
Step 0:	{R, B, Y}	{R, B, Y}	{R, B, Y}	{R, B, Y}	{R, B, Y}	{R, B, Y}
Step 1: **C ← red**	{B, Y}	{B, Y}	⟨**C**, R⟩	{R, B, Y}	{B, Y}	{B, Y}
Step 2: **B = blue**	{B}	⟨**B**, B⟩	⟨**C**, R⟩	{R, Y}	{Y}	{Y}
Step 3: **A← blue**	⟨**A**, B⟩	⟨**B**, B⟩	⟨**C**, R⟩	{R, Y}	{Y}	{Y}
Step 4: **E← yellow**	⟨**A**, B⟩	⟨**B**, B⟩	⟨**C**, R⟩	{R, Y}	⟨**E**, Y⟩	{Y}
Step 5: **F← yellow**	⟨**A**, B⟩	⟨**B**, B⟩	⟨**C**, R⟩	{R, Y}	⟨**E**, Y⟩	⟨**F**, Y⟩
Step 6: **D← red**	⟨**A**, B⟩	⟨**B**, B⟩	⟨**C**, R⟩	⟨**D**, R⟩	⟨**E**, Y⟩	⟨**F**, Y⟩

Solution: {⟨A, B⟩, ⟨B, B⟩, ⟨C, R⟩, ⟨D, R⟩, ⟨E, Y⟩, ⟨F, Y⟩}

Forward chaining and constraint propagation Assignment of a value to a variable obviously has its effects on the domains of the remaining variables. *Constraint propagation* is the process of propagating the implications of a constraint on the variables onto the other variables. Suppose, as an example, that in the first step of the map colouring problem, the region C has been assigned the value *red*. Since *A*, *B*, *E* and *F* are all involved with *C* through the constraints C_4, C_1, C_3, and C_8, respectively, the domains of all these variables reduces to {*blue, yellow*}. However, the domain of *D* remains {*red, blue, yellow*} as it is not involved with *C* through any constraint. This procedure, which, after an assignment is made, modifies the domains of the unassigned variables so that the modified domains are consistent with the assignment, is called *forward checking*. However, mere forward checking is not sufficient. Suppose, after assigning *red* to *C*, we assign *blue* to *E*. This will reduce the domain of *A* to {*yellow*} as *A* is adjacent to *E*. Moreover, since *D* is associated with *A* through the constraint C_6, the domain of *D* is in turn reduced from {*red, blue, yellow*} to {*red, blue*}. In this way the effect of a certain assignment is propagated to other unassigned variables through forward checking followed by further modification of the domains so that the values attain consistency with respect to the constraints.

The entire process can be illustrated with reference to the graph colouring problem. A trace of the progress of the algorithm is shown in Table 11.7 and the stepwise description is provided below.

Step 0. We start with the empty assignment {}. All the variables have the same domain {*red, blue, yellow*}, abbreviated as {*R, B, Y*}.

Step 1. We have to select a variable for assignment. Since all domains have the same number of values the MRV heuristic is not applicable. Therefore, the degree heuristic is to be followed. Consulting the constraint graph (Fig. 11.75(b)), it is found that *C* is involved with the maximum number of variables, 4 in this case, through constraints. Hence *C* is chosen for assigning a value. We make the assignment $C \leftarrow$ *red* and propagate the effect of this assignment on other variables. As a result of this propagation all the variables involved with *C* through constraints, i.e., *A, B, E* and *F*, remove red from their domains. However, the domain of *D* remains unchanged because it is not adjacent to *A*. The state of the problem after step 1 is {⟨*C, R*⟩}.

Step 2. Applying the MRV heuristic we find four candidates *A, B, E* and *F* for the next assignment. The number of unassigned variables these are attached to in the constraint graph are 2, 2, 2 and 1, respectively. Again there is a tie among *A, B*, and *E*. Let us resolve the tie by arbitrarily choosing B for assignment this time. We make $B \leftarrow$ *blue*, so that the state becomes {⟨*B, B*⟩, ⟨*C, R*⟩}. What about constraint propagation? As *E* and *F* are adjacent to *B*, blue is readily removed from the respective domains leaving both the domains {*yellow*}. As *A* is adjacent to *E yellow* has to be removed from the domain of *A* so that it becomes {*blue*} and this in turn reduces D_D to {*red, yellow*}.

Step 3. Now each of *A, E* and *F* have just one remaining value in their respective domains. So let us take the help of the degree heuristic to break the tie. A is attached to two of the still unassigned variables, viz., *D* and *E*. *E* is adjacent to only *A* and *F* is no more attached to any unassigned variable. Therefore *A* is the next candidate for value assignment and the only value in its domain, *blue*, is assigned to it. Now the assignment is {⟨*A, B*⟩, ⟨*B, B*⟩, ⟨*C, R*⟩}.

The subsequent steps, i.e., steps 4, 5, and 6 can be easily worked out and are depicted in Table 11.7. The final assignment is {⟨*A, B*⟩, ⟨*B, B*⟩, ⟨*C, R*⟩, ⟨*D, R*⟩, ⟨*E, Y* ⟩, ⟨*F, Y* ⟩}. Fig. 11.80 shows the solution tree corresponding to the heuristic recursive backtracking depth-first search described above.

Min-conflict local search The backtracking depth-first search strategy described above for solving a CSP starts with the empty assignment {} and incrementally proceeds to a complete assignment consistent with the constraints. An alternative approach is to start with a complete assignment, perhaps arbitrarily generated, and then employ some local search procedure which transforms this complete but non-solution assignment onto a complete and consistent assignment, i.e., a solution. **`Algorithm Min-Conflict-for-CSP`** (P_{CS}, MAX_{steps}) (Fig. 11.81) presents a pseudo-code for the procedure mentioned above. At each iteration, a variable is identified which is under conflict as per the given constraints (line 8). It is then tried with values other than the present one and the value for which the variable suffers minimum amount of conflict is chosen. The current assignment is then modified to that which incorporates this latest value. In this way newer variables are modified over and over again until either we get an assignment which satisfies all constraints and therefore offers a solution, or exceeds a predefined maximum number of iterations. The min-conflict local search process is illustrated with the help of the **8-queen problem** which is stated below.

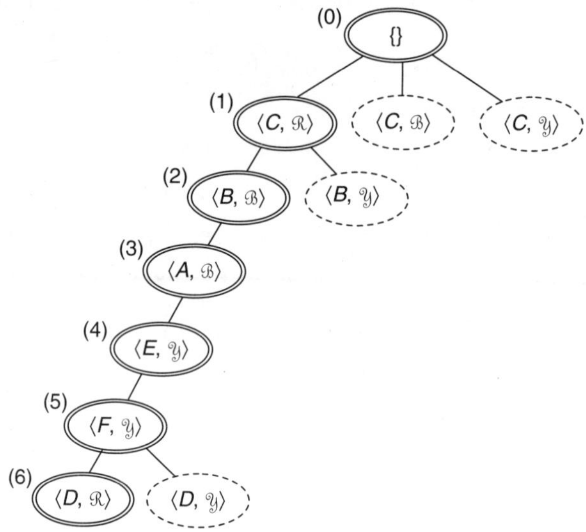

Fig. 11.80. *Solution tree corresponding to the heuristic recursive backtracking depth-first search to solve the map colouring CSP.*

Example 11.11 (The 8-queen problem)

Is it possible to arrange 8 queens on a chess board in a way such that none of them is in an attacking position with respect to any other?

The generalized form of the 8-queen problem is the ***n*-queen problem,** which states that given an $n \times n$ array, is it possible to arrange n number of queens within the array in a way such that none of them attack any other and if yes, then to find one such arrangement of the n queens.

Let us denote the eight queens by the variables Q_A, Q_B, Q_C, Q_D, Q_E, Q_F, Q_G, and Q_H. The queens corresponding to the variables Q_A, Q_B, Q_C, Q_D, Q_E, Q_F, Q_G, and Q_H are in the columns $A, B, \ldots, H$, respectively. As no queen is attacking any other all the queens must be in different columns. Let us number the 8 rows as 1, 2, 3, 4, 5, 6, 7, and 8. Then each variable mentioned above may take a value from the set {1, 2, 3, 4, 5, 6, 7, 8}. We are now in a position to formulate the 8-queen problem as a CSP.

CSP formulation of the 8-queen problem

1. Variables : $Q_A, Q_B, Q_C, Q_D, Q_E, Q_F, Q_G, Q_H$
2. Domains : $D_A = D_B = D_C = D_E = D_F = D_G = D_H$
   $= \{1, 2, 3, 4, 5, 6, 7, 8\}$
3. Constraints : For all pairs $Q_X$and Q_Y, $X, Y \in \{A, B, C, D, E, F, G, H\}$, $X \neq Y$, Q_X and Q_Y should be in non-attacking position, i.e. not in the same row, column or diagonal.

The initial arrangement of the 8 queens is shown in Fig. 11.82 (*a*). It corresponds to the assignment $\{\langle Q_A, 8\rangle, \langle Q_B, 5\rangle, \langle Q_C, 1\rangle, \langle Q_D, 6\rangle, \langle Q_E, 3\rangle, \langle Q_F, 7\rangle, \langle Q_G, 2\rangle, \langle Q_H, 4\rangle\}$.

However, this assignment is not consistent with the constraints because the queens at positions 8*A* and 2*G* are attacking each other diagonally. Similarly, the queens at 1*C* and 3*E* are also attacking each other. At this point we employ the min-conflict local search procedure and look for a better position for the queen presently at the position 8*A*. With this purpose in mind, for each other position of the queen in column *A* we find the number of queens in conflict if the current queen is placed in respective cell.

For example, if the queen is placed in cell 4*A* then it will be attacked by two queens at positions 4*H* and 5*B*. Hence the value (2) is associated with the cell 4*A*. Similarly the other values are found. Now there is a tie regarding the lowest conflict count. Both cells 1*A* and 5*A* are having the same minimum value 1. The tie is arbitrarily resolved in favour of cell 1*A*. The queen concerned is placed at this position so that the assignment after the first becomes {$\langle \mathbf{Q_A, 1} \rangle$, $\langle Q_B, 5 \rangle$, $\langle Q_C, 1 \rangle$, $\langle Q_D, 6 \rangle$, $\langle Q_E, 3 \rangle$, $\langle Q_F, 7 \rangle$, $\langle Q_G, 2 \rangle$, $\langle Q_H, 4 \rangle$} (the change is highlighted with boldfaces). After Q_A we focus our attention on Q_B. Fortunately, Q_B is already in a non-conflicting position with respect to other queens. Therefore, we leave it in the same position and proceed to find a better place for Q_C which is in conflict with Q_A and Q_E (Fig. 11.82(b)). It is found that at cell 8*C* the queen Q_C is in non-attacking position. Making this assignment we arrive at the state {$\langle Q_A, 1 \rangle$, $\langle Q_B, 5 \rangle$, $\langle \mathbf{Q_C, 8} \rangle$, $\langle Q_D, 6 \rangle$, $\langle Q_E, 3 \rangle$, $\langle Q_F, 7 \rangle$, $\langle Q_G, 2 \rangle$, $\langle Q_H, 4 \rangle$}, which satisfies all the constraints and therefore is a solution to the given problem.

```
Algorithm Min-Conflict-for-CSP (P_CS, MAX_steps)
INPUT: A constraint satisfaction problem P_CS consisting of the following
components:
    •  Variables X_1,…, X_n.
    •  Domains D(X_1),…, D(X_n) of allowable values for each variable.
       If the variable X_i may assume any of the values a_i1,a_i2,…, a_ip
       then D(X_i) = {a_i1,a_i2,…, a_ip}.
    •  Constraints C_1,…, C_k.
  MAX_steps is the number of times to try before giving up
  OUTPUT: SUCCESS or FAILURE, and if SUCCESS then an assignment
  S = {⟨X_1, v_1⟩,…, ⟨X_n, v_n⟩} where v_1∈ D(X_1),…, v_n∈ D(X_n) and all the con-
  straints C_1, …, C_k are satisfied.

BEGIN
   S ‹ A complete, perhaps arbitrary, assignment for P_CS
   FOR steps = 1 TO MAX_steps DO
   BEGIN
      IF S is a solution to the CSP P_CS THEN
         Return S as the solution to the CSP P_CS
      END-if
      X ← a variable which is under conflict as per assignment S
      v_X ← the value of variable X that minimizes the conflict
      Modify assignment S by setting ⟨X, v_X ⟩
   END-for
END-Algorithm-Min-Conflict-for-CSP
```

Fig. 11.81. *Algorithm Min-Conflict-for-CSP (P_{CS}, MAX_{steps}).*

(a) Initial state. The numbers in different cells of column *A* indicate the number of conflicts if the queen is placed in that cell.

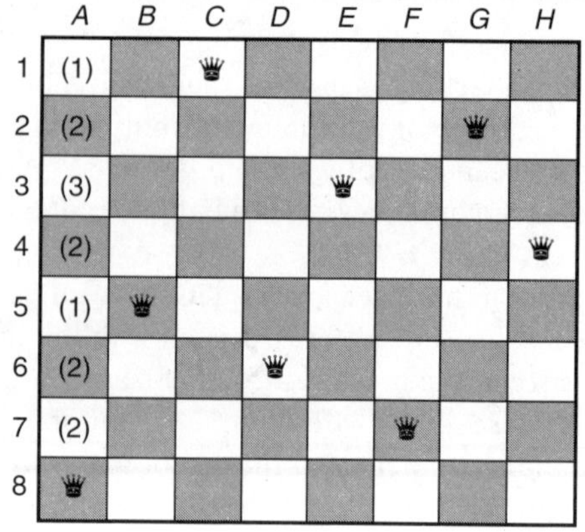

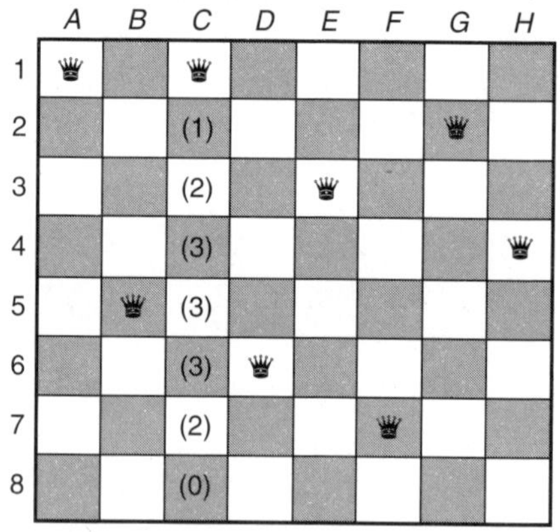

(b) The state after reassigning the queen at column *A*. The present target is to reassign the queen at column *C*.

(c) The final state obtained after reassigning the queen at column *C*. As no queen is attacking any other this is solution to the 8-queen problem.

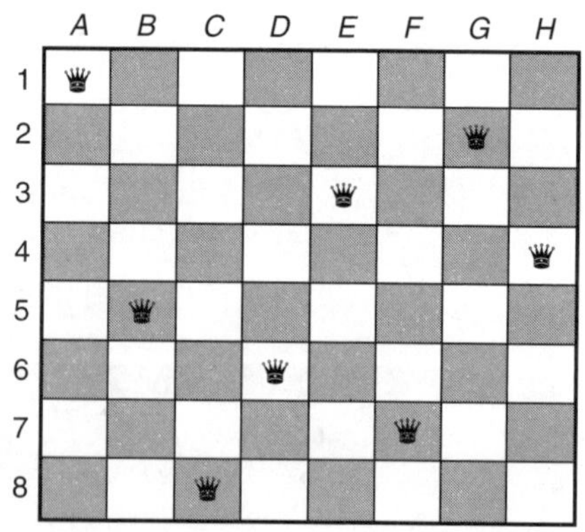

Fig. 11.82. *(a)-(c) A min-conflict local search procedure to solve the 8-queen problem*

11.4.9 Measures of Search

The efficiency of a heuristic search depends to a large extent on the quality of the heuristic evaluation function employed. Better heuristic results in less computational effort without compromising the success of the search process. However, it is hardly possible to make an estimation of heuristic power through direct calculation because it depends on too many factors.

Instead, certain computable measures of performance are frequently used to compare the performances of various search processes. Two of these are **penetrance** and **effective branching factor**.

Penetrance. P of a search process is defined as the ratio of the length of the path from the start state to the goal state reached through the search and the total number of nodes generated during the search, including the goal node but excluding the start node.

$$P = L / N \tag{11.11}$$

Here L is the length of the path from the start state to the goal state, and N is the total number of nodes generated during the search. Penetrance is the measure of how focused the search was towards the goal. In the ideal case, the search process has complete knowledge of the problem, and only those nodes are generated which are on the path from the start node to the goal node. The value of P for such an ideal search process is 1 which is obviously the maximum attainable value for P. Uninformed, or ill-informed, searches have much lower values of P.

Effective branching factor. The other measure, **effective branching factor** B, is relatively more independent of the length of the optimal path to the goal node and can be defined in the following way. Let N be the total number of nodes generated during the search that has successfully ended at some goal node and L be the length of the path to the goal node. Now consider a complete tree of depth L where each internal node uniformly has B number of children and total number of nodes in the said tree excluding the root is N. Then

$$N = B + B^2 + B^3 + \ldots + B^N \tag{11.12}$$

so that,

$$N = \frac{B \times (B^L - 1)}{(B - 1)} \tag{11.13}$$

The relation between the penetrance P and effective branching factor B is given by

$$P = \frac{L}{N} = \frac{L \times (B - 1)}{B \times (B^L - 1)} \tag{11.14}$$

It is easy to see that B is always greater than or equal to 1. A better search technique should give a value of B which is closer to 1. A value of B near unity corresponds to a search that is highly focused towards the goal with very little branching in other directions.

11.5 PRODUCTION SYSTEMS

Production systems are intelligent systems that are structured to facilitate a state space search procedure. There are three main components of a production system. These are

1. A **global database**
2. A set of **production rules**
3. A **control system**

Global database is the central data structure which is accessed, modified and manipulated throughout the problem solving process. Usually, the situation prevailing in the global database defines a state within the state space. A change in the global database corresponds to a move from one state to another state. The term global database should not be confused with the database of database management systems. The exact form of a global database depends on the application. It might be as simple as an integer, or as complex as an entire file structure.

A **production rule** is a transformation rule of the form $\alpha \rightarrow \beta$ where α and β are forms of the global database. In the rule $R : \alpha \rightarrow \beta$, α is called the **precondition** and β, the **postcondition**. A rule $R : \alpha \rightarrow \beta$ is said to be *applicable* to a global database *GDB* if the present condition of *GDB* matches with the precondition α. If applied, the production rule will transform *GDB* from α to β.

Usually at each step of the search process more than one rules are applicable on the global database though only one of them can be actually applied at a time. Therefore, a production system must have some knowledge to identify the appropriate rule to apply among a set of eligible rules. **Control strategy** is that component of the production system which, at each step, selects the rule to operate on the global database from a set of applicable rules. Moreover, it tests whether the current global database satisfies the termination condition and if so, takes appropriate action to terminate the search process.

```
Algorithm Production-System

Input: A set of production rules P = {R_1, ...., R_k}, and a termination
condition which when satisfied by the global database GDB would
indicate the successful completion of the search process.

Output: A solution to the given problem. Depending on the nature of
the problem, the goal state might be the global database itself, or
a path from the initial state to the goal state.

Begin
    /* Initialize the global database */
    GDB ← Initial state of the global database.
    /* Search for the goal */
    While (GDB does not satisfy the termination condition) Do
      Begin    /* Select a rule to apply on the global
                  database */
          R_i ← A rule that is applicable to GDB.
          GDB_new ← Resultant of applying R_i to GDB.
          GDB ← GDB_new
      End-while
      /* Return the solution */
      Return GDB, along with the path from the initial
            state to the goal, if required.
End-Production-System
```

Fig. 11.83. *Algorithm Production-System.*

The basic algorithm followed by a production system is thus very simple. Once the global database is initialized, an appropriate production rule is selected (by the control strategy) and applied on the global database to transform it to a new state. This selection and application of the rule, as well as the resultant transformation of the global database is repeated till the termination condition is satisfied by the global database. Depending on the requirement, either the final form of the global database, or the path from the initial global database to the final, is returned as the solution of the problem concerned. The outline of procedure is given in **`Algorithm Production-System`** (Fig. 11.83).

Example 11.12 (*A production system for parsing a sentence*)

Consider the task of parsing a given sentence on the basis of its grammar. The sentences of the language are made up of sentences made up of words from the set Σ= {***Hari***, ***Sam***, ***runs***, ***walks***, ***slow***, ***fast***}. In the theory of formal languages, Σ is called the **alphabet** and the members of Σ are called the **terminal symbols**. The grammar **G** specifies a number of transformation rules of the form $\alpha \rightarrow \beta$ where α and β are strings over members of Σ and some special symbols used only to describe the grammar. The grammar symbols used here are N= { ⟨**sentence**⟩, ⟨**subject**⟩, ⟨**predicate**⟩, ⟨**verb**⟩, ⟨**adverb**⟩ }. The transformation rules, which act as the production rules of the system, are given in Table 11.8.

Table 11.8. *Production rules*

Rule #	*Precondition*		*Postcondition*
(1)	⟨**Sentence**⟩	→	⟨**subject**⟩ ⟨**predicate**⟩.
(2a)	⟨**Subject**⟩	→	*Hari*
(2b)	⟨**Subject**⟩	→	*Sam*
(3a)	⟨**Predicate**⟩	→	⟨**verb**⟩
(3b)	⟨**Predicate**⟩	→	⟨**verb**⟩ ⟨**adverb**⟩
(4a)	⟨**verb**⟩	→	*runs*
(4b)	⟨**verb**⟩	→	*walks*
(5a)	⟨**adverb**⟩	→	*slow*
(5b)	⟨**adverb**⟩	→	*Fast*

To generate a sentence, one has to start with ⟨**Sentence**⟩ and progressively apply the rules until a string is generated that consists of only terminal symbols. The sequence of such transformations is called a **derivation** of the sentence. For example, derivation of the sentence "*Hari walks slow.*" is shown below:

⟨**Sentence**⟩	⟶	⟨**subject**⟩ ⟨**predicate**⟩.	(1)
	⟶	*Hari* ⟨**predicate**⟩.	(2*a*)
	⟶	*Hari* ⟨**verb**⟩ ⟨**adverb**⟩.	(3*b*)
	⟶	*Hari walks* ⟨**adverb**⟩.	(4*b*)
	⟶	*Hari walks slow.*	(5*a*)

The intermediate strings consisting of words as well as meta-words are called **sentential forms**. The grammar symbol of a sentential form on which a rule is applied is highlighted. The rule numbers are given on the right of the sentential forms within parentheses. In the derivation shown above, the leftmost grammar symbol of a sentential form is selected for replacement.

It is obvious that an arbitrary sequence of words may, or may not, be a sentence. Such a sequence of words is a sentence only if it is derivable from the start meta-word of the grammar with the help of the transformation rules. **Parsing** a string of words with respect to a grammar means trying to determine whether it is a sentence defined by the grammar or not. One way to parse a sentence is to try to derive it from the start meta-word. If the effort is successful then we conclude that the input string is really a sentence else not. The parsing problem can be formulated as a production system in the following way.

Global database. An array of words and meta-words from the set {⟨**sentence**⟩, ⟨**subject**⟩, ⟨**predicate**⟩, ⟨**verb**⟩, ⟨**adverb**⟩, *Hari*, *Sam*, *runs*, *walks*, *slow*, *fast*}.

Production rules. As given in Table 11.8.

Control strategy. At any step, only the leftmost grammar symbol will be targeted for replacement with appropriate production rule. If more than one rules are applicable, then rule that produces maximum match between the goal string and the newly produced string will be chosen. A tie will be resolved randomly.

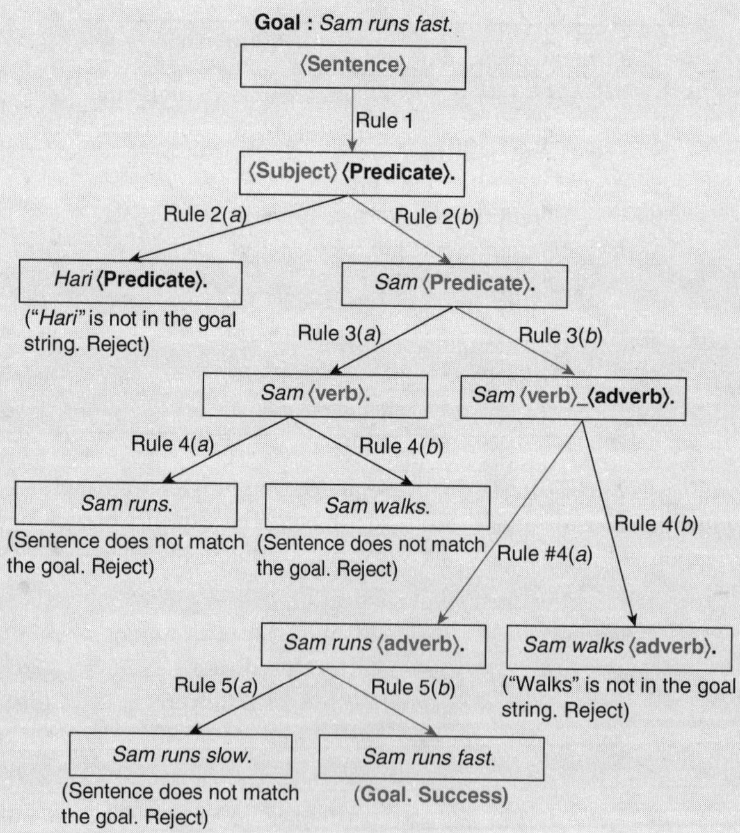

Fig. 11.84. *Parsing of a sentence.*

Let us trace the activities of the proposed production system while parsing the sentence "*Sam runs fast.*" The initial global database contains the starting grammar symbol ⟨**sentence**⟩. This is shown as the root node of the tree structure of Fig. 11.84. There is only one production rule, Rule 1, with the precondition ⟨**sentence**⟩. Hence there is no option other than applying it on the initial global database to obtain ⟨**subject**⟩ ⟨**predicate**⟩. In Fig. 11.84 this is shown as the child of the root node. As per control strategy the leftmost grammar symbol ⟨**subject**⟩ is to be replaced next. The candidate production rules for this purpose are Rules 2*a* and 2*b*. The resultant forms of the global database, *viz.*, *Hari* ⟨**Predicate**⟩ and *Sam* ⟨**Predicate**⟩, are shown as the nodes at level 2 (the root node is at level 0). Since *Hari* is not in the goal sentence, but *Sam* is, *Sam* ⟨**Predicate**⟩ matches better than *Hari* ⟨**Predicate**⟩ with the goal sentence. Therefore, the production system proceeds with *Sam* ⟨**Predicate**⟩. The subsequent steps are depicted in Fig. 11.84, which shows the entire parsing process where the correct parsing sequence is highlighted.

Control Systems. Step 5 of `Algorithm Production-System` selects a rule to operate on the global database but does not specify how this selection is to be made. The control strategy is equipped with the knowledge necessary to assess which rule, among a set of candidates, is the best. Moreover, it keeps track of the sequence of rules applied, as well as the corresponding states of the global database.

Primarily there are two kinds of control strategies, *viz.*, **irrevocable**, and **tentative**. An **irrevocable** control strategy does not undo the effects of a rule once it is applied. In contrast, a **tentative** control strategy may discard the effects of a certain rule once it is found wrong and then carry on with some other more prospective alternative. Tentative control strategies may further be divided into two categories, **backtracking**, and **graph-search control**. A **backtracking** control system a backtracking point is established at each step where a choice of a production rule is made from a set of alternatives. If at some further point of time it is discovered that the choice was wrong then the system returns to the latest backtracking point, selects a yet untried production rule, applies it to the global database existing at that point of time, and proceeds with the result. However, the technique followed by **graph-search** control is to maintain a data structure that keeps track of several alternative paths, sequence of production rules and the corresponding global database, simultaneously. During the search process, the best among these alternative paths is followed for further processing.

The production system proposed to solve the parsing problem in Example 11.12 can be cited as an instance of graph-search control strategy provided the system maintains the tree structure of Fig. 11.84. Incidentally, in Fig. 11.84, the leaf nodes of all abandoned paths are forms of the unacceptable global data structure, and hence rejected. But this need not be the case for other production systems. Instead, we may have some heuristic objective function to measure the quality of a node in terms of its vicinity to the goal. During the search process the most prospective node is chosen for further exploration. In other words, the production system then follows a best first search strategy. Example 11.13 cited below illustrates an irrevocable control strategy.

Example 11.13 (*A production system to solve CNF-satisfiability problem*)

A boolean function is said to be **satisfiable** if there is a truth-value combination of its variables that evaluates the function to True. For example, since the function $F(x_1, x_2, x_3) = x_1.(x_2'x_3 + x_2.x_3')$ attains a True value for the assignment $\{x_1 = \text{True}, x_2 = \text{False}, x_3 = \text{True}\}$, it is satisfiable. Conversely, there is no truth-value assignment that makes the function $F(x_1, x_2, x_3) = x_1.(x_1'.x_2 + x_3.x_1')$ True.

Hence it is not satisfiable. The problem of finding whether a given Boolean function is satisfiable or not is known as the satisfiability problem for that function. **CNF-satisfiability** is the satisfiability of a Boolean function given in **conjunctive normal form** (CNF), i.e., product-of-sum form. It can be stated as follows: *Given a Boolean function $F(x_1, \ldots, x_n)$ of n variables expressed in CNF, to determine whether it is satisfiable or not.* CNF-satisfiability is a well-known NP-complete problem. Presently we address the satisfiability of the function

$$F(x_1, x_2, x_3, x_4) = (x_1' + x_2) \,.\, (x_3 + x_4') \,.\, (x_1' + x_4') \,.\, (x_2 + x_3)$$

To store a certain truth-value assignment to the variables x_1, x_2, x_3, x_4, we define a **solution vector** X [1..4] where $X[i]$ contains the truth value assigned to the variable x_i, $i = 1, 2, 3, 4$. The given expression consists of four sum terms, $C_1 = (x_1' + x_2)$, $C_2 = (x_3+x_4')$, $C_3 = (x_1' + x_4')$, and $C_4 = (x_2 + x_3)$ so that $F(x_1, x_2, x_3, x_4) = (x_1' + x_2) \,.\, (x_3 + x_4') \,.\, (x_1' + x_4') \,.\, (x_2 + x_3) = C_1.C_2.C_3.C_4$. We define a **sum-term vector** as C [1..4] such that $C[i]$ denotes the truth value attained by max-term C_i under some assignment X. In order to satisfy F each of max-terms C_1, C_2, C_3, and C_4 are to be satisfied individually. Let $f(X)$ = number of max-terms attaining True value under the truth value assignment X. Then $f(X)$ expresses the quality of assignment X. We are now in a position to formulate the production system to solve the given satisfiability problem.

Global database. The *solution vector* X [1..4] and the *sum-term vector* C [1..4] jointly form the global database.

Production rules. At any instant, a new truth value combination may be obtained from the current combination by flipping (complementing) any one of the truth value. As there are four variables we have four production rules listed in Table 11.9.

Control strategy. We follow a simple *hill-climbing* strategy. A new truth value assignment is generated from the current assignment by flipping a randomly chosen truth value. The new assignment is accepted if it is better than the current one. Otherwise, the new assignment is rejected and yet another truth value combination is produced to repeat the same steps. Hence the role of the control strategy is described as follows.

1. Select a variable x_i randomly among x_1, x_2, x_3, x_4.
2. Flip its current truth value of x_i stored in X [1..4] to obtain a new X_1[1..4].
3. Evaluate C [1..4] for this new X_1[1..4].
4. Evaluate $f(X_1)$ = number of sum-terms attaining True value under the truth value assignment X_1.
5. If $f(X_1) \geq f(X)$ then make X_1 the current X and continue, else go to step 1.

For the present instance of the satisfiability problem, the starting point for the production system is the randomly chosen assignment X = [T, F, F, T], i.e., x_1 = True, x_2 = False, x_3 = False, and x_4 = True. It is easy to verify that none of the sum-terms are satisfied under this assignment, making the sum-term vector all False, so that C = [F, F, F, F]. Obviously, $F(X)$ = False, and $f(X) = 0$ in this case. Fig. 11.85 shows the trace of execution. As shown in figure, from initial state to the goal state the assignment vector follows the sequence [T, F, F, T] → [T, T, F, T] → [F, T, F, T] → [F, T, F, F]. Among all these only the last one satisfies the given Boolean function.

Table 11.9. *Production rules*

Rule	Precondition		Postcondition
1 (Flip x_1)	$X = [x_1, x_2, x_3, x_4]$	$\rightarrow$	$X = [x_1', x_2, x_3, x_4]$
2 (Flip x_2)	$X = [x_1, x_2, x_3, x_4]$	$\rightarrow$	$X = [x_1, x_2', x_3, x_4]$
3 (Flip x_3)	$X = [x_1, x_2, x_3, x_4]$	$\rightarrow$	$X = [x_1, x_2, x_3', x_4]$
4 (Flip x_4)	$X = [x_1, x_2, x_3, x_4]$	$\rightarrow$	$X = [x_1, x_2, x_3, x_4']$

$$F(x_1, x_2, x_3, x_4) = (x_1' + x_2)\cdot(x_3 + x_4')\cdot(x_1' + x_4')\cdot(x_2 + x_3)$$

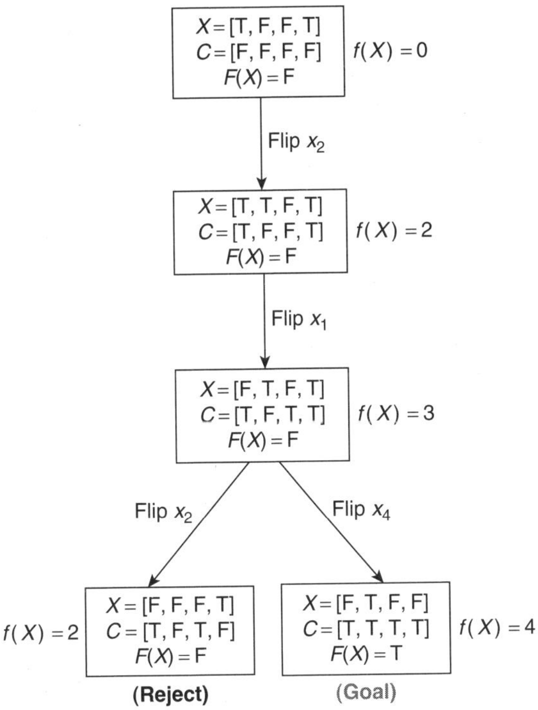

Solution Vector (i.e., truth value assignment):

$X = [x_1, x_2, x_3, x_4]$

Sum-term Vector:

$C = [C_1, C_2, C_3, C_4]$
where

$C_1 = (x_1' + x_2)$
$C_2 = (x_3 + x_4')$
$C_3 = (x_1' + x_4')$
$C_4 = (x_2 + x_3)$

***f*(*X*)** = Number of sum-terms attaining True value under the truth value assignment X.

Fig. 11.85. *Steps of an irrevocable production system to solve CNF-satisfiability*

Example 11.14 *(Solving n-queen problem through back-tracking strategy)*

A classical example of backtracking system refers to the 8-queen problem, or more generally, the ***n***-queen problem. In this example we describe a production system employing the backtracking control strategy to solve ***n***-queen problem.

Let us, for the sake of simplicity consider the 4-queen problem. The four queens are denoted by Q_1, Q_2, Q_3, and Q_4 where the *i*th queen Q_i is placed in the *i*th row of the chess board. Then a placement of the four queens is expressed with a vector $V[1..4]$ where $V[i]$, $i = 1, 2, 3, 4$, gives the column number in which Q_i is placed. For example, Fig. 11.86 shows the board position for the placement [2, 3, 1, 4].

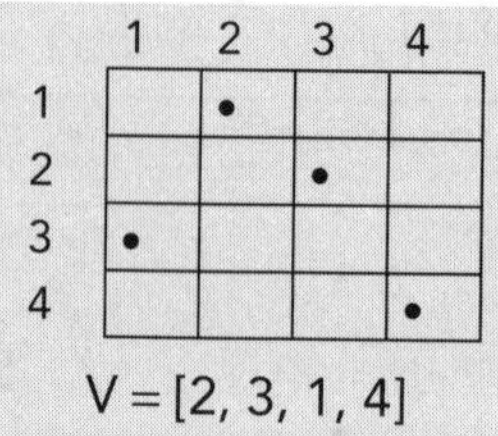

Fig. 11.86. *A placement of 4-queens and its representation*

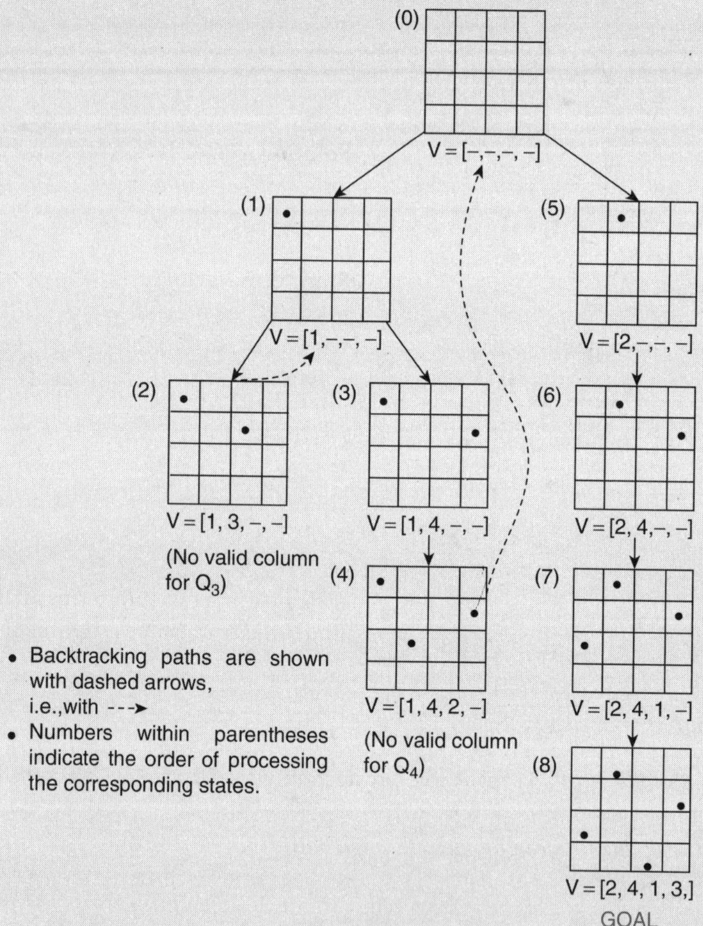

Fig. 11.87. *Backtracking strategy to solve the queen problem*

The successive steps of the backtracking search, when applied to solve the 4-queen problem are shown in Fig. 11.87 in a tree structure. Each node of the tree presents a board position and the corresponding $V[1..4]$ vector. The symbol '–' in V indicates that the corresponding queen is not yet placed. A recursive procedure to solve the n-queen problem through the backtracking strategy is described in **Algorithm Backtrack-n-Queen** ($V[c_1, \ldots c_k, -, \ldots, -]$) (Fig. 11.88).

The algorithm starts with the empty board and then tries to find suitable positions of the queens Q_1, Q_2, …, Q_n at successive steps. At each step, the algorithm looks for the possible positions of the current queen and makes a choice among the alternative locations. It then recursively calls itself for further progress. If, at some later point of time, it is found that there is no valid, i.e., non-attacking, position for some subsequent queen, it backtracks to the point of making the last choice, selects an alternative location (if there is any), and proceeds.

```
Algorithm Backtrack-n-Queen (V[c1,... ck, -, ..., -])
/* V[c1,... ck, -, ..., -] is a partial solution where the first
k queens Q1, ... Qk, k ≤ n, are placed at the columns c1,... ck
respectively, and the remaining n-k
queens are yet to be placed. */
 Begin
    If V is a solution Then return V.
    /* Find a suitable position for Qk+1 */
    For ck+1 ← 1 To n Do
    Begin
          If V[c1,... ck, ck+1, -, ..., -] is a non-attacking
              arrangement of the queens Q1, ... Qk, Qk+1 Then
          Begin
              Sol ← Backtrack-n-Queen (V[c1,... ck,ck+1, -, ..., -])
              If (Sol != NULL) Then Return End-If
          End
       End-If
    End-For
    /* No suitable position for Qk+1 in current
       arrangement of k queens */
    Return NULL
 End- Backtrack-n-Queen
```

Fig. 11.88. *Algorithm backtrack-n-queen ($V[c_1, \ldots c_k, -, \ldots, -]$).*

Let us now focus on the 4-queen problem. In order to solve the 4-queen problem **`Algorithm Backtrack-n-Queen`** would be invoked with the empty solution *V* [-,-,-,-] as its parameter. Fig. 11.87 shows a trace of the execution of the procedure where the successive arrangements of the queens are shown as the nodes of a tree structure. The sequence numbers of these arrangements are indicated within parentheses at the upper-left corner of the corresponding nodes. The position of a queen is indicated by a dot (•) within a cell of a 4 × 4 matrix. Backtracking paths are indicated with dotted arrows.

Initially the board is empty and the solution vector is *V* [-,-,-,-]. This forms the root node, node (0), of the tree. The task is to find a suitable column for the queen Q_1, where Q_1 is the queen belonging to the 1st row. There are four possible columns for Q_1, *viz.*, 1, 2, 3 and 4. We choose column 1 to start with. So the partial solution is now *V* [1,-,-,-], and the board configuration is as shown in node (1). Now we look for a suitable location for queen Q_2. Queen Q_2 belongs to row 2 and there are two positions in row 2, *viz.*, at column 3, and 4, at which Q_1 and Q_2 are not attacking each other. Therefore, we choose column 3 for Q_2. The resulting partial solution is shown as node 2 of Fig. 11.87. However, this assignment leaves no valid position for the third queen, Q_3. Therefore, the process backtracks to the latest backtracking point which is at node (1). The other position for queen Q_2 is now tried with. It is seen that this allows a valid position for Q_3 but leaves nowhere to place queen Q_4. Therefore, the algorithm has to backtrack. Since all alternatives out of placing queen Q_1 at column 1 are exhausted, the backtracking point is now the root node itself. Queen Q_1 is placed at column 2 (see node (5) of Fig. 11.87). The subsequent steps are shown at nodes (6), (7), and (8). The solution we eventually arrive at is $V = [2, 4, 1, 3]$, shown as the goal node in the said figure.

CHAPTER SUMMARY

The main points of the foregoing discussion are given below.

- A state space is defined by a directed graph $G(V, E)$ where each node $v \in V$ represents a state, and each edge e_{ij} from state v_i to v_j represents a possible transition from v_i to v_j. There is a designated state $s \in V$ known as the start state, or start node, of the state space. The search starts from this node. Moreover, there is a goal condition which must be satisfied to end the search process successfully. Usually one or more nodes of the state space satisfy this condition. Such nodes are called the goal nodes.
- A state space search is either uninformed or informed, i.e heuristic. An uninformedsearch do not apply any knowledge of the problem domain to guide the search for a goal node. However, an informed, or heuristic, search is guided by some knowledge which makes the search efficient.
- An exhaustive search tries to examine each and every node of the state space till a goal is reached or there is no way to proceed. Important exhaustive searches are breadth-first search, depth-first search, depth-first iterative deepening search, and bidirectional search.
- Breadth-first search explores the search space laterally. DFS does so vertically. Depth-first iterative deepening tries to combine the advantages of depth-first and breadth-first search. It is a version of depth-first search where the search is continued till a predefined depth d is reached. The value of d is incremented by 1 after each iteration until the goal node is reached. Bidirectional search proceeds in two opposite directions, from the start state towards the goal state (forward direction) and from the goal state towards the start state (backward direction), simultaneously. The search ends successfully when the two paths meet at a common node.
- Best-first search tries to identify the best node to advance the search. An evaluation function is used for this purpose. Hill climbing is a heuristic search technique that makes use of local knowledge in its attempt to attain global solution. An 'A' algorithm is guided by estimating an evaluation function $f(n) = g(n) + h(n)$ where $g(n)$ is the cost of a minimal-cost path from the start node to node n, and, $h(n)$ is the cost of a minimal-cost path from node n to a goal node. If the heuristic estimation $h_1(n)$ is a lower bound of $h(n)$ so that $h_1(n) \le h(n)$ for all n, then it is an A^* algorithm. Such algorithms are admissible in the sense that they are guaranteed to find a minimal-cost path from the root to a goal.
- In the problem reduction strategy a problem is repeatedly decomposed into subproblems until the subproblems obtained are readily solvable.It employs a special kind of graph called

AND-OR graph. The search through an AND-OR graph using some knowledge of the problem domain is known as AO* search. In AO* search the individual solutions of the subproblems are combined to obtain the solution of the given problem.

- Means-Ends Analysis (MEA) is a technique employed for generating plans for achieving goals. The MEA strategy is based on the concept of the *difference* between the start state and the goal state. The MEA process recursively tries to reduce the difference between two states until it reduces to zero. As a result it generates a sequence of operations or actions which transforms the start state to the goal state.
- Constraint satisfaction problems (CSPs) are characterized by three components, a set of variables, a set of values, called the domains, for each variable, and a set of relations, or constraints, involving variables that restrict their attainable values. The structure of a CSP, especially the constraints, can be represented as a graph, or hypergraph, known as the *constraint graph* (or hypergraph). Depth-first search with backtracking is commonly used to solve a CSP. Sometimes local search procedure guided by the minimum-conflict heuristic are also used.
- Games are typically multi-agent environments in which the agents are competitive rather than cooperative. Mini-Max search, a kind of adversarial search technique, helps to select a good move in s deterministic, two-player, turn-taking, zero-sum game. It uses a static evaluation function that returns a numeric value for each state of the game. Alpha-Beta pruning is a technique to make Mini-Max search efficient. It enables the search process to avoid parts of the game tree that do not contribute to decision making while the best move is selected.
- Production systems are intelligent systems that are structured to facilitate a state space search procedure. The main components of a production system are a global database, a set of production rules and a control system. Once the global database is initialized, an appropriate production rule is selected (by the control strategy) and applied on the global database to transform it to a new state. This is repeated till the termination condition is satisfied by the global database.

SOLVED PROBLEMS

Problem 11.1. (*Water-Jug Problem*) There are two water jugs, one of 4 litre capacity and the other of 3 litre. There are no marking on the jugs and they can be filled with water from a nearby tap. The only permissible operations are:

1. Filling an empty jug with water from the tap.
2. Emptying a fully or partially filled jug.
3. Transferring water from one jug to another.

Initially both the jugs are empty. Now, using the operations described above, is it possible to obtain exactly 2 litre of water in the 4-litre jug? If yes, then what is the sequence of operations to achieve this? Create the state space for the problem and show a solution path in it.

Solution 11.1. Let us denote the 4-litre jug as jug *A* and the 3-litre jug as jug *B*. A state of the problem can be presented as a pair of integers $[x, y]$ where x and y are the amount of water in litre in jug *A* and *B*, respectively. For the sake of simplicity let us assume that x and y are both integers and $x \leq 4$, $y \leq 3$. The rules to manipulate the state space are listed in Table 11.10.

Table 11.10. *Rules to solve the water-jug problem*

#	Pre-condition		Post-condition	Remark
1	$[x, y] \wedge (x < 4)$	$\rightarrow$	$[4, y]$	Fill the 4-litre jug.
2	$[x, y] \wedge (y < 3)$	$\rightarrow$	$[x, 3]$	Fill the 3-litre jug.
3	$[x, y] \wedge (x > 0)$	$\rightarrow$	$[0, y]$	Empty the 4-litre jug.
4	$[x, y] \wedge (y > 0)$	$\rightarrow$	$[x, 0]$	Empty the 3-litre jug.
5	$[x, y] \wedge (x + y \geq 4) \wedge (y > 0)$	$\rightarrow$	$[4, y-(4-x)]$	Pour water from 3-litre jug to the 4-litre jug till the 4-litre jug is full.
6	$[x, y] \wedge (x + y \geq 3) \wedge (x > 0)$	$\rightarrow$	$[x-(3-y), 3]$	Pour water from 4-litre jug to the 3-litre jug till the 3-litre jug is full.
7	$[x, y] \wedge (x + y \leq 4) \wedge (y > 0)$	$\rightarrow$	$[x + y, 0]$	Pour all water from 3-litre jug into the 4-litre jug.
8	$[x, y] \wedge (x + y \leq 3) \wedge (x > 0)$	$\rightarrow$	$[0, x + y]$	Pour all water from 4-litre jug into the 3-litre jug.

Initially both the jugs are empty so that the initial state is [0, 0]. At this stage we may either fill jug-A or jug-B resulting in the states [4, 0] or [0, 3], respectively. While in state [4, 0], we may either pour water from jug-A to jug-B to fill up the later or simply fill jug-B to its full. The corresponding states are [1, 3] and [4, 3]. Of course we can empty jug-A, and return to the initial state. Therefore [1, 3] and [4, 3] are the children of the state [4, 0]. Similarly the state [0, 3] has the children [4, 3] and [3, 0]. The entire state space is shown in Fig. 11.89. Two paths to reach the goal are highlighted in the figure.

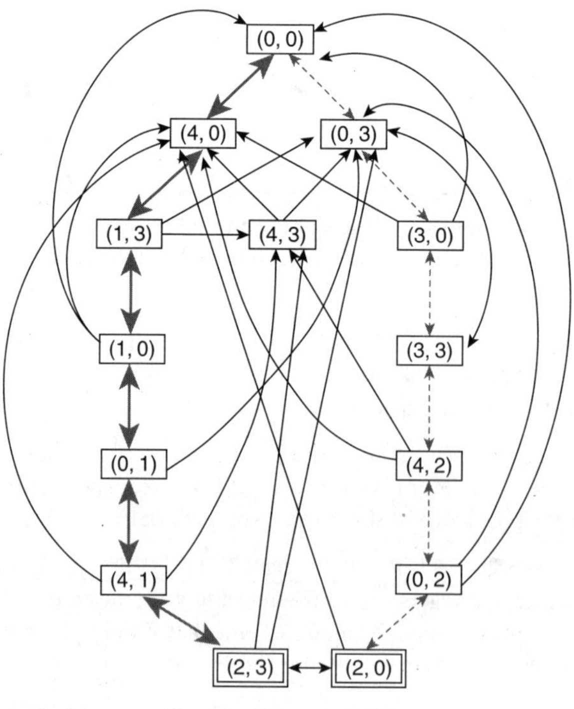

Fig. 11.89. *The state space for the water-jug problem*

Problem 11.2 (*Monkey-and-Banana Problem*) Here is the simple world of a monkey. There is a room with a door and a window. A box is placed at the window and a bunch of bananas is hanging from the ceiling at the middle of the room. The monkey is hungry but it can not hold the bananas as these are out of its reach. However, if the box is placed at the middle of the room just below the bunch of bananas and the monkey climbs the top of the box then it can catch the bananas and eat them. The monkey can walk, can push the box along the floor, can climb the box, and if within its reach, it can catch the bananas. Initially the monkey is at the door of the room. Can it catch the bananas? If yes, what is the sequence of actions to achieve this goal?

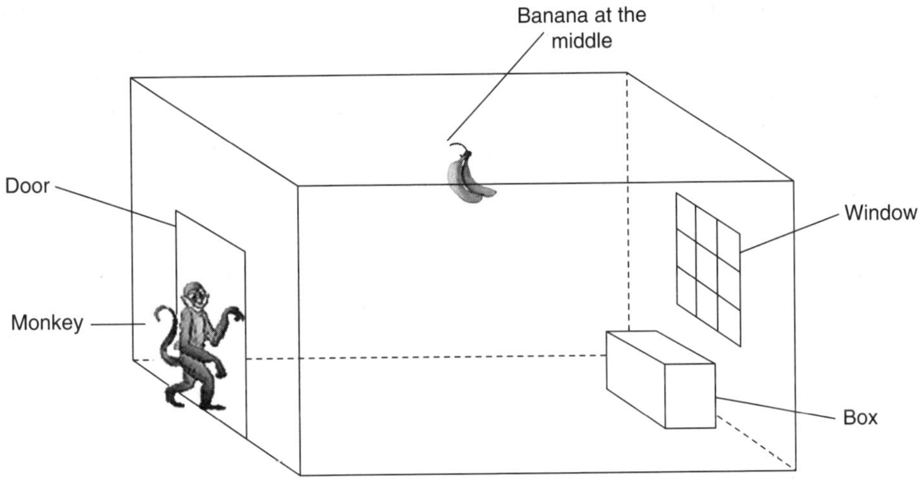

(a) **Initial State**

P = position of monkey = *Door*
Q = whether the monkey is on the floor, or on the box = *on Box*
R = position of the box = *Window*
S = whether the monkey holds the banana or not = *NO*

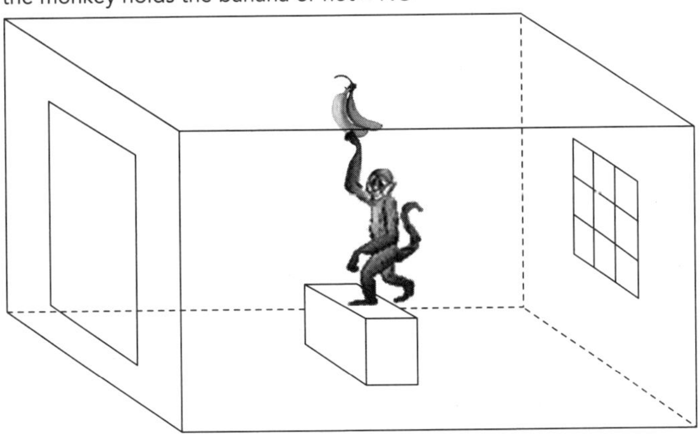

(a) **Final State**

P = position of monkey = *Middle*
Q = whether the monkey is on the floor, or on the box = *on Box*
R = position of the box = *Middle*
S = whether the monkey holds the banana or not = *Yes*

Fig. 11.90. *The Monkey-and-Banana problem.*

Solution 11.2. Fig. 11.90 shows the problem graphically. A problem state is expressed with a 4-tuple < *P*, *Q*, *R*, *S* > where

P is the position of the monkey
Q is whether the monkey is on the floor or on the box
R is the position of the box
S is whether the monkey has grasped the banana or not

For the sake of simplicity we assume that the monkey can be either at the door, or at the window, or at the middle of the room. Similarly, the box can be at one of these positions only. Hence the domains of *P*, *Q*, *R*, and *S* are defined as follows:

$P \in \{ Door, Window, Middle \}$
$Q \in \{ onFloor, onBox \}$
$R \in \{ Door, Window, Middle \}$
$S \in \{ Yes, No \}$

There are four activities of the monkey, *viz.*, it can walk from place to place, it can push the box from one place to another, it can climb the box, and if possible, it can grasp the banana. However, each of these activities requires certain conditions to hold good. These are described in Table 11.11. The initial state of the system is < *Door, onFloor, Window, No* > because in the beginning the monkey is at the door, on the floor, the box is at the window, and the monkey is not holding the banana. The final state is given by < *Middle, onBox, Middle, Yes* >.

Table 11.11. *Valid moves of the monkey*

Operation	Description and prerequisite conditions
Walk (X, Y)	The monkey walks from *X* to *Y*. Precondition : The monkey is on the floor, Q = *onFloor*.
Climb	The monkey climbs the box. Preconditions : i) The monkey and the box are at the same place, P = R. ii) The monkey is on the floor, Q = *onFloor*.
Push (X, Y)	The monkey pushes the box from *X* to *Y*. Precondition : i) Both the monkey and the box are at *X*, P = R = X. ii) The monkey is on the floor, Q = *on Floor*.
Grasp	The monkey grabs the banana. Preconditions : i) Both the monkey and the box are at the middle, P = Q = *Middle*. ii) The monkey is on the box, Q = *onBox*.

To estimate the distance of a given state $< P_1, Q_1, R_1, S_1 >$ from the goal state < *Middle, onBox, Middle, Yes* > we introduce a measure *d* between two states $n_1 = < P_1, Q_1, R_1, S_1 >$ and $n_2 = < P_2, Q_2, R_2, S_2 >$ as follows:

$$d(n_1, n_2) = \text{Number of mismatched parameters}$$

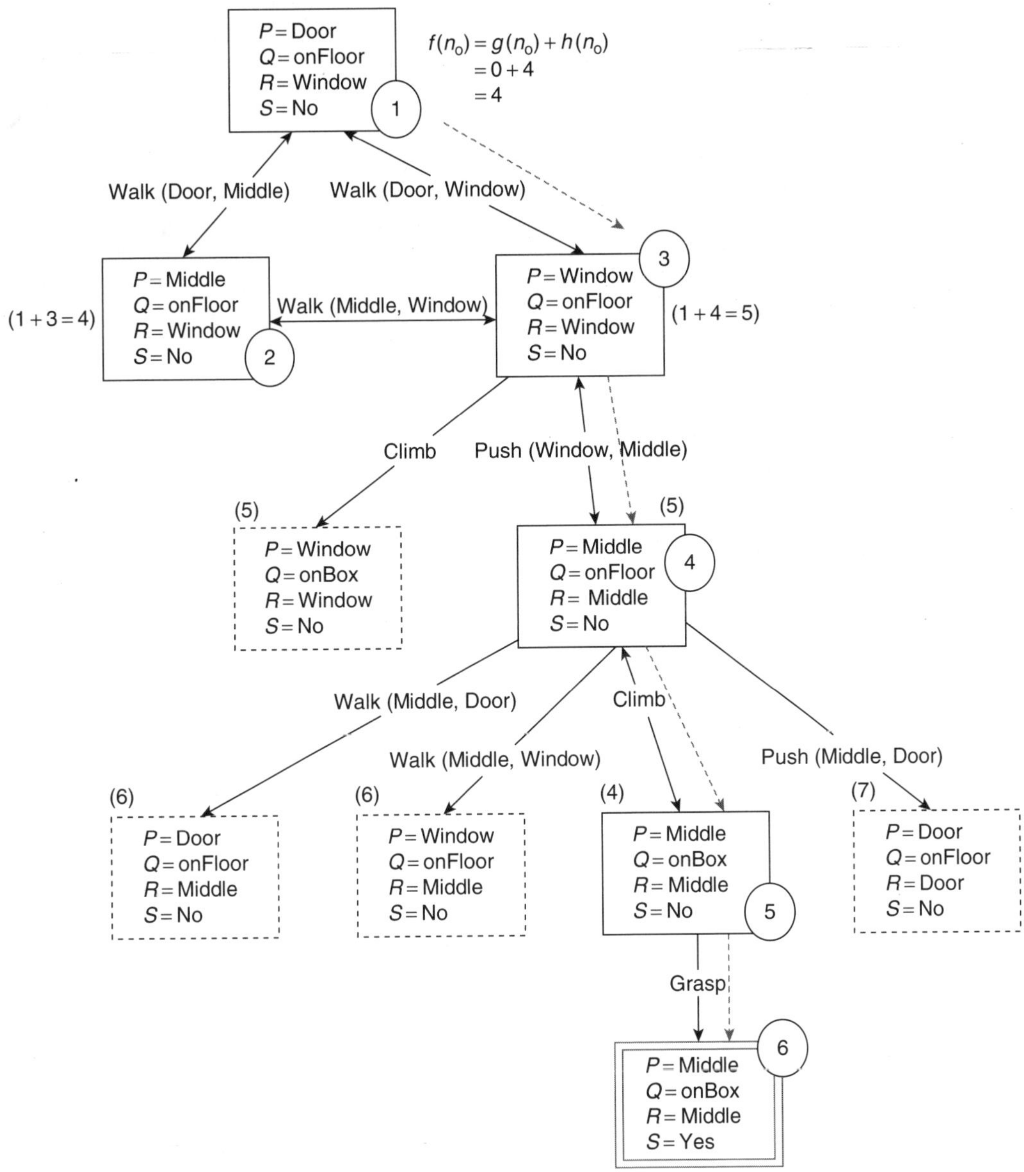

Fig. 11.91. *Search tree for the Monkey and Banana problem.*

For example, let n_0 = the initial state = < *Door*, *onFloor*, *Window*, *No* >, and n_f = the final state = < *Middle*, *onBox*, *Middle*, *Yes* >. Since none of the parameters *P*, *Q*, *R*, and *S* of n_0 and n_f have matched, the distance of the initial state from the final state is 4. For $g(n)$, the distance of node n from the start node along the path taken is considered. Hence for the start state the objective function has the value

$f(n_0) = g(n_0) + h(n_0) = 0 + 4 = 4$. This is shown in Fig. 11.91 which depicts the entire search tree. The nodes are shown in rectangular boxes and the values of the objective function for different nodes are given within parentheses. The encircled numbers adjacent to some nodes indicate the sequence in which the nodes are expanded. The nodes which are generated but never expanded are shown with dashed lines.

It is seen that from the initial state < *Door, onFloor, Window, No* > the only possible moves for monkey are to walk from the door to either the middle or to the window. Accordingly, the initial state has two children < *Middle, onFloor, Window, No* > (state 1) and < *Window, onFloor, Window, No* > (state 2). The heuristic estimates of state 1 and 2 are 3 and 4, respectively while each of them is at a distance 1 from the root. Therefore $f(n_1) = 1 + 3 = 4$ and $f(n_2) = 1 + 4 = 5$. Obviously, state 1 is chosen for further exploration at this point of time. However, it is found that there are only two possible moves from state 1, *viz.*, either return to state 0 or go to state 2. Consequently, state 2 is selected as the next node to be explored and expanded. Fig. 11.91 shows the entire search tree along with the sequence of nodes explored and expanded. Each transition edge is labeled with the corresponding action taken by the monkey. The chain of actions that leads from the start state to the goal is highlighted.

Problem 11.3 (*Farmer-Fox-Goose-Grain problem*) There is a farmer on one bank of a river. He has a fox, a goose and some grain with him and he want to cross the river with all his possessions. There is a boat to cross the river but it is too small to accommodate more than one possession at a time. Therefore each time the farmer crosses the river he can take at most one possession with him. In absence of the farmer, the fox will eat the goose. Similarly, if the goose is left with the grain then it will eat the grain. Formulate the problem as a state space search and show the state space.

Solution 11.3 Fig. 11.92 shows the state space of the given problem. A node is represented by a rectangular box containing two smaller boxes. The inner boxes represent two banks of the river. The direction of an arrow between two banks of the river indicate the direction of the movement of the boat in the next move. The labels attached to the edges between the nodes convey the entities being moved from one bank to the other in the present step. Suitable representation of a node as a state is left as an exercise.

Problem 11.4 (*Missionaries and Cannibals problem*) Three missionaries and three cannibals are standing at one bank of a river. They have to cross the river. There is a boat to cross the river which can accommodate at most two persons at a time. If the cannibals outnumber the missionaries at any bank they will eat the missionaries. How should the missionaries and the cannibals cross the river so that the cannibals can never eat any missionary?

Solution 11.4 Let us represent a state of the problem in the form (α) [R_l | R_r] (β) where α and β are strings of the form M^pC^q, $0 \leq p \leq 3$, $0 \leq q \leq 3$. Each M represents a missionary and each C represents a cannibal. For example, the string MMCCC represents two missionaries and three cannibals. The null string, M^0C^0, is indicated with '-'. The middle portion of the expression, i.e., [R_l | R_r] represents the position of the boat with respect to the river. The vertical line '|' stands for the river. One of R_l and R_r is 'B', indicating the boat in the corresponding bank, while the other must be '-', expressing the fact that the boat is not in that bank of the river.

So the string (MMCC) [- | B] (MC) expresses the following facts:

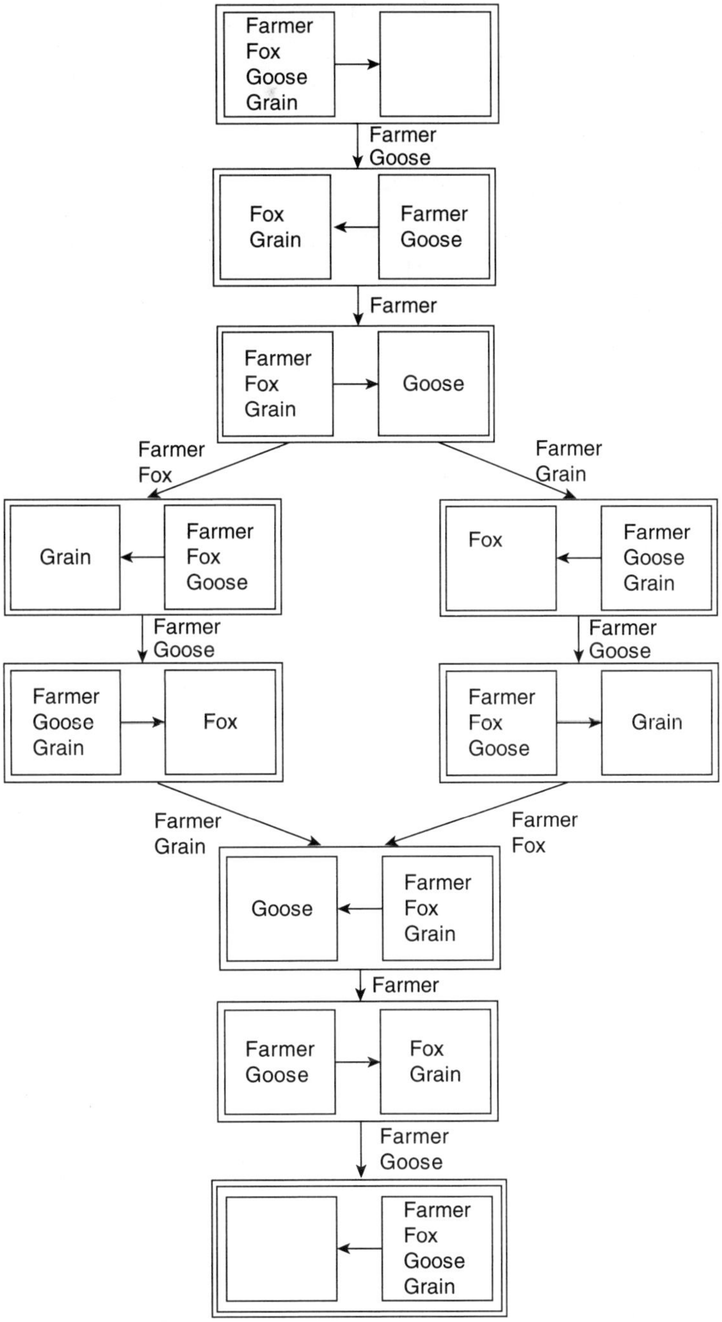

Fig. 11.92. *State space of the Farmer-Fox-Goose-Grain problem.*

Table 11.12. *Rules to solve the missionaries and cannibals problem*

#	Pre-condition		Post-condition	Remark
1a	(MMMCCC) [B|-] (-)	→	(MMMCC) [-|B] (C)	1 C goes to right bank.
1b		→	(MMCC) [-|B] (MC)	1 M and 1 C go to right bank.
1c		→	(MMMC) [-|B] (CC)	2 Cs goes to right bank.
2a	(MMMCC) [B|-] (C)	→	(MMCC) [-|B] (MC)	1 M goes to right bank.
2b		→	(MMMC) [-|B] (CC)	1 C goes to right bank.
2c		→	(MMM) [-|B] (CCC)	2 Cs go to right bank.
3	(MMMCC) [-|B] (C)	→	(MMMCCC) [B|-] (-)	1 C goes to left bank.
4a	(MMCC) [B|-] (MC)	→	(MC) [-|B] (MMCC)	1 M and 1 C go to right bank.
4b		→	(CC) [-|B] (MMMC)	2 Ms go to right bank.
5a	(MMCC) [-|B] (MC)	→	(MMMCC) [B|-] (C)	1 M goes to left bank.
5b		→	(MMMCCC) [B|-] (-)	1 M and 1 C go to left bank.
6a	(MMMC) [B|-] (CC)	→	(MMM) [-|B] (CCC)	1 C goes to right bank.
6b		→	(MC) [-|B] (MMCC)	2 Ms goes to right bank.
7a	(MMMC) [-|B] (CC)	→	(MMMCC) [B|-] (C)	1 C goes to left bank.
7b		→	(MMMCCC) [B|-] (-)	2 Cs go to left bank.
8a	(CCC) [B|-] (MMM)	→	(CC) [-|B] (MMMC)	1 C goes to right bank.
8b		→	(C) [-|B] (MMMCC)	2 Cs go to right bank.
9	(CCC) [-|B] (MMM)			*No possible move*
10	(MMM) [B|-] (CCC)			*No possible move*
11a	(MMM) [-|B] (CCC)	→	(MMMC) [B|-] (CC)	1 C goes to left bank.
11b		→	(MMMCC) [B|-] (C)	2 Cs go to left bank.
12a	(MC) [B|-] (MMCC)	→	(C) [-|B] (MMMCC)	1 M goes to right bank.
12b		→	(-) [-|B] (MMMCCC)	1 M and 1 C go to right bank.
13a	(MC) [-|B] (MMCC)	→	(MMCC) [B|-] (MC)	1 M and 1 C go to left bank.
13b		→	(MMMC) [B|-] (CC)	2 Ms go to left bank.
14a	(CC) [B|-] (MMMC)	→	(C) [-|B] (MMMCC)	1 C goes to right bank.
14b		→	(-) [-|B] (MMMCCC)	2 Cs go to right bank.
15a	(CC) [-|B] (MMMC)	→	(CCC) [B|-] (MMM)	1 C goes to left bank.
15b		→	(MMCC) [B|-] (MC)	2 Ms go to left bank.
16	(C) [B|-] (MMMCC)	→	(-) [-|B] (MMMCCC)	1 C goes to right bank.
17a	(C) [-|B] (MMMCC)	→	(MC) [B|-] (MMCC)	1 M goes to left bank.
17b		→	(CC) [B|-] (MMMC)	1 C go to left bank.
18	(-) [-|B] (MMMCCC)			*Goal*

- The left bank of the river contains two missionaries and two cannibals.
- The right bank of the river contains one missionary and one cannibal.
- The boat is on the right bank of the river.

Obviously, not all distribution of the missionaries and the cannibals over the two banks are valid. At any bank, number of cannibals can not exceed that of the missionaries, in case both kinds of people are there at the same bank. Hence the distribution (CC) [B | -] (MMMC), or (CCC) [- | B] (MMM) are valid but neither (CCM) [B | -] (MMC), nor (MMCCC) [B | -] (M) is a valid distribution. In order to define a production rule we need to specify the pre-condition and the post-condition which, in this case, are distribution of the missionaries and the cannibals over the two river banks and the position of the boat. For example, the rule

$$\text{(MMMC) [B | -] (CC)} \rightarrow \text{(MC) [- | B] (MMCC)}$$

states that if there are three missionaries and one cannibal on the left bank, two cannibals on the right bank, and the boat is one the left bank, then two missionaries may take the boat to the right bank so that after the move one missionary and one cannibal are left on the left bank while two missionaries and two cannibals remains on the right bank. The complete set of such rules is listed in Table 11.12. Solving the problem with the help of these rules is left as an exercise.

Problem 11.5. (*8-puzzle*) Consider an instance of the 8-puzzle for which initial and goal states are as shown in Fig. 11.93. Propose a hill climbing search algorithms to solve this problem.

1	4	2
8		3
7	6	5

Start state

1	2	3
8		4
7	6	5

Goal state

Fig. 11.93. *Another instance of the 8-puzzle.*

Solution 11.5. First we have to define an objective function to express the quality of a state with respect to the goal state. Let us consider the entire frame of the 8-puzzle as a 3×3 matrix. Then the successive cells can be designated by the ordered pairs (1,1), (1,2), (1,3), (2,1), (2,2), (2,3), (3,1), (3,2), and (3,3) (Fig. 11.94). Now, suppose a certain tile x is in cell (i, j) while as per configuration of the goal state it should be in cell (k, l). In order to bring tile x to its designated position it must be moved through at least $d_x = |i-k| + |j-l|$ number of cells. This d_x may be called the distance of tile x from its desired position.

For example, Fig. 11.95 shows a situation where a tile x is at position (1, 2) though its targeted position is at (3,1). Therefore, for this tile the displacement $d_x = |i-k| + |j-l| = |1-3| + |2-1| = 2 + 1 = 3$. This means, in order to place tile x at its proper position, it has to be moved through at least 3 cells from its current position.

(1,1)	(1,2)	(1,3)
(2,1)	(2,2)	(2,3)
(3,1)	(3,2)	(3,3)

Fig. 11.94. *Configuration of 8-puzzle as a 3×3 matrix.*

We are now in a position to define the objective function. The objective function $f(n)$, which estimates the distance of state n from the goal state can be defined as the sum over all d_x, $x = 1, \ldots, 8$.

$$h(n) = \sum_{x=1}^{8} d_x \tag{11.15}$$

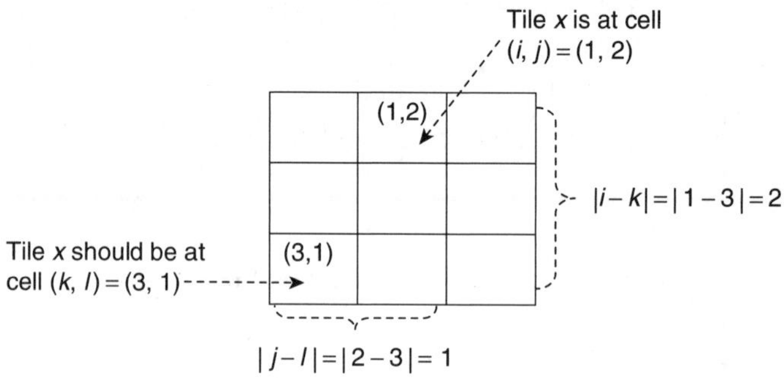

Fig. 11.95. *Computation of* d_x.

As an example, let us compare the state depicted in Fig. 11.96 (*a*) with the goal state shown in Fig. 11.96 (*b*).In the goal state tile 1 is at position (1, 1) while in state n it is actually at position (2, 3). Therefore, $d_1 = |1\text{-}2| + |1\text{-}3| = 1 + 2 = 3$. Similarly, the distances of the other tiles are computed as $d_2 = 1$, $d_3 = 4$, $d_4 = 2$, $d_5 = 0$, $d_6 = 2$, $d_7 = 4$, and $d_8 = 2$. Hence the distance of state n as a whole from the goal state is given by $f(n) = d_1 + d_2 + d_3 + d_4 + d_5 + d_6 + d_7 + d_8 = 3 + 1 + 4 + 2 + 0 + 2 + 4 + 2 = 18$ (Fig. 11.94). Now let us consider the initial state of the given problem. Here $f(n) = d_1 + d_2 + d_3 + d_4 + d_5 + d_6 + d_7 + d_8 = 0 + 1 + 1 + 2 + 0 + 0 + 0 + 0 = 4$.

(a) State n

2	4	7
6		1
3	8	5

(*b*) Goal State

1	2	3
8		4
7	6	5

$d_1 = 3, d_2 = 1, d_3 = 4, d_4 = 2, d_5 = 0, d_6 = 2, d_7 = 4, d_8 = 2$
$h(n) = d_1 + d_2 + d_3 + d_4 + d_5 + d_6 + d_7 + d_8 = 3 + 1 + 4 + 2 + 0 + 2 + 4 + 2 = 18$

Fig. 11.96. *Computation of the distance of a state n from the goal state.*

The four different new states that can be obtained from this initial state are shown as the children of the start state in Fig. 11.97. These states have $f(n)$ values 5, 5, 5, and 3 as indicated within a pair of parentheses adjacent to the respective nodes. The search will proceed along the state with $f(n)$ value 3 because that is the only value lower than 4, that of the current state.

However, the hill climbing procedure is not supposed to generate all these states at a time. Instead, it will generate only one among these. If the newly generated state happens to have $f(n)$ value less than 4, then that will be accepted. Otherwise, the hill climbing procedure will reject the newly generated state and produce a yet another state. Eventually it will generate the desired one, i.e., the state with $f(n)$ value 3, because such a state exists and is reachable from the current state. The progress of the hill climbing process can be traced by following the solid arrows in Fig. 11.97. The dashed arrows indicate the steps rejected by the hill climbing process.

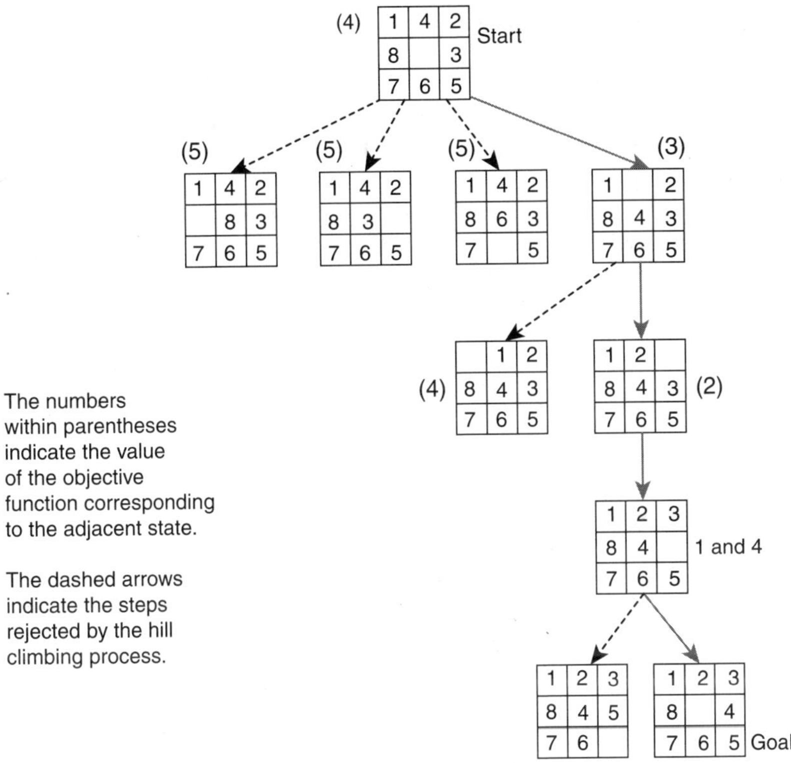

Fig. 11.97. *Solving 8-puzzle through hill climbing*

Problem 11.6. (*Solving 8-queen problem through steepest ascent hill-climbing*) Apply steepest ascent hill climbing method to solve the 8-queen problem.

Solution 11.6. The rows of the chess board are numbered as 0, 1, …, 7. Each of these queens is placed in a distinct column to ensure that the queens are not attacking each other. Thus a configuration of eight queens on the chess board can be expressed as a vector of eight elements [$r_0, r_1, r_2, r_3, r_4, r_5, r_6, r_7$] where r_i is row number of position of the queen in the ith column. Fig. 11.98 shows such a board configuration.

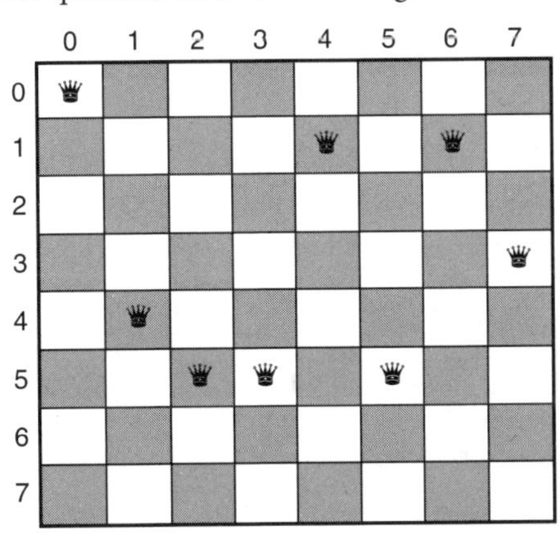

Fig. 11.98. *Board configuration: [0, 4, 5, 5, 1, 5, 1, 3].*

We consider the objective function for a given arrangement $n = [\, r_0, r_1, r_2, r_3, r_4, r_5, r_6, r_7 \,]$ of eight queens as follows:

$$F(n) = \text{Number of attacking pair in the arrangement } n \tag{11.15}$$

For example in the arrangement shown in Fig. 11.98, there are nine attacking pairs of queens, *viz.*, (Q_0, Q_5), (Q_1, Q_2), (Q_1, Q_4), (Q_2, Q_3), (Q_2, Q_5), (Q_2, Q_6), (Q_3, Q_5), (Q_4, Q_6), and (Q_5, Q_7), where Q_i denotes the queen in the ith column. Now, given an arrangement n of queens, we compute the value of $f(n)$ by placing each queen Q_i at various rows, remaining in its designated column i. For example, in Fig. 11.99 (*a*) if Q_0 is placed at row 1, instead of row 0, we would have 10 attacking pairs of queens. This is indicated by placing the number 10 within cell (1, 0) in the chess board. Similarly other cells contain the number of attacking pairs in case the queen of the respective row is placed at that cell. The values of the objective function for the arrangements shown in Fig. 11.99 (a)-(d) are indicated at the top of the respective boards. Obviously, each cell of the chess board that contains a queen should have exactly this value. For example, each of the cells (0, 0), (4, 1), (5, 2), (5, 3), (1, 4), (5, 5), (1, 6) and (3, 7) of Fig. 11.99 (a) contains the value 9.

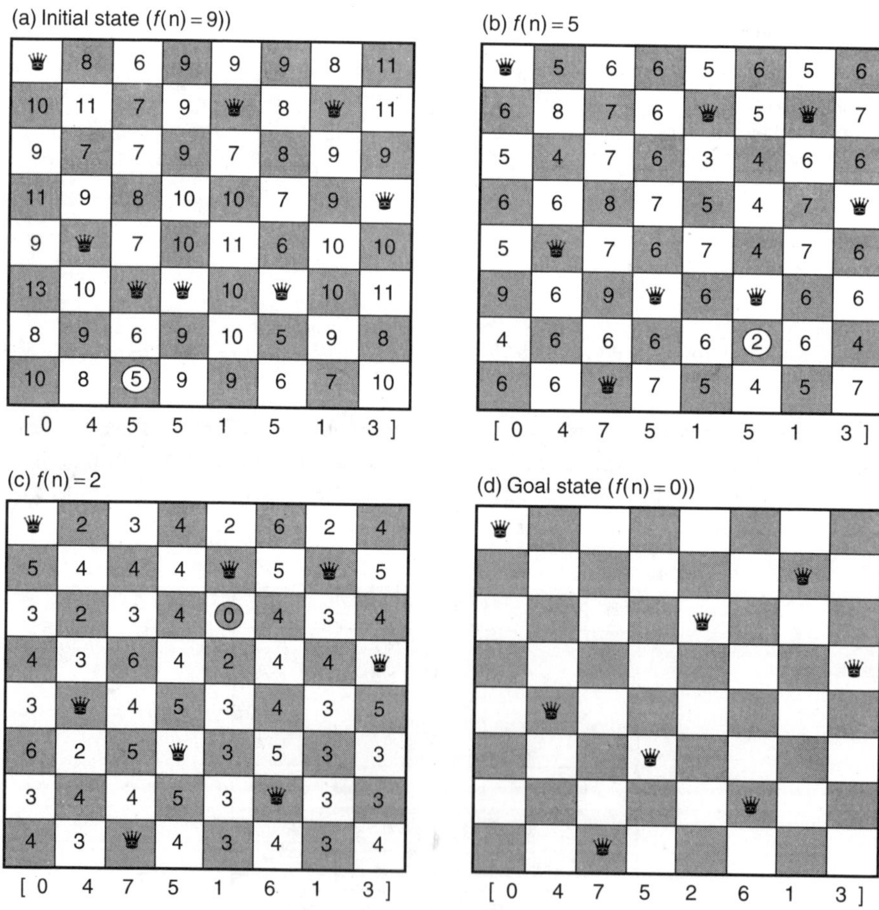

Fig. 11.99. *(a)–(d) Successive steps of hill climbing process for 8-queen problem*

The hill climbing strategy for 8-queen problem would start with a random arrangement of the eight queens in eight different columns. One such random arrangement is depicted in Fig. 11.99 (*a*). The objective function described above is then evaluated for each cell of the chess board. The minimum among these 64 values is then located, say at cell (*i*, *j*). If there is a tie then it can be resolved arbitrarily, or through some suitable manner. Then the new state of the 8-queen problem is obtained by moving queen Q_j to the ith row, i.e., to the cell (*i*, *j*). For example, the minimum $f(n)$ value for the configuration of Fig. 11.99 (a) is 5 and is located at cell (7, 2) and (6, 5). Therefore Q_2 is moved to (7, 2) position to obtain the new arrangement of eight queens as depicted in Fig. 11.99 (*b*). The process is repeated until we arrive at a state where there is a cell for which the objective function evaluates to 0. The progress of the hill climbing process from the initial state to a solution is shown in Fig. 11.99 (*a*) - (*d*). The minimum $f(n)$ values are indicated as encircled numbers.

Problem 11.7. (*Solving the satisfiability problem using AND-OR graph*) Using AND-OR graph search technique, find a combination of truth-values to the Boolean variables of the expression $(a + b'.c').c + (a' + b'.c').(c + c'.a)$ to satisfy the expression, i.e., to make the expression attain a truth-value True.

Solution 11.7. Starting with the given expression we go on decomposing it until we reach a literal, i.e., a Boolean variable either in the complimented or in non-complimented form. The basic principle of decomposition is shown in Fig. 11.100 where *x* and *y* are literals. The truth assignments to variables are made in a way that makes the terminal literals true. In other words, if $x = a$ then we assign $a =$ true and if $x = a'$ then $a =$ false.

The cost of a node is estimated by the total number of AND and OR operations in the corresponding expression, or sub-expression. Let *f* be the Boolean expression associated with a node *n*, then $h_1(n)$ is estimated as

$$h_1(n) = \text{Number of operators (excluding NOT) in } f.$$

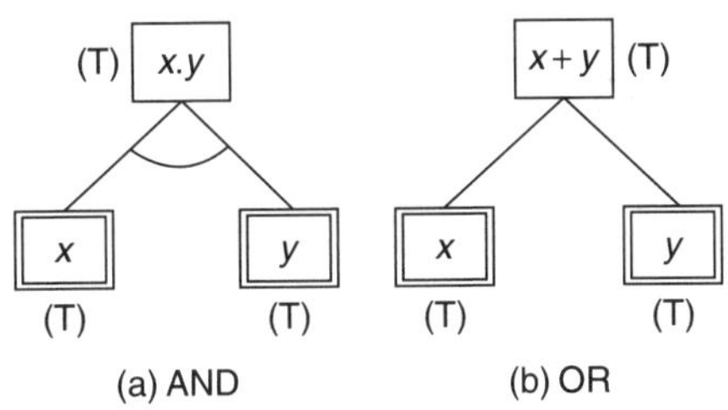

Fig. 11.100. *Truth value assignment to Boolean variables.*

For example, the root node of the given problem corresponds to the Boolean expression $f(a, b, c) = (a + b'.c').c + (a' + b'.c').(c + c'.a)$ which includes a total of 9 operators (excluding logical inversion, 4 ORs and 5 ANDs). Therefore its cost estimate is 9. Obviously, the cost of a node containing a single literal, i.e., a SOLVED node, is 0. Each link of the resultant AND-OR graph has a uniform cost of 1. The successive steps of the search process are shown in Fig. 11.101 (*a*)–(*d*). The solution offered by the process is the assignment $a =$ true, and $c =$ true. The truth value of *b* does not affect the satisfiability of the given expression for this assignment.

Problem 11.8 (*Game of Tic-tac-toe with mini-max search strategy)* The game of tic-tac-toe is widely used to illustrate the application of MiniMax search strategy for game playing. The game is familiar to most of us. It consists of a 3 × 3 board configuration as shown in Fig. 11.102 (*a*)–(*d*). Initially all compartments of the board are empty. The game is initiated by the player who puts a check mark (×) in one of the compartments. Let us call this player as the MAX player. The opponent, in his turn, puts a circle (O) in his chosen place. The two players go on putting their designated symbols on the board alternately till the end of the game. The game ends in one of the following three situations:

1. Three consecutive check marks in horizontal, vertical, or diagonal alighment (win by MAX).
2. Three consecutive circles in horizontal, vertical, or diagonal alignment (win by MIN).
3. There is no empty compartment, and none of condition 1, or 2 above, are satisfied (draw).

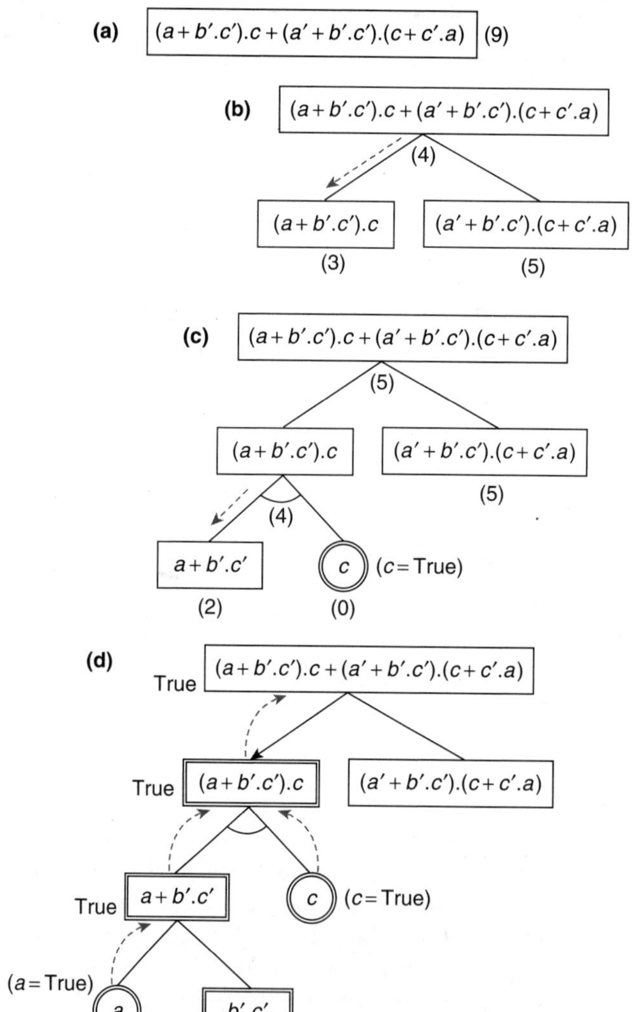

Fig. 11.101. *Satisfying a Boolean function through AND-OR search*

These are illustrated in Fig. 11.102(a)–(d). Now, it is required to design an AI system that may play a credible game of tic-tac-toe with a human opponent.

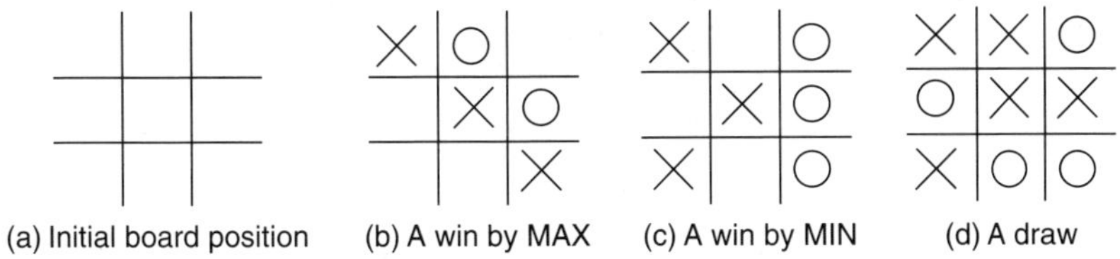

Fig. 11.102. *Board positions of tic-tac-toe*

Suppose our system employs 2-ply MiniMax search as the guide to select a move at its turn. The first thing we have to find is a suitable static evaluation function. Of course the function $e(N)$ shall return $+\infty$ or $-\infty$ if N, the board position, happens to be a winning position for MAX (playing $\times$) or MIN (playing O), respectively. But what about the other non-terminal situations? Let us consider that the total number of rows, columns, and diagonals still available for a certain player P (P is either MAX or MIN) as a measure of his scope for winning the game. We define $X(N)$ as the number of rows, columns, and diagonals in board position N still available for MAX. The same for MIN is expressed as $O(N)$. Then the static evaluation function may be defined as:

$$
\begin{aligned}
e(N) &= +\infty && \text{if } N \text{ is a winning position for MAX} \\
&= -\infty && \text{if } N \text{ is a winning position for MIN} \\
&= X(N) - O(N) && \text{otherwise.}
\end{aligned}
$$

Obviously, according to the heuristic knowledge employed here while designing the evaluation function, more scope a certain player have of winning better his chance of winning the game eventually. Fig. 11.103 and 11.104 illustrates two instances of computing the evaluation function for two different board positions.

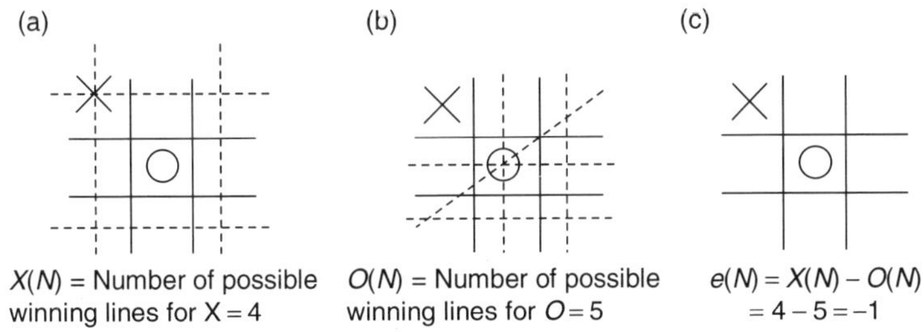

Fig. 11.103. *Computing the static evaluation function for tic-tac-toe, case #1.*

A positive $e(N)$ can be interpreted as indicative of higher chance for MAX to win the game. Similarly, negative $e(N)$ implies that given the current situation N player MIN has a greater chance of winning the game.

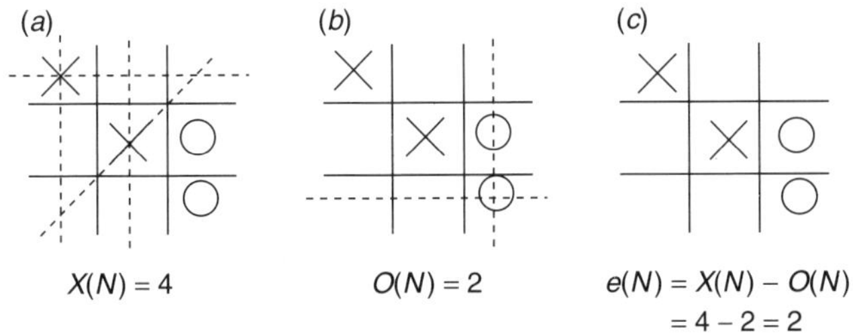

Fig. 11.104. *Computing the static evaluation function for tic-tac-toe, case #2.*

The first three moves on the basis of 2-ply MiniMax search employing the static evaluation function mentioned above are depicted in Fig. 11.105, Fig. 11.106 and Fig. 11.107. We assume that both the players are using the same technique and the same evaluation function as their strategy. In the initial empty board position, MAX may put the '×' mark at any of the nine compartments. However, taking symmetry into consideration, the resultant nine board positions boil down to only three distinct board positions. Hence the start node of the game tree representing the empty board position has just three children, not nine. This principle is followed in subsequent steps also.

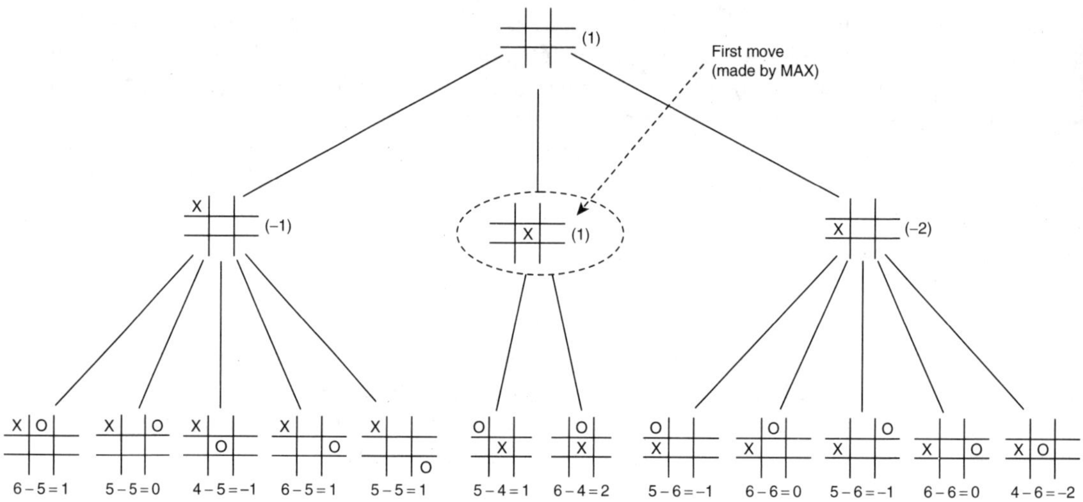

Fig. 11.105. *First move of tic-tac-toe by MAX player applying 2-ply Mini-Max.*

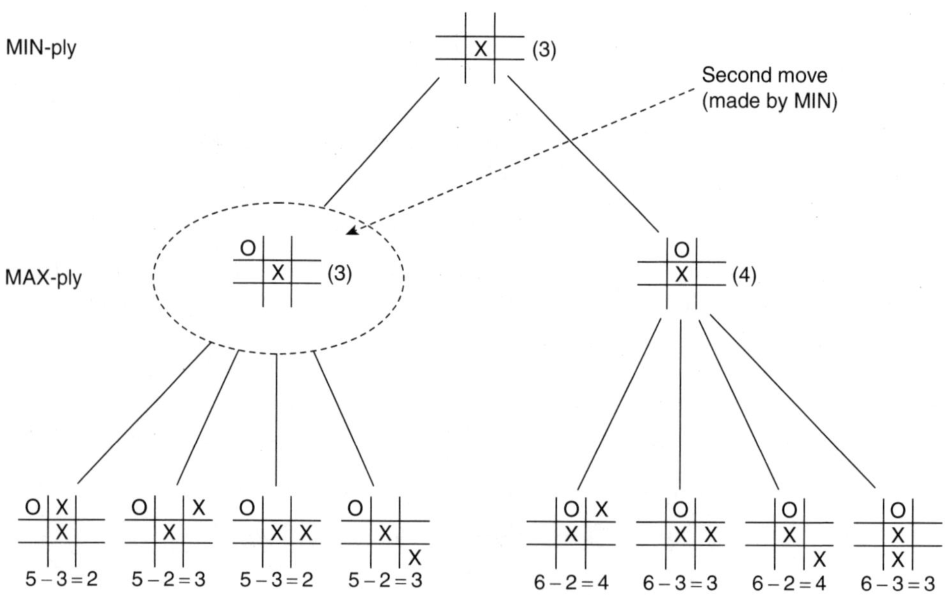

Fig. 11.106. *Second move of tic-tac-toe by MIN player applying 2-ply Mini-Max.*

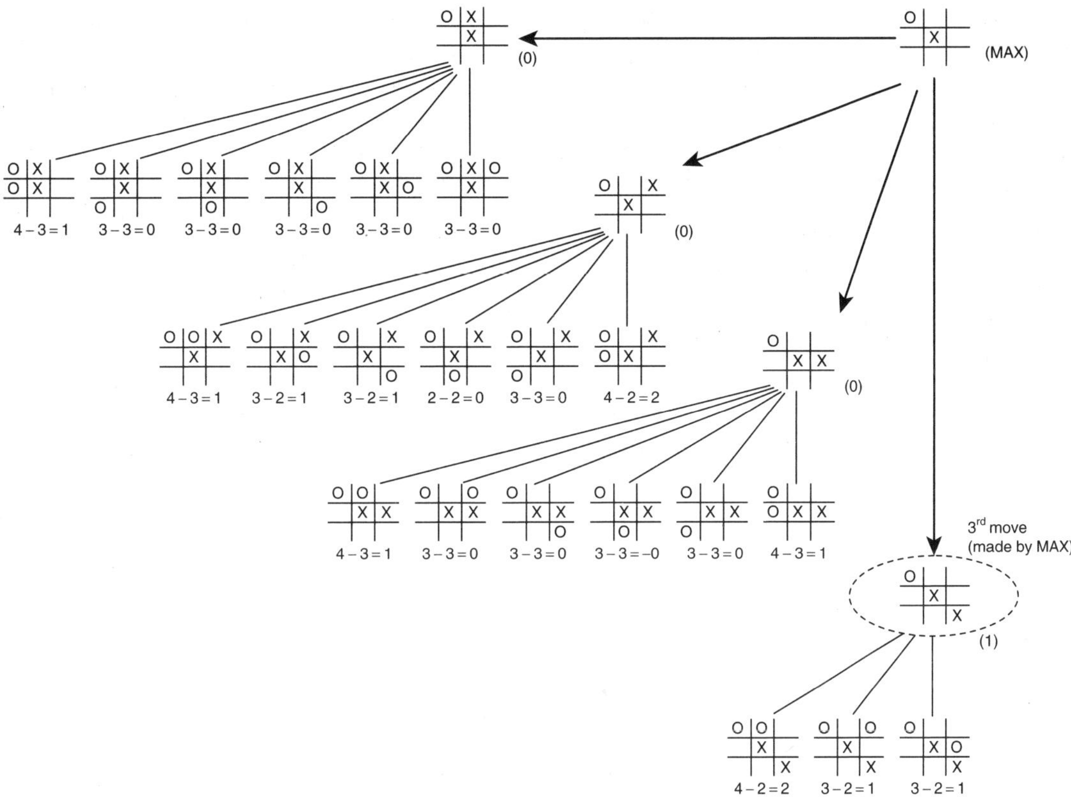

Fig. 11.107. *Third move of tic-tac-toe by MAX player applying 2-ply Mini-Max.*

Problem 11.9 (*Applying constraint satisfaction to solve crossword puzzle*) Crossword puzzles are excellent examples of constraint-satisfaction problems. The basic requirement of a crossword puzzle is words that cross each other must have the same letters in the locations where they cross. A simple crossword puzzle is given in Fig. 11.108. Five words are to be fitted in a 4×5 array. The words are to be chosen from the set { *COW*, *FOX*, *FROG*, *GOAT*, *RAT* }. The cells of the array that should not contain any letter are marked by a cross (×). The cells where the words should begin are indicated by the numbers 1, 2, 3, and 4. The cells marked by the numbers 1, 2 and 3 has to begin words across the array and the cells marked by 1 and 4 must begin words in downward direction. Formulate the problem as a CSP and solve it in appropriate manner.

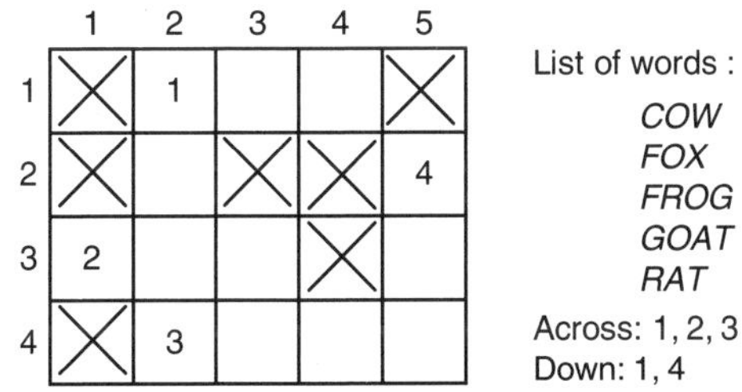

Fig. 11.108. *A crossword puzzle.*

Solution 11.9 Let A_1, A_2 and A_3 be the variables corresponding to the words starting at cells marked 1, 2 and 3, respectively across the rows of the array and D_1, D_4 be variables for the words starting at cells marked 1 and 4 in the downward direction. Among these variables A_1, A_2 and D_4 refer to three-letter words and A_3 and D_1 are four-letter words. If we adopt the conventional array notation then the constraint that the first letter of A_1 is identical to the first letter of D_1 also can be expressed as $A_1[0] = D_1[0]$. Considering these, the given crossword puzzle can be formulated as a CSP in the following way:

CSP formulation

1. Variables: A_1, A_2, A_3, D_1, D_4
2. Domains: $D(A_1) = \{COW, FOX, RAT\}$
   $D(A_2) = \{COW, FOX, RAT\}$
   $D(A_3) = \{FROG, GOAT\}$
   $D(D_1) = \{FROG, GOAT\}$
   $D(D_4) = \{COW, FOX, RAT\}$
3. Constraints: C_1 $A_1[0] = D_1[0]$
   C_2 $A_2[1] = D_1[2]$
   C_3 $A_3[0] = D_1[3]$
   C_4 $A_3[3] = D_4[2]$

Table 11.13 shows the details of the variables, the starting cells and the domains.

Table 11.13. *Details of the variables*

Variable (x_i)	Starting cell	Domain (D_i)
A_1	1	{COW, FOX, RAT}
A_2	2	{COW, FOX, RAT}
A_3	3	{FROG, GOAT}
D_1	1	{FROG, GOAT}
D_4	4	{COW, FOX, RAT}

The constraint graph is shown in Fig. 11.109.

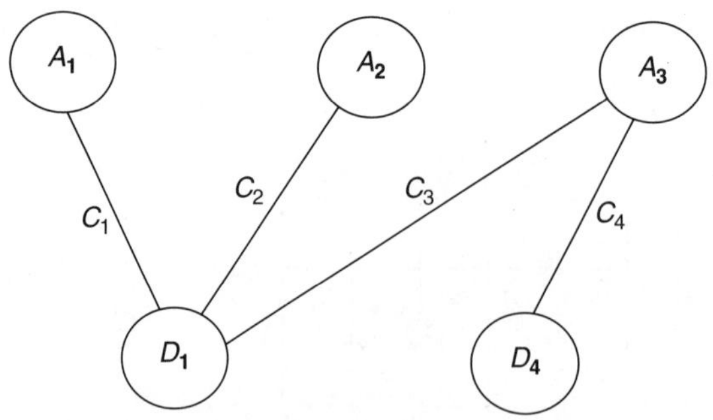

Fig. 11.109. *Constraint graph for the crossword puzzle.*

The step-by-step execution trace of the backtracking DFS for the problem is shown in Table 11.14. The columns of Table 11.14 contain the current domains of the variables. A value that has been assigned to a variable is shown inside an oval. For example, in the second row of the table (Step 1) the value *GOAT* in the column marked for the variable D_1 is inside an oval. This represents the assignment $\langle D_1, FROG\rangle$. The shaded ovals indicate the latest assignment made in the current step. Initially at Step 0 the state of the problem corresponds to the null assignment and all the domains are in their full capacities. The progress of the algorithm during the subsequent steps is described below.

Table 11.14. *Trace of backtracking DFS for crossword puzzle*

Step #	A_1	A_2	A_3	D_1	D_4
Step 0.	*COW, FOX, RAT*	*COW, FOX, RAT*	*GOAT, FROG*	*GOAT, FROG*	*COW, FOX, RAT*
Step 1. **D_1 ← GOAT**	*COW, FOX, RAT*	*COW, FOX, RAT*	*FROG*	(*GOAT*)	*COW, FOX, RAT*
Step 2. **A_3 ← FROG**	*COW, FOX, RAT*	*COW, FOX, RAT*	(*FROG*)	(*GOAT*)	*COW, FOX, RAT*
			$A_3[0] \neq D_1[3]$ Back track to Step2		
Step 3. **D_1 ← FROG**	*COW, FOX, RAT*	*COW, FOX, RAT*	*GOAT*	(*FROG*)	*COW, FOX, RAT*
Step 4. **A_3 ← GOAT**	*COW, FOX, RAT*	*COW, FOX, RAT*	(*GOAT*)	(*FROG*)	*COW, FOX, RAT*
Step 5. **A_1 ← COW**	(*COW*)	*FOX, RAT*	(*GOAT*)	(*FROG*)	*FOX, RAT*
	$A_1[0] \neq D_1[0]$ Back track				
Step 6. **A_1 ← FOX**	(*FOX*)	*COW, RAT*	(*GOAT*)	(*FROG*)	*COW, RAT*
Step 7. **A_2 ← COW**	(*FOX*)	(*COW*)	(*GOAT*)	(*FROG*)	*RAT*
Step 8. **D_4 ← RAT**	(*FOX*)	(*COW*)	(*GOAT*)	(*FROG*)	(*RAT*)

Solution: {⟨A_1, FOX⟩,⟨A_2, COW⟩,⟨A_3, GOAT⟩,⟨D_1, FROG⟩,⟨D_4, RAT⟩**}**

Step 1. To select the first variable for assignment of a value we first apply the MRV heuristic and find that both D_1 and A_3 are the candidates. To resolve the tie we apply the degree heuristic and find that D_1 is the candidate as it is involved with the highest number of variables (3) through constraints. Hence we select D_1 for assignment at this stage. Now, the current domain of D_1 is {*FROG*, *GOAT*}. Among these candidates the value *GOAT* is selected for D_1. Hence the assignment is now $\{\langle D_1, GOAT\rangle\}$. This assignment immediately removes the value *GOAT* from other domains. However, as $D(A_3) = \{FROG, GOAT\}$ is the only other domain containing *GOAT* as a member. Therefore $D(A_3)$ reduces to $\{FROG\}$ after this step.

Step 2. As A_3 has minimum number of remaining values, just one – *FROG*, it is the candidate for next assignment and we assign $\langle A_3, FROG\rangle$ making the current assignment state as $\{\langle A_3, FROG\rangle, \langle D_1, GOAT\rangle\}$. However, this assignment violates the constraint $A_3[0] = D_1[3]$ because in this case $A_3[0] = F$ and $D_1[3] = T$. Since A_3 does not have any other value to try, we have to reject this assignment and backtrack to step 1.

Step 3. We retrieve the assigned value of D_1 and try with the other alternative, i.e., *FROG*. Hence the state of the problem becomes $\{\langle D_1, FROG\rangle\}$. This assignment reduces the domain of A_3 to a single value $D(A_3) = \{GOAT\}$.

Step 4. A_3 is given the value *GOAT*. Now the constraint $A_3[0] = D_1[3]$ is satisfied because both $A_3[0]$ and $D_1[3]$ are now *G*. The assignment state is $\{\langle A_3, GOAT\rangle, \langle D_1, FROG\rangle\}$.

Step 5. A_1 is selected for the next assignment and we assign $\langle A_1, COW\rangle$. Accordingly *COW* is eliminated from both $D(A_2)$ and $D(D_4)$. But this assignment $\langle A_1, COW\rangle$ violates the constraint $C_1 : A_1[0] = D_1[0]$. Therefore we have to reject it and backtrack. This is done in Step 6 where we try with $A_1 \leftarrow FOX$ and this turns out to be the right choice.

The rest of the process as depicted in Table 11.14 is self-explanatory. Ultimately we get the solution $\{\langle A_1, FOX\rangle, \langle A_2, COW\rangle, \langle A_3, GOAT\rangle, \langle D_1, FROG\rangle, \langle D_4, RAT\rangle$. The solved crossword puzzle is shown in Fig. 11.110.

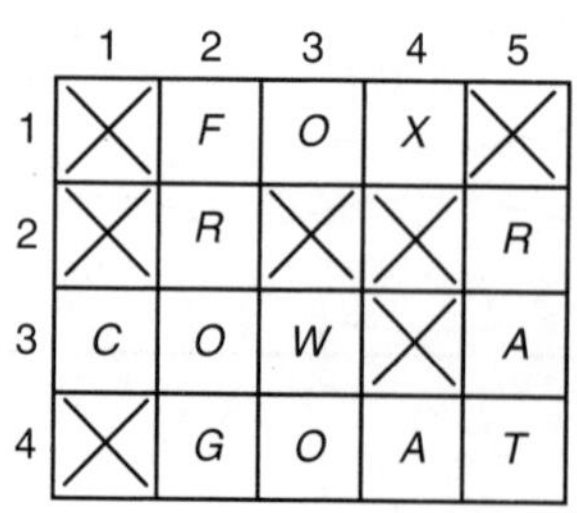

$\{\langle A_1, FOX\rangle, \langle A_2, COW\rangle, \langle A_3, GOAT\rangle, \langle D_1, FROG\rangle, \langle D_4, RAT\rangle\}$

Fig. 11.110. *Solution of the crossword puzzle.*

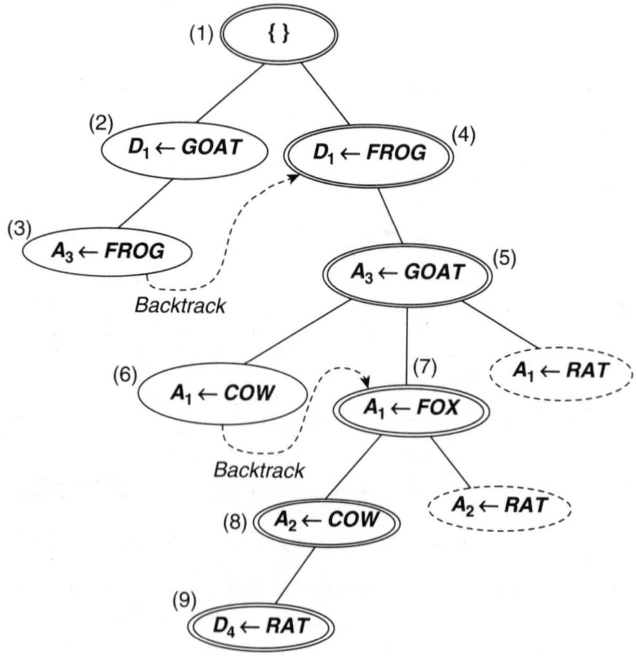

Fig. 11.111. *Solution tree for the crossword puzzle under backtracking DFS strategy.*

Fig. 11.111 represents the solution tree where the backtracking paths are indicated with dotted lines. The numbers in the parentheses give the sequence in which the nodes are explored.

Problem 11.10 (*Applying constraint satisfaction to solve cryptarithmetic puzzle*) Cryptarithmetic puzzles are typical CSPs with general constraints. Consider the following cryptarithmetic problem:

$$\begin{array}{r} O\,N\,E \\ +\;O\,N\,E \\ \hline T\,W\,O \\ \hline \end{array}$$

It is required to find values (taken from the set of 10 digits {0, 1, 2, 3, 4, 5, 6, 7, 8, 9} for the letters *E, N, O, T* and *W* such that their substitution into the above scheme results in a valid addition. Moreover, all the values of *E, N, O, T* and *W* should be different. Formulate the problem as a CSP and solve it.

Solution 11.10 First we present the CSP formulation then work for a solution to the formulated CSP. In this case, apart from the five variables *E, N, O, T* and *W* directly involved with the CSP we need to consider two more variables, say X_1 and X_2, corresponding to the two carries of addition. Let X_1 be the carry produced by adding the digits at the unit place and X_1 be the same for the 10's place. As it is seen from the scheme the last addition does not produce any carry.

CSP formulation

1. Variables: E, N, O, T, W
   Auxilary Variables: X_1, X_2
2. Domains: $D(E) = D(N) = D(O) = D(T) = D(W)$
   $= \{0, 1, 2, 3, 4, 5, 6, 7, 8, 9\}$,
   $D(X_1) = D(X_2) = \{0, 1\}$
3. Constraints:
   C_1: $E \neq N \neq O \neq T \neq W$
   C_2: $E + E = O + 10 \times X_1$
   C_3: $N + N + X_1 = W + 10 \times X_2$
   C_4: $O + O + X_2 = T$

As the constraints are general in nature, i.e., they involve more than two variables, we should have a constraint *constraint hypergraph* and not just a constraint graph. This hypergraph is shown in Fig. 11.112. Now we go for the solution. The trace of the solution process is depicted in Table 11.15. Successive steps described below.

Step 1. Applying the MRV heuristic, we identify X_1 or X_2 as the probable candidates for the first assignment of value. To resolve the tie, let us apply the degree heuristic. However, the degree heuristic does not help much because both the variables happen to be involved with 5 other variables through constraints (see Fig. 11.112). Therefore we resolve the tie arbitrarily and make the assignment $X_1 \leftarrow 0$. However this assignment has its implications on the domains of the other variables. Let us see how. If $X_1 = 0$ then according to constraint C_2 we have $E + E = O + 10 \times 0 = O$. As $2 \times E = O$, O must be an even digit. This makes $D(O) = \{0, 2, 4, 6, 8\}$. However, O can not be 0 because in that case E is also 0 and we would have $E = O$ which violates constraint C_1. Therefore 0 is eliminated from $D(O)$ to obtain $D(O) = \{2, 4, 6, 8\}$. In Table 11.15 this is shown in a sub-row demarked with dotted lines within the row for Step 1. Now as $2 \times E = O$, i.e., $E = O/2$, domain of E is reduced to $D(E) = \{1, 2, 3, 4\}$. Let us now focus on constraint C_4: $O + O + X_2 = T$. If $X_2 = 0$ then T can be either

4, or 8 depending on whether O is 2, or 4. Similarly, if $X_2 = 1$ then $T = 5$, or 9. The fact that T is a single digit eliminates 6 and 8 from the domain of O which in turn removes 3 and 4 from $D(E)$. Hence ultimately we get $D(E) = \{1, 2\}$, $D(O) = \{2, 4\}$, and $D(T) = \{4, 5, 8, 9\}$. All these are shown in the sub-rows within the row for Step 1 in Table 11.15.

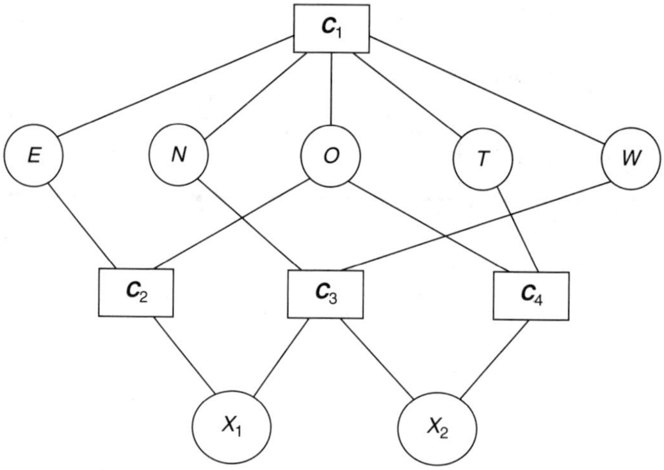

Fig. 11.112. *Hypergraph for the cryptarithmetic puzzle.*

Step 2. At the end of the first step the problem state is $\{\langle X_1, 0\rangle\}$ and the domains of the unassigned variables are $D(E) = \{1, 2\}$, $D(O) = \{2, 4\}$, $D(T) = \{4, 5, 8, 9\}$, $D(N) = D(W) = \{1\text{-}9\}$, and $D(X_2) = \{0,1\}$. The MRV heuristic offers three candidates, *viz.*, E, O and X_2, for assigning a value in the second step. The tie should be resolved through the degree heuristic. Now, consulting the hypergraph of Fig. 11.112 it is seen that the variables E, O and X_2 are involved with 4, 5 and 4 number of yet unassigned variables through the constraints. Therefore O is selected. The candidate values 2 and 4 have the same effect on the domains of other related variables. Hence we arbitrarily choose $O \leftarrow 2$. This immediately removes 2 from all other domains and 8 and 9 from the domain of T by virtue of constraint C_4. Hence the state of the problem at the end of Step 2 is $\{\langle O, 2\rangle, \langle X_1, 0\rangle\}$.

Step 3. At this point E has only one legal value left in its domain, and all other unassigned variables have more that one values in their domains. Hence the assignment $E \leftarrow 1$ is made resulting in the state $\{\langle E, 1\rangle, \langle O, 2\rangle, \langle X_1, 0\rangle\}$. The value of 1 is removed from all other domains, except X_2.

The rest of the steps can be traced similarly. Table 11.15 depicts the entire process.At each step the assignment made is highlighted with boldfaces. The blank cells indicate that the domains of the corresponding variables have remained unchanged.

Table 11.15. *Trace of backtracking DFS for cryptarithmetic puzzle*

	E	N	O	T	W	X_1	X_2
Step 0:	{0-9}	{0-9}	{0-9}	{0-9}	{0-9}	{0, 1}	{0, 1}

(continued)

Table 11.15. *Continued*

	E	N	O	T	W	X_1	X_2
Step 1:						$\mathbf{X_1 \leftarrow 0}$	
$\mathbf{X_1 \leftarrow 0}$			{2, 4, 6, 8}				
	{1, 2, 3, 4}			{4, 5, 8, 9}			
			{2, 4}				
	{1, 2}						
Step 2:	{1, 2}	{0–9}	$\mathbf{O \leftarrow 2}$	{4, 5, 8, 9}	{0–9}	$\langle X_1, 0\rangle$	{0, 1}
$\mathbf{O \leftarrow 2}$	{1}	{0–1, 3–9}		{4, 5}	{0–1, 3–9}		
Step 3:	$E \leftarrow 1$	{0–1, 3–9}	$\langle O, 2\rangle$	{4, 5}	{0–1, 3–9}	$\langle X_1, 0\rangle$	{0, 1}
$\mathbf{E \leftarrow 1}$		{0, 3–9}			{0, 3–9}		
Step 4:	$\langle E, 1\rangle$	{0, 3–9}	$\langle O, 2\rangle$	{4, 5}	{0, 3–9}	$\langle X_1, 0\rangle$	$\mathbf{X_2 \leftarrow 0}$
$\mathbf{X_2 \leftarrow 0}$				{4}			
		{0, 3}			{0, 6}		
Step 5:	$\langle E, 1\rangle$	{0, 3}	$\langle O, 2\rangle$	$\mathbf{T \leftarrow 4}$	{0, 6}	$\langle X_1, 0\rangle$	$\langle X_2, 0\rangle$
$\mathbf{T \leftarrow 4}$							
Step 6:	$\langle E, 1\rangle$	$\mathbf{N \leftarrow 0}$	$\langle O, 2\rangle$	$\langle T, 4\rangle$	{0, 6}	$\langle X_1, 0\rangle$	$\langle X_2, 0\rangle$
$\mathbf{N \leftarrow 0}$					{6} (C_3 violated. Backtrack)		
Step 7:	$\langle E, 1\rangle$	$\mathbf{N \leftarrow 3}$	$\langle O, 2\rangle$	$\langle T, 4\rangle$	{0, 6}	$\langle X_1, 0\rangle$	$\langle X_2, 0\rangle$
$\mathbf{N \leftarrow 3}$					{6}		
Step 8:	$\langle E, 1\rangle$	$\langle N, 3\rangle$	$\langle O, 2\rangle$	$\langle T, 4\rangle$	$\mathbf{W \leftarrow 6}$	$\langle X_1, 0\rangle$	$\langle X_2, 0\rangle$
$\mathbf{W \leftarrow 6}$							
Solution : {⟨E, 1⟩,⟨N, 3⟩,⟨O, 2⟩,⟨T, 4⟩,⟨W, 6⟩}							

Substituting these values into the given puzzle we get the following consistent solution. Obviously, the solution is not unique. Different solutions may be obtained by assigning different values to variables, wherever applicable.

$$\begin{array}{r} 2\,3\,1 \\ \underline{2\,3\,1} \\ 4\,6\,2 \end{array}$$

Problem 11.11 (*Transformation of propositional logic formulae through means-ends analysis*) Propositional logic formulae are converted from one form to other using standard rules, *e.g.*, *commutative* law, *associative* law, *distributive* law, *De Morgan's* law etc.Propose a Means-Ends Analysis system to automate such transformation and apply it to transform the formula $(P \rightarrow Q) \wedge (P \rightarrow R)$ to $(R \wedge Q) \vee \neg P$.

Solution 11.11 Equivalent propositional formulae may structurally differ in many ways. For example the formulae $A \wedge B$ and $B \wedge A$ differ in their relative positions. This difference can be removed by applying the commutative law. Similarly, the distributive law which states that $(P \vee Q) \wedge (P \vee R) = P \vee (Q \wedge R)$ can be applied to reduce the difference between the number of occurrences of a variable. Table 11.16 presents some of the fundamental operations, or rules, that can be used to reduce various such differences between an intermediate formula and a goal formula. The table indicates the pre-conditions as well as the post-conditions corresponding to these operations.

Table 11.16. *Difference Table for Transformation of Logical Formulae*

Difference	Operator	Precondition	Postcondition
Presence / absence of the implication sign (→)	*remove implication*	P→Q	¬P∨Q
Relative positions of the variables	*commutative law*	*i)* P∨Q	Q∨P
		ii) P∧Q	Q∧P
Number of occurrences of the variables	*distributive law*	*i)* (P∨Q)∧(P∨R)	P∨(Q∧R)
		ii) (P∧Q)∨(P∧R)	P∧(Q∨R)
		iii) (P∨(Q∧R)	(P∨Q)∧(P∨R)
		iv) P∧(Q∨R)	(P∧Q)∨(P∧R)
Presence / absence of parenthesis	*De-Morgan's law*	*i)* ¬(P∨Q)	¬P∧¬Q
		ii) ¬(P∧Q)	¬P∨¬Q
		iii) ¬P∧¬Q	¬(P∨Q)
		iv) ¬P∨¬Q	¬(P∧Q)

Fig. 11.113 (*a*) - (*b*) and Fig. 11.114 (*a*) - (c) together show the trace of an MEA process applied to the given formulae. Let the starting formula $(P \rightarrow Q) \wedge (P \rightarrow R)$ be denoted as the initial state S_i and the final form $(R \wedge Q) \vee \neg P$ as S_g, the goal state. S_i and S_g involve 3 variables P, Q and R. These variables have occurred a total of 4 times in S_i and 3 times in S_g.

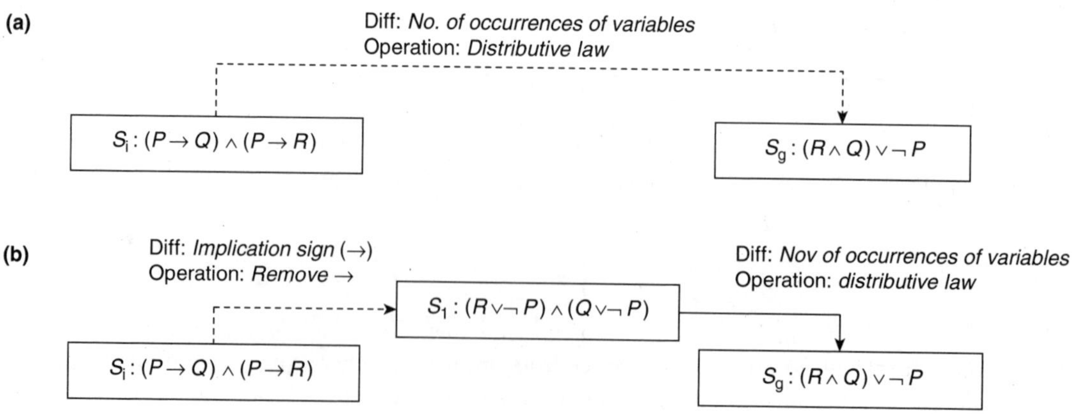

Fig. 11.113 *(a)–(b). First two steps*

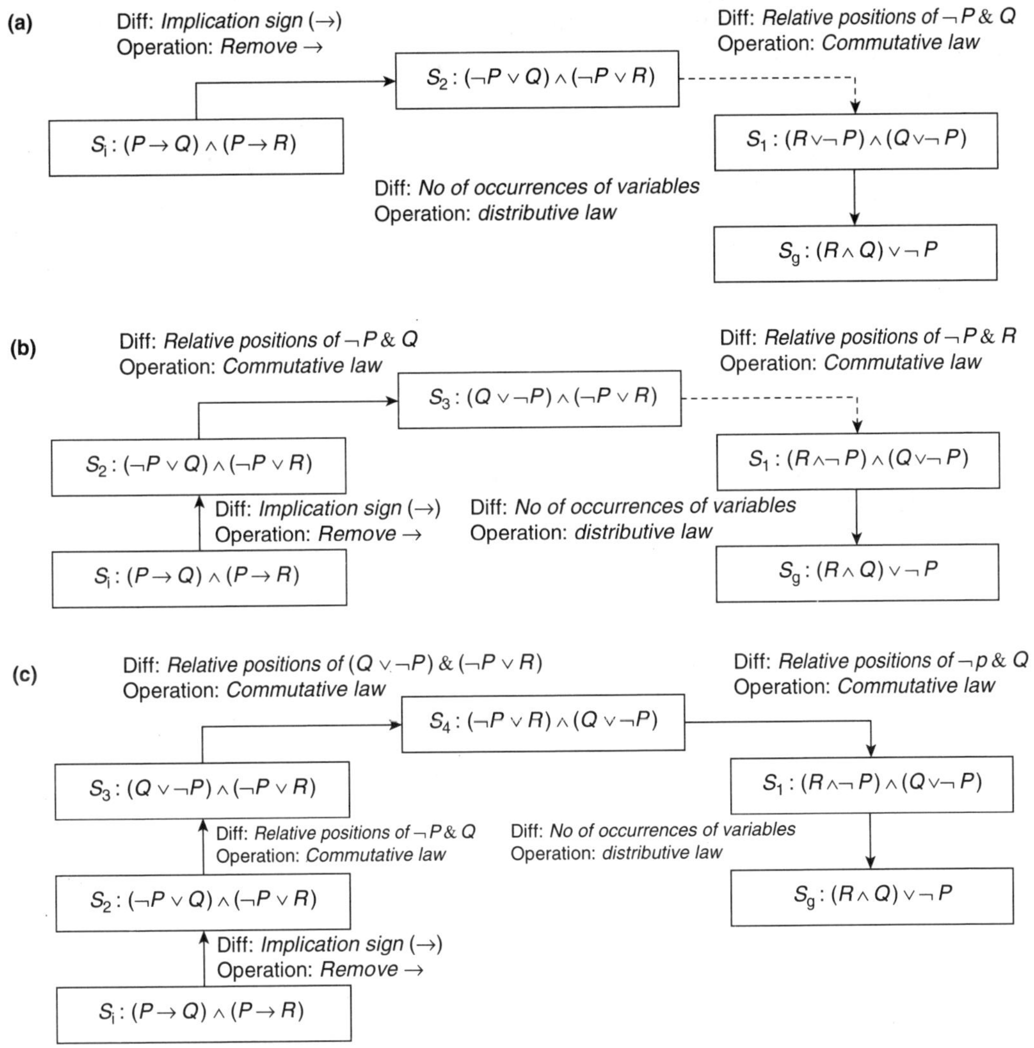

Fig. 11.114. *(a)–(c) Last three steps*

Let us suppose that the systems presently considers this to be the most important difference and identifies, with the help of the Difference-operator table, the distributive law $(P\vee Q)\wedge(P\vee R) = P\vee(Q\wedge R)$ as the appropriate operation for reducing the said difference. Moreover, consulting the pre-condition *vis-à-vis* the structure of the goal $S_g = (R\wedge Q)\vee\neg P$ the system creates a sub-goal S_1: $(R\vee\neg P)\wedge(Q\vee\neg P)$. These two steps are shown in Fig. 11.113 (*a*) - (*b*). The solid and the dashed arrows depict differences already addressed and differences yet to be addressed, respectively.

To reduce the gap between S_i and S_1, the system considers the main difference to be the presence and absence of the implication (→) sign in the respective formula, i.e., S_i and S_1. Therefore the operation to be applied is *remove implication* with the help of the rule $P\rightarrow Q = \neg P\vee Q$. The rest of the trace is given in Fig. 11.114 (*a*)–(*c*). The generated plan of actions as well as the gradual transformation of the formulae from the initial state to the goal state resulting from the application of these operations is shown in Fig. 11.115.

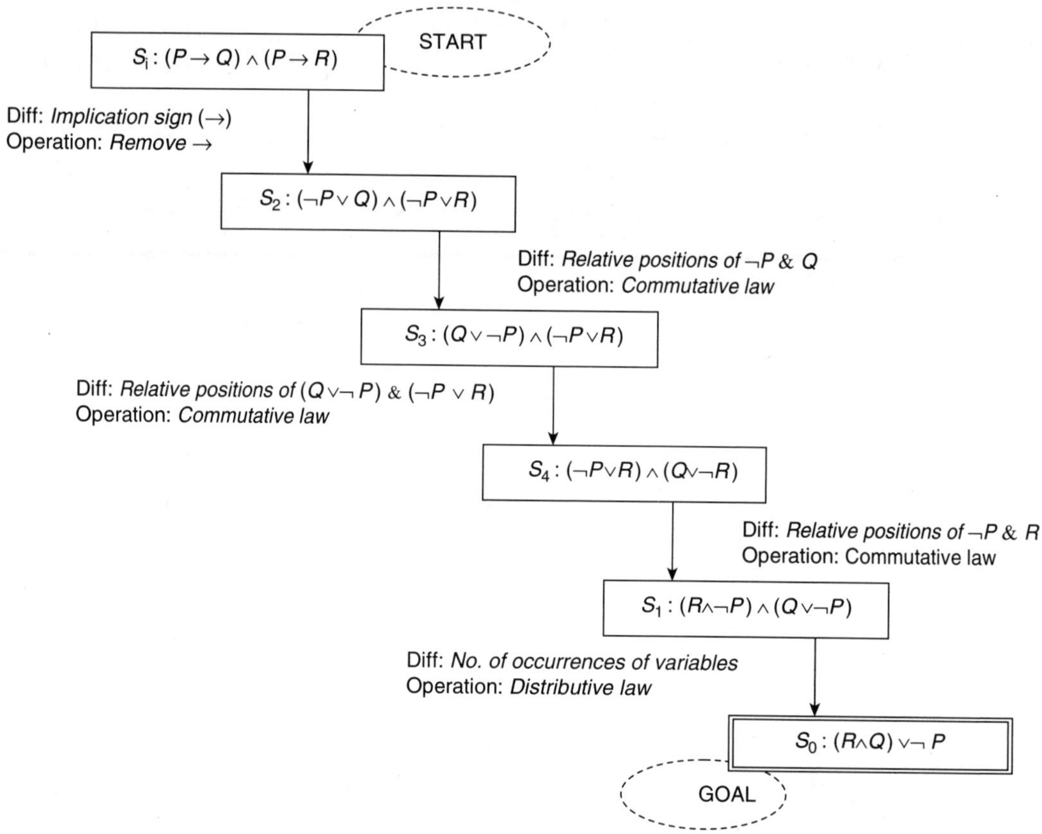

Fig. 11.115. *Plan generated through the MEA process for transformation of predicate logic formulae*

Problem 11.12 (*Solving the Monkey-and-Banana Problem applying means-ends analysis*) Consider the simple world of a monkey. There is a room with a door and a window. A box is placed at the window and a bunch of bananas is hanging from the ceiling at the middle of the room. The monkey is hungry but it cannot get the bananas as these are out of its reach. However, if the box is placed at the middle of the room just below the bunch of bananas and the monkey climbs the top of the box then it can grab the bananas and eat them. The monkey can walk, can push the box along the floor, can climb on the top of the box, and if within its reach, it can grab the bananas. Initially the monkey is at the door of the room. Can it catch the bananas? If yes, what sequence of actions must be taken to achieve this goal? Propose a Means-Ends Analysis system to solve this problem.

Solution 11.12 There are four significant parameters to characterize a state of the given Monkey-and-Banana problem, ***viz.***, the position of the monkey, whether the monkey is on the floor or on the box, the position of the box, and whether the monkey is holding the banana or not. Hence, a state of the system can be expressed as a 4-tuple $< P, Q, R, S >$ where

P is the position of the monkey
Q is whether the monkey is on the floor or on the box
R is the position of the box
S is whether the monkey has grasped the banana or not.

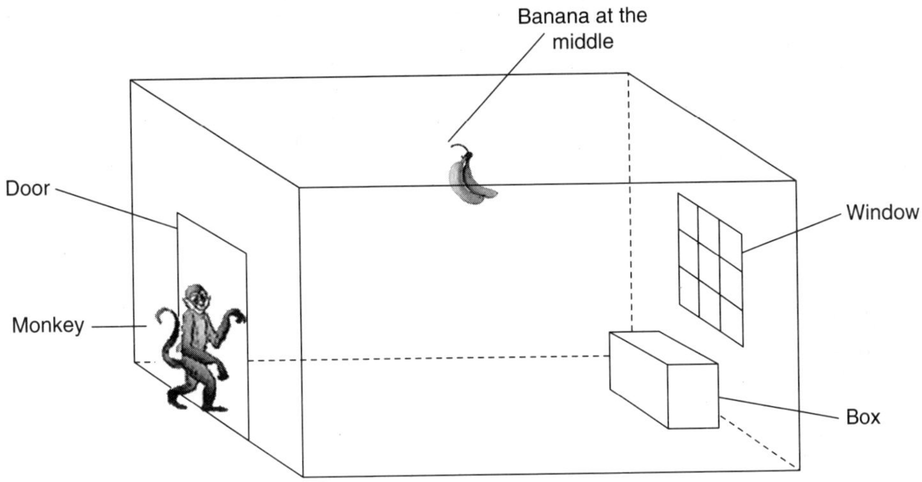

Initial State
P, i.e., position of monkey = *Door*
Q, i.e., whether the monkey is on the floor, or on the box = *Floor*
R, i.e., position of the box = *Window*
S, i.e., whether the monkey holds the banana or not = *No*

Fig. 11.116. *Initial state of the Monkey-and-Banana problem*

For the sake of simplicity we assume that the monkey can be either at the door, or at the window, or at the middle of the room. Similarly, the box can also be at one of these positions only. Hence the domains of *P*, *Q*, *R*, and *S* are defined as follows:

$P \in$ { *Door, Window, Middle* }
$Q \in$ { *Floor, Box* }
$R \in$ { *Door, Window, Middle* }
$S \in$ { *Yes, No* }

There are four activities of the monkey, *viz.*, it can *walk* from place to place, it can *push* the box from one place to another, it can *climb* the box, and if possible, it can *grab* the banana. However, each of these activities requires certain conditions to hold good. For example, in order to push the box from position *X* to position *Y* both the monkey and the box must be at position *X*. Moreover, the monkey should be on the floor to push the box. As a result of pushing the box from *X* to *Y* the monkey as well as the box will be at *Y*. The initial state of the system is < *Door, Floor, Window, No* > because in the beginning the monkey is at the door, on the floor, the box is at the window, and the monkey is not holding the banana. The final state is given by < *Middle, Box, Middle, Yes* >. Fig. 11.116 and Fig. 11.117 present the initial and the goal states of the given problem.

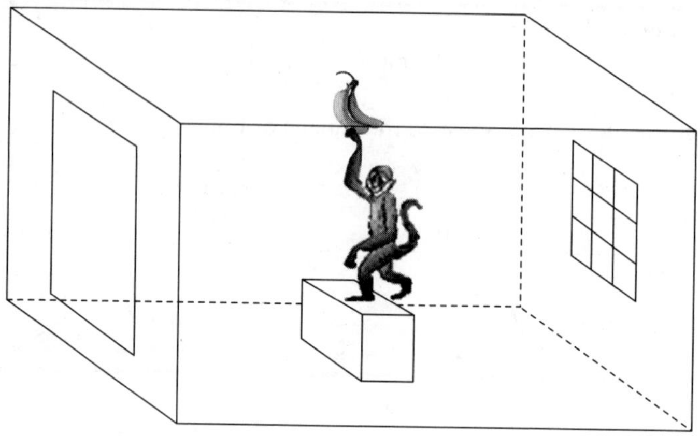

Goal State
P, position of monkey = *Middle*
Q, whether the monkey is in the floor, or on the box = *Box*
R, position of the box = *Middle*
S, whether the monkey holds the banana or not = *Yes*

Fig. 11.117. *Goal state of the Monkey-and-Banana problem*

Fig. 11.118 shows the Difference-Operator-Precondition table for this problem. Initially the system recognizes the most important difference between the start state and the goal state to be with respect to the status of the banana. Consulting the Difference-operator table it is found that the only operation capable of reducing this difference is *grab*().

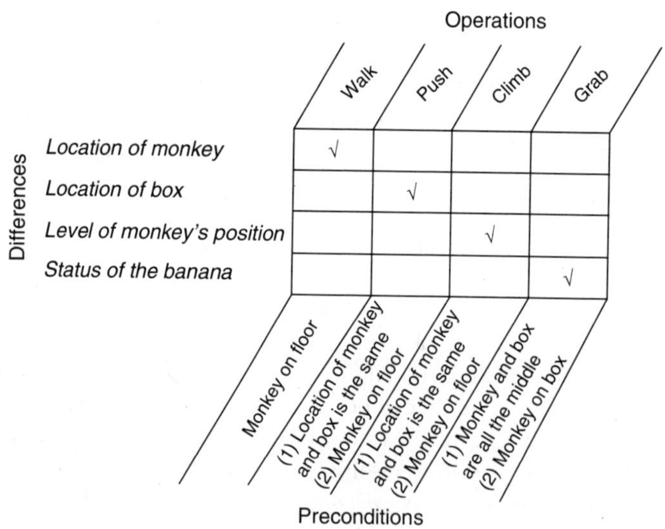

Fig. 11.118. *The Difference-Operator-Precondition table for the Monkey-and-Banana problem*

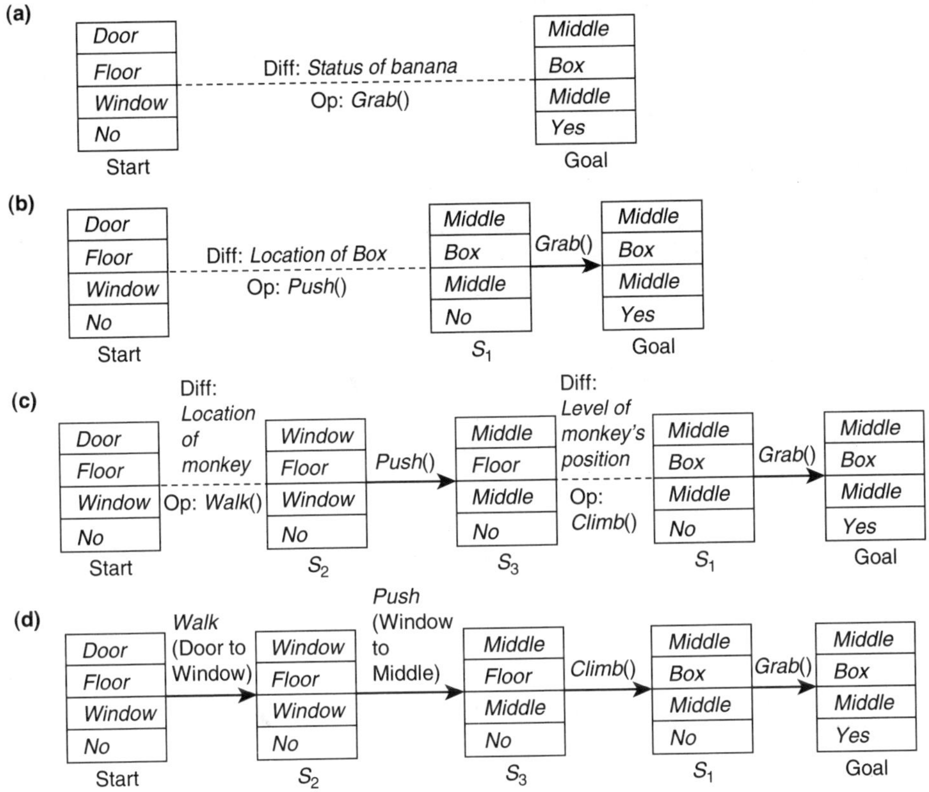

Fig. 11.119. *Solving the Monkey-and-Banana problem through Means-Ends Analysis*

However, in order to grab the banana both the monkey and the box should be in the middle and the monkey should be on the box. Therefore a sub-goal S_1 corresponding to such a state is created (see Fig. 11.119 (*a*) - (*b*)). As usual, the dashed lines represent the differences yet to be removed and the solid lines correspond to differences already addressed through appropriate operations.

The situation depicted in Fig. 11.119 (*c*) is noteworthy. The difference identified by the system between the start state and S_1 is *location of box* and the operation to remove that difference is *push* (see Fig. 11.119 (*b*)). However, application of the operation *push* results in creation of states S_2 and S_3 both of which are intermediate between the start state and S_1. Consequently, the gap between the start state and S_1 is fragmented into two gaps, *viz.*, one between the start state and S_2 and the other between S_3 and S_2. The operators employed to bridge these gaps are shown in Fig. 11.119 (*c*) - (*d*).

✓ TEST YOUR KNOWLEDGE

11.1 Which of the following search algorithm is not admissible?

a) Breadth-first search b) Depth-first search

c) A^* d) None of the above

11.2 For an ideal search process the *penetrance* P attains the value
a) 0 b) 0.5
c) 1 d) None of the above

11.3 Let P be the *penetrance* and B be the *effective branching factor* of an A* search. Then which of the following is true?
a) $P \leq 1$ and $B \leq 1$ b) $P \leq 1$ and $B \geq 1$
c) $P \geq 1$ and $B \leq 1$ d) $P \geq 1$ and $B \geq 1$

11.4 Let P be the *penetrance* and B be the *effective branching factor* of an A* search. Which of the following is true for an ideal A* search?
a) $P = 1$ and $B = 1$ b) $P = 1$ and $B \neq 1$
c) $P \neq 1$ and $B = 1$ d) $P \neq 1$ and $B \neq 1$

11.5 Let A_1 and A_2 be two A^* algorithms using the heuristic estimation functions h_1 and h_2 such that A_2 is more informed than A_1. Then for any node n of the search space which of the following holds good?
a) $h_1(n) \leq h_2(n)$ b) $h_2(n) \leq h_1(n)$
c) $h_1(n) \neq h_2(n)$ d) None of the above

11.6 If there exists a goal in the state space, an A^* algorithms will not terminate if
a) The state space is infinite b) The state space contains cycles
c) The state space is not fully connected d) None of the above

11.7 In which of the following situations, an A^* algorithms fails to return an optimal path from the start state to a goal state?
a) The state space is infinite b) The state space contains cycles
c) The state space is not fully connected d) None of the above

11.8 Which of the following may not be true for a state space?
a) It has many goals states b) It has no goal state
c) It has some start state d) None of the above

11.9 Which of the following is not an *exhaustive* search?
a) Depth-first search b) Breadth-first search
c) Best-first search d) None of the above

11.10 The possibility of reaching a goal by a depth-first search is high if the state space has
a) Only a few goal states b) Many goal states
c) No goal state d) None of the above

11.11 Which of the following is not an informed search?
a) A-algorithm b) A*-algorithm
c) Best-first search d) None of the above

11.12 Which of the following is not an un-informed search?
a) Depth-first search b) Breadth-first search
c) Bidirectional d) None of the above

11.13 Let A_1 and A_2 be two A^* algorithms using the heuristic estimation functions h_1 and h_2 such that for any node n of the search space $h_1(n) \geq h_2(n)$. Then which among A_1 and A_2 will explore more nodes?
a) A_1 b) A_2
c) Uncertain d) None of the above

11.14 Which of the following search procedures is not applicable when there are multiple goal states?
a) Bidirectional b) Iterative deepening
c) Depth-first d) None of the above

11.15 Which of the following search procedures has best time complexity?
a) Breadth-first
b) Iterative deepening
c) Depth-first
d) Bidirectional

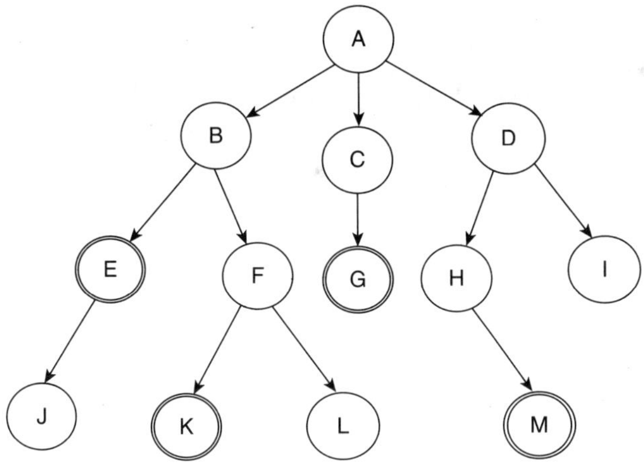

Fig. 11.120

11.16 Fig. 11.120 shows a state space with a number of goal states and the start state A. Which of the following search strategies is the most appropriate for such a state space?
a) Breadth-first
b) Depth-first
c) Either (*a*) or (*b*)
d) None of the above

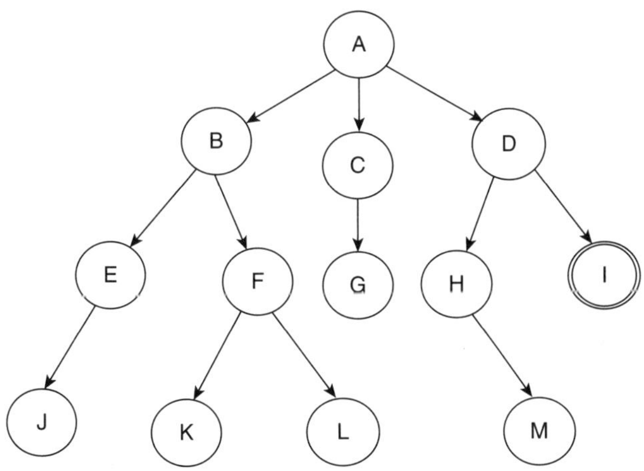

Fig. 11.121

11.17 Fig. 11.121 shows a state space with a single goal state I and the start state A. Which of the following search strategies is the most appropriate for such a state space?
a) Breadth-first
b) Depth-first
c) Either (*a*) or (*b*)
d) None of the above

11.18 Fig. 11.122 shows a state space with estimated costs attached to each state. Which set of states will remain open after the node marked B is expanded?

a) {A,B,C,D,E,F,G}
b) {E,F,G}
c) {D,E,F,G}
d) {E,F,G,H,I}

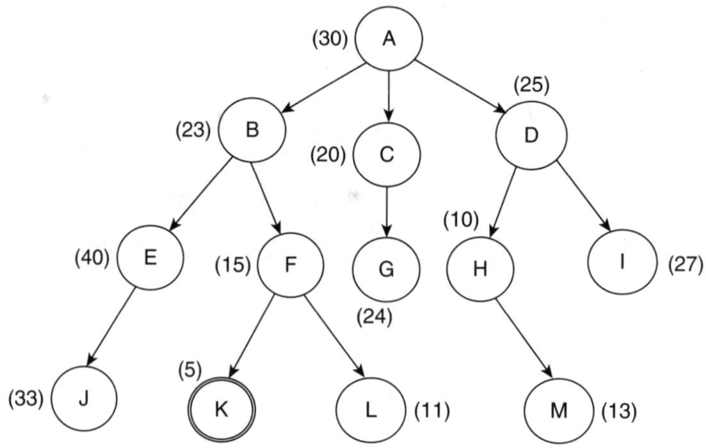

Fig. 11.122. *A state space with estimated costs of each state*

11.19 Fig. 11.122 shows a state space with estimated costs attached to each state. Which of the following states will be explored and expanded after B?
a) C
b) H
c) F
d) L

11.20 Fig. 11.122 shows a state space with estimated costs attached to each state. How many nodes will remain in the OPEN queue after reaching the goal state?
a) 1
b) 2
c) 3
d) 4

11.21 Which of the following describes hill climbing strategy best?
a) It is a local search
b) It is adversarial search
c) It is an admissible search
d) None of the above

11.22 Which of the following is not true for a hill climbing search?
a) It uses an objective function
b) It employs heuristic knowledge
c) It solves optimization problems
d) None of the above

11.23 Which of the following may cause a hill climbing process to return a sub-optimal solution?
a) The state space is too large
b) There are local optima in the state space
c) The objective function is not appropriate
d) None of the above

11.24 Among the following, whose existence within the state space does not hinder a hill climbing process in its progress towards the global optimum?
a) Plateaux
b) Local optima
c) Ridges
d) None of the above

11.25 Between regular hill climbing and steepest ascent hill climbing, which one is likely to return a better solution?
a) Regular hill climbing b) Steepest ascent hill climbing
c) Uncertain d) None of the above

11.26 Between regular hill climbing and steepest ascent hill climbing, which one is more likely to get stuck in a local optima?
a) Regular hill climbing b) Steepest ascent hill climbing
c) Uncertain d) None of the above

11.27 Which of the following problems is not suitable for hill climbing as a solution strategy?
a) Traveling salesperson b) 8-queen
c) CNF satisfiability d) None of the above

11.28 Which of the following structures in a state space may consist of a number of local optima?
a) Plateaux b) Ridges
c) Both (*a*) and (*b*) d) Neither (*a*) nor (*b*)

11.29 AND-OR graphs are suitable representations of problems that are
a) Irrevocable b) Decomposable
c) Intractable d) None of the above

11.30 Which of the following can be considered as a special case of AND-OR graphs?
a) State space b) Semantic networks
c) Both (*a*) and (*b*) d) None of the above

11.31 The sub-problems into which the problem corresponding to an AND-node of an AND-OR tree are decomposed should be
a) Independently solvable b) Further decomposable
c) Trivially solvable d) None of the above

11.32 In order to solve an OR node of an AND-OR graph we have to solve
a) Its parent node b) Any one of its successors
c) All of its successors d) None of the above

11.33 In order to solve an AND node of an AND-OR graph we have to solve
a) Its parent node b) Any one of its successors
c) All of its successors d) None of the above

11.34 Solution of a problem expressed as an AND-OR tree is represented by
a) A path b) A leaf node
c) The root node d) A sub-tree

11.35 In an AND-OR graph, the optimization criteria can be formulated by attaching costs/weights to the
a) Nodes b) Arcs
c) Both (*a*) and (*b*) d) None of the above

11.36 Let $h(n)$ be the value of the heuristic function at node n and $h_1(n)$ be the estimated value of $h(n)$. Which of the following conditions must be satisfied to make AO* algorithm admissible?
a) $h_1(n) \leq h(n)$ b) $h_1(n) \geq h(n)$
c) $h_1(n) \neq h(n)$ d) None of the above

11.37 In which of the following situations of AO* search a node is marked as FUTILE?
a) The estimated cost of the node becomes too high
b) The problem represented by the node is unsolvable

c) Either (*a*) or (*b*)
d) None of the above

11.38 Consider the partially created AND-OR graph of Fig. 11.123. Assuming a uniform cost of 1 for each link, which of the following nodes will be chosen for expansion in this situation?
a) x
b) y
c) z
d) None of the above

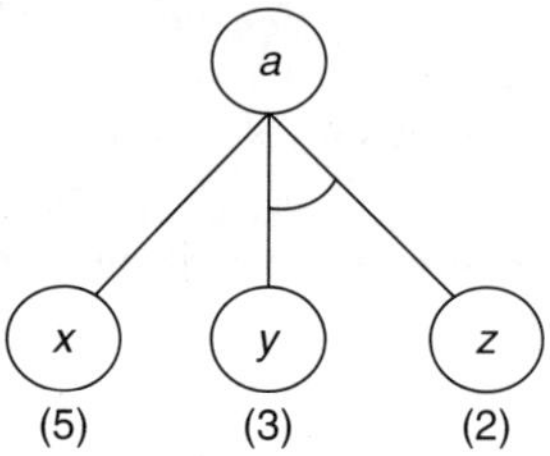

Fig. 11.123

11.39 Which of the following is a kind of best-first search?
a) A*
b) AO*
c) Both (*a*) and (*b*)
d) None of the above

11.40 Which of the following problems is neither *monotonic*, nor *partially commutative*?
a) Theorem proving
b) Chemical synthesis
c) Robot navigation
d) Playing a game of bridge

11.41 Which of the following problems is both *monotonic* and *partially commutative*?
a) Theorem proving
b) Chemical synthesis
c) Robot navigation
d) Playing a game of bridge

11.42 Which of the following is not a part of a AI *production system*?
a) Global Database
b) Production rules
c) Control strategy
d) None of the above

11.43 What kind of control system a *backtracking* control system is?
a) Irrevocable
b) Tentative
c) Both (*a*) and (*b*)
d) Neither (*a*) nor (*b*)

11.44 A *commutative* production system is one which is
a) Monotonic
b) Partially commutative
c) Both (*a*) and (*b*)
d) Neither (*a*) nor (*b*)

11.45 For a given problem, the way to decide which between BFS and DFS is more efficient is
a) By running BFS and DFS for the problem separately.
b) By analyzing the problem
c) By simulation
d) None of the above

11.46 Which among the following usually requires less memory ?
a) BFS
b) DFS
c) Undecidable
d) None of the above

11.47 Depth-first iterative deepening is a combination of
a) BFS and DFS
b) Best-first search and bidirectional search
c) A* search and AO* search
d) None of the above

11.48 Which among the following search techniques assumes the heuristic function as 0 for all nodes ?
a) BFS b) Branch and bound
c) Both (*a*) and (*b*) d) None of the above

11.49 Which of the following search techniques make use of AND-OR graphs ?
a) Branch and bound b) Problem reduction
c) Hill climbing d) None of the above

11.50 In state space search heuristic knowledge is employed to
a) improve the quality of the solution b) make the search faster
c) Both (*a*) and (*b*) d) None of the above

11.51 In which of the following problem solving strategies the path by which a solution is reached is irrelevant?
a) Means-Ends Analysis b) Minimax search
c) Constraint Satisfaction d) None of the above

11.52 Which of the following is not a *constraint satisfaction problem*?
a) Linear programming b) Graph colouring
c) 8-queen d) None of the above

11.53 In the context of *constraint satisfaction problems* which of the following statements is true?
a) All general constraints can be converted to binary constraints
b) All binary constraints can be converted to unary constraints
c) All general constraints can be converted to unary constraints
d) None of the above

11.54 Which of the following structures is used in a *constraint satisfaction problem* having constraints involving more than two variables?
a) Constraint graph b) Constraint hypergraph
c) Both (*a*) and (*b*) d) None of the above

11.55 Which of the following methods of solving a *constraint satisfaction problem* starts with an empty assignment and gradually proceeds towards a complete solution?
a) Backtracking DFS b) Min-conflict local search
c) Both (*a*) and (*b*) d) None of the above

11.56 Which of the following methods of solving a *constraint satisfaction problem* starts with a complete but inconsistent solution and then transforms it into a consistent complete solution?
a) Backtracking DFS b) Min-conflict local search
c) Both (*a*) and (*b*) d) None of the above

11.57 While solving a *constraint satisfaction problem* through backtracking DFS, which of the following is not used to select a variable for assignment?
a) Minimum remaining values heuristic b) Degree heuristic
c) Least constraining value heuristic d) None of the above

11.58 Which of the following methods of solving a *constraint satisfaction problem* involve constraint propagation?
a) Backtracking DFS b) Min-conflict local search
c) Both (*a*) and (*b*) d) None of the above

11.59 Consider the constraint hypergraph of Fig. 11.124. According to degree heuristic, which variable should be considered for assigning a value at the beginning of a backtracking DFS strategy?
a) *A* b) *B*

c) C

d) D

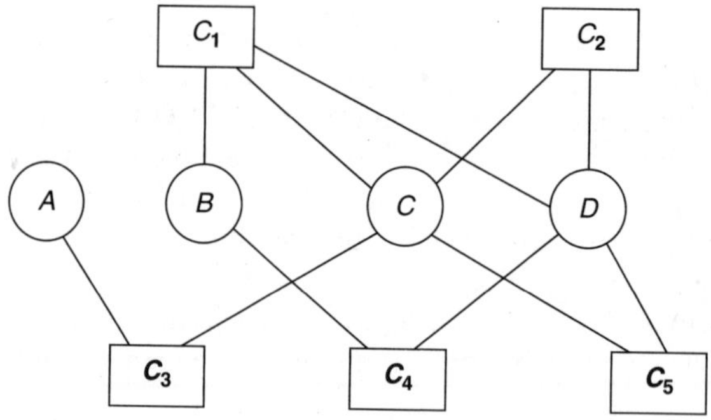

Fig. 11.124 *A constraint hypergraph*

11.60 Consider the constraint hypergraph of Fig. 11.124. Suppose that C has been assigned a value and the present domains for the remaining variables are as follows: $D(A) = \{v_1, v_2\}$, $D(B) = \{v_3, v_4, v_5\}$, $D(D) = \{v_6, v_8\}$.

a) A
b) B
c) D
d) None of the above

11.61 Which of the following kinds of problems is suitable for adversarial search?

a) Theorem proving
b) Game playing
c) Robot navigation
d) Language processing

11.62 Which of the following is an adversarial search procedure?

a) MiniMax procedure
b) Mean-Ends analysis
c) Constraint satisfaction
d) None of the above

11.63 In MiniMax search, *Alpha-Beta pruning* is used to

a) Limit the search to a fixed depth
b) Guide the search towards a goal
c) To avoid irrelevant parts of the game tree during search
d) None of the above

11.64 Which of the following is a technique to determine the depth to which MiniMax search should be conducted?

a) Alpha-Beta pruning
b) Waiting for quiescence
c) Secondary search
d) None of the above

11.65 The technique employed to avoid *horizon effect* in MiniMax search is

a) Alpha-Beta pruning
b) Waiting for quiescence
c) Secondary search
d) None of the above

11.66 Which of the following features of a depth-limited-MiniMax search embody heuristic knowledge to win the game?

a) Depth limit of search
b) Static evaluation function
c) Both (*a*) and (*b*)
d) None of the above

11.67 Fig. 53.16 presents a game tree showing the scores of the terminal nodes according to some static evaluation function. What is the Mini-Max value of node A?

a) $-\infty$
b) 0
c) 3
d) 5

11.68 On the basis of the game tree presented in Fig. 11.125, which node represents the best move for MAX in this turn?

a) B
b) C
c) D
d) None of the above

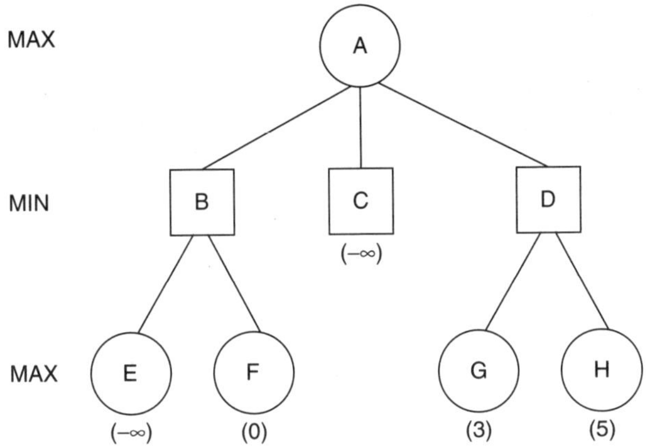

Fig. 11.125 *A game tree*

11.69 If the game tree presented in Fig. 11.125 is subject to Alpha-Beta pruning during a MiniMax search, which of the following nodes will be pruned?

a) E
b) F
c) G
d) H

11.70 According to the game tree presented in Fig. 11.125, which of the following nodes represent the worst move for MAX?

a) B
b) C
c) D
d) None of the above

11.71 Which of the following A.I systems first exploited Means-End Analysis technique of problem solving?

a) GPS
b) MYCIN
c) ELIZA
d) None of the above

11.72 Which of the following is not true for Means-End Analysis as a problem solving technique?

a) It is a recursive process
b) It can identify the difference between two problem states
c) It generates a plan of actions to solve a problem
d) None of the above

11.73 Which of the following A.I processes involve *operator subgoaling*?

a) Means-End Analysis
b) Hill climbing
c) Natural language processing
d) Pattern recognition

11.74 Which of the following A.I procedures makes use of a Difference-operator table?

a) AO*
b) Mini-max
c) Constraint satisfaction
d) Means-Ends Analysis

11.75 Which of the following best describes the Means-Ends Analysis process?

a) Its a top-down process
b) Its a bottom-up process
c) Its an iterative deepening process
d) None of the above

Answers:

11.1 (b)	11.2 (c)	11.3 (b)	11.4 (a)	11.5 (a)
11.6 (d)	11.7 (d)	11.8 (b)	11.9 (c)	11.10 (b)
11.11 (d)	11.12 (d)	11.13 (b)	11.14 (a)	11.15 (d)
11.16 (b)	11.17 (a)	11.18 (c)	11.19 (c)	11.20 (d)
11.21 (a)	11.22 (d)	11.23 (b)	11.24 (d)	11.25 (c)
11.26 (c)	11.27 (d)	11.28 (c)	11.29 (b)	11.30 (a)
11.31 (a)	11.32 (b)	11.33 (c)	11.34 (d)	11.35 (c)
11.36 (a)	11.37 (c)	11.38 (a)	11.39 (c)	11.40 (d)
11.41 (a)	11.42 (d)	11.43 (c)	11.44 (c)	11.45 (d)
11.46 (b)	11.47 (a)	11.48 (c)	11.49 (b)	11.50 (b)
11.51 (c)	11.52 (d)	11.53 (a)	11.54 (b)	11.55 (a)
11.56 (b)	11.57 (c)	11.58 (a)	11.59 (c)	11.60 (a)
11.61 (b)	11.62 (a)	11.63 (c)	11.64 (b)	11.65 (c)
11.66 (b)	11.67 (c)	11.68 (c)	11.69 (b)	11.70 ()
11.71 (a)	11.72 (d)	11.73 (a)	11.74 (d)	11.75 (b)

EXERCISES

11.1 Consider a mobile robot moving in the *x-y* plane among some obstacles. The obstacles are rectangular in shape and are aligned along the *x* and *y* axes. The movement of the robot is restricted in the *x* and *y* direction only and not along any oblique direction. On encountering an obstacle to robot can change its direction and the cost of changing the direction is equal to the cost of moving through a unit distance. Propose an A^* algorithm for the robot to plan a collision-free path from an initial position to a destination.

11.2 A branch-and-bound algorithm for the traveling salesperson problem assumes a uniform value of $h(n) = 0$ for every open node n. Can you suggest a non-zero estimation of $h(n)$ for this problem? Solve the same problem as given in Example 11.7 with your heuristic function and see the outcome.

11.3 Consider a modified version of the Monkey-and-banana problem in which there are two windows instead of one. Show how the state space representation of the problem changes due to this modification.

11.4 Solve the 8-puzzle cited in Example 11.5 through bidirectional search.

11.5 Augment the set of production rules given in Table 11.8 in such a way that it is possible to generate sentences similar to *Hari walks very slow*. Show the derivation process for this sentence with the help of the augmented set of production rules.

11.6 A Boolean expression is said to be satisfiable if there is a truth value assignment to its variable which makes the expression True. Construct an AND-OR graph to determine whether the Boolean expression $p.(q + r'.s') + r'.(r + s'.(s + p))$ is satisfiable or not. Also, show one solution graph for the given expression.

11.7 Construct an AND-OR graph for parsing valid sentences of the language defined by the following grammar.

Production Rules	**Rule #**
<sentence> → **<statement>**	(1)
<sentence> → **<question>**	(2)
<statement> → **<noun><verb><adverb><fullstop>**	(3)
<question> → *Who* **<verb><adverb><note-of-interrogation>**	(4)
<noun> → *Mita*	(5)
<noun> → *Gita*	(6)
<verb> → *talks*	(7)
<verb> → *walks*	(8)
<adverb> → *quickly*	(9)
<adverb> → *slowly*	(10)
<fullstop> → .	(11)
<note-of-interrogation> → ?	(12)

As usual, the symbols of the form <·> are the non-terminals of the grammar. Rest of the symbols, except '→' are terminals.

11.8 Fig. 11.126 shows a network of cities through which a river passes. Cities A, B, C and D are on one side of the river and E, F and G are on the other side. There are two bridges X and Y. The numbers adjacent to each arc shows the cost of the corresponding path between the cities. Construct an AND-OR graph to reach city G starting from city A. Moreover, show the solution graph for the minimal cost route from A to G.

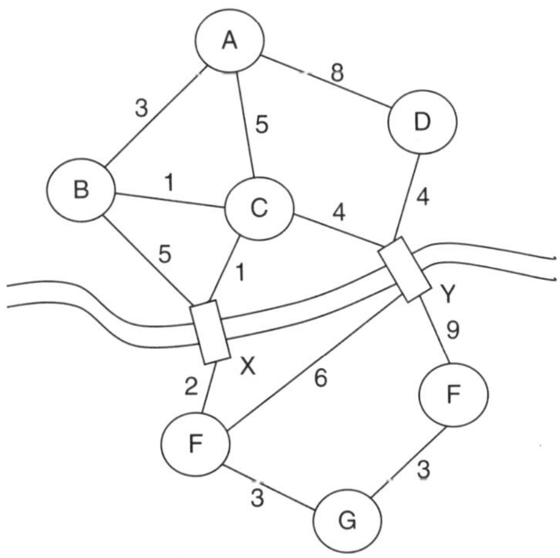

Fig. 11.126. *A network of cities separated by a river*

11.9 Consider the following set of rewrite rules

(1)	$E \to DA$	(2)	$E \to CB$
(3)	$D \to CA$	(4)	$D \to BB$
(5)	$C \to BA$	(6)	$B \to AA$

Using the AO^* algorithm find the sequence of steps to transform the letter *E* to a string of consecutive *A*s.

11.10 Formulate and solve the following cryptarithmetic puzzle as a constraint satisfaction problem.

```
  TWO
+ TWO
-----
 FOUR
-----
 FOUR
-----
```

11.11 Formulate and solve the following crossword puzzle as a constraint satisfaction problem.

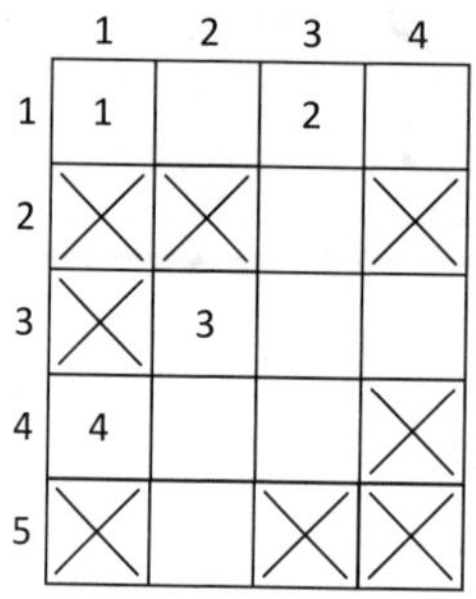

List of words :

ARMS
BOX
BUS
MOON
SUN

Across: 1, 3, 4
Down: 2, 3

Fig. 11.127. *A crossword puzzle*

11.12 Fig. 11.128 shows a map with 6 regions *A*, *B*, *C*, *D*, *E* and *F*. Prove that at least four colours are required to colour the map such that no two adjacent regions have the same colour. The available colours are *red, blue, green*, and *yellow*. Formulate the colouring problem of the given map as a constraint satisfaction problem and find a solution through a suitable technique to solve a CSP.

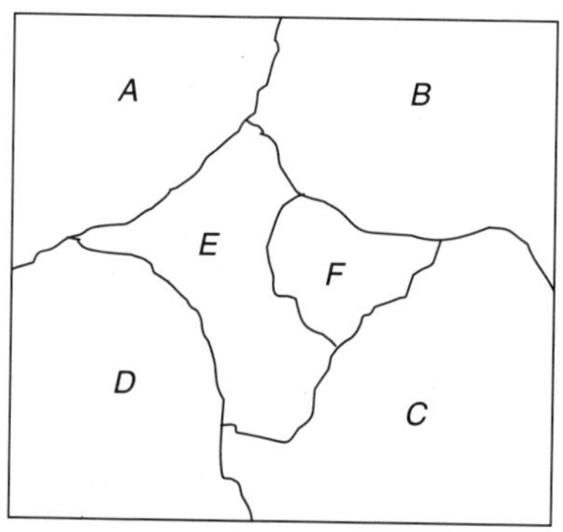

Fig. 11.128. *A map with 6 regions*

11.13 Another version of the game of NIM: There is a version of the game of NIM different from what is described in Example 11.10. Here, instead of a number of piles, the game starts with a single pile of an odd number of sticks. During the game, each player in his turn has to split a pile into two. The two piles thus created should consist of unequal number of sticks. There must be at least one stick in each pile. The game terminates when a player have no valid move. The player who fails to make a move loses the game and the other player wins.

Construct the complete game tree for NIM(7), i.e., the game which starts with 7 sticks in a single pile.

11.14 Consider the complete game tree constructed in problem 11.8 above. Assuming a perfect game, i.e., no erroneous move made by any of the players, is it possible to determine at the outset who will win the game? If yes, then find that player and show the technique through which you determine this.

11.15 A simple household robot can push, or carry an object from one place to another place, walk to a specified location from its current position, pick up an object, putdown an object it is presently holding, and place an object on another provided the top of the second object is not currently occupied by anything. The differences that may appear between the states of the robot world are with respect to the position of some object, position of the robot itself, whether or not the top of an object is clear, whether or not a specified object is on the top of another specified object, whether or not the robot arm is free, whether or not the robot is holding a specified object etc. The robot may pick a small, or light, object but not a big, or heavy, object. If the object is small, or light, it may pick it up and move to some place. However, if it intends to transfer a big, or heavy, object from one location to another, it has to push.

Propose a set of operations for the said robot with their pre-conditions and results expressed as predicate logic formulae. Construct the Difference-operator table to be utilized by a Means-Ends Analysis system and apply it to generate a plan for the robot to transfer a heavy object from one corner of a room to another corner.

BIBLIOGRAPHY AND HISTORICAL NOTES

State space search is a well-explored area in Artificial Intelligence. Many pioneering works have been done in this field from early days of AI. Some of the important works are cited below.

De Champeaux, D. and Sint, L. (1977). An improved bidirectional heuristic search algorithm. *Journal of the ACM*, 24(2), pp. 177–191.

Dechter, R. and Judea, P. (1985). Generalized best-first search strategies and the optimality of A*. *Journal of the ACM*, 32(3), pp. 505–536.

Freuder, E. and Mackworth, A. (ed.) (1994). *Constraint-based Reasoning*. MIT Press.

Guesguen, H. and Hertzberg, J. (1992). *A Perspective of Constraint Based Reasoning*, Springer.

Hart, P. E., Nilsson, N. J., Raphael, B. (1968). A formal basis for the heuristic determination of minimum cost paths. *IEEE Transactions on Systems Science and Cybernetics*, 4(2), pp. 100–107.

Hentenryck, V. P. (1989). *Constraint Satisfaction in Logic Programming*. MIT Press.

Judea, P. (1982). The solution for the branching factor of the alpha-beta pruning algorithm and its optimality. *Communications of the ACM*, 25 (8), pp. 559–564.

Judea, P. (1984). *Heuristics: intelligent search strategies for computer problem solving*. Addison-Wesley Longman Publishing Co., Inc.

Kahneman, D., Tversky, A., and Slovic, P. (eds.) (1982). *Judgment under Uncertainty: Heuristics and Biases*. Cambridge, UK: Cambridge University Press.

Klahr, D., Langley, P., and Neches, R. (1987). *Production System Models of Learning and Development*. Cambridge: The MIT Press.

Knuth, D. E. and Moore, R. W. (1975). An analysis of alpha-beta pruning. *Artificial Intelligence*, 6(4), pp. 293–326.

Knuth, D. E. (1997). *The Art Of Computer Programming*. Vol. 1. Boston: Addison-Wesley.

Newell, A. and Simon, H. A. (1959). *The Simulation of Human Thought*. Santa Monica, California: Rand Corp.

Newell, A. and Simon, H. A. (1961). *GPS, a Program that Simulates Human Thought*. Santa Monica, Calif: Rand Corporation.

Newell, A. and Herbert A. S. (1976). Computer science as empirical inquiry: symbols and search. *Communications of the ACM*, 19 (3).

Pohl, I. (1971). *Bi-directional search*. In *Machine Intelligence*, **6**, Edinburgh University Press, pp. 127–140.

Tsang, E. (1993). *Foundations of Constraint Satisfaction*. Academic Press.

Waterman, D.A. and Hayes-Roth, F. (1978). *Pattern-Directed Inference Systems*. New York: Academic Press.

12

ADVANCED SEARCH STRATEGIES

Key Concepts

Boltzman constant, Charles Darwin, Chromosome, Chromosome encoding/decoding, Convergence, Cooling schedule, Crossover, Crossover probability, DNA, Dominance relation, Elitism, Euclidean distance, Fitness function, GA parameters, Genetic algorithms (GAs), Initial population, Mating pool, Maximization, Minimization, Multi-cut-point crossover, Multi-objective fitness, Multi-objective GAs, Mutation, Mutation probability, Natural evolution, Natural selection, Niche count, Niche size, Normalized fitness function, One cut-point crossover, Optimization problems, Pareto-optimal front, Pareto-optimal ranking, Pareto-optimal solution, Population, Population size, Roulette wheel selection, Selection, Shared fitness value, Simulated Annealing (SA), Survival of the fittest, Termination condition, Tournament selection

Chapter Outline

An important class of problems encountered in real life is the so called optimization problems. Typically such a problem has numerous solutions of varying qualities where the quality of a solution is judged on the basis of certain criteria, presented in the form of a real valued objective function. Depending on whether the function is to be maximized or minimized, the optimization problem is further categorized as a maximization, or minimization, problem. Now, classical optimization techniques can be used only on continuous differentiable functions. In the realm of computational problems, possibility of the objective function being continuous and differentiable is quite low, and therefore classical techniques have limited scope. Moreover, often the classical techniques have the tendency of settling down at local minima or maxima points instead of the global best solutions. In reality, there are computational problems which require tremendous computational efforts to find the best solution. Intelligent search strategies like hill climbing may be employed to obtain reasonably good solutions to such problems. However, hill climbing suffers from the serious problem of settling to sub-optimal solutions remaining in the search space as local optimal points. Genetic Algorithms (GAs) and Simulated Annealing (SA) are two search strategies that are inspired by natural evolutionary processes and have the capacity to overcome the problem posed by the existence of local optima in large search spaces. GAs try to mimic the process of natural evolution through natural selection based on the Darwinian principle of survival of the fittest. It is essentially a maximization process. Simulated Annealing (SA) follows the process of physical annealing where a metal is first heated to a molten state and then gradually cooled to get a uniform crystal structure. This uniform crystal structure corresponds to a minimal energy level. Hence annealing is a minimization process. Both GAs and SAs have been extensively employed to solve complex problems of various fields including engineering, economics, biology etc. In the subsequent sections of this chapter, these two search techniques are discussed in greater details.

12.1 NATURAL EVOLUTION: A BRIEF REVIEW

Natural, or biological, evolution is the process of emergence of higher and complex life-forms from simpler, primordial, life-forms over billions of years. The scientific theory of evolution was proposed by Charles Darwin in 1859 through his celebrated work entitled *The Origin of Species by Means of Natural Selection*. Darwin's theory had a great impact on humanity. It is widely perceived as one of greatest intellectual triumphs achieved by man. Darwin's theory is one of the few scientific discoveries that have revolutionized man's world-view forever.

The mechanism Nature employs to realize evolution is called *Natural Selection*. The basis of Natural Selection is the principle of *Survival of the Fittest*, a phrase coined by Herbert Spencer. Darwin's theory of evolution is based on three observations: (a) a species on earth, in general, produce much higher number of offspring than possibly can survive, (b) the individual members of a species possess various traits resulting in varied probabilities of survival and reproduction, and (c) children inherit the traits of their parents. In a certain environment, individuals having traits favourable to live in that environment have higher chance of survival and procreate. On the other hand, individuals lacking such traits are likely to die earlier and thereby, have less opportunity to have children. This is natural selection. The effect of natural selection is the gradual increase in the relative number of individuals who are better adapted to survive and reproduce in a certain environment. Individuals who lack such traits become scares over successive generations and eventually die out. The phenomenon of mutation helps to introduce a random radical change in a species. If the change is favourable for survival then it is likely to continue in subsequent generations, otherwise it extinguishes in the process of natural selection. By way of natural selection, coupled with occasional mutation, Nature evolves higher forms of l ife on earth from lower ones. The main features of natural evolution that are significant from computational point of view are presented below.

12.1.1 Chromosomes

The traits of an individual are encoded and stored in each cell with the help of a structure called the chromosomes. For example, there are 23 pairs, or 46, chromosomes in human cells. Chromosomes are long strands of genes and the genes are made up of two long thin strands of DNA in a double helix structure. Roughly speaking, a gene may be thought of as encoding a trait, e.g., colour of eye, or the shape of the lips etc. The idea of chromosome as an encoded pattern of individual traits is used in Genetic Algorithms (GAs). In GAs, each feasible solution is of a given optimization problem is encoded as a string of bits, characters etc. The GA process consists of processing a number of such chromosomes over successive generations and then mapping the chromosome returned by the GA to its encoded solution.

12.1.2 Natural Selection

As mentioned earlier, natural selection is Nature's way to support and perpetuate 'good' qualities in a species against the 'bad' qualities. Consider the case of polar bears that survive under the harshest Arctic weather. The fur is different from all other members of the bear family and coloured white which not only helps in camouflaging but also contains body heat. It is also adapted to store more fat within, to beat the cold. This fat, accumulated mostly during summers, when the bears overfeed serves nutritional value during frozen winters when food becomes scarce. This kind of adaptability, seen in most animals, including man is an example of 'survival of the fittest'. Only those bears that could adapt, survived. Offspring of highly adaptable survivors over generations are passed on these survival traits and result in permanent changes in the genetic structure of the species.

12.1.3 Crossover

Crossover is a genetic operation, which results in exchange of genetic material between two chromosomes. In biological world, crossover occurs when the reproductive cells of the parents unite to form a zygote. It can be considered to be a string operation where two similar strings of same length swap partial contiguous contents. Crossover is the mechanism to ensure reshuffle of traits of the parents in their children.

12.1.4 Mutation

In genetics, a gene mutation is a permanent change that may occur in the DNA sequence constituting a gene. Such changes permanently alter the gene and thereby bring about variations in the lineage of a living organism. In biological sense, mutation can occur in one of the two following ways: inherited from parents (through crossover), or acquired by an individual during its lifetime due to altered environment, or habits of individuals, or some unforeseen circumstances like radioactive or cosmic radiation. Mutation is the main vehicle of evolving new species from old ones.

12.2 GENETIC ALGORITHMS (GAs)

Computationally, GA is a maximization process. The problem it addresses usually has a very large search space with probable multiple local maxima inside it. The GA process has to ensure that it is not trapped at local maxima, so that, at the end of the process it may find the global maxima. Even if the global maximum is not returned, we may expect a close approximation of it as the outcome of the GA process.

To achieve this, GA works on a set of solutions (perhaps suboptimal) to the given problem instance, and evolves it through a number of generations. The evolution process stops when some predefined termination condition is satisfied. At each intermediate stage, the old generation is replaced by the new generation. The individuals of the population of a generation are processed with the help of a number of GA operators in such a way that the quality of the new generation, in general, is improved in comparison with old generation. In this way we obtain better and better solutions as the search proceeds until the end of the search when we expect the best, or a near-best solution will be returned by the GA process. Fig. 12.1 and Fig. 12.2 present the outline of the procedure and the corresponding flow chart.

```
Procedure Basic-GA

Step 1.   Initialize the population. Call this the current population.

Step 2.   Repeat Step 3 through Step 5 till termination condition is satis-
          fied.

Step 3.   Apply selection operation on the current population to obtain the
          mating pool.

Step 4.   Apply crossover and mutation operators on the mating pool to gen-
          erate the new population.

Step 5.   Replace the current population by the new population.

Step 6.   Return the best solution of the current population.
```

Fig. 12.1 *Procedure Basic-GA*

There are certain features associated with a GA. These are

1. The chromosomes.
2. Procedures to encode a solution as a chromosome, and procedure to decode a chromosome to the corresponding solution.
3. Fitness function to evaluate each solution, i.e., each chromosome.
4. Population size.
5. Initial population.
6. The mating pool, i.e., the set of chromosomes selected from current population who will generate the new population/generation.
7. GA operators, e.g., selection, crossover, and mutation.
8. Various GA parameters, e.g., crossover probability (p_c), mutation probability (p_μ), population size etc.
9. Termination condition.

Chromosomes are usually one or multidimensional arrays of bits, digits, characters, or other suitable elements. A chromosome encodes a solution to the given maximization problem. There must be simple procedures to map the solution to the corresponding chromosome and vice-versa. Moreover, there must be a fitness function which helps us to evaluate a chromosome/solution. A population is a set of chromosomes. There is a predefined size of the population, say n. The population is initialized with n randomly generated chromosome. Each chromosome of population is evaluated with the help of the fitness function. The values of the fitness function for the chromosomes indicate the quality of the corresponding solutions.

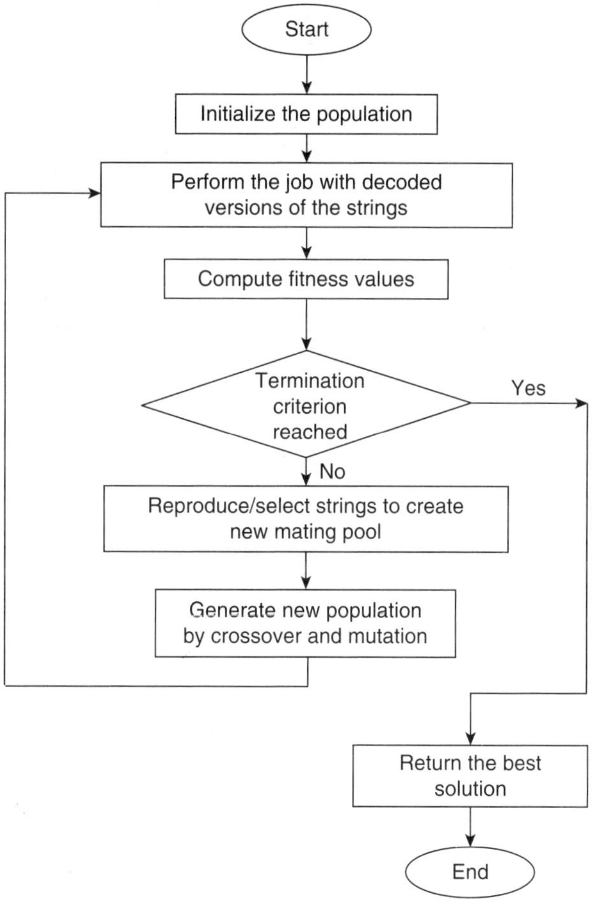

Fig. 12.2 *Flow chart of the basic genetic algorithm (GA) process*

During every iteration, a mating pool is created by selecting chromosomes from the population. The selection procedure is designed on the basis of the Darwinian principle of survival of the fittest. Therefore, better fit chromosomes are selected more often than the less fit ones. Consequently, the average fitness of the mating pool is usually higher than that of the current population.

Mating pool has the same size as that of the current population. The individual chromosomes in the mating pool act as parents for the next generation of chromosomes. Characteristics of the parents are reshuffled and propagated to the children with the help of the crossover operator. These children are subject to a mutation operator which helps to bring about a rare but random and unpredictable change in the chromosomes. The mutation operator helps the GA process to overcome the problem of getting stuck at local maxima. The process of obtaining a new generation of population from old are is shown in Fig. 12.3.

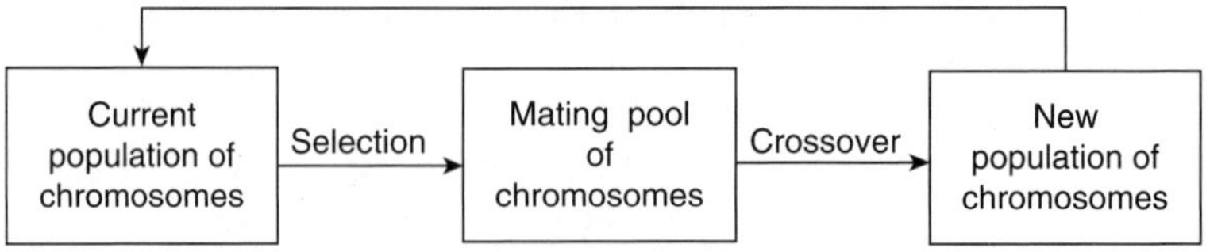

Fig. 12.3 *Formation of new generation from old one*

As the GA proceeds, the search is expected to converge. Usually, when the search space is sufficiently explored, the average fitness of the population, or the fitness of the best-fit chromosome of the population, does not improve over consecutive generations. However, this depends on how finely the GA parameters are tuned to appropriate values. The search may be terminated after a pre-defined number of generations, or, when the average fitness does not show any improvement over a pre-defined number of consecutive generations. The subsequent parts of this subsection present the details of various GA features.

12.2.1 Chromosomes

A feasible solution for a given maximization problem must be encoded as a chromosome. In its simplest form, a chromosome is a one-dimensional string of bits. However, various other types of chromosomes have been tries e.g., strings of denary digits, alphanumeric characters, real numbers and so on. The design has to select an appropriate encoding scheme on the basis of the nature of the problem to be solved. For example, the real number encoding scheme has been found to be ideal for function optimization.

The integer or literal permutation encoding is better suited for combinatorial optimization problems than others. However, these techniques are applicable only to one-dimensional strings as chromosomes. For more complex real world problems, it might be essential to have an appropriate data structure to capture the nature of the problem. Depending upon the structure of the encodings, the methods can be further classified as one-dimensional or multi-dimensional.

Though most problems are solvable using one-dimensional encoding, some more complex problems do need a multi-dimensional approach. Whatever the chosen encoding scheme, it is necessary that it builds an effective solution to the problem. There exist several criteria to decide the effectiveness of an encoding scheme. These include

- Requirement of space by the encoded chromosomes.
- The time to perform operations like crossover, mutation and fitness evaluation.
- All encoded chromosomes must map to feasible solutions.
- The chromosomes resulting from crossover and mutation must map to feasible solutions.

Example 12.1 given below illustrates the concept of a chromosome as an encoded form of a solution and the procedures to map a solution to the corresponding chromosome and vice versa.

Example 12.1 (*Chromosome for Travelling Salesperson Problem*)

Consider a tiny instance of TSP with five cities as shown in Fig. 12.4. For the sake of simplicity and brevity, the number of cities has been kept low. Moreover, the network of cities under consideration is fully connected. This ensures that any permutation of the cities represent a feasible tour by the salesperson. A network which is not fully connected can be easily converted to such one by adding appropriate number of extra edges and assigning infinite cost to each of these additional links. Each link between two cities is associated with a cost which must be incurred if the sales person traverses that link. The TSP problem is to find a minimal cost tour i.e., a cycle containing each node of the graph exactly once and total cost of the tour being minimal.

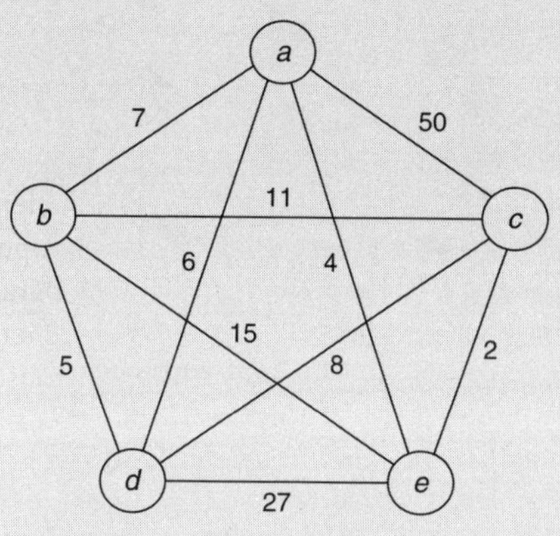

Fig. 12.4 *An instance of Travelling Salesperson Problem (TSP).*

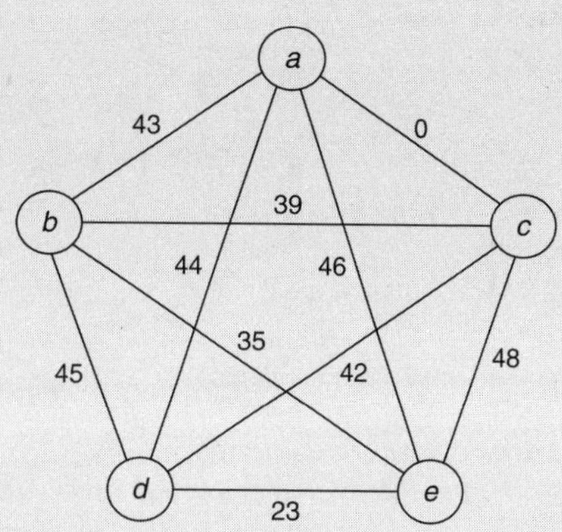

Fig. 12.5 *The TSP of Fig. 12.4 posed as a maximization problem.*

As we see, TSP is essentially a minimization problem. In order to apply a GA on it, we must transform it to a suitable equivalent minimization problem. For this purpose, the cost associated with a link is converted into a reward by subtracting it from the maximum cost. Then the tour with minimum cost will be the tour with maximum reward. The altered graph where each link is associated with a reward, instead of a cost, is shown in Fig. 12.5. The goal is now to find a tour with maximum reward.

For the network of cities shown in Fig. 12.5 where the cities are denoted by the letters *a*, *b*, *c*, *d* and *e*, a tour can be represented simply as a permutation of five letters *a*, *b*, *c*, *d* and *e*. Therefore, assuming that the permutation is circular, i.e., the last and the first node in the permutation are adjacent, any such permutation is a chromosome. However, if we prefer binary chromosomes, then this alphanumeric string must be transformed to its binary equivalent and vice-versa. This can be easily done by substituting each letter by its designated bit pattern. The technique is illustrated in Fig. 12.6.

Fig. 12.6(a) shows the tour $c \rightarrow d \rightarrow b \rightarrow a \rightarrow e$ in the network under consideration. The table shown in Fig. 12.6(b) contains the binary code for each node. The codes are chosen arbitrarily. Since there are 5 nodes, we need $\lceil \log_2 5 \rceil = 3$ bits to encode them. However, the remaining 3 (= 2^3 – 5) codes are unused. Fig. 12.6(c) depicts the mapping of the tour $c \rightarrow d \rightarrow b \rightarrow a \rightarrow e$ to its corresponding binary chromosome. Therefore, for this problem a chromosome is any binary string of length $3 \times 5 = 15$.

In order to decode a chromosome to its corresponding tour, the chromosome is partitioned into five segments each consisting of 3 bits. Each of these 3 bit codes is then substituted by the appropriate node. However, it may not be possible to convert an arbitrary 3 bit string to a node directly. For example, consider the chromosome *ch* = 101 011 001 110 001. Here the leftmost 3 bits are 101 which do not represent any node at all. The same is true for the fourth pattern 110. Moreover, the pattern 001 has occurred twice, though a node is allowed to be visited exactly once in a tour.

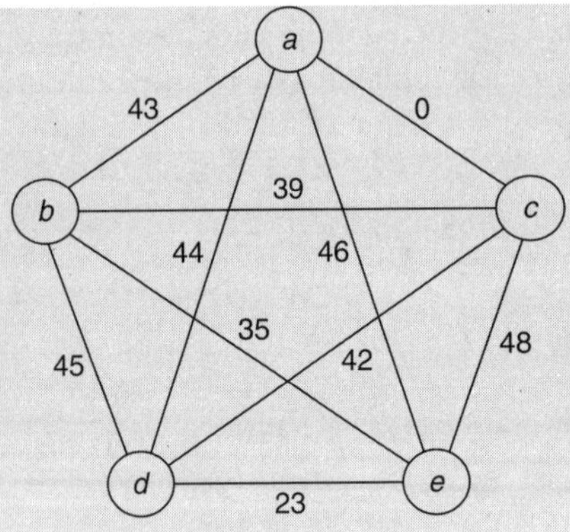

(a) Problem instance

#	Node	3-bit Code
0	*a*	000
1	*b*	001
2	*c*	010
3	*d*	011
4	*e*	100
5	Unused	101
6		110
7		111

(b) Encoding scheme

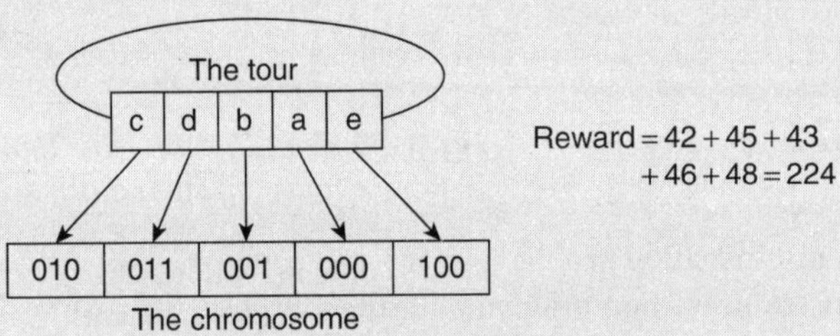

(c) Chromosome encoding

Fig. 12.6 *Encoding and decoding a chromosome*

Such issues may be resolved in various ways. Consider the following strategy. We arrange the set of nodes in a circular way. When a node is selected it is marked as visited. When we come across a code without any node assigned to it, we select the next available node in the list of nodes. We apply the same policy in case of a conflict, i.e., a code occurring more than once in a chromosome. Fig. 12.7 presents the pseudo-code for the technique described above. Accordingly, chromosome ch = 101 011 001 110 001 will be interpreted as the tour $a \rightarrow d \rightarrow b \rightarrow c \rightarrow e$.

```
Procedure TSP-Chromosome-Decode
Begin
   Partition the chromosome into a sequence of five 3-bit binary patterns.
   For (each 3-bit pattern p) Do
      If p has a node n associated with it Then
         If n is not already visited Then
               Select the node as visited.
         Else Select the next available node in the list of nodes
         End-If
      Else Select the next available node in the list of nodes
      End-If
   End-For
End-Procedure TSP-Chromosome-Decode
```

Fig. 12.7 *Procedure TSP-Chromosome-Decode*

12.2.2 Fitness Function

Fitness functions are objective functions that are used to evaluate a particular solution represented as a chromosome in a population. As GA is a maximization process, the fitness function is to be defined in such a way that higher fitness values may represent better solutions.

Two main types of fitness functions exist: the first one, the fixed type does not allow the fitness function to change. In the second case, the fitness function itself is mutable. The most important factor in deciding a fitness function is that it should correlate to the problem closely and is simple enough to be computed quickly. Speed of execution is very important because GA itself is quite computation intensive.

Example 12.2 (*Fitness function for TSP*)

Let us consider the TSP instance given in Fig. 12.5. Here the fitness function is simply the sum of the rewards associated with the links included in a tour. Hence for the chromosome *chr* = 101 011 001 110 001 which represents the tour $a \rightarrow d \rightarrow b \rightarrow c \rightarrow e$ is given by $f(chr) = w(a \rightarrow d) + w(d \rightarrow b) + w(b \rightarrow c) + w(c \rightarrow e) + w(e \rightarrow a) = 44 + 45 + 39 + 48 + 46 = 222$. On the other hand, the fitness of $a \rightarrow b \rightarrow c \rightarrow d \rightarrow e$ is $43 + 39 + 42 + 23 + 46 = 193$. Obviously the former solution is a better fit than the latter one.

12.2.3 Population

Usually, standard optimization algorithms consist of a sequence of computational steps which converge to the optimal solution. Most algorithms perform deterministic computational steps based on higher order derivatives of the objective function. The GA based approach differs from the standard approaches due to the fact that, while the standard approaches have single point initiations in the search space and move along the direction of descent, GA's employ multi-directional search by initiating the process through a population of possible solutions. While point to point approach suffers from the threat of local optima, the GA has higher probability of escaping it.

The GA starts with a group of chromosomes known as population. The size of the population is an important parameter that needs to be tuned by the designer of the GA. The complexity of the problem, which is reflected by the size of the search space, is a factor to be considered while fixing the size of the population. The initial population is normally randomly generated. This is illustrated in the next example.

Example 12.3 (*A small population for the TSP*)

Let us continue with the TSP instance cited in Example 12.1 and Example 12.2. Assuming a population size of 10, Fig. 12.8 presents a procedure to generate the initial population randomly. Table 12.1 shows the randomly generated population of 10 chromosomes along with the corresponding tours and the fitness values.

```
Procedure TSP-Generate-Initial-Population
Begin
    For i ← 1 To 10 Do
        /* Generate the ith chromosome */
        For j ← 1 To 15 Do
```

```
            Chr[i][j] = Random {0, 1} /* Assign a bit randomly*/
        End-For
    End-For
End-Procedure TSP-Generate-Initial-Population
```

Fig. 12.8 *Procedure TSP-Generate-Initial-Population*

Table 12.1 *Randomly Generated Initial Population*

#	Chromosome	Tour	Fitness
1	011 101 111 011 001	*d-e-a-b-c*	193
2	010 100 001 101 110	c-e-b-d-a	172
3	100 100 001 111 010	e-a-b-c-d	193
4	011 100 110 001 101	d-e-a-b-c	193
5	110 011 101 110 001	a-d-e-b-c	141
6	010 100 010 011 011	c-e-d-a-b	197
7	100 100 011 111 110	e-a-d-b-c	222
8	010 101 011 011 001	c-d-e-a-b	193
9	100 110 101 011 110	e-a-b-d-c	224
10	111 011 101 100 100	a-d-e-b-c	141

12.2.4 GA Operators

As in natural evolution, GAs employ three operators, viz. selection, crossover and mutation, on the population to evolve them towards the optimal solution of the target optimization problem. While the selection operator ensures continuation of good qualities in the solutions, the crossover and mutation operators help to explore the entire search space by providing reshuffle of individual traits and variations. Each of these operators is described below with greater details.

(a) Selection. The members of the mating pool are picked up from the current population with the help of the selection operator. There are various techniques to realize the selection process. All of them, some way or other, are based on the Darwinian principle of survival of the fittest. In other words, the selection operator is designed in such a way that chromosomes with higher fitness values have a greater chance of being selected for the mating pool. However, the lower fit chromosomes should also have their chance of producing offspring. They should not be blocked altogether. There are several selection techniques available in the literature. Two of the most widely used selection operators, viz., *roulette wheel* selection and *tournament* selection, are discussed below.

Population and fitness values

Chromosome #	1	2	....	PopSize
Fitness value	$f(chr_1)$	$f(chr_2)$	....	$f(chr_{\text{PopSize}})$

$$Sum\_fitness = \sum_{i=1}^{PopSize} f(chr_i)$$

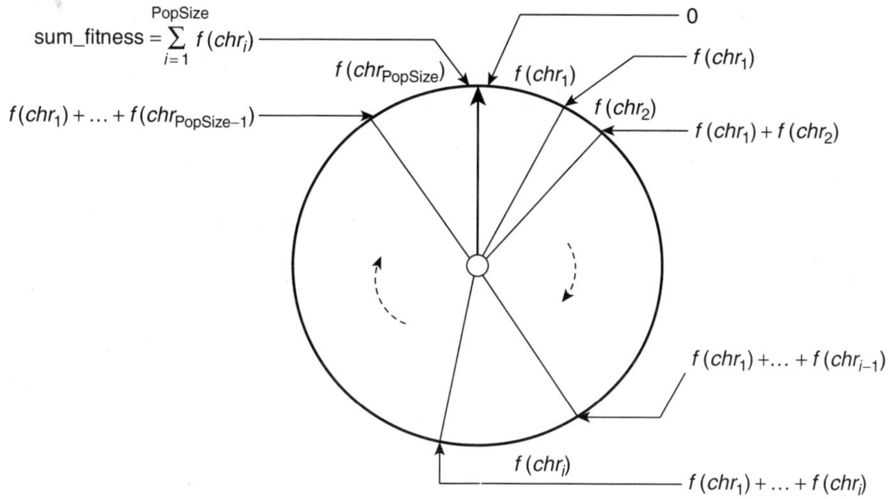

Fig. 12.9 *A roulette wheel*

Roulette Wheel. Roulette wheel selection was proposed by John Holland and is possibly the best known selection type. The technique ensures that the survival probability of a chromosome is proportional to its fitness value. Let us consider a population of *PopSize* number of chromosomes chr_1, chr_2, …, $chr_{PopSize}$, with fitness values $f(chr_1), f(chr_2), \ldots, f(chr_{PopSize})$ respectively. Now imagine a circular disk whose circumference has a length of

$$sum\_fitness = \sum_{i=1}^{PopSize} f(chr_i) \tag{12.1}$$

On the circumference, we demarcate successive regions of length $f(chr_1), f(chr_2), \ldots, f(chr_{PopSize})$ so that the successive regions correspond to the chromosomes chr_1, chr_2, …, $chr_{PopSize}$ respectively. This is the roulette wheel. Fig. 12.9 explains the structure of a roulette wheel graphically.

In order to select a chromosome from the current population for the mating pool, a random number is generated between 0 and *sum_fitness*. Let *x* be the random number generated in this way. We now locate the point *P* on the circumference of the wheel at a distance *x* from the starting point *S*. The chromosome within whose limits this point *P* is situated is selected for the mating pool. This procedure is repeated *PopSize* times. Since the regions on the circumference of the roulette wheel are proportional to the fitness values of the corresponding chromosomes, those with high fitness values are likely to get selected more often than those with low fitness values. The pseudocode for the roulette wheel technique is presented in Fig. 12.10.

```
Procedure Roulette-Wheel-Selection
Begin
   Sum_fitness ← 0
   For i ← 1 To PopSize Do
      sum_fitness ← sum_fitness + fitness (Chromosome (i))
   End-For
```

```
    For i ← 1 To PopSize Do
        /* generate a random number between 0 and sum_fitness */
        r ← random (0, sum_fitness)
        /* locate the point P */
        j ← 1, sum ← 0
        While (sum < r) Do
            sum ← sum + fitness (Chromosome (j))
            j ++
        End-While
        Select Chromosome (--j) and include it in the mating pool
    End-For
End Procedure Roulette-Wheel-Selection
```

Fig. 12.10 *Procedure Roulette-Wheel-Selection*

Example 12.4 *(Roulette wheel selection)*

Let us consider the roulette wheel for the population shown in Table 12.1. Here the $sum\_fitness = \sum_{i=1}^{10} f(chr_i) = 1869$. Let the random number generated in the range [0, 1869] be 1279.

Since $\sum_{i=1}^{6} f(chr_i) = 1089$, $\sum_{i=1}^{7} f(chr_i) = 1311$, and $1089 < 1279 < 1311$, 7th chromosome is selected.

(a) Tournament. In tournament selection, a *tournament* is run among the chromosomes of the current population. Winners of the tournament are selected and included in mating pool. So, at each step of this procedure, two chromosomes, say chr_1 and chr_2 are picked up randomly. Among these two, the chromosome with higher degree of fitness wins and hence selected. This is repeated *PopSize* number of times. The procedure is presented in Fig. 12.11.

```
Procedure Tournament-Selection
Begin
    For i ← 1 To PopSize Do
        p1 = random (0, PopSize)
        p2 = random (0, PopSize)
        If (fitness(chromosome p1) ≥ fitness(chromosome(p2) Then
            Select chromosome (p1) for the mating pool
        Else Select chromosome (p2) for the mating pool
        End-If
        Include the selected chromosome as the ith chromosome in the
        mating pool
    End-For
End Procedure Roulette-Wheel-Selection
```

Fig. 12.11 *Procedure Tournament-Selection*

Example 12.5 (*Tournament selection*)

Once again, we consider the population shown in Table 12.1. Let $p_1 = 4$ and $p_2 = 9$ be the random integers generated within the range [0, 10]. Since the fitness values of the 4th and the 9th chromosomes are 193 and 224 respectively, the 9th chromosome is selected.

(b) Crossover. The selection operation ensures that the quality of the solutions improve over successive generations. The purpose of the crossover operation is to share information among the chromosomes of a population. The reshuffled chromosomes become the offspring of the parent chromosomes and are propagated to the new generation of population. The significance of crossover is it enables the GA search process explore the search space adequately.

During the crossover operation, a pair of chromosomes, say chr_i and chr_j are randomly chosen from the mating pool. These two chromosomes act as the parents. There is a pre-defined probability p_c, called the crossover probability. Crossover probability is the probability that crossover takes place between two parent chromosomes. After selecting the parents, we have to decide if they would undergo the crossover operation at all. So a random number $r \in [0, 1]$ is generated. If $r \le p_c$ then crossover occurs otherwise the parent chromosomes are directly copied to the mating pool. When a crossover occurs, a *crossover point* is determined. The crossover point is a randomly generated integer in the range [1, *ChrLength*] where *ChrLength* is the length of a chromosome. The crossover operation consists of swapping the segments of the parent chromosomes from the crossover point to end. Fig. 12.12 provides the pseudo-code for this operation and Fig. 12.13 illustrates it graphically.

The crossover operator just described and illustrated in Fig. 12.12 and Fig. 12.13 is the basic crossover with one crossover point. This can be generalized to multi-point crossover. An instance of two-point crossover is shown in Fig. 12.14.

```
Procedure One-Cut-Point-Crossover
/* pc is the crossover probability. Size of the population is PopSize.
ChrLength is the length of a chromosome */
Begin
   For i ← 1 To PopSize/2 Do
      /* Select the parents */
      Randomly choose 2 chromosomes chrk and chrl from the mating pool.
      /* Decide if crossover should be performed */
      r ← random [0, 1]
      If (r < pc) Then
         /* Select the crossover point */
         c ← IRandom [1, ChrLength]
         For j ← c To ChrLength Do
            Swap the jth bits of chrk and chrl
         End-For
      End-If
      Include chrk and chrl in the new population.
   End-For
End Procedure One-Cut-Point-Crossover
```

Fig. 12.12 *Procedure One-Cut-Point-Crossover*

There are several crossover operators for real number encoding. These can be broadly grouped into four classes, viz., conventional, arithmetic, direction-based, and stochastic. The conventional operators are made by extending the operators for binary representation into the real-coding case. Such operators can further be divided by two categories namely the simple crossover (one-cut point, two-cut point, multi-cut point or uniform) and random crossover (flat crossover, blend crossover).

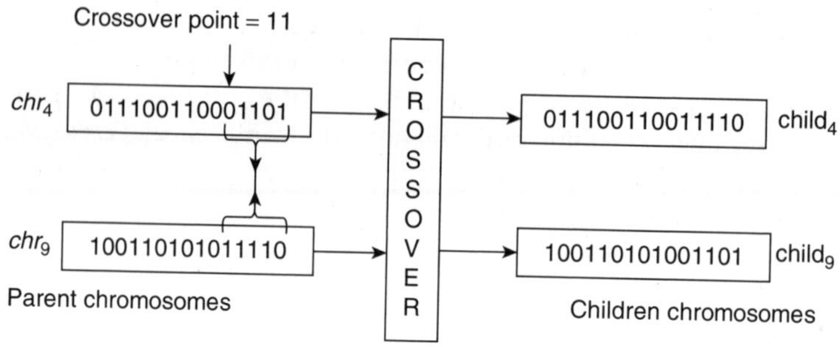

Fig. 12.13 *An instance of one cut-point crossover*

The arithmetical operators are constructed by borrowing the concept of linear combination of vectors from the area of convex set theory. Operated on the floating point genetic representation, the arithmetical crossover operators, such as convex, affine, linear, average, intermediate, extended intermediate crossover, are usually adopted. The direction-based operators are formed by introducing the approximate gradient direction into genetic operators. The direction-based crossover operator uses the value of objective function in determining the direction of genetic search. The stochastic operators give offspring by altering parents by random numbers with some distribution.

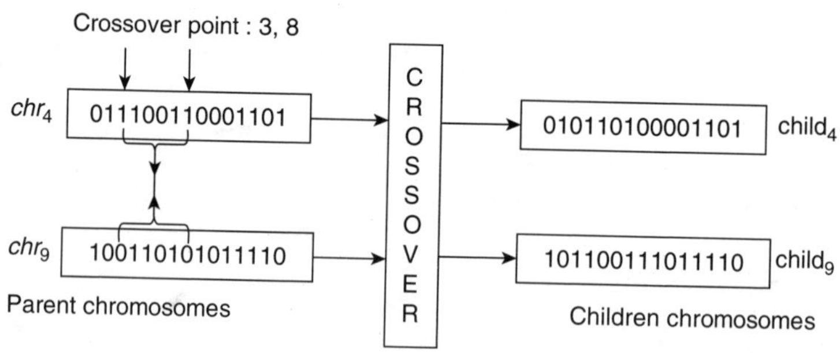

Fig. 12.14 *Two cut-point crossover*

Example 12.6 *(Crossover operation)*

Fig. 12.13 shows the crossover operation on two chromosomes chr_4 = 01110011000110 and chr_9 = 100110101011110 taken from the population in Table 12.1. Choosing 11 as the crossover point the resultant children are 011100110011110 and 100110101001101. Finding the corresponding tours and their fitness values are left as an exercise. Fig. 12.14 depicts an instance of two cut-point crossover on the same pair of chromosomes with 3 and 8 as the crossover points. This time we get 010110100001101 and 101100111011110 as the resultant children chromosomes. Again, finding the corresponding tours and their fitness values are left as an exercise.

(c) Mutation. The mutation operation imparts a small change at a random position within a chromosome. The intention is to empower the GA process to salvage from local optima and explore every region of the search space adequately. However, mutation should occur very rarely failing which the search process will be disturbed too much. A disturbed search finds it difficult to converge. Hence mutation probability p_μ is usually kept low.

```
Procedure Binary-Mutation
Begin
   For i ← 1 To PopSize Do
     r ← random [0, 1]
     If (r < pμ) Then
        mupt ← IRandom [1, ChrLength]
        Flip the bit at mupt in the ith chromosome
     End-If
   End-For
End Procedure Binary-Mutation
```

Fig. 12.15 *Procedure Binary-Mutation*

The pseudo code for mutation operation is given in Fig. 12.15. For each chromosome of the mating pool, a decision is taken on the basis of the mutation probability p_μ regarding whether that chromosome would undergo mutation or not. If the chromosome has to mutate, a mutation point is randomly chosen. The bit at the mutation point is complemented in case of binary chromosome. For other types of chromosomes suitable technique is adopted for mutation.

Example 12.7 *(Mutation)*

The mutation operation is illustrated in Fig. 12.16. The chromosome 011100110001101 is mutated at the 13th bit to obtain 011100110001001 as the mutated chromosome.

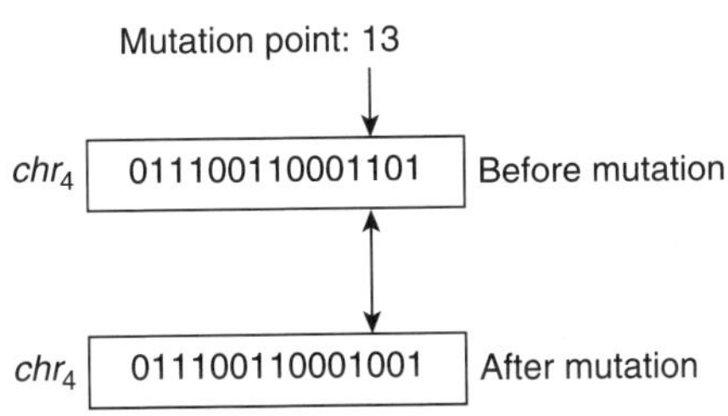

Fig. 12.16 *Mutation operation*

12.2.5 Elitism

Elitism is a strategy to ensure that the best chromosomes are not lost in the search process through generations. This is a legitimate concern because randomness plays a vital role in the GA process. So it is quite possible that a good chromosome, once generated, may get lost in subsequent generations. Therefore, it is logical to preserve the best chromosomes.

Elitism is implemented in various ways. A common technique is to define a special chromosome called the *best-till-date* chromosome. It is initialized with the best chromosome (i.e. the chromosome with the highest fitness value) of the initial population. In each subsequent generation the best chromosome of the current population is identified and its fitness is compared with that of the current best-till-date chromosome. The later is updated by the former in case the best of the current population happens to be better than the prevailing best-till-date chromosome. Alternatively, during the selection operation, we may directly transfer a few top-quality chromosomes (say, top 10% of the population) to the next generation.

12.2.6 GA Parameters

Success and efficiency of a GA process largely depends on how well the parameters of the GA are tuned to suit the targeted problem instance. The GA parameters include the size of population, number of generations through which the GA should be evolved, type of crossover to be used, crossover probability, and mutation probability.

There is no hard and fast rule to fix these parameters. However, long experience and wide experimentation by researchers has provided us certain ranges of values for these parameters. These are obeyed under normal circumstance. An indicative set of values is given below.

$25 \leq PopSize \leq 100$
$500 \leq$ Number of generations ≤ 1500
Number of crossover point(s) = 1, 2, 3, or 4
$0.6 \leq$ Crossover probability $(p_c) \leq 0.8$
$0.01 \leq$ Mutation probability $(p_\mu) \leq 0.02$

Once again, these are not rules. The actual values are to be tuned to the specific GA through experience and trial-and-error. However, some standard settings are reported in literature. One of the widely acclaimed standards was proposed by DeJong and Spears (1990) as given below:

Population size = 50
Number of generations =1000
Crossover type = two point
Crossover rate = 0.6
Mutation types = Bit flip
Mutation rate = 0.001 per bit

If single cut-point crossover, instead of two cut-points crossover, is employed, the crossover rate can be lowered to a maximum of 0.50.

The Grefenstette settings (1986) are usually tried when the complexity of the fitness function is high and the population has to be kept low compulsively, even at the cost of lower dimensionality. These are

Population size = 30
Number of generations = To be fixed through experimentation

Crossover type = Two point
Crossover rate = 0.9
Mutation types = Bit flip
Mutation rate = 0.01 per bit

The population size is another important issue. The size must be apt to represent the entire solution space over a number of generations without compromising on the speed of execution due to complexities of the fitness function.

12.2.7 Convergence

As the GA approaches a global optimum, the fitness's of the average and the best chromosomes approaches equality. This progression towards uniformity is termed convergence in GA. Generally, a GA is said to have converged when over 90% of the population share or have approximately the same fitness value.

While the GA population converges, the average fitness of the population approaches that of the best individual. However, since the GAs are subject to stochastic errors, the problem of genetic drift may occur. Even in the absence of any selection pressure (i.e. a constant fitness function), members of the population will still converge to some point in the solution space. This happens simply because of the accumulation of stochastic errors. If, by some chance, a gene becomes predominant in the population, then it is just as likely to become more predominant in the next generation as it is to become less predominant. If an increase in predominance is sustained over several successive generations, and the population is finite, then a gene can spread to all members of the population. Once a gene converges in this way, it is fixed; crossover cannot introduce new gene values. This produces a ratchet effect, so that as generations go by, each gene eventually becomes fixed. The rate of genetic drift therefore provides a lower bound on the rate at which a GA can converge towards the correct solution. That is, if the GA is to exploit gradient information in the fitness function, the fitness function must provide a slope sufficiently large to counteract any genetic drift. A method of reducing the genetic drift is by increasing the rate of mutation. Interestingly however, it must be remembered that a high mutation rate may turn the search random thereby leaving the gradient information of the fitness function unexploited.

Example 12.8 (*Convergence of GA*)

Given a connected graph $G(V, E)$, a *node cover*, or *vertex cover*, is a set of nodes $N \subseteq V$ such that for any edge $e \in E$, at least one end point of e is in N. The *minimal node cover problem* is to find a minimal node cover for a given graph. Minimal node cover problem have been proved to be NP-complete. A graph with 16 nodes and 25 edges has been considered (see Fig. 12.26 in the section 'Solved Problems'). A GA has been run on a search space of size $2^{16} = 65536$ for this instance of node cover problem. The convergence scenario over about 50 generations is shown in Fig. 12.17. The upper curve shows the progress made by the best fitness value in a generation over successive generations. The lower curve is the same for average fitness of a generation. It is seen from the figure that the GA converges in 21 generations of iteration. The best fit chromosome returned by the GA corresponds to a node cover of size 6 for the given graph. The GA parameters used are: population size = 64, crossover probability = 0.65, mutation probability = 0.04.

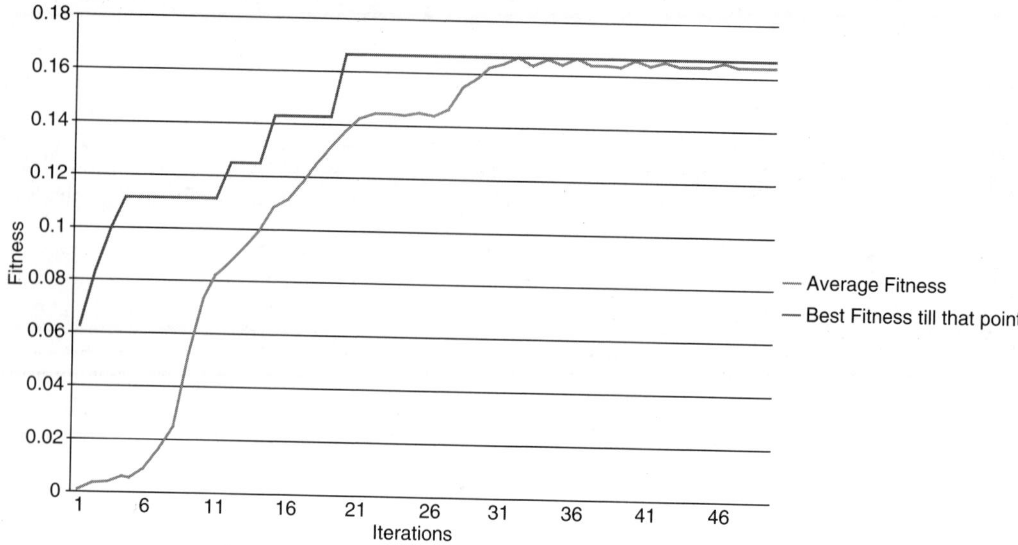

Fig. 12.17 *Convergence of GA process: a sample scenario*

12.3 MULTI-OBJECTIVE GENETIC ALGORITHMS

Discussions so far were limited to GAs that handled the optimization of a single parameter. The optimization criteria are represented by fitness functions and are used to lead towards an acceptable solution. A typical single-objective optimization problem is the TSP. There the sole optimization criterion is the cost of the tour undertaken by the salesperson and this cost is to be minimized. However, I real life, we often face problems which require simultaneous optimization of several criteria. For example, in VLSI circuit design, the critical parameters are chip area, power consumption, delay, fault tolerance etc. While designing a VLSI circuit, the designer may like to minimize area, power consumption, and delay while, at the same time, would like to maximize fault tolerance. The problem gets more complicated when the optimizing criteria are conflicting. For instance, an attempt to design low-power VLSI circuit may affect its fault tolerance capacity adversely. Such problems are known multi-objective optimization (MOO), multi-criterion optimization or vector optimization problems. Multi-objective optimization (MOO) is the process of systematically and simultaneously optimizing a number of objective functions. Multiple objective problems usually have conflicting objectives which prevents simultaneous optimization of each objective. As GAs are population based optimization processes, they are inherently suited to solve MOO problems. However, traditional GAs are to be customized to accommodate such problems. This is achieved by using specialized fitness functions as well as incorporating methods promoting solution diversity. Rest of this section presents the basic features of multi-objective GAs.

12.3.1 MOO Problem Formulation

Let us suppose that there are K non-commensurable objectives with no clear preference relative to each other among them. We may assume, without loss of generality, the objectives are to be minimized. Each of these objectives are represented by the functions $f_1(\vec{x}), f_2(\vec{x}), \ldots, f_K(\vec{x})$, where $\vec{x} = (x_1, x_2, \ldots, x_n)$ is an n-dimensional decision variable vector in the solution space X. We have to find a vector $\vec{x}_{\min}$ that minimizes the objective function vector $f(\vec{x})=\{f_1(\vec{x}), f_2(\vec{x}),..., f_K(\vec{x})\}$. Usually, the solution space X is subject to certain constraints.

As stated earlier, in many real life situations the objectives under consideration conflict with each other. Therefore a perfect multi-objective solution that achieves optimal values for each objective function is hardly feasible. A reasonable alternative is to search for a set of solutions each of which attains an acceptable level for each objective and having the optimal values for one or more objectives. Such a set of solutions is known as a pareto-optimal set. The concept of pareto-optimal solutions is explained in greater details in the nest sub-section.

12.3.2 The Pareto-optimal Front

The Pareto-optimal front is defined in terms of dominance relation between solution vectors. Assuming all the objective functions to be minimized, a solution vector $\vec{x}_1$ is said to dominate another solution vector $\vec{x}_2$ if all the objective functional values of $\vec{x}_1$ are less than or equal to those of $\vec{x}_2$ and there is at least one objective function for which $\vec{x}_1$ has a value which is strictly less than that of $\vec{x}_2$.

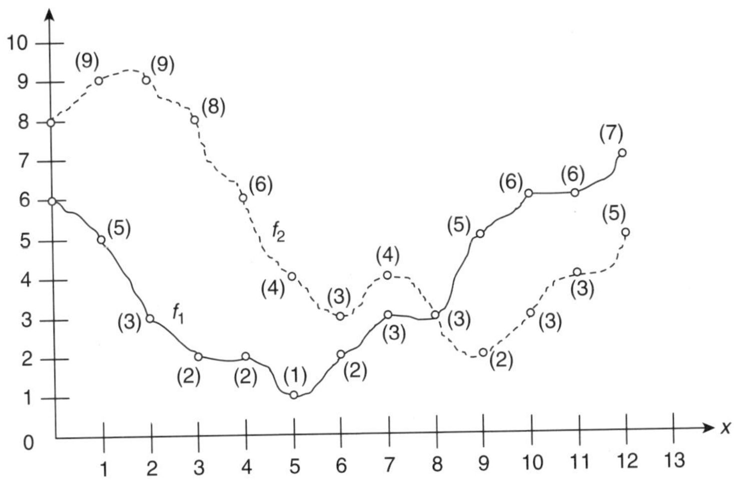

Fig. 12.18 *Two objective functions to be minimized*

Definition 12.1 (*Dominance relation between solution vectors*) Let $\vec{x}$ denote the vector of objective functions of a MOO problem with K objective functions. Without loss of generality we assume that the functions $f_1(\vec{x}), f_2(\vec{x}),..., f_K(\vec{x})$ all need to be minimized. We say that solution $\vec{x}_1$ dominates another solution $\vec{x}_2$, written as $\vec{x}_1 \prec \vec{x}_2$, if and only if

$$f_i(\vec{x}_1) \le f_i(\vec{x}_2) \quad \forall i \in \{1,2,...,K\}, \text{ and}$$
$$\exists i \in \{1,2,...,K\} \ni f_i(\vec{x}_1) < f_i(\vec{x}_2) \tag{12.2}$$

Example 12.9 (*Dominance relation between solution vectors*)

Let us consider an MOO with two objective functions f_1 and f_2 both to be minimized. For simplicity we assume that the solution vector consists of a single parameter x. The shapes of f_1 and f_2

plotted against x are shown in Fig. 12.18. The search process produces sample solutions at $x \in \{0, 1, 2, 3, 4, 5, 6, 7, 8, 9, 10, 11, 12\}$. It is evident from Fig. 12.18 that the minima for f_1 and f_2 do not coincide. In fact f_1 attains its minimum value of $f_1(x) = 1$ at $x = 5$, while $f_2(x)$ attains its minimal value of 2 at $x = 9$. Fig. 12.19 shows positions of the objective function vector $f(x)=(f_1(x), f_2(x))$ corresponding to various values of $x \in \{0, 1, 2, 3, 4, 5, 6, 7, 8, 9, 10, 11, 12\}$. Now consider the points e (3, 3) and g (3, 4). Here e dominates g. Similarly g dominates i, j, k, l and m. However, d (2, 6) and e (3, 3) are non-dominating with respect to each other. In fact, the points in the set $\{a, b, c\}$ are mutually non-dominating. Similarly $\{d, e\}$, $\{f, g, h\}$, $\{i, j\}$, and $\{k, l, m\}$ are non-dominating sets of solutions.

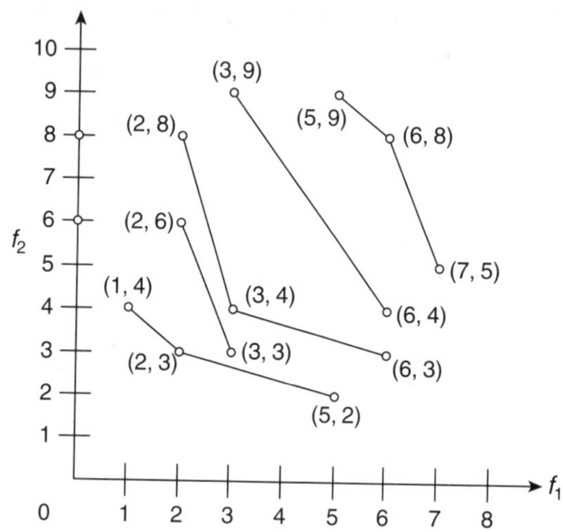

Fig. 12.19 *Two-objective function vectors*

Definition 12.2 (*Pareto-optimal Front*) Let P be a population of solutions to an MOO problem. The pareto-optimal front, F_{PO} is the set of all non-dominated candidates of P.

$$F_{PO} = \{\vec{x} \mid \neg \exists \vec{y} \ni (f(\vec{y}) \prec f(\vec{x}))\}$$

Example 12.10 (*Pareto-optimal Front*)

Consider the multi objective function vectors depicted in Fig. 12.19. It is easy to observe that the points a (1, 4), b (2, 3), and c (5, 2) are non-dominated by any other solution vectors. Therefore, this is the pareto-optimal front for the given population.

Example 12.11 (*Pareto-optimal Front*)

Let us consider the example of a car manufacturer who wishes to simultaneously reduce the cost of the car and the number of accidents involving the specific model. Table 12.2 presents the available data set. Here the pareto-optimal front is $F_{PO} = \{A, C, F\}$.

Table 12.2 *Car Dataset*

Model	(Cost, Accidents)	Dominated by
A	(3, 3)	
B	(8, 10)	*A, C, D, E, F, G, H*
C	(2, 5)	
D	(4, 6)	*A, C*
E	(5, 7)	*D*
F	(7, 2)	
G	(6, 4)	*A*
H	(9, 4)	*A*

12.3.3 Pareto-optimal Ranking

In order to carry out the selection operation on a population, the chromosomes of the population must be assigned an overall fitness value. Therefore, the multi-objective vectors should be mapped to some suitable fitness values so that these can be utilized by the selection operator. Pareto-ranking is an approach to achieve this. It exploits the concept of pareto-dominance for this purpose.

The technique is to rank the population on the basis of dominance relation. The rank of a solution is further utilized to assign its fitness value other than the actual values of the objective functions. The basic pareto-ranking technique was proposed by Goldberg. It involves finding of successive pareto-optimal fronts of a population. Fig. 12.20 shows the pseudo-code as **Procedure Pareto-Ranking**.

```
Procedure Pareto-Ranking
/* F_POi is the i^th pareto-optimal front. P is the population and PP is the
remaining part of the population yet to be ranked. */
Begin
    i ← 1, PP ← P
    /* Find the pareto-optimal fronts */
    While (PP ≠ φ) Do
        F_POi ← The pareto-optimal front of PP.
        PP ← PP - F_Poi
        i++
    End-While
    /* Assign pareto-ranks using the pareto-optimal fronts */
    For (each x⃗ ∈ P ) Do
        r(x⃗) ← i, if x⃗ = F_POi
    End-  For
End Procedure Pareto-Ranking
```

Fig. 12.20 *Procedure Pareto-Ranking*

Example 12.12 (*Goldberg's Pareto-Ranking*)

Applying **Procedure Pareto-Ranking** on the objective function vectors shown in Fig. 12.18 and Fig. 12.19 we get the following pareto-optimal fronts.

$F_{Po1} = \{a\,(1, 4), b\,(2, 3), c\,(5, 2)\}$, $F_{Po2} = \{d\,(2, 6), e\,(3, 3)\}$,
$F_{Po3} = \{f\,(2, 8), g\,(3, 4), h\,(6, 3)\}$, $F_{Po4} = \{i\,(3, 9), j\,(6, 4)\}$,
$F_{Po5} = \{k\,(5, 9), l\,(6, 8), m\,(7, 5)\}$

Accordingly, the ranks assigned to the solutions are $r(a) = r(b) = r(c) = 1$, $r(d) = r(e) = 2$, $r(f) = r(g) = r(h) = 3$, $r(i) = r(j) = 4$, and $r(k) = r(l) = r(m) = 5$. This ranking is shown in Fig. 12.21.

The pareto-ranking method described above is often improvised to obtain other ranking schemes. For example, Fonseca and Fleming (1993) followed a ranking method that penalizes solutions located in the regions of the objective function space which are dominated, or covered, by densely populated sections of the pareto-fronts. They used the formula

$$r(\vec{x}) = 1 + nd(\vec{x}) \qquad (12.3)$$

Here $nd(\vec{x})$ is the number of solutions who dominate $\vec{x}$.

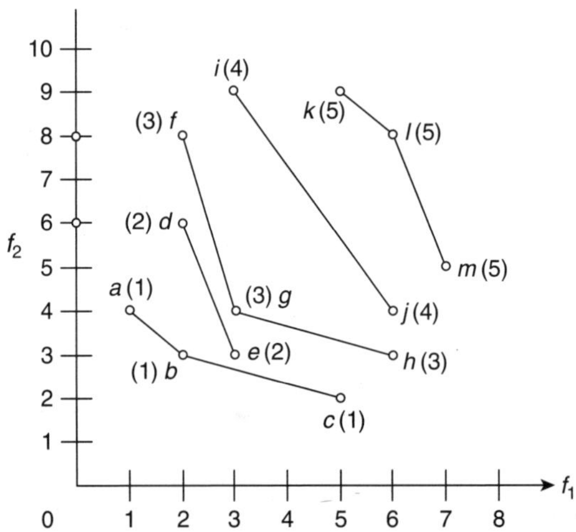

Fig. 12.21 *Pareto-Ranking as per Goldberg's method*

Example 12.13 *(Pareto-Ranking by Fonseca and Fleming)*

Fig. 12.22 shows the pareto-ranking on the objective function vectors shown in Fig. 12.18 and Fig. 12.19 using Formula 12.3.

Accumulated ranking density strategy, proposed by Lu and Yen (2003) too penalizes redundancy in population sue to over-representation. They have used the formula

$$r(\vec{x}) = 1 + \sum_{\substack{\vec{y} \in P, \\ \vec{y} \prec \vec{x}}} r(\vec{y}) \qquad (12.4)$$

Therefore, the ranks of the solutions dominating $\vec{x}$ must be available to compute that of $\vec{x}$. Fig. 12.23 shows the ranks of the same set of solutions obtained in this method.

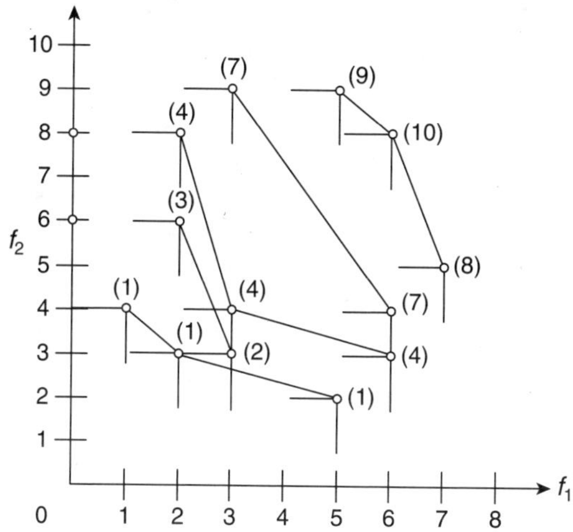

Fig. 12.22 *Pareto-Ranking as per Fonseca and Fleming method*

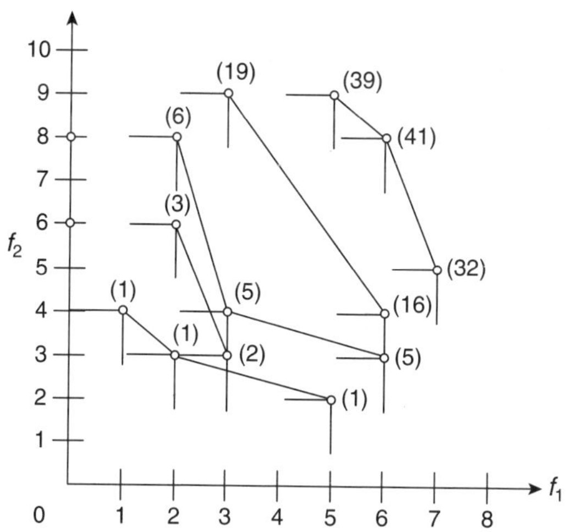

Fig. 12.23 *Pareto-Ranking through Lu and Yen method*

12.3.4 Multi-objective Fitness

Suppose an MOO problem has K number of objective functions $f_1(\vec{x}), f_2(\vec{x}),..., f_K(\vec{x})$. One obvious way to tackle the situation is to combine all objective functions into a single one by taking the weighted sum of the individual functions as below.

$$f(\vec{x})=w_1 \times f_1(\vec{x})+w_2 \times f_2(\vec{x})+ ...+ w_K \times f_K(\vec{x}) \tag{12.5}$$

Here $\vec{w}=(w_1,w_2,...,w_K)$ is the weight vector. The MOO problem then boils down to yet another single-objective optimization problem and solving such a problem will yield a single solution as usual. However, if multiple solutions are necessary with varied importance of different objectives, the problem must be solved multiple times with different weight vectors. The critical aspect of this weighted sum approach is selection of appropriate weight vector for each run. Moreover, combining a number of apparently unrelated objective functions in the form of a weighted sum is often undesirable.

So, instead of forcefully combining a number of non-commensurable objectives into a single one, multi-objective GA tries to return a set of good solutions. To achieve this, the individual solutions of a population need to be assigned some fitness value that reflects the relative status of the candidate with respect to various competing objectives. The pareto-ranking techniques described above can be used directly as the fitness values to individual solutions. However, these are usually combined with various fitness sharing techniques so that a diverse and uniform pareto-front is obtained. Maintaining a diverse population is a matter of concern for multi-objective GAs. This is because, unless preventive measures are taken the population is prone to form a few clusters instead of being distributed uniformly throughout the solution space. This is called *genetic drift*. There are several approaches to prevent genetic drift. Among them, *niche count* is a popular and widely applied one.

Niche Count. The motivation is to encourage search in unexplored sections of a pareto-front by suitably reducing fitness of solutions in densely populated areas. This is achieved by identifying such areas and penalizing solutions located there.

Given a solution $\vec{x} \in P$, the niche count for $\vec{x}$, denoted as $nc(\vec{x})$, is the number of solutions $\vec{y} \in P$, with the same rank as that of $\vec{x}$, in the neighbourhood of predefined size around $\vec{x}$. The niche count of the solutions in a population P is calculated in the following way.

1. Between every pair of solutions $\vec{x}, \vec{y} \in P$, calculate the Euclidean distance $df(\vec{x}, \vec{y})$ in the normalized objective space using the formula

$$df(\vec{x}, \vec{y}) = \sqrt{\sum_{i=1}^{K} \left(\frac{f_i(\vec{x}) - f_i(\vec{y})}{f_i^{max} - f_i^{min}} \right)^{2}} \tag{12.6}$$

   In Formula 12.6, f_i^{max} and f_i^{min} are the maximum and the minimum values of the objective function f_i observed so far in the search.

2. For each $\vec{x} \in P$, calculate the niche count $nc(\vec{x})$ using the formula

$$nc(\vec{x}) = \sum_{\substack{r(\vec{x}) = r(\vec{y}) \\ df(\vec{x}, \vec{y}) \le \sigma}} \frac{\sigma - df(\vec{x}, \vec{y})}{\sigma} \tag{12.7}$$

   Here σ is the size of the niche. The value of σ is to be supplied by the user.

Fitness of a chromosome is initially calculated with the help of Formula 12.8 given below.

$$f(\vec{x}) = PopSize - \sum_{i=1}^{r(\vec{x})-1} n_i - \frac{n_{r(\vec{x})} - 1}{2} \tag{12.8}$$

In Formula 12.8, n_i is the size of the ith pareto front, and $r(\vec{x})$ is the rank of $\vec{x}$. Then *shared* fitness of an individual solution is computed using the niche count as per Formula 12.9.

$$f'(\vec{x}) \leftarrow \frac{f(\vec{x})}{nc(\vec{x})} \tag{12.9}$$

Finally, the *normalized* fitness values are calculated using the shared fitness with the help of Formula 12.10.

$$f''(\vec{x})=\frac{f'(\vec{x})\times n_{r(\vec{x})}}{\sum_{\substack{\vec{y}\in P\\ r(\vec{y})=r(\vec{x})}} f'(\vec{y})}\times f(\vec{x}) \tag{12.10}$$

```
Procedure Multi-Objective-GA
Step 1.   Generate the initial population randomly.
Step 2.   Determine the pareto-optimal fronts F_Po1, F_Po2, ..., F_PoK.
Step 3.   If stopping criteria is satisfied then Return the pareto-optimal
          front F_Po1 and Stop.
Step 4.   For each solution x ∈ P, evaluate the fitness as follows:
          Step 4.1. Assign a rank r(x) using Goldberg's method, or Formula
                    12.3 (Fonseca and Fleming), or Formula 12.4 (Lu and Yen).
          Step 4.2. Compute the basic fitness value using Formula 12.8.
          Step 4.3. Compute the shared fitness value using Formula 12.9.
          Step 4.4. Compute the normalized fitness value using Formula 12.10.
Step 5.   Generate the mating pool MP from population P applying appropriate
          selection operator.
Step 6.   Apply crossover and mutation operations on the chromosomes of the
          mating pool to produce the next generation P' of population from
          MP.
Step 7.   Replace the old generation of population P by the new generation
          of population P'.
Step 8.   Goto Step 2.
```

Fig. 12.24 *Procedure Multi-Objective-GA*

The fitness value obtained through Formula 12.10 is used to select chromosomes for the mating pool. Niche count based fitness sharing has the overhead of selecting an appropriate value for the parameter σ. Researchers have proposed methods to settle this issue. Another issue is the computational overhead of calculating the niche counts. However, the cost of the extra computational effort is usually fairly compensated by its benefits.

12.3.5 Multi-objective GA Process

Multi-objective GA is designed by incorporating pareto-ranked niche count based fitness sharing into the traditional GA process. This is presented as **`Procedure Multi-Objective-GA`** (Fig. 12.24).

```
Procedure Simulated Annealing
Begin
     S_cur ← Initial solution; /* generate initial solution */
     E_cur ← energy level of S_cur
     T ← T_max  /* Set T to maximum temperature */
     While (T ≥ T_min ) Do
          For i = 1 To N Do /* iterate at constant T */
               Generate S_new from S_cur by perturbing S_cur
               Let E_new be the energy level of S_new
               If (E_new<E_cur) Then /* new solution is better */
                    S_cur ← S_new
               Else /* new solution is not better */
                    ΔE = (E_new−E_cur)
                    P =1/(1+e^(-ΔE/T)) /* find acceptance probability */
                    Generate a random number r ∈ [0,1]
                    If (r < p) Then S_cur ← S_new
                    End-If
               End-if
          End-For
          T = α × T /* α is a constant, 0 ≤ α ≤ 1 */
     End-While
End Procedure Simulated Annealing
```

Fig. 12.25 *Simulated Annealing procedure*

12.4 SIMULATED ANNEALING

Simulated annealing (SA) is a technique for finding good solutions to minimization problems. It simulates the physical annealing process of solidifying a metal to a uniform crystalline structure. In order to achieve this uniform crystalline structure, the metal is first heated to a molten state and the gradually cooled down. The critical parameter of this process is the rate of cooling. If the cooling takes place too quickly, energy gaps will be formed resulting in non-uniformity in the crystalline structure. On the other hand, if the cooling takes place too slowly, then time is wasted. The optimal cooling rate varies from metal to metal.

As a search process, SA is similar to hill climbing. The difference is, in hill climbing, a solution worse than the current solution is outright rejected and we look for a solution which is better than, or at least as good as, the current solution. However, in SA, a worse solution too has a finite probability of being accepted. This probability is inversely proportional to the extent of degradation in the quality of the new solution. Moreover, as the SA process approaches convergence, this probability gradually decreases.

In Simulated Annealing, an energy function is associated with the feasible solutions of the given minimization problem. Quality of a solution is determined in terms of this energy function. Lower the energy level, better the solution. In SA, a parameter called temperature, denoted by T, is used. As in physical annealing, temperature T is high in the beginning and is gradually lowered as the annealing process advances. Given, the current solution S_i with energy E_i, the next configuration S_{i+1} (with energy E_{i+1}) is generated by perturbing S_i. Then $E_{i+1} - E_i$ is difference in the energy levels of the new solution and the current solution. If $E_{i+1} - E_i < 0$, then S_{i+1} is better than S_i and the current solution is directly updated by S_{i+1}. Else, it is accepted with a probability $exp\ (-\ (E_{i+1} - E_i)\ /\ (k_\beta T))$, where T and k_β are the temperature and the Boltzmann's constant respectively. If the lowering of the temperature is done slowly enough, the crystal reaches equilibrium at each temperature. In SA, this is achieved by applying a number of perturbations at each T. Simulated annealing starts from a random initial configuration at high T. It then proceeds by generating new states and accepting/rejecting them according to a probability that depends on the current T and $E_{i+1} - E_i$. Initially, the probability of accepting an uphill move is high. As the search proceeds, the temperature cools down, the probability of taking an uphill move diminishes and the process converges to a global minima. The purpose of allowing some uphill moves at the earlier phases is to overcome the problem of getting stuck at a local minimum. The logical steps of a simulated annealing process are shown in **`Procedure Simulated Annealing`** (Fig. 12.25).

CHAPTER SUMMARY

The main points of the foregoing discussion are summarised below.

- Genetic Algorithms are complex search processes inspired by natural evolution. These are essentially maximization processes.
- In a GA, a feasible solution is encoded as a chromosome. In its simplest form, a chromosome is a one-dimensional string of bits though various other types of chromosomes have been tries.
- Fitness functions are objective functions used to evaluate a particular solution or a chromosome. The fitness function of a GA is defined in a way so that higher fitness values may represent better solutions.
- *Selection* is an important GA operator used to decide which chromosomes of the current population will be included in the mating pool. The selection operators are based on the Darwinian principle of survival of the fittest. Most widely used selection operators are the roulette wheel selection and tournament selection.
- The crossover operation helps to share information embedded in the chromosomes. During crossover, portions of the parent chromosomes are exchanged and are passed to the children. This operation helps the GA to explore the entire search space.
- Another GA operator, *mutation*, imparts a small change at a random position inside a chromosome. The purpose is to salvage the search process from local optima and explore every region of the search space adequately. Compared to crossover, mutation occurs rarely.
- In the elitist model of GA, the best chromosomes are preserved to ensure that at the end of the search process these are not lost.
- Multi-objective genetic algorithms are employed to solve problems having several non-commensurable objectives with no clear preference relative to each other among them. In real life situations the objectives under consideration may conflict with each other. Hence, instead of a perfect multi-objective solution that achieves optimal values for each objective function, a set of solutions each of which attains an acceptable level for each objective and having the optimal values for one or more objectives is returned by a multi-objective genetic algorithm. Such a set of solutions is known as a Pareto-optimal set.
- As a search process, Simulated Annealing (SA) is similar to hill climbing. However, in SA, unlike in hill climbing, a worse solution has a finite probability of being accepted. This probability is inversely proportional to the extent of degradation in the quality of the new solution. Moreover, as the SA process approaches convergence, this probability gradually decreases.

SOLVED PROBLEMS

Problem 12.1 Given a connected graph $G(V, E)$, a *node cover*, or *vertex cover*, is a set of nodes $N \subseteq V$ such that for any edge $e \in E$, at least one end point of e is in N. The *minimal node cover problem* is to find a minimal node cover for a given graph. Minimal node cover problem have been proved to be NP-complete. Fig. 12.26 shows a graph with 16 nodes and 25 edges. Apply a GA to find a minimal node cover for this graph.

Solution 12.1 The nodes of the graph are numbered 1 through 16 and the edges are also numbered 1 through 25, as shown in Fig. 12.26. The adjacency matrix for this graph is given in Table 12.3. The $(i, j)^{th}$ entry of the adjacency matrix is 0 if there is no edge between node i and node j, else it is k if edge numbered k connects these nodes. The chromosome for this problem is a binary string of length 16. The encoding/decoding scheme is rather simple. The ith bit of a chromosome is 1 if node i is included in the set of nodes under consideration, else it is 0. For example, the chromosome 1000 1011 0000 0100 represents the set {1, 5, 7, 8, 14} and the chromosome 0010 0110 0011 1101 corresponds to the set {3, 6, 7, 11, 12, 13, 14, 16}. The fitness function employed is $1 / n$ where n is the number of nodes in the set.

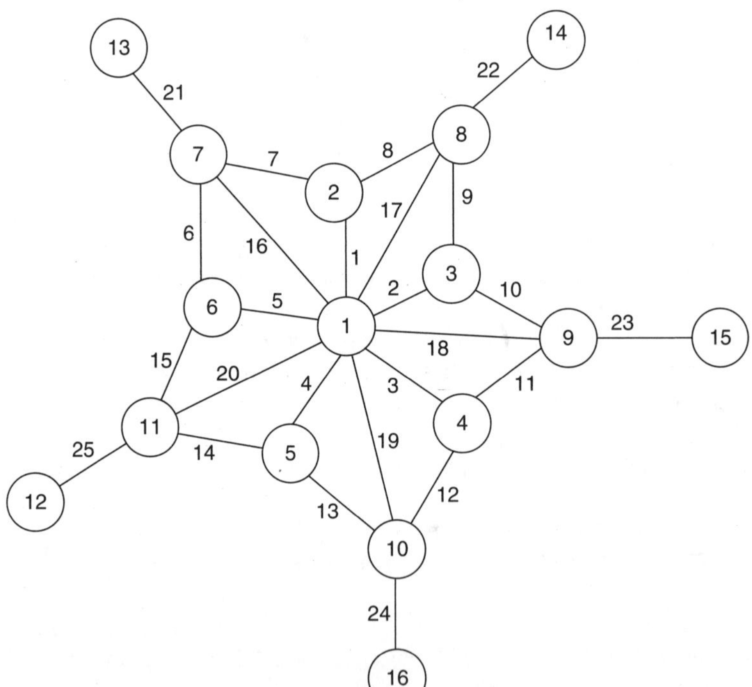

Fig. 12.26 *Sample graph with 16 nodes and 25 edges*

Writing the program for the GA is left as an exercise. After some experimentation, we settled on the following parametric values: population size = 64, crossover probability = 0.65, mutation probability = 0.04. Initial population was generated randomly. The first three chromosomes are 0 1 1 1 1 1 1 1 0 1 0 0 1 1 1 1, 0 1 1 0 0 0 1 0 1 0 1 1 1 0 1 0, and 0 0 0 1 0 1 0 1 1 1 0 0 0 1 0 1. The GA was terminated when there was no improvement in the best fitness over 10 consecutive generations. The convergence scenario over about 50 generations is shown in Fig. 12.17. The upper curve shows the progress made by the best fitness value in a generation over successive generations. The lower curve is the same for average fitness of a generation. It is seen from the figure that the GA converges in 21 generations of iteration.

Table 12.3 *Adjacency Matrix for Graph Shown in Fig. 12.26*

	1	2	3	4	5	6	7	8	9	10	11	12	13	14	15	16
1	0	1	2	3	4	5	16	17	18	19	20	0	0	0	0	0
2	1	0	0	0	0	0	7	8	0	0	0	0	0	0	0	0
3	2	0	0	0	0	0	0	9	10	0	0	0	0	0	0	0
4	3	0	0	0	0	0	0	0	11	12	0	0	0	0	0	0
5	4	0	0	0	0	0	0	0	0	13	14	0	0	0	0	0
6	5	0	0	0	0	0	6	0	0	0	15	0	0	0	0	0
7	16	7	0	0	0	6	0	0	0	0	0	0	21	0	0	0
8	17	8	9	0	0	0	0	0	0	0	0	0	0	22	0	0
9	18	0	10	11	0	0	0	0	0	0	0	0	0	0	23	0
10	19	0	0	12	13	0	0	0	0	0	0	0	0	0	0	24
11	20	0	0	0	14	15	0	0	0	0	0	25	0	0	0	0
12	0	0	0	0	0	0	0	0	0	0	25	0	0	0	0	0
13	0	0	0	0	0	0	21	0	0	0	0	0	0	0	0	0
14	0	0	0	0	0	0	0	22	0	0	0	0	0	0	0	0
15	0	0	0	0	0	0	0	0	23	0	0	0	0	0	0	0
16	0	0	0	0	0	0	0	0	0	24	0	0	0	0	0	0

A partial picture of the evolutionary progress is given below. The best fit chromosome returned by the GA corresponds to the node cover {1, 7, 8, 9, 10, 11} of size 6 for the given graph. A close scrutiny of the given graph reveals that this a minimal node cover for the graph.

FITNESS	GENERATION	CHROMOSOME
0.062500	1	1 1 1 1 1 1 1 1 1 1 1 1 1 1 1 1
0.083333	2	1 1 1 0 1 1 1 1 1 1 1 1 0 0 1 0
0.100000	3	1 0 0 1 0 0 1 1 1 1 1 1 0 0 1 1
0.111111	4	1 0 0 1 0 0 1 1 1 1 1 1 1 0 0 0
0.125000	12	1 1 0 1 0 0 1 1 1 1 1 0 0 0 0 0
0.142857	15	1 0 0 1 0 0 1 1 1 1 1 0 0 0 0 0
0.166667	20	1 0 0 0 0 0 1 1 1 1 1 0 0 0 0 0

Problem 12.2 Genetic Algorithms have been successfully applied to many areas of computation. Here we present a case study of the application of Genetic Algorithms to *grammar induction*, a problem in natural language processing. Grammar induction stands for deciding or finding out a grammar from a set of sample strings collected from the language generated by the grammar. However, the problem of grammar induction from legal and illegal strings is known to be NP-complete even for finite state grammars. Automatic grammar induction has found applications in the areas of natural language processing, speech recognition, automatic computer program synthesis to name a few.

Given a set of positive and negative sentences as samples, the problem is to find out the grammar that can generate the positive samples. Simply put, given a set of similar sentences some of which have been generated using the same grammar (i.e. they belong to the same language/ positive strings) and some which differ from those generated using the target grammar (negative strings), and a set of equivalent and non-equivalent grammars the primary aim is to generate an equivalent grammar using genetic algorithm for the positive strings. Use the following set of correct / incorrect sentences as samples.

Sample Sentences	Comment
the dog chases the cat in the house	correct
the cat the dog the house in chase	incorrect
dog the cat house in chases the in	incorrect
in dog cat house chases the the the	incorrect
house cat the dog chases in the the	incorrect
chases the dog the cat house in the	incorrect
in the the the house chases dog cat	incorrect
house chases the dog cat in the the	incorrect
the the the in dog cat house chases	incorrect
dog cat house chases the in the the	incorrect

Solution 12.2 The input to the genetic algorithm would be the initial gene pool with equivalent and non-equivalent grammars only. The task of the GA would be to generate after each iteration a new set of grammar's which will be tested for fitness value and depending on the result would replace lesser fit members of the generating pool, or die.

The process would continue generation of the grammars until it arrives at one which satisfies the terminating condition. The terminating condition should ideally be correct identification of all the test sentences. In other words, the generated grammar should positively identify and classify the sentences as positive or negative strings.

Fitness Evaluation The evaluation of the fitness function would depend on the ability of the grammar to successfully and correctly identify the positive and negative strings. Identification would mean parsing of a string using the respective grammar. A reward-punishment scheme has to be implemented wherein the grammars score count increases on correctly identifying a positive string as positive and a negative string as negative. The same score count will be decremented on identification of the positive strings as negative and negative strings as positive. The termination condition is therefore decided on the score.

$$F(\alpha) = r\,C(\alpha) - p\,W(\alpha)$$

The fitness of the individual α is determined based on the number of sentences correctly identified, $C(\alpha)$, and the number of sentences wrongly identified, $W(\alpha)$. The associated reward and penalty values are r and p respectively and may be tuned suitably.

Encoding the chromosome When it comes to representational issues there are two broad categories involved. The first is the grammar issue, which has at least two degrees of freedom, the formalism used, and the encoding of the grammar. The second category covers the representational issues of the Genetic Algorithm itself, which concerns the choice of genetic operators, the fitness function and the grammar representation style. So for the grammar $\{S \rightarrow AB, A \rightarrow a, B \rightarrow b\}$ an encoding may be *SAB Aa Bb*. To ease operation of crossover on the strings, it would be wise to keep markers to distinguish between the LHS and RHS of a production. So, the strings may be encoded finally as *S-AB A-a B-b*.

A sample grammar used in the initial population is $\{Start \rightarrow S, S \rightarrow VP\ NP, NP \rightarrow DT\ NP, VP \rightarrow NP\ NN, VP \rightarrow V\ NP, PP \rightarrow P\ DT, DT \rightarrow the, DT \rightarrow a, NN \rightarrow dog, NN \rightarrow cat, NN \rightarrow house, V \rightarrow likes, V \rightarrow chases, P \rightarrow in\}$. The grammar returned by the GA process is $\{Start \rightarrow S, S \rightarrow NP\ VP, NP \rightarrow DT\ NN, VP \rightarrow V\ NP, VP \rightarrow V\ NP\ PP, PP \rightarrow P\ NP, DT \rightarrow the, DT \rightarrow a, NN \rightarrow dog, NN \rightarrow cat, NN \rightarrow house, V \rightarrow likes, V \rightarrow chases, P \rightarrow in\}$

Problem 12.3 Implement a multi-objective GA using MatLab to solve the following MOO problem: Minimize $f(x) = [f_1(x), f_2(x)]$, where $f_1(x) = (x + 1)^2 - 30$, and $f_2(x) = (x - 1)^2 + 30$.

Solution 12.3 To solve this multi-objective minimization problem using Genetic Algorithms on MatLab, we need to use the GAMULTIOBJ function. The function must be supplied with the following variables:

- The Fitness Function
- Number of variables
- Linear inequality constraints *A* and *b*.
- Linear equality constraints *Aeq* and *beq*.
- The lower and upper bounds *lb* and *ub* respectively.

The successive steps of the solution process are described below:

Step 1. Open a blank .m file.
Step 2. Write the following code into it:

```
function y = sample_mult_ga(x)
y(1) = (x + 5)^2 - 30;
y(2) = (x - 5)^2 + 30;
```

Step 3. Save the file as sample_mult_ga.m
Step 4. Open another blank .m file.
Step 5. Write the following code into it:

```
f_fn=@sample_mult_ga; %Fitness Func as in sample_mut_ga.m.
num_var = 1;
A=[]; b=[];            % Linear inequality constraints kept
empty
Aeq = [];
beq = [];              %Linear equality constraints kept empty
lb = -5;               % Lower bound of the variable.
```

```
ub = 0;                    % Upper bound of the variable.
x = gamultiobj(f_fn,num_var,A,b,Aeq,beq,lb,ub);
options=gaoptimset('PlotFcns',{@gaplotpareto,@gaplotscoredi-
versity});                 % Visualization options
gamultiobj(f_fn,num_var,[],[],[],[],lb,ub,options);
```

Step 6. Save the file as simmulti.m.

Step 7. Run it.

The output of the multi-objective GA is a set of three pareto-optimal objective vectors (–29.76, 32.25), (–29.3, 31.35) and (–29, 31). The output generated by MatLab is shown in Fig. 12.27.

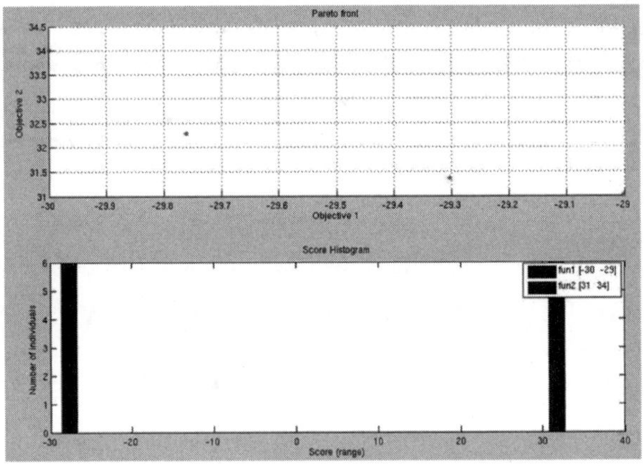

Fig. 12.27 *MatLab output for Problem 12.3*

Problem 12.4 Minimize the function $y = e^{x_1} + \sin(x_2^{\,2})$ by applying Simulated Annealing search technique provided in MatLab.

Solution 12.4 The steps-by-step is given below. This is followed by a list of various parameter values used in the SA employed. However, these are inbuilt in MatLab.

Step 1. Write the following piece of code into a Matlab file and save it as example_objective.m:

```
function y = example_objective(x)
y = exp(x(1)) + sin(x(2)^2);
```

Step 2. Open another file by the name of myfun.m and write the following into it:

```
clear;
clc;
ObjectiveFunction = @example_objective;
X0 = [0.5 0.5]; % Starting point
x = simulannealbnd(ObjectiveFunction,X0)
% The simulannealbnd function takes as input the Objective
Function and the
% starting point and returns the local minimum x to the
objective
```

```
% function specified by the function handle.
```

Step 3. Run myfun.m

The following output will be displayed on the Matlab prompt:
Optimization terminated: change in best function value less than options.TolFun.
x = *−182.3034 −249.2520*

Parameters

The function *simulannealbnd* uses the *saoptimset,* which creates a structure called *options* that contains the *parameters*, for the simulated annealing algorithm, with all parameters set to []. Some of the important parameters and their default values are as below:

AnnealingFcn	Function used to generate new points for the next iteration. The default is @ annealingfast.
TemperatureFcn	Default is @temperatureexp -- (InitialTemperature*0.95^i).
AcceptanceFcn	This function is used to determine whether a new point is to be accepted or not. The default function is @acceptancesa
TolFun	Tolerance value (non-negative scalar). Default is 1e-6
MaxFunEvals	Maximum number of evaluations of the objective function (positive integer). Default is 3000*numberOfVariables.
TimeLimit	Maximum time allowed(positive scalar). Default is Infinity.
MaxIter	Maximum number of iterations allowed(positive integer). Default is infinity.
ObjectiveLimit	The functions stopping criterion. The function stops if the value of the objective function is less than or equal to this. Default value is -Infinity.
HybridFcn	A hybrid function is another minimization function that runs during or at the end of iterations of the solver. The default option is [].
HybridInterval	This value determine the interval after at which the hybrid function is called.
InitialTemperature	The initial temperature (positive scalar). Default is 100.

✓ TEST YOUR KNOWLEDGE

12.1 In order to apply GA, an optimization problem should be formulated as
a) Maximization problem b) Minimization problem
c) Decision problem d) None of the above

12.2 Genetic Algorithms are inspired by
a) Statistical mechanics b) Big bang theory
c) Natural evolution d) None of the above

12.3 Which of the following genetic operators is based on the Darwinian principle of *Survival of the fittest*.
a) Selection b) Crossover
c) Mutation d) None of the above

12.4 Which of the following selection techniques never selects the worst-fit chromosome of a population?
a) Roulette wheel b) Tournament selection
c) Both (*a*) and (*b*) d) None of the above

12.5 Which of the following GA operators helps the search process overcome the problem of getting stuck at a local optima?
a) Crossover b) Mutation
c) Both (*a*) and (*b*) d) None of the above

12.6 If p_c and p_μ be the crossover probability and the mutation probability of a GA then which of the following relations is true?
a) $p_c < p_\mu$ b) $p_c > p_\mu$
c) $p_c = p_\mu$ d) None of the above

12.7 Which of the following properties is not guaranteed by a GA?
a) Admissibility b) Convergence
c) Both (*a*) and (*b*) d) None of the above

12.8 Which of the following GA operators do not help in exploring the various parts of the search space?
a) Selection b) Crossover
c) Mutation d) None of the above

12.9 Usually a multi-objective GA returns
a) The optimal solution b) A number of pareto-optimal solutions
c) One optimal solution per objective d) None of the above

12.10 Niche count in multi-objective GA is used to penalize
a) Sub-optimal solutions b) Solutions in sparsely populated areas
c) Solutions in densely populated area d) None of the above

12.11 The pareto-front of a population in multi-objective GA consists of
a) A set of non-dominated solutions b) A set of dominated solution
c) A set of semi-dominated solutions d) None of the above

12.12 In multi-objective GA, the rank of a solution in a population may be assigned on the basis of
a) Relative position of the pareto-front to which it belongs
b) Number of solutions dominating it
c) Number of solutions dominated by it
d) All of the above

12.13 Which of the following parameters of a GA is not user-defined?
a) Size of population b) Crossover probability
c) Mutation probability d) None of the above

12.14 Let $A = (10, 20)$, $B = (5, 15)$, $C = (15, 15)$ be three solution points in the objective space of a 2-objective minimization problem. Which of the following statements is true?
a) *B* dominates *A* and *C* b) *A* and *C* are mutually non-dominating
c) Both (*a*) and (*b*) d) None of the above

12.15 In Simulated Annealing (SA), the probability of accepting a solution worse than the current one
a) Increases as the temperature decreases
b) Decreases as the temperature decreases
c) Remains constant throughout
d) None of the above

12.16 In order to apply Simulated Annealing (GA), an optimization problem should be formulated as
a) Maximization problem b) Minimization problem
c) Decision problem d) None of the above

Answers

12.1 (a)	12.2 (c)	12.3 (a)	12.4 (b)	12.5 (c)
12.6 (b)	12.7 (c)	12.8 (a)	12.9 (b)	12.10 (c)
12.11 (a)	12.12 (d)	12.13 (d)	12.14 (c)	12.15 (b)
12.16 (b)				

EXERCISE

12.1 Let G (V, E) be a connected graph with $|V| = n$ number of nodes. Each edge e (i, j) between two nodes i and j has a weight w (i, j). If we want to assign a binary code to each node then we need $k = \lceil \log_2 n \rceil$ number of bits. For example, if there are 6 nodes in the graph, we need $\lceil \log_2 6 \rceil = 3$ bit code to assign. Out of the $2^3 = 8$ possible codes 6 will be actually assigned and the rest will remain unused. Optimal code assignment problem is to assign a set of codes to the nodes of a graph such that the function

$$f = \sum_{(i,j)\in E} w_{ij} \times h(C_i, C_j)$$

where C_i, C_j are the codes assigned to the nodes i and j respectively, and h (C_i, C_j) is the Hamming distance between C_i, C_j, i.e., the number of bits in which C_i and C_j differ. Optimal code assignment problem is NP-hard. Design a GA to solve this problem for a given graph. Apply it to the graph shown in Fig. 12.26.

12.2 Solve the optimal code assignment problem mentioned above with the help of a Simulated Annealing. Compare the solutions returned by the two methods.

12.3 The minimal edge cover problem for a given graph G (V, E) may be stated as to obtain the minimal set of edges E' such that for each node $v \in V$ there is at least one edge $e \in E'$ of which v is an end point. Design a GA to solve this problem for a given graph. Apply it to the graph shown in Fig. 12.26.

12.4 Solve the minimal edge cover problem mentioned above with the help of a Simulated Annealing. Compare the solutions returned by the two methods.

BIBLIOGRAPHY AND HISTORICAL NOTES

Ever since the development of Genetic Algorithms by John Holland and his students and colleagues at the University of Michigan, innumerable works have been reported on the application and development of this technique. A number of scientists, e.g. Scott Kirkpatrick, C. Daniel Gelatt, Mario P. Vecchi, Vlado Černý made fundamental contribution to the development of the Simulated Annealing method of minimization. A very brief list of some significant literature on GAs and SAs is given below.

Aarts, E. And Korst, J. (1989). *Simulated annealing and Boltzmann machines: A stochastic approach to combinatorial optimization.* John Wiley and Sons, Chichester, UK.

Baker, J. E. (1985). *Adaptive selection methods for genetic algorithms.* In Grefenstette, J. J. (ed.). *Proceedings of the First International Conference on Genetic Algorithms and Their Applications,* Erlbaum.

Davis, L. (1987). *Genetic algorithms and simulated annealing.* Pitman, London.

Fogel, L. J., Owens, A. J., and Walsh, M. J. (1966). *Artificial Intelligence through Simulated Evolution.* Wiley.

Goldberg, D. E. (1989). *Genetic algorithms in search, optimization and machine learning.* Addision–Wesley.

Goldberg, D. E., and Deb, K. (1991). *A comparitive analysis of selection schemes used in genetic algorithms.* In Rawlins, G. (ed.) *Foundations of Genetic Algorithms*, Morgan Kaufmann.

Goldberg, D. E., Korb, B., and Deb, K. (1989). Messy genetic algorithms: Motivation, analysis and first results. *Complex Systems*, Vol. 3, pp. 493–530.

Goldberg, D. E., Richardson, J. (1987). *Genetic algorithms with sharing for multimodal function optimization.* In *Genetic algorithms and their applications: Proceedings of the second international conference on Genetic Algorithms*, Cambridge, MA, USA.

Goldberg, D.E., and Segrest, P. (1987). *Finite Markov chain analysis of genetic algorithms.* In Grefenstette, J. J. (ed.) *Genetic Algorithms and Their Applications: Proceedings of the Second International Conference on Genetic Algorithms*, Cambridge, MA, USA.

Holland, J. H. (1975) '*Adaptation in natural and artificial systems*,' Ann Arbor: University of Michigan Press.

Horn, J., Nafpliotis, N., Goldberg, D. E. (1994). A niched Pareto genetic algorithm for multiobjective optimization. In *Proceedings of the first IEEE conference on evolutionary computation. IEEE world congress on computational intelligence*, Orlando, FL, USA.

Kirkpatrik, S., Gelatt, C. D. and Vecchi, M. P. (1983). Optimization by simulated annealing. *Science*, Vol. 220, pp. 671–680.

Lu, H., Yen, G. G. (2003). Rank-density-based multiobjective genetic algorithm and benchmark test function study. *IEEE Transaction on Evolutionary Computation*, Vol. 7(4), pp. 325–343.

Monseca, C. M., Flemming, P. J. (1993). *Multiobjective genetic algorithms.* In IEE colloquium on "Genetic Algorithms for Control Systems Engineering"

Murata, T., Ishibuchi, H., Tanaka, H. (1996). Multi-objective genetic algorithm and its applucations to flowshop scheduling. *Comput Ind Eng*, Vol. 30(4), pp. 957–968.

Rawlins, G. (ed.) (1991). *Foundations of Genetic Algorithms.* Morgan Kaufmann.

Schaffer, J. D., Caruana, R. A., Eshelman, L. J., and Das, R. (1989). *A study of control parameters affecting online performance of genetic algorithms for function optimization.* In Schaffer, J. D. (ed.) *Proceedings of the Third International Conference on Genetic Algorithms.*

Schaffer, J. D. and Morishima, A. (1987). *An adaptive crossover distribution mechanism for genetic algorithms.* In Grefenstette, J. J. (ed.) *Genetic Algorithms and their Applications: Proceedings of the Second International Conference on Genetic Algorithms.* Cambridge, MA, USA.

Syswerda, G. (1989). *Uniform crossover in genetic algorithms.* In Schaffer, J. D. (ed.) *Proceedings of the Third International Conference on Genetic Algorithms.* Morgan Kaufmann.

Zitzler, E., Thiele, L. (1999). Multiobjective evolutionary algorithms: a comparative case study and the strength Pareto approach. *IEEE Transaction on Evolutionary Computation*, Vol. 3(4), pp. 257–271.

13

Hybrid Systems

Key Concepts

AND fuzzy neuron, Action selection network (ASN), Action-state evaluation network, Adaptive neuro-fuzzy inference system (ANFIS), Approximate reasoning based intelligent control (ARIC), Auxiliary hybrid systems, Backpropagation of error, Embedded hybrid systems, Fuzzy-genetic hybrid systems, Hybrid neural networks, Hybrid systems, Implication-OR fuzzy neuron, Innovation number, Interval of performance, Link chromosome, Multi-layer feed-forward nets, Mutate add connection, Mutate add node, Neuro-evolution of augmenting topologies (NEAT), Neuro-fuzzy-genetic hybrid systems, Neuro-fuzzy hybrid systems, Neuro-genetic hybrid systems, Node chromosome, OR fuzzy neuron, S-conorm, S-norm, Sequential hybrid systems, Sugeno fuzzy model, T-conorm, T-norm

Chapter Outline

The three main pillars of soft computing are fuzzy logic, artificial neural networks, and evolutionary search – particularly genetic algorithms. All of these have been successfully applied in isolation to solve practical problems in various fields where conventional techniques have been found inadequate. However, these techniques are complementary to each other and they may work synergistically, combining the strengths of more than one of these techniques, as the situation may occasionally demand. Hybrid systems are systems where several techniques are combined to solve a problem. Needless to say that such amalgamation must be used only if it returns better results than any of these techniques in isolation. Based on how two or more systems are combined, hybrid systems have been classified into three broad categories, viz., sequential (where the techniques are used sequentially, i.e. the output of the first is the input to the later), auxiliary (where one system calls the other as a subroutine, gets some results and uses it for further processing) and embedded hybrid systems (where the systems are totally amalgamated). Three primary types of hybrid systems are briefly discussed in this chapter. These are, neuro-genetic (combining neural networks and genetic algorithm), neuro-fuzzy (combining neural network and fuzzy logic) and fuzzy-genetic hybrid systems. Hybrid systems integrating all three techniques, viz., fuzzy logic, neural networks, and genetic algorithms, are also implemented in several occasions.

13.1 NEURO-GENETIC SYSTEMS

Neuro-genetic systems are combinations of artificial neural networks and genetic algorithms. Two such hybrid systems, a neuro-genetic system for weight determination of multi-layer feedforward networks, and a technique that artificially evolves neural network topologies using genetic algorithms are discussed in this section.

13.1.1 GA-based Weight Determination of Multi-layer Feed-forward Net

The weights in a multi-layer feedforward net are usually determined through the backpropagation learning method. In backpropagation of errors the interconnection weights are randomly initialized during network design. The inputs travel across the interconnections to the output node through the nodes of the hidden units. During training, the actual output is compared with the target output and the error, if any, is backpropagated for adjustments of the interconnection weights. The error is calculated as $E=\frac{1}{2}\sum_i (TO_i - AO_i)^2$, where TO_i is the target output and AO_i is the actual output at the ith output unit. During backpropagation of the error, the network adjusts its weights to return better results in the next iteration. This error backpropagation follows a gradient descent technique and therefore, is vulnerable to the problem of settling down at local minima. Another limitation of the gradient descent technique is that it is slow since the number of iterations needed to properly train the network is usually considerably high. In this section, we discuss a genetic algorithm based method for weight determination of multi-layered networks. The distinctive features of the system are briefly described below.

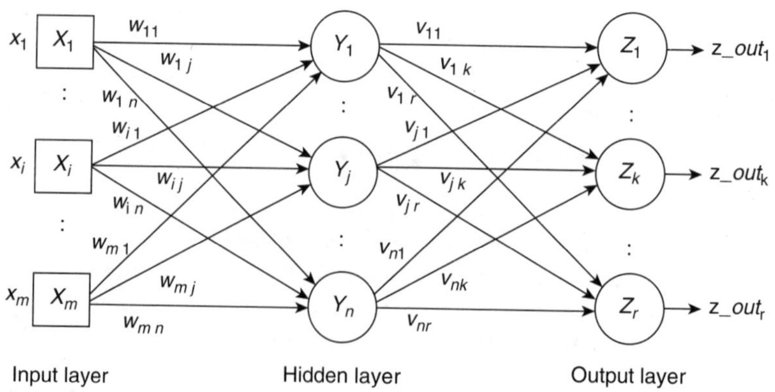

Fig. 13.1 *A multi-layer feed forward network with one hidden layer*

Let us consider a single hidden layer network having $m + n + r$ number of nodes, where m is the number of input nodes, n is the number of hidden nodes, and r is the number of output nodes. Therefore, the total number of interconnecting weights in the network is $(m + r) \times n$. Now, if each weight is represented by a gene, a chromosome having $(m + r) \times n$ number of genes can be used to encode the entire network. However, the scheme assumes that the topology is known to the encoding–decoding process. Let us recall the topology of an m-n-r single hidden layer network shown in Fig. 6.26, which is reproduced here as Fig. 13.1.

Each gene, representing an interconnection weight, consists of a 5-digit number $d_1d_2d_3d_4d_5$ where the most significant digit d_1 is used to determine the sign and the rest four, $d_2d_3d_4d_5$, the interconnection weight. The decoding can be done is the following manner: the sign of the interconnection weight is '+' or '–' depending on whether d_1 is even or odd. The magnitude is obtained by dividing $d_2d_3d_4d_5$ by 100, i.e., the real number $d_2d_3.d_4d_5$. A chromosome is then a linear array of $(m + r) \times n \times 5$ digits. The method is explained in Example 13.1.

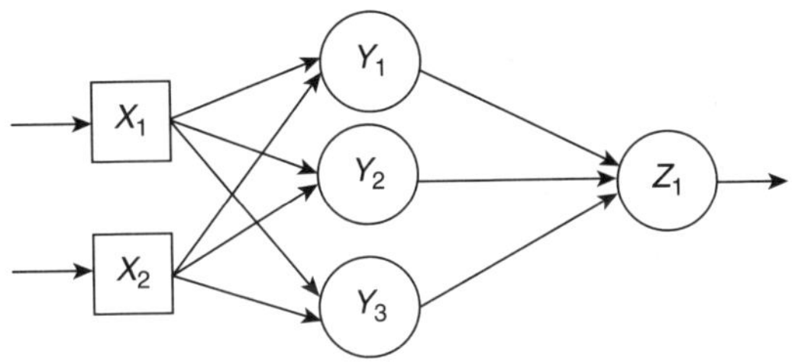

Fig. 13.2. *Sample backpropagation network*

Example 13.1 *(Chromosome for weight determination of BPN through GA)*

Figure 13.2 shows a 2-3-1 multi-layer network. As per notational convention followed here, the interconnection weight between the input unit X_1 and the hidden unit Y_1 is denoted as w_{11}. The other weights between the input layer and the hidden layer are w_{12}, w_{13}, w_{21}, w_{22}, and w_{23}. Similarly the weights between the hidden layer and the output layer are v_{11}, v_{21}, and v_{31}. Therefore, a chromosome for this network corresponds to an arrangement of weights as given by:

w_{11}	w_{12}	w_{13}	w_{21}	w_{22}	w_{23}	v_{11}	v_{21}	v_{31}

In the present case, the chromosome is an array of $(2 + 1) \times 3 \times 5 = 45$ digits. For instance, let 1434590 765432107654304567135092468094785625 89 be a chromosome. The mapping between the chromosome, weights and interconnections are shown below.

14345	90765	43210	76543	04567	13509	24680	94785	62589
–43.45	–07.65	+32.10	–65.43	+45.67	–35.09	+46.80	–47.85	+25.89
w_{11}	w_{12}	w_{13}	w_{21}	w_{22}	w_{23}	v_{11}	v_{21}	v_{31}

The initial population consists of a set of randomly generated chromosomes. Fitness is measured in terms of the error term $E = \frac{1}{2}\sum_i (TO_i - AO_i)^2$. In order to compute the error, a chromosome is mapped to its corresponding BPN net. The network is then tested by applying the input of a test pair and computing the actual output for the said input. This actual output when compared with the target output as in $E = \frac{1}{2}\sum_{i}(TO_i - AO_i)^2$ gives the error for that training pair. The same is computed for every training pair and the average is considered for fitness calculation. Since the aim is to minimize the error whereas GA is a maximization process, we cannot directly use the error E as the fitness measure. An obvious way out is to take the reciprocal of E as the fitness.

$$F = \frac{1}{E} \tag{13.1}$$

The rest of the process is usual GA. It may be noted that the GA-based learning of multi-layer nets does not involve any backpropagation of error. The journey towards the minimum error multi-layer network is now controlled by the GA instead of the backpropagation learning method process.

13.1.2 Neuro-evolution of Augmenting Topologies (NEAT)

Determination of interconnection weights of multi-layer feedforward networks using GA, discussed in the last subsection, was based on the tacit assumption that the topology of the network is finalized at the outset. Here GA is employed to evolve the appropriate combination of interconnection weights only. However, performance of the net is greatly influenced by the topology of the net. Therefore, finding an optimal network topology, along with the weights, is an issue that needs to be addressed in certain situations. Evolution of artificial neural networks using GA, referred to as neuro-evolution (NE), is the process of searching for such suitable network topology that carries out a given task efficiently.

Neuro-evolution of augmenting topologies (NEAT) was proposed by K.O. Stanley and R. Miikkulainen in 2002. It employs a GA that simultaneously evolves artificial neural network topologies along with their interconnection weights. An interesting feature of NEAT is its ability to optimize and *complexify* solutions simultaneously. The rest of this subsection presents the salient features of this methodology.

(a) Genetic encoding. An important issue in problem solving using GA is the effective encoding of the solution for the GA to operate on it. In NEAT the issue is rather complex due to a phenomenon called the *competing conventions* problem. The problem is illustrated in Fig. 13.3. Fig. 13.3(a) and (b) show two networks with the same set of nodes. The nodes in the hidden layer are arranged in different order in the two nets. It is clear from the diagram that a single point crossover over the two networks results in two children each of which loses one of the three components of the hidden layer. In NEAT, this problem is solved with the help of an *innovation number*. The concept of an innovation number and its role in NEAT will be explained in subsequent sections.

NEAT employs two types of genes, the *node* genes and the *connection* genes, sometimes referred to as the *link* genes. The *node* genes contain information about each node, their number and type, viz. input, hidden or output. The link genes store information about the links, the *in* node number, the *out* node number, the weight of the link, the status (*enable/disable*) of the link and a number called the *innovation number* of the link.

The *innovation number* is a unique number that is used to track the historical origin of the link. This number is incremented by one and assigned to a gene on creation through structural mutation and is passed on to its children. It therefore represents the chronology of appearance of every link. The innovation number of a link never changes. It helps to overcome the competing convention problem during the crossover operation. This will be explained later in this subsection. The structure of the chromosomes in NEAT is illustrated in Example 13.2.

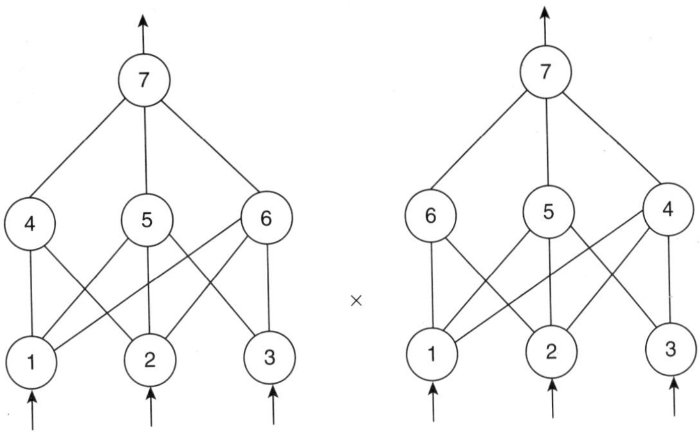

(a) (b)

Crossover	[4, 5, 6]	×	[6, 5, 4]
Children	[4, 5, 4]		[6, 5, 6]

Fig. 13.3. *The competing conventions problem*

Example 13.2 *(Structure of NEAT chromosomes)*

A 3-1-1 multi-layer neural net along with its chromosomes is shown in Fig. 13.4. The node gene is shown in Fig. 13.4(b). It consists of a list of nodes and their nature. In this specific case, nodes #1, 2, 3 are inputs, node #5 is a hidden node, and the node #4 is the output node. This information is incorporated in the node gene.

The structure of the *connection* chromosome, also referred to as the *link* chromosome, is more complex because a greater amount of information is accommodated here. A closer scrutiny of this chromosome will reveal some evolutionary history of the network, and the constituent genes. First, notice that each entry of the connection chromosome has a *disable/enable* field that indicates whether the link is still alive or not. For the chromosome shown in Fig. 13.4(c), the link 2 → 4 (i.e. *in* node 2, *out* node 4) is disabled, while all other nodes are enabled. This implies that once there was a direct link from node #2 to node #4, which is now disrupted due to the intervening new node #5. At some point of the evolution process node #5 was inserted between the nodes #2 and node #4 so that the link 2 → 4 is replaced by the pair 2 → 5 and 5 → 4. Since the innovation numbers of the links 2 → 5 and 5 → 4 (4 and 7 respectively) are larger than that of the disabled link 2 → 4 (innovation number = 2) we know that these links were formed later than the link 2 → 4. It may be noted that the links link 1 → 5 and link 3 → 5 were created even later than 2 → 5.

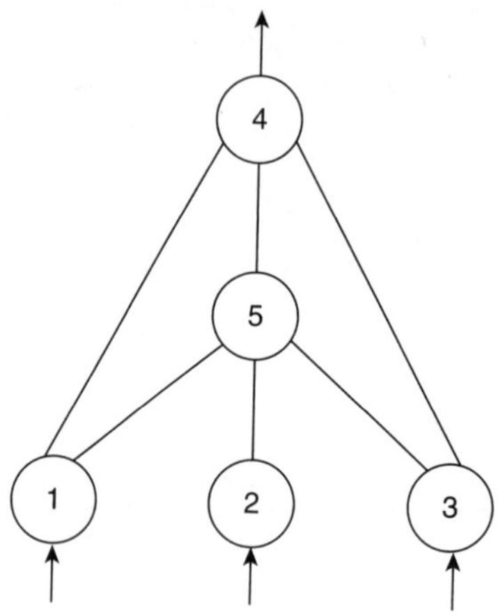

(a) The network

NODE #1 INPUT	NODE #2 INPUT	NODE #3 INPUT	NODE #4 OUTPUT	NODE #5 HIDDEN

(b) Node chromosome

IN = 1 OUT = 4 W = 0.5 ENABLD INOV. = 1	IN = 2 OUT = 4 W = 0.86 DISABLD INOV. = 2	IN = 3 OUT = 4 W = 0.67 ENABLD INOV. = 3	IN = 2 OUT = 5 W = 0.32 ENABLD INOV. = 4	IN = 1 OUT = 5 W = 0.9 ENABLD INOV. = 5	IN = 3 OUT = 5 W = 0.68 ENABLD INOV. = 6	IN = 5 OUT = 4 W = 0.66 ENABLD INOV. = 7

(c) Link chromosome

Fig 13.4 *The NEAT chromosomes*

(b) Mutation. There are two kinds of mutation operators in NEAT, one for adding a new connection, which is called *mutate add connection* and the other for adding a new node, which is termed as *mutate add node*. It may be recalled that the NEAT process progresses from simple network structures to complex networks. The two kinds of mutations are explained in Examples 13.3 and 13.4.

Example 13.3 *(Mutate add connection operation)*

Figures 13.5(a) and (c) show a network with 6 nodes and 6 connections and the corresponding link chromosome. The structure of the link chromosome is made simple by symbolically expressing a link as $p \rightarrow q$ where p is the *in* node and q is the *out* node. Moreover, the weights are not shown. Figures 13.5(b) and (d) show the topology and the link chromosome respectively of the network after being mutated by adding a new link $2 \rightarrow 6$. This addition of the new connection is reflected in the altered connection gene which contains a new link gene with innovation number 7.

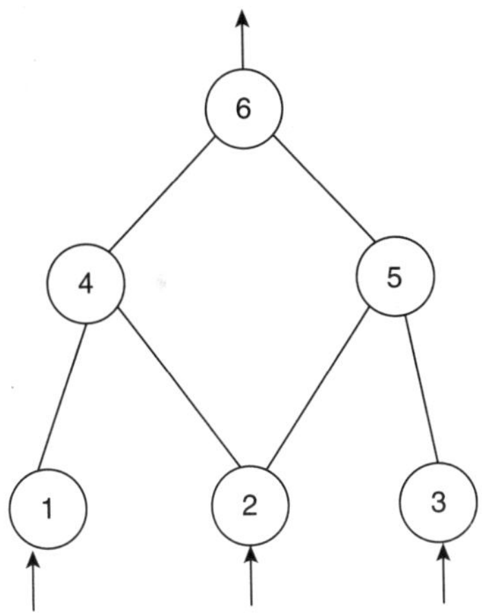

(a) The network before mutate add connection

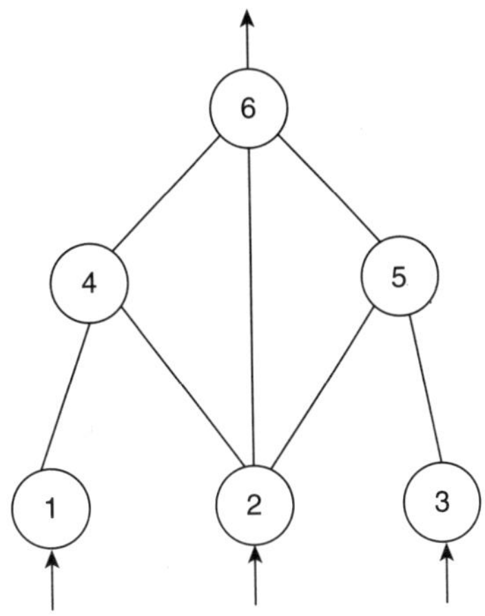

(b) The network after mutate add connection

1 → 4 ENABLD INOV. = 1	2 → 4 ENABLD INOV. = 2	2 → 5 ENABLD INOV. = 3	3 → 5 ENABLD INOV. = 4	4 → 6 ENABLD INOV. = 5	5 → 6 ENABLD INOV. = 6

(c) Link chromosome of network before mutate add connection

1 → 4 ENABLD INOV. = 1	2 → 4 ENABLD INOV. = 2	2 → 5 ENABLD INOV. = 3	3 → 5 ENABLD INOV. = 4	4 → 6 ENABLD INOV. = 5	5 → 6 ENABLD INOV. = 6	2 → 6 ENABLD INOV. = 7

(d) Link chromosome of network after mutate add connection

Fig 13.5 *The mutate add connection operation*

Example 13.4 *(Mutate add node operation)*

Figure 13.6(a) depicts the network structure of Fig. 13.5(b) after mutate add node operation in which the node 7 is added between nodes 2 and 6. As a result of this operation, the structures of both the node chromosome and the link chromosome have changed. Fig. 13.6(b) shows the node chromosome which reflects the change by introducing node #7 as a hidden node. Similarly, Fig. 13.6(c) shows the link chromosome which is obtained by appropriately modifying the chromosome in Fig. 13.5(d). The modifications are: inclusion of two new connections 2→7 and 7→6, with innovation numbers 8 and 9, respectively, and disabling the link 2→6, of innovation number 7. It is interesting to note that the link is not discarded, but *disabled*.

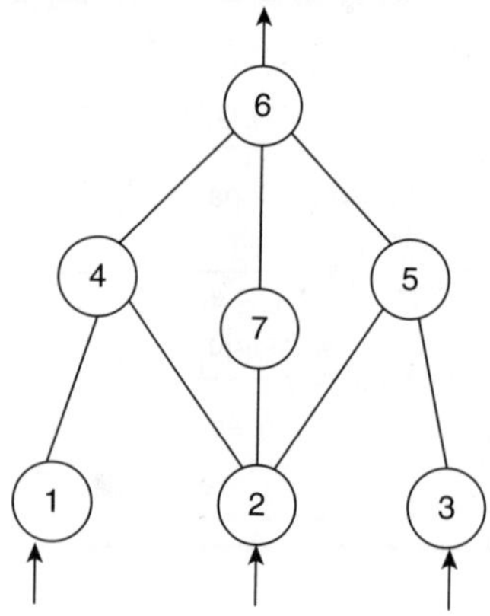

(a) The network of Fig. 13.5 (b) after mutate add node operation

NODE #1 INPUT	NODE #2 INPUT	NODE #3 INPUT	NODE #4 HIDDEN	NODE #5 HIDDEN	NODE #6 OUTPUT	NODE #7 HIDDEN

(b) Node chromosome of network after mutate add node

1 → 4 ENABLD INOV. =1	2 → 4 ENABLD INOV. =2	2 → 5 ENABLD INOV = 3	3 → 5 ENABLD INOV. = 4	4 → 6 ENABLD INOV. = 5	5 → 6 ENABLD INOV. = 6	2 → 6 DISABLD INOV. = 7	2 → 7 ENABLD INOV. = 8	7 → 6 ENABLD INOV. = 9

(c) Link chromosome of network after mutate add node

Fig. 13.6. *The mutate add node operation*

(c) Crossover. Crossover is probably the most complex operation in NEAT. This is because it involves matching up of chromosomes of various network topologies suitable for crossing over. The concept of innovation number helps to achieve this. The innovation numbers enable the NEAT process to identify the portions of two parent chromosomes that match even without direct analysis of the topologies of the networks. The technique of NEAT crossover is explained in the Example 13.4 presented below.

Example 13.5 *(Crossover operation in NEAT)*

Consider the network structures (a) and (b) as shown in Fig. 13.7. They seem to have a common ancestor from which they were generated through mutation. The corresponding node chromosomes are shown at the top and the link chromosomes are shown below the nets. The offspring is generated by adding to the common genes, the disjoint genes and the excess genes from the parents. In the present case the genes for the links 1→4, 2→4, 2→5, 3→5, 4→6, 5→6 are the common genes. A *disjoint gene* is a gene that is not included in the other parent but has innovation number less than the greatest innovation number.

In the figure, the link gene 1→5, having innovation number 8 is a disjoint gene, since it is present in network (a) but not in network (b) and its innovation number (8) is less than the greatest innovation number (10) included in network (b). An *excess gene* is a gene that is part of one parent and has innovation number greater than the greatest innovation number of the genes of the other parent.

NODE #1	NODE #2	NODE #3	NODE #4	NODE #5	NODE #6
INPUT	INPUT	INPUT	HIDDEN	HIDDEN	OUTPUT

Node chromosomes of network (a)

NODE #1	NODE #2	NODE #3	NODE #4	NODE #5	NODE #6	NODE #7
INPUT	INPUT	INPUT	HIDDEN	HIDDEN	OUTPUT	HIDDEN

Node chromosomes of network (b)

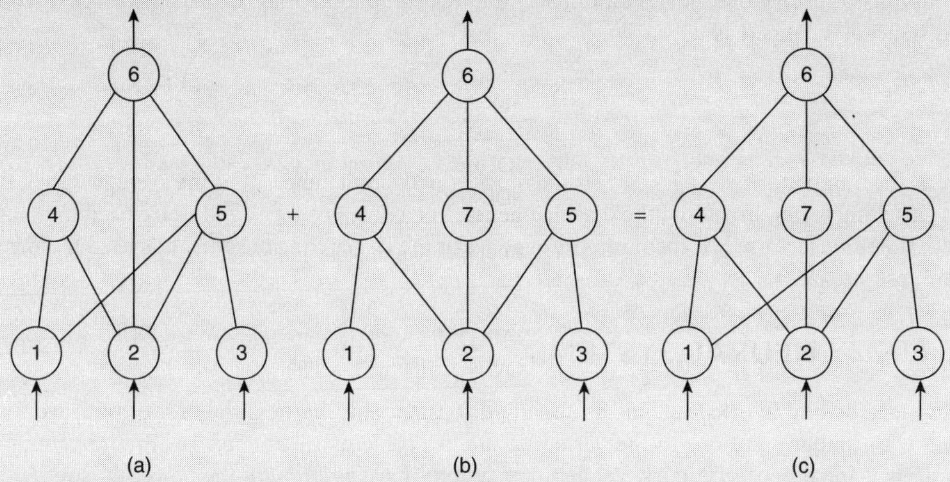

(a)	1 → 4 ENA INO = 1	2 → 4 ENA INO = 2	2 → 5 ENA INO = 3	3 → 5 ENA INO = 4	4 → 6 ENA INO = 5	5 → 6 ENA INO = 6	2 → 6 ENA INO = 7	1 → 5 ENA INO = 8		
(b)	1 → 4 ENA INO = 1	2 → 4 ENA INO = 2	2 → 5 ENA INO = 3	3 → 5 ENA INO = 4	4 → 6 ENA INO = 5	5 → 6 ENA INO = 6	2 → 6 DISA INO = 7		2 → 7 ENA INO = 9	7 → 6 ENA INO = 10
(c)	1 → 4 ENA INO = 1	2 → 4 ENA INO = 2	2 → 5 ENA INO = 3	3 → 5 ENA INO = 4	4 → 6 ENA INO = 5	5 → 6 ENA INO = 6	2 → 6 DISA INO = 7	1 → 5 ENA INO = 8	2 → 7 ENA INO = 9	7 → 6 ENA INO = 10

(a) Parent #1, (b) parent #2, (c) offspring

Fig. 13.7. *The NEAT crossover operation*

In Fig. 13.7, the link genes 2 → 7 (INO = 9) and 7 → 6 (INO = 10) are excess genes because they are part of network (b) only and have innovation numbers greater than 8, which is the highest innovation number of network (a). After crossover, the offspring inherits all the nodes of both parents and the links including excess and disjoint ones from both parents which is shown in network (c) and the corresponding chromosome in Fig. 13.7.

(d) NEAT process. Conventional neuro-evolution process starts with an initial population of random network topologies so that diversity is introduced from the very beginning. NEAT, in contrast, starts with a uniform population of networks with no hidden units. This is to facilitate the search for minimal network capable of performing the given task. As the networks mutate over time, new structures are incrementally introduced into the pool. Fitness evaluation ensures that only those structures survive who are useful for the designated task.

A relevant question for this scheme is how the NEAT process identifies the compatible networks for processing? A natural measure of compatibility distance of two chromosomes (and the underlying nets) is the number of excess and disjoint genes between them. The more disjoint two chromosomes are, the less evolutionary history they share, and hence, the less compatible they are. The measure of compatibility distance δ is defined as

$$\delta = \frac{c_1 E}{N} + \frac{c_2 D}{N} + c_3 \overline{W} \tag{13.2}$$

where E is the number of excess genes, D is the number of disjoint genes, $\overline{W}$ is the average weight difference of matching genes, including the disabled genes. The constants c_1, c_2, and c_3 are used to adjust the weight of the three factors. N is the numbers of genes in the larger chromosome. It is used to normalize the chromosome size.

13.2 FUZZY-NEURAL SYSTEMS

The basic idea behind hybrid systems, as already discussed, is to harness the best of both worlds and come up with unique solutions to the varied nature of problems we are faced with and cannot solve satisfactorily using other techniques. While fuzzy systems have as strength the power to work with imprecise information and vagueness, they cannot adapt, cannot learn from experience, cannot generalize or exploit parallelism. On the other hand, artificial neural networks are tools that cannot deal with uncertainty but can learn and adapt, generalize and being massively parallel can use the synaptic weights to store information that acts like memory. Fuzzy-neural systems are systems obtained by integrating fuzzy logic with neural networks to exploit the advantages of both.

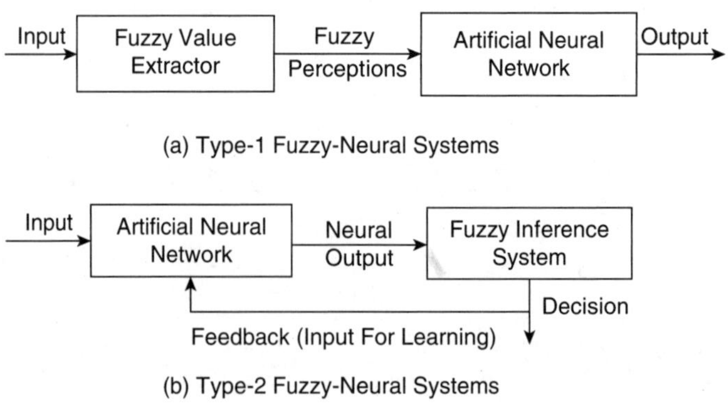

Fig. 13.8. *Types of neuron-fuzzy system*

Fuzzy-neural systems have been classified into two broad categories, depending upon how the two techniques are merged. These are the type-1 and type-2 fuzzy-neural systems. In type-1 systems, the input is fed to the fuzzy value extractor, where, based on the truth value of the input, an input vector is generated for the artificial neural network. The neural network then generates the output as decisions. In type-2 fuzzy-neural systems the output of the neural network is fed to the fuzzy inference system whose decision is fed back to the neural net to facilitate learning. The schematics of these tow types of neuro-fuzzy systems are depicted in Fig. 13.8(a), (b).

A typical example of a fuzzy-neural system is the *approximate reasoning based intelligent control* (ARIC) system proposed by H. R. Berenji. This system uses a neural model of a fuzzy controller that can learn by updating the behavioral prediction of the physical system and changes the predefined control logic database accordingly. ARIC basically comprises two modules that work together. The first module, called the *action selection network* (ASN), is a neural model of a fuzzy controller which consists of two networks. One network acts as the unit doing the fuzzy inference and the second is used to calculate the confidence associated with the fuzzy inference value generated by the first. The second module of ARIC apart from ASN is the *action-state evaluation network* (AEN). This is a feed forward network with one hidden layer and tries to predict the system behavior. The inputs to the AEN are the system state and an error signal from the physical system. The output of the network is a prediction of future reinforcement. In the subsequent parts of this section two neuro-fuzzy systems, viz., *fuzzy neuron*, and *adaptive neuro-fuzzy inference system* (ANFIS), are briefly described.

13.2.1 Fuzzy Neurons

Artificial neural networks are discussed in detail in Chapters 6 to 10. Figure 13.9 depicts the structure of an elementary 2-input 1-output neuron without any hidden nodes.

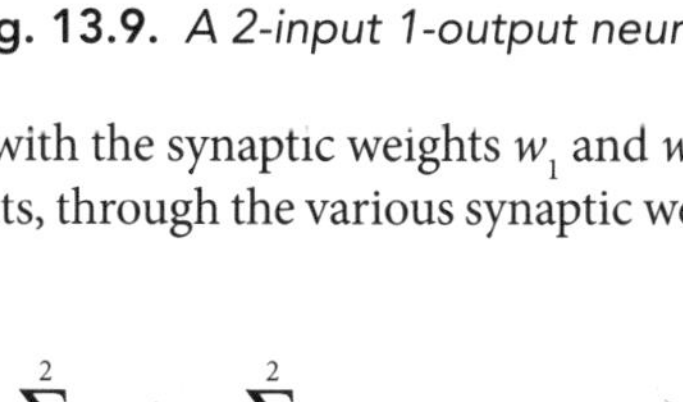

Fig. 13.9. *A 2-input 1-output neuron*

The input signals x_1 and x_2 interact with the synaptic weights w_1 and w_2 to give intermediate results $w_1 \times x_1$ and $w_2 \times x_2$ respectively. All the inputs, through the various synaptic weights, are aggregated to produce the net input *y_in* to the output unit *Y*.

$$y\_in = \sum_{i=1}^{2} y\_in_i = \sum_{i=1}^{2} w_i \times x_i = w_1 \times x_1 + w_2 \times x_2 \tag{13.3}$$

If $f(\cdot)$ is the transfer function that the network uses, the neuron computes its output as $y\_out = f(y\_in)$. The operations discussed above are all crisp. However, it is possible for a neuron to perform fuzzy operations on the input and weight. Such neurons are called *fuzzy neurons*. Therefore, a *fuzzy neuron* is a neuron that applies fuzzy operations on incoming data.

A ***t-norm*** (T-Norm) is a binary operator that represents conjunction in logic. Used specifically in fuzzy logic, it can be defined as a function $\mathbf{T} : [0, 1] \times [0, 1] \rightarrow [0, 1]$ which is commutative ($\mathbf{T}(\mathbf{a}, \mathbf{b}) = \mathbf{T}(\mathbf{b}, \mathbf{a})$), monotonic ($\mathbf{T}(\mathbf{a}, \mathbf{b}) \leq \mathbf{T}(\mathbf{c}, \mathbf{d})$ if $\mathbf{a} \leq \mathbf{b}$ and $\mathbf{c} \leq \mathbf{d}$), associative ($\mathbf{T}(\mathbf{a}, \mathbf{T}(\mathbf{b}, \mathbf{c})) = \mathbf{T}(\mathbf{T}(\mathbf{a}, \mathbf{b}), \mathbf{c})$. The neutral element of a ***T***-Norm is 1. The dual notion of ***T***-Norm is ***T***-Conorm (also known as ***S***-Norm) which has a neutral element 0. A few well known ***T***-Norms and ***T***-Conorms (***S***-Norms) are listed below.

Drastic product ($\mathbf{t}_w$)	: $\mathbf{t}_w(\mathbf{a}, \mathbf{b}) = \mathbf{min}\{\mathbf{a}, \mathbf{b}\}$ ***if max*** $\{\mathbf{a}, \mathbf{b}\} = 1$, ***else*** 0.
Drastic sum ($\mathbf{s}_w$)	: $\mathbf{s}_w(\mathbf{a}, \mathbf{b}) = \mathbf{max}\{\mathbf{a}, \mathbf{b}\}$ ***if min*** $\{\mathbf{a}, \mathbf{b}\} = 0$, ***else*** 1.
Bounded difference ($\mathbf{t}_1$)	: $\mathbf{t}_1(\mathbf{a}, \mathbf{b}) = \mathbf{max}\{0, \mathbf{a}+\mathbf{b}-1\}$.
Bounded sum ($\mathbf{s}_1$)	: $\mathbf{s}_1(\mathbf{a}, \mathbf{b}) = \mathbf{min}\{1, \mathbf{a}+\mathbf{b}\}$.
Minimum ($\mathbf{t}_3$)	: $\mathbf{t}_3(\mathbf{a}, \mathbf{b}) = \mathbf{min}\{\mathbf{a}, \mathbf{b}\}$.
Maximum ($\mathbf{s}_3$)	: $\mathbf{s}_3(\mathbf{a}, \mathbf{b}) = \mathbf{max}\{\mathbf{a}, \mathbf{b}\}$.
Product ($\mathbf{t}_p$)	: $\mathbf{t}_p(\mathbf{a}, \mathbf{b}) = \mathbf{a} \cdot \mathbf{b}$.
Product t-conorm ($\mathbf{S}_p$)	: $\mathbf{S}_p(\mathbf{a}, \mathbf{b}) = \mathbf{a} + \mathbf{b} - \mathbf{a} \cdot \mathbf{b}$.

Fig. 13.10 *T-norms and T-conorms*

Neural networks that use fuzzy neurons as building blocks are called *hybrid neural networks*. Such neural networks use crisp signals, crisp transfer functions and crisp weights, but have certain properties that distinguish them from usual crisp neural networks. These properties are mentioned below.

(a) The inputs and the weights can be combined using fuzzy operations, e.g., fuzzy AND, fuzzy OR, implication, *T*-Norm, or *T*-Conorm. Fig. 13.10 shows certain details about *T*-Norm, or *T*-Conorm operations.
(b) The results of such combinations can be aggregated using *T*-Norm, or *T*-Conorm or some other continuous function.
(c) The function $f(\cdot)$ is a continuous function that maps input to output.

It must be clearly understood that the weights, inputs and the outputs of a hybrid neural network are real numbers in the interval [0, 1]. The processing units of hybrid-neural networks are fuzzy neurons. Descriptions of a few variants of fuzzy neurons are presented here. All examples are modeled on the neural structure of Fig. 13.9.

(a) *AND Fuzzy Neuron.* The input x_i and weight w_i are combined using fuzzy OR to produce the intermediate result. If y_in_i denotes the combination of input x_i and weight w_i then

$$y\_in_i = OR_f(x_i, w_i) = max\{x_i, w_i\}, i = 1, 2 \tag{13.4}$$

The intermediate results are then transformed to the output using fuzzy AND, $y\_out = AND_f(y\_in_1, y\_in_2)$. Hence the output of the neuron $y\_out = f(y\_in)$ is obtained according to the formula

$$y\_out = min\{ max\{w_1, x_1\}, max\{w_2, x_2\} \} \tag{13.5}$$

Alternatively, the inputs x_1, x_2 and weights w_1 and w_2 are combined by a triangular conorm S to produce the intermediate result

$$y\_in_i = S(x_i, w_i), i = 1, 2 \tag{13.6}$$

The intermediate results are then aggregated using a triangular norm T to produce the output as formulated below.

$$y\_out = AND_f(y\_in_1, y\_in_2) = T(y\_in_1, y\_in_2) = T\{ S(x_1, w_1), S(x_2, w_2) \} \tag{13.7}$$

So, if $T \equiv min$ and $S \equiv max$ then the *AND* neuron realizes the min-max composition.

(b) *OR Fuzzy Neuron.* In an OR fuzzy neuron, the input x_i and weight w_i are combined using fuzzy AND to produce the intermediate result. Therefore, in this case

$$y\_in_i = AND_f(x_i, w_i) = min\ \{x_i, w_i\},\ i = 1, 2 \tag{13.8}$$

The intermediate results are then transformed to the output using fuzzy OR, so that $y\_out = OR_f\ (y\_in_1, y\_in_2)$. Hence the output of the neuron $y\_out = f\,(y\_in)$ is obtained according to the formula

$$y\_out = max\ \{\ min\ \{w_1, x_1\},\ min\ \{w_2, x_2\}\ \} \tag{13.9}$$

Alternatively, the inputs x_1, x_2 and weights w_1 and w_2 are combined by a triangular norm T to produce the intermediate result

$$y\_in_i = T\,(x_i, w_i),\ i = 1, 2$$

The intermediate results are then aggregated using a triangular conorm S to produce the output as formulated below.

$$y\_out = OR_f\ (y\_in_1, y\_in_2) = S\ (y\_in_1, y\_in_2) = S(\ T\ (x_1, w_1),\ T\ (x_2, w_2)\ ) \tag{13.10}$$

So, if $T \equiv min$ and $S \equiv max$ then the *OR* neuron realizes the max-min composition.
It may be noted that while fuzzy AND, OR neurons perform logic operations on the membership values, the connections play the role of differentiating the impact levels of the inputs on the aggregation result. In fact, higher values of w_i have stronger impact of x_i on y_out of an OR_f neuron, and lower values of w_i have stronger impact of x_i on y_out of an AND_f neuron.

(c) *Implication-OR Fuzzy Neuron.* In an implication-OR fuzzy neuron the input x_i and weight w_i are combined using fuzzy implication to produce the intermediate result. Hence, for an implication-OR fuzzy neuron,

$$y\_in_i = IMP_f(x_i, w_i) = x_i \rightarrow w_i,\ i = 1, 2 \tag{13.11}$$

The input information y_in_i, $i = 1, 2$, are then aggregated by a triangular conorm S to produce the output

$$y\_out = S\ (y\_in_1, y\_in_2) = S\ (x_1 \rightarrow w_1, x_2 \rightarrow w_2) \tag{13.12}$$

Hybrid neural nets can be used to realize fuzzy rules in a constructive way so that the resultant nets are computationally equivalent to fuzzy expert systems and fuzzy controllers. These nets do not learn anything, they do not need to. Hybrid neural nets cannot directly use the backpropagation algorithm for learning. However, in order to determine the parameters of the membership functions representing the linguistic values in the rules, they may exploit steepest descent method, assuming that the outputs are differentiable functions of these parameters.

13.2.2 Adaptive Neuro-fuzzy Inference System (ANFIS)

The *adaptive neuro-fuzzy inference system*, quite often referred to as the *adaptive network based fuzzy inference system* (ANFIS) is a class of adaptive networks that can function in the same way as a fuzzy inference system. ANFIS uses a hybrid learning algorithm and represents the Sugeno and Tsukamoto fuzzy model which is described below.

(a) *Sugeno Fuzzy Model.* Developed by Takagi, Sugeno and Kang and popularly known as the Sugeno model, this method generates fuzzy rules from a set of data. A typical rule in the Sugeno Model has the form:

$$\text{If } (x \text{ is } A) \text{ AND } (y \text{ is } B) \text{ Then } z = f(x, y) \tag{13.13}$$

Considering $f(x, y)$ to be a first-order polynomial, we get the first-order Sugeno fuzzy model and can be described with the help of the following rules.

$$\begin{aligned}&\text{Rule 1. If } (x \text{ is } A_1) \text{ and } (y \text{ is } B_1) \text{ then } f_1(x, y) = p_1x + q_1y + r_1\\&\text{Rule 2. If } (x \text{ is } A_2) \text{ and } (y \text{ is } B_2) \text{ then } f_2(x, y) = p_2x + q_2y + r_2\end{aligned} \tag{13.14}$$

(b) *ANFIS architecture.* Fig. 13.11 shows the ANFIS architecture for two input first order Sugeno fuzzy model with two rules. It consists of five layers including the input and output layers.Each layer has a specific job to do. The task performed by every layer is explained below. Here O_{ki} is the output of the ith node of the layer k.

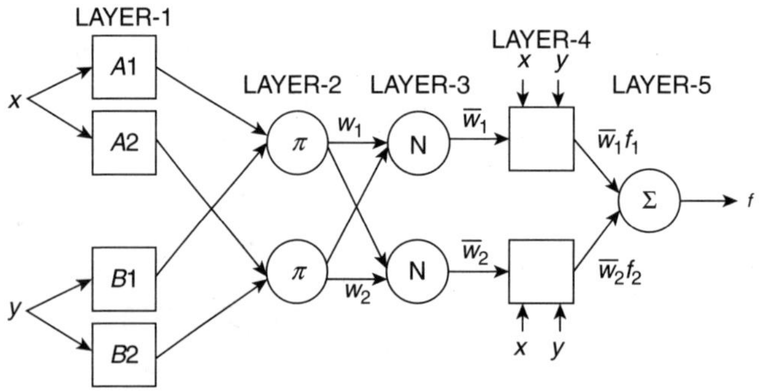

Fig. 13.11 *ANFIS architecture for 2 input first order Sugeno fuzzy model with 2 rules*

Layer 1. Every node in this layer is an adaptive node with a node function as described below.

$$O_{1,i} = \begin{cases} \mu_{A_i}(x), for\, i=1,2 \\ \mu_{B_{i-2}}(y), for\, i=3,4 \end{cases} \tag{13.15}$$

Here x (or, y) is the input to node i and A_i (or B_{i-2}) is a linguistic label associated with this node. Therefore $O_{1,i}$ is the membership grade of a fuzzy set A_1, A_2, B_1, or B_2. Needless to say that the membership functions can be any parameterized function like the *bell, triangular*, or *trapezoidal.*

Layer 2. This layer consists of a number of nodes each of which is labeled *Prod* and produces the product of all the incoming signals on it as its output.

$$O_{2,i} = \mu_{A_i}(x) \cdot \mu_{B_i}(y), for\, i = 1,2 \tag{13.16}$$

The output from each of these nodes represents the fire strength of the corresponding rule. Alternatively, any other T-norm operator that performs as the AND operator can be used.

Layer 3. Nodes in layer 3 are fixed nodes labeled *Norm*, and in this layer, the ith node calculates the ratio between the ith rule's firing strength and the sum of the firing strengths of all the rules.

$$O_{3,i} = \overline{w}_i = \frac{w_i}{w_1 + w_2}, for\, i = 1,2 \tag{13.17}$$

The outputs of these nodes are referred to as the *normalized firing strengths*.

Layer 4. The node function of each node in this layer is presented below.

$$O_{4,i} = \bar{w}_i f_i = \bar{w}_i (p_i x + q_i y + r_i) \tag{13.18}$$

In expression 13.17, w_i is the normalized firing strength from layer 3 and $\{p_i, q_i, r_i\}$ is the parameter set of the ith node and is referred to as *consequent parameters.*

Layer 5. This single node layer computes the output of the network by summing all incoming signals. The output is expressed as

$$O_{5,1} = \sum_i \bar{w}_i f_i = \frac{\sum_i w_i f_i}{\sum_i w_i} \tag{13.19}$$

Training the ANFIS is accomplished by using the hybrid learning algorithm presented by Jang. This algorithm uses least squares method to identify the consequent parameters on the layer 4 during the forward pass. During backward pass the errors are propagated backward and the premise parameters are updated using gradient descent technique.

13.3 FUZZY-GENETIC SYSTEMS

As the name suggests, fuzzy-genetic systems are hybrid systems that combine fuzzy systems with genetic algorithms in order to exploit the advantage of the both. As a typical instance of the synergy between fuzzy logic and GA, we present a scheme for tuning a fuzzy logic controller (FLC) with GA. Fuzzy logic controllers are discussed in details in Chapter 4. These systems try to simulate a skilled operator controlling a complex ill-defined process without knowledge of the underlying dynamics. The expert knowledge of the operator is embedded in the fuzzy logic controller in the form of a set of fuzzy rules, usually referred to as the fuzzy rule base.

GA based tuning of fuzzy logic controllers. In an FLC, the fuzzy rules are IF-THEN rules formulated in linguistic terms where the linguistic terms refer to certain fuzzy sets. Performance of the FLC depends to a large extent on the correct choice of the membership functions of the linguistic labels. The difficulty lies in representing the expert's knowledge suitably by linguistic control rules. The rest of this section discusses the essential features of a GA that tries to modify the fuzzy set definitions, i.e., the shape of the fuzzy sets defining the linguistic values. The purpose is to determine the membership functions for best FLC performance. The main features of this GA are briefly explained below.

Chromosomes. The rule base of an FLC consists of a number of rules with the form

$$\text{If '}x_1 \text{ is } A_{i1}\text{' AND '}x_2 \text{ is } A_{i2}\text{' AND ...AND '}x_n \text{ is } A_{in}\text{' Then '}y \text{ is } B_i\text{'} \tag{13.20}$$

where $x_1, x_2, \ldots, x_n$ and y are linguistic variables representing the process state variables and the control variables respectively. $A_{i1}, A_{i2}, \ldots, A_{in}$ and B_i are the linguistic values of the linguistic variables $x_1, x_2, \ldots, x_n$ and y respectively.

For instance, a typical fuzzy rule may look like: If '*Blood pressure is large positive*' AND '*Blood sugar level is small positive*' AND '*Calorie consumption is small negative*' Then '*Insulin dose is small positive*'. Here each of the variables *Blood pressure, Blood sugar, Calorie consumption*, and *Insulin dose* are measurable quantities. The corresponding linguistic values e.g. *large positive* etc. are fuzzy sets on these variables with predefined membership functions. Assuming that the linguistic labels $A_{i1}, A_{i2}, \ldots, A_{in}, B_i$ for $i = 1, 2 \ldots,$

a trapezoidal membership function is parametrically represented by a 4-tuple $\langle c, a, b, d \rangle$ which characterize the said membership function.

Example 13.6 *(Parametric representation of trapezoidal membership function)*

Let us consider the linguistic value '*Small positive*' with respect to the variable '*Blood sugar level*'. A probable membership profile for this fuzzy set is shown in Fig. 13.12. The parametric representation of this membership function is, obviously, $\langle c, a, b, d \rangle = \langle 125, 150, 175, 225 \rangle$.

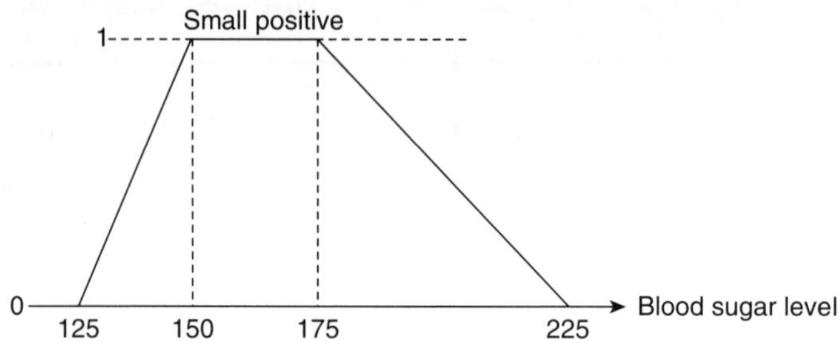

Fig. 13.12 *< 125, 150, 175, 225 > Trapezoidal function*

In the GA under consideration, a chromosome represents an encoding of a fuzzy rule base. Each rule of the form given in Expression 13.19 is included in the chromosome as a gene G_{ik}, denoting the kth gene (i.e. the kth rule) of the ith chromosome (the ith candidate rule base in the GA population). This G_{ik} must contain information about the fuzzy sets $A_{i1}, A_{i2}, \ldots, A_{in}$, and B_i. Let $\langle c_{ik1}, a_{ik1}, b_{ik1}, d_{ik1} \rangle, \langle c_{ik2}, a_{ik2}, b_{ik2}, d_{ik2} \rangle, \ldots, \langle c_{ikn}, a_{ikn}, b_{ikn}, d_{ikn} \rangle$, and $\langle c_{ik}, a_{ik}, b_{ik}, d_{ik} \rangle$ be the corresponding parametric representations. Then the kth gene of the ith chromosome is given by

$$G_{ik} = c_{ik1}\ a_{ik1}\ b_{ik1}\ d_{ik1}\ c_{ik2}\ a_{ik2}\ b_{ik2}\ d_{ik2} \ldots c_{ikn}\ a_{ikn}\ b_{ikn}\ d_{ikn}\ c_{ik}\ a_{ik}\ b_{ik}\ d_{ik} \quad (13.21)$$

Accepting this notation, the entire i^{th} fuzzy rule base consisting of m number of rules is represented by the chromosome C_i where

$$C_i = G_{i1}\ G_{i1} \ldots G_{im} \quad (13.22)$$

Finally, a population P of R number of fuzzy rule bases is given by

$$P = \{C_1, C_2, \ldots, C_R\} \quad (13.23)$$

The GA process evolves this population for the purpose of finding the appropriate rule base suitable for the designated control activity.

Interval of performance. The initial population is created from a rule base suggested by the domain expert. Let us denote the chromosome for this seed rule base as C_1. In order to enable the GA process to tune the rules, an *interval of performance* is defined for each fuzzy set parameter. Suppose $\langle c_1, a_1, b_1, d_1 \rangle$ be the parameters suggested by the expert for the fuzzy set corresponding to a particular linguistic value and this is included in the seed chromosome C_1. Then the subsequent values $\langle c_i, a_i, b_i, d_i \rangle$ in further chromosomes evolved by the GA must lie within certain pre-defined intervals $c_i \in [c_L, c_H]$, $a_i \in [a_L, a_H]$, $b_i \in [b_L, b_H]$ and $d_i \in [d_L, d_H]$ where c_L is the lower bound and c_H is the upper bound for c, and so on for the rest of the parameters. These intervals are defined below.

$$\begin{aligned} c_i &\in [c_L, c_H] = \left[c_1 - \frac{a_1 - c_1}{2}, c_1 + \frac{a_1 - c_1}{2} \right], \\ a_i &\in [a_L, a_H] = \left[a_1 - \frac{a_1 - c_1}{2}, a_1 + \frac{b_1 - a_1}{2} \right], \\ b_i &\in [b_L, b_H] = \left[b_1 - \frac{b_1 - a_1}{2}, b_1 + \frac{d_1 - b_1}{2} \right], \\ d_i &\in [d_L, d_H] = \left[d_1 - \frac{d_1 - b_1}{2}, d_1 + \frac{d_1 - b_1}{2} \right] \end{aligned} \tag{13.24}$$

These intervals are diagrammatically shown in Fig. 13.13.

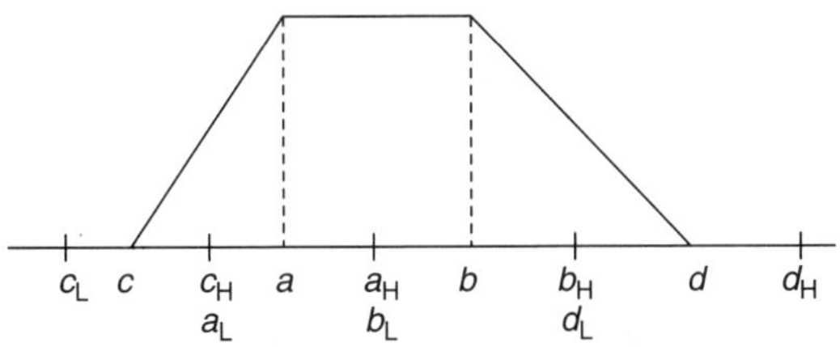

Fig. 13.13 *Intervals of performance*

Fitness. Fitness is measured on the basis of the performance of a candidate solution with respect to a set of training input-output data. Let the training data consists of a set of K number of such input-output pairs.

$$\{(x_i, y_i) = (x_{i1}, x_{i2}, \ldots, x_{in}, y_i), i = 1, 2, \ldots, K\}$$

The error of inference committed by a fuzzy rule base S, is calculated as

$$E(S) = \frac{1}{2} \sum_{i=1}^{K} [y_i - S(x_i)]^2 \tag{13.25}$$

The objective is to minimize the error $E(S)$ formulated above. Keeping this in mind, $E(S)$ can be used to define a suitable fitness function to guide the GA. The other GA operations are defined suitably and various GA parameters, e.g., population size, crossover probability, mutation probability, selection procedure etc., are set and tuned as per requirement of the problem instance.

CHAPTER SUMMARY

The main points of the forgoing discussions on hybrid systems are given below.

- Soft computing techniques are complementary to each other and they may work synergistically, combining the strengths of more than one of these techniques, as the situation may occasionally demand. Hybrid Systems are systems where several techniques are combined to solve a problem.
- The primary types of hybrid systems are, neuro-genetic (combining neural networks and genetic algorithm), neuro-fuzzy (combining neural network and fuzzy logic) and fuzzy-genetic hybrid

systems. Hybrid systems integrating all three techniques, viz., fuzzy logic, neural networks, and genetic algorithms, are also implemented in several occasions.

- Genetic algorithm based method for weight determination of multi-layer networks, or neuro-evolution of augmenting topologies (NEAT) are examples of neuro-genetic systems. In the former, instead of learning the interconnection weights of a multi-layer feedforward neural net through the technique of backpropagation of error, a GA is used to evolve these weights. In NEAT, genetic algorithm is employed to evolve the network topology, along with the weights, in order that the optimal net to carry out designated is obtained. In NEAT, the concept of an *innovation number* is introduced to resolve the competing conventions problem. The innovation number is a unique number that is used to track the historical origin of a link in the genetic evolution process.
- A *fuzzy neuron* is a neuron that applies fuzzy operations on incoming data. Various kinds of fuzzy neurons, e.g., fuzzy AND neuron, fuzzy OR neuron, fuzzy implication-OR neurons etc., are there that are used as building blocks of hybrid neural nets.
- The *adaptive neuro-fuzzy inference system*, quite often referred to as the *adaptive network based fuzzy inference system* (ANFIS) is a class of adaptive networks that can function in the same way as a fuzzy inference system. ANFIS architecture with first order Sugeno fuzzy model as input consists of five layers including the input and output layers. Each layer has a specific job to do.
- Fuzzy-genetic systems are hybrid systems that combine fuzzy systems with genetic algorithms in order to exploit the advantage of the both. Tuning a fuzzy logic controller (FLC) with GA ia a typical fuzzy-genetic system. Such a system employs a GA to evolve the fuzzy set definitions, i.e., the shape of the fuzzy sets defining the linguistic values. The purpose is to determine the membership functions for best FLC performance.

✓ TEST YOUR KNOWLEDGE

13.1 Hybrid systems are formed by combining
   a) Soft computing with hard computing
   b) Two or more soft computing techniques
   c) Embedding soft computing in hardware
   d) None of the above

13.2 A hybrid system that totally integrates two or more soft computing techniques is called
   a) Sequential hybrid system b) Auxiliary hybrid system
   c) Embedded beg hybrid system d) None of the above

13.3 In a neuro-genetic system, GA can be used to determine
   a) The interconnection weights b) The topology of the network
   c) Both (*a*) and (*b*) c) None of the above

13.4 Which of the following is a hybrid system to evolve the topology of a neural network?
   a) NEAT b) ANFIS
   c) Both (*a*) and (*b*) d) None of the these

13.5 In NEAT hybrid system, the innovation numbers in a chromosome is used to express the
   a) Degree of a node b) Historical origin of a link
   c) No of hidden units d) None of the above

13.6 Which of the following is not used in NEAT?
   a) Node chromosomes b) Link chromosomes
   c) Both (*a*) and (*b*) d) None of the above

13.7 Which of the following chromosomes in NEAT is affected by the Mutate Add Node operation?
   a) Node chromosomes b) Link chromosomes
   c) Both (*a*) and (*b*) d) None of the above

13.8 In NEAT crossover operation, which of the following is not inherited by the offspring from the parents?
   a) Disabled links? b) Excess links
   c) Disjoint links d) None of the above

13.9 How may layers are there in adaptive neuro-fuzzy inference systems(ANFIS)?
   a) 3 b) 4
   c) 5 d) None of the above.

13.10 While tuning fuzzy logic controllers by GA, the membership functions of the fuzzy sets corresponding to various linguistic values are taken as
   a) Gaussian b) Trapizoidal
   c) S-function d) None of the above

13.11 In a hybrid system for tuning fuzzy logic controllers by GA, the first set of fuzzy rules is generated
   a) Randomly b) By consulting experts
   c) Any of (*a*) and (*b*) d) None of the above

13.12 In a hybrid system for tuning fuzzy logic controllers by GA, the interval of performance indicate the interval in which
   a) The fitness values must lie b) Fuzzy rule parameters must lie
   c) Population size must lie d) None of the above

Answers

13.1 (b)	13.2 (c)	13.3 (c)	13.4 (a)	13.5 (b)
13.6 (d)	13.7 (c)	13.8 (d)	13.9 (c)	13.10 (b)
13.11 (b)	13.12 (b)			

BIBLIOGRAPHY AND HISTORICAL NOTES

Literature on hybrid systems is quite rich as this is a well-explored area of soft computing. A selected list of some interesting articles is given below.

Adeli, H. and S. L. Hung. (1995) '*Machine Learning – Neural Networks, Genetic Algorithms, and Fuzzy Systems*,' John Wiley and Sons, New York.

Carpenter, G. A., Grossberg, S., Markuzon, N., Reynolds, J. H., and Rosen, D. B. (1992). Fuzzy ARTMAP: A neural network architecture for incremental supervised learning of analog multi-dimensional maps. *IEEE Transaction on Neural Networks*, Vol. 3, No. 5, pp. 698–713.

Herrera, F., Logano, M., and Verdegay, J. L. (1994). Tuning fuzzy logic controllers by Genetic Algorithms. *International Journal of Approximate Reasoning*, Vol. 12, pp. 299–315.

Herrera, F., Logano, M., and Verdegay, J. L. (1995). Applying genetic algorithms in fuzzy optimization problems. *Fuzzy Systems and A.I. Reports and Letters*, Vol. 3, No. 1, pp. 39–52.

Mamdani, E. H. (1977). Application of fuzzy logic to approximate R\reasoning using linguistic synthesis. *IEEE Transactions on Computers*, Vol. C-26, No. 12, pp. 1182–1191.

Maniezzo, V. (1994). Genetic evolution of the topology of weight distribution of neural networks. *IEEE Transactions on Neural Networks*, Vol. 5, No. 1, pp. 39–53.

Rajasekaran, S. and Vijayalakshmi Pai, G. A. (2007). *Neural Networks, Fuzzy Logic and Genetic Algorithms: Synthesis and Applications*. Prentice-Hall India, New Delhi.

Stanley, K. O. and Miikkulainen, R. (2002). Evolving neural networks through augmenting topologies. Evolutionary Computation, Vol. 10, No. 2, pp. 99–127, MIT Press.

Takagi, H. and I. Hayashi. (1991). NN driven fuzzy reasoning. *International Journal of Approximate Reasoning*, Vol. 5, No. 3, pp. 191–212.

Wu, Y., Zhang, B., Lu, J. and Du, K. -L. (2011). Fuzzy logic and neuro-fuzzy systems: a systematic introduction. *International Journal of Artificial Intelligence and Expert Systems* (IJAE), Vol. 2, No. 2.

INDEX

M

N

O

P

Q

R

S

T

U

V

X